PREHISTORIC EUROPE
AN ILLUSTRATED HISTORY

Barry Cunliffe is Professor of European Archaeology at the University of Oxford. The author of over 40 books, including *The Ancient Celts*, published by Oxford University Press, he has served as President of the Council for British Archaeology and the Society of Antiquaries, and is currently a member of the Ancient Monuments Board of English Heritage.

CONTRIBUTORS

Barry Cunliffe
UNIVERSITY OF OXFORD

Clive Gamble
UNIVERSITY OF SOUTHAMPTON

Anthony Harding
UNIVERSITY OF DURHAM

Paul Mellars
UNIVERSITY OF CAMBRIDGE

Steven Mithen
UNIVERSITY OF READING

M. R. Popham
UNIVERSITY OF OXFORD

Andrew Sherratt
UNIVERSITY OF OXFORD

Timothy Taylor
UNIVERSITY OF BRADFORD

Malcolm Todd
UNIVERSITY OF DURHAM

K. A. Wardle
UNIVERSITY OF BIRMINGHAM

Alasdair Whittle
UNIVERSITY OF WALES

PREHISTORIC EUROPE

AN ILLUSTRATED HISTORY

EDITED BY

BARRY CUNLIFFE

Oxford   New York

OXFORD UNIVERSITY PRESS

Oxford University Press, Great Clarendon Street, Oxford OX2 6DP

Oxford New York

Athens Auckland Bangkok Bogota Bombay
Buenos Aires Calcutta Cape Town Dar es Salaam
Delhi Florence Hong Kong Istanbul Karachi
Kuala Lumpur Madras Madrid Melbourne
Mexico City Nairobi Paris Singapore
Taipei Tokyo Toronto Warsaw
and associated companies in
Berlin Ibadan

Oxford is a trade mark of Oxford University Press

© Oxford University Press 1994

First issued as an Oxford University Press paperback 1997

British Library Cataloguing in Publication Data
Data available

Library of Congress Cataloging in Publication Data
Data available
ISBN 0–19–288063–2

3 5 7 9 10 8 6 4

Printed in Hong Kong

CONTENTS

LIST OF COLOUR PLATES

LIST OF MAIN MAPS

ACKNOWLEDGEMENTS

The editor and authors wish to thank the very many colleagues who have helped them by providing information and illustrations and by reading texts in manuscript. In particular, they would like to thank Sandra Assersohn, who collected the half-tone illustrations from all corners of Europe. In addition, Steven Mithen would like to thank Dr Peter Rowley-Conwy, Dr Chris Scarre, Dr Bill Finlayson, and Dr Petra Day, all of whom read drafts of his manuscript (or parts of it), and Clive Gamble wishes to record the name of Dr Nick Ashton of the British Museum, who helped with the photographs. Timothy Taylor wishes to thank colleagues and scholars in Eastern Europe whose work made this overview possible and, in Britain, Anders Bergquist, Ralph and Barbara Hoddinott, Rachel Pilkington, and Sarah Wright. The editor would particularly like to thank Lynda Smithson for her support at all stages in the production of this volume.

Introduction

BARRY CUNLIFFE

EUROPE is a kaleidoscope of subregions and microclimatic zones tightly juxtaposed creating, at first sight, a bewildering variety of niches for its human communities to occupy. Like a kaleidoscope its perspectives constantly change. From one viewpoint Europe can be seen as simply one of the land fringes of the Mediterranean, from another it is little more than the western extremity of the great plain of Asia edged along its southern side with a more mountainous zone continuing, in pale reflection, the great chain which begins in the Himalayas. Yet from the perspective of world history it is central—central that is to the development and dissemination of Western culture.

How this should have come about—by what processes the varied landscape was peopled, how the resources were exploited and distributed and how the social and political complexity of the early medieval world developed, are the themes of this book. We begin with a bare ice-scarred landscape and end with the turmoil of the migrations from which the polities of western Europe were to emerge in the early Middle Ages. It was the entrepreneurs born of these political systems and their successors that were to explore, exploit, and briefly colonize much of the world. Our story, then, can fairly be said to form a significant chapter in world history.

Why the seas and lands of Europe should have provided the stage for such spectacular developments is a complex—and dangerous—question to approach: there can be no simple answer, but it is a question that cannot be avoided. One factor of crucial importance is the incredible variety of the landscape. One moment you can be lost among the snow-covered pastures of the Alpes-Maritimes and a couple of hours later (by car) be sitting in the sun outside a restaurant enjoying the aromatic smells of the Nice vegetable and fruit market while eating sea urchins. In a mere half hour you can travel from the wooded, silver-rich mountains of the Sierra Morena to the baking heat of the interminable olive groves of the Guadalquivir valley. The European landscape is an intricate patchwork of environments, each with its own range of resources, closely interlocked in such a way that, however isolated the communities were geographically, networks of interaction and exchange were inevitable. As the population grew and the landscape filled up, the intensity of these interactions increased.

Over and above these essentially local systems lay the broader, crucial divide between the Mediterranean and the land mass of temperate Europe. The Mediterranean is far more than just a collection of conjoined seas—it is a vastly convoluted littoral zone—a coastal strip of great complexity composed of islands, headlands, fjords, plains, and deltas sharing one sea in common and providing a congenial environment where olives, vines, and wheat could be grown with ease, and sheep and goats reared on the neighbouring hills. It was in the eastern part of this zone, in the Aegean and its fringes, that the earliest food producing economies took root and where, by the third millennium BC, great advances were being made in cultural and political development leading to Europe's earliest civilization—that of the Minoan-Mycenaean world. By the twelfth century this cycle of development was at an end and after a period of social turmoil—known as the Greek Dark Ages—new centres of innovation began to appear. On the Greek mainland and the Aegean coast of Asia Minor Greek civilization was emerging by the eighth century and over the next two centuries the politico-cultural system of the city state was transported to the Black Sea and the west Mediterranean to be transplanted in similar environmental niches on distant littorals. Meanwhile the cities of the Phoenician coast of the Levant were busy exploring the mineral resources of the western Mediterranean.

These intrusive probings and the networks of exchange which developed from them inspired indigenous communities in Italy (the Etruscans) and Spain (the Iberians) to evolve their own sophisticated cultural systems. Thus by the fourth century BC, as the Greek world of the Aegean entered a state of decline, the western Mediterranean became a hive of activity and innovation. From this Rome emerged to dominate not only the shores of the Mediterranean but much of temperate Europe beyond.

It is perhaps worth taking the story a little further, beyond the strict chronological confines of this volume. After the later Dark Age, which followed the collapse of the Roman Empire, the Mediterranean again emerged briefly into the limelight as the coastal cities of Venice, Genoa, Pisa, and others attempted to re-create maritime empires and indeed achieved a degree of success. But by the middle of the second millennium AD the Mediterranean was too constricted an environment any longer to provide an adequate power base in the new world order that was emerging. It was those countries with an Atlantic interface, Portugal and Spain at first and Britain, France, and Holland later, that were able to grow rich and powerful on the potential available to those willing to traverse the world's oceans.

To see the Mediterranean and its varied cultures as an entity complete in itself is to misunderstand prehistory and history. The Mediterranean world was at all times part of a much broader system which embraced temperate Europe, the Near East, and the plains of Russia.

The successive civilizations of the Near East and Egypt for the most part impinged only indirectly upon the European world through a network of coastal cities stretching from Alexandria in the south to Antioch in the north. Some of these, in particular the Phoenician towns of Tyre and Sidon, served as the bases of middlemen in complexes of exchange which transported raw materials from the Mediterranean to the East and brought various consumer luxuries out in return. Only occasionally did Near Eastern populations attempt to move westward, as in the case of the Persians who managed to penetrate deep into Greece by the late sixth century; yet the cultural impact of these areas of high civilization, as a spur to innovation and change in the West, was considerable.

North of the Caucasus the situation was rather different. Here a vast expanse of steppe, extending from China to Europe, provided a corridor for constant movement and migration throughout time. This zone of open steppe with forest steppe to the north was dissected by the great rivers, the Volga, Don, Dnepr, Bug, Dnestr, and the lower reaches of the Danube. Through this zone moved bands of horsemen-pastoralists, unnamed in deep prehistory but later appearing in a variety of historical texts as Cimmerians, Scythians, Sarmatians, Alans, Huns, Magyars, Bulgars, and Mongols. All made some cultural impact on Europe threading their way along the Danube corridor or being deflected northward around the Carpathian mountains to the plains of northern Europe. The intensity and nature of that impact especially in the prehistoric period provides an opportunity for lively debate! None, however, will deny the significance of the steppe communities on developing European culture.

This brings us, finally, to that contorted sea-girt peninsula with its numerous offshore islands which we know today as Europe—joined to Asia by the Russian steppes and washed on one side by the warm, congenial, innovating Mediterranean and on the other by the harsh, stormy, unending Atlantic. It is a peninsula divided by mountain ranges and joined by its systems of great rivers. Areas of old, hard, and, often infertile, rocks yielding a rich array of metals contrast with younger fertile plains. Wine and oil produced in the sun on the southern side of the peninsula find their way to the forest communities of the north while amber and furs are passed south to be admired by the populations of the Mediterranean coasts. The variety is immense: the contrasts are endless.

Why then did Europe develop as it did? Could the answer not lie simply in the interplay of this variety: ample mineral resources, contrasting but congenial ecologies, demanding climates, barriers and communications, and, above all, the constant interaction of its rich ethnic mix, proliferating in their restricted peninsular home?

At the end of this second millennium AD, as Europe achieves a degree of political unity it has never before experienced and frontiers become increasingly irrelevant, we have an unprecedented opportunity to experience and to cherish the environmental, ethnic, and cultural variety that is and always has been the essence of Europe. This book, we hope, will provide some understanding of the genesis of that variety.

1

The Peopling of Europe 700,000–40,000 Years before the Present

CLIVE GAMBLE

Understanding Cave-Men

IN 1905, forty years after Sir John Lubbock, in his landmark book *Pre-Historic Times*, had first used the term Palaeolithic to describe an old Stone Age era, Henry Knipe celebrated the achievements of prehistoric science in his illustrated poem *Nebula to Man*. He accompanied a specially commissioned picture of early humans with these lines:

> A master force, a subtle influence new
> Is here to leaven life, and through and through.
> More nervous strength than brute life can command
> Now plays a part upon this western land.
> For here has wandered Nature's latest birth,
> The crown and glory of her work on earth.
> Primeval men are now upon the scene—
> Short, thick-boned hairy beings of savage mien,
> With ape-like skulls: but yet endowed with pride
> And power of mind to lower brutes denied.

In his depiction of such low-life scenes Knipe neatly summarized the thrust of nineteenth-century prehistory which was to demonstrate the law of progress. Humans assumed their place at the pinnacle of creation through the development of mental powers. In the imperial world of the turn of the century the exercise of these same powers provided adequate explanation to those in the Western world for the 'natural' arrangement of political and social reality on a global scale.

More than eighty years later it is still common to find similar conclusions about progress and the brutish nature of our ancestors. 'Neanderthal' is not a term of endearment and stone tools are often thought to indicate primitive qualities among those who

BUCKNALL'S SKETCH OF EARLY PALAEOLITHIC MEN commissioned in 1905 and frequently copied.

continue to use them. Technology is still the measure of progress to the extent that it is not a question of whether you can drive, but rather *what* are you driving? Our earliest ancestors are still portrayed as hairy, near-naked, club-clutching children of nature. This is an interesting amalgamation of symbols, well seen in Bucknall's picture, but for which there is no archaeological evidence. We *still* await the discovery of the first wooden club and fur wrap from the old Stone Age.

I mention these pictures and the original purpose of prehistoric studies for a very good reason. Our images of cave men are so strong that alternative views based on evidence rather than fancy are all too easily brushed aside. Therefore, before presenting an account of 700,000 years of European prehistory it is worth pausing to ask where these dominant ideas came from and what need did they fulfil? The answers vary and include the experience of empire as it met, classified, and ruled the indigenous peoples of the world. The philosophers of the eighteenth century put forward the idea that many peoples in the world were examples of living prehistory. Adam Smith, in 1762, set out a graded system that archaeologists embraced in the next century in order to organize their stones, pots, and bronzes into a developmental, progressive sequence: 'There are four distinct states which mankind pass thro: 1st, the age of hunters, 2dly, the age of shepherds, 3rdly, the age of agriculture; and 4thly, the age of commerce.' Geographical remoteness from Paris and London was translated directly into remoteness in time. Hunters and gatherers lived at the uttermost ends of the western earth in places such as Alaska, Tierra del Fuego, Tasmania, and the Cape. They made stone tools and were readily used by Lubbock and many others to flesh out early European prehistory.

A second strand is more difficult to trace since it goes deeper into the Western past. This is the distinction between civilized and uncivilized people drawn in the classical world and incorporated into the medieval. Pliny provided a catalogue of monstrous races who inhabited the edges of the world, and one in particular, the Blemmyae, are important. They lived in the deserts of Libya and had their faces on their chests. These were freely incorporated in the largely fictitious, but best-selling, *Travels of Sir John Mandeville* that appeared in 1356. Here we learn that in the Andaman Islands there are a great many different types of people, among whom, 'There are ugly folk without heads, who have eyes in each shoulder; their mouths are round, like a horseshoe, in the middle of their chest'. The Blemmyae were frequently illustrated in medieval manuscripts where the symbols which revealed their uncivilized state were nakedness, clubs, and living in wild landscapes. They never failed to impress as Othello recalled:

A MEDIEVAL BLEMMYAE which helped set the artistic tradition that was later adopted in scientific reconstructions of Neanderthals and other prehistoric outsiders.

A CLASSIC IMAGE OF THE NEANDERTHALS drawn by Charles R. Knight to the American palaeontologist Henry Fairfield Osborn's specifications in 1915. This powerful, and much reproduced, image endorsed the expulsion, by scientists, of Neanderthals from human ancestry. The visual argument relies, however, on techniques borrowed from western art to portray outlaws, wild men, and those outside civilization rather than use archaeological evidence.

It was my hint to speak. Such was my process,
And of the cannibals that each other eat,
The Anthropophagi, and men whose heads
Do grow beneath their shoulders. These things to hear
Would Desdemona seriously incline.

When combined with the long folk tradition of Wild Men (the source of modern Yetis and Almas who also live at the edge of the 'civilized' world) we can see what helped the first scientific artists like Bucknall and Knight to make their reconstructions of the earliest Europeans intelligible to their public. The pictures owed little to scientific fact, even though they were both closely supervised by leading authorities such as Duckworth, Smith Woodward, and Osborn, and everything to medieval traditions of knowledge which the industrial and scientific revolutions had supposedly driven through like a runaway train. The creation of prehistory as a discipline in the nineteenth century involved incorporating more recent traditions of understanding people and the world which, ironically, the science of the day was bent on consigning to the realm of superstition.

The drawing by Charles Knight that appears as the frontispiece to Osborn's *Men of the Old Stone Age* (1915) is most interesting in this regard. In the ten years since Bucknall's picture a number of key fossil finds had been made in Europe. Of these, by far the most important was the excavation in August 1908, by three clerics, of a nearly complete skeleton of a male Neanderthal from the small cave of La Chapelle-aux-Saints in the Corrèze region of France. On the advice of Abbé Breuil, who later became the doyen of Palaeolithic studies, it was sent for analysis to Marcellin Boule at the Museum of Natural History in Paris. The choice was deliberate since it kept this important fossil away from the anti-clerical group, once led by Gabriel de Mortillet, at the École d'Anthropologie which had always argued that the earlier but often fragmentary finds of Neanderthals should be included in human ancestry. Boule disagreed and produced a highly detailed report, published between 1911 and 1913, presenting anatomical evidence expelling the Neanderthals from human ancestry. Knight's picture endorsed this interpretation which became the orthodoxy for many years. He achieved this by using time-honoured symbols to show the lack of civilization. For example, Boule's reconstruction of Neanderthal posture as slumped, is faithfully reproduced as a quasi-Blemmyae with his face moving downward to his chest.

The timing of this image is significant. Boule's expulsion of the Neanderthals came during the psychological prelude to the Great War which questioned the belief in mental and moral progress. Knight's picture is an attempt to deny the retention of the unthinkable in spite of contemporary evidence for primitive qualities among those engaged in the slaughter. As Hendrik Van Loon explained to a new generation in 1925:

We modern men and women are not 'modern' at all. On the contrary we still belong to the last generations of cave-dwellers. The foundation for a new era was laid but yesterday. The human race was given its first chance to become truly civilized when it took courage to question all things and made 'knowledge and understanding' the foundation upon which to create a more reasonable and sensible society of human beings. The Great War was the 'growing pain' of this new world.

Historical Background

The irony, of course, was that the battlefields of the Somme had also been the areas where seventy years before Boucher de Perthes and later, in 1859, Sir John Evans and Joseph Prestwich had established the great antiquity of mankind through their demonstration that in the same geological deposits stone tools occurred with extinct animals. For many years Boucher de Perthes' claims had been regarded with suspicion, and his drawings of artefacts ridiculed. We now see that they are tolerably accurate when compared with a systematic treatment of the main characteristics of flint-flaking including striking platforms, bulbs of percussion, and secondary retouch around the edges of flakes. But Boucher de Perthes, in an interesting parallel with the English antiquary William Stukely who, in the eighteenth century gave us field archaeology *and* the Druids, also secured his position as a paid-up member of the lunatic fringe. Alongside his perceptive observations of stratigraphy and artefacts in the gravel pits of Abbeville and Amiens he also illustrated many stone sculptures. His claims for heads of birds and humans in natural lumps of gravel undoubtedly delayed the full acceptance of his scientific observations.

Whereas Boucher de Perthes was treated with suspicion, John Frere was simply ignored. In 1797 he wrote to the Society of Antiquaries of London who, in 1800, published his brief account of stone tools from Hoxne in Suffolk. Today these would be

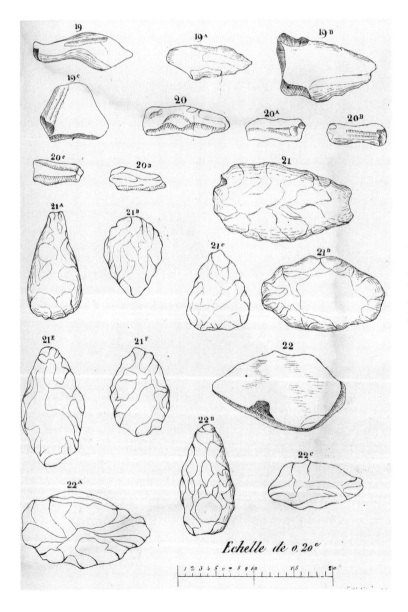

STONE TOOLS FROM ABBEVILLE on the Somme (*left*), drawn by Boucher de Perthes in 1847. These would now be classified as Lower Palaeolithic.

JOHN FRERE'S HANDAXE FROM HOXNE (*right*). His description in 1800 noted that 'the situation in which these weapons were found may tempt us to refer them to a very remote period indeed; even beyond that of the present world'.

classed as Acheulean handaxes, large implements flaked on both sides (bifacial), and which come in a wide range of sizes, shapes, and degrees of finishing. The specimens that Frere illustrated were especially well finished and pointed.

By 1872 the pace of discovery in the river terraces of north-west Europe and the caves of southern and central Europe was such that Gabriel de Mortillet was able to subdivide Lubbock's Palaeolithic into various phases based on the shapes of stone tools. Chronology was provided by the implements themselves and their progressive character as well as the epochs established by the animals with which they were discovered. His major division was between the Acheulean and Mousterian and the later stone cultures of what is now the Upper Palaeolithic where bone tools first appeared. The number and chrono-

A LEVALLOIS CORE (*left*) and typical levallois flake. The remnant core is often described as a tortoise core.

logical position of these gradually became clearer as more stratigraphic sequences from the caves of south-west France became available. This led Breuil, in 1912, to propose a major reclassification of the Upper Palaeolithic.

By this time a tripartite division had been agreed. The *Lower Palaeolithic* marked primarily by Acheulean handaxes and coming predominantly from the river terraces in the London and Paris basins; the *Middle Palaeolithic* or Mousterian, by points and scrapers made on flakes, from caves and rock shelters in the Dordogne, southern Germany and central Europe; and the *Upper Palaeolithic* by its art in the form of engraved bone and ivory objects and, most sensationally, painted caves in Cantabria (northern Spain), the Pyrennes, and the Périgord.

The next fifty years saw the addition of many other regional sequences from all over Europe. The typological study of the stone tools became the major concern, and the leading figure was undoubtedly Bordes, who developed a scheme, in 1953, for classifying assemblages of stone tools from discrete stratigraphic horizons. He did this by means of a list of types which, for the Middle Palaeolithic, consisted of sixty-three repeated forms of flake tools and a further twenty-one handaxes. The flake implements ranged in shape from side-scrapers to points, and included other less formal types such as notched pieces and denticulates (gap-toothed). These could be counted and assemblages compared according to how many of each type they contained. Bordes, who was an expert stone-knapper, also devoted part of his analysis to the study of flint technology, where observations on various proportional indexes, including platform type and Levallois technique, were taken into account. The latter technique was important since it represented an approach to stoneworking that was far removed from a concept of bashing rocks together to produce struck flakes. Named after the Paris suburb from whose gravel pits the original artefacts came, it is designed to produce flakes and blades of predetermined dimensions from a flint nodule. These may be triangular, elongated, or squat, but the important point is that they are not randomly produced.

Bordes' typology has been extremely influential and was adapted to the Upper Palaeolithic. It still represents the standard way in which Lower and Middle Palaeolithic materials are presented in reports. However, its basis is now under serious attack. This has arisen from two directions. In the first place there has been a shift towards technological rather than typological studies. This has been backed by the functional analysis of stone artefacts by experimental means with attention focused on the shape and damage to edges rather than whole pieces. High-powered microscopy has also identified traces of use wear in the form of polishes on these edges—not unlike the better-known sickle gloss from later prehistory. One major finding has been that many flakes and chips, which Bordes would classify as waste, were in fact used to cut meat, whittle wood, and shred plant materials. Concentrating on the retouched 'tools', therefore, biased the analysis to what *we* thought were important finished products.

Among the so-called tools there have been surprises when the 'biography' of such pieces has been reconstructed. In a recent paper Dibble has shown how, due to resharpening, a flint-scraper can at different times of its use life be classified as three different types of scraper from Bordes' list. He presents a dynamic model of tool use and technological organization rather than the static picture of formal implement types locked in

AN EXPERIMENTAL RECONSTRUCTION to show how continued retouching to an artifact changes its shape from straight to convex and finally to transversal edge. The artifact's 'biography' is summarized in (*d*).

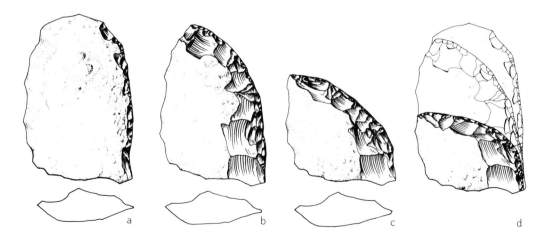

the mind of the prehistoric flint-knapper. The end result of Bordes' analysis of many hundreds of Middle Palaeolithic stone-tool assemblages was to show that the proportions of types and frequency of technological indexes combined to produce only five principal variants. His explanation for these was very straightforward. The five assemblages which recurred in time and place were five cultures belonging to five Neanderthal tribes. Their culture was fixed and knapped in stone. At a site like the Combe Grenal rock shelter, with no less than fifty-five Middle Palaeolithic layers and where all five types were present, Bordes explained this as local replacement of one group by another as they

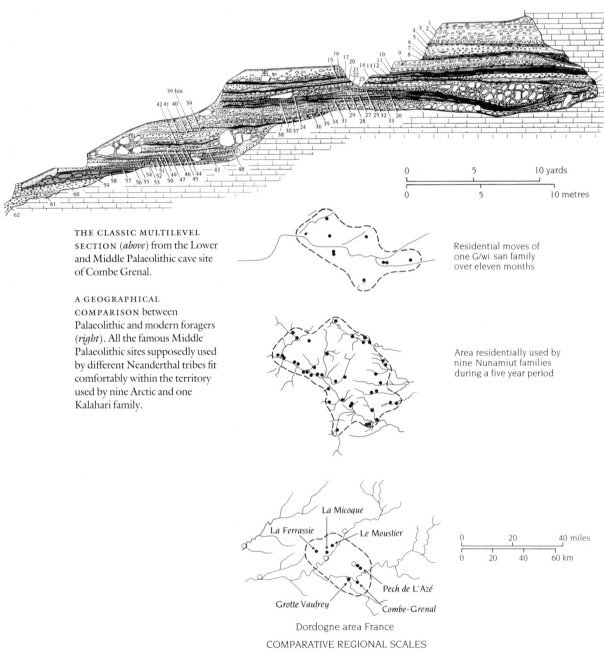

THE CLASSIC MULTILEVEL
SECTION (*above*) from the Lower
and Middle Palaeolithic cave site
of Combe Grenal.

Residential moves of
one G/wi san family
over eleven months

A GEOGRAPHICAL
COMPARISON between
Palaeolithic and modern foragers
(*right*). All the famous Middle
Palaeolithic sites supposedly used
by different Neanderthal tribes fit
comfortably within the territory
used by nine Arctic and one
Kalahari family.

Area residentially used by
nine Nunamiut families
during a five year period

Dordogne area France
COMPARATIVE REGIONAL SCALES

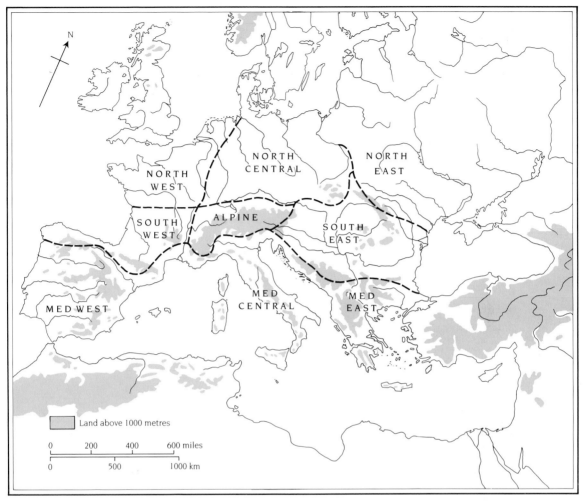

A REGIONAL MAP TO STUDY PALAEOLITHIC EUROPE. The divisions mark important differences in the structure of food resources and the impact of environmental conditions on survival. These differences are reflected in how the archaeology of the nine regions is structured.

competed for such desirable residences within Palaeolithic Périgord—no doubt to his mind as the British today are buying up holiday homes in the same area.

The second direction complements the dynamic view of stone technology. First proposed by the Binfords, in 1966, it points out that these caves and rock shelters formed part of a settlement system. In contrast to Bordes' view that people lived in the same rock shelter for many thousands of years, the alternative emphasized that in order to survive people would be mobile; moving around their landscapes according to a seasonal round and exploiting resources as they became available. Different seasons and the activities of either getting or processing the raw materials of existence required different tool-kits. Therefore, any variability in the proportions of tool types between assemblages was related to the organization of survival on a regional scale rather than to the expression of five cultural identities. These ideas have since been modified. Tool-kits, as Dibble's work shows, are impossible to determine archaeologically since what today is a 'screwdriver' might tomorrow become a 'chisel'. Furthermore settlement systems among mobile peoples are infinitely more complex than originally thought. But the importance of the Binfords' analysis was to expand the scale and suggest links between sites as a result of adaptation to conditions and the organization of survival.

Gamble has recently proposed that Palaeolithic evidence can be examined profitably against a regional framework where, irrespective of the climate, ecological conditions are expected to have varied in consistent ways between the major regions of Europe. These conditions are dependent on latitude, longitude, and relief. When combined, these affect the key plant and animal resources by controlling their distribution and abundance. As a result, the human use of these regions would have varied considerably and this would show up in a comparison of the quantities of archaeological materials and the nature of the history of settlement they contain. This is an important conceptual development. Rather than studying progress through the refinement and elaboration of technology we have turned instead to investigating past survival behaviour through measureable variation in the materials which have been preserved.

Ice Age Climate

This regional model predicts different human adaptations as a response to harsher conditions with more scattered resources in the northern and eastern parts of the Continent. But to complete the picture we must assess the climatic conditions of the Ice Ages.

We have now had to abandon the four-Ice-Age system of the Pleistocene which was created in 1909 by Penck and Brückner following their work in the Alpine foreland. For many years this provided a relative chronology, but has now been found to be grossly inadequate. The current pattern of the Ice Ages comes not from the evidence of moraines, raised shorelines, and changes to river terraces but from the sediments on the bottom of the ocean floors. These muds and oozes contain the tiny skeletons of marine creatures, foraminifera, which, when alive, lived at its surface. Their skeletons consist of calcium carbonate which absorbs the oxygen isotopes present in sea water. This sponge effect has proved very useful in establishing the number and rhythms of the Ice Ages. Two of these isotopes are critical, oxygen 16 and oxygen 18. As their numbers indicate, the latter is heavier than the former and the ratio between the two, preserved in the tiny skeletons, is the key to unlocking Pleistocene chronology.

During a glacial phase when ice sheets built up on Scandinavia and the British Isles and extended out from the Alps, Carpathians, and Pyrenees, moisture was drawn from the oceans. With this moisture went the lighter oxygen 16 leaving the world's oceans isotopically heavy and much smaller in size. When they dropped to their minimum, *c.*150 metres below present sea level, the continental shelves were exposed, linking England to France and producing a large plain in the northern Adriatic. During glacial retreat and

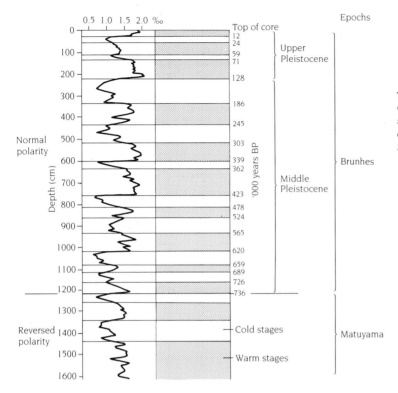

THE LAST 730 000 YEARS
OF ICE AGE CLIMATE
as reconstructed in deep sea
core V28-238 taken from the
Solomon Plateau.

the appearance of warmer, interglacial conditions the increased ocean size led to a lighter isotopic count. The procedure is to core these muds and then measure the ratio of oxygen 16 to oxygen 18 at intervals in the core. This produces a saw-toothed curve against depth and shows the sharp alternation between large and small ocean conditions. What this demonstrates is the number of repeated interglacial/glacial cycles in a *continuous* sequence which has now replaced the observations from the *discontinuous* terrestrial sequences pieced together from various sources.

But the major breakthrough with the deep-sea Ice Age record is that it can be dated. At 1200 centimetres in core V28–238 the sediments show a magnetic reversal when the North and South Poles adopted their present positions. Before this they were completely reversed. This major reversal at the Brunhes/Matuyama boundary has been measured in rocks which can be dated by isotopic decay methods. In this instance it is the measurement of the decay between potassium and argon (K/Ar). This has fixed the Brunhes/Matuyama boundary at 730,000 BP and this is regarded as the division between the Lower and Middle Pleistocene. It is a significant date for European prehistory as we shall see later. With this date fixed in the core the ages of each cycle can be determined by dividing depth into age. In the past 730,000 years there have been eight full cycles. Initially these were completed every 70,000 years but after 450,000 BP they extend to a span of 100,000 for the last four. This change in the duration of cycles may have had a major impact on settlement in the Continent as we shall see below.

A division of the last cycle for which the details about landscape, fauna, and flora are

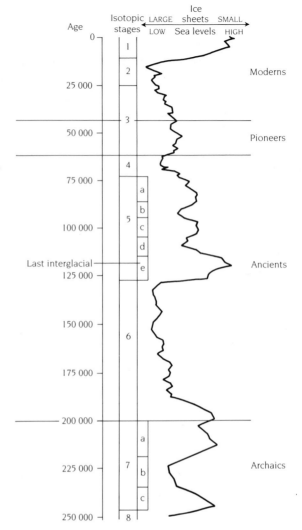

A CLIMATIC CLOSE-UP of the last 250,000 years. The isotope curve shows how rapid were the transitions between low and high sea level — large and small ice caps. Moreover, the last interglacial, sub-stage 5e, was short lived and very extreme when compared to stage 7, the penultimate warm period.

best known shows that the extremes of warm, forested interglacial and arid, cold full glacials were comparatively short-lived. Using this as a rough guide to the earlier cycles, it is apparent that over half of the Ice Ages were neither full glacials nor interglacials, but instead somewhere in between. Neither were these intermediary conditions static, but show a major division between broken woodland conditions followed by very open, unglaciated landscapes. In both situations herds of animals would have thrived but particularly in the open-steppe tundra conditions where herds of bison, horse, red deer, and reindeer were supplemented by mammoths and woolly rhinos, giant deer, musk ox, aurochs, and in some areas ibex, chamois, and wild sheep. The social carnivores were also abundant, lion, hyena, and wolf, while huge cave bears, their increased size an adaptation to cold stress, were also common.

In the last interglacial which began 130,000 years ago, the fauna was rather different to these more open conditions when large herds and animal biomass was at its peak.

Instead we find the woodland rhino, straight-tusked elephant, hippopotamus, and fallow deer. At the glacial maximum, the last of which occurred only 18,000 years ago, resources were thinned out in more continental regions and especially in central Europe, pinched between the two ice sheets. The upshot of these discoveries about the Pleistocene world is that we can no longer regard cold as the major limiting factor for the earliest colonizers. The more complicated picture of changing landscapes is matched by a pattern of population ebb and flow between the regions in the Continent. Coping with ever more seasonal environments emerges as the key to hominid colonization and, in particular, the settlement of northern latitudes in Europe.

Earliest Arrivals

There is still some uncertainty about when the Continent was peopled. There are claims from the Mediterranean for artefacts dated to between one and 1.8 million years old. The main claims are for a few worked pieces from the cave of Vallonnet near Nice and Chillac in the Auvergne. The material is typologically similar to stone tools from Olduvai Gorge in east Africa and consists of very simple flakes and some pebbles flaked into chopping tools. There are no hominid remains with the material. The age of these tools is important since in recent years the appearance of *Homo erectus* outside sub-Saharan Africa, in China, and in south-east Asia has been dated to little more than a million years. The very early claims for artefacts in Europe do not fit with this pattern. One thing is quite certain. Assigning great antiquity to such pebble tools and simple flakes on the basis of their primitive appearance is no longer possible, as such simple notions of technological progress will no longer stand up. A good reason for abandoning such schemes rests on the appearance of the Acheulean with its handaxes and cleavers made on large flakes in east Africa and dated by absolute methods to 1.6 million years old. If these are regarded as an advanced technology when compared to the Oldowan pebble tools and flakes, then how can such later material, when found in Europe, be assigned an age on the basis of what it looks like?

In Europe the earliest site with abundant artefacts and cross-checked by different methods of absolute dating is Isernia La Pineta south-east of Rome. The importance of this site rests in its stratigraphic position just beneath a volcanic horizon in which the Brunhes/Matuyama boundary occurs and which K/Ar dating confirms as at least 730,000 years old. The site is rich in fauna with the remains of extinct bison accumulated in stream deposits. Among these bones are many thousand flakes and pebble tools. Unfortunately there are no hominid (early humans) remains, but on this evidence, which compares with the chronological estimates from China and Java, the pioneers from sub-Saharan Africa possibly reached the Mediterranean province between one million and 700,000 years ago. The lakeside site of Soleihac in the Auvergne, where a few flakes and pebble tools have been dated to 900,000 years old, provides a glimpse of the fragmentary evidence that such pioneers would have left.

Within the broader picture of human evolution this seems very recent. The earliest hominids are found in east Africa about four million years ago while genetic evidence points to the separation of chimpanzee and hominids about a million years before these oldest fossil finds. Between two and four million years ago there is a radiation of hominid species and genera in eastern and southern Africa. This includes the southern 'ape-men', the australopithecines, who come in gracile, robust, and super robust forms. The widespread *Australopithecus africanus* is currently thought to be the founding fossil in the gracile lineage which leads to *Homo habilis* (handy person) and through to *Homo erectus* by at least 1.6 million years. The robust 'ape-men' persist until about 1.3 or perhaps even 1.1 million years ago. What is interesting to note, however, is that *Homo erectus*, with a brain whose size falls among the lower values for modern humans, a stature that in a recently discovered 12-year-old skeleton from Kenya was 1.68 metres tall, and an apparently advanced stone technology in the shape of the Acheulean, should take half a million years to move out of sub-Saharan Africa and into the rest of the Old World. This strongly suggests that long legs, large heads, and technology had little to do with initiating dispersal.

One argument currently favoured to explain this timing comes from the deep-sea record. A number of palaeontologists have pointed to bursts in fossil species, both animal and hominid, which coincides with the onset of the first weak glaciations 2.5 million years ago. A further pulse, but this time linked to dispersal, is thought to correlate with the change in duration of climatic cycles at about 900,000 BP. These arguments give the environment a very deterministic role in forcing the pace of speciation and dispersal. However, before such correlation can be considered as causal it is necessary to demonstrate a time-lag between the onset of new climatic rhythms and conditions and a biological or behavioural response.

In contrast to such determinism, the alternative view, bearing in mind the long period of waiting by *Homo erectus* in sub-Saharan Africa, is that they created their own opportunities. In other words they remained below the Sahara because of some behavioural and social constraints which made passage through such resource-poor areas north of the tropical savannahs impossible. Rather than wait for a friendly environment to open a window and allow them through, it is more plausible to argue that *they* opened the window by evolving new behavioural strategies. This undoubtedly involved expanding the scale of society which involved intensity of interaction, communication, and the ability to cope with extended periods of absence, by individuals and small groups, from the main group in increasingly seasonal environments.

Fossil Hominids

The earliest human presence in Europe is known from artefacts alone. Our first, dated, glimpse of what they looked like is some 300,000 years later than the abundant chipped stones found at Isernia in the Mediterranean province. By this time the earliest Europeans had, as Stringer has shown, undergone their own regional evolution. As a result the fossils from Steinheim and Bilzingsleben in Germany, Petralona in Greece, and Swanscombe in England are no longer regarded as *Homo erectus* but instead a new species, *Homo sapiens*. The main developments have been not only in the increased size of the head, and with it brain size, but also in the reduction of the teeth. The skulls, however, are still massively robust with thick cranial walls and sturdy brow ridges. Very little is known about the rest of the skeleton. As a result these fossil skulls, which are not well dated but range in age from 400,000 to 200,000 BP are grouped as 'archaic' *Homo sapiens* to differentiate them from later developments in Europe and the earlier African populations of *Homo erectus* from which they are believed to derive. Only one specimen from Europe is generally thought to belong to *Homo erectus* and, according to some but unsupported by an absolute date, may be as much as 600,000 years old. This is the massive mandible from a gravel pit at Mauer, near Heidelberg, that was recovered in 1907.

This single find has always been enigmatic. H. G. Wells in *A Short History of the World* (1929) regarded this jaw-bone as:

One of the most tormenting objects in the world to our human curiosity. To see it is like looking through a defective glass into the past and catching just one blurred and tantalizing glimpse of this Thing, shambling through the bleak wilderness, clambering to avoid the sabre-toothed tiger, watching the woolly rhinoceros in the woods. Then before we can scrutinize the monster, he vanishes.

Here is the Yeti, the Alma, and the Bigfoot come to life. Alas, such imagination is as ill-founded as beliefs in Blemmyae, Hairy Wild Men, or the fantastic Piltdown fraud perpetrated just before the Great War and which produced a brainy Englishman to run beside the massive, tooth-grinding German from Mauer. But like Humpty-Dumpty, Piltdown eventually came crashing down in 1953 when J. S. Weiner, K. P. Oakley, and W. E. Le Gros Clark unmasked him as a crude forgery that planted bits of a medieval skull with the stained and filed-down jaw of an immature orang-utan. This means that for almost ninety years the Mauer jaw has been the oldest fossil in the European collection.

Compared with the wealth of fossil finds that have been made in cave and open sites in Africa during the last thirty years the earliest European evidence is meagre indeed. This situation only changes after 200,000 years ago when we see the development from these archaic *Homo sapiens* of the Continent's best-known fossil hominid *Homo sapiens neanderthalensis*. There is widespread agreement that the Neanderthals of Europe and the Near East were derived directly from the archaic Europeans of the Middle Pleistocene. Later archaic finds such as Arago in southern France and Pontnewydd in North Wales show, respectively, the evolution of the Neanderthal face and the thickening of tooth roots which is an ancestral trait found in later populations. But despite these changes the Neanderthals continue to have very robust skulls, now matched by skeletal evidence for massive musculature and very thick limb-bone shafts.

Larger skulls also mean bigger brains. These fall within the top end of the size range for modern humans at 1600 cubic centimetres. Part of this size may be explained by biological scaling to climatic factors since today it is common to find an increase in head size away from the Equator. Such variation is to be expected due to the effect of thermoregulatory mechanisms designed to reduce metabolic expenditure in regulating the temperature of such a costly organ as the brain. The long, low Neanderthal cranium is rounded off by what is known as an occipital bun while at the front end the jutting face sits beneath massive brow ridges and above a chinless jaw. The teeth were large as were the noses which would have acted to warm the air inhaled and so protect the brain. The number of Neanderthal finds are considerable. It is worth emphasizing that most of them fall this side of the last interglacial when preservation in caves and rock shelters in the south-western region were particularly good. Finding complete skeletons means that we can search for any reflections of lifestyle that carried through to the skeleton.

The Neanderthal skeleton is short and stocky. Males were on average 1.65 metres tall with big shoulders, while the females were ten centimetres shorter. The degree of sexual dimorphism was not as pronounced as among earlier hominids such as the Chinese *Homo erectus*. However, both sexes were very robust with characteristically short legs and long bodies, whereas among the later European populations of anatomically modern humans the females have a much more gracile anatomy. Using modern populations as a guide, these limb proportions are best explained as adaptations, developed over a long period of time, to cold stress. They may also have developed the capacity for prolonged fasting endurance where large body size, as indicated by the robust skeleton, was one way of coping with seasonality and in particular the dearth of food resources in winter. Living on fat reserves accumulated during seasons of plenty might have been one way to overcome shortages in the absence of fully developed systems of food storage.

In this respect it would be more accurate to interpret the Neanderthal face and physique as adapted to fluctuations in seasonality, which would have occurred with increasing latitude and longitude in Europe, rather than to the cold alone. Indeed the Neanderthals appear well adapted to a range of climatic conditions. A study of their settlement histories in parts of the northern and southern provinces reveals, however, that their populations ebbed and flowed as the climatic cycles ran their repetitive course. As a result we can see that they were absent during the warmest phases of the last interglacial in some areas of western Europe and were not present during the extreme glacial troughs. Conditions ranged from cold to arid and temperate, and where the controlling factors seem to have been either the balance between forest and the open grassland conditions which produced large mixed herds of locally dense abundant animal resources or the thinning of such resources due to the disruption to vegetation that intense periglacial regimes bring.

Their skeletons bear the marks of a strenuous and robust lifestyle as they procured their food in such habitats. Trinkaus showed that among the Neanderthal skeletons from the Shanidar cave in Iraq there were several healed fractures on the shoulders and

STONE POINTS which were probably hafted. These could be made by either levallois or non-levallois techniques.

arms. Using this evidence Valerius Geist has portrayed the Neanderthals as hunting large animals at close quarters. This would have been achieved with short stabbing spears tipped with large, lethal, triangular stone points which would produce massive haemorrhaging in bison, horse, and deer when wielded with ferocious power in such confrontational encounters. He even suggests that the powerful grip of the large Neanderthal hand would allow them to cling to the long wool coats of the mammoth as they strove to kill it by keeping with their prey. While this interpretation is less convincing, Neanderthal skeletons do bear clear evidence of a bruising lifestyle, and one which is common to both males and females. The strong possibility emerges that both sexes fed themselves and that largely separate feeding economies were practised.

Questions for Early Humans

What else does the archaeological record tell us about these earliest Europeans? How did they use technology and material culture to survive and how similar or different was their behaviour from ours?

A necessary first step towards answering such questions depends on our control over the archaeological dimension of time in the organization and understanding of our evidence. The last section showed that several conclusions can be drawn from the anatomical evidence of the later European hominids which fall mostly this side of the last inter-glacial warm period. The chronological position of these finds in cave and open sites between 120,000 and 40,000 BP has depended upon major advances in dating burnt flint and sediments by thermoluminescence (TL) measurements. At the same time a preliminary chronology is emerging for the more widespread stone tool assemblages of the Middle Palaeolithic that extends back to about 250,000 BP and which includes some of the archaic *Homo sapiens*.

This improved chronology is beginning to show that during the immense period from 730,000 to 40,000 years ago there were considerable developments. This was not a time of stagnation although skulls and technology seem to change imperceptibly. The major chronological markers can be placed at 200,000 BP, by which time the Middle Palaeolithic is established, and after the last interglacial between 60,000 and 40,000 BP, when there is a distinct pioneer phase that in several, but not all, ways prefigures the Upper Palaeolithic that follows (Chapter 2).

Our problem is interpreting what these chipped stones and butchered animal bones signify in terms of past behaviour. Did earlier patterns of behaviour differ drastically from a modern pattern and if so, how? Just because they made stone tools is no sure guide to differences, since factors of preservation have interposed in the succeeding mil-lennia and the possibility remains that these early populations had the potential for tech-nological behaviour equivalent to that contained in the archaeology of the Upper Palaeolithic, and which most archaeologists agree is equivalent to any modern person, but they chose not to use it. This would not make them inferior or different in the sense that chimps are different to people, but instead *very* human in that they varied in essen-tial details as a result of local and regional histories and circumstances. Certainly these early populations were successful, as their long-term survival in the regions of Pleis-tocene Europe shows.

Resolving these questions from what initially looks like unpromising evidence is the task that faces the Palaeolithic archaeologist. The answer must be to concentrate less on the stones and bones as objects of comparison and points of discussion about relative levels of intelligence and potential and instead to devise a means of investigating how these ancient populations were organized. This type of behaviour which we might call social organization, or study as economic and subsistence strategies, is, of course, invis-ible to the archaeologist. Stones do not tell stories however hard they are squeezed or however accurately they are dated. The reconstruction of behaviour depends on putting the surviving evidence into a context where it can be interpreted. The way this is achieved is to use the archaeologist's second dimension of space.

Fossil Humans in Time and Space

Let us start at the small scale with the evidence for camp-sites in three periods which, for convenience, I will label Archaic, Ancient, and Pioneer.

730,000–200,000 BP	Archaic
	for example Swanscombe, Petralona, Steinheim, Arago
200,000–60,000 BP	Ancient (early Neanderthal)
	for example Pontnewydd, La Cotte, La Chaise
60,000–40,000 BP	Pioneer (late Neanderthal)
	for example Saint-Cesaire, Le Moustier, Molodova

The spatial arrangement of stones and bones in sediments contains a great deal of information about how sites were formed and the range and complexity of past behaviour. What we find when looking at the well-preserved sites of the Archaics, dated to the Middle Pleistocene, is the absence of the familiar features which make up a camp-site. These would include built hearths, post holes, indicating where the poles of a tent might have been pitched, and well-segregated areas of rubbish disposal for flint and animal bone. Across Europe at sites such as Vertesszollos in Hungary, Terra Amata in Mediterranean France, and Hoxne in England there is evidence for burning in the form of burnt flints and pieces of charcoal, but no conclusive evidence for fireplaces, huts, or the sort of zonation on a living surface which comes from people living in a place for any appreciable length of time. What these sites show instead is a fairly low density scatter of

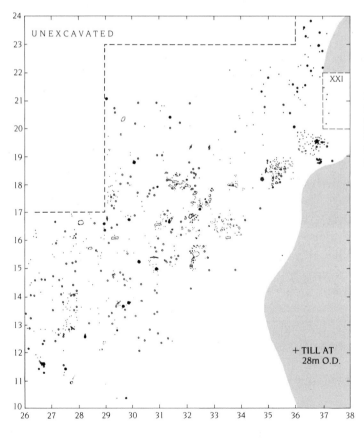

THE PLAN OF EXCAVATIONS AT HOXNE, SUFFOLK. This detailed plot of animal bone and stone material brings home the lack of sensible camp-site structure in well preserved sites of this period.

chipped stone, animal bones—some of which are butchered and carry stone tool marks on their surfaces—and other debris including unworked stone nodules. It is often very difficult to see any clear structure or patterning in the distribution of this material to the extent that we are often left asking—where were the camps?

Neither can poor preservation be blamed in this case. Although these sites are very old they are also some of the best preserved in the whole of European prehistory. At Swanscombe in the Thames Valley or Boxgrove on the marine sands in front of a former sea cliff on the southern coast of England the preservation is exceptional. The fine-grained sediments have not moved the material more than a few millimetres at most as shown at Swanscombe where the footprints of extinct deer are preserved in the same soft silts which contain stone tools. Compared with the post-depositional destruction of Neolithic to Iron Age living sites where most of our evidence comes from secondary contexts such as pits and ditches where it was shovelled as refuse, these Middle Pleistocene sites and landscapes are a cause for astonishment and a remarkable archaeological resource. If tents and huts had been built, then the chances of finding their sub-surface features in the form of post holes, scoops, and even pits would be very good indeed.

On most of these sites all that can be said from the remains lying in primary context, exactly where they were abandonned between 500,000 and 200,000 years ago, is that flint and other stone was knapped and animal carcasses dismembered, partitioned, and the flesh cut off and marrow extracted. The current interest in technology, referred to earlier, has led to considerable investment in piecing together the sequence of nodule reduction and artefact manufacture. This lithic jigsaw puzzle has revealed a number of individual knapping events and, where excavations have been large enough, has shown that different stages in the sequence from selecting a nodule to roughing it out, producing flakes, finishing a bifacial tool such as a handaxe, using the flakes and discarding them took place within a relatively short distance. The preliminary indications at the site of Boxgrove are that flint nodules were grubbed from the collapsed sea cliff and some initial trimming undertaken. Then the lumps were carried some 500 metres away where they were further reduced, used, and dropped. The implications are that the entire sequence was measured in minutes, at most hours, and that longer-term planning, which involved stone tools, was not a regular part of the Archaics behaviour. It is worth pointing out that these raw materials are always local. Distances of up to 10 to 15 kilometres are normal and would be within a daily foraging range. In one exceptional case a distance of 100 kilometres is known. Hence in areas which lack fine-grained rocks such as flint or chert, with their predictable patterns of fracture and razor-sharp edges, we find coarse-grained basalts and quartzites being used.

Among the Ancients at the end of the Middle Pleistocene this pattern begins to change. There is now evidence for the transport of raw materials over much larger distances from their known geological sources. The absolute distances are still not vast, the largest are usually between 80 and 150 kilometres with an absolute maximum of 300 kilometres, but clearly beyond the hours and minutes picture that is suggested by the evidence from the Archaic sites. Moreover, there are developments in the structure of their living spaces. At the site of Lazaret, a cave near Nice, there are two well-defined hearths near the side wall of the cave, just in from the entrance. Surrounding them are the expected patterns of debris including chips of stone and animal bone. These form

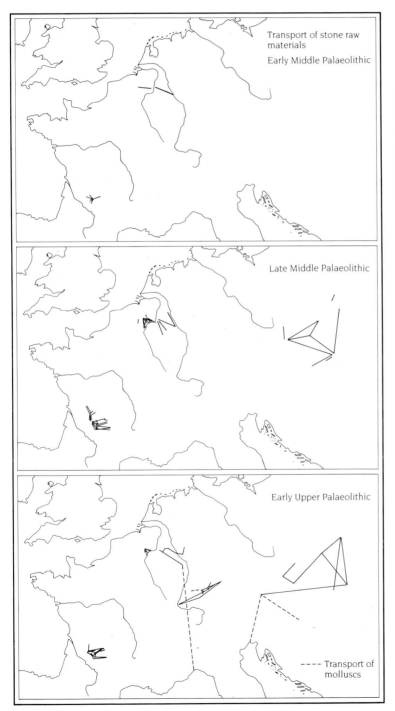

Transport of stone raw materials

Early Middle Palaeolithic

Late Middle Palaeolithic

Early Upper Palaeolithic

- - - - Transport of molluscs

THE GEOGRAPHY OF EARLY EXCHANGE. The big difference in the distances over which raw materials were obtained comes with the Upper Palaeolithic when shells, amber, and other items were widely traded.

semicircular rings, and, although the excavator favoured an interpretation of a skin tent inside the cave with its walls acting to make these patterns as material was swept into its corners, it is more probable that people sitting in a ring around the hearth were responsible.

Such patterning is not present in all rock shelters. At level VIII in the Grotte Vaufrey, located in the Dordogne and dated to older than 120,000 BP, the lack of hearths produced a very unstructured pattern to the distribution of the flint material. A detailed analysis by Simek has shown that the combinations of tool types and their spatial distributions point to unspecific and spatially unfocused behaviour. From this evidence it is difficult to argue that they went to that location with a particular activity in mind, such as hunting horses. Instead they made do with what they found when they arrived.

The structure of most of the sites from this period is still reminiscent of the previous period. The greater use, or perhaps preservation, of materials in caves and rock shelters does on occasion provide evidence that, as with the evidence from the transport of raw materials, the system of land use and the scale of existence has been extended. The gran-

ONE OF THE BONE PILES AT LA COTTE. The mammoth skulls are clearly visible in front of the rock wall.

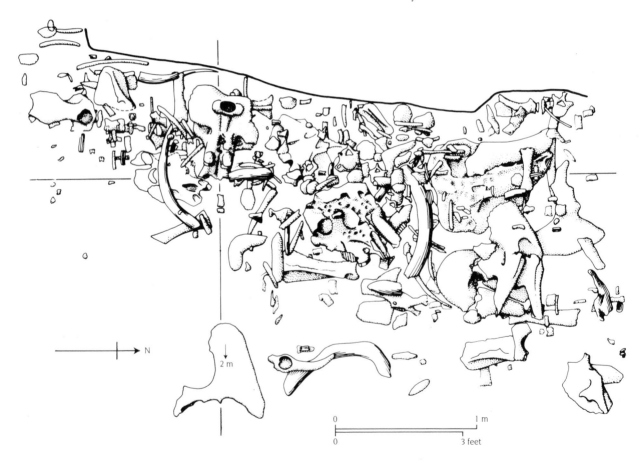

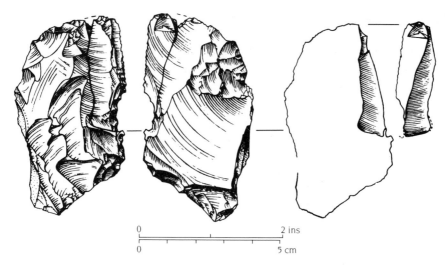

0   2 ins

0   5 cm

AN EXAMPLE OF A REFITTED FLAKE, struck to re-sharpen an edge, from the site of La Cotte.

ite headland site of La Cotte, on the island of Jersey, provides a good example of the new evidence. This fissure site contains a huge series of deposits, the oldest dates of which are provided by thermoluminescence on burnt flint at 238,000 ± 35,000 BP. This puts levels C and D in the site into an interglacial, stage 7, and on my scheme towards the end of the Archaic phase. At this time there is nothing exceptional about either the stone industries or the patterning of materials in the sediments. The changes come in the next isotope stage 6 at about 180,000 years ago when in levels 3 and 6 two remarkable piles of animal bones have been recovered from beneath the protective overhang. These consist of selected parts of mammoth and woolly rhino. Mammoth skulls, shoulder blades, and pelves are the most common elements, although the composition of the two piles differs quite considerably. It is thought that they were dragged into position after small herds of these animals had been stampeded over the cliff of which the site forms a part. When occupied at this time by the Ancients, La Cotte would have been a prominent landmark on the dry plain which joined Jersey and mainland France.

While the significance of these bone stacks is still unclear—if they were stores then why abandon them?—their presence, which indicates accumulation and positioning of bulky items, stands in marked contrast to the archaeological record of the Archaics. It is also the case that in the period after 200,000 BP there is growing evidence for more elaborate reduction sequences involving stone resources. On the one hand there is the increased use of Levallois, or prepared nodule, technique. On the other is the greater economy of raw material as is also well shown in the later levels at La Cotte. A detailed study of the flake artefacts reveals resharpening behaviour where a long sharpening flake has been carefully struck so as to rejuvenate the working edge. It is most common in those assemblages at the site dated to isotope stage 6 and is increasingly employed as the quantities of flint to coarser stones declines. Such economizing behaviour is combined at this time with the first 'biographies' of stone tools as outlined earlier.

HOUSE OR WIND-BREAK? This structure from Molodova I in the Ukraine represents some of the earliest evidence for artificial construction.

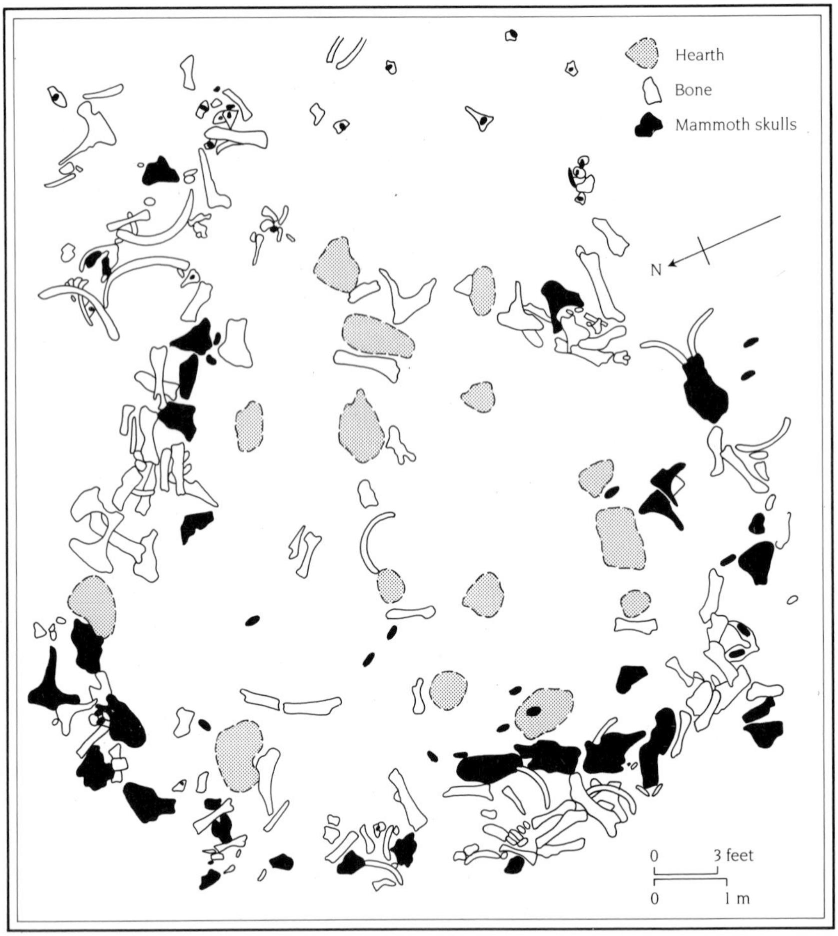

Legend:
- Hearth
- Bone
- Mammoth skulls

0   3 feet

0   1 m

The final, Pioneer stage, is so named because camp-sites are now more commonly found with the sorts of feature *we* expect to see on them, and many other aspects of technology bear close comparison with what we shall find accompanying the moderns in the Upper Palaeolithic (Chapter 2). Well-built hearths are known from open sites such as Vilas Ruivas in Portugal and Molodova I along the Ukrainian bank of the Dnestr. At this site a series of large surfaces have been excavated to reveal arrangements of mammoth skulls and reindeer antlers that many regard as evidence for hut foundations. A more parsimonious explanation is that they acted as windbreaks with fires lit right up against, or sometimes in, the walls. Whatever the final verdict the structure and patterning on this site represents a quantum leap over the earlier evidence from living space.

As might be expected the wider scale of contact and movement as indicated by the transfer of raw materials is again greatly increased. These distances are much larger in the continental regions than in the less seasonally extreme climates of the early last glacial of the south-western region. Such differences can be understood in the context of a regional model which stresses the impact of resources on the relative scale of behaviour.

In this instance we are seeing the greater movements in search of game in some parts of the Continent and such pointers are a productive way of examining Palaeolithic data.

Another way to use this regional framework is to examine the number and size of occupations. When the Ancient and Pioneer collections of artefacts are compared between the caves and rock shelters of the northern and southern regions, some striking differences can be seen. In the north, collections are seldom large and multiple levels in a single site are also rare. In order to recover enough artefacts to conduct a typological study (100 is usually considered the minimum requirement), huge quantities of deposit have to be dug. This only emphasizes, as excavations in Kents Cavern in England, the Bockstein in southern Germany, or the Kulna cave in the Moravian karst of former Czechoslovakia confirm, that the presence of Archaics, Ancients, and Pioneers was small and infrequent. This should come as no surprise since these northern and more continental regions were those most affected by the constant turn of the interglacial/glacial climate as it went through a full cycle every 70,000 then 100,000 years. This would principally have affected the density of prey species through such controls as depth of winter snow cover over forage, alternative woodland foods for the grazing species at such times, and the effect during interglacials of forest cover on the abundance and herd forming of key species such as bison, horse, and red deer.

By contrast the cave and rock-shelter sites from the southern and Mediterranean regions have a rather different story to tell. The examples of sites with multiple horizons, each containing more than the magic number of 100 retouched artefacts, are more numerous. At the same time there are more assemblages with very large numbers of retouched implements and chipped stone generally. Finally, the size of excavation trenches is often smaller, which reflects the greater density of artefacts deposited in the sediments. However, when these figures are compared, the conclusion must be that over the long periods of time represented by the Pleistocene cycles these southern and Mediterranean regions were occupied almost continuously.

The 'biography' of individual stone tools is very marked in the Pioneer period although this is a feature that generally characterizes all the Mousterian assemblages this side of the last interglacial. One novel feature among the retouched artefacts is the appearance of highly distinctive projectile points. Previously these had been restricted to such ubiquitous forms as the triangular Levallois point or the retouched Mousterian point. In many parts of Europe are found small collections of well-made points known collectively as leaf points, since they are often pointed at both ends, and date between 60,000 and 40,000 BP. These leaf points were made with knapping techniques that are entirely Middle Palaeolithic in character, and the other flakes and retouched pieces in the assemblages can be classified as Mousterian. Some of the best-known examples come from the caves at Mauern and Ursprung in the limestone uplands of southern Germany. These are small collections which, in the case of Mauern, numbers only 113 retouched pieces from level F of which, as Allsworth-Jones shows, almost half are leaf points. Similar forms are restricted both geographically and chronologically.

A BOUT-COUPÉ HANDAXE OR KNIFE from the late Middle Palaeolithic.

The interest in these distinctive artefacts is that broadly similar forms, dating immediately after 40,000 BP, are found in some of the earliest Upper Palaeolithic industries such as Kents Cavern, Jerzmanowice in southern Poland, and Istallöskö in the Bükk mountains of Hungary. The blade rather than flake industries and the presence of worked bone tools, also in the form of projectile points, suggest a transition from one set of technological traditions to another. These collections are also small in size and regionally distinctive, which suggest that the organization behind their production and use may also have been similar.

Distinctive artefacts, known after the geological term *type fossil* is a notable feature of the Upper Palaeolithic. Whatever the reason for their stylized shapes, it is the case that a whole range of such type fossil artefacts were produced at particular times and places so that archaeologists can be fairly sure about assigning undated and even unprovenanced material to a specific culture such as the Aurignacian or Magdalenian. What is noticeable is that in the Archaic and Ancient periods this is not possible. There were distinctive artefacts such as the twenty-one types of handaxe or the various forms of flint side-scrapers. But these could have been made almost anywhere in Europe and at any time. The site of Grotte Vaufrey provides a good example of an assemblage of typical Mousterian in level VIII which, before absolute dating by TL, would have been dated to this side of the last interglacial. Now we know it belongs to stage 6 and lies well on the other side. For a long time the Middle Palaeolithic appearance of some of the retouched end-scrapers from High Lodge in East Anglia caused considerable debate about the age of this site, which has now been established as at least 500,000 BP.

Neither are the leaf points the only distinctive artefacts in the Pioneer period. Mellars originally made the case against Bordes and the Binfords (see above) that in key sequences such as Combe Grenal it was possible to see chronological ordering for some of Bordes' five variants. In particular, the Mousterian of Acheulean Tradition (MTA), which comes in two forms, A and B, was always late in the stratified sequences. The earlier MTA A is characterized by triangular handaxes, which live up to their name by being stylish and intensively worked (Chapter 2). Of all handaxe shapes these are the only ones which follow the type fossil rule and can be tied down to time and place with some degree of accuracy.

There are then elements in the Pioneer phase which foreshadow the behaviour governing the use and manufacture of stone technology in the Upper Palaeolithic. This does not make it modern behaviour as we shall see below but does distinguish it from the earlier Archaic and Ancient periods. These in turn are differentiated from each other by the consistent groupings, first identified by Bordes, among assemblages of flake tools. This occurs after 200,000 BP and has been described by Bosinski as a threshold in the development of cultural behaviour. It is seen more widely in China as well as in Africa where Clark has established, as a feature of the Middle Stone Age, the appearance of recurrent groupings of artefacts in assemblages from sites, and sometimes with a regional focus. Coinciding with this change in the patterning of archaeological materials in Europe is a noticeable increase in range. Bosinski also points out that it is at this time that the inhospitable North European Plain is first settled at sites such as Salzgitter Ledenstedt, southeast of Hanover. It is worth noting, however, that this use of the plain lies towards its western arm. We have to wait until the Pioneer phase when the plains of the Ukraine and Russia were first used and settled, as at the site of Khotylevo on the Desna near Briansk. Here large bifacially worked points made with the Levallois technique are abundant. It is also the case that the finds of leaf points in the uplands of the northern regions and in the south-eastern region may well represent an extension of range into areas which would previously have been abandoned as resources dwindled towards the middle of the glacial cycle. It is for these reasons that I have dubbed this interesting period between 60,000 and 40,000 BP the Pioneer phase.

This same period also sees the recovery of a large sample of complete Neanderthal skeletons. The dating for many of them is poor but at Le Moustier, where the two skeletons are thought to have come from level J, a recent TL date has been obtained for this level of 40,300 ± 2600 BP. The Kebara skeleton from Israel has been dated by a series of TL samples to the other end of the Pioneer phase at 60,000 BP. The indications are that the complete skeletons from La Ferrassie and Chapelle-aux-Saints may date to the same chronological bracket. Even if they are older, they are unlikely to exceed 70,000 BP, as Mellars has recently argued.

The possibility that these complete skeletons are a feature of the Pioneer phase is most intriguing when we come to try and solve the question of whether they were burials or just fortunate preservation events. The evidence in favour of intentional burial is that the bodies were laid in scooped-out pits and on occasion protected by stones and other large objects. The position of the bodies varies greatly so that no clear pattern can be seen, but at La Ferrassie the presence of more than one individual in the same layer is noteworthy as the graves respect each other. Claims of grave goods in the form of tools and joints of meat are very difficult to evaluate since such items occur as part of the general archaeological signature of the layers in which these skeletons are found. Flowers laid on the corpses were once claimed from work on the pollen grains in the earth surrounding the Shanidar Neanderthals in Iraq. However, caution is necessary here since it has recently been demonstrated by Turner that pollen grains can percolate through sediments and so may be much later additions.

The argument against intentionality rests on the age of the burials—if the TL dates continue to support a relatively narrow and late time window—and where they were found. Most of the Neanderthal skeletons in Europe come from the south-western region. The only exceptions are the Spy caves in Belgium and the original find in 1856 in a cave in the Neander valley near Düsseldorf. Elsewhere Neanderthal remains are literally bits and pieces at sites such as the Hortus and Krapina caves in the Mediteranean province. The intense fragmentation has led, over the years, to suggestions of cannibalism, but it seems more likely that carnivores such as hyena, leopard, and wolf, which also used such caves, were responsible for the damage to skulls and long bones. What is noticeable about the south-western region is that the bones of these carnivores are generally very rare in the rock shelters where complete Neanderthal skeletons have been dug up. Perhaps the milder, oceanic climates did not require the use of rock shelters as carnivore dens and so the increased chance of destruction once the humans had moved on was much less. This same pattern of few carnivore remains is also found in the caves of Israel and the Near East, the other areas where complete skeletons have been found.

The final observation which diminishes the argument for intentional burial comes from the fact that no complete skeletons have ever been found in an open site from either the Ancient or the Pioneer phases. As we shall see in the next chapter Upper Palaeolithic burials after 40,000 BP do occur in open settlements as at Sunghir, near Moscow, and Dolní Věstonice, close to Brno in former Czechoslovakia. These occur at times when carnivores were abundant in the open plains environments, but the arrangements to dispose of the dead in well-dug graves was sufficient to thwart disturbance.

Weighing the evidence, my conclusion is that the Neanderthal burials have survived through good fortune in protected locations in climatically favoured regions which kept carnivores and corpses apart long enough for the latter to survive as intact skeletons. The intention of those who did the burying is unknown but was probably concerned more with carcass disposal than with the numinous qualities of preservation, afterlife, spiritual and symbolic motivation that is frequently claimed for these interesting finds. Of course, the similarity of complete Neanderthal bodies in shallow graves to Western burial traditions led to the alternative conclusion by those who first found them in the early years of this century. It must be remembered, however, that these same archaeologists also looked outside the Western tradition to affirm, on the basis of the stone tools being used, that the Australian Aborigine was the equivalent, if not the living representative, of people like the Neanderthals who made the European Mousterian. Support for the Palaeolithic examples as burials was not, however, sought from the many and highly varied means by which the Native Australians intentionally dispose of their dead.

These burials introduce us to the whole issue of symbolic behaviour and whether this existed prior to modern behaviour in the Upper Palaeolithic. The Pioneer phase is the appropriate span over which to discuss it since, as I have shown, there are undoubtedly aspects such as widespread transfers of raw materials and type fossil artefacts that foreshadow the full Upper Palaeolithic to come. If symbolic behaviour can also be demonstrated then this sets the tone for this phase as one of transition towards the later developments of the Upper Palaeolithic rather than of replacement by a system of behaviour imposed from outside the European peninsula.

Apart from the burials, the claims for symbolic behaviour rest on three lines of evidence—organic artefacts, arrangements of bones in open sites and caves, and the style of stone tools. The first group consists of an heterogenous collection of material from sites scattered in time and space. Pierced reindeer toe bones, scratched ribs, shells, and a polished lamellar from a mammoth tooth from the Hungarian site of Tata. In nearly all cases, as Davidson and Noble have argued, these can be explained by more parsimonious means as puncture marks by carnivore teeth or the action of roots on buried bone. Butchery with stone tools can also leave traces which seem more regular than they should, but which does not mean that the marks were symbolically informed. The polished Tata tooth emerges as the only item which merits serious consideration, and mainly because no obvious functional explanation presents itself. It is a unique object and therefore difficult to interpret. But does one object make the case for behaviour organized according to a set of symbolic principles which constituted and guided action?

The arrangements of bones can be more easily discounted. In the Archaics site of Torralba, in Spain, lines of elephant long bones were once thought to have been deliberately placed, but a re-examination of their rolled condition suggests that river action produced their 'intentional' alignment. The oft-quoted 'chests' of cave-bear skulls in several high-altitude Swiss caves must also be ignored. The frequent use of deep caves as hibernation dens produced many weird and wonderful arrangements as the bears swept aside the skeletons of previous occupiers who had died in their sleep. While the filling of specially built stone cupboards by Neanderthals, with the skulls of cave bears, is one of the most endearing and enduring images of Palaeolithic life there is unfortunately no supportable evidence for the claims. This is one 'cupboard' that when opened was bare.

The last line of evidence comes from the stone tools and their restricted and often repeated shapes. Oakley pointed out that some handaxes contain fossil shells within the flint and these were carefully knapped around. Respect for such pretty objects and sticking to a lithic pattern book are sometimes put forward as powerful arguments for the existence of symbolically communicated ideas. However, it must be remembered that we are primates with those special qualities of imitation where learning occurs through copying what we can see rather than being instructed by what we are told. Such aping behaviour would be entirely sufficient to manufacture stone tools while existing artefacts left in caves and at stopping places along the rivers would serve as ready-made blueprints for action. The idea championed by Bordes that each of his five Neanderthal tribes made its allotted proportions of stone tools because they wished to express in stone their ethnic identity seems an unnecessary transposition into the past of the English rolled umbrella and the French baguette.

Consequently, as Davidson and Noble have argued these early hominids in Europe are best regarded as tool-assisted hominids. This is in contrast to culture-using humans and where material culture in the form of tools, dress, ornaments, houses, and so on is a vehicle for the codification and transmission of information. This has meaning only in that it operates according to a symbolically approved set of rules. I do not see this ability existing before the Upper Palaeolithic since in the Pioneer phase it is unaccompanied by items such as drilled fox teeth, perforated shells, and other objects for display either as body ornaments or sewn on to clothing. Such items are universal after 40,000 BP and mark what Pfeiffer once referred to as the creative explosion. It is at this time that artefacts assume, through their stylistic treatment, that passive voice of additional information. It is also the moment when art objects in the form of figurines, carved pendants, and schematized scratches on limestone blocks also appear (Chapter 2).

How did they survive?

I have come full circle from the myths and stories which surround the peopling of Europe. It is now time to provide a general interpretation of these 700,000 years and to examine what light can be shed on the earlier question of whether their behaviour differed from ours. It is clear to me that the answer must be *yes* for the entire time span although there are significant changes during the period. The question of language ability and intellect will be discussed in the next chapter, but the conclusion that these earlier populations did not possess fully articulate speech, or language as we know it, is now widely held. This absence would obviously make a critical difference to society and sur-

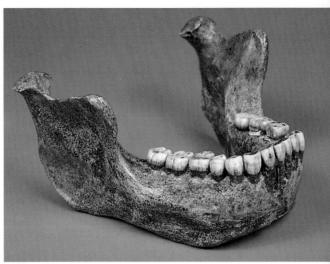

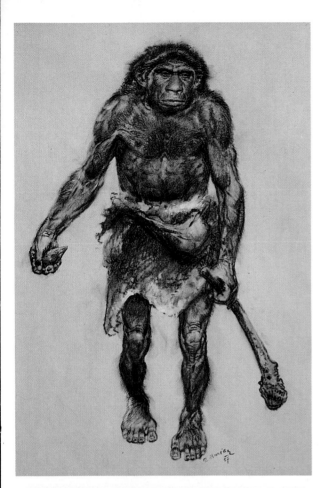

THE JAW OF *Homo erectus* from Heidelberg (*above*).

A TEXTBOOK RECONSTRUCTION of a Neanderthal (*left*) drawn by Burian. It owes more to the medieval imagination of wild men in wild places than archaeological discovery.

THE NEANDERTHAL SKULL from the Grotta Guattari, one of the Circeo caves, in Italy (*below*). The discovery of this isolated skull on the surface of a cave floor, whose entrance had been sealed by a landslip in prehistory, led to theories of skull cults, cannibalism, and Neanderthal ritual. The presence of hyenas in the cave suggests another non-human reason to account for the presence of the skull. Note the heavy brow ridges and cheek bones, low forehead, and occipital bun—all hallmarks of Neanderthals.

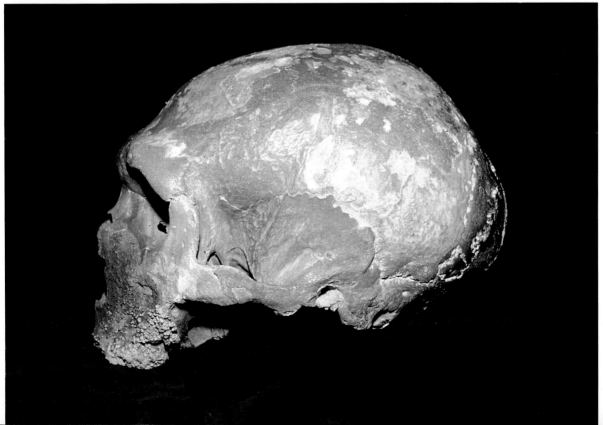

vival. But how would this help to explain the form of the archaeological record I have described above?

Language is culture with all its associated symbolism and manipulation of time in the form of memory and forward projection. As Whallon has cogently argued, the addition of past and future tenses transforms what humans can do in terms of social organization and has repercussions for subsistence and settlement. Understanding the effect a lack of language would have is not just a matter of saying that no art would be produced or that flint tools would be highly repetitive. It has to be understood in terms of those invisible systems of organization which are the archaeologist's goal to measure and unravel.

This might open the door to a very subjective interpretation of the past as we try to 'think primitive' and imagine what life would be like without one of the key elements of modern humanity. We need to avoid the sort of approach favoured by H. G. Wells who, in 1921, sealed the popular fate of the Neanderthalers in a famous short story: 'The grisly folk we cannot begin to understand. We cannot conceive in our different minds the strange ideas that chased one another through those queerly shaped brains. As well might we try to dream and feel as a gorilla dreams and feels.' In order to avoid such pitfalls I will concentrate on issues of survival and the extension of population into new habitats.

The Archaics could only live in Europe if they solved the problems of a seasonal environment. It has traditionally been supposed that this was achieved by hunting large animals, and there are many artists' reconstructions showing mammoths being stoned to death and bison being beaten to their knees with clubs. It is undoubtedly the case that animals were killed by Archaics, although such feats of machismo against three-tonne pachyderms and one-tonne charging bulls are unlikely. But making this simple demonstration misses an important point. Hunting, whether it is qualified as big, medium, or small game, individual or communal, is not just about killing animals. That may be the most visible part and the one which attracts the most prestige in any society which hunts, and it is, of course, not without its skills and dangers. But killing animals is generally the easy part, whether it is by spear or bow, by trap or a drive over a cliff. The difficult part lies instead in the organization of personnel so that they are in the right place at the right time and with the right gear to ensure a better-than-average chance of success. The stakes increase rapidly in seasonal environments as animal movements and numbers become less predictable and hence their availability is restricted. Under such conditions 'better than average' is not good enough. Nothing must be left to chance since the penalties for failure are starvation and extinction. Nor, in the seasonal environments of Pleistocene Europe would there be abundant alternative supplies of plant foods, nuts, and berries to tide over a missed hunting opportunity or an unexpectedly lean season.

Hunters and gatherers today, and Palaeolithic societies after 40,000 BP, take such

THE CAVE SITE OF LA COTTE in the granite headland of St Brelade's Bay on the island of Jersey. Were mammoths and rhinos intentionally driven over these cliffs 180,000 years ago?

environmental challenges in their stride. Indeed they act as a hone on behaviour applying selection for particular behavioural solutions. Consequently technology is improved to reduce the chances of failure and social networks are established through
alliance, kinship, visiting, and feasting so that should the unthinkable happen there is a
regional insurance policy that can be cashed by calling on neighbours in times of need.
Such forms of social storage are commonplace and are one means of survival in harsh
environments. But at the same time as spreading the risk across the region, the local
solution, when faced by marked seasonal conditions, is to set up stores of food at one
time of the year and budget them to cover subsistence over the lean times. Such
behaviour produces a very distinctive type of regional archaeology since it is ultimately
at this scale that survival takes place. One of the signatures would be the persistence of
settlement, albeit in reduced form, as seasonality increased and resources were diminished during the roll of the Pleistocene climate cycles. The ebb and flow of both Archaic
and Ancient populations from regions, particularly in the northern province, is clear
evidence that such 'hunting' behaviour had not yet developed. The lack of art and the
rarity of hafted, multi-component light tools, which are common in the Upper Palaeolithic, support this conclusion.

But this still leaves the problem of how they made a living. Among the Archaics there
were undoubtedly variations in the scale of their social groupings throughout the eight
European regions which were occupied (the north-east was not). One way to answer the
question is to concentrate on the limiting factor that would have faced them in several of
these regions. This would have been what to eat during the winter period when the environment shut down for five to six months and the large herds of bison, horse and reindeer, and red deer migrated long distances in order to solve the same problem. The
distances would often be too great for Archaics to follow and there are no artefacts suggesting they possessed even rudimentary transportation. Storage would be the answer
although there is no evidence for the social networks which guide and articulate such
behaviour and the planning it implies. A possible alternative is that instead of hunting,
they foraged for carcasses which had either died as winter mortalities or been brought
down by carnivores before they, too, left the area at winter's onset. The large numbers of
prey in these mid-latitude grasslands would ensure a supply scattered over the landscape, but concentrated along rivers and around lakes since it is here that most mortalities occur. Frozen carcasses of mammoths and other Pleistocene fauna from Siberia and
the Yukon indicate the effectiveness of a natural deep-freeze even though when thawed
the meat and marrow would not meet our requirements of filet mignon. But we are discussing survival here rather than gourmet dinners. Finding whole, or partial, carcasses
which still contained important fat reserves would act as a basic resource in getting
through those winter months until the large herds returned from their winter feeding
grounds, and the Archaics could make a living killing and scavenging among them.
Scavenging for megafauna with their huge reserves of fat and marrow makes more sense
than trying to stone them to death.

This winter strategy would be aided by two factors. Large group size would be important at this time of the year in order to have enough people to find some carcasses in the local landscape. Local groups might have numbered as many as 150 who would have been in regular contact and from which most marriage partners were drawn. This social grouping which involved considerable mobility would not require elaborate methods of remembering who people were since absence from the main group for many weeks or even months on a specialized hunting trip did not occur. These face-to-face societies did not need to rely on either language or the symbolical content of artefacts to organize their interpersonal relations. Selection for planning and the use of the past and present in the form of memory and negotiation were therefore linked to the development of relationships within society rather than simply the circumstances of obtaining food and the means of survival in a hostile environment.

The second factor was fire. This not only kept people warm, but also helped defrost the carcasses. This was assisted by taking the carcasses, where possible, into caves where the temperature could be more easily raised. Searching would require a minimal technology and what at one time of the year saw service as a spear—as recovered from the Clacton channel—could at other times have been a probe or chisel used for searching beneath snow banks and through ice. These two aspects would open up an economic niche unavailable to other carnivores. Such a strategy to get them through the winter would depend on many factors in the environment, for example, the abundance of herd animals, the distance they moved, the temperature, and the depth of snow cover. As these fluctuated year by year and over the much longer-term cycles of the Pleistocene, so some areas rather than others within a region would become attractive for settlement as the risks of failing to meet the dietary needs of the group from local resources varied. A feature of this strategy was that few skills and little knowledge were needed to make it work. It could be readily transferred from one valley to another as circumstances dictated. Over many thousands of years, however, some valleys would be better placed than others and it is for this reason that we find variation in the numbers of artefacts contained in their gravels and other sediments.

This solution to survival may well have developed in Europe after a considerable period of occupation. The earliest date for Archaics in the northern province is *c.*500,000 at sites such as Westbury, Boxgrove, High Lodge, and Stranska Skala in former Czechoslovakia. This is possibly associated with the shift at this time towards those longer Pleistocene cycles of 100,000 years' duration, which would have increased the

THE TIP OF A SIMPLE, but possibly multi-purpose, yew artifact from Clacton.

amount of open dry/cold conditions when herd size was greatest, and this strategy most advantageous. It suggests that the older occupations in the Mediterranean province depended more on following herds over the shorter distances they would migrate seasonally as well as making more use of plant resources.

In the same way the Ancients, as already mentioned, increased their range by moving on to parts of the North European Plain. The larger distances involved in their raw material transfers point to expanded territories over which groups now foraged and which was a consequence of living in such open environments. Foraging continued to play its part as indicated perhaps by the use of La Cotte as a convenient defrosting chamber. At the same time studies, by Chase, of the faunal remains from sites such as Combe Grenal and La Quina show clearly that horse and bison were being killed directly. While meat storage is difficult to prove, I strongly suspect that some local stores were now being created from such events, although the evidence for social networks that underpinned such behaviour on a regional scale is still lacking. Close-quarter killing seems very possible and the most likely scenario is that both males and females were engaged in such activities. Individuals were largely responsible for their own provisioning, and consequently both sexes exhibited strength and robust features as an anatomical sign of how they insured their security.

The clearest indication of how limited were the survival strategies of the Ancients comes, however, from their regional history of settlement. During the last interglacial in England they are absent, even though this large island was then stocked with straight-tusked elephants, narrow-nosed rhinoceros, hippopotami, bison, and the products of the oak-mixed forests. But for all the megafauna and warm climate the 'big game hunters' are missing. The reason can only be that they never survived by such means, and the large size but low density of animals in temperate forest settings was something their social organization could not cope with since it required greater planning to reduce risk and almost certainly longer periods of group fissioning. This would have shattered for ever the face-to-face basis of their society. A similar situation is reported by Hoffecker for the Russian plain during the last interglacial, when population is also absent.

It is also the case that during the early part of the last cold period, when there was considerable glacial activity during stage 4, the population, which had reappeared in the plains' environments of the north-east and north-central regions during the temperate stages 5 a–d, disappeared. This would be a reaction to the thinning of resources to a point where survival became unviable under existing strategies. By contrast, the Upper Palaeolithic response to such climatic deterioration, whether warm or cold, would have been to intensify. The Ancients responded by quitting the regions altogether.

The only sign that they did otherwise comes from the Pioneer phase. The evidence from those numerically small leaf-point sites indicates the emergence of wider social networks in the inhospitable environments of northern, central, and eastern Europe. The networks supporting the hunters in the hills allowed groups to fission more often and for longer periods of time and could only result from increased ability for planning and social organization. As a result, the geographical areas they covered grew considerably and the need for regulating contact and dealing with strangers would be greater. Whether such developments were due to the appearance elsewhere in Europe of another pattern of behaviour, which had already dealt with these problems and so prompted the Pioneers into realizing their latent potential, or whether such artefacts and the systems of organization they betoken were made entirely by newcomers operating from novel behavioural premises is something to be examined in the next chapter.

Note In discussing periods prior to 10,000 years ago it is customary to quote radiocarbon dates not in 'BC' terms, but rather as dates 'Before Present' (i.e. 'BP'), using AD 1950 as the conventional 'present'. Consequently, 'BP' is employed for dates in the first three chapters of this book, after which 'BC' takes over. It has recently become clear that radiocarbon dates before 10,000 years ago may in fact be significant underestimates of *time* ages—probably by around 1,000 years at *c*.10,000 BP, and perhaps by as much as 3,000 years at 30,000 BP. (All dates in these chapters are based on radiocarbon measurements.) For more on the subject of dating, see M. J. Aitken, *Science-Based Dating in Archaeology* (London: Longmans, 1990).

2

The Upper Palaeolithic Revolution

PAUL MELLARS

Introduction

THE period centred on *c*.40,000–35,000 BP marks one of the critical turning points in European prehistory. Over this period we can identify two major developments which, in one form or another, were clearly fundamental to the whole of the subsequent development of European society. On the one hand, this period witnessed the effective replacement (in the very broad sense of the word) of the earlier 'archaic' or Neanderthal populations of Europe by populations which are, in most biological respects, apparently identical to ourselves. And over essentially the same time span we can identify a wide range of changes in the archaeological records of human behaviour which collectively define the transition from the Middle to the Upper Palaeolithic periods. The question of how far these two developments may have been related in some kind of direct, cause-and-effect way, poses a range of intriguing issues which will be discussed at a later point in this chapter. Collectively, however, there can be no doubt that this combination of changes in both the 'biological' and 'behavioural' records of human development represents one of the most significant events in the prehistory of Europe since the initial colonization of the Continent almost one million years ago.

The Environmental Background

Arguably, one of the most striking features of this transition is that it took place not during one of the more dramatic episodes of climatic and environmental change within the long time span of the Pleistocene period, but during a period of relative climatic stability. At this time, the more northerly and central parts of Europe were in the grip of a harsh glacial climate, probably not too different from that experienced at the present day in areas such as southern Alaska or northern Scandinavia. Estimates suggest that during the most severe parts of the glaciation (around 18,000 to 20,000 years ago) average year-round temperatures in most areas of Europe are likely to have fallen to at least 10 °C below present-day levels. At this time extremely cold currents of sea water flowing from the polar regions of the north Atlantic would have extended down the Atlantic coast of Europe to the latitude of northern Spain. A combination of these ocean currents and

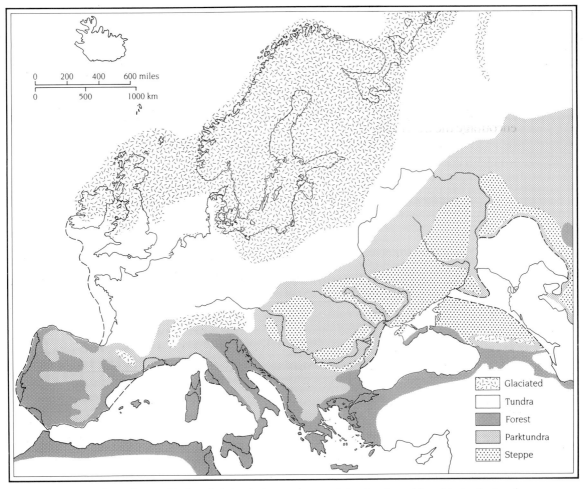

MAP OF EUROPE at the maximum of the last glaciation (*c*.18,000–20,000 BP) showing the position of the ice sheets and major vegetation zones. The dashed coastline reflects the lower sea level conditions of the last glaciation.

associated wind circulation patterns would have created a more continental pattern of climate in most areas of Europe than at the present day, leading to greater contrasts in temperature between the summer and winter months. Even if some of the summers in glacial Europe may have enjoyed temperatures not too dramatically different from those of today, the winters would have been bitterly cold, with local temperatures that could easily fall to below –10 °C for weeks at a time. Heavy snowfall would have been an inevitable feature of these long glacial winters, posing major obstacles to the mobility of the human groups during the colder months of the year. Under the impact of these conditions, the glaciers expanded rapidly from the principal mountainous regions of Europe (i.e. from the Scandinavian mountains, the Scottish highlands and, to a more limited degree, from the Alps and Pyrenees) spreading ice sheets over large areas of northern and central Europe, extending from the latitude of the English midlands to the southern foothills of the Alps.

The living conditions of human groups occupying the periglacial environments of Europe would, therefore, have been far from comfortable in a climatic sense (at least during the winter months) but nevertheless afforded some crucial compensations in certain other respects. The most direct effect of these glacial conditions was to eliminate significant tree growth from all except the most southerly zones of Europe, and to encourage the development of vast areas of open landscape, dominated by rich growths of grasses, mosses, and other herbaceous plants. Even if heavy snowfall may have impeded the movements and hunting activities of the human groups during the winter half of the year, the human populations would not have had to contend with the dense, impenetrable forest of the kind which clearly posed such a major obstacle to the activities of later, Mesolithic communities, during the earliest stages of the postglacial era (see Chapter 3).

From an economic point of view, the effect of these open, treeless conditions was even more profound. The extremely rich and productive tundra and steppe-like environments which extended over large areas of eastern, central, and western Europe provided, in many ways, ideal conditions for numerous species of cold-adapted herd animals, such as the reindeer, wild horse, and steppe bison, as well as the larger 'pachyderm' species such as mammoth and woolly rhinoceros. To envisage these steppe and tundra-like landscapes of last-glacial Europe as a kind of Serengeti game park would no doubt be an exaggeration, but not necessarily on an over-imaginative scale. Certainly, many of these species are known to have formed large, roaming herds (amounting in some cases probably to several hundreds if not thousands of animals), which followed more or less regular migration trails between summer and winter pastures, at regular and largely predictable periods of the year. There can be no doubt that the Upper Palaeolithic communities of Europe were keenly aware of these seasonal migrations and (as discussed below) frequently located their settlements directly astride these migration trails in order to anticipate and intercept the movement of the animal herds. Under the impact of these highly productive environments it would seem that Upper Palaeolithic communities in some of the more ecologically favourable regions of Europe (such as south-western France, the Cantabrian coast, and the loess-covered plains of Austria, former Czechoslovakia, and southern Russia) may well have attained overall population densities which were perhaps not far below those of some of the earliest agricultural communities in the same regions.

One further direct consequence of glacial conditions was a substantial lowering of sea levels. From estimates of the total extent and thickness of the ice sheets it can be calculated that world-wide sea levels must have dropped by at least 100 metres at the time of the maximum of the last glaciation, around 18,000 BP. Similar estimates can be made from studies of the oxygen-isotope record of sea-water conditions (clearly reflected in the skeletons of foraminifera and other marine organisms preserved in deep-sea sediments), which suggest that corresponding quantities of isotopically 'light' sea water (i.e. water composed of the isotopically lighter oxygen 16 as opposed to the heavier oxygen

18) must have been removed from the oceans at the time of the glacial maximum. All of this, of course, would have had a significant effect on the coastal geography of Europe. In most regions of Europe this led simply to an expansion in the extent of the coastal plains — usually by not more than perhaps 20–50 kilometres beyond their present limits. In some other regions of very shallow seas, however, the results were much more dramatic. The most significant effects were experienced in northern Europe, where the effects of the maximal lowering of sea level would have exposed large areas of both the English Channel and the North Sea basin as dry land, and effectively integrated Britain with the main land mass of Europe. It was not until well after the end of the Ice Age that the final insulation of Britain from the European mainland took place, probably in the region of 6,000–8,000 years ago. For much of this period, no doubt, most of the northern fringes of Europe (including Britain) would have been far too bleak and inhospitable for any kind of permanent or even semi-permanent occupation by hunting groups. Nevertheless, it is clear that during one or two brief, warmer 'interstadial' episodes, Upper Palaeolithic groups did extend to southern Britain, as, for example, during the period of the 'Arcy' interstadial at around 30,000 BP, and certainly during the closing stages of the glaciation around 12,000–13,000 BP. As we shall see, these brief incursions leave no doubt that Upper Palaeolithic communities were well equipped to exploit these brief 'windows' of ecological opportunity, when temporary improvements in climate made this kind of territorial expansion possible.

The Nature of the Transition

Whatever significance one may eventually attach to the complex of behavioural changes which marked the emergence of fully Upper Palaeolithic communities in Europe, there can be no doubt as to the scale of these changes, nor to some of the striking ways in which these behavioural shifts are reflected in many different aspects of the archaeological evidence. The problem of how these behavioural changes originated, and how far they may have been associated with the dispersal of new human populations from regions beyond the European continent, will be taken up in the following section. Before embarking on these highly contentious issues, however, it is important to have a clear idea of exactly what patterns we can recognize in the archaeological evidence, and what significance these patterns may have for understanding some of the underlying changes in human technological, economic, and social organization. Reduced to their simplest terms, the changes can perhaps be summarized as follows.

First, we can identify certain basic changes in the patterns of stone tool production — changes which, in one form or another, have always been seen as the principal diagnostic features for differentiating between the Upper Palaeolithic and the preceding Lower and Middle Palaeolithic stages. In reality, these changes are not quite as clear-cut as some of the earlier textbook discussions have suggested. Even if earlier, pre-Upper Palaeolithic communities relied mainly on the use of various Levallois and related techniques

the face of the core is trimmed to shape in order to control the form and size of the intended flake. The preparatory flaking is directed from the periphery of the core towards the centre. The residual core is shaped rather like a tortoise, with one face plane and the other domed.

for the production of fairly broad, relatively heavy flakes, it is now clear that in at least some contexts Middle Palaeolithic groups had developed surprisingly sophisticated techniques for the production of much thinner, more elongated, and highly regular forms of 'blades'—i.e. slender, tapering flakes produced from specially prepared conical or barrel-shaped cores. The most striking feature of the Upper Palaeolithic lies in the sudden *proliferation* of these blade forms, which now effectively dominate stone tool production—at least in areas where local supplies of flint and other stone were of sufficient quality to allow these rather demanding flaking techniques to be applied. Several potential explanations for this shift have been suggested, ranging from the simple need to achieve greater economy in the use of local raw material supplies, to the demands of new patterns of stone tool production (such as, for example, the large-scale hafting of knife blades, scraping tools, or projectile points) which put a new premium on the production of more elongated and regular forms of flake blanks. Whatever the explanation, there can be no doubt that the production of these blade forms suddenly took on a new prominence over wide areas of Eurasia, on a very different scale from that documented during the earlier stages of the Palaeolithic sequence.

Arguably the most significant shifts in stone tool production can be seen in the much greater dynamism and innovation shown by Upper Palaeolithic communities in creating a much wider and more diverse *range* of tool forms than those produced during the earlier periods. From the start of the Upper Palaeolithic sequence one can document the appearance of many new forms of stone tools ranging from the emergence of new forms of skin-scraping tools (the so-called 'end-scrapers') and tools designed specifically for working bone and antler materials (notably, the gouge or chisel-like 'burins' or 'gravers') to a remarkable diversity of knives, piercing tools, and (most strikingly) various forms of tips of spears or other hunting weapons. Much of this increased diversity of stone tool production no doubt reflects a substantial increase in the range of other, related, technologies which almost certainly emerged during the earliest stages of the Upper Palaeolithic—for example, the more elaborate shaping of bone and antler, greater use of wooden artefacts, more elaborate forms of skin clothing, and new forms of hunting technology. But it seems equally clear that not *all* of the documented changes and diversification in the production of stone tools can be explained in these simple economic or functional terms. Several authors have recently argued that many Upper Palaeolithic tools seem to reflect a degree of investment in the shaping of tools to a relatively high degree of standardization and a clearly preconceived form, which seems to go beyond anything as yet documented clearly in the earlier periods. It is as though the *shapes* of stone tools were now taking on some kind of more explicit symbolic significance, which in one way or another had some clear meaning to the human groups

EXAMPLES OF NEW 'TYPE FOSSIL' FORMS, mostly manufactured from elongated blades, characteristic of the earlier stages of the European Upper Palaeolithic. Nos. 3 and 12 are 'end scrapers'; nos. 2, 7, 9, and 14 are 'burins'; the remainder probably represent either missile heads or inserts of hafted knives.

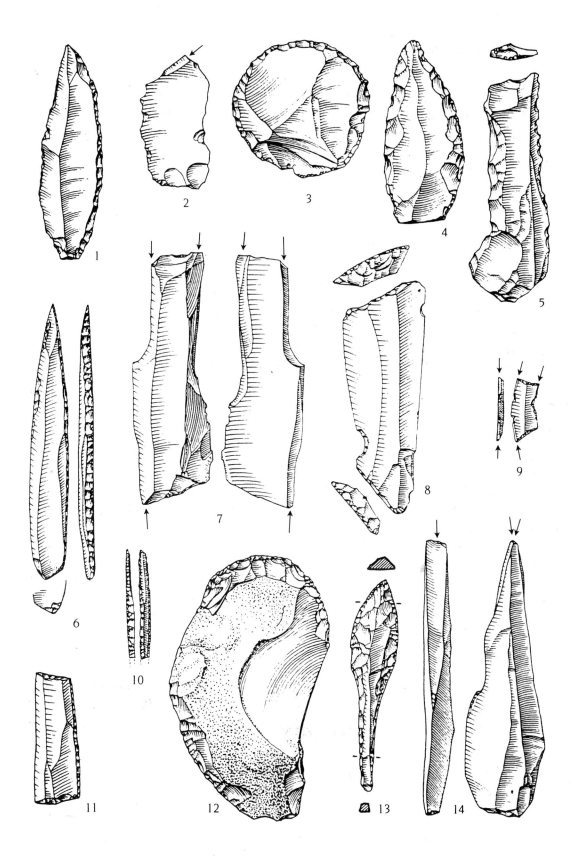

1   2   3   4   5

6   7   8   9

10   11   12   13   14

who produced them. One of the most intriguing possibilities (as discussed further below) is that this could reflect the emergence of much more highly structured forms of *language* among Upper Palaeolithic groups, which dictated that the shapes of stone tools (and no doubt most other artefacts) should conform to some clearly defined 'mental templates'—associated, presumably, with the linguistic and conceptual labels attached to the tools themselves. An alternative (though by no means mutually exclusive) interpretation is that the sharply varying forms of stone tools were now being used

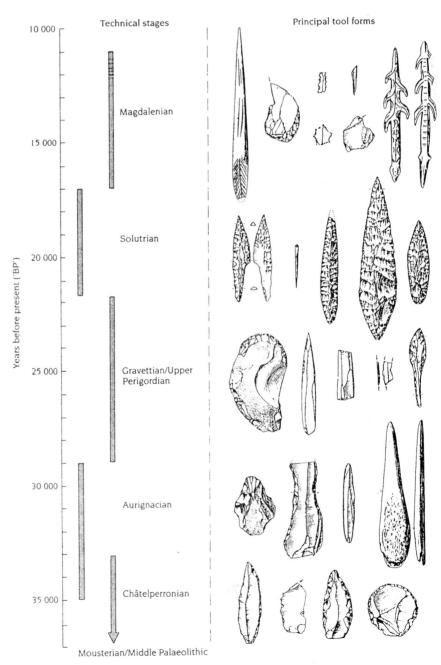

PRINCIPAL TECHNO-LOGICAL STAGES of the Upper Palaeolithic in Western Europe, with characteristic tool forms. The sequence shown here is based on the 'classic' region of south-western France, and differs in certain respects from that found in other regions of Europe.

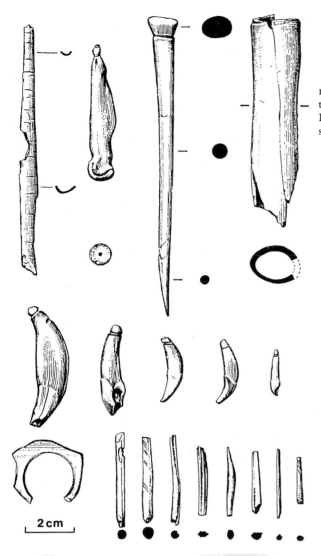

RANGE OF BONE IMPLEMENTS and animal-tooth pendants from the earliest Upper Palaeolithic ('Châtelperronian') levels at Arcy-sur-Cure (central France), c.33,000– 34,000 BP.

2 cm

in some way to symbolize the social or ethnic divisions of Upper Palaeolithic society. The latter interpretation has the attraction that it would help to explain the striking variations in the forms of stone tools encountered in the different regions of Europe and also (perhaps) the equally striking way in which the forms of the stone tools changed— rapidly and repeatedly—at many different points throughout the Upper Palaeolithic sequence (see Figure). Whatever the correct explanation, there can be no doubt that the whole spectrum of stone tool production in Upper Palaeolithic communities shows a degree of dynamism and creativity which contrasts sharply with the much more uniform and conservative patterns of technology documented throughout the long time ranges of the Lower and Middle Palaeolithic periods.

All of the features documented above in the production of stone tools by Upper Palaeolithic groups are reflected equally, if not more strikingly, in the production of

SEMI-STYLIZED FIGURE OF A
HORSE, (*above*) carved from mammoth ivory, from the early Upper Palaeolithic (Aurignacian) levels of the Vogelherd cave, south Germany, *c.*30,000–34,000 BP.

MALE HUMAN FIGURE WITH
LION'S HEAD (*right*), of mammoth ivory from the early Aurignacian levels in the Hohlenstein-Stadel cave, south Germany, *c.*30,000–34,000 BP.

bone, antler, and ivory artefacts. It is here, perhaps, that the real creativity and innovation of Upper Palaeolithic technology reveals itself most explicitly. As Clive Gamble has pointed out in the preceding chapter, there is no doubt that Middle Palaeolithic groups occasionally *utilized* fragments of bone and antler for a variety of purposes, and in some cases would seem to have modified the forms of these materials by, for example, localized grinding of the ends of naturally pointed bones to improve their use as awls, or occasional flaking of pieces of dense bone into simple imitations of stone side-scraper or even handaxe forms. What is conspicuously *lacking* in the Lower and Middle Palaeolithic is any clear appreciation that bone, antler, and ivory could be used as essentially 'plastic' materials, which could be carved and transformed into a wide variety of contrasting and closely controlled forms. This sudden burst of bone and ivory technology can be documented from the earliest stages of the Upper Palaeolithic sequence in Europe—most strikingly perhaps in the wide variety of awls, pins, bone tubes, bone rings, and so on recovered from the Châtelperronian levels (*c.*33,000–34,000 BP) at Arcy-sur-Cure in central France, and in the even more elaborate forms of bone and ivory spearheads and perforated antler 'batons' recovered from early Aurignacian sites. As in the case of stone tools, we can see the same emphasis on the high degree of standardization and clearly imposed form in the shaping of the tools, and the same remarkable tendency for the specific *shapes* of the bone and antler tools to change repeatedly at many points throughout the Upper Palaeolithic sequence. The whole technology of bone-, antler-, and ivoryworking reflects mastery of a wide range of new technological procedures; from the deep grooving of large fragments of bone and antler to produce workable splinters of raw material (the so-called 'groove and splinter' technique—almost certainly involving the use of flint burins or gravers) to the systematic sawing, grinding, and polishing of the worked surfaces to achieve neat, regular forms. Whatever significance one may attach to the few rather sparse traces of boneworking in Middle Palaeolithic contexts, this does seem to reflect some kind of almost quantum leap in the range and complexity of technological behaviour among Upper Palaeolithic groups.

The whole question of aesthetic or 'artistic' creativity in Upper Palaeolithic groups will be discussed more fully in a later section of this chapter. The main point to be emphasized here is that the remarkable proliferation of artistic or decorative behaviour is by no means confined to the later stages of the Upper Palaeolithic sequence, even if some of the more impressive manifestations of this creativity are reflected in sites (such as Lascaux in southern France, or Altamira in northern Spain) which date from around the time of the last glacial maximum, between *c.*20,000 and 15,000 BP. As Randall White, Joachim Hahn, and others have pointed out, some of the very earliest Upper Palaeolithic communities in both central and western Europe were clearly highly accomplished artists in every sense of the word. Explicit evidence for this can be seen, for example, in the remarkable range of animal statuettes carved from mammoth ivory recovered from the early Aurignacian levels at the Vogelherd cave in south Germany, the extraordinary lion-headed human figure from the nearby Hohlenstein-Stadel cave, and some of the highly stylized representations of animals and female 'vulvar' symbols from early Aurignacian sites in southern France. All of these artistic manifestations can now be traced back to at least 30,000–32,000 BP and perhaps in some cases to around 35,000 BP.

Even if less impressive in a strictly artistic sense, one should hardly attach less significance to the remarkable proliferation of what would seem to be clearly 'personal' decorative items recorded from a variety of early Upper Palaeolithic contexts throughout Europe. The majority of these consist of simple animal teeth (mainly those of fur-bearing species, such as fox, bear, and wolf) which were perforated for suspension by drilling through the root of the tooth. Well-documented examples of these perforated teeth have been recorded from levels dating back to at least 33,000–35,000 BP in both France and northern Spain, and perhaps as early as 40,000 BP at the Bacho Kiro cave in Bulgaria. The most striking proliferation of these personal ornaments, however, seems to occur slightly later in the Upper Palaeolithic sequence at around 30,000–34,000 BP. Thus Randall White has pointed out that in the earliest Aurignacian levels at the Abri Blanchard, La Souquette, and Abri Castanet in the Castelmerle valley of south-west France there is evidence for what would seem to be almost factories for the production of various forms of beads and pendants, involving complicated sequences of incising, grooving, and splitting of carefully shaped ivory rods, designed explicitly for the large-scale production of a variety of beads and pendant forms. In some cases these beads were apparently shaped and decorated in various ways to resemble particular species of marine shells. White estimates that the two sites of Abri Castanet and La Souquette alone have yielded over 500 of these deliberately manufactured pendants, while similar centres of production can apparently be identified in some of the Belgian and south German Aurignacian sites, at roughly the same date. As Gamble has pointed out in Chapter 1, convincing traces of artistic or decorative productions of this kind are at present virtually lacking from Lower and Middle Palaeolithic contexts in Europe—with the possible exception of the partially engraved cross on a nummulite fossil from Tata (Hungary)

IVORY BEAD, possibly decorated to resemble a sea shell, from the early Aurignacian levels in the La Souquette rock shelter (south-west France), *c*.32,000–34,000 BP.

and the apparently perforated bones of wolf and swan from the Bocksteinschmiede cave in south Germany.

The various lines of evidence discussed above leave no doubt that a wide range of essentially novel, and in some ways quite dramatic, patterns of behaviour can be identified over large areas of Europe during the earliest stages of the Upper Palaeolithic sequence—certainly well before 30,000 BP, and in some cases apparently as early as 38,000–40,000 BP. How far similar changes can be documented in some other spheres of human organization, such as the exploitation of animal populations, levels of human population density, or the internal social organization of the Upper Palaeolithic groups, will be taken up further in a later section. From the evidence cited above, however, it must be clear that the period of the conventional 'Middle to Upper Palaeolithic transition' does indeed reflect some kind of major watershed in cultural development, which is probably no less significant than that documented over the period of the so-called 'Neolithic revolution', or during the development of early metal-using communities. The critical question, of course, hinges on how these developments originated, and how they came to spread—apparently very rapidly—over such large areas of the European continent. As will be seen, this stands at present as one of the most central and controversial issues in understanding the overall development of human communities throughout the enormous time range of the Pleistocene period.

The Problem of Origins

The challenge of explaining the appearance of Upper Palaeolithic culture in Europe hinges at present on two central questions. First, what was the *demographic* context in which this transition took place? In other words, should we envisage the whole complex of behavioural and archaeological changes which define the Middle–Upper Palaeolithic transition as occurring, essentially, within the context of purely local, gradually developing populations, or does the transition reflect a much more dramatic process of population replacement, brought about by human groups who originated outside Europe, and effectively colonized the European continent over a relatively short span of time? And second, regardless of any issues of population replacement versus population continuity, how do we account for the specific *origins* of the various cultural and behavioural innovations which the archaeological record of the Upper Palaeolithic clearly reveals?

Both of these questions raise a number of highly controversial issues which, in one form or another, have largely dominated research in the European Palaeolithic throughout the greater part of the twentieth century. The majority of earlier workers (extending back to the time of Marcellin Boule in 1908) seem to have favoured the idea of some kind of major population replacement—at least for the more central and western parts of the European continent. Throughout the same period, however, there have been occasional voices of protest against this 'colonization' scenario, from anthropologists who would prefer to see the whole pattern of biological and cultural development as part of a gradual working out of evolutionary and behavioural processes within the context of purely local populations.

While the issue still remains subject to lively controversy, a number of recent discoveries seem to have shifted the balance of evidence fairly strongly towards the long-advocated view of population replacement. Three developments are especially relevant in this context. In the first place there has been the discovery of a highly typical Neanderthal skeleton at the site of Saint-Césaire in western France, which can be clearly dated on a variety of lines of evidence to a surprisingly recent date of around 35,000 BP. The archaeological associations of this skeleton pose some particularly intriguing questions, which will be discussed further below. What is now well established, however, is that this particular skeleton can hardly be more than (at most) 3–4,000 years earlier than discoveries of several other specimens of typically Cro-Magnon (i.e. *Homo sapiens sapiens*) skeletons which are to all appearances virtually identical to those of later Upper Palaeolithic and even modern European populations. Advocates of the population replacement hypothesis would argue that in this situation there was simply not enough *time* for typically Neanderthal populations (of the type represented at Saint-Césaire) to have evolved into fully 'modern' populations, within the time span available. A second crucial development has come from the recent dating of a range of essentially 'anatomically modern' skeletons from the sites of Skhul and Qafzeh in Israel to the remarkably early date of around 90,000–100,000 BP. These discoveries of course lie only shortly beyond the limits of Europe, and clearly demonstrate that in these adjacent areas of Eurasia, essentially modern populations (in an anatomical sense) had already emerged, apparently 50,000–60,000 years *before* their eventual appearance over most areas of Europe. Third, there have been the recent developments in molecular biology (particularly studies of the patterns of mitochondrial DNA in *modern* populations) which seem to point to the conclusion that all of the present-day populations throughout the world were most probably derived from a single common ancestor, within the span of the past 200,000 years. If the conclusions of the latter research are taken at face value, they would imply that the earlier 'archaic' populations of Europe (as represented by both the *Homo erectus* and later Neanderthal populations) made little if any genetic contribution to the Upper Palaeolithic and later populations of Europe.

As indicated above, all of these interpretations are currently subject to a great deal of debate, and have been challenged from several different aspects of the biological and skeletal evidence. My own impression, however, is that this scenario of some form of fairly rapid population dispersal would not only accord well with the overall pattern of the archaeological evidence from most regions of Europe, but would help to explain some of the more puzzling features of the evidence which have always been difficult to reconcile with the notion of a simple, essentially linear pattern of evolutionary development over the whole of the Middle to Upper Palaeolithic transition. One of the most striking features in this respect, for example, is the remarkable uniformity of the technology which has been documented for some of the earliest stages of the Upper Palae-

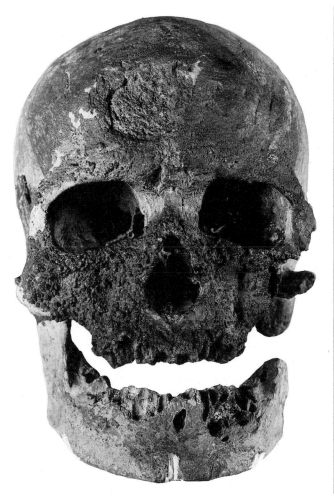 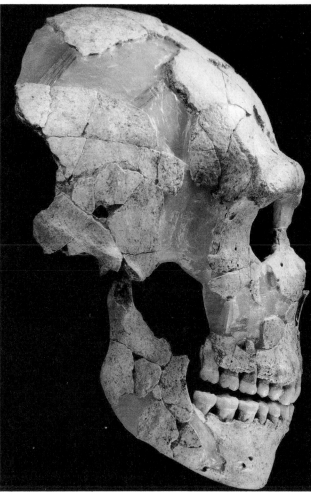

HUMAN SKULL (*left*) from the Cro-magnon rock shelter (south-west France), *c*.30,000 BP. The skull is more heavily built than that of modern Europeans, but is otherwise of typically modern anatomical form.

NEANDERTHAL-TYPE SKULL (*right*) from the Châtelperronian levels at Saint-Césaire (south-west France), *c*.35,000 BP. This is probably the latest Neanderthal skull known from Europe, and is probably contemporaneous with the earliest anatomically modern populations in the same region.

olithic sequence, in areas ranging from southern Israel to the north-west coast of Spain. This is the so-called Aurignacian phenomenon, characterized not only by a highly distinctive range of stone tool forms (various types of steep, nosed, and 'carinated' scrapers, small retouched bladelets, continuous, edge-retouched blades, and so on) but also by a range of equally characteristic bone and ivory tools (most notably the various forms of 'biconical' and 'split-base' bone points). The extraordinary uniformity of this technology, extending over a span of at least 4,000 kilometres, has always been difficult to explain by any pattern of purely local development in so many different regions of Eurasia, and would clearly accord much better with the notion of a rapid population disper-

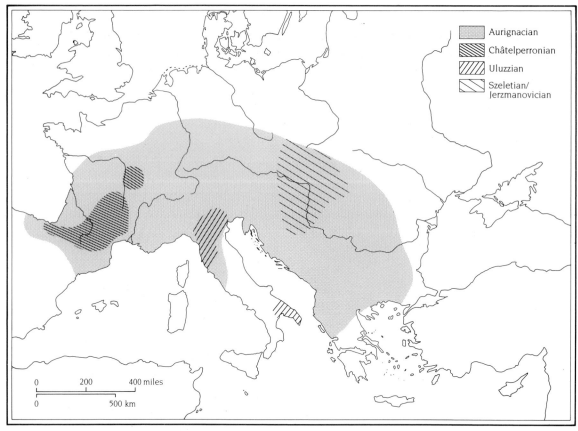

GEOGRAPHICAL DISTRIBUTION of the major varieties of early Upper Palaeolithic industries in Europe, *c*.30,000–40,000 BP. Whereas the Aurignacian is distributed over most of eastern, western and central Europe, the Châtelperronian, Uluzzian, and Szeletian industries are confined to much smaller areas, and probably represent survivals from the earlier Middle Palaeolithic/Neanderthal populations in the same regions.

sal throughout these regions. This notion is supported by the fact that Aurignacian industries seem invariably to be associated with the earliest well-documented occurrences of fully modern anatomical forms (as for example at Mladeč in former Czechoslovakia, Vogelherd in Germany, and Cro-Magnon and Les Rois in France) and also—equally if not more significantly—with the earliest clear-cut manifestations of fully Upper Palaeolithic technology in the form of elaborately shaped bone tools, the earliest well-documented occurrences of bone and tooth pendants, and the earliest manifestations of sophisticated, representational art. The fact that typically Aurignacian industries would seem to occur slightly earlier in south-eastern than in western Europe, would seem to add further support to this hypothesis. In any event, it has been clearly demonstrated from recent applications of radiocarbon accelerator dating that fully developed Aurignacian technologies were being produced in areas ranging from the northern Lebanon to the Cantabrian coast by at least 35,000–40,000 BP.

Perhaps one of the most intriguing issues raised by this scenario of rapid demographic dispersal of *Homo sapiens sapiens* populations centres on the nature of any contact or interaction between the expanding modern populations and the local archaic (i.e. Neanderthal) populations within the different regions of Europe. Zubrow has recently argued that even if we envisage some kind of direct competition between these two populations, this need not necessarily have taken any very dramatic form. On the basis of various simulation-modelling experiments of population dynamics, he has shown that a simple imbalance in relative birth-over-death ratios between the two populations could quite easily have led to a process of effective replacement of one population by the other, within a relatively short space of time—perhaps no more than a thousand years or so. If we envisage Neanderthal populations who were fairly thinly distributed over most areas of Europe, in relatively small, highly mobile social units, one could easily visualize a scenario of eventual population replacement without any notion of mass genocide, or even direct conflict between the two populations.

Interestingly, there may well be some direct evidence for this kind of coexistence, and at least partial interaction, of the two populations in certain specific features of the archaeological evidence. As discussed above, there is now clear evidence that some Neanderthal groups continued to survive in parts of western Europe until at least 35,000 BP, apparently alongside the earliest populations of anatomically modern form. The clearest evidence of this is provided by the very late dating of the typically Neanderthal skeleton from Saint-Césaire, and by a number of other sites where we can observe a direct interstratification of early Aurignacian industries with other industries of the so-called 'Châtelperronian' type (i.e. the type of industry associated with the Neanderthal skeleton at Saint-Césaire). There is now fairly general agreement that the Châtelperronian industry is, in fact, a direct product of the final Neanderthal populations in France, with a clear technological ancestry which can be traced back directly to the latest Mousterian industries in the same region. Despite these obvious Neanderthal associations, and clear Middle Palaeolithic origins, there is nevertheless equally clear evidence that the Châtelperronian populations were beginning to adopt some very specific features of Upper Palaeolithic technology—in the form, for example, of typical blade techniques, distinctive forms of Upper Palaeolithic stone tools, and (in at least certain contexts) simple forms of both shaped bone and antler tools, and perforated animal-tooth pendants. The most significant factor in this context is that all of these distinctively Upper Palaeolithic features of the Châtelperronian industries can be shown to have developed at a relatively late date (probably around 35,000 BP), which was demonstrably *later* than the earliest appearance of typically Aurignacian technologies in western Europe. The most economical view would therefore be to see any specifically Upper Palaeolithic features in the Châtelperronian industries as reflecting—either directly or indirectly—some form of interaction and associated 'acculturation' between these latest representatives of the local Neanderthal populations and the earliest populations of anatomically modern type.

Apparently similar patterns of contact and acculturation between the latest Neanderthal and earliest modern populations can be detected in several other parts of Europe—as, for example, in the appearance of the Szeletian and related 'leaf-point' industries of central Europe, in the Bohunician industries of former Czechoslovakia, and in the Uluzzian industries of Italy. As in the case of the French Châtelperronian, all of these industries show a curious blend of both Middle Palaeolithic and Upper Palaeolithic technological features and, significantly, all of them would seem to be broadly contemporaneous with the presence of early Aurignacian industries in the same or closely adjacent regions. Unfortunately, none of these industries have as yet yielded any clearcut associations with human skeletal remains, and it is only in the case of the Châtelperronian that we can demonstrate conclusively that these apparently 'acculturated' industries were, in fact, the product of Neanderthal populations. Nevertheless the evidence as a whole suggests that in many regions of Europe there was indeed a period of significant overlap between the two populations, and that during this period some form of interaction between the two populations occurred. As Zubrow and others have argued, all of this suggests that the process of apparent demographic replacement of one population by the other need not have been nearly so dramatic, sudden, or potentially violent as some earlier writers have tended to imply.

Leaving aside this question of demographic replacements and interactions, the issue of exactly when, where, and, above all, *how* the distinctive features of Upper Palaeolithic culture may initially have developed remains far more enigmatic. All that can be said with any real confidence at present is that there is clear evidence that at least *many* of the distinctive hallmarks of Upper Palaeolithic technology had already developed in several parts of both western Asia and Africa, by at least 45,000–50,000 BP—that is, at least five or ten thousand years before their appearance in most areas of Europe. There is clear evidence for this, for example, in the archaeological sequences documented at Ksar Akil and Boker Tachtit in the Middle East and, much further afield, at Klasies River Mouth and Border cave in South Africa. The ultimate *stimulus* for these developments remains for the present far more enigmatic. Various potential scenarios have been suggested, ranging from the effects of local climatic and ecological changes in stimulating significant shifts in human social and economic patterns, to more prosaic explanations relating simply to the effects of dwindling raw material supplies in promoting more economical approaches to the flaking of flint nodules. None of these interpretations can at present be regarded as more than highly speculative, and certainly none of the different models can be adequately tested against the available archaeological evidence. A more intriguing possibility is that the development of Upper Palaeolithic culture may have been linked in some way with the emergence of much more complex and highly structured patterns of language—a development which, according to Bickerton and others, could have emerged relatively suddenly at some specific point in human development. If this suggestion *does* have any validity, then, of course, it could potentially explain most of the dramatic developments in human culture, ranging from the emergence of more highly organized patterns of economic exploitation and the internal social organization of human groups, to the appearance of various forms of explicit symbolism in the production of stone and bone tools and—ultimately—the appearance of art and personal ornamentation. The problem, of course, is that language must presumably rank as one of the least archaeologically 'visible' of all aspects of human behaviour. The widely canvassed link between Upper Palaeolithic symbolic culture and language is intriguing, and is perhaps the most plausible explanation, overall, for the dramatic spectrum of changes in the technological, economic, social, and aesthetic aspects of human behaviour reflected in the archaeological record of the Middle–Upper Palaeolithic transition. But it can hardly rank at present as more than a suggestion, inevitably difficult to evaluate in any very direct or rigorous way against the archaeological data.

Upper Palaeolithic Economy and Society

Whatever view one may adopt regarding the ultimate origins of Upper Palaeolithic populations, there can no longer be any doubt that some of the distinctive behavioural hallmarks of these populations involved not only the more technological aspects of culture discussed in the preceding section, but also several aspects of the economic and social organization of the human groups. The scope of the hypothetical 'Upper Palaeolithic revolution' seems, in other words, to have extended through all aspects of human culture and organization, reaching far beyond the scope of the purely technological or even 'aesthetic' realms.

At a purely economic level, of course, Upper Palaeolithic communities in Europe were clearly dependent on essentially the same range of food resources as their Middle Palaeolithic and Neanderthal predecessors. Climatic and ecological conditions during the later stages of the last glaciation were not dramatically different from those during the earlier part of the glaciation, and the human communities would have been confronted by essentially the same range of economic opportunities, in both the total range of food resources available, and their distribution throughout the landscape. The potential wealth of these resources, to groups who were properly organized and equipped to exploit them, has already been emphasized. The massive and concentrated herds of reindeer, wild horse, bison, and mammoths that roamed over the open tundra and steppe-like landscapes of the middle latitudes of Europe would have provided an exceptionally rich, and potentially reliable, resource base for groups who had the necessary technology to intercept and kill these herds and (perhaps more importantly) possessed the degree of social organization and integration necessary to exploit the animal herds in a focused and co-ordinated way.

It is in this level of co-ordination and organization of hunting activities that Upper Palaeolithic communities seem to have shown significant advances over the subsistence behaviour of earlier Palaeolithic groups. As Clive Gamble has discussed in the preceding chapter, there is still a good deal of debate as to how far Neanderthal communities in

Europe can, in fact, be regarded as systematic hunters in the full sense of the word. Lewis Binford, in particular, has argued that the Neanderthals, in common with earlier Palaeolithic populations, may have played the role primarily of scavengers, exploiting mainly the abandoned residues of animal carcasses that were killed by carnivores, such as the hyaena or wolf. These interpretations remain highly controversial, and strong arguments have been advanced by Philip Chase and others that most of the animal species encountered on Middle Palaeolithic sites almost certainly result from deliberate hunting—perhaps oriented mainly towards the driving of small groups of animals over cliffs or similar natural obstacles. Even so, there are strong indications that the overall hunting strategies of Middle Palaeolithic groups were in at least some significant respects less highly organized, less efficient, and less sharply focused than those which emerged during the Upper Palaeolithic.

One of the most striking features of many of the faunal assemblages recovered from Upper Palaeolithic sites is their strong orientation towards a *single* species of game. All hunters are, by necessity, opportunists, and the particular species of animals selected for these highly specialized hunting activities varied in different regions of Europe. In the tundra-dominated landscapes of western Europe, the most heavily exploited animals seem to have been either the reindeer or (in certain contexts) the wild horse. Further to the east in central and eastern Europe, however, the emphasis frequently shifts on to other, more steppe-adapted species such as the steppe bison, the wild ass, or, in some cases the woolly mammoth. Further to the south, in the more forested areas of southern and Mediterranean Europe, the focus is usually on red deer combined (in more mountainous areas) with species such as the ibex or chamois. In many if not all these sites, however, it is clear that the central focus of hunting activities was concentrated very heavily on one or other of these major game animals.

Some of the clearest evidence for this high degree of specialization in hunting activities can be seen in the various cave and rock-shelter sites of the classic Périgord region of south-west France. In these sites it is not uncommon to find that reindeer remains account for well over 90 per cent of the total faunal assemblages from Upper Palaeolithic levels, and in some cases as high as 99 per cent. These overwhelming frequencies of reindeer are by no means confined—as has sometimes been suggested—to the later stages of the Upper Palaeolithic sequence, and can be traced back in several sites (such as the Abri Pataud, La Gravette, Le Piage) to some of the earliest Aurignacian levels, dated to between 32,000 and 35,000 BP. In this region at least there can be no doubt that Upper Palaeolithic groups practised a far more selective pattern of specialization on this particular species than can be documented from any of the abundant Middle Palaeolithic sites in the same region. Even where Mousterian sites show a clear predominance of reindeer remains, the overall frequencies of this species rarely exceed 70–80 per cent, and are invariably accompanied by a wide range of other species (horse, bison, red deer, and so on) which clearly reflect a more wide-ranging and 'eclectic' pattern of faunal exploitation among the Neanderthal groups. However the data are interpreted, the Middle

Palaeolithic groups appear to have played the role of much more 'generalized' foragers within this particular environment.

Several other aspects of the evidence seem to bear out this general pattern of shift towards a more selective and specialized exploitation of animal resources in the Upper Palaeolithic period. In several regions of Europe, for example, it can be seen that Upper Palaeolithic sites tend to be heavily concentrated in certain specific locations—or particular river valleys—which clearly served as major migration trails for one or more species of game. In the south-west region of France, the valleys of the Vézère and the Dordogne almost certainly served this function, channelling the seasonal migrations of the reindeer from the high-level summer pastures of the Massif Central to the more low-lying winter pastures of the Atlantic plain. Significantly, it is precisely these areas which contain by far the highest densities of Upper Palaeolithic sites, and which reflect the most specialized level of exploitation of reindeer resources. In central and eastern Europe, similar concentrations of sites seem to be apparent in the valleys of the Rhine and Upper Danube in south Germany, and along the course of the Don and Dnestr valleys in southern Russia. All of these concentrations seem to reflect the sharp focus of Upper Palaeolithic groups on particular animal species and—perhaps more significantly—the clear capacities of the Upper Palaeolithic hunters to predict the movements of the animal herds along these major migration trails. Middle Palaeolithic sites tend to be less sharply concentrated in these regions, and more widely distributed over a broader range of the available habitats.

As noted above, part of this tendency to focus so heavily on the exploitation of particular species of game probably reflects the ability of Upper Palaeolithic communities to *predict* reliably the movements of animals, and to anticipate these movements by locating the major settlements directly astride these major migration trails. This capacity may well tell us something about the patterns of communication maintained between different social units in Upper Palaeolithic society, and their detailed understanding of seasonal and ecological conditions within their local environments. But there can be little doubt that the tendency to rely so heavily on particular species of game also reflects something of the internal *social* organization of Upper Palaeolithic communities, and their ability to organize the exploitation of the migrating animal herds in a highly integrated and co-ordinated way. One reflection of this internal organization can perhaps be seen in some of the remarkably large settlements occupied by many Upper Palaeolithic groups, clearly suggesting the aggregation of relatively large, multi-family human groups. Again, numerous examples of these very large settlements could be cited, ranging from some of the massive rock-shelter occupations in southern France (Laugerie Haute, Abri Pataud, Laussel, La Madeleine) to some of the equally if not more extensive open-air settlements at sites such as Pavlov and Dolní Věstonice in former Czechoslovakia, Willendorf in Austria, and Kostenki in southern Russia. The perennial problem posed by these very extensive sites is whether they do indeed reflect the activities of very large, co-residential groups, or simply 'palimpsests' of repeated

RECONSTRUCTION OF HOUSE constructed from the jaws, bones, and tusks of mammoths, from the Ukrainian site of Mezhirich, *c*.14,000 BP.

occupations on the same site by much smaller groups. The overall degree of internal structure and organization documented in many of these Upper Palaeolithic sites, however (reflected, for example, in the distribution of hearths, paved areas, storage pits, and—in some cases—well-defined huts or other living structures), seems to leave little doubt that in many cases they must indeed have been occupied by relatively large social units, probably amounting to at least tens if not hundreds of occupants. Leaving aside these interpretative problems there is, in any event, a clear pragmatic contrast with the patterns documented in the majority of Middle Palaeolithic settlements from the same regions. In the various cave and rock-shelter sites of south-western Europe, for example, it is difficult at present to document any occupation deposits which can compare—either in total area, or in the massive concentrations of occupation debris—with those recorded at many of the Upper Palaeolithic sites such as Laugerie Haute, Abri Pataud, and La Madeleine. Overall, there seems little doubt that the individual social units of Upper Palaeolithic groups did, in many contexts, greatly exceed those of the earlier, Lower and Middle Palaeolithic communities in the same areas.

Some of the best-documented examples of these relatively large and highly structured Upper Palaeolithic settlements come not from the well-known cave and rock-shelter

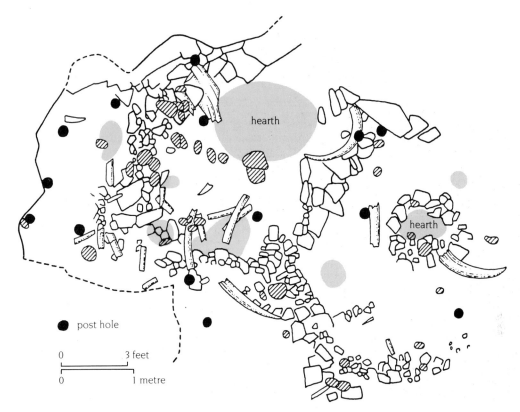

hearth

hearth

● post hole

0　　　　　3 feet

0　　　　　1 metre

CIRCULAR HUT STRUCTURES, built with stones and mammoth tusks, from the earliest Upper Palaeolithic (Châtelper-ronian) levels at the Grotte du Renne cave (Arcy-sur-Cure) in central France, c.33,000–34,000 BP.

sites of western Europe, but from many of the open-air encampments on the exposed, loess plains of central and eastern Europe—at sites such as Pavlov and Dolní Věstonice in former Czechoslovakia, or Pushkari, Kostenki, Mezhirich, and Mezin in southern Russia. At these sites we have evidence for the construction of substantial houses, consisting of either major pitlike depressions excavated into the subsoil (usually focused on a large, central hearth), or clearly defined circular or oval arrangements of stone settings or post holes which appear to mark the foundations of substantial huts or similar living structures. In some of the sites in Eastern Europe (such as Mezhirich, Mezin, and Pushkari) these hut foundations may incorporate large accumulations of tusks, jaws, or leg bones of mammoths which apparently served as major components in the architecture in regions where local supplies of wood were effectively lacking. Simple forms of these circular or sub-circular hut foundations can be traced back to some of the earliest stages of the Upper Palaeolithic sequence—as, for example, in the two juxtaposed hut structures documented in the Châtelperronian levels at Arcy-sur-Cure in France, clearly dated to around 33,000–34,000 BP. In some of the later 'Gravettian' settlements (such as Dolní Věstonice and Pavlov in former Czechoslovakia, or Vigne-Brune in France), we seem to have clear evidence that several different hut structures were in use on the same site at the same time, presumably indicating the aggregation of several family units within a single settlement. In other cases (as at Pushkari or Kostenki site I) there would seem to be indications of clearly linear arrangements of hearths within a single living structure, perhaps suggesting the formation of more extended, multi-family units. All of these sites would seem to indicate a far more highly structured pattern in the organization of human settlements (and, by implication, the internal social organization of the human groups who occupied the sites) than anything which can at present be documented from the earlier, Middle Palaeolithic sites of Europe.

Lastly, any assessment of the overall shifts in economic and social patterns between the Middle and Upper Palaeolithic periods must take account of the evidence for a very substantial increase in overall population densities coinciding at least broadly with the transition from the Middle to the Upper Palaeolithic. Here again, of course, the archaeological evidence must be treated with due caution, and we must always allow for the possibility that occupation sites of the earlier periods have been subject to a higher degree of selective destruction than those of the later periods. Even allowing for this caveat, however, the documented contrast in the *total numbers* of Middle and Upper Palaeolithic sites recorded in several regions can hardly be dismissed. Within the heavily explored region of south-west France, for example, it is now clear that there are at least four or five times as many cave and rock-shelter sites with substantial traces of Upper Palaeolithic occupations as there are for the preceding Middle Palaeolithic period. These contrasts become even more striking if we recall that the duration of the Upper Palaeolithic period is substantially less than *half* that of the Middle Palaeolithic period— implying a rate of formation of Upper Palaeolithic sites (per unit of time) at least ten times higher than that during the earlier periods. Similar contrasts in the total numbers of Middle and Upper Palaeolithic sites have been documented in central Europe, Cantabria, and the south Russian plain. Allowing for all possible caveats, these figures can only indicate a fairly massive increase in the overall densities of human populations in many regions of Europe, coinciding broadly with the transition from the Middle to the Upper Palaeolithic.

How far these changes in population density and the overall sizes of human groups may have impinged on some other aspects of the social organization of Upper Palaeolithic communities is inevitably more difficult to decipher from the archaeological evidence. One fairly obvious possibility is that the formation of relatively large social units would have encouraged—and perhaps even *required*—a more complex level of separation and specialization in the economic or social roles occupied by particular individuals within the societies. It seems almost certain, for example, that the production of some of the more elaborate and impressive forms of cave art (discussed below) must have been the work of specialist artists. Similarly, it could be argued that some of the highly sophisticated forms of both stone- and boneworking encountered in many Upper Palaeolithic industries are likely to be the products of specialist craftsmen. On a more general level it could no doubt be argued that almost any social system which involved the regular formation of relatively large and stable social units would have required some form of division of authority or ranking within the societies, if only to provide the necessary degree of integration and co-ordination of the activities of the groups as a whole (as, for example, in the organization of communal hunting activities). It is tempting, perhaps, to see some of the elaborate ceremonial burials recorded from sites such as Dolní Věstonice in former Czechoslovakia, Sungir in Russia, and Arene Candide in Italy, as a direct reflection of this kind of increased social 'status' or 'ranking' now being accorded to particular individuals within Upper Palaeolithic society.

There would seem to be equally clear indications that in some of the ecologically richer environments, the human populations may have been living in overall densities which involved various forms of 'crowding stress' in the relationships between the separate social and residential units. Several authors have argued that under these conditions of relatively high population densities, the emergence of some kind of clear recognition and demarcation of discrete 'social territories' may have been essential to avoid recurrent conflicts between the occupants of adjacent areas over access to particular economic resources, such as game or even raw material supplies. The sharp demarcation and delimitation of these social territories could, in turn, have fostered the emergence of specific forms of self-identification for the individual social units, which could well be reflected, for example, either in the particular styles of art or ornamentation produced in particular communities, or even in the specific forms of more utilitarian artefacts, such as spearheads or hunting knives. In short, the combined effects of population crowding within sharply prescribed ecological territories could well have led to the emergence—probably for the first time in prehistory—of distinct, self-conscious 'ethnic' groups. As discussed in an earlier section, this would seem at present to provide the most convincing and economical interpretation for the highly diverse and contrasting forms of artefacts which can now be documented throughout the Upper Palaeolithic universe—both in different locations in Europe, and at different periods throughout the Upper Palaeolithic sequence.

Even if Upper Palaeolithic populations in many areas were divided into relatively discrete territorial and ethnic units, however, it is debatable how far these units could have acted as completely independent, self-sustaining units under the rather brittle and unpredictable ecological conditions of the last glacial period. It is well known, of course, that highly specialized ecosystems of the kind represented by the periglacial tundras and steppes are inherently unstable and unpredictable (at least in the short term) and are thus susceptible to local fluctuations in the availability and abundance of specific resources—particularly in the case of highly mobile and migratory resources such as herds of reindeer or wild horse. Periods of exceptionally heavy or prolonged snowfall, or occasional periods of heavy overgrazing of forage resources (or even temporary destruction of forage resources by fires) can easily disrupt the movements and migration patterns of the individual animal herds in ways which might well be catastrophic to individual social groups heavily dependent on a single, highly specialized source of food. As Gamble and

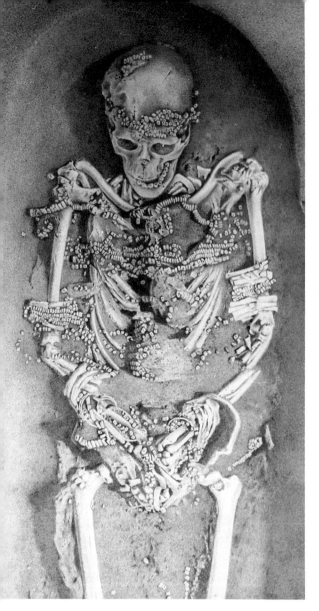
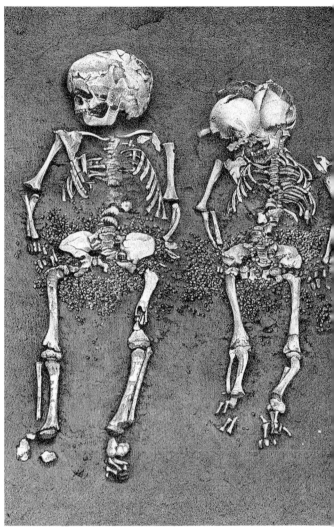
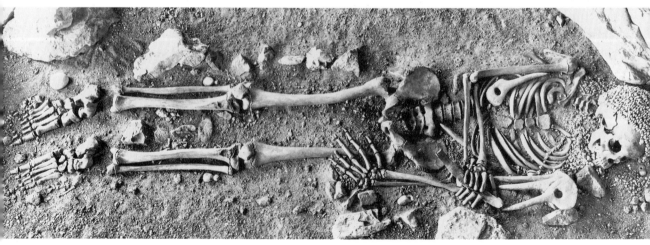

others have pointed out, it would almost certainly have been essential in these contexts for the human groups to maintain some form of wide-ranging contacts with other social groups as a hedge against these periods of local food-resource failures. One possible reflection of this kind of wide-ranging alliance system is perhaps seen in some of the extensive trading or exchange networks which can now be documented in many areas of Upper Palaeolithic Europe. In both western and central Europe, for example, there is evidence that several species of sea shells were traded or exchanged over vast areas—as, for example, between the Mediterranean coast and the Périgord region (a distance of *c*.250 kilometres) or between the Black Sea coast and the Don valley (*c*.500 kilometres). Similar networks can be seen in the distribution of certain, high-quality types of flint or other raw materials—for example, between the Holy Cross mountains of southern Poland and western former Czechoslovakia, or between the Dordogne valley and the Pyrenees. While exchange networks of this kind can be documented from most stages of the Upper Palaeolithic sequence (extending well back into the Aurignacian), Gamble argues that these patterns seem to become especially conspicuous over the period of the last glacial maximum (around 15,000–25,000 BP), when the degree of unpredictability and relative insecurity of economic resources would probably have been most acute.

Upper Palaeolithic Art

It is hardly possible to do justice to the immense topic of Upper Palaeolithic art in the scope of a few pages. Recently, a number of excellent surveys of this topic have been published, including André Leroi-Gourhan's *The Art of Prehistoric Man in Western Europe*, and the beautifully illustrated *Images of the Ice Age* by Paul Bahn and Jean Vertut. As noted earlier, the art stands in many ways as the most impressive and enduring testimony to the creativity of Upper Palaeolithic culture—not only in terms of the sheer skill and aesthetic flair of the artists themselves, but also in their capacity to convey highly sophisticated, symbolic messages in a remarkable variety of forms. Ultimately, perhaps, the art may provide more insights into the mental and social dimensions of Upper Palaeolithic society than we can derive from any other aspects of the archaeological evidence.

At the outset, a basic distinction must be made between the broad categories of 'parietal' art (paintings and engravings preserved on the walls of caves) and that of 'mobiliary' art (depictions found on small portable objects, excavated directly from archaeological

HUMAN BURIAL (*above, left*) elaborately ornamented with carved ivory beads—probably originally attached to skin clothing—from the site of Sungir, near Moscow, *c*.25,000 BP.

DOUBLE BURIAL (*above, right*) of two young children from the later Upper Palaeolithic levels in the 'Grotte des Enfants' cave, north-west Italy, *c*.20,000 BP. The burials are associated with large numbers of sea shells.

HUMAN BURIAL (*left*) from the Upper Palaeolithic levels in the Arene Candide cave in northern Italy, *c*.20,000–25,000 BP. The body is decorated with sea shells and a number of perforated deer-antler implements placed near the shoulders.

occupation levels). The study of portable art poses fewer problems than that of cave art, since the objects themselves can be accurately dated from their association with other archaeological material, and can be related directly to the overall cultural context in which they were produced. As noted earlier, one of the most striking features of the mobiliary art objects is their occurrence throughout almost all stages of the Upper Palaeolithic sequence, extending back to some of the earliest Aurignacian levels in both France and parts of central Europe, dating to around 30,000–35,000 BP. The remarkable animal and human statuettes recovered from Vogelherd, Geissenklösterle, and Hohlenstein-Stadel in south Germany, and the simpler outline engravings of both animals and female vulvar symbols recorded from a range of sites in south-west France (La Ferrassie, Abri Blanchard, Abri Cellier) provide impressive testimony to this sudden burst of artistic creativity coinciding closely, it would seem, with the first appearance of anatomically 'modern' human populations in the central and western parts of Europe.

Broadly similar patterns of mobiliary art can be traced, to varying degrees, throughout most of the later stages of the Upper Palaeolithic sequence. From the Upper Périgordian and Solutrian periods we have a variety of engraved animal outlines (for example, La Colombière, Parpallo) and in some cases more deeply incised low-relief engravings of similar species—as, for example, from the Solutrian levels of the Roc de Sers rock shelter in the Charente. From the so-called Gravettian sites of central and eastern Europe (Dolní Věstonice, Pavlov, Kostenki) we have small statuettes of animal figures—carved in stone or ivory or, in some cases, modelled in fired-clay—which are strongly reminiscent of those recovered from the earlier Aurignacian levels at Vogelherd and Geissenklösterle. The greatest proliferation of these mobiliary art objects, however, derives from some of the latest stages of the Upper Palaeolithic sequence around 15,000 to 12,000 BP—most notably from some of the later Magdalenian levels in the Franco-Cantabrian region and from the contemporaneous sites in south Germany. The repertoire of motifs recovered from some of the later Magdalenian sites is particularly impressive, ranging from highly naturalistic depictions of reindeer, horse, ibex, and mammoth, through to similar representations of fish, birds, seals, and (in some rare cases) much more schematic representations of simple human forms. The animal figures may be either engraved on fragments of stone or bone, or (more rarely) carved in the round either on individual fragments of the same materials, or incorporated into the forms of some of the larger bone or antler artefacts, such as spear-throwers or perforated

HEAVILY STYLIZED FEMALE 'VENUS' FIGURINE (*above, left*), carved from mammoth ivory, from the Gravettian levels at Lespugue (Haute Garonne, southern France), *c*.25,000 BP.

APPARENTLY BISEXUAL 'VENUS' FIGURINE (*above, right*) carved from translucent calcite, from the Upper Perigordian levels of the Abri du Facteur rock shelter (Tursac, south-west France), *c*.25,000 BP.

BONE CARVING OF A BISON (*right*), apparently licking its flank, from the later Magdalenian levels of the La Madeleine rock-shelter (south-west France), *c*.14,000 BP.

antler batons. All of these 'naturalistic' depictions are accompanied by a wide range of more enigmatic 'symbolic' motifs, ranging from simple lines of incisions along the edges of bone fragments, to complex arrangements of dots, lines, and zig-zags. One of the most intriguing possibilities, which has recently been argued at great length in the publications of Alexander Marshack, is that some of these more or less linear arrangements of notches and indentations on bone and stone fragments could represent some system of calendrical 'notation', structured in some way around closely observed lunar cycles. These interpretations inevitably remain highly controversial, and are perhaps not quite as easy to decipher from the artefacts themselves as Marshack's interpretations would imply. Nevertheless, there is nothing inherently implausible in the idea that Upper Palaeolithic groups may have been involved in close observations of lunar patterns or other cyclical patterns in the environment and (as Steven Mithen and others have suggested) that they could have used this kind of knowledge of natural environmental rhythms in planning various forms of economic and social activities throughout the annual cycle.

Some of the most intriguing reflections of mobiliary art are embodied in the so-called 'Venus' figurines, which can now be documented across a remarkably broad arc of eastern, central and western Europe extending from southern Russia to the Pyrenees. These consist of small statuettes of rather well-developed (in some cases obese) female figures, with heavily accentuated sexual features and, usually, very attenuated or schematic representations of the heads, arms, and feet. The figures range from comparatively naturalistic forms (such as those from Willendorf in Austria and Kostenki in south Russia) to highly stylized forms which in some cases could be seen as having bisexual connotations (as, for example, in the specimen from Tursac in south-west France). Chronologically, most, if not all, of these figures seem to be confined to a relatively narrow time horizon centred on *c*.25,000 to 23,000 BP, and usually associated with industries of the Upper Périgordian or Gravettian groups. Not surprisingly, these figures have generated a variety of imaginative interpretations, ranging from an emphasis on the central role of women in Upper Palaeolithic society, to suggestions that the figures could have served as items of ritualistic exchange between communities who (for various economic and environmental reasons) were dependent on wide ranging social and 'alliance' networks across large areas of the European continent. Gamble, for example, has argued that these figures seem to show their widest distribution precisely at the time when environmental and ecological conditions in Europe would have been most unstable and unpre-

ONE OF THE COMPOSITE PAINTED PANELS (*above*) at Lascaux, incorporating superimposed figures of wild cattle, horses, and red deer, painted in red ochre and black manganese dioxide (*c*.17,000 BP). The overall length of the panel is over four metres.

PRESUMED HUNTING SCENE (*below*) of a wounded bison, from the Lascaux cave (south-west France) *c*.17,000 BP. This is one of the few examples of Upper Palaeolithic cave art involving a human figure. The entire structure and composition of the scene suggests a highly 'ritualistic' or 'symbolic' treatment, perhaps only loosely connected with the hunting component of the picture.

ANIMAL FIGURE (possibly representing a young feline), carved from reindeer antler, from the later Magdalenian levels of the Laugerie Basse rock shelter (south-west France) *c*.12,000–14,000 BP.

dictable, and when (as discussed earlier) various forms of interaction and exchange between the occupants of different regions would have been most essential to the survival of the human groups.

All of the issues entailed in the interpretation of the various forms of mobiliary art become even more controversial when extended to the analysis of the so-called 'parietal' or 'cave art'. The basic features of the cave art are now well documented. The art consists, overwhelmingly, of representations of animals, comprising both the major economic species (such as reindeer, red deer, horse, bison, wild cattle, ibex, and mammoth) and (more rarely) representations of some of the predator species such as lion, bear, and wolf. With a few very rare exceptions (such as the curious 'sorcerer' figures from Les Trois Frères, and a few highly schematic human representations at Pech-Merle, Lascaux, and Les Combarelles) explicitly human figures are almost lacking in the documented repertoire of cave art. Most of the art occurs deep inside the caves, often in relatively inaccessible and narrow passages at distances of up to a kilometre or more from the entrances. The representations may consist of either linear engravings, presumably made with stone tools, such as flint blades or burins, or elaborate paintings, made with either iron ochre (to produce a range of colours from yellow to deep maroon) or black manganese dioxide—or quite often a combination of both pigments. Almost invariably the animals are shown in silhouette and almost equally invariably as single individuals, rather than as associated groups or scenes (with some rare exceptions, such as the friezes of horse figures, and an apparent group of swimming deer at Lascaux). In addition to the animal figures, there are frequently representations of various 'schematic' signs, ranging from negative imprints of human hands, to purely abstract symbols such as linear 'macaroni' engravings, triangular or rectangular 'tectiform' designs, or various meandering arrangements of dots and circles. The designs are distributed at various points over the available walls and ceilings of the caves, and are frequently superimposed directly on top of *earlier* drawings in such a way that the outlines of the individual figures may be almost impossible to decipher. In this situation, of course, it is difficult to escape the impression that the principal motivation which underlay the production of the art lay in the original act of *depicting* the animals, rather than in the overall visual or artistic effect of the finished composition.

SHAPED AND ENGRAVED BONE PLAQUE from the early Aurignacian levels of the Blanchard rock shelter (south-west France), *c.*32,000–34,000 BP. The sequence of engraved dots has been interpreted by Alexander Marshack as representing a possible lunar 'calendar', showing different phases of the moon over a monthly cycle.

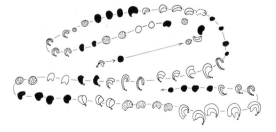
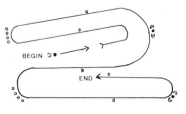

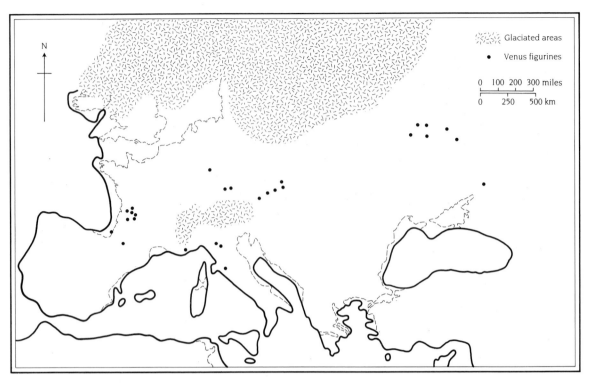

GEOGRAPHICAL DISTRIBUTION of 'Venus' figurines of the Gravettian/Upper Perigordian period in Europe, *c*.22,000–27,000 BP.

The challenge of explaining the deeper motivation which lay behind the creation of cave art has preoccupied successive generations of Palaeolithic specialists since the initial discovery of cave paintings in the 1870s. The original, rather attractive notion of 'art for art's sake'—created by artists who had the time and leisure to engage in aesthetic pursuits well beyond the demands of day-to-day food gathering activities—was inevitably soon demolished by some of the specific features of the art discussed above (particularly the effects of superpositioning, which effectively obliterated any overall visual impact of the art). Later interpretations focused on the potential role of art as reflecting certain 'totemic' symbols, associated with specific human communities, or, (perhaps more plausibly) on the use of painting as a form of 'sympathetic magic', designed to secure control over particular species of animals which were crucially important in the human food supply. The fact that many of the animals seemed to be depicted with spear-inflicted wounds or (in one interpretation) in the form of dead carcasses rather than as living animals, was frequently held to support this interpretation. More recent interpretations have drawn on anthropological notions of structuralism to suggest that the whole spectrum of Palaeolithic art might be seen as reflecting some fundamental 'binary opposition' in Upper Palaeolithic society, structured (perhaps predictably) around the opposition between male and female components of society. This view—propounded mainly in the publications of André Leroi-Gourhan—assumes that all of the major species of animals represented in the art can be seen as a reflection of either 'male' or 'female' symbols, which were distributed differentially throughout the various areas of the caves (the female symbols in the more central parts, and the male symbols in the more peripheral parts), often in association with supposedly male or female abstract signs in the form of various line or arrow-like figures (male) and broader triangular or tectiform designs (female). The most recent interpretations (advanced by John Pfeiffer, Steven Mithen, and others) have tended to emphasize the potential role of cave art as carrying explicit 'information' about the contemporary environment of Upper Palaeolithic groups, by reflecting factors such as various seasonal changes in the behaviour or movements of the animal herds, or the particular behavioural features of the animals that were most relevant in the organization of hunting activities. A more imaginative interpretation is that much of the art could represent so-called 'entoptic' images, produced during drug-induced trance-like states in the artists!

Overall, perhaps, three features are clear: first, there is almost no limit to the range of potential hypotheses which can be invoked to account for the deeper 'significance' or 'psycho-social' motivation of cave art; second, virtually none of these interpretations are at present capable of being systematically tested or evaluated in any very rigorous or controlled way against either the individual details or the broader context of the art itself; and third, allowing for the enormous variety and overall spatial distribution of the art, there is clearly room for a wide range of *complementary* interpretations, which may have varying degrees of credibility at different times and places throughout the Upper Palaeolithic universe as a whole.

In some ways perhaps the most productive approaches to the analysis and interpretation of Upper Palaeolithic art have come not from attempts to delve into the conscious or unconscious motivation which underlay the specific features of the art itself, but from studies of the more general distribution of the art in different social and economic contexts in Upper Palaeolithic Europe. Arguably the most striking feature of the cave art is its remarkable concentration in certain very localized regions of Europe—particularly in the Périgord and adjacent areas of south-west France, and in the neighbouring areas of the Pyrenees and north-west Spain. Even a rapid survey of the distribution patterns will show that well over 90 per cent of the documented occurrences of cave and rock-shelter art derive from this relatively localized zone of western Europe. Admittedly, one can hardly expect to find traces of cave art in regions such as the loess plains of central and eastern Europe, or the similar landscapes of north-western Europe. But, of course, there are many other regions of Europe (such as southern Germany, parts of the Balkans, and northern Italy) where limestone caves and rock shelters suitable for preserving art are comparatively abundant, and have been repeatedly surveyed for traces of art over the past century. The extremely sparse occurrences of art in these regions—compared with the massive concentration in the classic Franco-Cantabrian area of south-west Europe—must clearly tell us something about the nature of Upper Palaeolithic social and cultural patterns within the different regions of Europe.

Most workers are now agreed that the extraordinary concentration of cave art within these particular regions of western Europe must be related in some way to the overall density and concentration of human populations within these areas, which must be equally clearly related in some way to the particular economic and ecological opportunities provided in these regions. The arguments hinge largely on the fact that these particular areas served as the most southerly regions of essentially open tundra or steppe environments within last-glacial Europe, and would, therefore, have supported some of the highest concentrations of animal populations within the European continent as a whole. Crucial supporting factors would have been the highly migratory behaviour of the animal herds (particularly those of reindeer and red deer), which were almost certainly channelled along specific, largely predictable route-ways by the major river valleys which flow westward from the Massif Central and northward from the Cantabrian mountains. The combination of these factors, it is argued, would have provided ideal conditions for the aggregation (at least seasonally) of relatively large human groups, intended specifically to exploit these rich and concentrated herds of migrating game.

DISTRIBUTION OF MAJOR OCCURRENCES of Upper Palaeolithic cave and rock-shelter art in western Europe, showing a strong concentration in south-west France, the Pyrenees and north-west Spain. The coastline shown here reflects the reduced sea-level conditions of the last glaciation.

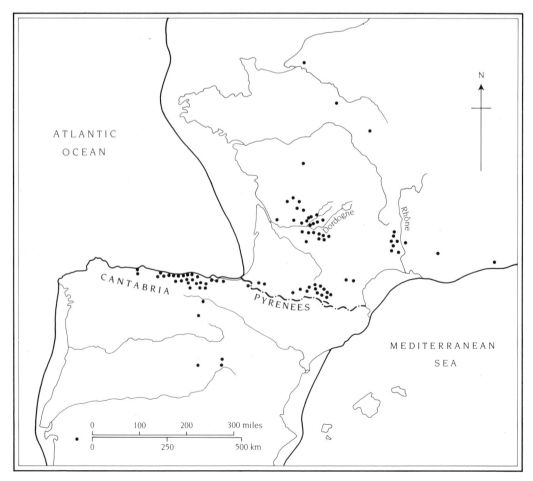

The remainder of the arguments relate to the various issues of population 'crowding stress', social differentiation, and the need for clearly defined and differentiated social territories which—as argued in the preceding section—would almost inevitably have been generated by these exceptionally large, dense concentrations of human population. Seen in these terms, the production of the cave art could be viewed as just one further response to these constraints of population crowding (with its inevitable social consequences), which created a clear, essentially functional need for various forms of ritualistic or ceremonial activities which could be used to integrate and co-ordinate the individual territorial groups. Exactly *how* the art would have functioned in this context remains more speculative. One possibility is that some of the major centres of art production (such as Lascaux in south-west France, or Altamira in northern Spain) served as major ritualistic or ceremonial centres—perhaps the scene of important ceremonies during regular annual gatherings by the human groups. Alternatively (or in addition) the production of the art could have been in the hands of particular chiefs or religious leaders who used the creation of the art, and associated ceremonial, to reinforce and legitimate their particular roles of power or authority in the societies. Clearly, all this lies in the realm of speculation. What *is* clear is that cave art is not uniformly distributed throughout Europe, and is concentrated in areas which (on other, independent archaeological grounds) are known to have contained some of the highest and densest concentrations of human populations. Viewed in these terms, the art may well provide some crucial insights into the varying patterns of social organization among Upper Palaeolithic groups in the different geographical provinces of Europe.

The End of the Ice Age

The end of the Palaeolithic world came fairly abruptly. The critical factor in this context was, of course, the rapid warming in climatic conditions which marked the end of the last glacial period, and which transformed the environment of Upper Palaeolithic communities in Europe in radical and irreversible ways. The initial stages of this warming process can be detected as early as 13,000 BP. Progressively, the ice sheets retreated from their maximum positions, world-wide sea levels began to rise (as water was returned to the oceans from the melting glaciers), and the forests began to expand northward from their glacial refuge areas in southern Europe. While these were all relatively gradual processes, it is clear that the most rapid environmental changes occurred around 10,000 years ago, when the overall rate of climatic change was at its peak. Conventionally, the period centred on 10,000 years ago (in terms of the current radiocarbon time-scale) is taken to define the end of the Upper Palaeolithic period and the start of the ensuing Mesolithic stage.

From the human standpoint, there can be little doubt that the most significant factor was the replacement of the open tundra and steppe-like landscapes of the central and northern latitudes of Europe by densely forested conditions. Inevitably, the precise date at which this critical threshold was crossed varied in different regions of Europe, and occurred rather earlier in the southern parts of the Continent (*c*.12,500 BP) than in the more northerly regions (*c*.10,000 BP). Regardless of precise timing, the effect of this crucial ecological transition could hardly have been more profound. Purely at the level of hunting activities, the pursuit of animals in a heavily forested landscape is very different from that in an open periglacial environment, and requires very different kinds of strategies and tactics in the organization of hunting groups. But the arrival of the forests would have entailed even more significant changes in both the overall densities and local biomass of the animals in particular regions, and their patterns of migration between different ecological zones. From studies of animal populations in modern environments it is clear that forested habitats can support only around 20–30 per cent of the total biomass of animal populations which can be maintained in open environments. Similarly, it is clear that the kinds of animals encountered in forested environments tend to be much less migratory in their seasonal habits, and to be distributed in smaller, more widely dispersed groups. In other words, the human groups would have needed to accommodate their behaviour not only to a sharply *reduced* overall food supply, but also to the pursuit of animals whose behaviour was very different from that of the earlier glacial species.

The response of the human populations to these ecological changes can be documented in two different ways. One of the obvious reactions to the encroachment of the forests was, of course, for the human groups themselves to retreat northward, and to colonize the new environments which were beginning to emerge in northern Europe as the ice sheets receded. From around 13,000 years ago we can document precisely this pattern of population expansion into northern Europe, in areas ranging from northern France and southern Britain to southern Scandinavia. From the settlements excavated at various sites in the Paris basin (Pincevent, Etiolles, Marsangy, La Verberie) and northern Germany (Meiendorf, Stellmoor) it is clear that by adopting this option the human groups were able (at least temporarily) to maintain their grip on essentially open environments, and to continue to exploit the same species of animals (mainly reindeer and horse) which had provided the mainstay of their economic activities throughout the earlier stages of the Upper Palaeolithic. Even if some of these sites were only occupied during the summer months, it is clear that these newly emerging landscapes in northern Europe provided an extremely rich environment for human occupation, which required only minimal kinds of economic and social adaptations on the part of the human groups.

The second option, of course, was for the human groups to remain within the previously occupied regions, and to adapt their behaviour and organization to the new, forested conditions. One of the clearest illustrations of this kind of adaptation can be seen in the classic region of south-west France, at the time of the archaeological transition from the Magdalenian to the Azilian period—now clearly dated to around 12,500 BP. The most direct reflection of this ecological transition can be seen in the composi-

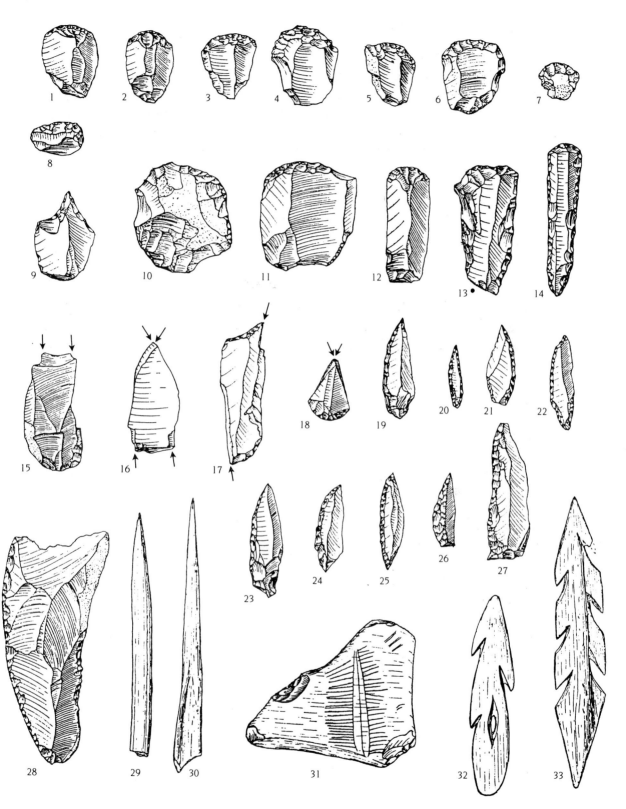

STONE AND BONE/ANTLER TOOLS, typical of the Azilian period (*c*.11,000–12,500 BP), from sites in south-west France.

tion of the associated faunal assemblages. Over a remarkably short space of time the heavily reindeer-dominated faunas associated with the late Magdalenian were replaced by assemblages consisting almost entirely of red deer, wild boar, wild oxen, and other typically forest-living species. At almost exactly the same time we can document a sharp reduction in the total *numbers* of occupied sites (from around seventy to eighty sites during the late Magdalenian period to around twenty to thirty sites in the Azilian phase) and an equally conspicuous reduction in the overall size of the occupied sites. From this evidence alone there can be no doubt that the overall levels of population within this region had suffered a dramatic decline, and that the human groups were now living in much smaller and more widely dispersed social units.

But some of the most striking reflections of these changes can be seen in the character of the archaeological assemblages themselves. Compared to the wealth and complexity of the material equipment recovered from the late Magdalenian levels, the kinds of stone, bone, and antler artefacts recovered from Azilian levels are not only much simpler and less varied in a 'typological' sense, but also in general much smaller and less carefully made. This can be seen, for example, in the form of the double-barbed harpoon heads recovered from Azilian levels, which provide only a pale reflection (in terms of size, morphological complexity, investment in workmanship, degree of decoration) of those recorded from late Magdalenian levels. Most striking of all is the virtual disappearance of art at the end of the Magdalenian period. From the Azilian sites, we have only a handful of incised representations of animal figures, accompanied (in some sites) by a range of enigmatic 'painted pebbles' embellished with a range of simple geometrical designs in red ochre. Despite these radical changes in the whole spectrum of material culture, there can be little doubt that the Azilian populations of south-west France were descended directly from the earlier Magdalenian populations in the same region.

Exactly how one should explain these curious correlations between changes in environmental conditions, economic activities, and technological patterns is open to debate. The most obvious implication (as discussed earlier) would seem to be that the human groups were now living not only in much lower population densities but also, apparently, in the form of very much smaller, more widely dispersed groups. Under these conditions it could be argued that most of the essential social mechanisms which had previously supported the production of elaborate technology, art, and probably associated ceremonial activities, had effectively disappeared—to be replaced by much simpler and less structured forms of social organization. Whatever the explanation, there can be no doubt whatever as to the dramatic character of these changes in the archaeological record, or to the intimate correlations between these changes and the simultaneous shifts in the character of local environmental and ecological conditions. It is this phenomenon which marks the end of the Upper Palaeolithic universe in Europe, and the onset of the various forest adaptations of the ensuing Mesolithic period.

3

The Mesolithic Age

STEVEN J. MITHEN

Introduction

TH E Mesolithic denotes the period following the end of the last Ice Age and prior to a predominantly farming economy. Both of these time boundaries are extremely fuzzy. The late-glacial interstadials (*c*.13,000–12,000 BP) provided a 'false start' to the post-glacial during which hunter-gatherers adapted to warmer environments. They then had to re-adapt to a final period of intense cold before warmer conditions returned. Consequently, quite where one draws the line between the Palaeolithic and Mesolithic is to some extent arbitrary—a date of 10,000 BP is often chosen. Rather than seeing any clear separation in the archaeological record between the behaviour of Palaeolithic and Mesolithic hunter-gatherers, we see a process of continuous behavioural change stretching back into the last glacial as foragers explored and exploited a series of ever-changing landscapes. The same underlying process of human adaptation to the environment structured both Mesolithic and Palaeolithic societies. Moreover, many of the traditionally diagnostic features of the Mesolithic, such as microlithic technology and the exploitation of coastal resources, are now firmly traced back into the Palaeolithic.

The juncture between the Mesolithic and Neolithic is similarly blurred. The use of pottery, sedentism, and complex social organization were once thought to be the sole domain of Neolithic populations. These are now known to have been prevalent in the later Mesolithic. Similarly the economy of many early Neolithic groups is now recognized to have been based on wild rather than domesticated resources. They are perhaps more appropriately described as 'complex hunter-gatherers' rather than farmers. While it is impossible to specify precisely when the Mesolithic began or finished, it is nevertheless one of the most critical periods in European prehistory. At the end of the Pleistocene (10,000 BP) populations were living in a manner that had not changed in its essence since the first arrival of biologically modern humans in Europe 30,000 years previously. They were characterized by an egalitarian social organization and highly mobile lifestyles. Within 5000 years three irreversible events had occurred that underwrite the developments of later prehistory: ranked societies had appeared; agricultural economies had been adopted; man had interfered with, and dramatically altered, the natural environment.

Aggersund
Ertebølle
Dyrholmen • Meilgaard
Ringkloster •
Norslund • Vængo So
Ulkestrup • Vedbæk/Vægnet Nord
Tybrind Vig • Øgaarde
Flaadat • Holmegaard
Svaerdborg

Staosnaig
Oronsay
Lussa Bay
Gleann
Mor
Bolsay
Farm

Tverrvikraet
Varanger
Fjord

Sanna
Vega

Vis I •

Oleneostrovski Mogilnik
Nizhneye Veretyre 1

'148' Øvre Storvatnet •

Mount Sandel • Morton
Newferry
Star Carr
Dunford
Broomhead

Ageröd V
Sjöholmen
Bare Mosse
Skateholm

Duvensee
Friesack •
Poznan-Staroleka
Calowanie

Oakhanger
Hengistbury Head

Hoëdic, Téviec

Rouffignac
La Riera
Grotte des Fieux •
Balma Aberuador
Arene Candide
Urtiaga
Mas d'Azil

Lepenski
Vir Iconana
Vlasac

Moita do Sebastão
Cueva Remigia
Cueva de la Arana •
Barranco de los Grajos •

Grotta del'Uzzo

Francthi
Cave

0   200   400 miles

0   500 km

MAP OF EUROPE showing principal Mesolithic sites mentioned in the text.

    Yet we discredit the Mesolithic if we only see it as a period of transition and study it for that sake alone. While many of its social and technological traits are found in the Palaeolithic and Neolithic, their particular constellation and interplay in the Mesolithic was unique. It was a period of significant cultural achievement in the spheres of technology, subsistence, and art. Indeed many view the Mesolithic as a period when the engagement between humans and their environment was pushed to its ultimate limit. In this sense we have in the archaeological record the finest testimony to the capacity of humans to become part of, rather than simply to exploit, the natural world.

In this chapter we will consider the Mesolithic Age by drawing on data from sites as far afield as northern Norway and southern Greece and seek to identify the defining characteristics of this phase of European prehistory. We will recognize similarities between all Mesolithic societies, principally deriving from constraints imposed by the hunting and gathering way of life. But our primary focus will be on social and economic variability arising from different cultural traditions and environmental conditions across Europe. Our study must start by briefly reviewing the environmental background of the Mesolithic. Then we will gradually construct a picture of settlement and subsistence by beginning with the artefacts, the faunal remains, and the features excavated from sites. We will consider how these may be integrated to interpret the nature of individual settlements and then how these may be related to build models of Mesolithic settlement-subsistence systems. We will then need to discuss aspects of demography, social organization, and art, and conclude with general models for the process of culture change during this critical phase of European prehistory.

The Environmental Background

The prehistory of the Mesolithic Age is intimately tied to the sequence of environmental changes that ensued following the end of the last Ice Age. The increasing warmth changed the extent of land and sea, the distribution of vegetation and of animals. The most dramatic and well-researched environmental changes occurred in northern Europe in the immediate vicinity of the retreating glaciers. In this area the physical geography, flora, and fauna underwent a series of dramatic changes, at least on a geological time-scale. Whether or not these were perceptible to the Mesolithic peoples themselves is open to debate. One may well imagine that folk memories existed about times when there were large hunting lands available that had become drowned by the sea.

Land/sea relations Two processes occurred in northern regions to create new sizes and shapes for the land masses; isostatic rising of the land, which had been depressed by the weight of the ice, and eustatic rising of the sea level due to melted water from the glaciers. Isostatic recovery was limited to the land which had been beneath the ice sheets, and was so dramatic in the far north so as to leave relic post-glacial shorelines over 250 metres above the present sea level. This unwarping of the land was a slow and time-lagged process; land in northern Scandinavia is still rising today. In such areas this isostatic land recovery created much larger areas of land to be claimed by spreading vegetation and exploited by Mesolithic hunter-gatherers. Working in the opposite direction, was the eustatic rise of the sea level. In contrast to isostatic land recovery this was a rapid process affecting all areas. It led to the drowning of glacial, and early post-glacial coastlines and in some areas, such as southern Scandinavia, the loss of large areas

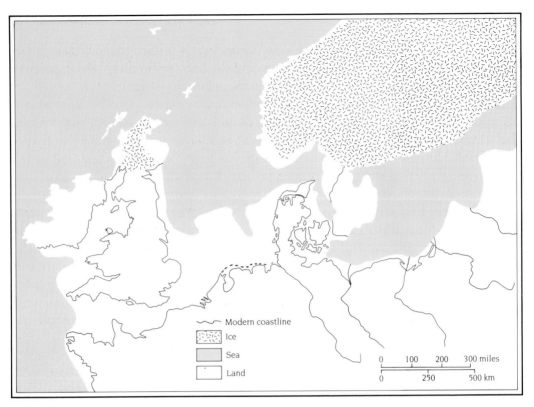

LAND, SEA, AND ICE IN NORTHERN EUROPE at *c*.10,500 BP. Britain was joined by extensive lowlands to the continent which became progressively flooded during the course of the Mesolithic due to the continued retreat of glaciers.

of land and hence the reduction in hunting territories. Britain became cut off from the Continent at around 8500 BP. One can appreciate that the combination of these two processes, together with variable rates of deglaciation, created considerable variability across northern Europe in the specific alteration in shorelines.

The Gulf of Bothnia illustrates the complexities of these environmental changes. During the last glacial this area was filled by an ice-dammed lake that spread over what is now southern Sweden, the Baltic islands, Estonia, and Finland. As the ice retreated, salt water penetrated the basin bringing in marine organisms. Delayed isostatic recovery of the land, however, soon outstripped the eustatic rise of the sea level and a freshwater lake was once again created, the Ancylus lake. At *c*.7000 BP the land barrier to the south-east was once again breached by rising sea level to return the area to a marine environment, the Litorina Sea.

Vegetational change   While these changes in land–sea relations were occurring there was a transition from open, tundra landscapes to those dominated by trees. Pollen cores from northern Europe show a succession of tree varieties resulting in the formation of thick forest. We can construct 'isopoll' diagrams to show the spread of specific species across Europe, such as lime and oak. The spread and succession of different tree types was determined by a complex interplay of factors involving increasing warmth, processes of soil formation, tree migration rates, and the location of refugia. Evidence from beetle remains shows that many areas had been sufficiently warm for tree species for many years prior to their arrival from refugia in south and east Europe. In northern Europe the earliest post-glacial landscape was dominated by herbs of open land with the cold-tolerant species of birch, aspen, willow, and juniper. As the temperature increased, pine, and then hazel, rose to prominence followed by warm-loving, broad-leaved species eventually to form the mixed forest of the mid-post-glacial composed predominantly of oak, lime, and elm, with alder on less well-drained soils. A consequence of the increasing warmth and vegetational succession was the infilling of lakes with organic sediments. This process began immediately after the melting of the ice and many shallow lakes became completely filled in during the course of the Mesolithic.

In southern Europe, away from the former edge of the ice sheets, the vegetational changes were less dramatic. Here the lack of moisture, rather than low temperature, was probably the critical limiting factor for late Pleistocene vegetation. In southern France and the Iberian peninsula there was sparse tree vegetation of pine and juniper at the end of the Pleistocene. During the early post-glacial, pine spread to the higher ground while deciduous oak-dominated forest spread throughout the lowlands. The composition of the oak forest appears to have been rather different to that of northern Europe with

THE DRAMATIC CHANGES IN VEGETATION during the Mesolithic can be inferred from the frequencies of pollen grains in sediment cores. This sequence from Denmark between *c.* 13,000 years ago and the present day shows a pattern common to large areas of northern Europe. The Roman numerals to the left refer to specific 'zones' of vegetation development.

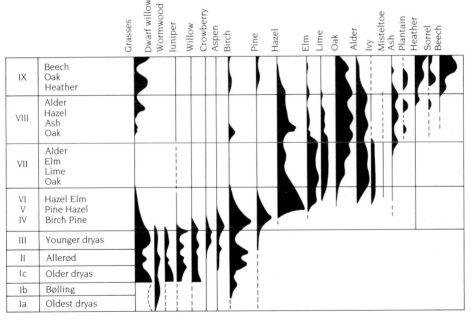

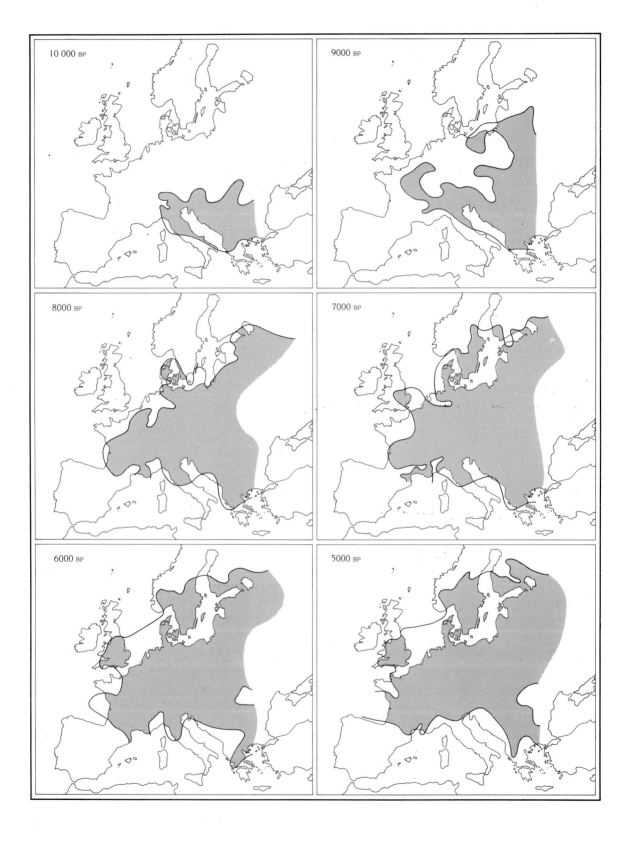

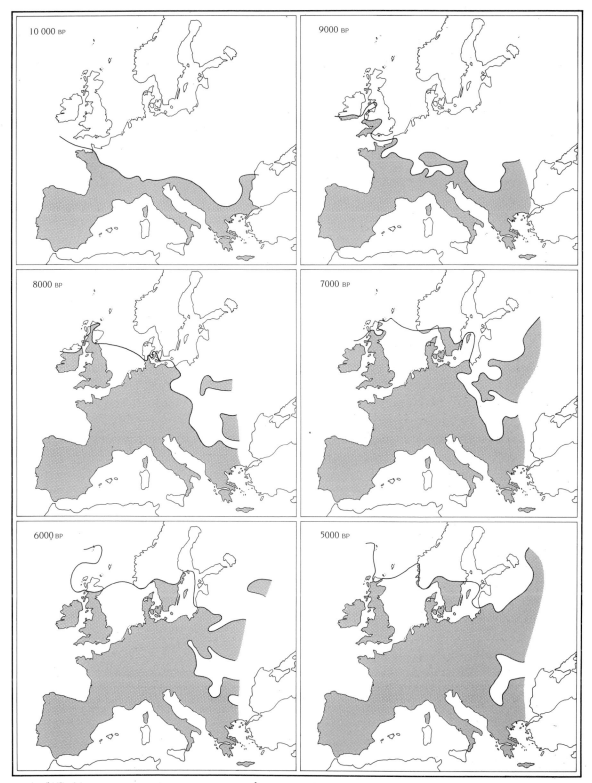

ISOPOLL MAPS can be used to describe the spread of specific plant species across Europe. The diagrams illustrate (*left*) the spread of lime (*Tilia*), and (*above*) the spread of oak (*Quercus*), by denoting the area in which they constitute at least 1% and 5% respectively of the total tree and shrub pollen.

much less elm, lime, and alder. In the eastern Mediterranean there were pockets of woodland at the height of the last glaciation, within a predominantly steppe environment. As the climate improved, first pine, and then oak, spread rapidly. Further increases in temperature and precipitation led to the spread of other tree species such as beech and hornbeam. In the drier areas, such as southern Greece, it is unlikely that woodland would ever have been substantial and the environment is most appropriately described as an open parkland.

The post-glacial fauna   Along with the vegetation, the post-glacial fauna showed marked contrasts with that of the late glacial. Several large mammal species, such as woolly rhino, mammoth, and giant deer, became extinct. Reindeer and elk were forced into the most northerly latitudes. The large migratory herds of reindeer and horse, which had inhabited the open tundra landscapes, were now replaced with a more diverse set of ungulates which lived in smaller groups and lacked marked migratory behaviour. Pre-eminent among these were red deer, roe deer, wild pig, auroch, and elk. The small mammal fauna also increased in numbers and diversity, notably in the thick forest of the mid-post-glacial. The particular character of the post-glacial fauna in any one region was, like that of the vegetation, dependent upon a broad range of climatic and ecological factors which caused considerable variability throughout Europe. The fauna continued to change during the course of the Mesolithic. This was due partly to the continuing climatic and vegetational changes, and partly to human activities. For instance, auroch and elk appear to have become extinct in eastern Denmark during the later Mesolithic. This is likely to have been caused partially by overhunting by Mesolithic foragers. It is very difficult, however, to make detailed reconstructions of past environments as the majority of animal and plant remains are recovered from archaeological sites and hence pass through a 'cultural filter'. If a particular species is absent, it is often unclear as to whether it was not present in the early post-glacial environment or simply not exploited by the Mesolithic hunter-gatherers.

The marine biotopes were also much richer in number and diversity of species during the post-glacial period than in the preceding glacial. Marine vertebrates ranged from whales and sharks to porpoises and dolphins. A wide range of salt-water fish became available for exploitation together with many species of shellfish. Many of these resources would have been migratory, becoming available for exploitation at specific and limited times of the year. The freshwater lagoons, lakes, and rivers also came to possess a very rich variety of animal life. Wildfowl were prolific as were the many species of freshwater fish such as pike, tench, and bream.

Landscape evolution   While it is easiest to treat the changes in physical geography, flora, and fauna as separate entities, these were, in fact, intimately connected and we should think of the environmental changes at the start of, and throughout, the post-glacial, and a process of landscape evolution. This is well illustrated by the changes in the Argolid peninsula of southern Greece, an area exploited by the late Pleistocene and Holocene inhabitants of Franchthi cave. At 20,000 BP there was an extensive coastal

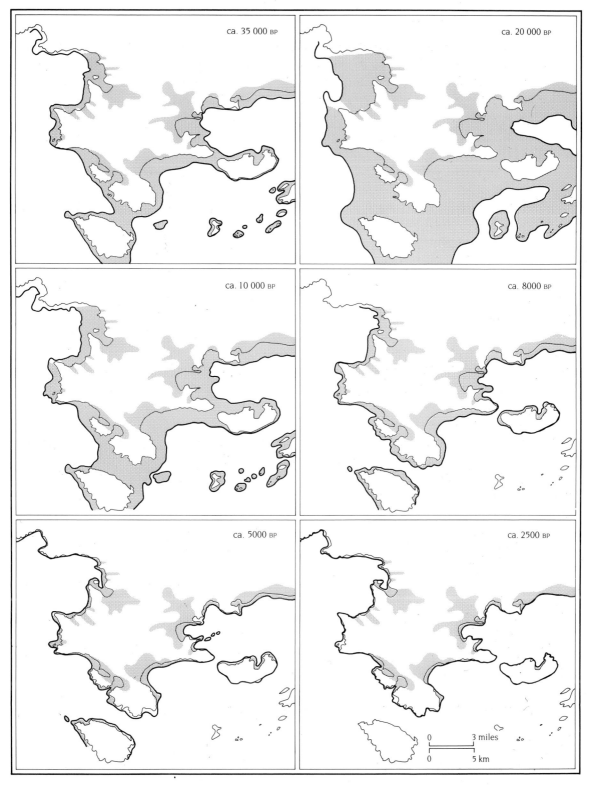

PALAEOGEOGRAPHY OF THE COAST of the southern Argolid in the late Quaternary showing the changing relationship between land and sea. The shaded areas denote coastal plains and lower valleys.

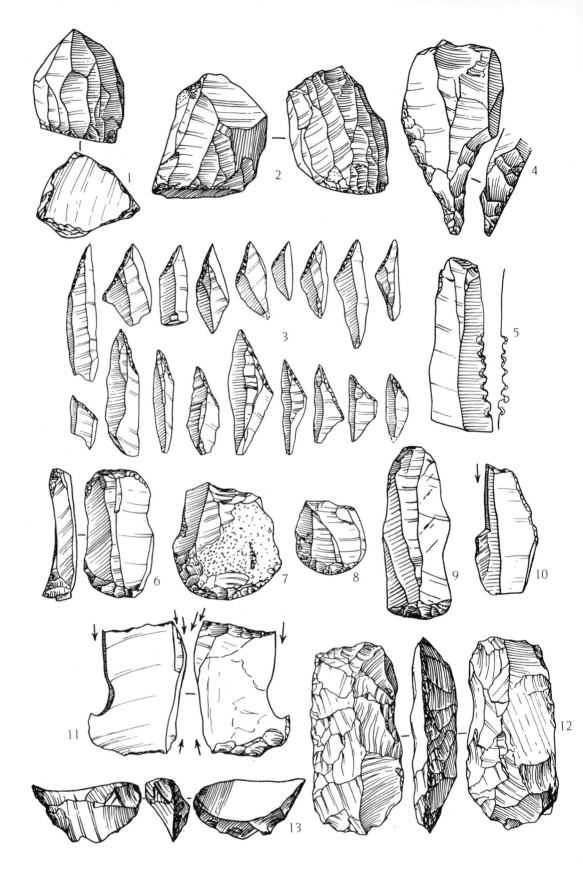

plain with sea levels more than 120 metres lower than today. This plain would have been covered with a steppe vegetation, though patches of trees are likely to have been present particularly around oases and watering holes. Large herds of horse and most probably bovids grazed on this plain. As the sea levels rose, this plain, and the resources it provided, were gradually reduced in extent until by 8000 BP there was only a narrow strip of sandy beach and marsh. This is lost today and the coastline is a series of rocks and cobbles set against steep buffs. Consequently, the Holocene hunter-gatherers had continuously to adapt their subsistence strategies to cope with a rapidly evolving landscape. These adaptations are reflected in the sequence of archaeological remains from Franchthi cave, as we will see below.

Environmental structure   The floral and faunal changes should not only be noted in terms of the number and diversity of species. The whole structure of the post-glacial ecosystem was markedly more complex and less stable than that of the late glacial. Each species, including man, was involved in many more connections with other animal and plant species in terms of predator–prey and competitive relationships. The ecosystems became more susceptible to periodic, but unpredictable, fluctuation in species composition and numbers. The environment was also characterized by marked seasonal changes in vegetation and animal populations. In addition to this temporal variability, an important feature of the post-glacial landscapes was their spatial patchiness. Certain regions, and certain locations within those regions, were particularly abundant in resources, notably rivers, lakes, and the coast. Interior regions had a lower biomass and less diverse resource set. In understanding the Mesolithic lifestyle we need to take into account this temporal and spatial patchiness as well as the numbers and types of species. The technology used to exploit this environment, to which we will now turn, can be seen as geared to coping with the structure, as much as with the content, of the environment.

Technology

As with the earlier prehistoric periods, stone tools dominate the archaeological record of the Mesolithic. Flint was available in the majority of areas, and from this elegant arrowheads and other tools were fashioned. The preservation of organic materials in the bog sites of northern Europe provides a glimpse into the diverse and very sophisticated use of antler, bone, and wood. We also have a few instances from which larger items of technology have been preserved—those for shelter and transport.

FLINT WAS THE MOST IMPORTANT RAW MATERIAL during the Mesolithic and used to fashion a wide range of stone tools. The specific types vary considerably from site to site due to the nature of the flint (size of nodules, texture, location of source), functional considerations relating to the activities at the site, and the cultural context of those making the tools. These tools from Star Carr provide a typical range of the artifacts one finds on Mesolithic sites. 1–2: blade cores used for producing the blanks to be later retouched into tools; 3: microliths which were probably used in projectiles; 4: an awl; 5: a denticulate; 6–9: scrapers; 10–11: burins probably used for working bone and antler; 12: an adze and 13 a flake detached to a sharpened adze.

The use of stone   Flint quarries dating to the Mesolithic are rare and probably absent in many parts of Europe. An exception are those found on the northern slopes of the Swietokrzyskie (Holy Cross) mountains on the southern edge of the Polish plain. From here a high-quality chocolate-coloured flint was quarried and this is found over a wide area, probably reflecting mobility patterns rather than exchange networks. In most areas, surface outcrops of flint were sufficient for the needs of the Mesolithic stone-knappers. These may have been primary deposits, such as from the chalk of southern England, or secondary deposits in the form of either erratic nodules in glacial sediments or beach pebbles. Such deposits may have been exploited either by special visits or by embedding the procurement of stone in other activities, such as hunting trips. Some primary workshops are known. For instance at Poznan-Staroleka in Poland a primary knapping site is known at an abundant source of erratic flint. The assemblage here typifies such a site in having very high frequencies of cores and primary cortical flakes and very few retouched tools.

Flint was not the only stone used during the Mesolithic. In areas where it was unavailable, or when inappropriate for the task in hand, the Mesolithic foragers turned to a wide range of other stones. Quartz and quartzites could also furnish sharp flakes for either scrapers or arrowheads. Excavations at the sites of Gleann Mor, Staosnaig, and Lussa River in the Hebridean islands of Scotland indicate the increasing use of quartz in Mesolithic tool-kits, as one moves further away from the flint sources. Slates lent themselves to splitting and polishing and slate knives are an important part of the Mesolithic tool-kit in northern Scandinavia. Fine-grained greenstones were also flaked while gneiss and a variety of rock types were worked by pecking to produce a range of artefacts such as axes and adzes. It is characteristic of the Mesolithic that a wide range of local raw materials were used.

In certain areas of Europe we can document a change in the types of raw material used through time, which may reflect important changes in socio-economic organization. For instance, there is a marked difference in the raw materials used during the earlier and later Mesolithic of northern England, the boundary falling in the ninth millennium BP. In the earlier period, tools were made from a high-quality white/grey flint. Through time this was replaced by a variety of low-quality cherts and translucent flint. This change may reflect the failure of the high-quality flint to meet demand, perhaps due to a rising population, the exhaustion of its source, or its loss caused by a rising sea level. Alternatively, it may reflect a change in mobility patterns. The later Mesolithic foragers may have covered smaller distances when conducting their economic activities and hence had to rely on more local, and poorer quality, materials. Similar reasons may explain the change from the use of obsidian to quartz and quartzite at *c.*8000 BP by Mesolithic populations in the Danube gorges.

Many of the flint tools from the Mesolithic were made on small bladelets produced from pyramidal cores. An extraordinary level of flint-knapping skill is often evident as these cores are frequently very small and beautifully worked. It is likely that some wooden supports may have been used to hold the cores in place when detaching the blades. In certain areas, such as Scandinavia, handle cores were produced. These are elongated cores so that the knapper could keep a firm hold at one end while detaching blades from the other. While such blade technology dominates the Mesolithic, a range of other reduction methods for producing flakes were also used. In areas where raw material nodules were small and/or of poor quality, bipolar working was used to produce thin and razor-sharp flakes and blades.

When the level of recovery and analysis is sufficient, considerable information about Mesolithic knapping strategies can be acquired. This is particularly the case when refitting of debitage and tools is used to reconstruct the 'biography' of a core. For instance at Bare Mosse II, an early Mesolithic site in Scania, 48 per cent of the 817 artefacts have been refitted to produce seven principal clusters of flakes and blades. From these, the specific knapping stages used on each core can be reconstructed. These include

LEAF-SHAPED SLATE POINTS
from Mesolithic Finland.

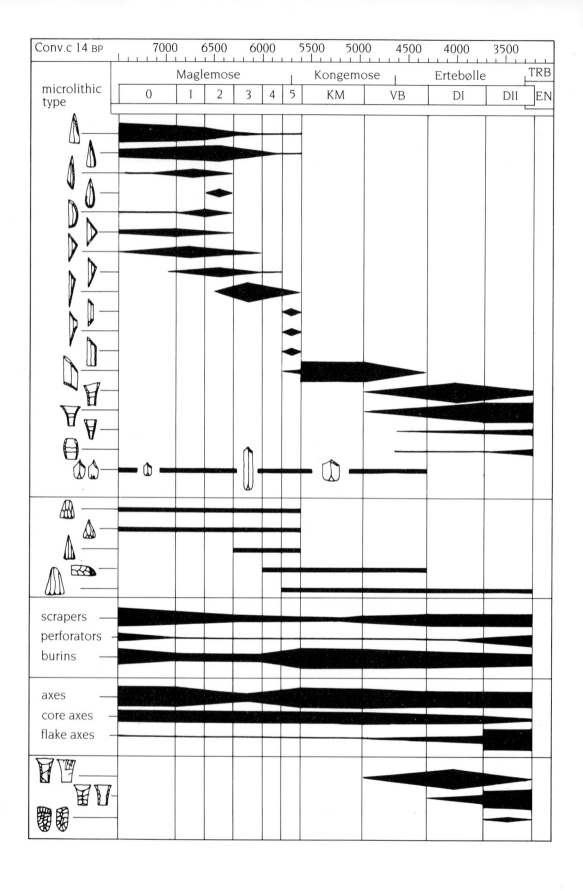

the removal of cortex and irregularities, the preparation of platforms, the removal of flake and blade blanks, and the retouching of these into tools. Some of the pieces from the refitted groups, such as the cores themselves, were missing suggesting that these had been kept and carried to other settlements. At Bare Mosse II one can recognize a consistent method of reduction and tool manufacture applied to each core. This probably reflects factors such as the constraints imposed by raw materials, similar functions for the tools, and traditions of tool manufacture within the group. Moreover, spatial patterning could be detected in the distribution of debitage types indicating that different stages of tool production were undertaken at different parts of the site. In general, the study of debitage in terms of reconstructing knapping strategies has become a central part of Mesolithic studies in recent years, overriding a more old-fashioned concern with typology.

The microlith The Mesolithic is often directly associated with the use of microliths — small retouched blades or blade segments. This relationship is not absolute however; some Mesolithic industries, such as the Larnian (the later Mesolithic) of Ireland used a large blade technology—a 'macrolithic Mesolithic'. In addition microliths are found in several Late Pleistocene industries such as the Magdalenian (*c.*17,000–11,000 BP). Nevertheless the microlith is at least symbolic of the Mesolithic Age.

Microliths come in a diverse set of shapes and sizes. It has been, and remains, one of the principal concerns of archaeologists to classify these into types based on morpho-

CHRONOLOGICAL SEQUENCE of microliths and other lithic types during the Mesolithic period in Denmark (*left*).

THE SUCCESSION OF PROJECTILE-POINT TYPES during the five phases of the late Mesolithic in north-east Denmark (*below*). (1) Villingebaek phase (early Kongemose); (2) Vedbaek phase (late Kongemose); (3) Trylleskov phase (early Ertebølle); (4) Stationsvej phase (middle Ertebølle); (5) Aalekistebro phase (late Ertebølle).

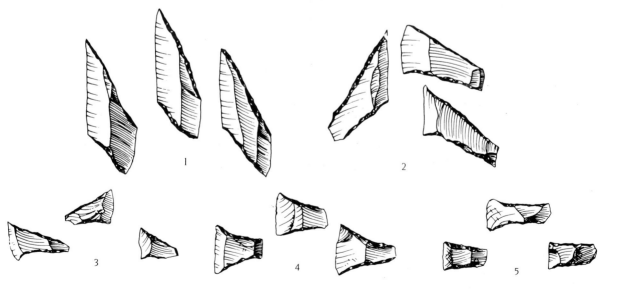

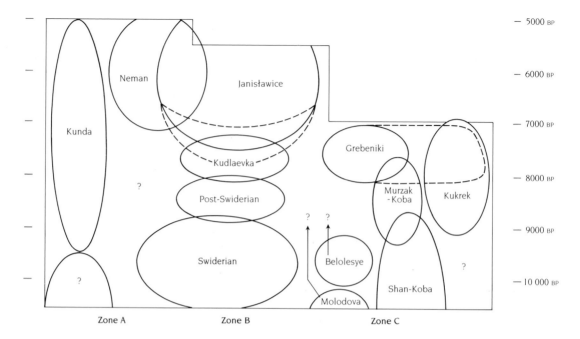

ARCHAEOLOGICAL INDUSTRIES and cultures of the Mesolithic (and other periods) have been defined on the basis of artifact types and their associations. The resulting patterns are often complex, as illustrated by those from the western part of the East European Plain. At least nine different taxonomic divisions have been made in this area. The three zones refer to the latitudinal/ecological subdivisions of this area. Zone A: northern lowlands and lakes; Zone B: central lowlands and river valleys; Zone C: the southern upland-lowland steppe. The meaning of such 'cultural variation' in space and time remains unclear.

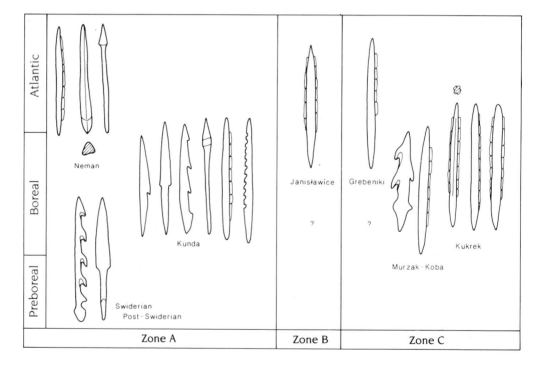

Zone A — Kunda, PostSwiderian, Neman

Zone B — Kudlaevka, Janisławice, Shan-Koba (Locally)

Zone C — Murzak-Koba, Grebeniki, Kukrek

logical characteristics. Their frequences in lithic assemblages are then measured and assemblages grouped into industries and cultures. Quite what the cultures represent in terms of past populations remains unclear, but some form of ethnic identity is often assumed. The best illustration of this typological approach is from southern Scandinavia where a rich archaeological record, a long history of fieldwork, and a quickly changing past technology combined to provide a wide set of microlith types. By 1973 these microlith types, together with other artefactual evidence, were used to identify ten industrial phases of the Mesolithic which could then be grouped into three cultures — the Maglemose (*c*.9500–7600 BP), the Kongemose (*c*.7600–6500 BP), and the Ertebølle (*c*.6500–5200 BP). More recently even finer distinctions have been drawn. The data sets from east Denmark have been used to divide the Kongemose and Ertebølle periods into five different phases based on changes in the shape of microliths. Elsewhere in Europe similar cultural historical sequences have been established. For instance, the Mesolithic data from north-east Europe has been classified into a complex series of cultures varying through time and space in their typical artefacts.

If we stand back from these regional sequences, three main phases of the Mesolithic for Europe can be established on the basis of microlith form and radiocarbon dating. The first phase is characterized by obliquely blunted points. Star Carr is the classic British site of this period, which ends at around 9000 BP. The second phase witnesses an immense diversification of microlith forms made on smaller blades, often referred to as 'narrow blade' or 'geometric' industries. They contain a range of forms such as scalene triangles, lancelots, and rods, and the earliest dates for these industries appear to be in southern France at the sites of Grotte des Fieux and Rouffignac during the tenth millennium BP. In the first half of the ninth millennium BP they are found at other French sites and in Holland and Britain; by 8500 BP they are widespread. These industries last about a millennium, and are in turn replaced by those dominated by rhomboids and trapezes made on broad blades. The latter industries appear almost synchronically across Europe, although, perhaps due to its isolation from the Continent, they are not found in Britain.

If we are to ask what caused this change in microlith types we must first consider what they were used for. The most likely answer is that they were a standardized element for a wide range of multi-component tools. One of their uses, perhaps the most important, was as points and barbs for hunting weapons. There are several lines of evidence for this. Numerous arrows have been found with microliths still attached to a wooden haft by resin and twine. Some microliths also show characteristic fracture patterns caused by impact with meat or bone. There have also been numerous finds of animal (and human) bones with microliths still embedded, indicating that they had been the cause of death. As such they would have killed either by slicing muscle and arteries to cause severe bleeding or by penetrating organs to cause almost immediate death.

Experiments with replica bows and arrows have suggested that microliths can have great penetrative power. Such replicas can be made due to finds of bows from sites such

as Ageröd V, Holmegaard, and Ringkloster. All of these were made from elm and measure between 150 and 190 centimetres long. Three qualities make for a particularly
efficient arrowhead: the ability to penetrate, the capacity to produce sharp cuts, and
symmetry to ensure maximum directional stability of the arrow. The variation in shape
of microliths through time and space may well relate to a continuous interplay between
these variables. Some would argue that the trapeze and rhomboid microliths made on
broad blades characterizing cultures such as the Ertebølle provided particularly good
combinations of these three variables. The increased hunting efficiency from their use
may have been a major factor for their rapid adoption throughout Europe.

It must be stressed, however, that microliths may have been used in many tools not
associated with hunting activities, notably in those used for processing plant materials.
The large numbers often found on sites may be due to their use as the cutting parts of
implements such as graters. Microliths from the Scottish site of Gleann Mor have been
found with a circular wear pattern around the tip, rather than longitudinal striations,
indicating they had been used as borers, or possibly drill bits. Hence, some of the variation in microlith shape may simply relate to the wide variety of tasks for which they were
employed. Alternatively, it may have had little functional significance of this type. Other
factors may have been important. The shape of a microlith may have had symbolic value
denoting that it belonged either to a particular individual or to a member of a particular
group. Such signalling may have been significant when retrieving carcasses by indicating who had killed the beast.

Other stone artefacts Microliths were just one of many different artefact types manufactured during the Mesolithic. Flaked flint axes and adzes are also characteristic of the
period. These were made by bifacially working large flakes or nodules and then detaching a flake from one end by a blow either transversely or obliquely to the axis of the
implement. This produced a sharp edge. More flakes of this type were removed when
the axe/adze required sharpening and these characteristic resharpening flakes are often
found on Mesolithic sites. Other stone artefacts from Mesolithic assemblages include
scrapers—retouched flakes or blades coming in a wide variety of shapes and sizes; borers—artefacts with a convergent backing to produce a stout point; and burins—artefacts from which a spall has been detached to create a chisel-like edge. Artefacts of these
types are found in most assemblages throughout Mesolithic Europe with varying
degrees of refinement and standardization.

Some sites provide quite unusual artefacts for the Mesolithic. For instance, from the
boreal period site of Nizhneye Veretye I (*c.*8520–9050 BP) in northern Russia five flint
'hoes' have been recovered. These have broad working edges, rounded sides, and short
handles carefully finished by transverse chipping. Similar artefacts are found in
Neolithic assemblages from eastern Europe and the Near East, where they are assumed
to have been used for tilling land. These Mesolithic artefacts are likely to have had a different function. They may have been made to imitate artefacts created from elk antler.

The function of the more regularly found, mundane flint tools is also not easy to elu-

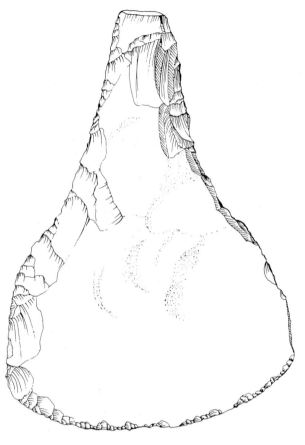

FLINT 'HOE' (*left*) from Nizhneye Veretye. The maximum width of the artifact is 17.5 cm.

DURING THE MESOLITHIC there was an extensive use of organic materials for the manufacture of tools (*right*), deriving from an understanding of natural materials that probably far outstrips ours today. These have been preserved at numerous sites, particularly the waterlogged sites of northern Europe.
1. Barbed points from Star Carr, probably used for hunting large game. Both are made from red-deer antler, 28.7 cm & 31 cm long. Note that on one of them the tang is heavily incised, which may have been to create a rough surface to facilitate binding. 2. Bone projectile heads inset with micro-blades of flint from south Scandinavia, *c.*22 cm. 3.Wooden bolt heads for shooting birds or small furred animals from Danish Mesolithic sites, half size. 4. Mattock head from Star Carr made from lower part of an elk antler. The working edge has been carefully shaped, but is not sharp, 20.7 cm. 5. Bone fish hooks from Mesolithic sites in Denmark and north Germany, two-thirds actual size. 6. Knives/daggers from Nizhneye Veretye I made from elk bone. These were probably personal weapons and usually show careful manufacture and extensive decoration, *c.* 24 cm and 34 cm. 7. Small wooden bow from Vis I. While the function of this and other similar objects remains unknown, the most likely possibility is that they were used for boring or for making fire, *c.* 25 cm. 8. A birch-bark container from Nizhneye Veretye I, *c.* 18 cm. This was made from a single strip of birch bark, with the sides bent to form the walls and the ends the lid. Eighteen cores, 9 flakes, one scraper and an implement for flaking were found inside. 9. Fragments of a net made from plant fibres from Friesack.

cidate. It is difficult to imagine any other function that an artefact with a sharp point could be used for other than boring. However, the catch-all term 'scraper' is applied simply to flakes or blades retouched in a particular manner and coming in a wide variety of forms, and not to imply that they were necessarily used for scraping. Microwear analysis can give us some information concerning function—although the results are often controversial. A study of the flint tools from the site of Star Carr in northern England (*c.*9500 BP) showed that there were very few clear patterns between tool form, the material it had been used upon, and the manner in which it had been used. For instance fifty-six of the 374 scrapers from the site were examined for wear patterns. Only thirty-six (64 per cent) showed traces of use, representing fifty-five use episodes. These were mainly of scraping/planing actions and directed against hide (40 per cent), bone (22 per cent), antler (22 per cent), wood (13 per cent), and either bone or hide (*c.*4 per cent). There did appear to be some difference in the morphology of the artefacts used on different materials. The tools used on antler tended to be longer and more curved than those used against bone, wood, or hide.

Wooden, antler, and bone tools The bog sites of northern Europe, which preserve organic materials, demonstrate that the Mesolithic hunter-gatherers had an immensely

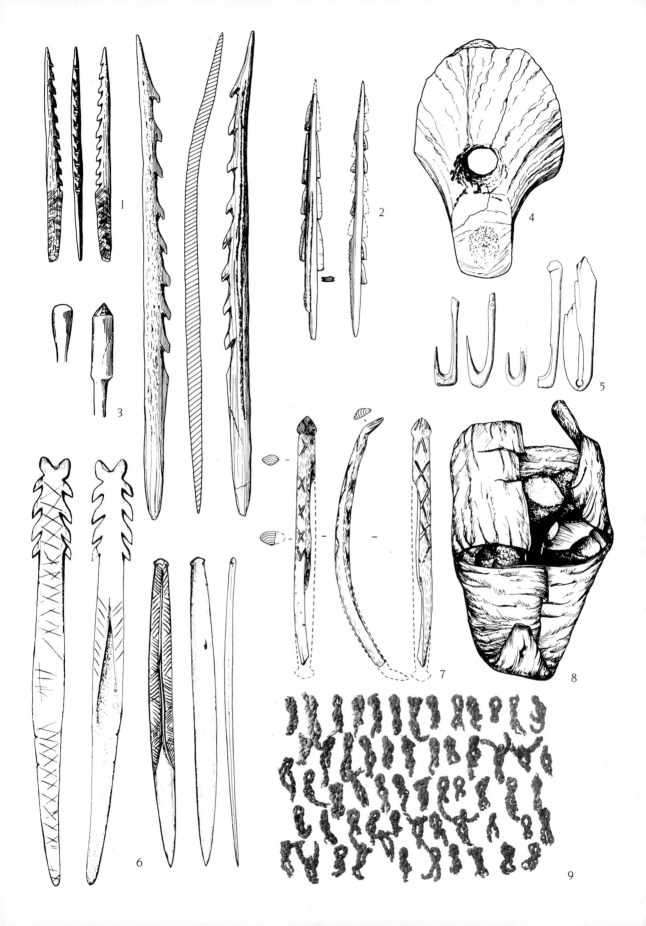

diverse tool-kit made from antler, bone, and wood to complement that of stone. These artefacts can be divided into two classes—those forming hand-held implements and those forming traps and facilities which worked without human presence. Of the first type, the diversity in the form of arrows, spear points, and harpoons is vast. Arrow shafts were fashioned from a variety of wood types. These had either stone tips attached by the use of resin or blunted tips so that they would not damage the pelts of birds and mammals when killed. Bone was also used as a support for microliths. Narrow grooves were made in the bone and microliths inset by using resin. Long, narrow pieces of antler were produced by using a groove and splinter technique, and were fashioned into various forms of barbed points. A great variety of forms was created with either small or large barbs placed either close together or far apart on one or both sides of the harpoon. These harpoons have been used by archaeologists in a similar way as microliths to create industries and cultures.

Another type of artefact that was made from either red deer or elk antler was the mattock. In the earlier Mesolithic, mattocks were produced by removing the palmate part of the antler and then obliquely piercing the remainder so that a wooden handle could be inserted. A variation on this was to use part of the antler shaft and perforate through the stump of the trez tine which could then be used for the socket for the handle. Mattock heads were also manufactured from the limb bones of auroch and elk.

FRAGMENT OF A WICKER CAGE from Agerod V, likely to have been part of an eel or fish trap. This is the largest (82 cm × 52 cm) of several examples from the site. Eight separate rows of bindings made from pine roots had been used to join at least 48 branches of cherry and alder wood. These had been cut during the winter months when the branches were one or two years old.

ERTEBØLLE VESSEL from Tybrind Vig. Charred food remains were found encrusted on the inside of this vessel which gave a radiocarbon date of *c.*5640 BP. The pot measures *c.*30 cm from the pointed base to the rim.

The other class of artefact made from wood, antler, and bone is best represented by wickerwork baskets, which are most likely to have been eel and fish traps. Several examples of these have been found and they display immense technical skill. A range of different raw materials was used to construct the frame and the bindings. The examples from Ageröd V were made from cherry wood while that from Nidløse was made of birch twigs and bound by using split pine roots. Both the frame and bindings of an example from Magelby Long were made of lime.

Plant material was put to a great number of other uses during the Mesolithic, although for many of these we have only minimal evidence. The submerged Ertebølle site of Tybrind Vig, on the west coast of Fyn, Denmark provides some of our best evidence for Mesolithic plant use. From here we have a fish hook with a short length of twine still attached and a few pieces of textiles. These had been woven using plant fibres that had been spun together to form a yarn. Similarly, from the site of Friesack in the Potsdam district of Germany fragments of a net have been found dating to the early boreal period occupation of the site (9050–8800 BP). It remains unclear whether these nets had been used for carrying or fishing.

Pottery   Pottery has traditionally been seen as a product of the Neolithic. Yet in recent years it has become apparent that many late Mesolithic communities were manufacturing and using pottery vessels, first appearing in southern Scandinavia at *c.*5600 BP. This is often taken to indicate that those communities had established a semi- or wholly

FEATURES DENOTING MESOLITHIC HUT and associated structures at Mount Sandel. These are found within an artificially enlarged hollow and are likely to represent a substantial dwelling constructed from posts driven into the ground. This hut appears to have had a large central hearth, from which burnt hazelnuts and bone were recovered. Large pits outside of the dwelling are likely to have been used for storage.

sedentary lifestyle. In the Ertebølle of Denmark two types of vessels were made; pots with pointed bases and oval bowls. Examples of each have come from Tybrind Vig; some contained charred-food residues, which were analysed, and found to be composed of grass and fish.

Dwellings Many Mesolithic sites have post holes, which indicate past structures ranging from simple windbreaks to substantial huts. Evidence for the first of these are found on many sites—a few post holes making a straight line or arc. For instance, the site of Morton, Scotland (*c.*6700–6300 BP) is interpreted as a location repeatedly visited for short periods and has several sets of post/stake holes which are likely to derive from rather flimsy windbreaks.

A rather larger structure is found within the massive shell midden of Moita do Sebastiâo in the Muge valley of Portugal (*c.*7080–7350 BP). Here sixty-one post holes were found in one area of the site, forming a half circle with an opening to the south. This appears to represent a light shelter providing protection from northerly winds. The roofing may well have been made from rushes and stems of *Gramineae* and then water-proofed with clay, since numerous fragments of clay with imprints of *Gramineae* have been found nearby. Associated with it were numerous pits and features representing cooking, storage, and disposal pits. At Mount Sandel, an early Mesolithic site in Ireland (*c*.8960–8440 BP), an exceptionally large number of post holes provides clear evidence for a substantial dwelling. Some of these were over 20 centimetres deep and sloped inwards at a slight angle from the vertical. Others were cut by hearths and pits to suggest that there had been extensive reoccupation on the site.

In Arctic Norway several Mesolithic sites have been found with substantial remains of stone walls and foundations. At Tverrvikraet in Gamvik on the outer coast of Finnmark there are the remains of a small rectangular house. Similarly on the island of Saana, Traena the remains of a house, dating somewhere between 8000 and 6000 BP, have been found with stone foundations, post holes along the interior of the walls, and a single, centrally placed hearth. Even further north around the Varanger Fjord there is evidence for several different types of dwelling structures including pit houses and tents, indicated by circular arrangements of post holes.

In Denmark several sites have been excavated which preserve the remains of hut floors, such as the Maglemosian sites of Ulkestrup Øst I, Holmegaard IV, Duvensee, and Sværdborg I. These floors were made from interlaced bark sheets and split logs of birch and pine. At Ulkestrup I a line of branches was found stuck into the ground along part of the floor edge, which may be the remains of the superstructure. The huts themselves had been either rectangular or trapezoidal in plan ranging from 2.5 × 2.5 metres to 4 × 6 metres. The roofs and walls are likely to have been made from bark and/or reeds. At Holmegaard and Duvensee superimposed birch bark floors suggest either reoccupation or repair during a long period of use. One of the problems with interpreting these 'hut floors' is illustrated by the site of Sværdborg I. Here the remains of nine huts were found and while one was demonstrably earlier than the others it was not possible to identify whether the remaining eight had been in contemporary use or relate to separate visits to a favoured hunting location.

Of course, it is extremely rare that structural remains of dwellings survive in the archaeological record. But the character of past dwellings may be inferred from the distribution of stone tools. Concentrations of worked stone may indicate where people had sat, and the spatial arrangement of such concentrations may indicate the size and shape of a structure in, or beside, which they had been sitting. For instance two adjacent crescent-shaped concentrations of microliths at Flaadat, a Maglemosian site in Denmark, may mark the location of a large dwelling 7–8 metres in diameter. Similarly, cobbled surfaces have been found at sites such as Eskmeals in Cumbria, England and may trace the presence of past structures. Such inferences are highly contentious, however, and we require further studies of the spatial structure of ethnographically documented campsites before they can be verified.

The best preserved dwellings come from the site of Lepenski Vir, in the Danube valley (*c*.7750–6250 BP). This is a very complex and important site at which Mesolithic hunters had 'settled down' to live sedentary lifestyles. The dwellings were trapezoidal in plan varying in size from 5 to 30 metres square. They were built on terraces which had

THE BEST PRESERVED MESOLITHIC DWELLINGS
come from Lepenski Vir in the Danube valley.
Above: one of these trapezoidal structures during
excavation. *Right*: detailed reconstructions
of these structures have been proposed.
The roof is likely to have been made
from two inclined planes of
branches and may have been
covered with hides.

been cut into the sloping banks of the Danube and conformed to regular proportions and internal arrangements. All had their wide ends pointing towards the river. The floors were made of hard limestone plaster and these were surrounded by post holes which must have supported a wooden structure. Inside, large, elongated pits lined with limestone blocks functioned as hearths. In some houses human burials had been made close to these pits while in almost every house there was a large rounded block of limestone carved into a human/fish image.

Transport technology Efficient water transport would have been essential for the Mesolithic communities of Europe for various subsistence activities, to move between different habitats, and for communication between groups. During the Mesolithic,

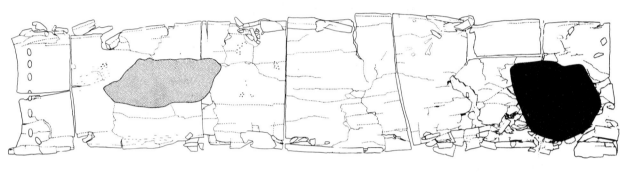

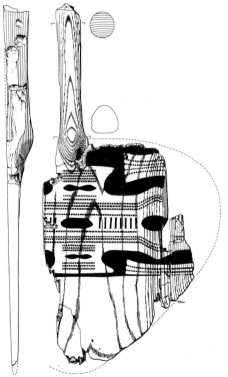

BOAT AND PADDLE from Tybrind Vig. A fireplace and a large stone for ballast (dark) have survived in the stern of the boat. The design on the paddle was created by filling carved incisions with a brown substance. This is just one of ten paddles from Tybrind Vig, all of which were carved to the same heart-shaped design from ash wood. Only two appear to have been decorated.

many offshore islands were colonized, such as the Hebrides and those of the Mediterranean, and substantial boats would have been necessary for the sea crossings. The remains of ling at settlements in western Sweden indicate that deep-sea fishing had been undertaken, probably requiring substantial crafts.

The best preserved Mesolithic boats come from Tybrind Vig. Here the remains of two canoes were found along with decorated paddles. The largest measures 9.5 metres long and 0.65 metres wide and is estimated to have been able to carry six to eight people together with their gear. Within it was a large stone weighing 30 kilograms, which had probably acted as ballast. The sides of the canoes were smooth and rounded and the stern cut into a square. Both of the boats had the remains of a small fire placed at the stern. This may have been related to eel fishing.

From the site of Vis I (8300–7000 BP) in the north-east of the CIS fragments of skis have been preserved. These had been cut from massive hardwood logs. They tapered towards the front end while the lower surface became increasingly convex. On one of them an elk head had been carved to prevent reverse movement of the ski through the snow and to act as a stabilizer. While these are unique finds from the Mesolithic, they closely resemble the skis of the Yakut people of Siberia as documented in the seventeenth century.

Subsistence Activities

The economic basis of Mesolithic societies varied with the nature of their environment. As a whole, the archaeological record reflects an immense flexibility by the Mesolithic hunter-gatherers to exploit diverse environmental types and to cope with the short- and long-term fluctuations in resources availability. This flexibility would have been based upon an exhaustive knowledge of their surroundings and a constant monitoring of the changes in resource distribution.

Hunting terrestrial game   Large terrestrial mammals have, for many years, been assumed to be the essence of Mesolithic economies. Their pre-eminence is gradually being eroded, however, as the productivity of the marine and freshwater environments are appreciated and as studies of human bone provide direct evidence for a significant amount of aquatic foods in the diet. Nevertheless, the hunting of large terrestrial mammals remains central to the Mesolithic, for, even if they were not the staple food supply in all areas, they may have required the greatest time to exploit, and they had considerable social significance. Throughout Europe the faunal assemblages attest to the exploitation of a mix of large ungulates; varying frequencies of red deer, wild pig, roe deer, elk, and auroch are found. It is very rare for any assemblage to be dominated by just one of these ungulates. The Danish site of Ringkloster (*c.*5630–5230 BP) is one exception as remains of pig dominate the faunal assemblage.

Hunting of these large mammals appears to have been predominantly by an encounter strategy, and hunters are likely to have searched in forests for tracks and trails of deer and pig. Having found and inferred information about their makers' age, sex, state of health, and direction of travel, a stalk may have been initiated. If the animal was large, a hunter may have elicited help from other members of the group. Once located, an attempt would have been made either to kill the animal outright or to wound it so it would bleed and could be tracked until it collapsed. The tracking of animals may have been facilitated by the use of dogs. The burial of dogs in Mesolithic cemeteries, generally of animals like German shepherd dogs, indicates that these had been domesticated and were held in much esteem. Pits and traps were also used for hunting large game. Microliths embedded in the bones of an auroch found in a bog at Vig in northern Zealand indicate that it had been shot by arrows released from a trap. In northern Scandinavia there are many pit traps that had been used for hunting large game, notably reindeer.

In those parts of Europe which were not covered by thick forests, and where animals may have aggregated in larger numbers, other types of hunting strategies may also have been employed. From the Levantine art of Spain (which we will discuss below) we have a scene depicting a red deer drive towards an ambush of archers. The picture is at Cuevo de los Caballos and depicts twelve hunters. Eight act as beaters to drive a herd of deer towards four waiting archers. The herd appears to be a group of females with their young—a typical pattern of herd structure for the summer months. Such drives may well have also taken place in northern Europe on particular occasions, but the weight of evidence points towards a more individual stalking pattern.

In addition to large mammals, smaller terrestrial game were also available and exploited during the Mesolithic. Rabbits, badger, otter, and pine marten would have provided furs as well as a source of meat. It is likely that such animals were principally trapped using snares rather than actively hunted. Some sites appear to have been locations where particular species of small game were targeted; Ringkloster has a particularly high frequency of pine marten remains.

The exploitation of aquatic resources   The hunting of large terrestrial game was just one element of the diverse subsistence base of the Mesolithic. For those living along the coast or by large lakes and rivers, aquatic resources would have rivalled, if not surpassed, the large terrestrial mammals in their productivity. Sea birds may have been an important source of food. Recent history indicates the potential food value of those birds which nest in colonies; the 180 inhabitants of St Kilda are reputed to have made an annual harvest of 22,600 gannets. Some Mesolithic sites have a bird fauna dominated by just one or two species. At Aggersund and Øgaarde, Ertebølle sites, the avian fauna is dominated by single species, whooper swan and white-tailed eagle respectively. At other sites, such as Ertebølle itself, many different species are found, often in large numbers. Wholesale slaughter appears likely at such sites, perhaps by driving birds into nets. Inland birds were also regularly hunted mainly for their feathers although these may also have provided a valuable source of food.

The bones of large sea mammals—seals, dolphins, porpoises, and whales—have been

AN IMAGE FROM THE ROCK ART of the Spanish Levant depicting a red-deer hunting drive. The picture is in the Cueva de los Caballos and shows a herd of animals being driven towards a party of archers. The schematic figures and depiction of hunting activity are typical for this rock art tradition.

found in many of the coastal shell middens of the late Mesolithic. These animals may have been actively hunted by using boats, as illustrated in rock engravings from Arctic Norway. Alternatively, beached animals may have been killed. This would almost certainly be the case for the larger animals such as the blue and sperm whales which are occasionally represented in the middens. Many species of seals are also found in the shell middens, and indeed seal bones are found at inland sites such as Ringkloster.

Fish bones are frequently found on well-preserved sites and both salt-water and freshwater fish must have been a valuable source of food. This is particularly the case when migratory species were exploited, since these can provide spectacular harvests. Sites in southern Scandinavia show that a wide range of freshwater species was exploited including eels, pike, tench, bream, and perch. These would have been caught by various techniques including hook, leister, trap, and net. Many coastal sites also have a high representation of salt-water fish. For instance, excavations of the middens on the small Scottish island of Oronsay (*c.*6300–5200 BP) indicate that marine fish, notably saithe, had been systematically exploited and probably exceeded shellfish in their contribution to the diet. Fish remains from the massive shell midden of Ertebølle are predominantly (71 per cent) of freshwater species caught in nearby lakes. Consequently, the coastal location of a site does not necessarily imply that marine species were of principal significance.

At the bottom of the aquatic resource spectrum are shellfish such as oysters, limpets, and periwinkles. These appear to have been an essential source of food in the later Mesolithic when large shell middens are found in many coastal areas. They are, however, very costly to exploit; it has been calculated that 52,267 oysters, 156,800 cockles, or 31,360 limpets would be needed to supply the same calorific value as a single red deer carcass. However, such resources can be gathered by the very young, the old, and the infirm. Also, they are always available and hence could have been relied upon when other resources failed.

The increasing importance of coastal and aquatic resources in the diet during the early post-glacial is clearly shown at the site of Franchthi cave in southern Greece. When this cave was first occupied at 20,000 BP it lay some 5–6 kilometres from the coast. With the rise in sea level, this distance fell to only 1 kilometre by 8500 BP. The faunal remains in the cave show a concomitant increase in the amount of fish and shellfish in the Mesolithic diet.

Plant foods   Plant foods are likely to have been an essential part of the diet during the Mesolithic Age. The post-glacial forests would have provided a rich variety of edible plants, berries, fungi, nuts, and roots. Grass seeds could have been collected from the more open landscapes of southern Europe. While impressive lists of potentially edible species can be made, it is very rare that any plant remains are actually preserved on Mesolithic sites; it is rarer still that these can be confidently identified as a source of food. It is impossible to evaluate the contribution made by plant material to the diet. Studies of wear patterns on human teeth from sites in the Danube gorges suggest this may have been substantial.

Hazel nuts are by far the most common plant material. These are often found at British Mesolithic sites, usually in small quantities but occasionally in larger numbers suggesting extensive exploitation and perhaps storage. For instance, at Oakhanger VII in Hampshire, broken hazel-nut shells were found scattered across the whole of an occupation floor. Some people have suggested that the high frequency of hazel in early post-glacial pollen diagrams may indicate a deliberate encouragement of this species. Acorns are surprisingly scarce on Mesolithic sites in light of their significance as a plant food in other periods. Possibly the need to remove their tannic acid by leaching prior to consumption reduced their attractiveness as a food source. Other edible plant remains include water chestnuts from sites in north-east Europe, fat hen, nettle, and yellow water lily at Star Carr; raspberry at Newferry; and grass (maybe cereal) pollen in copralites from Icoana and Vlasac in the Danube gorges. From 11,000 BP the occupants of Franchthi cave exploited a wide range of plant species including wild almond, pear, bitter vetch, lentils, oats, and barley. The apparently increasing use of plant resources may be compensating for the loss of hunting territories for large game due to rising sea level. All of these plants would have been found growing wild in the valley floors and gentle hill slopes.

Important botanical remains have also been acquired from the site of Balma Abeurador, a cave on the southern margins of the Massif Central and about 50 kilometres from the present Mediterranean coast. The carbonized remains of lentils, chick-peas, and peas have been found in stratified contexts dating between 10,000 and 8,000 BP. These are morphologically similar to the cultigens from early Neolithic sites in south-west Asia. The increasing use of plant material in west Mediterranean sites such as Balma Abeurador appears to be associated with an increase in the exploitation of fish and birds.

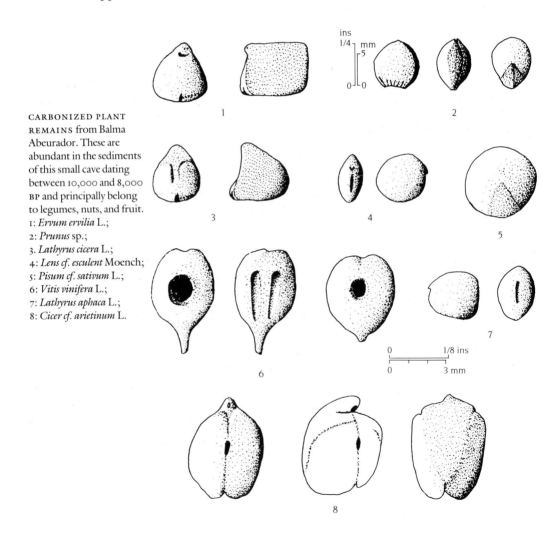

CARBONIZED PLANT REMAINS from Balma Abeurador. These are abundant in the sediments of this small cave dating between 10,000 and 8,000 BP and principally belong to legumes, nuts, and fruit.
1: *Ervum ervilia* L.;
2: *Prunus* sp.;
3: *Lathyrus cicera* L.;
4: *Lens cf. esculent* Moench;
5: *Pisum cf. sativum* L.;
6: *Vitis vinifera* L.;
7: *Lathyrus aphaca* L.;
8: *Cicer cf. arietinum* L.

It is clear that the Mesolithic foragers had a detailed knowledge of the vegetal resources they exploited for food and that the adoption of domesticates at the start of the Neolithic did not present any major transformation in their economies. Indeed, it is a matter of debate as to whether the occupants of Balma Abeurador and of Franchthi caves could have exploited such legumes over the long term by a simple collecting strategy. Incipient cultivation may have been necessary using techniques such as burning, weeding, and irrigation.

In addition to the acquisition of foodstuffs Mesolithic foragers appear to have interfered with the natural vegetation in other ways. In Britain there is considerable evidence of burning, particularly in upland areas. This implies that large areas of vegetation were burnt, but the extent to which this results from human activity, or from natural events, remains unclear. If Mesolithic foragers were burning large areas, it may have been to encourage the growth of young shoots either to exploit for food or as a means to attract deer. If the latter, they would have been increasing the numbers of deer, and the extent to which their location in the landscape could be predicted. Consequently, foraging efficiency would have been improved.

Settlement

We have seen that the post-glacial environments provided the Mesolithic foragers with many different resources to exploit for food and raw materials. This exploitation was not random or haphazard but pursued with great skill and organization. We cannot doubt that the Mesolithic foragers were like the hunter-gatherers recorded in the ethnographic record in having an immense knowledge about their natural environment, the habits of the game, and the changing seasons. Such knowledge would have been used to organize their subsistence activities in an efficient manner so that they were positioned at the appropriate places in the landscapes to exploit those resources which were 'in season'. In addition, however, they needed to be able to take advantage of, or guard against, the unpredictable events of the natural world—the lucky find of a beached-whale or the failure of a migratory resource to arrive. In exploring this aspect of the Mesolithic we can begin by recognizing the many different varieties of settlement types.

Site types and interpretation The diversity of site types during the Mesolithic is immense. At one end of the scale are small campsites which represent a single occupation for perhaps just a few hours by a small group of hunters. At the other, we have large site complexes which have settlement remains indicating occupation throughout the year by large groups of people. Between these extremes we have various types of hunting camps, raw material extraction sites, and specialized activity locations. Much of the research in recent years has been concerned with inferring the function and season of occupation of such settlements. We can appreciate this diverse range of site types, and the means by which they are interpreted, by looking at a selection from Mesolithic Europe.

The most common Mesolithic site is a small discrete scatter of worked-flint with no organic preservation. These may denote short-term camps, perhaps just overnight stops by hunting parties, or even events during the course of a hunt such as the field butchering of a killed animal. Many of these sites are scattered throughout the highland areas of Europe. Typical examples are the flint scatters from the Pennines of Britain, such as Dunford A and Broomhead 5, which have microliths making up over 90 per cent of the retouched tools. Such sites often command prominent positions with extensive views over the countryside and are assumed to relate to the hunting of red deer. Similar sites in the Norwegian highlands would have been concerned with reindeer exploitation. For instance site '148' (*c*.5870 BP) in the Ryfylke-Setesdal mountains is found on a slight slope just above the edge of standing water and near to a path used by modern reindeer. Just seven flint artefacts were found, six of which fitted back into one nodule. This site appears to represent just a single event, perhaps a butchering episode or the remains of a hide.

When interpreting flint scatters, which are larger than those from '148', the main difficulty is knowing how many occupation events are represented. Are they simply palimpsests from many short-term occupations by a few hunters or from a more extensive period of occupation by a relatively large group? Acquiring a series of radiocarbon dates from such sites can help decide. For instance, flint scatters at the open-air site of Calowanie, near Warsaw, had once been interpreted as representing individual occupation units. But new radiocarbon dates indicate that each individual flint scatter had formed over as much as 1000 years between *c*.9400 and *c*.8300 BP and are therefore palimpsests from a series of reoccupations.

When radiocarbon dates cannot be attained, the refitting of flakes, which are horizontally or vertically dispersed, is another way to demonstrate that an assemblage relates to just one occupation, or, at least, a limited number. This has been used at the Mesolithic site at Hengistbury Head in southern England. This site is a dense spread of flint artefacts stratified in wind-blown sand deposits which have been heavily podzolized. Excavation of over 78 square metres yielded 38,000 flint artefacts. Refitting has not only shown that the site consisted of a series of overlapping knapping clusters but also that the considerable vertical distribution of artefacts is purely a result of post-depositional processes. Artefacts have been refitted from vertical intervals of up to 39 centimetres. When all the rejoined items are combined, they form a series of interlocking fits spread over a vertical distance of 60 centimetres. Processes such as trampling, bioturbation, drift, and deflation would have been responsible for the vertical distribution. Had it not been for refitting, this site might easily have been interpreted as one of multiple occupations within a gradually accumulating sand deposit. At other sites, the possibilities for either numerous radiocarbon dates or refitting are limited due to preservation and the character of the raw materials. Often, however, the sheer quantity of artefacts and knapping debitage suggests that the sites had been reoccupied many times. For instance, at Bolsay Farm on the Isle of Islay in western Scotland, excavations

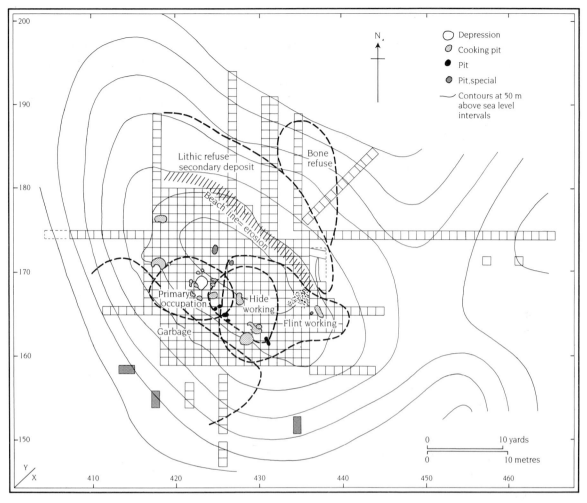

Labels on map: Lithic refuse secondary deposit, Bone refuse, Beach line = erosion, Primary occupation, Hide working, Flint working, Garbage

0   10 yards
0   10 metres

EXCAVATION PLAN AND ZONATION of activity areas of Vaenget Nord. The activity areas have been defined by the distribution of artifacts, features, and wear analysis on stone tools. The 'primary occupation' area is likely to have been where the hut(s) were placed. Just to the north of this, and at the highest part of the island, a single burial likely to have been of an adult male was made.

suggest that several million pieces of worked stone were originally present, including many thousands of microliths. The quality of preservation is low, but it is most likely that such quantities of material had built up gradually from many occupations of the site, probably due to its excellent location as a hunting site.

The reconstruction of activity areas within sites can be achieved by wear analysis. One of the most successful examples of this has been at the site of Vænget Nord, an Ertebølle site at Vedbæk dated to c.7000 BP. This is one of a whole complex of sites that have been discovered in the Vedbækfjord area of Zealand, Denmark. Wear analysis has shown that the site can be divided into two distinct areas. One is characterized by burins for working bone or antler and the other by tools which had been used for hide working, such as end-scrapers and unretouched blades. The first of these has been referred to as the area

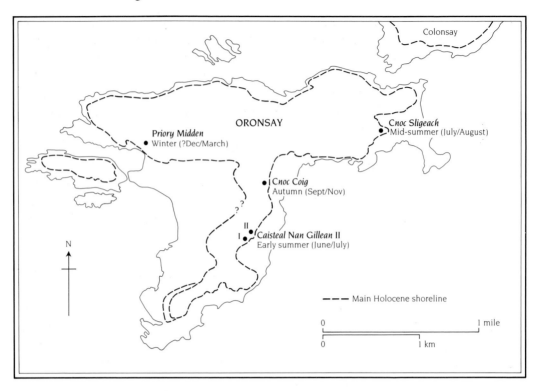

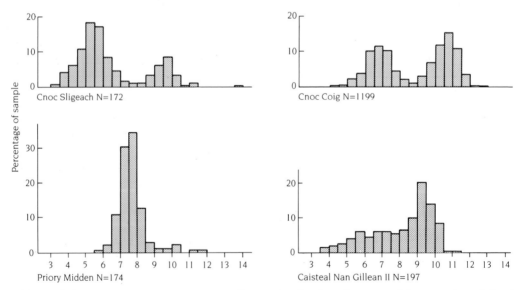

LOCATION OF MESOLITHIC SHELL MIDDENS on Oronsay showing the main seasons of site occupation as inferred from the size distribution of otoliths of saithe, shown below. Saithe was the most important species of fish exploited from Oronsay and, due to its rapid growth, its size as estimated from otolith length can provide a direct indication of the season in which the fish had been caught.

of primary occupation since it coincides with the concentration of features, rhomboid points, and microburins. Around the hideworking zone is an area of flintworking and behind these a waste dump, which was an area dark in colour and rich in charcoal and fire-cracked rocks. In some places individual dumps have been located such as a flint scatter containing all the debitage from the manufacture of an axe, except for the axe itself and the tiny chips, which would presumably have remained at the knapping location when the waste was cleared up.

When faunal remains are preserved, many more inferences about the seasonality and the function of a site can be made. For instance, at the Ertebølle site of Aggersund in northern Denmark, the faunal remains are dominated by the migratory whooper swan. These would only have been available in that area between November and March. Consequently, the site is interpreted as a specialized winter swan-hunting camp. The faunal remains from Star Carr provide a classic example of attempts to infer site season and function. These remains have been intensively studied and frequently reinterpreted. Current views suggest that they indicate a late spring/early summer occupation for the site. This is indicated by the dentition from red deer and roe deer jaws and the numerous red deer skulls with shed antlers—something that occurs in April and May. The loose antlers at the site, which on prima-facie evidence would indicate an autumn occupation, could have been collected throughout the year. Since the skeletal elements at the site are those which hunters typically dispose of after initial butchery, because they bear little meat, this spring/summer occupation appears to have occurred at a temporary hunting camp rather than at a more permanently occupied base camp to which the meat-bearing bones would have been returned.

Faunal remains from the shell middens on the tiny island of Oronsay in the southern Hebrides are also worthy of mention. Here five middens are found on an island that would have been no more than 4 kilometres square when occupied. As mentioned above, saithe was a very common fish species and the otoliths (ear bones) of these have been used to calculate the season during which each midden was occupied. This is possible since during the first two to three years of life the growth of young saithe is very rapid and its size, as measured by otolith length, indicates the season in which it was killed. By using this technique it appears that each midden on Oronsay had been occupied in a different season. Presumably, the particular topographic location of the midden made it particularly favourable for one specific season. Two alternative interpretations could be made for this pattern. Permanent, year-round occupation might be proposed with foragers moving from one midden to another as a seasonal round. However, this seems unlikely on such a small island in this part of Europe where other resources (such as deer) may have been unavailable. The middens may, therefore, represent a very gradual accumulation over many years by short-term visits to the island for fishing and sealing. The Mesolithic foragers would have used their knowledge of the landscape, tides, and prevailing winds to choose the most favourable location on each visit.

More likely candidates for year-round permanent occupation are the large midden and settlement sites of southern Scandinavia. Many of these are found at the interface of several different ecological zones and would have provided the foragers with an array of seasonally overlapping resources. For instance, in the north of Denmark we find the massive shell midden of Ertebølle (*c.*5800–5100 BP), which gave its name to the Ertebølle culture. It has been suggested that the inhabitants of this site would have relied upon the produce from large terrestrial animals during the summer and autumn months, while migratory and breeding sea mammals would have been the mainstay during the winter. A possible 'spring gap' would have been filled by the oyster, the shells of which constitute the bulk of the midden. Similarly, the site of Skateholm (*c.*7000–5400 BP) in the south of Sweden appears to be located at the interface between the terrestrial, lagoon, and marine biotopes because of the variety of resources such a mix of environments provided. The faunal assemblage from this site, or rather sites since three periods of occupation are known, testify to an amazing diversity of resources exploited from each of these biotopes. Seasonality indicators are dispersed throughout the year.

Subsistent-settlement systems   We have so far discussed site types as individual entities, but the thrust of much recent research has been to make associations and hence reconstruct the 'subsistent-settlement' system. Now, it is very rare for an archaeologist to be able to state confidently that two sites were sufficiently contemporary to have been used by the same group of people, even with the rather fine chronological resolution we have for the Mesolithic. Consequently, the settlement systems we reconstruct are often amalgams using sites which may not have been precisely contemporary and hence represent idealized models, rather than detailed reconstructions, for any particular region or phase of the Mesolithic.

The simplest type of Mesolithic settlement system is that involving movement between low and high ground. Among many historically documented hunter-gatherers, people aggregated in lowland areas during the winter months, when many communal activities were undertaken, and then dispersed into the upland areas in smaller groups during the summer. It is most likely that such a pattern of fission and fusion extended back into the Mesolithic. Often one can detect differences in the lithic assemblages from highland and lowland areas which suggest different activities had been undertaken and which relate to past mobility patterns. For instance, in Britain, Mesolithic sites in upland areas tend to have a high frequency of microliths, suggesting the repair/manufacture of hunting equipment. In contrast, those in more lowland areas often have much higher frequencies of tools such as scrapers which would have been used in base-camp activities, for example, in the preparation of skins. It is very likely that the small flint scatters in the Norwegian highland relating to reindeer hunting derive from spring-autumn hunting parties who moved up from either the western or eastern lowlands. The artefacts found at these sites are made of flint, which could only have come from coastal sites.

The excellent preservation of Mesolithic sites in Denmark allows us to reconstruct settlement systems which were more sophisticated than a simple aggregation/dispersion cycle. For the Ertebølle period we have several sites which, by virtue of their location, the faunal remains, and artefact inventories, are thought to have been seasonal camps used for very particular subsistence activities. We have already mentioned Aggersund which was devoted to the hunting of swans during the winter. The site of Vængo So is at a location that is particularly suitable for the standing of whales, a species that figures prominently in its faunal assemblage. The catching of eels is likely to have been the main activity undertaken at the site of Dyrholm, which was only occupied during the autumn and winter. Ringkloster appears to have been a winter camp-site where hunters specialized in hunting wild piglets and pine marten. The occupation of these sites is likely to have been by hunters making special forays from their base camps. These were large coastal midden sites, such as Ertebølle, Meilgaard, and Norslund, in locations suitable for a range of different activities, and contain evidence of occupation throughout much of the year.

It is rare to find high levels of organic preservation throughout an entire region enabling the reconstruction of a spatially extensive settlement system using faunal remains to infer site function and seasonality. When such remains are absent, one must rely on factors such as site size, features, and the character of lithic assemblages. Such variables can be used with great effect. For instance on the island of Vega in northern Norway a series of sites have been classified as to their respective roles in the Mesolithic settlement system. Åsgarden is the largest site with a lithic assemblage of over 250,000 pieces, a diverse range of tools and a large house structure. This has been interpreted as a residential base. From here Mesolithic foragers may have visited satellite field camps, such as at Hesvik where the sites are smaller in area and the structures less substantial. A further class of site, smaller still in area and in the size of the lithic assemblage, may represent 'boat stations'—temporary landing places around the coast, or 'stops', locations where a single activity had taken place. Quite whether such reconstructions are correct is questionable, but there is no reason why the settlement systems in areas with poor organic preservation need have been any less complex than those in areas such as southern Scandinavia.

An example of reconstructed settlement systems from southern Europe is useful in that it shows the demise of the 'culture' concept as a valid explanation for assemblage variability. Along the coast of northern Spain two 'types' of Mesolithic sites are found within the same period (9500–8500 BP) and which have been given different 'cultural' labels, the Asturian and the Azilian. For instance, the term Asturian is applied to the material from level 29 at La Riera dating to 8650 ± 300 BP while that from level C at Urtiaga dated to 8700 ± 170 BP (i.e. contemporary in archaeological terms) is referred to as Azilian. The differences lie partly in the tool assemblages. Asturian assemblages have fewer retouched pieces and backed bladelets than Azilian assemblages together with a much higher frequency of heavy duty tools such as picks and choppers. Asturian sites are found predominately at lowland locations and in estuaries, while Azilian sites are found throughout lowland and highland areas. The faunal remains also vary;

Asturian assemblages are always dominated by red deer with low frequencies of roe deer and wild pig, while Azilian assemblages show much greater variation. In upland areas, they are dominated by ibex. Traditionally, the Azilian and Asturian sites have been attributed to different groups of people, different cultures. More likely, however, they are two components of a single subsistent-settlement system. Asturian sites are probably the bulk disposal of garbage from base camps while the Azilian sites represent the locations where various hunting, gathering, and fishing activities were carried out. Other elements of this settlement system, such as the base camps, have yet to be discovered.

Foraging decisions　We must be very careful when 'reconstructing' these subsistent-settlement systems not to lose the view of Mesolithic foragers as extremely flexible in their subsistent behaviours by forcing them into a regular seasonal round. Although much of their subsistence pattern may have been routinized—waiting for the migrating fish in spring, and moving to the inland sites in summer—the efficiency of their foraging behaviour had to have been based on a readiness to respond to new opportunities or to cope with unexpected shortfalls in resources. To do this they would have depended on their knowledge of the surroundings and have had a continuous updating of their 'information banks' about the availability and location of different resources. Hence, rather than thinking of Mesolithic subsistence in terms of a seasonal round, a more appropriate perspective is to view it as a series of choices made by individuals and groups as to what resources to exploit at which time of year.

We can think of such decisions as either 'patch choices' (which type of biotope to move to, such as inland forest or the coast) or 'prey choices' (which specific resources to exploit once within those patches). In making such decisions foragers would have gathered and processed much information concerning their current needs and the likely returns from different patch/prey types. They would have been trying to make a balance between the cost, benefit, and risk of exploiting different resources. Cost concerns the amount of energy and time invested into hunting or gathering them; benefit is the return in terms of meat and raw materials; the risk is the chance that much effort will be invested for no return. For instance, if a hunter successfully kills a red deer then the yield in terms of meat, hide, and antler will be substantial; but hunting red deer is a risky activity—one may not find the tracks, fail to strike it when a shot is made, or fail to find the carcass after a wounded and dying animal has fled. In contrast, gathering molluscs has no risk associated with it for they are easy to find in large quantities. However, one must invest much back-breaking work if a sufficient amount is to be gathered for a decent meal!

Ageröd V　Much of the Mesolithic subsistence behaviour and technology can be understood from this decision-making, cost–benefit–risk perspective. As an example we might finish this look at Mesolithic subsistence and settlement with a brief consideration of the site of Ageröd V (*c.*6860–6540 BP), an early Atlantic settlement in central Scania. The faunal remains from this site testify to a wide range of animals being exploited.

Red deer, elk, roe deer, and pig are represented and the site appears to have been a hunting camp where hunters went in search of these animals on the encounter basis described above. The number of individual carcasses of each of these represented at the site suggests that considerable effort was placed in hunting and much meat and raw materials acquired. Preference appears to have been for the larger and more difficult to find species such as red deer; many opportunities for hunting the smaller roe deer are likely to have been passed over. In light of this focus on terrestrial hunting it initially appears strange that the site is placed on a small island in a marshy area about 400 metres to the nearest firm land. However, such placement would have been very appropriate for the setting of fish traps to catch the perch, bream, and tench represented at the site. On a daily basis these fish traps may have been far more regular in supplying food than hunting large terrestrial game as there was little risk associated with them. Hence, the foragers could afford to go off in the risky pursuit of red deer—and return home empty-handed on many occasions—for the fish traps assured a supply of food.

Population and Society

The Mesolithic is widely regarded as a period of rapid population growth. Estimates for population densities vary markedly, not surprisingly in light of the difficulties in making such estimates and the likely pattern of variability across Mesolithic Europe. Population densities between 0.50 and 0.005 people/kilometres square are probable and are relatively high for hunter-gatherers. The difficulty in estimating past population sizes and rates of change can be illustrated with the Mesolithic of southwest Germany. Here we see a marked reduction in the number of sites at *c.* 8000 BP, the boundary between the earlier and later Mesolithic. This may reflect a reduction in the size of the human population. However, as there were considerable environmental changes at this time, such as increasing vegetational diversity, the reduction in site numbers may reflect a change in settlement pattern. It is possible that the hunter-gatherers responded to their new environment by living in fewer, but larger, residential camps, or by restricting the location of these to specific areas.

On analogy with documented hunter-gatherers, the social organization of populations are likely to have been hierarchically structured with three principal tiers. At the base would have been the family group. For much of the year families would have congregated to form groups ranging in size from twenty-five to a hundred individuals. These would then have been associated into networks stretching over extensive regions. Contact between groups and individuals in this network would have been made by visiting and periodic aggregation, at which time information, goods, and marriage partners may have been exchanged. However, as with subsistence patterns and technology, one must also recognize that considerable variability in social organization is likely to have existed across Mesolithic Europe. In part this is because social organization, like technology, is a means by which the Mesolithic foragers adapted to their natural environments. Speculation on the nature of Mesolithic populations and social organization is easy; hard evidence is more difficult to find. One of the best sources comes from the burial of the dead.

It is during the Mesolithic Age that the first cemeteries were created in Europe. Throughout the Upper Palaeolithic, and perhaps even in the Middle Palaeolithic, individuals had been buried with varying amounts of ritual. But it is only during the Mesolithic that formal burial grounds were created, with the largest containing several hundred individuals. The existence and contents of these cemeteries provides many insights into the Mesolithic; we can re-create the demographic structure of the society; learn about the state of health; make inferences about the social structure and the symbolic meaning of artefacts, which are placed with the dead.

Cemeteries   Cemeteries are a late Mesolithic phenomenon with a mean age of *c.*6250

DISTRIBUTION OF MESOLITHIC CEMETERIES in Europe showing preference for coastal, lake, and riverine locations. This may partly be a factor of discovery, although most likely reflects a true pattern of social complexity and incipient territoriality in these areas of high resource abundance and diversity.

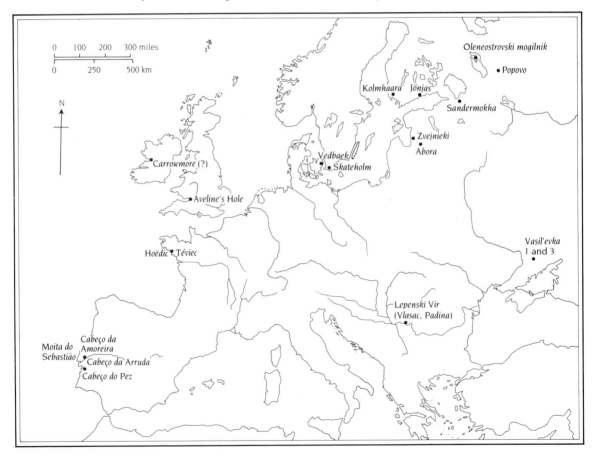

BP. During the earlier Mesolithic, burial continued to be of an individualistic nature — at least no cemeteries have yet been discovered. Their appearance seems to represent a distinct event in European prehistory; perhaps the passing of a demographic threshold at *c*.6500 BP. Cemeteries, and the 'complex' societies they reflect are predominantly found in coastal areas or adjacent to large lakes or rivers. There is good reason for this, as such areas would have been the most productive and hence best able to support the largest populations. Some believe this led to the need to mark, perhaps defend, territory achieved by many traditional societies through the use of ancestor presence, i.e. by burial.

The cemeteries show a marked variation in size: the two largest are Oleneostrovski Mogilnik, in Karelia, and Cabeço da Arruda, in Portugal. From each of these over 170 graves have been excavated. Most cemeteries, however, have between twenty to sixty burials each. There are many difficulties in trying to calculate the actual size of a cemetery and to make appropriate comparisons. It is often hard to estimate how long a cemetery was in use and the rate at which people were added to it. Are some larger simply because they were used over a longer period or because they relate to a much larger population? Similarly, comparisons are confounded by the marked variability in the quality of preservation between cemeteries, as well as with the extent and detail of excavation.

Palaeopathology   One of the most interesting types of datum from the skeletal remains concerns the state of health of past populations. Many types of disease and injury are represented in the skeletal material. Particularly common are arthritis and caries, but other pathologies include porotic hyperostosis, enamel hypoplasia, rickets, and osteomalacia. Some patterning in the intensity and types of pathology between different populations is evident. Cemeteries relating to more sedentary groups, such as Skateholm, Vedbæk, and Vlasac, contain individuals who have few caries but a wide range of other pathological conditions and had been in poor states of health when alive. In contrast, the populations from cemeteries relating to more mobile groups, such as at Grotta dell'Uzzo, Arene Candide, and Moita do Sebastiâo, have high frequencies of caries, as much as 50 per cent in some cases, but otherwise had been much healthier when alive, with little evidence for pathologies in the skeletal material. No doubt this pattern relates to the greatly increased exposure to parasites and infectious diseases that arise due to hygiene problems created in permanent settlements.

Numerous skeletons from these Mesolithic cemeteries have injuries caused by projectile points. These are often still embedded in the bone and are likely to have been the cause of death. For instance, grave 19A at Vedbæk contains a male with a bone point embedded between the second and third thoracic vertebrae, while that in grave 7 has a trapeze embedded in a long bone. At Skateholm, the remains of an adult man, which had been deposited in a pit, now labelled grave 13, had a transverse arrowhead embedded in the pelvis indicating that death was caused by a projectile which had pierced the abdomen. Several different scenarios are possible to interpret these injuries. They may

GRAVE FROM SKATEHOLM I.
This Mesolithic burial contains an
elderly man to the left in a supine
position, and a young female in a
slight hocker position.

have been caused by hunting accidents, when a group of hunters were slaying a large ungulate such as an adult red deer. Alternatively they may relate to fighting between individuals. A third possibility is that they may derive from organized warfare between groups, as illustrated in the Spanish Levantine paintings discussed below.

Grave goods and burial ritual Moving from the skeletons to the grave goods and the manner of burial we again find considerable variability within and between cemeteries. The variation within cemeteries may relate to the past social organization of the groups, whereas that between cemeteries may relate to the particular traditions of the groups concerned. We might contrast Vedbæk and Skateholm I. At the former, all seventeen graves were of the same simple type—a trough-shaped excavation 0.5–1.0 metres below the surface. They had been laid out in parallel rows and all but three contained just one individual. With the exception of one grave, the deceased had been placed in the supine position with their feet close together and arms along their sides. At Skateholm I, however, there was immense diversity in burial customs, including cremation, and bodies were found sitting up, lying outstreched on their back or stomach, in the hocker position (sideways with knees folded up below the chest), and in a range of contortions.

In addition to the variation in burial ritual across space we can also use the multiple cemeteries at Skateholm to monitor changes through time, for significant differences in burial ritual used in cemeteries I and II are evident. Whereas the hocker position was the most commonly used at Skateholm I, it is absent at Skateholm II, as is the sitting position. The number of grave goods increase at Skateholm II and the burials appear to be laid out according to a more rigid plan, in contrast to the apparent randomness in the earlier cemetery. Moreover, dogs are no longer accorded the same degree of burial ritual at Skateholm II. Previously they appear to have been treated in very similar ways to people. Another fascinating find at Skateholm II is the remains of a large ceremonial structure: a rectangular area demarcated by a belt of red ochre and containing deposits of various parts of different animals.

The burial of dogs at Skateholm deserves further comment. Dogs are likely to have been extremely valuable to the Mesolithic hunters and this is likely to account for the ritual often associated with dog burials. Certain dogs have been found buried individually and with very rich grave goods, such as antlers and flint blades, positioned as if the dog had been a human. Others appear to have been killed to accompany their masters in death, their skeletons being found within the backfill of the grave. In other cases, single canine skeletal elements have been found within graves, implying dismemberment. As a whole, the treatment of dogs, as of humans, appears to have been complex and variable.

We might note, also, other evidence for ritual behaviour during the Mesolithic. Although many of the artefacts found in the bogs of northern Europe, such as the arrows from Loshult, may have been chance losses, others are likely to have been votive depositions. Some of these finds appear to have been deliberately destroyed prior to deposition. Flint nodules have also been found with lines engraved into the cortex prior to being reduced to chips without any intention of manufacturing tools. At Dyrholm

N

| 0 | 5 | 10 | 15 | 20 m |

| 0 | 10 | 20 yds |

traces of cut marks and fractures on human bones suggest the extraction of marrow and cannibalism.

Social organization The very existence of cemeteries suggests a more complex social organization among hunter-gatherer populations than that found during the early post-glacial and the preceding glacial period. Insights into the nature of this social organization can be gained by examining the relationship between grave goods, the age and sex of those interred, and the variation in burial ritual. Two types of social differentiation can be searched for in the data. The first, horizontal, refers to the status attached to a person due to their intrinsic characteristics—age, sex, personal achievements—and is typical of an 'egalitarian' society. The second, vertical, is that by which status is acquired by virtue of birth—i.e. hereditary inequality—and is the basis of 'ranked' society. The classic indicator for this is the burial of children with great wealth that could not possibly have been obtained by their own actions.

In the majority of cases, social differentiation appears to have been of the horizontal type. Most of the variability in the distribution of grave goods and burial ritual can be accounted for by referring to age and sex alone. Other features, such as the distribution of ochre, are uniform within cemeteries. In these societies status may well have derived from one's success at hunting large game, notably red deer and wild pig, since antler and tooth pendants figure prominently in the repertoire of burial goods. Three cemeteries contain evidence for vertical social differentiation, indicating that the first ranked societies of Europe appeared during the Mesolithic. At Hoëdic and Téviec on the Brittany coast, children had been buried with a very elaborate graveside ritual and many grave goods. These cemeteries are also notable for having multiple burials, in contrast to the otherwise almost universal pattern of single burials, implying that graves were periodically re-opened and resealed to inter members of a single descent group. Complex burial structures are also found at Téviec involving slab-lined graves covered by small mounds.

The cemetery of Oleneostrovski Mogilnik in Karelia has evidence for the most complex social organization currently known from the Mesolithic. Hereditary social positions and economic ranking were prevalent. The 170 graves excavated—roughly a third of the total number in the cemetery—showed marked variability in the quantity of grave goods. Twenty per cent of the graves had no items while others had more than 400 items. Much of this variability can be accounted for by horizontal social differentiation, that is, by reference to age and sex alone conforming to the pattern found elsewhere in Mesolithic Europe. For instance, there were few child burials, suggesting that the inheritance of wealth was limited. Males and females were regularly associated with different types of grave goods: bone points, slate knives, and bone pins with males and carved

THE CEMETERY AT OLENEOSTROVSKI MOGILNIK. This cemetery has a diverse range of burial types including upright internments marked here by bold stipples. The finer stipples represent ground surface irregularities, primarily depressions. Some 170 burials have been excavated leading to the recovery of more than 7000 artifacts, the majority of which were pendants made from the perforated teeth of elk, beaver, and bear.

beaver incisors with females. The wealth possessed by an individual was apparently expressed through the type and quantity of pierced animal tooth pendants with which they were interred. These were of bear, elk, and beaver—just three of the many animals that were hunted and, which one can presume had symbolic importance. Individuals in their prime of life had the greatest number of these pendants, probably reflecting their greater abilities as hunters versus the young or old.

Cross-cutting this horizontal social differentiation are patterns which suggest that certain individuals had social positions independent from achieved social status. Nine graves contained carved effigies of snakes, elks, and humans, suggesting that those individuals had some special social position. In addition there were four shaft graves in which the deceased assumed a standing position. These are likely to be the graves of shamans. A third type of social distinction at Oleneostrovski Mogilnik is division of the entire cemetery into two grave clusters, probably reflecting a bipartite division of the society, perhaps into two clans. Elk effigies were restricted to graves in the northern cluster, whereas snake and human effigies predominated in the southern cluster. We can describe Oleneostrovski Mogilnik as an incipient ranked society. Together with Téviec and Hoëdic, Vedbæk and Skateholm, and the many smaller cemeteries we can readily appreciate that the hunter-gatherer societies of the later Mesolithic had reached a level of social complexity greater than that of any preceding society in prehistoric Europe.

Social boundaries   A further aspect of social organization concerns ethnic boundaries between groups marked by distinctive changes in artefact types and styles. Identifying such stylistic variability requires that we hold other variables, such as raw material types and function, constant. Rarely is this possible, and much of the artefactual variability across Europe is most readily explained by reference to utilitarian factors, rather than to style and ethnicity.

A recent study has attempted to investigate whether any regional patterning can be detected in the many different shapes of microliths found which may be considered functionally equivalent to each other. By using sophisticated statistical techniques, the majority of variation in microlithic shape was shown to be random. However, some patterning was apparent in the later Mesolithic. Certain regions seemed to have a clear preference for specific shapes of microlith. This may well relate to the establishment of socio-cultural boundaries and territoriality in the later Mesolithic period. By studying the distribution of other artefact types, it appears that southern Scandinavia was divided into three major areas each having distinct traditions during the later Mesolithic: Jutland, the east Danish islands, and Scania. A boundary between west and east Denmark is indicated by different artefact distributions: certain harpoon types, bone combs, T-shaped antler axes, and decorative motifs are not found east of Funen. Other artefacts, such as certain types of stone axe are not found in Jutland. Scania is noticeably different in its mortuary practices, as discussed above, and in the designs found on bone harpoons and Ertebølle pottery.

Social boundaries can also be detected at a smaller spatial scale. Flake axes from Erte-

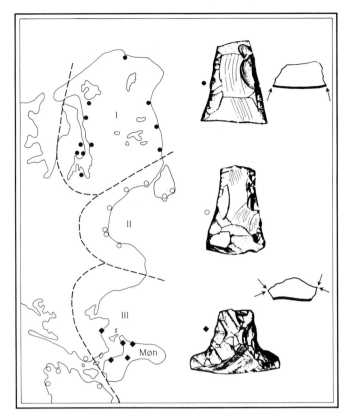

DISTRIBUTION OF FLAKE AXES in the late Ertebølle culture in eastern Zealand. In each of the three groupings one specific type of axe prevails. Such variation over a small spatial area may derive from a variety of factors including raw material availability for axe manufacture, contrasting activities for which axes were used, and stylistic differences relating to discrete social groups and perhaps reflecting territoriality. The latter is generally preferred for this specific example.

bølle sites in eastern Zealand come in a range of different shapes varying with respect to symmetry and the breadth of cutting edge. Three principal variants show clear spatial patterning, and this may well reflect the boundaries of social groups. We clearly have not only a complex social organization but also the emergence of a complex social geography in the later Mesolithic.

Art

As in any period, it is difficult to draw a line between what is, and what is not, an object of art. As we have seen, the tools of the Mesolithic often display a skill that teeters on the edge, if not falls into, the realm of creativity that we call art rather than craft. The finely worked flint objects and the houses of Lepenski Vir all demonstrate that an aesthetic sensibility was involved in the manufacture of even the most utilitarian of objects.

It is often only when we have little idea of the function of an artefact that we describe it as art. This is illustrated by the Azilian painted pebbles which come principally from sites in France and Spain at around 11,000 BP. These are small, flat or ovoid pebbles mainly of a blue-grey schist which were selected from a river and then painted. This decoration is in the form of dots, lines, and, occasionally, more complex motifs such as chevrons and crosses. There are no depictions of animals or indeed of any representa-

AZILIAN PAINTED
PEBBLES from Mas
d'Azil. Such pebbles
tend to be rather small,
c.2–3 cm in length.

tional figures. The majority of these pebbles come from the cave/tunnel of Mas d'Azil in the foothills of the Pyrenees and were discovered at the same time as Palaeolithic cave paintings. Although we describe these as art, they have none of the elegance or craftsmanship that we find in the antler harpoons or woven fishtraps that convention required us to discuss under 'technology'. But these pebbles have their own beauty, part of which is contained in the mystery as to what they were used for. Perhaps they were markers in a game, or constitute an early counting system; possibly they were used in cult or ritual activities. The idea that they were just playful doodlings has been falsified by a recent study which demonstrated that there is order and pattern in these designs. For instance, sixteen different motifs have been identified but only forty-one of the 246 possible binary combinations were ever used. The pebble collections from different sites have markedly different frequencies of motifs: for example, dots dominate on those from Mas d'Azil while lines are most common on the pebbles from Rochedare.

From Lepenski Vir we have another Mesolithic art tradition based on rounded stone, but one of impressive proportions. Found among the ruins of the trapezoid houses, we have a striking series of carved sandstone boulders varying from 20 to 60 centimetres in height. Many of these have purely abstract designs of either a geometric or a more amorphous nature. Others are anthropomorphic—haunting faces with heavy eyebrows, ears, noses, and wide, large lips. They are often described as half human and half fish. The power of these simple designs is immense and provides a glimpse into the mythological world of the Lepenski Vir hunter-fishers.

For the art produced on organic materials we must once again return to the waterlogged sites of northern Europe. The most significant find of recent years is the wooden paddle from the submerged settlement of Tybrind Vig. An elegant geometric design had been either engraved or pressed into the face of this paddle and then filled with a brown pigment. The design itself is unique from the Mesolithic and provocatively suggests the visual riches that we only glimpse at through such lucky finds.

Throughout southern Scandinavia there have been many finds of decorated antler and bone objects. Engraving or pitting was used to build up geometric designs. Most of these were constructed from basic shapes such as rhomboids, squares, lozenges, and barbed lines. More complex mesh images are sometimes found, and, occasionally, representational imagery. Some spatial and temporal patterning in decorated objects can be identified. In the Maglemosian, bone objects and pointed antler tools were the main items decorated. In the Kongemose and Ertebølle, antler axes and long antler shafts were also decorated. Likewise, some designs had limited geographical distribution as noted in the discussion above on social boundaries.

An artefact from the site of Sjöholmen in southern Sweden is part of a red deer antler that had been extensively ground down to prepare the surface for engraving and to exaggerate the Y formed by the beam and a tine. The surface is covered with a complex of shapes involving rhomboids and hexagons. Amid this complexity, two zoomorphic forms are present which appear to be images of fish. They have long, slender bodies and oblique lines which may be fins. Whether this artefact was once part of a functional object is difficult to decide; there are the remains of a shaft hole opposite the Y suggesting it was part of a multi-component object, but no wear is apparent on the engraved surface.

Engraved animals are rare and, as with the supposed fish on the above example, may be so schematized that they are difficult to identify. A few engravings of deer are known, such as the red deer on the mattock head from Ystad, Scania. Anthropomorphic designs are rather more numerous and often intermixed; indeed they grade into, geometric designs. A few carvings of animals are known from southern Scandinavia. There is a small set of objects carved in amber including a wild boar (or bear) and a duck. The boar once again shows the pervasiveness of geometric designs since these are engraved on its side, while the bird has an elegance that matches any Brancusi. From further north a tradition of carving elk heads existed. There is a splendid series of these from the cemetery of Oleneostrovski Mogilnik. Whether such objects had any utlitarian value is unknown. They may have been symbols denoting power or wealth and were possibly involved in

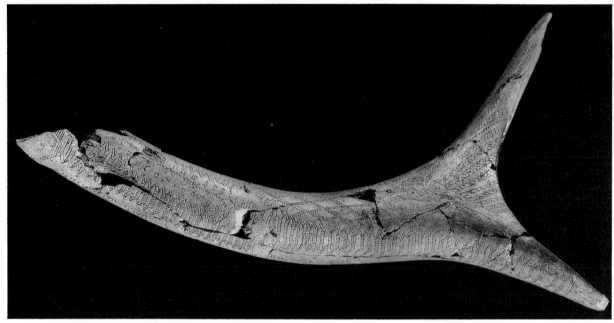

exchange networks. They certainly testify once again to the observational and creative skill of the Mesolithic hunter-gatherers. A beautiful elk head carving in wood has been recovered from the site of Vis I. As noted above, this carving had acted as the brake on a wooden ski. Once again we are reminded of the foolishness of trying to demarcate between that which is utilitarian and that which is art during the Mesolithic.

For a final glimpse of Mesolithic art we return to southern Europe and briefly look at the rock art of the Spanish Levant. Whether this art can be described as 'Mesolithic' is a bone of contention. More probably, it was created after agricultural economies had become established in the coastal lowlands of Spain. But in the high, rugged mountains, where we find this art, it is most likely that the Mesolithic hunting and gathering way of life was continued either by those same farmers during particular seasons or by separate populations. Hence to call the art Neolithic and not mention it in this chapter would be to fall foul of the terminological distinctions that recent research has shown to have such little meaning in terms of past lifestyles. A further reason for discussing it here is that the predominant subject of the art is hunting and gathering activities and hence it informs on many aspects of this way of life in prehistoric Europe, for which we have no other evidence. Rather than attempt a summary of this tradition, I shall briefly outline four paintings to appreciate both the beauty and academic significance of this art.

The first is the scene of a red deer drive from Cueva de los Caballos that was mentioned above when considering hunting techniques. Most of the hunting scenes are of this type—small schematic stick men with bows and arrows hunting herds of deer, horse, or wild boar. The scenes are vibrant with the excitement of the chase. Often the hunters are seen herding animals towards an ambush of archers. From Cueva Remigia in the Gasulla gorge, a painting may depict a wounded bull chasing the hunter who had failed to slay his game. From the Cueva de la Arana there is a depiction of a man or woman gathering honey. He/she is climbing a tree or possibly a rope ladder. One arm is outstretched to collect honey from a hive and is surrounded by swarming bees while the other holds the collecting jar. For Mesolithic foragers throughout Europe such honey gathering must have been a regular, perhaps mundane activity; here we have our only glimpse. A wonderful dance scene is depicted at the Barranco de los Grajos. Here twenty women and a few men are shown in a variety of poses; some women are swaying from their hips; others throw their arms into the air; all appear to keep their feet quite still. A third type of communal activity is illustrated at Les Dogues—a confrontation between

THIS RICHLY DECORATED ARTEFACT (*above and far left*) from Sjöholmen is 31.7 cm long and 3.5 cm thick at its midpoint and made from the beam of a red-deer antler. Although originally found broken into several pieces, its is complete except for minor parts. Traces of a shaft hole, *c.* 2 cm wide, survive at the end of the Y, and except for the concave part the whole surface is covered with shallow incisions.

EFFIGY OF AN ELK HEAD (*left*) from Oleneostrovski Mogilnik. Such elk figures were only found in six burials, all of which were in the northern cluster of graves (*see p. 124*). As such they may relate to both individual status and group identity. The elk was an important economic resource for northern hunters and, on the basis of such carvings, is likely to have had some mythological status.

two groups of archers. One group, which appears to have a leader wearing a hat with plumes, is sustaining an attack from a larger group of archers of much slighter build. It is unclear whether this depicts ritualized warfare or bloody combat for the defence of territory. Whatever it is, this scene, along with that of communal dancing and co-operative hunting, gives us rare insights into the social life of the Mesolithic communities of Europe.

Socio-economic Organization and Change

In reviewing the Mesolithic archaeological record I have had to separate the data into different categories—technology, subsistence, settlement, society, and art. Such divisions are, of course, artificial since all of these areas are intimately tied up with each other. It is very unlikely that a Mesolithic forager would have made the same divisions that we draw today for academic expediency. The connections between these different areas are most apparent when we consider socio-economic change during the Mesolithic. In providing an overall picture of the Mesolithic I have purposefully combined material from different areas and phases. But it must be appreciated that the Mesolithic was not a period of stasis in European prehistory; rather it was a time of considerable socio-economic change. This is particularly the case for northern Europe. In the south, continuity rather than change appears to be the key to the Mesolithic, as apparent from the long, continuous sequence of occupation in sites such as Franchthi cave.

The evidence from southern Scandinavia provides us with a picture of a very dynamic socio-economic organization in a continuous process of adjustment. If we compare the earlier (Maglemose and Kongemose phases) with the later (Ertebølle phase) Mesolithic, many contrasts can be drawn. There appears to be an intensification of subsistence practices; an increase in the number and diversity of resources exploited. In particular, there are indications of a far greater concentration on coastal and marine resources in the later period, many very 'costly' to exploit, such as shellfish. A problem here, however, is that much of the early post-glacial shoreline is now submerged and hence coastal resources may have been more heavily exploited in the earlier Mesolithic than is currently believed. Underwater surveys around the coast of southern Scandinavia are beginning to locate submerged early Mesolithic coastal settlement for future excavation.

Related to this subsistence intensification is an increase in the diversity and specialization of the tool-kit. The range of arrowheads is greater in the later Mesolithic, with each appearing to be dedicated to specific tasks. Similarly, there is an increase in the technology that relates to aquatic resources such as fish hooks, nets, weirs, and leisters. A third related change is the number and range of site types. There are quite simply many more known sites belonging to the Ertebølle than to the earlier periods. This is likely to reflect both an increase in population and the diversification of subsistence practices so that many more specialized types of site are created, each dedicated to the exploitation of a specific resource at a specific season.

SCULPTURE FROM LEPENSKI VIR. *Above*: These stone sculptures were closely associated with the architecture of the site and often embedded in the foundations of dwellings. As such, they have been described as a 'magic stone' and the 'navel of the world'. That on the left was found from the frontage, and the other, which has been described as the first monumental 'portrait' in the history of European Sculpture, in the rear wall of the sanctuary of dwelling XLIV at Lepenski Vir II.

A MESOLITHIC BURIAL FROM VEDBAEK. *Below:* This is grave 8 and contains a woman with a new-born baby. Beside the skull are a series of pendants, possibly a necklace, made from the teeth of red deer and wild pig. Substantial quantities of red ochre are found in the grave and a single, large flint blade is associated with the baby.

FEMALE ANTHROPOMORPHIC
FIGURINE (*left*) in fired clay from the
tell at Nea Nikomedeia, Macedonia,
north-east Greece.

AN UNUSUAL DOUBLE POT
(*below*) decorated in the Cardial style,
from the Cova de l'Or, Alicante,
eastern Spain.

A further set of changes concerns social organization. The spatial area of style zones, defined by the distribution of specific artefact types, appears to decrease throughout the Mesolithic, perhaps suggesting that territories were becoming smaller and/or required clearer definition. Similarly the phenomenon of cemeteries occurs only in the late Mesolithic and is likely to relate also to increasing territoriality.

By drawing all this information together and combining it with our knowledge of environmental change, we can suggest a likely scenario for the process of culture change in southern Scandinavia. The dramatic fall in available land area and an expanding population may have seriously increased population densities. To cope with this the foragers may have needed to diversify their subsistence base and, in particular, exploit those resources which had previously been ignored. This would have required a new range of technology. A further result of this pressure would have been the reduction of mobility and definition, and perhaps more intense defence, of territory.

Such scenarios of change forced on the Mesolithic hunters by increasing resource stress should be complemented by change deriving from the internal dynamics of Mesolithic society that occurred irrespective of environmental change. In the resource-rich areas of southern Scandinavia it is likely that there was intense social competition for prestige and power. This may have been the motor behind the innovation of new technology that allowed additional resources to be exploited so that surpluses could be created. Investing time and energy in this technology, such as construction of weirs, and the storing of food, is likely to have led to the delimitation of territorial boundaries. It is probable that both of these processes of change—stress imposed by population/resource imbalances and internal competition for power—were occurring simultaneously and were intermixed in a rather complex manner. This may also be the case for regions of Mesolithic Europe other than southern Scandinavia, such as the Morbihan area of Brittany where the cemeteries of Hoëdic and Téviec are found. At the heart of these processes of change we can envisage the individual Mesolithic forager making decisions about how to behave. The goal would have been to maintain the achieved standard of living in the face of continuous change in the physical and social environment. Such decision-making was equally at the heart of the process that denotes the end of the Mesolithic Age: the adoption of agricultural economies.

Summary

How can we summarize the Mesolithic Age? Was it the glorious finale to hunter-gatherer adaptations in Europe or the prelude to the social and economic systems of later prehistory? Or, was it a play within itself, requiring reference neither to what went before, nor after, for its identity. Perhaps we should try to see it as all three; a period with many complex threads which we are only just beginning to unravel and understand. If we need a single image to characterize the Mesolithic we cannot choose a particular environmental type, settlement system, or socio-economic organization. These all var-

IMAGES FROM THE ROCK ART of the Spanish Levant. (*a*) The honey gatherer, Cueva de la Arama; (*b*) Dance scene, Barraco de los Crajos; (*c*) Combat between two bands of archers, Les Dogmes. The interpretation of rock-art images such as these is extremely difficult as, on the basis of the work of recent hunter-gatherers such as Australian Aborigines, any image may contain multiple symbolic meanings which are impossible to infer without knowledge of the mythology of the group. At face value, however, they show, by a masterful use of line and form, some of the likely activities of Mesolithic hunter-gatherers that would otherwise be difficult to infer from the archaeological record.

ied markedly across Mesolithic Europe and through time. The only constant we have is at the level of the individual forager making decisions about which tools to produce, which resources to exploit, and which social alliances to form. Such decisions were made on the basis of imperfect information about the options available, under the influence of the society's traditions, and with the creativity that is inherent to the human mind. It was from such decisions, from the many intended and unintended consequences, that the social and economic structures of the Mesolithic emerged. It was these day-to-day, indeed minute-to-minute, decisions—made as Mesolithic foragers went about their daily business—that created one of the most critical periods of transformation in European prehistory.

I thank Dr Chris Scarre, Dr Peter Rowley-Conwy, and Dr Bill Finlayson for reading and commenting on the whole of an earlier version of this chapter and Dr Petra Day for commenting on those sections concerning vegetation and plant resources.

4

The First Farmers

ALASDAIR WHITTLE

Dramatis Personae

THE establishment of farming societies across Europe, from south-east to north-west, lasted some three thousand years, from around 7000 to 4000 BC. The last thousand years, in the complicated mosaic of northern and western Europe, are dealt with in other chapters. This chapter covers the initial processes by which farming societies were established over much of Europe, as far north as the southern edge of the North European Plain, by about 5500–5000 BC. The story of this transformation is complicated, and varies from area to area. Three main regions of distinctive development can be defined and these will be treated in turn: south-east Europe up to the Hungarian plain; the Mediterranean from Italy and Sicily westward; and central and western Europe from the edge of the Hungarian plain to the river valleys of northern France, but excluding the North European Plain, southern Scandinavia, and the British Isles.

The physical layout of Europe around 7000 BC recalls one of those maps of childhood imagination with examples of all conceivable geographical features crammed into it— inland seas, jutting peninsulas, high mountains, rivers and plains, and offshore islands of improbable shape. At this time the land was largely clothed in forest or woodland. It was also peopled, in varying densities, by numerous Mesolithic groups who lived by hunting, fishing, and gathering. These native inhabitants must have known intimately the territories over which they moved, some perhaps extensively, others within a much more restricted territory. Hobbes's seventeenth-century verdict on the life of the primitive—that it was 'solitary, poor, nasty, brutish, and short'—is wide of the mark. These were sophisticated people, in the sense of being expert technically in the arts of foraging and hunting, of being able to manipulate and perhaps control the native resources of animals and plants at their disposal, and of living intensely social lives.

Into this scene, from about 7000 BC onward, came new elements, which changed the nature of the map for ever. These were staples which were not native to Europe, wheats and barleys, sheep and goats, and at least as important, a new set of values and opportunities. Early farming or Neolithic societies can be defined in part by their cultivation of cereals and their husbandry of domesticated animals (with cattle and pigs native to Europe as well as sheep and goats), although older practices and resources remained in

use as well. They must also be defined by their social values based around sedentary existence, the acquisition and storage of produce and goods, close kin groups and descent
from ancestors, and a symbolic division of the world into constituent and often opposing parts.

That agricultural staples came from outside Europe is in little doubt. Farming societies had already become established in the Near East by 7000 BC; that is itself a complicated story, but one which must be taken as given for the purposes of this one. While
there have been claims that sheep could have survived in the west Mediterranean in the
late glacial and early post-glacial periods as relicts from earlier populations, most scholars now argue that sheep were reintroduced by people from east Mediterranean or Near
Eastern sources. Likewise it is possible that the wild ancestors of wheats and barleys
originally extended into south-east Europe, but it is most likely that cereals and their
cultivation were introduced by people from Near Eastern sources. Cattle and pigs,
however, could have been locally domesticated right across Europe, because they were
part of the native fauna. For such initial contacts and transfers to have taken place, people must have moved around. Distance and geography may have been lesser barriers
than we now suppose in our map-bound world. The great problem is to unravel who,
native or incomer, was moving.

The establishment of farming societies in Europe could have been the result of colonization by incoming people, seeking new land for increasing populations, or it could
have been the result of transformations of native society, already technically developed
and predisposed to further change, with new staples adopted and adapted from outside
to suit local needs and wants. There does not, in fact, appear to have been a uniform process, either in the establishment or in the subsequent development of farming societies.
In south-east Europe, colonization is likely, and by around 5000 BC there was a complex
physical and social landscape. In the central and west Mediterranean, the picture is less
clear, but it is likely that the role of native communities was substantial in the spread of
agriculture and in social transformation; the pace of change, however, was probably
much slower than in south-east Europe. In central and western Europe, colonization is
again likely, from about 5500 BC onward; the farming communities that pioneered the
temperate woodlands established a distinctive network of hamlets and small villages
that was to endure in essence until the period covered in the next chapter.

Greece and the Balkans, c.*7000 to after 5000 BC*

The establishment of the Neolithic and the role of native communities We know far too little
about native communities in the period from roughly 10,000 to 7000 BC. One recognized and well-explored Mesolithic occupation is at the Franchthi cave in the north-east
Peloponnese. Here foragers exploited a wide range of large and small game and native
grasses and other plants from about 10,000 BC. In the eighth millennium BC tunny were
fished from the site—of a size large enough to have been caught offshore—and obsidian

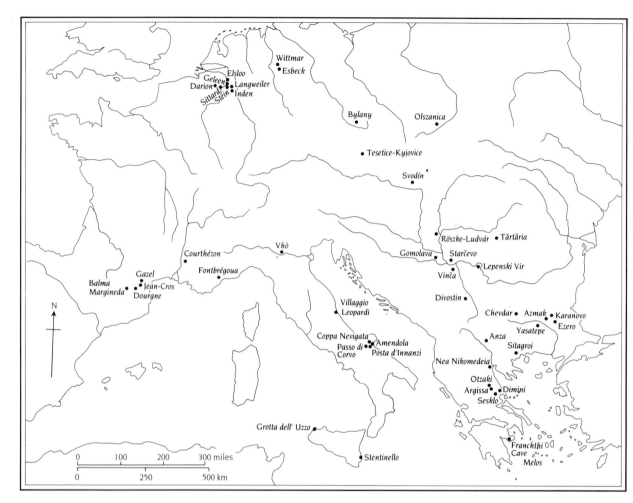

MAP OF PRINCIPAL SITES discussed in Chapter 4.

(a volcanic glass which can be worked like flint) was obtained from the island of Melos. Change came at the cave, apparently rapidly, around 7000 BC. Emmer wheat and barley and sheep and goats now appeared, together with polished-stone artefacts and simple pottery; at the same time the size of the occupation increased, extending beyond the cave. Simple stone tools continued to be made in the same way as before. The evidence could be taken to show a rapid transformation of both its economic base and its cultural identity by a native community, predisposed to change and in touch by sea with village farming communities in Anatolia. Population could have surged as a result of new resources and a perhaps more sedentary lifestyle.

Another candidate for native transformation is a group of Mesolithic sites in the Danube gorges between Serbia and Romania, south of Belgrade. Here local populations exploited rich river and forest resources and built clusters of huts beside the Danube, at Lepenski Vir and other sites. The occupations may have been permanent, and there are shrines and graves. By about 6000 BC agricultural staples were introduced, as in Greece, and the apparent success of the existing population could have been the basis for adoption of new resources.

It is doubtful, however, whether this argument can be sustained for the whole of this region. The evidence for a Mesolithic population in Greece and the Balkans is sparse. It is possible that this reflects an inadequate level of research as well as the destructive and masking effects of changing sea levels and land forms, but it is also possible that hunter-gatherers were, for various reasons, not thick on the ground in this region. Colonizing populations from Anatolia and the Near East could have occupied a relatively empty landscape. Neolithic sites are defined by the presence of wheat and barley, sheep and goats, cattle and pigs, polished-stone artefacts, pottery (though some of the earliest sites in Greece may have been aceramic), fired-clay figurines, and timber-framed buildings arranged in small clusters. Sites of this general character are found from Greece to the southern part of the Hungarian plain and either side of the Carpathians. Radio-carbon dates, admittedly inadequate in number, suggest that the more northerly sites, in Romania, northern Serbia, Croatia, and southern Hungary, are a little later than those in Greece, Bulgaria, and southern Serbia. This is compatible with a northward expansion by increasing farming populations. Expansion in another direction is documented by the appearance of Neolithic communities in Crete and Cyprus, which were probably largely empty before about 7000 BC. (One newly discovered site on Cyprus may show a slightly earlier population of hunters who exploited, and perhaps hunted to extinction, pygmy hippopotami, but there is no evidence of continuity through to the Neolithic.) Actual colonization, therefore, seems to have been a major feature of this early period of the establishment of agricultural communities in south-east Europe. Indeed, much of the emphasis on shrines and ritual at Mesolithic sites like Lepenski Vir in the Danube gorges could be seen as native reaction to the threat of encroachment by a different way of life and a new set of attitudes.

The first phase, c.7000–5500 BC   The Neolithic way of life must have included short-term camps, impermanent herding bases, and other specialized activity sites. The earliest features at some locations, like Argissa in Thessaly, are ill-defined pits and scoops, which could reflect sites of this nature. At most sites, however, the focus of settlement shifted to houses, solidly built and available for permanent occupation, and arranged in clusters which we can call hamlets and villages. The basic architectural unit was the single-room house, squarish to rectangular, usually wooden framed with a daub or clay covering, but stone footed with mud-brick on occasion in Greece and southern Serbia. Examples up to 12 metres long are known, but smaller sizes are common. There was usually a single entrance, and a clay oven on the back or side wall. By the developed Sesklo phase in northern Greece some houses had basements and others two storeys. Some houses may have been painted. Buildings were usually free-standing, though some mud-brick examples were interconnected, as at Anza near Skopje. It is extremely difficult to interpret the nature or size of the social unit involved from a building alone, but the evidence can be taken to suggest individual families (or other groupings), whose individuality was buttressed by their separate living space and concentrated in a very real sense around the domestic hearth. As far as can be seen, however, isolated buildings were rare. Houses were commonly closely spaced. At Nea Nikomedeia in Macedonia six houses were clustered around a larger building. At some sites houses were clearly arranged in rows, separated by narrow lanes, as at Otzaki in Thessaly and Karanovo in southern Bulgaria. The individual social unit belonged to a larger whole. Site size varied, both in area and in the number of buildings. Over sixty houses have been estimated in one phase of Karanovo, which is likely to have been one of the larger sites. Actual buildings and clay models of buildings suggest that some of these structures were shrines; one candidate is the central and larger building at Nea Nikomedeia. A common system of beliefs may have held together communities within which there is little sign of differentiation. Most known graves come from within the settlement area, often in pits beside houses. The dead appear to emphasize the importance of the household.

A feature of many areas is the careful siting of settlements to take advantage of a range of soils for cultivation and grazing. Major sites in the Maritsa valley of southern Bulgaria were spaced a few kilometres apart, each with areas of different soils close by. On the southern Hungarian plain, ribbons of settlement are known along the edges of the flood plains, taking advantage of terrace soils for cultivation, and the flood plain and other areas for grazing, fishing, and hunting. Another major feature is the duration of sites. Far more sites are known than in the Mesolithic period, but many of these may have been occupied for short periods only. For example, the ribbons of Hungarian plain valley-edge settlement probably reflect a shifting succession of individual occupations. In Greece and the southern parts of the Balkans, however, there are many sites which were repeatedly used for occupation, and the accumulation of decayed building material and other detritus resulted in the formation of settlement mounds or tells. Within a tell are usually distinguishable various phases of occupation and occasionally phases of abandonment. Some tells are modest in both area and height, particularly in the more northern parts of the region. Others reached impressive sizes. Karanovo, which was in use until the Early Bronze Age, reached a total height of 12 metres and covered an area around 250 by 150 metres. In its first main phase, three identified building levels were 0.6 to 1 metre thick and in its second main phase two building levels left 1.75 to 2 metres of build-up. These phases cover a span of centuries or more in the seventh to sixth millennia BC. There is a long roll-call of other large tells, including Argissa, Sesklo, and Sitagroi in Greece, Azmak, Ezero, and Yasatepe in Bulgaria, and Starčevo and Vinča in Serbia. This litany of classic names highlights not only the amount of research in the area since the nineteenth century, but also the successful nature of the settlements which ended as tells.

The first farmers cultivated cereals and kept domesticated stock. They grew wheats (emmer, einkorn, bread, and club) and barleys (two-row and six-row hulled and naked). They used, and probably deliberately grew, legumes such as peas, lentils, and vetches.

REMAINS OF A HOUSE in one of the Copper Age levels on the tell at Durankulak, Doleric district, north-east Bulgaria.

They also used acorns, olives, pistachios, cherries, and plums, and probably many other wild plants as well. Our knowledge of cultivation and plant use will be much improved when techniques appropriate for the recovery of plant residues become regularly employed in excavations. Samples were recovered in excavations at Anza by wet sieving and flotation. There emmer wheat appears to have been the basic mainstay, supplemented by smaller amounts of einkorn and hulled six-row barley, and by peas and lentils. Club wheat was found in one early deposit at the site. Sheep, goats, cattle, and pigs were the main domesticated animals at virtually all sites; dogs were also kept. Large wild game such as red deer continued to be exploited, and there are many finds of bones of small game and birds. Our knowledge of fishing derives best from the more northerly sites, of the Starčevo-Körös group, where bones of catfish and pike are well represented. At one site, Röszke-Ludvár, fish appear to have been cleaned and dried in great quantities. The list of species from just one site, that of Starčevo near Belgrade, illustrates the great diversity available. As well as the domesticates, there were red and roe deer, wild cattle, horse, and boar; beaver, fox, wolf, bear, badger, otter, and wild cat; wild ducks, geese, swans, and predators; and pike, catfish, bream, and carp.

While knowledge gradually accumulates of the resources in use, their relative importance remains hard to establish. Crude counts of bones, without making any allowance for the effects of butchery or disposal practices on bone survival, suggest that domesticated animals far outnumbered wild game, especially in Greece and the southern Balkans. There is no simple pattern in the representation of the domesticates. At some sites sheep and goats appear to be numerically dominant, at others cattle and pig, while at yet others they appear to be in balance. However, it is probably true that sheep and goats were more important in the southern Balkans and in Greece than further north. At Anza, sheep and goats gradually declined in numerical importance through the sequence of occupation. At Sitagroi in northern Greece, another tell with properly recovered samples, sheep and goats were again dominant in early phases, but less so than in other northern Greek sites such as Argissa or Nea Nikomedeia. Domesticated animals could have supplied meat, hides, and wool (though the latter probably only becomes important much later), milk and blood. They may have been important possessions in their own right. It is likewise not clear which plants provided the most food, though it is usually assumed that wheats and barleys were the most important. Cultivated cereals could have yielded high returns on favourable soils, and provided bread, biscuits, and gruel for daily consumption, as well as a storable resource for lean times. Club and bread wheat are hexaploid, or genetically more complex. Such hexaploid wheat was better suited for baking than emmer and einkorn, which lack gluten in their flour and cannot be baked into anything lighter than biscuits. We do not know whether cultivation or husbandry was more important for subsistence. It is likely, however, that the subsistence economy was unspecialized. There would have been considerable advantage in exploiting a range of domesticated staples and some wild resources, diversity acting as a buffer against the risk of failure of individual staples. In this respect, the early Neolithic economy may only have accelerated existing Mesolithic trends, rather than have represented something completely new.

The resources at the command of the first farmers were varied, adaptable, and productive. It is not clear, however, on what scale or on what basis they were used. The evidence from settlements for groupings of individual houses may suggest that the basic human unit through which agriculture was organized was the household, perhaps of individual families. The existence of village settlements implies also an ethos of co-operation, which may have extended to the tasks of clearance, cultivation, harvesting, breeding, herding, and butchery. Much of Neolithic life may have been lived within a relatively small radius around settlements, within which the needs of the annual farming cycle could have been satisfied, though herding and hunting could have taken individuals further afield. We do not know whether the first farmers lived at some basic subsistence level or were willing or able to intensify their agricultural production. The evidence is fragmentary and contradictory. Such pollen analyses as are available for the region suggest that the scale of woodland clearance was limited at this stage, and there are few heavy-duty stone tools for such a task. Yet high cereal yields could have been

obtained from favourable, well-watered soils, and forest herding, too, could have allowed a considerable density of stock. There is evidence from a few sites, such as Chevdar and Azmak in Bulgaria, for more or less pure crops of individual cereal and legume species, and there is circumstantial evidence at Chevdar for crop rotation involving emmer wheat, barley, and legumes; more or less pure crop samples contain stray remains of other species, which can be interpreted as the previous crop from the same land. There would, therefore, have been the capacity for individual households or settlements to have intensified the level of agricultural production. In a very real sense, the largest settlements may also have been the most successful.

Although some of the earliest Greek sites were aceramic, the presence of well-made pottery is characteristic of the Neolithic in the region. The Greek sequence shows that pots—simple bowls and jars, all handmade—were initially plain, but were later decorated with a great range of geometric motifs. Other crafts included the working of flint and obsidian for cutting tools, and of shell for ornaments. Apart from their intrinsic technical and artistic interest, these crafts reveal much about the social relations of the first farming communities. Pottery styles may be some sort of clue to the nature of social identity. Styles of decoration were very varied from site to site in northern Greece, but can be contrasted at a broader scale with the pottery of other regions. Thus red-on-white wares were popular in northern Greece, while white-on-red wares were more dominant in the early levels of the Karanovo sequence in Bulgaria. Pottery could have been an emblem of both local and wider identities. Settling down and living in more or less permanent settlements involved contrasting social needs: on the one hand, the need to define membership of the immediate social group with access to key resources; and on the other, the need to avoid isolation and create contacts over wide areas, not least for the maintenance of open breeding networks. The obsidian on sites in northern Greece was not obtained locally, but probably from the island of Melos well to the south. Beads and bracelets made from the *Spondylus* shell are found on sites right through the region. The shell came from the Aegean. We do not know whether such raw materials were deliberately obtained at long range or whether they (or goods made from them) were acquired by a series of shorter-range transactions, for example by gift exchanges. What is important is the further demonstration of the reality of long-range contact among the first farming communities.

Many sites have yielded fired-clay figurines. These are both anthropomorphic, mainly of female figures, and animal. The figurines are varied. The female figures are generally rather small, usually standing, squatting, or sitting. Their arms can be folded, on their hips, or outstretched. The faces are normally rather bland, some perhaps even representing masks; some heads are elongated or rod-like. By contrast, the lower limbs and sexual parts are often exaggerated. By the Sesklo phase in Thessaly, in the sixth millennium BC, figurines were more elaborate, with eyes in the form of grains of corn, details of hair and face, and more decoratively painted. In very general terms, similar figurines can be found over the whole region. Some styles were widespread, such as rod-headed figurines with decorative head-dress, which have been found as far apart as Nea Nikomedeia in Macedonia and Starčevo in northern Serbia. There are also various animal figurines, as well as miniature tables or altars, and house or shrine models. Some very well-preserved examples are known, though the archaeological reality is often less glamorous. At the site of Divostin in Serbia, for example, all the Starčevo phase anthropomorphic and animal figurines were recovered in a fragmentary state.

Such figurines are usually interpreted as ritual or cult objects, rather than as mere toys, and their 'mythical imagery', as one authority has put it, can be seen as part of a very widespread and important set of religious or spiritual beliefs. It is not possible with such material and often fragmentary evidence to gain anything like a full insight into the world symbolized by figurines, despite some attempts to reconstruct a very specific pantheon, but certain themes stand out. The world is categorized into constituent parts, human and animal, and perhaps human and divine and wild and tame. There is an emphasis on female reproduction. Figurines are often found beside or sometimes in houses within settlements, such as in a larger building at Nea Nikomedeia, and appear to reinforce the identity of the household. At this phase the cult appears to have been accessible to all. The wide distribution of figurines implies some kind of spiritual or conceptual unity among early farming communities in the region. Such a world-view may have been at least as important as the practice of agriculture in the success of the Neolithic way of life.

Developments, c.5500 to after 5000 BC It is a measure of the success of the Neolithic way of life in Greece and south-east Europe that there are several discernible developments by the last centuries of the period covered here. Within a span of perhaps fifty generations or more, Neolithic communities had become well established in the landscape. By the later sixth millennium BC, the archaeological map of their distribution is populous. Many sites are known. Some are older foundations—from the phase of establishment—which were still occupied. The Karanovo tell provides a classic example of such continuity. Other important and large tells were foundations from this sort of date, such as Gomolava in the Sava valley to the north-west of Belgrade. Large sites, whether new or old, may have become pre-eminent in this phase, both for the concentration of people and productive capacity, and for their control of ritual and other important social roles. There is no clear evidence that most tells were defended or enclosed, and the superficial picture is still of a well-ordered social landscape. While the size of houses increases, with some subdivision of interiors, there is generally no sign from tell layouts, such as Karanovo, for internal differentiation within settlements. One exception may be Sesklo in Thessaly in the sixth millennium, where a central higher area contains an inner enclosure with one large building surrounded by smaller ones. Dimini in Thessaly in the fifth millennium BC represents a further development, with a well-defined, perhaps fortified stone-walled central area in the site, containing a large central building or megaron with surrounding courtyard. The pattern of settlement was not everywhere stable. In the southern Hungarian plain, settlements of the Tisza phase in the early fifth millennium BC are more aggregated. Fewer but larger sites are now found, and the first true tells in this area appeared at this time. Another sign of development is the taking up, for agricultural settlement, of areas previously avoided or little used. Examples include the lower Danube or Dobrogea area of Romania, the more westerly parts of Bosnia, the fringes of the Carpathian basin around the Hungarian plain, and the river valleys on the edge of the steppe zone to the north-east of the Carpathians. In the Dobrogea, for example, settlements appear in a previously sparsely occupied region. Accompanying them were separate cemeteries. Some of the graves were notable for anthropomorphic figurines; one exceptional male figure is sitting with head in hands. Some of this infilling may be due to the acculturation of native people, while the rest must represent continued colonization.

In the sphere of subsistence, there were fewer discernible changes. The list of animal species from a site such as Gomolava is rather similar to that from Starčevo at an earlier date. Domesticates dominate, but there are also large and small wild game, birds, and fish. One trend seen at many sites, however, is for larger numbers of cattle bones. An increase in the number of cattle could represent several different changes: in the worth or value of species, in dietary preference, in continued adaptation to the European environment or to increased skills in domestication of the local fauna. Domestication has been studied in particular on and around the Hungarian plain. Cattle were less numerous at an earlier date. By the Tisza phase of the early fifth millennium BC cattle predominate, hunting of wild cattle was locally important and there are signs of local domestication being undertaken on the fringes of the plain. Essentially the same crops were cultivated, but we know too little about changes in the scale of clearance or the intensity of cultivation.

Copperworking began in this phase. Its development reflects increasing craft skill and perhaps also the beginnings of craft specialization. Early worked copper objects, however, were modest. They include beads, hooks and pins, or awls, beaten from native copper or smelted from ores and then beaten into shape. The rapid development of large-scale ore extraction and of casting in moulds is followed in the next chapter. Equally important were the continuation of potting, and the circulation by exchange of imported items and raw materials. Tisza sites on the Hungarian plain, for example, were able to acquire, from the upland fringes up to 150 kilometres away, flint, obsidian, stone axes, and fine pottery made by the neighbouring Bükk group.

The tradition of ritual paraphernalia was continued and elaborated. Figurines were more varied from region to region. In the Vinča culture of Serbia, named after the Vinča tell near Belgrade, anthropomorphic figurines were often modelled with stubby arms

FIRED CLAY HEAD
of a very large figurine
from the Vinča culture site
at Predionica, Serbia.

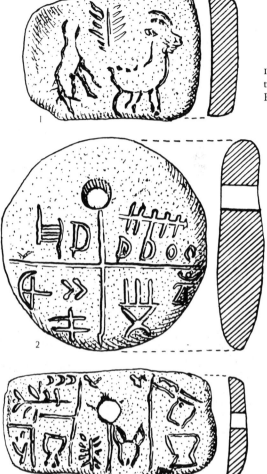

INSCRIBED CLAY TABLETS from the tell at Tărtăria, Transylvania, western Romania.

and schematic legs; many figures are seated. The body has incised and painted decoration and there are holes for attachments. The face is exaggerated, often almost triangular in shape, with prominent nose and large eyes, giving a catlike appearance. In the Tisza culture there were also elaborate figurines, some prominently decorated with cut or incised adornment, and there were similarly decorated anthropomorphic vessels. At Tărtăria in Transylvania in central Romania three unbaked clay tablets, from a pit containing also anthropomorphic figurines, bore on them a series of enigmatic symbols and representations of one or more animals. These items appear to reflect an increased emphasis on cult and ritual. Not only were the paraphernalia more complex, but there are signs that the practice and control of ritual were increasingly concentrated on particular sites. In the Tisza case, this coincides with large, aggregated settlements; in the Vinča case and elsewhere, the larger tells appear to have the greatest concentration of ritual items.

This development may be a further clue to the changing nature of early agricultural

DECORATED ANTHROPOMORPHIC POT (*left*) of the Tisza culture from Szegvár-Tüzköves, south-east Hungary.

ANTHROPOMORPHIC POT (*below*) of the Tisza culture from Kökénydomb, south-east Hungary. The seated female figure is elaborately decorated and is wearing arm ornaments.

communities. Settlements do not appear to show internal differentiation, and a common tradition of religious or spiritual belief, as well as links expressed in pottery styles and the exchange of other goods, could have continued to serve to project a conceptual unity among widely scattered communities. But in a landscape increasingly settled, and with enormous productive capacity available in the blending of domesticated cereals and animals backed by wild plants and game, there were opportunities for difference. This seems to find expression in the creation of larger sites. It is possible that some villages took a leading role at a regional level both in the support of population and agricultural production, and in the practice of important ritual and the maintenance of exchange. A combination of household and village may have remained dominant, however. There is little sign yet of further social difference. Most burials continue within settlements. The cemeteries of the Dobrogea are one exception, and small cemeteries beside large Tisza sites on the Hungarian plain could suggest the emergence of separate lineages.

The Central and West Mediterranean, c.7000 to after 5000 BC

The native background   By contrast with Greece and the Balkans, there is good evidence more or less throughout the central and west Mediterranean for native Mesolithic populations. At the Grotta dell'Uzzo on Cape S. Vito in north-west Sicily hunters and fishers were present from about 9000 BC. Plant foods were used as well as game. There was an increase in fishing at the site (though not certainly off shore) from about 6500 BC. Many other sites are known in parts of the Italian peninsula, southern France, and areas of Iberia. Shell middens in the Tagus and Sado estuaries of Atlantic Portugal were occupied from about 6500 BC, and may show a well-established population with limited annual movement. Islands such as Corsica, Sardinia, and the Balearics were colonized from about 9000 BC, documenting the use of sea-going craft. However, we know too little about developments along the north African coast; further research there may change our perspectives radically. The sea-level rose and vegetation changed to a more wooded environment. Resources of game (including deer and ibex), fish, shellfish, and plants in varied coastal and inland locations, with regular abrupt changes in relief, appear to have supported well-established populations. Only in the west Mediterranean islands was the resource base more restricted, the native fauna of the Balearics being the dwarf antelope-like ruminant *Myotragus balearicus* and of Corsica and Sardinia the hare-like *Prolagus sardus* and the deer *Megaceros cazioti*, which became extinct after about 7000 BC.

The introduction of agriculture into this area is even harder to unravel than elsewhere. Research has been uneven, and sea-level rise and land-form changes may have drowned or masked sites or areas of critical relevance. The picture in the present state of evidence is of the introduction of settled life and the agricultural staples, by sea-borne colonization, into southern Italy and eastern Sicily at some point after 7000 BC, but of a much more gradual adoption of Neolithic staples in areas to the north and west, in a drawn-out process lasting from after 7000 BC to at least 5500 BC. Sheep, goats, cattle, pigs, and even red deer were introduced to Corsica and Sardinia, but further west sheep and goats may have preceded the other domesticates. Cereal cultivation appears to have been adopted even more slowly. Pottery was quickly adopted over the whole area, but indigenous traditions of flintworking were maintained. This all implies that elements of the Neolithic way of life were adopted gradually by native communities.

Southern Italy and eastern Sicily   There are many early Neolithic sites in southern Italy, in Apulia and Calabria, and in eastern Sicily; recent surveys in Calabria have increased the number of known sites dramatically. Some sites are open occupations, and as in the Balkans there must have been a range of short-stay and specialized camps. The most obvious and so far best-known sites, however, are a numerous series of ditched enclosures. These are centred on the Tavoliere plain of Apulia, but Stentinello and other sites in eastern Sicily seem to be analogous. These sites are defined by an outer ditch or ditches within which are grouped smaller circular ditched compounds, 10 metres and more in diameter, which contained timber-framed houses, perhaps rectangular. Most of these sites have been discovered from the air. They are very varied, in the number and circumference of the ditches and in the number of compounds within. Rather few have been properly excavated, although current research is beginning to make good. Passo di

VERTICAL AIR PHOTO of the multiple ditched enclosure at Passo di Corvo on the Tavoliere plain, Apulia, southern Italy. Smaller ditched enclosures within the perimeters probably defined compounds which contained houses and other features.

Corvo is a maximum of 540 by 870 metres across and had three or more ditches and over 100 compounds within. La Quercia had not less than eight concentric ditches. Other vast sites such as Posta d'Innanzi and Amendola can be contrasted with much smaller enclosures and with sites which have compounds but not encircling ditches. There is some evidence that the largest sites were later than the rest.

One study has found enclosure sites to be placed on the edge of patches of light, fertile soil, but with alluvial and heavier soils also available near by. Such evidence as is available seems to show the introduction of cultivated cereals and of sheep, goats, cattle, and pig, but too little is known of the details of the agricultural economy in this region. One indication, however, of the nature of the introduction of agricultural staples was their simultaneous appearance in the sequence of the Grotta dell'Uzzo. There this could be due to the native population; other activities like fishing continued, now with the catching of whales. This indicates an improved seafaring capability. It is possible that cereals and domesticated animals were collected, rustled, or otherwise acquired by native populations from across the Adriatic and the Ionian Sea, but the probability of sea-borne colonization is at least as strong. Southern Italy and eastern Sicily would join Crete and Cyprus as niches colonized by sea at the beginning of the Neolithic. A further resemblance may be the relative absence in southern Italy and eastern Sicily of Mesolithic population. The few known examples include the south-east coastal site of Coppa Nevigata, which has stone tools in indigenous style along with early pottery; its precise date is uncertain.

It is not clear just how early the Neolithic began in this area. More sites belong to the sixth than to the seventh millennium BC. Many Neolithic sites are characterized by the presence of pottery. Over the whole of the central and west Mediterranean is found Impressed Ware, a very varied assortment of handmade bowls, dishes, and jars decorated with diverse impressions. In south-east Italy there was red-painted and finely incised pottery as well. The sequence of development is not firmly established, but it may well be that painted wares were introduced around 6000 BC, some time after the appearance of impressed pottery, and that they subsequently became increasingly elaborate. This may well show some craft specialization and also perhaps continued contact with Greece and the Balkans, where painted pottery was in common use, but it helps little in the search for origins.

The central and west Mediterranean excluding southern Italy and Sicily   It is unlikely that the Neolithic way of life spread to the rest of the Mediterranean by continued sea-borne colonization, unless all the relevant early sites were coastal and have been submerged by sea-level rise. Sea-borne contact, however, is likely, for there are a series of innovations which cannot easily be explained as having spread around the shores of the Mediterranean. Native communities were probably responsible for adopting Neolithic staples and material items, but gradually. Local traditions of flintworking were maintained in nearly all areas. Sheep, goats, cattle, pigs, and even red deer, as well as impressed pottery, were introduced in the seventh millennium BC to Sardinia, and sheep, goats, and pigs to Corsica, but beyond those islands sheep and goats appear to have been the first domesticated animals to have been introduced, to be followed by the others later. The use of pottery was taken up over wide areas in the seventh millennium BC, but cereals were not in widespread use until the end of the sixth millennium BC or even later; their early use on Sardinia and Corsica is unclear, due to lack of botanical samples from excavations. It must, however, be stressed that the evidence in the western Mediterranean, perhaps more than in any other area, is confusing. Research has been uneven. Far more excavation has been carried out in rock shelters and caves, generally in the uplands, than on open sites on lower ground. The stratigraphy of particular rock shelters may be confused and some radiocarbon sequences may be doubtful. It is not clear whether the situation at upland sites accurately reflects developments in an area as a whole. There has been intensive research in parts of southern France and northern Italy, but less in parts of central Italy and Iberia; the lack of knowledge of north African developments is serious.

In central Italy most early Neolithic sites belong to the sixth rather than the seventh millennium BC. Agriculture seems to have become established rather gradually on either side of the Apennines, for example at the Abruzzo lowland site of Villaggio Leopardi, but numbers of sites were still oriented to animal exploitation including that of native species. In north Italy, upland caves and rock-shelter sites show the continuation of local flintworking, the adoption of impressed pottery, and the gradual incorporation of sheep and goats into animal economies, but the area may have been relatively sparsely inhabited and was probably not a significant corridor for the landward transmission of innovations. Pottery was also adopted in other traditional areas, such as the Adige valley. Agricultural staples were introduced into the Po valley only from the later sixth millennium BC onward, at sites such as Vhò. Here red and roe deer, pigs and small game were hunted; cattle and very small numbers of sheep and goats were kept; and fish, shellfish, and birds were also exploited. A single wheat grain was recovered from the site and it is possible that cereals were not locally grown at this particular site.

In southern France there has been much research in both Provence and Languedoc. Once again, flintworking continued in local style, suggesting continuity of population. Sheep and goats were probably introduced early in the seventh millennium BC, before cattle and pigs. The use of cereals only becomes well documented in the later sixth millennium, for example at the inland site of Fontbrégoua, Var. Some open sites are known, such as Courthézon, Vaucluse, or the submerged coastal site of Leucate, but their relative importance is unclear. Much of the most detailed research has been carried out on sites at quite high altitude. In the Aude department of Languedoc, excavations at the inland foothill shelters of Gazel and Jean-Cros have shown the hunting of wild cattle, deer, and boar, and the gradual introduction of sheep from the seventh millennium BC onward, to reach higher numbers in the sixth, along with the introduction of goats, cattle, and pig. At the high level Abri de Dourgne ibex were an important quarry, along with other large wild and small game. Higher still at the Balma Margineda in Andorra, at about 1000 metres above sea-level, ibex were the main prey of hunters, but here too sheep and goats were introduced in small numbers.

In Iberia, the record is more patchy. The very arid south-east may have been among the last areas to see the introduction of a Neolithic way of life. Shell middens in the Tagus and Sado estuaries show a locally well-established native population in the seventh to sixth millennia BC, which hunted deer, pig, wild cattle, and small game such as hares and rabbits, fished, and collected shellfish and perhaps plants. The middens may have been occupied for seasons at a time, and burials in the middens may have reinforced the significance of these bases. In the caves of eastern Spain, impressed pottery and sheep and goats, together with small numbers of cattle, can be documented from after 6000 BC, though claims for earlier dates have been made. The role of north Africa in the transmission of innovations remains unclear. Cereals can also be documented from the sixth millennium BC, and open sites of this date are gradually being recognized.

The smaller Mediterranean islands saw innovation at a later date than the larger ones. Malta, for example, was probably first colonized in the later sixth millennium BC, and innovations probably came relatively late to the Balearics. Sardinia and Corsica, by contrast, saw change much earlier, and may have been important in the transmission of innovation to the West. Sheep and goats and pigs were introduced to both in the seventh millennium BC, but cattle evidently did not reach Corsica till later. Cereals were not certainly in use in the early Neolithic on Corsica, but may have been on Sardinia.

Sea-borne contact may, therefore, have been at least as important as landward transmission of innovations. Sardinia and Corsica could have acted as filters in this process, their inhabitants, previously reliant on a restricted range of resources, adopting and passing on a selected range of new resources. Sea-going capacity in the seventh millennium BC has already been discussed. Judging by the upland evidence of northern Italy, southern France, and eastern Spain, native communities did not feel compelled to adopt the agricultural package as soon as it became available. Evidence from inland shelters and caves shows how sheep and goats, and later, the other domesticates were gradually taken up. They may have been incorporated at first as a minor element in traditional strategies of hunting and annual cycles of movement. It is much less clear how actual transmission of innovation took place. People must have transported animals by sea. Contact and exchange may have taken place in coastal areas, and we know too little of the role in and impact on lowland economies of the first sheep and goats.

Another indication of the reality of long-range movement, including by sea, comes from obsidian. There are four main sources, on Sardinia, Lipari, Pantelleria near Malta, and Palmarola in the Pontine Islands. Sardinian obsidian is found on Corsica at an early date, and later in north Italy. Lipari and Pontine obsidian is found in central and southern Italy. We do not know whether exchange, trade, or direct acquisition was responsible for this movement, but it does show contact over considerable distances.

The adoption of pottery may also have social as well as purely technical and functional importance. The use of breakable pottery may indicate the existence of long-stay bases

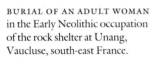

BURIAL OF AN ADULT WOMAN
in the Early Neolithic occupation
of the rock shelter at Unang,
Vaucluse, south-east France.

rather than a very mobile pattern of settlement, but its significance is likely to have been wider still. Impressed Ware was very varied over its distribution across the central and western Mediterranean. Decoration in the north and west, for example, was dominated by shell impressions. Pots could have been adopted as emblems of local identity and position. Adoption of innovations in general may have been generated in part by local social conditions including inter-group competitiveness and rivalry. Pots could also have symbolized participation in a wider interchange of contacts and ideas.

Outside southern Italy there were no clear signs of differences between sites in this long phase of slow change. Individual burials are known from shelters and caves. They may be significant for reinforcing the importance to their inhabitants of particular resources and territory, but such burials do not appear to signify a formal recognition of descent from particular ancestors.

Central and Western Europe, c.5500 to after 5000 BC

The spread of farmers in the temperate forest   The Neolithic way of life started much later in central and western Europe than in the Mediterranean, but became established much more rapidly. Its spread beyond the Carpathian basin and the Hungarian plain is associated with a culture known after its decorated pottery as the Linear Pottery culture. Sites of the Linear Pottery culture are found from northern Hungary to northern France, southern Belgium and the southern Netherlands, through Slovakia and the Czech Lands, northern Austria, central and southern Poland, and central and southern Germany to the southern edge of the North European Plain (roughly as far north as Hannover). This culture also extended around the northern side of the Carpathians into the Ukraine and Moldavia and was part of the process of expansion into the steppe zone referred to in the earlier section on the Balkans, but the eastern Linear Pottery culture will not be further discussed here. The distributions of changing styles of decorated pottery suggest that agricultural communities spread westward in stages: first to the upper Danube, upper Rhine and Neckar rivers, and northward to between Hannover and Magdeburg; then down the Rhine, into the southern Netherlands and southern Poland; and finally to southern Belgium, northern France, and other parts of the North European Plain. Radiocarbon dating at first suggested that this spread was extremely rapid, but more carefully chosen dating samples may indicate a more gradual, though still swift, expansion westward, beginning in the later sixth millennium BC.

THE DISTRIBUTION of the Linear Pottery culture (LBK). The dashed lines suggest principal stages of expansion.

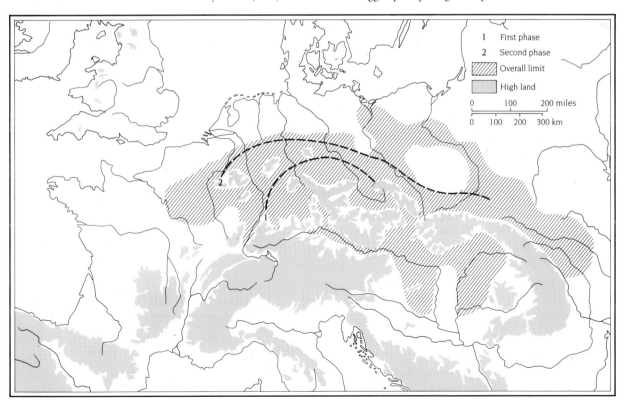

EXCAVATION OF A SETTLEMENT of the earliest phase of the Linear Pottery culture, at Schwanfeld, Ldkr. Schweinfurt, northern Bavaria, Germany.

The first farming settlements of central and western Europe are found above all on the edge of river valleys and on fertile soils, particularly loess. Thousands of sites are known, representing a succession of scattered homesteads, hamlets, and small villages. The distribution of sites is not even, but clustered into a series of regional groups. Most scholars see the Linear Pottery culture as the result of continued agricultural expansion from the Carpathian basin, but the process is poorly understood in detail. Some have seen the agricultural spread across Europe as essentially a steady, if slightly variable, advancement of the frontier with each generation. It is possible that there was a pause in the northern Balkans·in the later seventh and earlier sixth millennia BC and we know little about the conditions for a surge in human numbers in the probable source area of further colonization; much more needs to be known about the rate of expansion in northern Serbia, Croatia, western Romania, and southern Hungary. Once under way, colonization could have been self-sustaining, with pioneers taking up what could have been essentially empty environments, and experiencing high population growth under conditions with few constraints other than those of distance and newness. It is theoretically possible that the Linear Pottery culture represents a sudden or rapid transformation of native

Mesolithic communities around the fringes of initial agricultural colonization into the Balkans, but there are no obvious native antecedents for artefact styles, house building techniques, or, indeed, a settled way of life. As in the Balkans, Mesolithic populations are poorly documented across much of central and western Europe, and it is possible that they were genuinely sparse on the ground, in what would have been an environment of closed forest without the diversity of plant and animal resources favourable to the most successful foraging and hunting. Rather different environments and apparently much more numerous Mesolithic populations were to be found around the Atlantic and northern coasts of western Europe, and a different role for native populations in that region in the adoption of agriculture is discussed in other chapters. In central and western Europe, however, little more is likely than contact between pioneer farmers and established native communities. According to anthropological observation, farmers and hunters often exchange foodstuffs and goods, and there is some evidence from the southern Netherlands and the Main valley for Neolithic adoption of Mesolithic flintworking techniques. Contact may not always have been friendly. In southern Belgium, it has been suggested that the small agricultural hamlet at Darion in the Hesbaye, right on the limit of the Linear Pottery distribution, was enclosed by a ditch as defence against hostile native hunter-foragers. Farmers and hunter-foragers could have been in direct competition for resources including territory.

Households, hamlets, and villages   The basic unit of settlement in this area was the rectangular post-framed longhouse, the timber for which would have been freely available in the surrounding forest. The longhouse ranged from about 6 to 45 metres in length, with many in the range of 15 to 30 metres, and was usually 6 to 7 metres wide. Its construction could have been a demanding task for small pioneering groups, and even for small kin-groups in more established communities. It is usually considered as a single-level building, though its five rows of posts might be compatible with a storeyed structure, and as permanently inhabitable. It is possible that both people and stock were housed in the same buildings, with goods and produce stored in attics, which are suggested by those structures which have more posts at one end. In the larger buildings, the layout of posts suggests a tripartite internal division of space. Such interiors are tantalizing, because the conditions of survival of the evidence make it frustratingly hard to reconstruct the use of space. The ground-plans survive well, because of the depth below ground to which the original posts were sunk, but the contemporary surface has, in nearly every case, been eroded or cultivated away. Artefacts and debris, therefore, rarely survive *in situ*, and it is difficult to compare house with house in terms of use and occupants. At Olszanica in southern Poland, two longhouses were distinguished by the concentration around them respectively of polished-stone tools and of obsidian and fine imported pottery; one house was very large, the other rather small. Many buildings could have housed a basic family unit, but other households, organized by different rules of age or sex, would have been possible, and some smaller buildings could have been stalls or workshops. Most sites have some variation in the size of houses. In one phase of the settlement at Elsloo in the southern Netherlands, for example, houses ranged from 12.5 to 25 metres in length. It has been suggested that the largest buildings could have functioned as clubs or meeting-houses, or even as shrines. Social position, the ability to mobilize kin and allies to help in the building task, and the duration of households in a given area could also be factors which influenced house size.

The grouping of longhouses varied. Structural timbers probably did not survive more than two or three generations, and so any concentration of houses is likely to represent a succession of buildings over time. Some extremely large concentrations are known, even making allowance for this factor. Bylany, near Kutna Hora in eastern Bohemia, is one such example; rather smaller are Elsloo and Sittard in the Maas valley of the southern Netherlands. In these villages, there are no clear signs of streets or lanes as in some Balkan tells, and the individual houses were not built to a standard length. The houses were slightly spaced, and even though buildings must have been replaced, there are comparatively few examples of directly overlapping ground-plans. This suggests, at the least, an ordered set of rules governing space within the village, and may also suggest the independence of individual households within the village. Smaller concentrations could be seen as hamlets, again consisting of slightly spaced houses, replaced at intervals. Examples include southern Dutch sites such as Stein and Geleen in the Maas valley. We do not know if occupation of such sites was continuous. At Bylany a succession of five main phases has been proposed, each covering a slightly different area. Some concentrations of houses were partially bounded by or contained within lengths of palisade, but most sites were essentially unbounded.

Another form of settlement is the dispersed pattern of single longhouses. This has been highlighted particularly by area excavation in advance of open-cast extraction of lignite in Germany, to the west of Cologne. Linear Pottery houses have been discovered in numbers in small valleys which form a tributary system for larger rivers running into the Rhine. In one small valley, the Merzbach, there were spaced clusters of houses. Each of the sites, named after the local village of Langweiler, could be broken down into smaller numbers of houses in contemporary occupation. Only Langweiler 8 may have represented a hamlet or small village. The other sites represent ribbon-like settlements along both sides of the small valley, with distances between individual houses ranging from less than 50 metres to more than 100 metres. House sizes also varied in this dispersed pattern of settlement. Such a pattern may have been common in many other areas, though the extent of excavation is generally too small for this to be seen easily.

Burial grounds   Beside some settlements, particularly in western regions, were small cemeteries of individual graves. At Wittmar near Braunschweig, for example, there were graves of men and women and some children. The dead were laid in simple earth-cut graves, their bodies generally lying on one side and slightly flexed. Pottery, stone tools, and simple ornaments accompanied some graves. The graves were arranged in rough lines on a common orientation, a few metres apart. Their positions must, therefore, have been marked or known. Accompanying the Langweiler sites only one cemetery has

AERIAL VIEW of the Merzbach valley from the north-west. Arrows indicate the positions of Linear Pottery culture and other sites along the stream valley. The scale of lignite mining is self-evident; the overlying soil is loess.

so far been discovered, and it seems that the scattered households of the area used a central or common burial place. However, not all the dead of the area can have ended up in the cemetery, because of its relatively small size. Formal burial may have been reserved for certain people within the wider community.

Characteristic of the overall distribution of these early farming communities was the

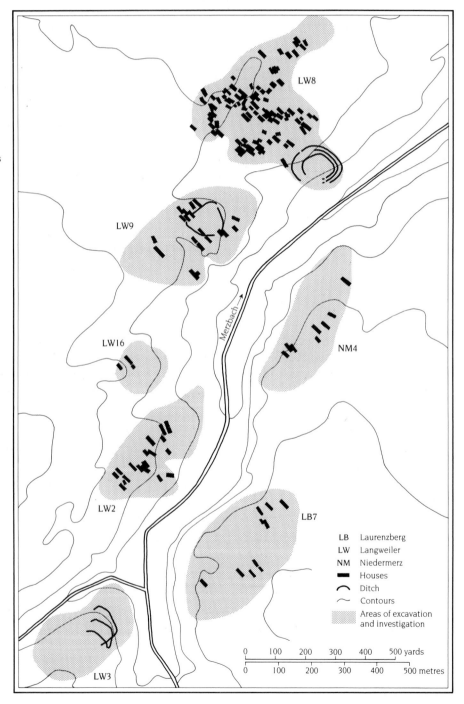

THE MAIN DISTRIBU-TION of LBK houses and ditched enclosures in the Merzbach valley. At any one phase there were considerably fewer houses in use; Langweiler 8 may have been the principal focus. There was a cemetery at Niedermerz. The enclosures came late in the sequence.

LW8

LW9

Merzbach

LW16

NM4

LW2

LB7

LB	Laurenzberg
LW	Langweiler
NM	Niedermerz
▬	Houses
⌒	Ditch
∼	Contours
▒	Areas of excavation and investigation

0   100   200   300   400   500 yards

0   100   200   300   400   500 metres

LW3

clustering of sites, forming what have been called 'settlement cells'. The explanation of this feature may lie with the conditions of swift expansion into the new environments of central and western Europe. There may have been a more or less free choice of areas to settle, and river valleys and areas of fertile soil were usually selected. None the less the newness and size of the region may have encouraged communities and households to reduce risks, to share common tasks such as clearance, and to minimize social distance from kin and neighbours, by settling in preferred areas.

Cultivators and herders   In settling on well-watered and highly fertile soils, such communities were well placed both for cereal cultivation and for grazing animals on both cleared and forested land. Wheats, barleys, and legumes were cultivated, and the common domesticates kept, especially cattle. However, we still know too little of subsistence practices. This is due partly to the failure to recover adequate residues in excavations, partly to the eroded condition of house floors, and partly to the present chemical state of loess soils in which bones often survive poorly. We are not certain whether cultivation was practised in fixed plots over long spans of time or rotated through clearings in the forest in a system of forest fallowing; and the balance between cereals and domesticated animals, as also between wild and tame resources, is not clear. A model commonly proposed, however, is of quite intensive cereal cultivation in small, fixed plots or gardens on cleared or partially cleared ground close to settlements. Animals could have been herded further afield or even allowed to browse freely by themselves. They could have been used to manure plots or gardens, and could have been a source of meat, milk, and hides, as well as a token of wealth in their own right. Such a model fits well with the choice of loess soils and with the observed pattern of settlement. Some game was killed, perhaps as much to keep deer and other animals out of plots and gardens as a deliberate strategy for an alternative source of meat; deer and other game may have been in relatively low densities in the contemporary forests. Such a pattern of subsistence may have been prone to shortages or even occasional acute failures, but since it endured for some centuries it may be regarded as a successful strategy for occupying the empty niche of the temperate forest. Risk could be countered by careful choice of settlement location, by keeping social distance to acceptable intervals, and by exploitation of a diverse package of resources, cereals imposed on environments new to them, and cattle husbanded in environments long familiar to them.

Questions of crafts and community   Linear pottery consisted of a range of bowls and cups, variously decorated with impressions and incisions, but not painted, as they were further east and south. The changing distributions of its styles can be seen to chart the development and perhaps in part the nature of the culture. The first styles show, as already noted, the process of expansion westward and northward. Middle-phase styles show very wide similarity over great distances, while late styles become much more regionalized. Pottery may have been used, at first, to signal affinity and solidarity between widely scattered communities, and, later, to define more restricted identities as the social landscape filled up. Various styles of polished-stone axe and adze were in use.

CUPS, BOWLS, AND JARS (*above*) of the Linear Pottery culture. These vessels are from sites in the Merzbach valley.

OBLIQUE AIR-VIEW (*right*) of excavations at the Lengyel culture ditched and palisaded enclosure at Svodín, southern Slovakia. The enclosure had four entrances. The west entrance features exposed here belonged to two phases of construction; the first phase consisted of the two palisades and ditch closest to the camera.

Some could have been used for tree clearance and woodworking, some as weapons, and some even as hoes for cultivation. In many cases a fine-grained rock called amphibolite was the raw material. Its source is uncertain, but may have been somewhere in central Europe. Amphibolite tools used in the Rhine or Maas valleys could have been transported hundreds of kilometres. Whether by trade or gift exchange, such movement over considerable distances must reflect socially very important transactions, perhaps creating an aura of the exotic as well as establishing affinity and alliance over broad areas. That pottery and stone tools are found regularly in graves, both of men and women, must reinforce their social rather than their purely functional importance. In life, both sets of items would have been part of the daily scene, pottery in longhouses and hafted stone tools carried by adults, and so could have been powerful symbols beyond their immediate use.

Both house size and the contents of graves have been used to suggest the existence of differences in status and position within Linear Pottery communities, but the results of such analyses are uncertain. As we have seen, house size was very varied and could have several different explanations. In some cemeteries older adults were buried with more and more varied grave goods than younger people, but there is considerable variation, and grave rites do not show clearly distinct social personae. The possibilities for social difference may have been fluid and contradictory. On the one hand, there were opportunities for individual households—many physically distanced from immediate neigh-

bours—to intensify agricultural production. The focus of competition, if it existed, could have been between communities or settlement areas, some becoming bigger and lasting longer than others. On the other hand, the very conditions of colonization and settlement would have militated against the consolidation of social difference. The availability of space would have allowed settlements to break up and re-form if tensions built up; this may, indeed, be one explanation of why relatively few sites were occupied right through the span of the Linear Pottery culture. The ethos of co-operation and solidarity, perhaps engendered in the initial conditions of forest pioneering, could also have served to reduce the overt expression of household or community aspirations.

Continuity and development into the fifth millennium BC   In many ways there was considerable continuity into the early fifth millennium BC. The general nature of houses, settlements, and subsistence practices, for example, remained little altered. There were, however, developments. One was the appearance of ditched enclosures in the settlement pattern. Some may have first appeared earlier in the Linear Pottery culture, but most belong to its late stages and after. Deep, often narrow, V-sectioned ditches were dug in circuits, single or multiple, enclosing a few acres. Banks probably accompanied the ditches. One example is the three-ringed enclosure at Langweiler 8. On loess soils the ditches would have quickly silted up. Many of these enclosures occur in the same locality as longhouses, but appear not to have contained buildings, though exceptions which did enclose contemporary houses are known, as at Darion, already mentioned, or Esbeck near Braunschweig. The latter can be seen as defensive or, at the least, more nucleated settlements than had existed before. The others could have served various roles. If for the penning or control of stock, they imply larger herds. If for gatherings or ceremonies, they may represent a formalization of the communal space found between longhouses in earlier periods and, therefore, an intensification of ritual. This kind of explanation finds support in the enclosures of the early Lengyel culture, which followed the Linear Pottery culture in Moravia, Slovakia, eastern Austria, and northern Hungary. At Těšetice-Kyjovice, in southern Moravia, a broad circular ditch 55–60 metres in diameter was broken by four opposed entrances and backed by two internal palisades. House remains were found only outside the enclosure, whose ditch contained many broken figurines. This, like other early Lengyel enclosures, may have been a ritual arena within a pattern of settlements and contemporary cemeteries. Some ritual practice may now have passed from households to other agencies, and perhaps into the hands of particularly important settlements or groups. The site of Svodín in southern Slovakia is even more elaborate. Houses again lay outside an enclosure, which began as a ditch with two internal palisades and was remodelled with two external ditches and three internal palisades. Here, defence could have been combined with extreme ritual elaboration. The nucleation of settlements and ritual elaboration have already been noted in the neighbouring area of the Tisza culture at this date.

Some studies, as in southern Poland, have shown that there was a gradual expansion of settlement out of the river valleys after the Linear Pottery culture. Further west, the

RESCUE EXCAVATION (*left*), in advance of opencast lignite mining, of a house in one of the Langweiler settlements of the Linear Pottery culture, in the small Merzbach stream valley west of Cologne, Nordrhein-Westfalen, Germany. (The area is also known as the Aldenhoven plateau.)

THE TELL OR SETTLEMENT MOUND (*below*) near Yunatzite, Pazardjik region, central-southern Bulgaria, during excavation. The tell was occupied in both the Neolithic period and the Bronze Age.

POTS AS PEOPLE: two decorated vessels from Bulgaria, making explicit the symbolism of pottery containers and their identification with the human form. The example on the left is earlier Neolithic, *c.*6000 BC, Gradeshnitsa near Vraca; the one on the right is Copper Age, *c.*4000 BC, from Hotnica near Veliko Turnovo.

evidence is more contradictory. Slightly fewer sites in some areas are found on loess soils, and parts of the North European Plain are colonized; in addition, many finds of polished-stone tools on the plain north of the loess indicate, at the least, increased contact with indigenous foragers, and very probably stock herding over wider areas. This suggests that the zone of agricultural settlement was gradually extended, but in several already settled areas the number of known sites does not actually increase. Several recently discovered sites of the Roessen culture, such as Inden near Langweiler west of Cologne, are different to those of the Linear Pottery culture. There are longhouses, but trapezoidal rather than rectangular in ground-plan; some are substantially larger. The houses are more closely grouped, and the settlement area is bounded by palisades. What caused this shift to nucleation is unclear, but it may reflect a fuller landscape, perhaps more competitive and more hostile than in earlier times. Regionalized pottery styles from the late stages of the Linear Pottery culture onward have already been discussed in this respect. A final example of settlement expansion comes from the western periphery. Neolithic sites in the river valleys of northern France were first established in the later part of the Linear Pottery culture. They have been particularly well studied in the Aisne valley in recent years. Within the Aisne valley, there appears to be the same long-term trend to change and expansion. Into the fifth millennium BC, more sites become known on the fringes of Normandy and Brittany, in the lower Seine and middle Loire. This brought agricultural communities into contact with indigenous foragers on the Atlantic coast, and the resulting fusions are followed in other chapters.

Conclusions: A New World

The first farmers present a series of contrasts. Neither the process of the spread of an agricultural way of life nor its subsequent development were uniform. Greece and the Balkans were probably colonized gradually from south to north, while the colonization of central and western Europe, though in stages, may have been swifter. In the Mediterranean, there may have been sea-borne colonization of southern Italy and Sicily, as there had been, further east, of Crete and Cyprus. Further west in the Mediterranean, the Neolithic way of life spread by other means, and more slowly; indigenous hunters and foragers determined the selection of new staples and new ways of doing things, and the rate at which they were taken up. Over nearly two thousand years of development in south-east Europe, there were considerable changes, while in the briefer span covered here in central and western Europe the degree of change, though significant, was smaller. By the early fifth millennium BC in much of the central and western Mediterranean, by contrast, Neolithic changes had only just been fully absorbed.

Despite these differences, the result by 5000 BC and after was a completely altered map. This was not just a question of adding new figures to the scene, but of a physical and social landscape altered forever, both by incomers and the indigenous population. New resources brought from outside, clearance and alteration of the natural vegetation, permanent settlements and zones of settlement with an increased sense of place, diverse material culture which could signal complex messages, an elaborate mythical imagery and perhaps a heightened sense of time, the beginnings of reverence of the dead as ancestors and as a principle for descent, and different possibilities for social relations, all contributed in varying ways to a new mental outlook. Despite the difficulties of recovering and understanding the prehistoric evidence, this was one of the great transformations in the history of Europe.

5

The Transformation of Early Agrarian Europe: The Later Neolithic and Copper Ages 4500–2500 BC

ANDREW SHERRATT

Introduction: The Diversification of Europe

THE pioneer farming groups which had become established in Europe over the millennia from 6000 to 4500 BC occupied only a tiny part of the European land mass. Their exotic crops, and the new village communities in which they lived, long remained an intrusive element in a continent still largely populated by hunters and foragers. During the next two millennia, however, features of the farming economy were adopted much more widely by the indigenous inhabitants, so that this contrast began to break down. In its place there grew up a series of regional cultures which resulted from the fusion of natives and later arrivals, and brought about the more general appearance of agriculture and the virtual disappearance of the foraging way of life.

The pattern that was produced by this process was not a uniform one: quite the reverse. Although it created broad areas of similar cultural phenomena such as the belt of megalithic monuments along the Atlantic coastlands or the round burial mounds (tumuli) of eastern Europe and the steppes, each of these areas had its own distinctive character; indeed, this regional differentiation was a prime result of the merging of farming and native populations, and the resultant appearance of specific ways of life appropriate to these distinctive contexts and their environmental settings. The emergence of these new groupings produced a greater diversity of European cultures than at any other period of prehistory—even if, in terms of social complexity, they were variations on a theme, and none could be described as more than tribal societies or simple chiefdoms. Nevertheless, increasing diversity provided new opportunities both for contact and for the self-conscious definition of group and individual identity, reflected in the archaeological record by a whole range of new monuments and types of artefacts.

Down to 3500 BC, this process can be seen as taking place largely in isolation from the developments that were occurring in the areas where farming began. Population

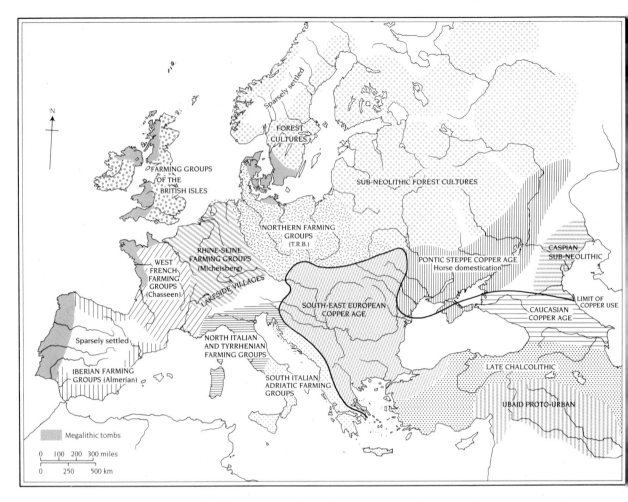

EUROPE IN THE LATER Neolithic and earlier Copper Age, 4500–3500 BC. Copper working was largely confined to south-east Europe, with occasional imports both into northern Europe and the Pontic steppes, where horse domestication was beginning. Megalith-building began in four separate foci on the western fringe, where Neolithic and indigenous (Mesolithic) groups interacted.

growth and interaction between horticulturalists and native groups, and the slow transformation of the temperate environment through forest clearance, gradually altered the conditions of European existence. Livestock rearing, especially in the more open parts of eastern Europe, provided some new opportunities for economic change. Although in the Near East the use of irrigation and the plough were producing the preconditions for the emergence of the first urban societies in Mesopotamia at that time, Europe was unaffected by these developments. After the spread of farming itself, Europe remained virtually closed to Near Eastern innovations for many millennia. Instead, it developed its own traditions on the basis of the common Neolithic craft skills of architecture, weaving, and potting. Timber architecture predominated in a forest setting, with villages of free-standing rectangular houses, rather than the complex mud-brick agglomerations

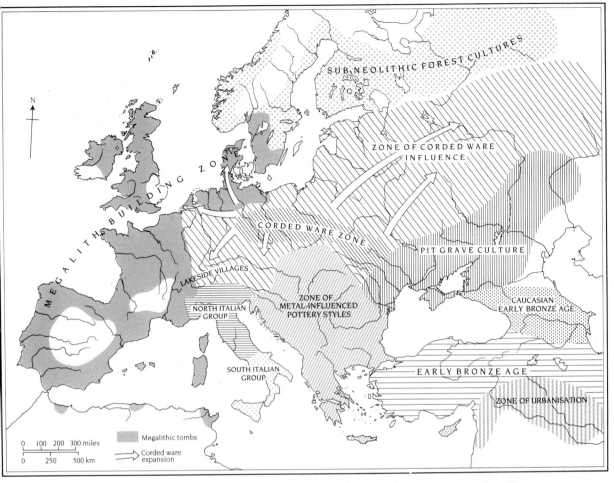

Map labels:

SUB-NEOLITHIC FOREST CULTURES

ZONE OF CORDED WARE INFLUENCE

CORDED WARE ZONE

MEGALITH BUILDING ZONE

PIT GRAVE CULTURE

LAKESIDE VILLAGES

NORTH ITALIAN GROUP

ZONE OF METAL-INFLUENCED POTTERY STYLES

CAUCASIAN EARLY BRONZE AGE

SOUTH ITALIAN GROUP

EARLY BRONZE AGE

ZONE OF URBANISATION

N

0 100 200 300 miles
0 250 500 km

Megalithic tombs
Corded ware expansion

EUROPE IN THE LATER Neolithic, later Copper Age, and Aegean Early Bronze Age, 3500–2500 BC. Outer Europe remained stone-using while copper working spread in central Europe and bronze came into use in the urbanizing Near East and its periphery. Megalith-building became widespread in the west, but more mobile ways of life developed on the steppes and in central Europe, and the expansion of this pattern affected surrounding regions.

typical of the Near East. Stone, too, was used—both for domestic structures (especially in the Mediterranean), and for funerary and ceremonial monuments which often employed massive megalithic blocks as well as timber, earth, and turf. Textile production (using linen and other vegetable fibres, since the sheep of Neolithic Europe were not wool-bearing) achieved considerable sophistication, with the use of the upright, warp-weighted loom; though woven clothing was slow to displace skins in the outer parts of the Continent. Pottery, too, showed great regional diversity in its sophistication, with elaborate painted wares (often decorated in textile patterns) being produced in south-east Europe, and more rustic styles predominating elsewhere in the Continent.

The experience gained by potters in the transformation of natural materials by heat lay behind the innovation which distinguishes this period in the eyes of archaeologists: the beginning of metallurgy. Two metals came into use during this time, copper and gold. Copper was obtained by smelting the rich, chemically simple ores which occur fairly abundantly in parts of south-east Europe; gold was obtained from riverine (placer) deposits in other parts of the same area. Both were cast or hammered into simple shapes—often forms which already existed in stone. These technologies were at first confined largely to south-east Europe, but they developed there without the more sophisticated techniques of alloying and complex casting then in use in the Near East, and it seems likely that metallurgy initially grew up independently in the two areas on the basis of similar common skills and the availability of simple ores. Its initial effects, however, were more symbolic than practical. While metal became a desirable status symbol, often traded over vast distances, it did not in itself bring about any revolutionary change in other aspects of life such as forest clearance or woodworking, or even in weaponry. Copper, like gold, was a medium of display rather than a means of changing the material world.

A similar role was played by varieties of fine stone, though here the practical usefulness was more apparent. Obsidian and flint blades were widely prized. Stone axes, too, were a vital element of the economy of the Neolithic and Copper Ages, and sources of good stone were exploited and traded on an increasing scale. Here again, however, the element of display was prominent, especially in those parts of western Europe where metallurgy was slow to penetrate: fine axes of jadeite were useful only for display, and might be considered as items of jewellery, in the same way as bracelets of valuable stone or imported *Spondylus* shell. These were the kinds of objects increasingly made of copper; but 'Copper Age' societies differed in no fundamental material way from their 'Neolithic' predecessors. The contrast was less one of technology than of behaviour: objects of social prestige were increasingly used as grave goods, perhaps in a more explicit form of competitive display as the old village community lost its coherence in the face of factional groupings, and as increasing diversity led to new roles and social opportunities.

These processes were accelerated after 3500 BC by spin-off from the emergence of urban societies in the Near East, and the much larger scale of economic transactions which they generated. The appearance of cities in Mesopotamia affected a huge hinterland, drawing desirable materials, such as metals and precious stones, over vast distances, and generating a bulk demand for consumable commodities. Technological change was enormously accelerated, both in the esoteric craft skills of luxury production and in the transport of goods. These changes affected a wide area, even beyond the societies immediately involved in such exchanges, since products and techniques permeated beyond the urban economies to reach their economically less advanced neighbours in the steppes and forests. These influences can be most easily traced archaeologically in the field of metallurgy. The use of copper-arsenic alloys and of the two-piece mould revolutionized the casting of large objects, and was apparent in the new design of axes which appeared in Europe in the third millennium BC. Even before that, however, the shapes of pottery types in south-east Europe in the later fourth millennium demonstrate the influence of metal vessels produced at nearby Anatolian centres such as Troy; and the types of vessels—which are principally jugs and cups—testify to new tastes in the consumption of what was arguably an alcoholic drink: vines are among the new crops to appear in the Aegean at this time. Other Near Eastern innovations with both a practical and a prestige element which now appeared in Europe include the first wheeled vehicles; and these can be linked to a more fundamental transformation of European agricultural practices involving the light plough, as well as new varieties of livestock such as wool-bearing sheep. All these innovations profoundly altered the scope for the construction of cultural difference in European societies, through novel media and materials for display, and changing patterns of work and consumption.

The area where these new elements had their most immediate impact was in south-east Europe—already the most sophisticated in terms of technology and in the far-flung character of its trading links, which carried copper items as far as Denmark in the north and eastward among the steppe communities which had already accomplished the domestication of the horse. Inter-island traffic in the Aegean introduced Anatolian features to the inhabitants of Greece, and connections across the steppes to the Caucasus gave north Balkan and Carpathian populations an independent, landward, link to the increasingly complex societies on the periphery of the Near Eastern world system. Small-scale opportunistic movements of population accompanied exchanges and the transfer of new technologies along these routes. From south-east Europe, the spread of these innovations can be traced into central Europe, and also—more slowly—along the Mediterranean to Italy and southern France. From these axial routes, they gradually permeated the fabric of European societies over the course of the millennium from 3500 to 2500 BC.

Important as these innovations were, it should not be imagined that they spread instantaneously or universally—or that they had the same significance wherever they were adopted. New forms of husbandry only slowly displaced earlier forms of horticulture, especially in those parts of Europe which had only recently adopted farming. Even the use of the plough, which can be demonstrated as far north as Denmark by shortly after 3500 BC, did not immediately bring about a marked alteration of cultural pattern. The contrasts in regional cultures created in the preceding millennium provided the structures within which these novelties were incorporated; and these structures were sufficiently robust to absorb or reject elements according to their compatibility with what was already in existence. When change occurred, it was often rapid and catastrophic in character. In northern Europe, fundamental changes which incorporated the full potential of plough farming and pastoralism only took place after 3000 BC with the spread of the Corded Ware complex—and they were accompanied by evident signs of tension between the old and new patterns, as archaic structures based on a static pattern of stone mortuary shrines were rapidly replaced by more mobile ways of life. Even greater disruption can be traced in the further spread of these innovations, associated with the Bell-Beaker complex, down the Atlantic sea-ways and rivers of western Europe. This final extension of the new European pattern is more appropriately considered in the chronological context of Chapter 7; but it must be mentioned here as the last episode in the events which we have been following. It completed the transformation of European societies begun in the mid-fourth millennium; and the inclusion of western Europe in a continent-wide configuration provided the preconditions for the increasing convergence of European cultures during the Bronze Age.

The later Neolithic and Copper Ages, therefore, represent one of the most complex and interesting phases of European development, during which the implications of the first spread of farming worked themselves out, to be rapidly followed by a second generation of agricultural and livestock-rearing innovations that followed hard on their heels. The indigenous inhabitants of the Continent were increasingly locked into an agricultural existence, in a bewildering diversity of cultural patterns; but the common conditions of their existence and the increasing contacts between them began slowly to re-assert the unity of the Continent. These themes are examined further in this chapter on a regional basis, chronologically divided by the point at which European developments were linked again to events outside the Continent, around 3500 BC.

South-east Europe, 4500–3500 BC

The areas in which farming had gained its first European foothold, in the Balkans and the lands around the Carpathian mountains, continued their distinctive culture into the Copper Age. These were the most sophisticated regions of the Continent, preserving their oriental inheritance without dilution from aboriginal ways of life, since farming appeared too early for a Mesolithic population to grow up in parallel with the introduced economy. Early horticulturalists occupied the most fertile enclaves, in the river valleys and old lake basins of this fragmented landscape, where dense populations could be sustained from small patches of easily tilled soil.

Each community occupied a site which would be lived in by further generations: a cluster of mud-and-timber houses whose remains would form the platform for their successors, until a series of artificial mounds marked the points of human habitation. The mound at Karanovo in Bulgaria is 12 metres deep, built up from successive settlements over 2000 years. These tells (each Balkan language has its equivalent word—*mogila, măgura, halom*) were more than accidental by-products of a sedentary economy, with each village intensively working the land within its immediate reach: they were the fixed points of human existence, the location of hearth and home, where life had its beginning and end—for the dead were often buried where they had lived, next to the family house. Each building, each artefact, was pregnant with symbolism, from the carefully painted tablewares (the tables themselves are shown in clay models), the elaborate hearths and ovens or decorated clay fittings, to the more explicit pottery images of female procreativity whose shapes they echoed; or the fine greenstone axes or flint

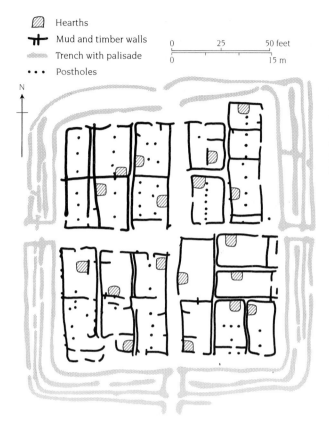

Hearths
Mud and timber walls
Trench with palisade
Postholes

0   25   50 feet
0   15 m

N

PLAN OF THE EXCAVATED settlement mound of Polyanitsa, north-east Bulgaria, in first building phase *c*.4500 BC. This regular plan, with four opposed entrances aligned on the cardinal points of the compass, is typical of the planned layout of Balkan Neolithic and Copper Age communities, even though later rebuildings necessarily departed from the regularities of plan.

blades of the men. Each object had its place, for not only are the houses themselves replications of a common plan, but whole villages were often laid out as exemplifications of a cosmological scheme, oriented on the cardinal points and enclosed by square palisades with central entrances, like Ovcharovo and Polyanitsa in north-east Bulgaria.

This was the model: but increasingly this pattern was transformed by attempts to break out from this introverted world and explore the exciting possibilities which lay beyond it. Hunting and herding provided one such outlet; so also did the winning of new minerals and their mutation into metals, or the opportunities for travel and trade which an abundance of such desirable items gave to those with access to coasts or passages through the mountains. Beside the hand-to-hand traffic that circulated good grinding-stones or the products of specially proficient potters, there developed a longer-distance trade in rare and valuable items: commodities such as salt or furs, and perhaps honey or resins, that leave little trace in the archaeological record, but increasingly, too, in fine flint suitable for long blades, pigments such as graphite for pottery or for body paints, and pre-eminently in the gleaming gold or copper ornaments, and in axes and woodworking tools made of the precious new materials.

In Balkan Europe, metalliferous mountains lay only a short way beyond the tamed world of the villages and gardens; and in the hills behind the settlements deep shafts were excavated to follow the veins of attractive green minerals and provide quantities of copper ore for smelting, as at Rudna Glava in Yugoslavia or Ai Bunar near to Karanovo. These operations were approached with due ritual, and offerings of fine pottery and their contents were left in the mines as propitiation or exchange for wealth taken from the earth; but once extracted, these materials could be traded with communities far distant, on the edges of the world where farming was practised, and even beyond, among the fishing and cattle-keeping groups clustered along the rivers flowing down to the Black Sea across the flat, open country of the Pontic steppes.

The network of farming villages had extended since Neolithic times out from the Balkans, in a north-eastward direction, following the belt of light woodland between the Russian forests and the Ukrainian steppe, as far east as Kiev. These pioneers maintained all the traditions of their Balkan origins, living in similar sorts of rectangular houses and using the same kinds of artefacts, including elaborately painted pottery and figurines. In the more open landscapes of the eastern frontier, however, the houses were not concentrated into closely packed settlements like tells, but occupied defensible promontories protected by deeply cut ditches. One reason for this was the existence of other populations with a different way of life, descendants of the indigenous Mesolithic inhabitants of this region who had adopted the use of pottery and some domestic livestock, but had not abandoned their seasonal mobility in favour of permanent villages. These groups lived within the interstices of the clusters of farming communities, and dominated the extensive areas further east as far as the Volga. They and the farmers lived in uneasy symbiosis: exchanging their complementary products, but also potentially in conflict. Both groups, however, were eager to acquire ornaments of copper traded from the Balkans.

The scope and effects of Copper Age trade were dramatically demonstrated in 1972, when a Bulgarian tractor-driver unearthed the first graves from a 6000 year-old cemetery on the shore of the Black Sea by the inlet of Varna. In subsequent excavations, not only were plentiful copper artefacts recovered, but also 6 kilograms of gold, mostly in the form of sheet-ornaments originally sewn on to clothing, but also including gold sceptres and shaft-hole axes. Other such cemeteries—though none so rich—are known from eastern Bulgaria. They mark a break from the previous pattern of mud-walled villages with household burials, and at Varna seem to be associated with wooden 'pile-villages' on the shores of the inlet, perhaps a special form of settlement connected with coastal trading activities. The goldwork is striking, and was certainly available in abundance; but it cannot be compared with later gold-rich burials such as the Mycenae Shaft Graves, since there were fewer commodities for which it could be exchanged in such a simple economy: indeed, it may not have belonged to individuals, since most of the graves in which it was found were not human burials, but symbolic interments with clay masks. Copper Age societies were profoundly different from those of historical Europe, and require an anthropological imagination.

In any case, the wealth of Varna seems to represent a temporary episode, for important changes soon occurred which reflect a changing balance of power on the steppes. Fundamental to this was the beginning of horse domestication by the Copper Age inhabitants of the steppe region, supplementing riverine resources by the taming and riding of wild horses, which were then used to exploit the wild herds. A settlement of this type has been excavated at Dereivka, on the Dnepr. These peoples began to develop a distinctive culture, ornamenting their simple pottery with cord impressions—perhaps the hempen ropes which would have been important in controlling the animals themselves—and creating distinctive forms of objects such as stone zoomorphic sceptres and small pottery braziers, which could have been used for burning cannabis seeds as did the Iron Age Scythian tribes of this region. Where they came into contact with the substantial houses and settlements of cultivators, at the western end of the Pontic steppes, these hunting and herding groups began to build circular burial monuments—giving focal points to an existence otherwise spent in mobile tents. This way of life expanded westward into some of the areas formerly controlled by horticulturalists, and some groups even seem to have penetrated in small numbers along the Danube into Romania, where their typical burials and artefacts occur. This incursion had its impact on neighbouring farmers, for later Copper Age settlements were now commonly located on promontories and hilltops, and on the eastern frontier of farming near Kiev, at sites like Dobrovody or Majdanetskoe, there were massive agglomerated villages of up to 200 houses, grouped together for defence.

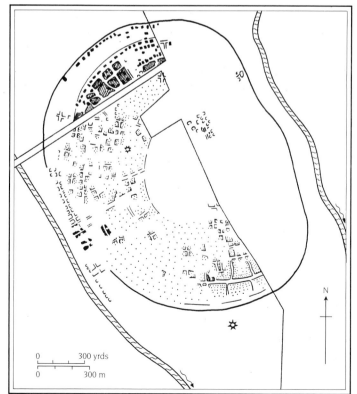

PLAN (established largely through surface investigations and magnetometry) of the massive Copper Age settlement (*c*.3700 BC) of Dobrovody, Ukraine. This is one of a number of such giant aggregations of settlement in the forest-steppe zone. Its area is roughly equivalent to that of medieval York and it may have housed a population of around 2,000 people.

0   300 yrds

0   300 m

In the Carpathian basin a comparable, but more peaceful, set of changes occurred, without the perturbations of historical incident. The large settlements and tells of the fifth millennium, with their wealth of decorated pottery, obsidian blades, and green-stone axes, and their modest burials within or near to the settlement, gave way to a new pattern. Smaller, more dispersed settlements became common; and at the same time cemeteries of up to several hundred burials, like that of Tiszapolgár-Basatanya in eastern Hungary, took on a more prominent role in the organization of the social landscape. These larger cemeteries probably served several of the small settlements, and the burials became more formal, with graves set out in rows (probably marked by posts) and with larger quantities of grave goods. The character of material culture also changed: domestic pottery became less elaborate and regionally distinctive, but new items of ostentatious male equipment made their appearance in metal, along with flint blades also imported over long distances. As the visibility of the immediate, living, community declined, so the symbolic importance of burials and signals of individual status increased. The cemeteries mapped out relationships that now had to be explicitly defined.

Each of these regions, in a different way, exemplifies the differentiation of the simple horticultural economies of the Neolithic, and the new spheres of activity opened up: in herding, winning new materials, and trading.

Central and North-western Europe, 4500–3500 BC

The pioneer horticultural groups, who had spread across the forested loess-lands of central Europe from the mid-sixth millennium onward, initially formed an equally intro-verted cultural community; even though they came increasingly into contact with the indigenous peoples of the forests and coasts. From the Rhine to the Vistula, their typical timber longhouses, 'shoe-last' adzes, and characteristic round-bottomed pottery (decorated with a spiral or meander ornament of incised lines and dots) maintained a homogeneity which suggests that they preserved their internal links and probably formed a relatively closed breeding network, or at least emphasized the distinctiveness and exclusiveness of their way of life. By 5000 BC these farmers had reached as far as the Paris basin, and in the following centuries spread further west to reach the Channel coasts and the edges of Brittany.

By this time, however, their unity was beginning to fragment: groups in central Europe were increasingly influenced by the copper-using societies of the Carpathian basin and the Balkans, while on the outer margins there were signs of accommodation and interaction with the native communities, which existed in greater numbers on the Atlantic coastlands and the Alpine fringe. In the central area, the village remained the primary unit of social life. Houses increased in size and complexity, developing a characteristic trapezoidal plan with a wide entrance area and more secluded rear portion. An especially large example from Bochum in Germany was more than 65 metres long. The scattered groups of longhouses which often characterized the pioneer phase now came together in nucleated settlements of larger buildings, enclosed by a palisade—perhaps to separate kitchen gardens from cattle which could graze in larger numbers in the cleared land round about. Influences from southern, Copper Age, groups are evident in more elaborate designs of pottery, figurines, and imported copper beads, as well as in the appearance of round earthwork enclosures (like the famous example from Köthing-eichendorf in Bavaria) with two sets of opposed entrances that recall the layout (and perhaps cosmology) of the tell sites. Near to the villages, these may have served as dancing-grounds and places for communal ceremonies. This model of village life was adopted in the Alpine foreland, in southern Germany, Switzerland, and Austria, where Mesolithic groups around the morainic lakes took up farming and livestock-keeping and built simple timber settlements on piles on the swampy margins of the lakes. Preserved in peat, these sites have yielded some of the most vivid evidence of Neolithic existence—birch-bark containers, wooden bowls and implements, linen textiles, piles of fodder and manure (complete with fly pupae!), and even a piece of resin 'chewing gum' with tooth-marks, along with the pottery and small stone axes which are all that usually survive on inland sites.

A rather different pattern of interaction with the older, indigenous, populations of Europe took place around the western and northern fringes of the loess. This process began earliest in western France, where distant central European influences began to give way to an accommodation to native ways of life, as material culture became less elaborate and farming was supplemented by hunting and collecting. As with the development of more mobile lifestyles in the Carpathian basin or coastal Bulgaria, emphasis shifted from the house and village to burials as a symbolic marker of community; but rather than the subtle messages of grave goods and complex artefacts, monumental tombs became important in the definition of group identity in western and northern Europe. In western France (as, somewhat later, in southern Britain and in northern Poland and Germany) timber or stone mortuary houses, enclosed in long (and often trapezoidal) earthern mounds, became the focal points of community life: such monuments to the ancestors became prominent features of the landscape at the same time as the houses and domestic sites became less substantial and long-lasting.

The emergence of these symbolic monuments characteristically took place where the central European farming tradition encountered dense native populations, and the farming population was enlarged by the incorporation of these earlier communities. Permanent monuments, whether houses or tombs, were fundamental to the organization of a farming existence and the longer perspective of planting and harvesting. But the initiative did not rest solely with the incomers: very rapidly, a diversity of built tomb types shows that this stimulus evoked a creative response from the indigenous inhabitants. The stone-built long mounds with burial cists which appeared in Normandy were echoed in a rather different design of stone-built tombs in many parts of the Atlantic façade: burial-chambers set in round mounds and approached by a long corridor which

A NEOLITHIC DOOR (*right*). This famous nineteenth-century find, from the lakeside settlement of Robenhausen on the Pfäffikersee south of Zürich, Switzerland, is 1.45 m high and dates to around 4000 BC. Made from a single piece of split timber, it was originally attached to the door-post by four thongs, probably of leather. (The frame is a modern reconstruction.)

FLOOR OF AN EXCAVATED NEOLITHIC HOUSE (*below*), *c.*4000 BC, preserved in peat at a lakeside settlement at Egolzwil, Canton Lucerne, Switzerland. The corduroy arrangement of logs was covered by bark, and clay platforms served as fireplaces. The structure was divided into several rooms, and probably sheltered animals as well as human inhabitants.

allowed repeated access and the insertion of new burials define a type known as the passage grave, which was to proliferate as the chief mark of native farmers in the far west. At first constructed mainly of dry-stone walling and with a corbelled vault, like the magnificent example on the Île Longue off the southern coast of Brittany, larger and larger stones came to be used in the construction of such tombs. A novel tradition of architectural construction emerged, which, for the next two thousand years, was to be the characteristic of the indigenous early farmers of Atlantic Europe, leaving huge perched blocks of stone which would survive to stimulate the imagination of early antiquarians some six thousand years later.

More complex than the processes by which farming had previously spread across Europe—either by migration or by the selective adoption of elements such as pottery and livestock—this dialectic between colonists and indigenes was worked out on a small scale over large areas of north-west Europe. Competition within and between these different groups accounts for the proliferating diversity of differing types of monument, and their growing complexity. In the British Isles, for example, it seems likely that the stimulus to farming came from small groups crossing the Channel from nearby Flanders, building timber mortuary houses (to be encased in long mounds) while themselves still living in simple huts scarcely different from those of the surrounding natives.

PLAN AND SECTION of the magnificent passage grave on Île Longue in the Morbihan, southern Brittany, France, dating to the later fifth millennium BC. The corbelled chamber underneath a circular mound was once compared to the tholos tombs at Mycenae, though these are in fact 2,500 years later.

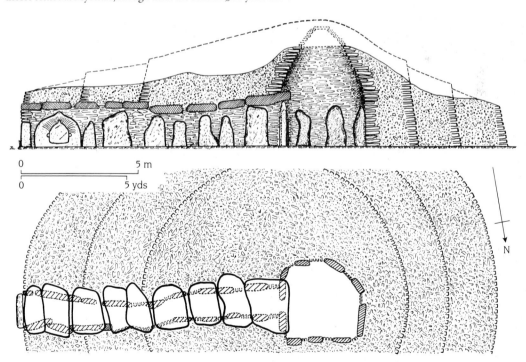

Stone-built cists with funnel entrances (called 'portal tombs') with circular covering mounds then appeared in western Britain and Ireland, and may be evidence of a native response; and such structures are sometimes found underneath the long mounds of the Cotswolds, which incorporate their own forms of stone-built chambers and thus synthesize both aspects—perhaps indicating a syncretic fusion. Simple earth-and-timber long mounds are found all the way up to Scotland, and stone-built varieties were introduced to northern Ireland. In Ireland and Scotland, however, the tradition of stone portal tombs and more developed passage tombs in circular mounds survived side by side with long cairns, especially in areas of native resistance to the introduced pattern. All these types bear witness to the struggle for distinctive identities as old landscapes were slowly transformed into new social patterns.

Similar patterns of regional distinctiveness and fusion occurred over a wide area from southern France to the North European Plain. The loess-lands themselves seem to have been affected by this process, as the old social exclusiveness broke down, and larger social and cultural units appeared. Older patterns of small-scale horticulture gave way to more extensive forms of slash-and-burn cultivation, and settlements often moved up out of the valleys to more commanding positions overlooking them. The increased demand for flint axes for forest clearance led to the opening up of mines in areas of suitable Cretaceous or Jurassic deposits, notably in Belgium and central Poland. New types of ceremonial monuments (often with concentric, interrupted ditches) appeared as local or regional centres within this more fluid pattern of settlement and regional trade.

The process of small-scale penetration and reaction was replayed in northern Europe, where long mounds echoing the longhouses of the northern loess-lands appeared over an area from the middle Vistula to Jutland, to be answered by another outburst of megalith-building (of types called *dysser* or 'dolmens') on the coasts and islands of the Baltic, as the dense Mesolithic populations of these areas converted to a farming existence. The vast numbers of flint axes known from this area are evidence of the substantial numbers of people involved, and the effort involved in clearing even small areas of heavy woodland for crops. As in south-east Europe, the tools of labour were also symbols of wealth; and the finely polished axe blades were sometimes deposited as offerings in bogs.

The types of pottery used by these northern and western Neolithic groups, although simple by comparison with their Copper Age contemporaries in the Balkans, nevertheless showed greater variety of types (and thus perhaps of cuisine) than the large, coarse, point-based forms (for one-pot meals) used by the late Mesolithic inhabitants of Scandinavia; and in northern Europe the assemblage soon included a combination of drinking-vessels ('funnel-necked beakers') and distinctive collared flasks, no doubt used in some drinking ceremony. In France the ceramic repertoire included highly decorated small burners, with a very widespread distribution; it has been suggested that these may have been used for burning some aromatic or narcotic substance—again, probably as the accompaniment to ritual and ceremony.

GRAVE GROUP from Tovstrup, near Ringkøbing in west Jutland, Denmark, c.3600 BC. This complementary set of vessels—the tall-necked amphora, collared flask, and drinking cup—frequently occurs together in tombs in this region, and seems to have formed the equipment for mixing a potent drink.

This phase of European prehistory has left some of the most remarkable memorials to the efforts of early farmers, and their ideological struggles. Monuments, once erected, were endowed with a sanctity and power that could be captured or subverted. In southern Brittany recent archaeological work has demonstrated that some time around 3800 BC a remarkable phase of reconstruction took place, in which existing megalithic structures were taken apart and re-erected in new positions. Great sculptured monoliths were broken and used as capstones for new, large passage graves such as the remarkable tomb of Gavrinis in the Morbihan, with its twenty-eight massive wall-slabs covered in profuse but enigmatic ornament, laboriously pecked and carved in granite. As with the golden graves of Varna, we can only dimly discern the motivations which dominated the lives of these remote Europeans; but the arrival of agriculture brought with it more than just changes in subsistence.

North-east Europe, 4500–3500 BC

By contrast with these spectacular archaeological phenomena in limited areas of the Continent, it is salutary to survey the vast areas of Boreal forests, in central and northern Scandinavia and reaching eastwards to the Urals, over which a slower and more uniform set of changes took place. Mesolithic cultures had appeared here from the beginning of the Holocene, living in semi-subterranean huts and gaining a living by collecting water chestnuts and fishing in the lakes and meres, by hunting elk, pig, and other animals in the forests and seals on the shores of the Baltic. They made wood and birch-bark containers, and their equipment included canoes and skin boats, floats, nets and traps, as well as skis. From the fourth millennium onward, the use of pottery spread from the later Neolithic groups of eastern Europe to the communities of the Pripyat' Marshes, and thence along the upper Dnepr and Volga rivers to the area of Moscow. No fundamental economic changes accompanied its adoption, which does not imply the use of cereals or domestic livestock, though population may have increased and become more concentrated: some sites may have been inhabited by up to one hundred people all year round.

This picture is important in giving perspective to the rest of Europe, for this is the pattern that would have prevailed more generally had farming not spread so rapidly from the Near East. Even more relevantly, it was a pattern which survived in those areas which farming failed to penetrate—especially over quite large parts of the North European Plain in the interstices of farming groups, but even in the mountainous areas and plateaux of western Europe, where pottery was rarely used and such hunting sites are harder to date. In such places, Mesolithic populations survived side by side with early farmers down to the third millennium. In Poland the users of 'pit-and-comb' ornamented pottery, with a non-agricultural way of life, occupied an extensive area around Warsaw with outliers as far west as the Oder. The arrival of farming did not initially oust the alternatives.

The Central and Western Mediterranean, 4500–3500 BC

The sharp contrasts between farming and foraging ways of life, which are notable in other parts of Europe, were less evident in the Mediterranean. The greater continuity between Mesolithic and early Neolithic populations, and the early arrival of farming in the east Mediterranean, meant that indigenous communities had tended to select certain aspects of the farming package and integrate them with existing ways of life. Pottery-making and small-scale livestock-rearing preceded cultivation in many areas of the western Mediterranean, without radically altering the patterns of settlement. Except perhaps in southern Italy, the spread of farming did not, therefore, create notable distinctions between villagers and mobile hunters, since farming communities were mostly small and foragers often themselves largely sedentary. Evidence of occupation comes as much from caves as from built habitation structures, and it would be misleading to expect elaborate architecture on the central European pattern. Nevertheless the later Neolithic period does mark an important change, since it was at this time that cereal cultivation caught up with the precocious spread of pottery and livestock, and new features spread both from the Balkans and central Europe.

In Italy, open-air sites (rather than caves or rock shelters) became more general, especially in the circum-Alpine lakelands of the north or the coastal plains of Sicily and Calabria; though hunting and foraging continued to be an important component of the economy. In Apulia, facing the adjacent coasts of Albania and Epirus, trichrome painted pottery in Balkan textile patterns made its appearance; in Liguria the characteristic square-mouthed pottery with incised decoration has central European analogies, while the Alpine fringes came to participate in the more general pattern of 'lake-village' cultures. In southern France the general adoption of farming by indigenous populations, as part of the wider pattern described in the previous section, is marked by the widespread appearance of querns and polished axes, as well as new forms of pottery with multiple lugs for suspension. A particular concentration of settlements occurs in the area around Toulouse, where riverside sites, with long spreads of cobble flooring with plentiful traces of burning, defy easy interpretation, but may represent some kind of sauna or communal facilities at sites of ceremonial significance. The best known example is at St Michel-du-Touche, at the confluence of the Touche and the Garonne.

IMAGINATIVE CONTEMPORARY DEPICTION of the discovery by nineteenth-century miners of a burial-cave of *c*.4000 BC (Cueva de los Murciélagos – "Bat Cave") high in the side of a gorge in Granada, southern Spain. The still clothed skeletons had esparto-grass sandals and coiled baskets, some containing poppy-heads.

The central Mediterranean volcanic islands became prominent in this phase because of the sources of obsidian on Sardinia, Lipari, and the Pontine Islands. Permanent farming villages permitted a sustained exploitation of sources such as Monte Arci in west-central Sardinia, and the products of these collecting centres were traded around the shores of the Tyrrhenian Sea, and up to southern France and the Alpine fringe. Fine pottery, too, travelled by such coastal traffic, spreading new styles such as the attractive red-slipped wares of the Lipari Islands. In Malta this phase is also notable for the beginnings of rock-cut burials, paralleled by the use of caves and built stone cists elsewhere.

Iberia at this time presents a somewhat isolated appearance, though here, too, open sites with a farming economy became more common and appeared in new regions; they are characterized by simple, round-based pottery and polished-stone axes. In the arid south, esparto grass (*Stipa*) fibres were used for the manufacture of clothing and containers, and cave burials preserve remarkable examples of such Neolithic textiles. One such remarkable find, made by quarrymen in the last century in the Cueva de los Murciélagos in the side of a gorge in Granada, contained a series of still-clothed skeletons accompanied by globular baskets containing poppy-heads. Were they simply symbols of fertility, or were the narcotic properties of opium already appreciated? Further west, in Portugal—where (as in Denmark) substantial coastal populations are indicated by shell mounds—the spread of farming over the surrounding inland areas was marked by the first appearance of megalithic tombs, in the form of simple passage graves.

By 3500 BC, therefore, Europe presented a diversity of cultures: most sophisticated in the south-east, and along an axis lying to the north-west; less closely linked to the south-west, and preserving older ways of life almost untouched in the north-east. These differences were to be exaggerated rather than diminished by the new eastward contacts that were already taking place.

South-east and Central Europe, 3500–2500 BC

The beginning of a new era is marked by the transformation of the Aegean from what was effectively a peninsula of Balkan Europe, typified by the mud-built villages and painted pottery of the plains of Thessaly, into a network of coasts and islands dominated by stone-built fortifications and clustered settlements looking down from the hilltops. Many factors contributed to this: new tree crops such as vines and olives; ploughs and donkeys to open up the countryside, and woolly sheep to graze the pastures; new metallurgical techniques for alloying and casting copper, and for extracting silver from lead, or working marble using emery; longboats to travel from island to island, fishing, trading, and raiding—all these were made possible by the new role which adjacent Anatolia had acquired in the international division of labour of the east Mediterranean Bronze Age.

The site of Troy conveniently epitomizes the nature of this transformation. This palace–fortress with its great halls and workshops, controlling the entrance to the Dar-

MAGNIFICENT TREASURE OF PRECIOUS METAL (*left*) from the second citadel of Troy (Hissarlik) in north-west Turkey, destroyed *c.*2300 BC, discovered by Heinrich Schliemann. It contained gold ornaments, gold and silver drinking-vessels (echoed in local pottery forms), and silver ingots. Such wealth is rarely preserved except by catastrophe, or in royal burials.

HANDLED DRINKING-CUP (*right*) in grey polished ware from Vinča, Serbia, belonging to the Baden culture, *c.*3400 BC. The surface treatment, shape, strap-handle, channel decoration and dimpled base echo features of contemporary forms in silver (like those preserved in the Troy II treasure), which were presumably imported into south-east Europe from Anatolian or Aegean palace workshops.

danelles and looking out to island towns like Poliochni on Lemnos, preserved in the conflagration of its second phase (at the end of our period) not only vast numbers of spindle whorls that testify to its industrial base, but also the rich metal equipment of its rulers: gold and silver jugs, cups, and dishes; bronze bowls; silver ingots; oriental types of bronze lanceheads; and fine gold jewellery with filigree and granulation work. This is a different world from the peasant cultures of the Neolithic and Copper Ages, and was linked by trade and emulation to the urban cultures of Syria and Mesopotamia. It held its place in this system by virtue of its maritime links to the Aegean Islands, whose raw materials included argentiferous lead that could supply the silver-hungry economy of growing cities.

The élite lifestyle of wine-drinking Anatolia was soon copied, in simpler fashion, by the suppliers of her raw materials. Silver vessels appeared on the Greek islands and mainland, too, along with their more plentiful copies in slipped and burnished pottery. Local centres on the Cyclades and the east coast of the Peloponnese copied the bastion walls and the large central buildings, and local workshops attempted to reproduce the skills of expert goldsmiths. Middlemen in the Cyclades profited from their control of inter-island routes, and created their own culture mirrored in marble figures of drinkers and lyre-players.

The rest of south-east Europe lay beyond these immediate influences; but even as far north as the Carpathian basin, the new pottery style of the later fourth millennium echoed the metal drinking sets of the Aegean, with its high-swung ribbon handles, dimpled bases, channelled ornament, and lustrous grey surface. Rustic élites are also in evidence, for these status items (now used for drinking some local brew, since

EXCAVATED PIT-GRAVE BURIAL beneath a round mound at Plachidol, northern Bulgaria, with wooden waggon wheels, *c*.3000 BC. This tomb is an outlier of the main distribution of such burials on the steppes north of the Black Sea, where they give their name to the Pit-grave culture.

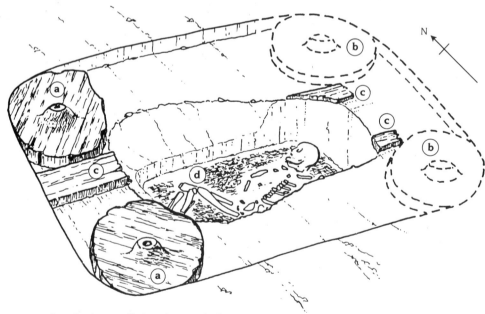

a Wooden wheels (actually found)   c Planks covering pit
b Wooden wheels (conjectured)   d Remains of organic (felt?) covering under skeleton

domesticated grapes were not to be grown here for another three millennia) occur in the same graves as other expensive accompaniments to eternity: women or pairs of cattle (or both) that are known from a few burials of this date in cemeteries in central Hungary. That these goods and chattels formed an ideological unity is shown by the ultimate fourth-millennium status symbol: a drinking cup in the shape of a model wagon, known from examples at Budakalász and Szigetszentmárton. The oxen used for pulling wheeled vehicles could also be used for ploughs, and new agricultural methods are reflected in the colonization of further territories on the edges of the lowlands and on the drier interfluvial areas within them.

The spread of paired draught technology for wheeled vehicles and light ploughs had an even greater effect in the dry landscapes north of the Black Sea, where complex societies on the edges of the Near Eastern network, such as Maikop in the northern Caucasus, opened relations with the pastoral horse-raisers of the steppes. The combination of horses and ox-drawn wagons gave the full mobility necessary for the exploitation of the pasture lands, and a powerful new culture developed, characterized by pit graves covered by wooden beams and marked by a round mound or *kurgan*. These monuments, sometimes topped by a stone anthropomorphic stela and occasionally containing wooden wheels or even whole wagons, appeared over the entire area from the lower Danube to the Ural river, flowing south to the Caspian. Small groups of these peoples penetrated along the Danube into northern Bulgaria and up into eastern Hungary, where they established an enclave on the increasingly saline lands in the seasonally dry flood plain of the Tisza and Körös rivers. Their burials—the skeleton on its back with knees drawn up, sprinkled with red ochre, and lying on a painted felt mat in a pit beneath a *kurgan*—form an exotic contrast to the local cemeteries of flat graves. It was through such eastward connections that ultimately Near Eastern features found their way into Europe other than via the Aegean: wool-bearing breeds of sheep, and a metalcasting technology using the two-piece mould.

Meanwhile, the earlier, Aegean, influences spread into those parts of central Europe around the Carpathian basin: Bavaria, former Czechoslovakia, southern Poland. In these areas the characteristic rounded, metal-influenced pottery shapes appeared, often associated in upland areas with promontory sites defended by ditches. Besides bringing a cultural unity to a large area of south-east and central Europe, further influences can be detected over a large part of Germany and Poland—including the surprising occurrence of pottery forms copying metal vessels in a megalith at Oldendorf in Lower Saxony, and paired cattle burials in Kujavia. These direct influences are indicative of more fundamental movements, including transmission of the plough and wheeled vehicles.

Northern and Western Europe, 3500–3000 BC

These further impulses from the south caused a rapid series of reactions and accommodations in the North European Plain and neighbouring areas to the west. In general, new elements were absorbed within existing social and ritual systems; but the larger scale of cultivation made possible by the plough, and the growing diversity of contacts, stored up the potential for radical change in the succeeding period.

The scale of economic change is indicated by the expansion of flint mining on an industrial scale at sites like Krzemionki in Poland, where up to 1000 shafts were sunk through softer rocks to the seams of hard, banded flint suitable for axes. The products of these mines travelled up to 500 kilometres to supply the growing needs of forest clearance required by cultivation with the plough. Dense clusters of find-spots of such tools pick out the areas of most rapid expansion, notably the area of Kujavia on the Vistula, where settlements of small, square houses and cemeteries, including animal burials (for instance cattle with a bone disc and 'sunburst' motif between the horns), are symptomatic of the growing importance of the pastoral component in subsistence and ideology, made possible by more extensive clearance of the forest. The pottery of this area includes large, globular vessels with suspension loops (somewhat inappropriately termed 'amphorae'), which spread eastward as far as Kiev, abutting the distribution of the pit-grave peoples of the steppes. From this source they acquired the ornament of twisted cord—and perhaps other habits—though not yet the practice of erecting round burial mounds. The first domestic horses reached central and northern Europe by this route. Globular amphorae with cord decoration are found in other areas of Poland and

ENGRAVED SIDE-SLAB from a later Neolithic cist-grave (*c.*3000 BC) at Leuna-Göhlitzsch, Merseburg, Sachsen-Anhalt, Germany. Originally painted in red, it seems to represent the interior of a room: a quiver of arrows (*left*) and a strung bow (*centre top*) hang up next to a set of four geometrically decorated strips of matting. (A similar representation is known from a contemporary grave in the northern Caucasus.)

METICULOUSLY EXCAVATED II m long stone cist (gallery-grave or *allée couverte*) with successive interments of more than 250 individuals at la Chausée Tirancourt, Somme, France, *c.*3100–2600 BC. The skeletons occur in layers, corresponding to phases of use. The collective tomb would have served hamlets scattered over the area of a modern parish.

Germany, where they seem to belong to specialist herders who existed alongside agricultural groups. A further element in the cultural mix was provided by hunting groups using pottery with pit-and-comb decoration, who seem to have penetrated in small numbers from central Scandinavia and the Baltic coasts to occupy a specialized niche among surrounding farmers and graziers.

Cultivation, now including ploughing, was carried out on a larger scale in the older heartlands of the loess belt and in the megalith-building zone which adjoined it to the north and west. Hilltop sites and ceremonial centres remained in use (or appeared in new areas, such as Denmark), while groups of substantial timber houses came to replace the simpler settlements which had previously predominated beyond the loess. In central Germany—the area of the middle Elbe and Saale rivers—a new feature was the appearance of mass collective graves in mortuary houses: recalling the megalithic tombs of the west, but usually built of timber or smaller blocks of stone. Pottery drums were used in ceremonial, and sometimes left in tombs. At Leuna-Göhlitzsch near Merseburg in Sachsen-Anhalt, in an unusual interior scene, an especially elaborate stone-built grave was carved with representations of decorative matting and of a bow and quiver hung on the wall. Timber cult-houses, with special forms of pedestalled pottery and clay spoons, appeared in Denmark, where larger megalithic tombs with entrance passages (called *jaettestuer* or 'giant's graves') were built for the first time. They typically contain large numbers of burials, often differentiated into skulls and longbones, which were placed in different compartments. These huge monuments were also built for the first time in the northern Netherlands.

Similar timber, stone, or subterranean collective graves were built over a vast area of western Europe, linking up the older megalithic centres on the coasts. These long stone cists are known from Hesse, the Paris basin, central Brittany, and the Loire valley, where they are known as 'gallery graves' or *allées couvertes* and contain large numbers of collective burials. They are associated with a new form of settlement, called the 'expanded village', in which the central megalithic tomb formed a focus for a scatter of hamlets round about. This pattern of probably plough-based settlement appeared extensively on inland plateaux where Mesolithic groups had survived in small numbers, and this phenomenon seems to represent the final absorption of these marginal populations. The impact of this new pattern on older established megalithic groups in western France is indicated by new forms of monument combining the features of passage graves and gallery graves, such as the so-called angled passage graves (*allées coudées*) which are concentrated in the Morbihan.

The pottery of this period shows a great diversity of types, especially in the decorated vessel forms appropriate to formal ceremony and display. They record a tension between conflicting models of appropriate behaviour, particularly the socially expressive consumption of food and drink. These include the rounded, southern shapes of drinking vessels, angular northern shapes of food containers, and the larger containers for liquids in eastern Europe, as well as the simplified 'flower-pot' shapes that predominated in the areas of Mesolithic incorporation in the west. Each type of pottery reflects regional modes of food preparation, and echoes the variety of monuments and settlements.

In all these varied regional expressions, certain common features stand out. Chief among them is the importance of *place*. Neolithic social structures were anchored in permanent physical forms, whether timber houses and villages, earth-built ceremonial centres or stone mortuary shrines. Where farming predominated over the raising of livestock, these marks of community were fundamental to the continuity of cultivation and social reproduction. They were the scene of regular rituals and ceremonies, and were erected in the expectation of permanence, lasting through the yearly cycles of everyday existence until eternity. What was to follow, and was already prefigured in eastern Europe, was a new mobility: a less rooted, more opportunistic, way of life in which societies were less closely tied to the soil and to symbols of stability.

Northern and Western Europe, 3000–2500 BC

The subdivision of this regional section at 3000 BC is emblematic of the rapid pace of change in the outer parts of the Continent as the contradictions of accumulated innovations ruptured traditional societies and ways of life. Whereas the previous five centuries had witnessed a growing elaboration of ritual structures and types of monument, this trend was suddenly reversed by the spread of new forms of material culture, in which portable wealth was to be more important than megaliths and ceremonial centres. The focus shifted from places to people and their personal possessions.

The symbol of this change was the type of pottery known to archaeologists as Corded

Ware. Decoration using impressed cords had been known before, on the steppes and more latterly in the eastern half of the North European Plain: but it now took the characteristic form of a drinking-vessel known as a beaker—a tall, handleless pot with an everted rim, holding a litre or so of liquid, and decorated in horizontal bands on its upper half. Such pots are typically found in male graves, accompanied by a stone axe with a shaft hole and single, drooping blade, often called a 'battleaxe'. Similar axes had also been made earlier, in imitation of the later Copper Age shaft-hole axes of the Carpathian basin: but now they occurred in much larger numbers, taking over the prestige which had formerly been associated with the polished axes used in clearing forest. Graves containing these items now lay in the centre of a circular mound.

This set of personal equipment and individual burial rite integrated elements both of

EARLY, MIDDLE, AND LATE EXAMPLES (3000–2400 BC) of the typical pottery drinking-vessel and stone battle-axe characteristic of male graves of the Corded Ware culture. These examples are from Denmark, but comparable artifacts are found over an area from Switzerland to Moscow. The burials (initially in a pit, later on the ground surface) were usually covered by a circular mound.

southern and eastern origin. The emphasis on drinking had reached southern Europe from Anatolia, and now, in rustic northern mugs, dimly echoed the sophistication of the silver wine cups in use in the Aegean. These were no empty containers, and to fill them with the appropriate stimulant required a concentration of scarce resources. The corded decoration may hint that its contents contained more than the weak alcohol obtainable from forest honey and wild fruits, for if cannabis was smoked on the steppes it could have been infused by neighbouring drinking cultures. This much is speculation; but the adoption of round burial mounds is another symbolic feature which is of more than trivial significance, perhaps reflecting the circular huts or tents of more autonomous family groups, that had its origins in the East. The battle axes, too, are charged with meaning, for they express the ideal of a society whose self-image was not work but warfare.

Nor were the changes confined to matters of ideology and style. The settlement patterns of Corded Ware peoples were an inversion of previous practices, and consisted of small, scattered groups of dwellings (of a less substantial kind, and thus hard to reconstruct from flimsy post-hole scatters, but probably small), and with no equivalents to the central earthworks and ceremonial centres of the previous pattern. They were appropriate to more rapidly changing social landscapes, in which habitations were less permanent features and social groupings more fluid. So, too, with the tombs: burial was a once-for-all event, witnessed only by those at the graveside; but the dead were interred as personalities, showing off the equipment of life and their personal position in a final *coup de théâtre*, rather than joining a more anonymous community of ancestors. The mounds marked specific lines of ancestry and inheritance which were of interest to the world of the living. These phenomena were not new in European prehistory, for they had earlier analogies in the Carpathian Copper Age and parallels on the steppes. Their novelty lay in their appearance in forested northern Europe, where pasture land had been slowly carved out of climax woodland by earlier farmers, and where the larger areas of arable and fallow now made possible a reorganization of existence according to new principles, where livestock rather than land was the basis of wealth, and artefacts—as symbols of authority and power—held sway above the flux.

Where did this pattern begin? Archaeologists, using typological analysis and a (so far) inadequate number of radiocarbon dates, have defined a primary group, an 'A-horizon' of initial Corded Ware beakers and battleaxes in pits under low mounds from Jutland to the Northern Bug. On the outer margins of this distribution, these communities were clearly intrusive, and for two centuries lived alongside the builders of megaliths and the makers of globular amphorae. Perhaps they had always been outsiders, growing up on the margins of existing cultures and gradually subverting their populations. Soon, however, they formed the dominant element in long-tilled plains such as those of the central German loess lands, or the easily cleared outwash-sands (not then the heathlands currently used for army manœuvres) of the Lüneburger Heide, and soon penetrating to comparable areas of light soil over large parts of the North European Plain. From there the pattern spread to the Rhineland, and down to Switzerland; over much of Scandinavia; eastward to absorb both farmers and foragers in the east Baltic and onward toward Moscow: rolling up previous patterns of culture and reformatting huge areas to create a cultural bloc which rivalled the steppe pastoralists and the more sedentary farmers of south-east Europe. It was one of the largest and most revolutionary transformation of European prehistory.

The British Isles, 3500–2500 BC

While these great events were taking place on the Continent, Britain experienced a more insular trajectory of change, in which older patterns survived longer and without direct subversion from these new ideas. The plough arrived here as early as in Denmark, however, and its use defines a later Neolithic which saw important changes of settlement pattern, though without radical changes of ideology. Plough-marks have been preserved under the South Street long-barrow, one of a new generation of 'short' long mounds (often not covering burials at all) that appeared on the chalklands of Wessex around 3500 BC. Settlement, now taking the form of larger and more stable domestic sites, was no longer confined to such loess-rich calcareous soils and began to expand more widely on the gravel-covered river terraces of major rivers such as the Thames. Here, and in other parts of eastern Britain such as Yorkshire, new types of individual burials made their appearance, with distinctive artefacts such as maceheads, flint axes, and knives, or adornments such as bone pins or jet belt fittings. These developments paralleled the changes taking place on the Continent at this time; but they seem to have been resisted in western England by the creation of new and more elaborate ceremonial monuments, for instance the long earthworks composed of parallel banks and ditches called *cursus* monuments (after an eighteenth-century whimsy that they represented racetracks), which have some analogies with the contemporary stone alignments of Brittany—although no direct contacts are implied. Signs of direct conflict are evident in south-west England, where hilltop ceremonial sites like Hambledon Hill and Crickley Hill were fortified, and indeed assaulted by attackers armed with bows and arrows.

In northern Britain and Ireland, the native round passage graves proliferated, and in Ireland—where the long mound tradition continued in adjacent areas—grew to major tribal centres, clustered on the hills like Carrowkeel or Loughcrew, or dominating the bend of the River Boyne with the great sculptured cruciform passage tombs of Newgrange, Knowth, and Dowth, within three kilometres of each other, each set in a huge conical mound. Here the esoteric interest in astronomy and the calendar of the seasons, hinted at in earlier passage graves, became explicit in the sundial engravings of the kerbstones and the sensitive alignments of the passages, which directed the beams of the rising sun at winter solstice so that they illuminated the carvings in the chamber beyond. Half a millennium after the erection of Gavrinis, megalithic art and architecture reached another climax in the far west of Europe where it was unaffected by continental conflicts. In other parts of Ireland, where the long-mound tradition prevailed, equal

AIR-PHOTOGRAPH of excavations in progress at the massive conical passage-grave (90 m in diameter) of Knowth, County Meath, Ireland, *c.*3200 BC — one of three similar adjacent monuments (the others being Newgrange and Dowth) in the bend of the River Boyne. The perimeter is marked by decorated kerbstones; inside are two long passages with cruciform chambers. Smaller passage graves cluster around.

efforts (though spread out over many generations) went into constructing the long lines of stone field-walls enclosing the rich pastures of Co. Mayo around Behy-Glenulra, where they were to be preserved by the growth of peat.

Another northern area to rise to prominence at this time was the fertile cluster of islands of Orkney. First colonized by plough-using farmers and fishermen around 3500 BC, they are notable not only for the elaboration of their main tombs (some of which, like Maes Howe, have similarities with Newgrange in their plan and orientation), but also in the complementary construction of stone-built settlements like Skara Brae, with its cluster of sub-rectangular huts joined by passages, and with stone fittings for beds, dressers, and hearths. At the recently excavated site of Barnhouse, next to Maes Howe itself, a comparable group of huts was arranged round a central circular building whose entrance faced the rising sun at summer solstice: a light which gladdened the living, just as the rays of winter solstice pierced the realm of the dead. Orkney is also outstanding for another group of monuments, on opposite sides of the Loch of Harray below these two sites. These are the remarkable ditched and banked stone circles of Brodgar and Stenness, with their ceremonial entrances, which are examples of a type of monument that is widely distributed in northern Britain and has later examples further south. The stone circles seem to be a further development (perhaps initially in north-west Scotland) of the round passage graves, with their stone kerbs; and it may well be that such stone circles enclosed circular timber structures for the kinds of rituals which previously took place in the tombs, now admitting larger numbers of people than could gather in the stone chambers. Such circles are often aligned on the summer solstice, like the large building at Barnhouse, rather than the winter solstice like the tombs. Of their esoteric rites we have no direct knowledge, but certain carefully made objects of hard stone, in the shape of ornamented spheres or platonic solids with carved stone bosses and facets (that were perhaps used for divination), argue for a sophisticated understanding of geometry at this time.

Northern Britain in this period seems to have had a particularly flourishing culture, drawing on an indigenous background not present further south, and its influence reached down as far as Wessex. It is indicated by the appearance there of a distinctive pottery known as Grooved Ware, probably the appropriate vessels for consuming a particular sort of food in a ceremonial meal, which had its origins in the north. In Wessex this occurs in 'henge' monuments—earthen and sometimes also stone circles like the Orkney examples—consisting (as at Avebury) of a bank and interior ditch, with opposed entrances, which surround a setting of stones. The huge adjacent mound of Silbury Hill echoes the shape of the great northern passage graves. At Durrington Walls, a circular banked and ditched enclosure surrounded large circular timber buildings; while at nearby Stonehenge—the last monument in the sequence, *c.*2000 BC—the circle of stone uprights and lintels replicates in lithic form the construction of a wooden wall and ring-beam. And this great monument is, of course, precisely oriented on the rising midsummer sun. Thus England's most famous prehistoric monument preserves an echo of the calendric rituals associated with the first northern farmers, and perhaps even with their Mesolithic ancestors on Europe's twilight fringe.

The Western and Central Mediterranean, 3500–2500 BC

The Mediterranean during this period exhibits the whole range of social forms which have been defined above, from the urban sophistication of the East, through the individualistic, copper-using groups with their weapon burials in the central area, to the collective burials of monument-building societies in the West. All of them used plough-based systems of agriculture, with herding coming to play a more important role in Italy and southern France, and interregional contacts beginning to bring into prominence otherwise largely barren islands; but these wider linkages should not be exaggerated, and the friction of distance in days before the sail prevented any long-distance development of trade. While certain features did spread from East to West, it had the character of slow diffusion rather than colonization or purposive exploration.

Iberia at this time witnessed a remarkable florescence of tomb-building and ritual activity, along with the growth of a simple copper metallurgy based on the exploitation of rich local ore sources and the production of fine stonework such as long flint blades and carefully engraved schist plaques. Although fine artefacts included personal items such as ivory combs and sandals, they were still interred in collective tombs without being used to distinguish the burials of individuals. The use of materials such as ostrich eggshell imply contact with adjacent north Africa, where chambered stone burial mounds were also built. Pottery was decorated with the same range of symbolic motifs that appear on the schematic anthropomorphic plaques and curved objects called 'croziers', and alongside geometrical and sun or eye motifs that are more representational elements such as stick-figures of stags. As well as monumental tombs, elaborate settlements or regional centres were also constructed in some areas, surrounded by elaborate defensive walls incorporating complex entrances and bastions. These have some analogies with the earthen 'camps' known from aerial photography in western France at this time, though the bastions seem to be a specifically Mediterranean element that may imply links with Sardinia, Sicily, and the Aegean, reaching back to the cities of the southern Levant. These common elements linked Atlantic Iberia, and its famous sites such as Zambujal and Vila Nova de São Pedro in Portugal, with the arid lands of Almería. Here intensive flood-water agriculture and simple irrigation sustained nucleated communities such as Los Millares with its adjacent cluster of some one hundred corbelled chamber tombs and outlying bastioned forts on nearby hills. The architectural sophistication of these tombs was echoed in more megalithic construction at the Dolmen de Matarru-

GRAVE 43 in the Copper Age cemetery at Varna, on the Black Sea coast of Bulgaria, *c.*4000 BC (reconstituted as a museum display); a man of about 45 years, buried with 990 separate gold objects (together weighing 1,516 grammes) and copper and flint weapons. Note the gold penis-sheath.

CORNER OF THE FAÇADE of the Neolithic temple (*left*), *c.*3000 BC, at Ggantija, Xaghra on Gozo, northernmost of the Maltese islands. One of a dozen such structures scattered across Malta, this one is built of exceptionally large limestone blocks. It encloses a series of interior chambers in a cinquefoil plan.

A VIEW (1861) of the Late Neolithic passage grave (*below*) of Maes Howe (*c.*3200 BC) and its later ditch, with the stone circles of Stenness (*left*) and the more complete Ring of Brodgar (*right*) in the background, on opposite sides of the lochs. A late Neolithic domestic site has recently been excavated near the Barnhouse (white building, *left*).

POTTERY BOWL with four feet, bearing panels of incised ornament including the 'eye motif' shown here, and schematic stags on the other side. From a Copper Age passage-grave in the cemetery of around 100 such communal tombs at Los Millares, Almería, southern Spain, c.3000 BC.

billa near Seville, and reproduced in simpler form in hundreds of tombs, some with incised and painted geometrical decoration, along the Atlantic coasts. On the opposite coastlands of the Spanish Levant, the tradition of rock art with painted hunting scenes shows that earlier ways of life continued.

In southern France there was a great extension of settlement on the dry limestone plateaux of Languedoc and Provence. Two, spatially distinct, forms of material constructions are associated with this movement: round cairns of stones covering stone cists or chambers, known as *dolmens simples*, and groups of oval, stone-built houses that were sometimes enclosed by stone walls with bastion-like projections, best known from the site of Lébous in Hérault. Although these constructions are commonly attributed to the *pasteurs des plateaux*, crop-raising with the light plough is likely to have been the pioneer mode of subsistence in these newly settled landscapes; although sheep may have been herded in larger numbers than previously, and many caves show evidence of occupation; while simple megalithic tombs in the valleys of the Pyrenees may be associated with the beginnings of transhumance. This extension of agricultural life has many analogies with the filling-in of inland areas by the builders of *allées couvertes*, which was occurring at the same time. The *dolmens simples* of the adjacent region of Quercy share the eastern orientation of the *allées couvertes*, although similar monuments in the Midi have a preferred orientation to the West, to the setting sun. Both were associated with anthropomorphic stelae or statue menhirs, not unlike the female figures engraved in the soft chalk of underground collective graves in the Paris basin. In areas of softer rock in

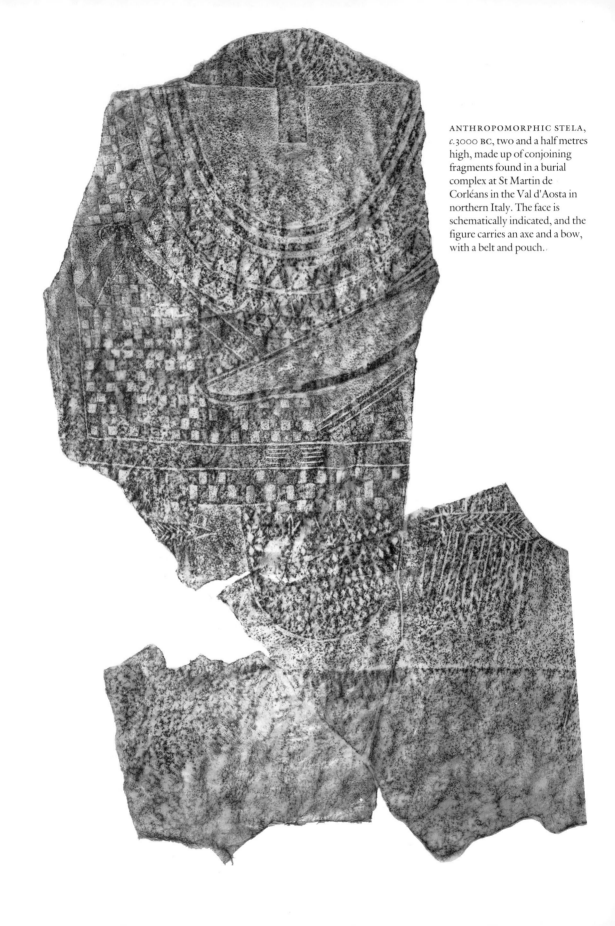

ANTHROPOMORPHIC STELA, *c.*3000 BC, two and a half metres high, made up of conjoining fragments found in a burial complex at St Martin de Corléans in the Val d'Aosta in northern Italy. The face is schematically indicated, and the figure carries an axe and a bow, with a belt and pouch.

the south, similar long subterranean tombs were excavated, some with side chambers like the famous Grotte des Fées near Arles, containing large numbers of collective burials. The material culture of these tombs and settlements includes long flint blades and fine arrowheads, as well as beads of green mineral and carefully worked limestone or marble and small objects of copper.

The more restricted island landscapes of Corsica, Sardinia, Malta, and, to some extent, Sicily showed a more introverted pattern of expansion, which may account for the elaboration of particular ritual centres rather than the more fluid patterns of the adjacent continental areas. Each of these areas shows the florescence associated with the introduction of plough cultivation to hitherto underpopulated islands, with limited evidence of inter-island contacts. The most extreme case is Malta, where, over the period in question, a quite remarkable series of half a dozen major temple complexes came into existence and became progressively more elaborate. These seem, in origin, to have been hypertrophied versions of underground tombs with several compartments, and the characteristic trefoil or cinquefoil plans of structures built of large, shaped (and often spiral-decorated) limestone blocks is echoed underground in the rock-carved, red-painted, mass burial vault or hypogaeum near to the main centre at Tarxien. The temples themselves grew and were often enlarged or duplicated, and provide evidence of closed sanctuaries, oracle holes, and a stone of sacrifice where a flint knife was kept in a concealed niche. The temples also contain huge representations of a steatopygous 'mother goddess', and smaller figures of sleeping (entranced?) 'priestesses'. As in Ireland, relative isolation nurtured a more extreme form of monumental principles exemplified in other areas; though the Maltese centres must be imagined as competing one with another, rather than with other groups, since there was apparently no alternative local ideology. Somewhat similar manifestations occur in the rock-cut tombs of Sardinia, which may copy above-ground structures in wood, and other surface monuments such as the collective burials of the Tombe di Giganti with their horned forecourts, and the notable pyramid mound of Monte d'Accodi near Sassari. In Corsica, a more dispersed pattern of stone cists and menhirs, some anthropomorphic and others grouped in lines, suggests a less centralized focus to social life in a wooded, montane environment.

Sicily and southern Italy exemplify the other end of the spectrum of Copper Age cultures, in which rock-cut or cist tombs contained personal drinking equipment and metal weaponry, and demonstrate wider connections. The decorated bossed bone plaques of the Castelluccio cemetery, from the end of the period, have analogies in the Aegean and at Troy; but they come from local types of rock-cut tombs with blocking slabs bearing carved spirals in relief. Their pottery, decorated in geometric painted designs, nevertheless consists of metallic shapes of strap-handled and dimple-based cups which show the impact of Aegean habits. On the Italian mainland, at Gaudo in the south, Rinaldone in the centre, and Remedello in the north, individual burials in cemeteries of rock tombs or pit graves contain drinking equipment and weaponry, either copper daggers or long stone arrowheads and lanceheads, rare battleaxes, and also occasional ornaments of silver. These artefacts indicate generalized affinities both with the Aegean and with central Europe, through the Alpine passes. In the Alpine fringe the rock engravings in the Val Camonica, and also the ritual settings of statue menhirs in the Val d'Aosta (overlying plough-marks) and just across the Alps at Petit-Chasseur near Sion in Switzerland, show two generations of engravings—the first with necklaces like the figures of the Paris basin and the Midi, the second with male equipment such as decorated belts and copper spiral pendants and sometimes carrying daggers and bows. There are hints here of a shift of image, from the female, 'mother goddess' representations of old Europe and the far west, to the new, male qualities associated with warrior values. In the world that was to follow, it was the latter values that would prevail.

Further east, on another Mediterranean island, these values would survive for longer. Crete in the Neolithic had been a relatively isolated community, dominated by a single large centre at Knossos, which nevertheless produced its own varieties of decorated pottery and female figurines. Initially unaffected by the growth of metal-using societies in the rest of south-east Europe, its culture was transformed by the arrival of new farming practices and tastes from Anatolia, and its new role in the inter-island exchange systems that followed. As contacts with the east Mediterranean were strengthened by long-distance voyaging from Syria in boats with sails, Knossos and other sites were to grow into palatial centres that participated in the urban intercourse of advanced societies. Still, however, its religious life and rituals were centred on a female deity; and this aspect continued to permeate its life and art.

Conclusion: The Social Life of Things

How can these multifarious developments be summarized in social terms, and what sense can we make of the Copper Age kaleidoscope? In emphasizing the unity of the phenomena under discussion, we may think of the relatively small sizes of the communities involved, and the low densities at which they lived. Even where population was concentrated in a few sites, or came together occasionally for the construction of major communal works, the landscape as a whole was still rather empty, the greater proportion untilled and ungrazed. The environmental impact of such small human groups was still relatively slight, and the quantities of materials moved from their place of production were tiny. How could it be otherwise, without large numbers of pack animals and sailing ships? What was important was the constructed environment, the small world of houses and things. This is why the organization of the domestic sphere, and its replication in tombs, absorbed so much of the energies of early farmers; why everyday material objects were so invested with meaning, and why alterations of the material world, and the extension of the artificial, were so important. Early farmers, especially in forested Europe, were constrained by this small scale of activity; and their efforts were often narrowly focused on fixed points within the world which they had created, bringing together local populations in larger groupings at sites which celebrated this permanence and continuity of existence. Supernatural sanctions were sufficient to bring order to such a universe, itself highly structured and constrained. Their ideals were expressed in images of female procreation and abundance—even if women themselves bore most of the burdens of everyday life, and died after short lives exhausted by the work of cultivation and child-bearing.

Where the social stage was wider, however, either in the more open country of eastern Europe or in the increasingly cleared landscapes carved from the forests by generations of agricultural effort, wider networks of social interaction became possible. Order was maintained not by a common allegiance to place, but by human action: the potential of independent segments of society to combine in opportunistic fashion for temporary goals—for the exchange of goods and livestock, to meet the threat of aggression, or to control deviance from common norms of behaviour. New ideals—of leadership, of hospitality, and of negotiation with the implicit threat of force—became prominent and found their expression in the artefactual repertoire. Control of men, animals, and the powers of nature became the paths to social and material success; and the transmission of this success to further generations became the object of those who were able to attain such power.

Both principles were exemplified in the societies of fifth-, fourth-, and third-millennium Europe, but the balance shifted gradually towards the latter type. This trend was markedly accelerated by the remaking of connections with the older and more advanced societies of the Near East, which both through the transmission of new technologies and materials and, on a smaller scale, through direct social interaction, promoted changes throughout the Continent. It was a pattern that was to be repeated many times in the millennia that were to follow.

6

The Palace Civilizations of Minoan Crete and Mycenaean Greece
2000–1200 BC

K. A. WARDLE

The Discovery of the Palace Civilizations

LITTLE over a hundred years ago our knowledge of the Greek Bronze Age was based only on the great Cyclopean walls of Mycenae and Tiryns and their tenuous link with the Homeric legends of Agamemnon's expedition against Troy and the ill-fated return of many of the Greek heroes. By the mid-nineteenth century scholars doubted whether these epic stories had any historical basis. The Palace civilizations of Crete and mainland Greece, the magnificence of their architectural and artistic achievements, and the complexity of their economic and social order were unknown. It was the obsessive determination of Heinrich Schliemann to discover Troy and to explore Mycenae and Tiryns which first laid bare the monuments of mainland Greece. The gold and weapons of the Shaft Graves at Mycenae, the tholos tombs outside the walls and the ruins of a great palace at Tiryns were to him enough proof that legend was history, that Agamemnon, barbarous enough to sacrifice his own daughter, ruled by force of arms over a great realm, amassed wealth beyond the dreams of avarice, and was buried amidst heaps of gold and silver vessels with a gold mask over his face.

Orally transmitted epic is not noted for its accuracy about time and place, for the individual hero transcends his background. Schliemann, in his turn, was less perceptive than a more detached scholar about the relative dates of his discoveries. For him, his major discoveries were all of a single period—that of the expedition against Troy, set according to tradition in the thirteenth century BC. Only after his death did his architect, Wilhelm Doerpfeld, continue the work at Troy and find the true 'Homeric' city. Not for a few more years were stratigraphy and chronology sufficiently understood for others to see that the Shaft Graves and the 'face of Agamemnon' were older by centuries than the great fortresses of the mainland and the reputed date of the Trojan War.

Arthur Evans started the exploration of the Cretan palaces at Knossos in 1900. He was

THE THRONE ROOM at Knossos in 1900. Sir Arthur Evans found the intact throne just below the ground surface soon after he started excavation.

attracted more by the carved sealstones and fragments of clay sealings with a primitive form of writing than by the legends of King Minos and the monstrous Minotaur which had persistently been associated with the area. His discoveries were as astonishing as the Shaft Graves at Mycenae. The barren hilltop at Knossos concealed a massive palace complex with lavishly decorated 'state' rooms, extensive granaries and oil stores, and archives of clay tablets in at least two unknown scripts (Linear A and B). His finds revealed a standard of craftsmanship and artistic talent equalling anything known from classical Greece. Italian and French excavators working at Phaistos and Mallia, soon showed that this brilliant 'Minoan' civilization extended over much of Crete.

At first these Bronze Age civilizations appeared so alien that they were regarded as the product of a pre-Greek population. It was only in 1952 when Michael Ventris deciphered the inscribed 'Linear B' clay tablets and showed them to be an early form of Greek, that the Mycenaean civilization, if not the Minoan, was recognized as a direct ancestor of classical Greece. Even with this decipherment, the picture of these societies remained only a partial one. The tablets were administrative records, not historical or literary texts, in contrast to those from Egypt or the Near East. The buildings were ruinous and the wall paintings only shattered fragments. In 1967, however, a very different kind of site was revealed by excavation at Akrotiri on the volcanic island of Thira. Here was a town preserved with buildings three storeys high and frescos still on the walls. As at Pompeii, a moment in the distant past had been captured by a dramatic fall of volcanic ash and pumice.

The sophisticated literate societies, which archaeology has revealed in Crete and on the mainland, were unknown to Homer, and unsuspected even by Schliemann. Both would be astonished at the detailed records of the Palace economies, issues of rations to workers, and the receipt of finished products. Today we have a better, if still imperfect, perspective on the importance of these civilizations with their wide-ranging trade and contact with neighbours on the shores of the eastern Mediterranean or with southern Italy and Sicily. It is this contact with the eastern Mediterranean and particularly with Egypt, which provides the current chronology of events in Greece and the Aegean. Datable objects, such as Egyptian scarabs in Greece, or Cretan and Mycenaean pottery in well-dated Egyptian contexts, have enabled a chronological framework to be established which is still more accurate than one based on carbon 14 determinations. On this basis the volcanic eruption of Thira is set at around 1525 BC. New scientific methods of dating the eruption, however, suggest a date as much as one hundred years earlier. The question is not yet resolved but the debate has drawn attention to the fragility of the conventional chronology. If the new dates are confirmed, the whole framework summarized in the following account will need adjustment both before and after this key event, although the date of one stage relative to another will remain unchanged.

The Old Palace Period in Crete, *2000–1600 BC*

The foundations of the Cretan 'Palace economy' lie in the stable and prosperous development of Early Bronze Age society. The clearest sign of this continuity is seen in the unbroken use of communal tombs, to which extra chambers for burials or offerings were regularly added. Large, almost urban, settlements had grown up towards the end of the third millennium BC and the first palatial complexes appeared soon after. Today, it is difficult to examine the remains of these first palaces and the towns around them since they were repeatedly reconstructed and the ruins we see are those of their successors destroyed two hundred years later. The term 'Palace' is convenient to denote, in Crete, a substantial architectural complex, with spacious 'public' rooms, prestigious building materials, and provision for large-scale food storage. The finds often include 'luxury goods' which required imported raw materials and days, even weeks, of skilled craftsmanship for their production. In addition, lumps of clay with seal impressions (sealings) and inscribed tablets, in the 'Linear A' script, record the details of an administrative system. We cannot, however, see beyond these material remains to the individuals or groups who controlled the population and the economy, and 'Palace' should not automatically bring to mind the image of a 'king'.

Three early palaces, each built round a central courtyard, have been found at Knossos, Mallia, and Phaistos while traces of another have been recognized below modern Chania. Each was the centre of a distinct geographical region. The best preserved is to be seen at Phaistos, where a monumental paved courtyard, flanked to the north with stepped stone benches and crossed by raised walkways, belongs to this phase. Clay storage jars (pithoi) as much as 1.5 metres high, still survive in the west wing of this palace. A similar courtyard was laid out in stages at Knossos, and raised walkways were used there for the 'Royal Road' and at Mallia for the streets around the palace. These palaces formed the focal point of large communities, as at Knossos, where the town had an area of 450,000 square metres and an estimated population of between 15,000 and 50,000. Although these towns are largely buried under the equally extensive towns of the New Palace period, excavation, particularly at Mallia, has revealed several houses of this date, including a large two-storey building with a seal-cutter's workshop, and smaller houses with potter's or metalsmith's workshops. Administrative records in the 'hieroglyphic

THE WEST COURT AT PHAISTOS, laid out about 2000 BC when the Old Palace was built. When it was destroyed, perhaps by an earthquake, the courtyard was covered with debris and the New Palace was built further back. The remains of the Old Palace can be seen as a low platform in front of the steps and the facade of the New Palace. (Photo K.A. Wardle.)

THE HEIGHT of the Minoan potters' skill can be seen in the Kamares ware pottery from the Old Palace period. The fabric was often eggshell thin and colourfully decorated in red, yellow, and white on a black ground.

script' and in 'Linear A', which developed from it, were used in these 'private' houses as well as in the palaces. Other towns flourished at Palaikastro, Gournia, Archanes, and Mochlos.

The development of communities the size of the town at Knossos could hardly have taken place without the exploitation of a large agricultural hinterland and the aid of pack animals or wheeled vehicles to bring the produce to the consumers. It is even more difficult to conceive of a Palace society in Crete, with its scattered, if fertile, agricultural land, before transport was available and it is no coincidence that donkeys, horses, and wagons were in use by the beginning of the Old Palace period. The link between the palace complexes and agricultural production is beyond question since the storage provisions are so extensive and the archives regularly list agricultural produce. One of the major roles of the palaces may well have been the maintenance of a reserve of food in a central place where it could be stored in safety and made available in a year of bad harvests, not unknown in the uncertain climate of Crete. In times of scarcity, the palace authority could distribute its reserves in return for labour on 'public works' of one kind or another. The construction of the vast palaces, for example, required a large labour force as well as skilled builders and carpenters, who must have been supported during their work by rations or goods in this pre-monetary society. As the community came to rely more on the central storage of reserves of food, the more closely it was bound to the prosperity of the palaces.

Pottery is by far the commonest surviving product of the Old Palace period. It ranges from the superb Kamares Ware, with eggshell-thin walls and polychrome decoration, to large painted pithoi and thousands of plain household conical cups. The varying styles of pottery from each part of the island emphasize the independence of each region with its own palatial centre. The palaces may have controlled the production of more sophisticated luxury goods such as bronze rapiers with stout mid-ribs like that from Mallia, a silver crinkle-edged cup from Gournia made in imitation of an Anatolian prototype, or the gold bee pendant with delicate granulation found in the 'Royal Ossuary' of Chrysolakkos at Mallia. Stone vessels were made in large numbers, and the same skills were employed for other items such as a stone shaft-hole axe in the form of a leopard from Mallia. Seal cutters used hard stones but designs are still relatively simple and often only geometric. A recurrent motif is a boat with sails, rather than the galley depicted earlier. This could reflect a development which gave new impetus to trade and exploration, seen in increasing quantities of imported ivory and Egyptian scarabs and in the export of Minoan pottery, which reached Egypt as well as the Argolid and coastal Thessaly.

In small communities, craftsmen can be part-timers, cultivating their own land and selling or bartering their goods for 'luxuries' they do not themselves possess. When they are attracted to larger communities, because of the larger 'market' and better supply of raw materials of different kinds, they cannot produce their own food and become full-time workers supported by the produce of others. At Mallia, the artisans whose houses and workshops were found outside the palace, may still have been independent, even though they relied on the palace as a major customer. Gradually this situation changed so that the craftsmen were controlled directly by the palace authorities, and issued with rations in return for a quota of work, as can be shown from the more extensive archives of the New Palace period. The more complex the transactions and the more formal the relationship between craftsman and palace, the greater was the need for a system of records to keep track of obligations outstanding or fulfilled. Several groups of clay 'tokens' are impressed with a seal and incised with a character in addition. These tokens were never attached to anything and served as some kind of docket or tally. A craftsman might receive one for each finished item handed over, and after a period could show that he had fulfilled a quota by producing the dockets, or could exchange them for rations or raw materials. Another requirement, particularly when dealing with precious commodities, was for a system of weights and measures of agreed value, and it is no surprise that weights have been found, though there are not enough to determine their relative values. The amount of bulkier commodities, such as cereals, could be checked by the use of storage pithoi of standard size.

Many communities had their own hilltop 'peak sanctuaries', sometimes with a small shrine building, where votive offerings were made in quantity, as at Petsofa, overlooking Palaikastro. Elsewhere caves, such as the Kamares, Diktaean, or Idean, were popular centres for cult offerings. The offerings that have survived were generally of clay and simply, even crudely made. They include male and female figures, parts of the body, animals such as bulls or sheep, and small vessels. The range is very similar to the votives of an archaic Greek temple, or the plaques attached to ikons in recent times to draw attention to someone or something that needed protection, or as a thank-offering for a successful appeal for help. Some sites have produced such vast numbers of ithyphallic figures that a fertility cult seems certain.

At Anemospelia, on the slopes of Mt. Juktas to the south of Knossos, is an isolated building with three entrances, leading to a single cross hall and three rooms beyond, which matches later illustrations of 'tripartite shrines'. The building had been destroyed by earthquake and then burnt. In the central room was a pair of clay feet, presumably the only durable part of a statue, perhaps a 'cult image'. Large numbers of storage jars and bowls suggest regular offerings of agricultural produce. The western room contained the strangest discoveries. In the centre was a low platform of stone and clay and lying on it the skeleton of a young man with legs doubled up and a dagger across his ribs. Further in were two skeletons, an adult male wearing a ring made of iron and other metals and a younger female, while a third, male skeleton was found outside the door. Was this the rare practice of human sacrifice, replacing for some urgent purpose the ritual of slaughtering animals depicted on sealstones and in the painted scene on the later stone sarcophagus from Agia Triada? Any explanation of this unique discovery raises as many problems as it answers, but there is no doubt that the building at Anemospelia was normally used as a temple, even if the particular circumstances in which it was destroyed were extraordinary.

The palaces must have had many roles within the society controlled by them, but it is impossible to tell as yet whether they developed in Crete in response to the needs of a growing and increasingly sophisticated population or whether they were innovations from outside Crete which established new patterns of activity. The administrative system and monumental architecture had been in use in Syria and the Near East for generations. Once established, these palaces formed the basis for the continuing prosperity of Cretan society. Even though all the palaces were destroyed by an earthquake, or a series of earthquakes, around 1600 BC, they were promptly rebuilt on the same scale and with as much magnificence.

The New Palace Period in Crete, 1600–1425 BC

Unlike their predecessors, the New Palace buildings are relatively well preserved, thanks to abandonment after their destruction *c*.1425 BC, and they provide a vivid picture of the complexity of Minoan society and the abilities of architects and craftsmen. The palaces are the best-known sites, but parts of several towns have also been explored together with many smaller rural sites usually called 'villas'. Excavation has concentrated on the grander sites and little is known of the basic unit of the Cretan economy, the village community. The collective burial chambers had gone out of use after nearly 1000 years, and we do not know what replaced them.

The largest of the palaces is that at Knossos (13,000 square metres), which survived for thirty-five years or more after the other sites were destroyed. The Knossos palace, like those at Phaistos, Mallia, and Zakros, was arranged around a central courtyard, as in the Old Palace period. Apart from Zakros, the palaces are organized in a very similar way. In each case the ground floor of the west wing is devoted to agricultural storage, in pithoi in long, narrow 'magazines' at Knossos, in circular granaries at Mallia, or in well-built chambers at Phaistos. The upper floor had grander rooms, shown by stairs of ashlar (sawn) masonry leading up to it, fallen pillar bases, and fragments of gypsum facings. Other important rooms opened off the central courtyard to west and north through elegant porches created by rows of wooden columns and multiple doorways. These had double doors, which folded back into recesses in the jambs and enabled rooms to be opened up, or divided off as needed or as the changing seasons required. Some of the rooms on the west may have been used for cult purposes, to judge from the figurines and other curious objects found at Knossos or from the large number at Zakros of elaborate stone 'rhyta' (decorative funnel-like vases perhaps used for libations).

The eastern and southern wings of the palaces have fewer similarities. At Mallia, there was another storeroom with rows of oil-jars set in benches, while at Zakros there were cisterns and bathing pools with steps leading into them. At Knossos, the 'domestic quar-

THE WEST MAGAZINES at Knossos soon after discovery. The clay jars—pithoi—stand nearly 2 m high and were used for the storage of wine, olive oil, and grain. The lead-lined stone chests set in the floor once stored more valuable commodities.

ter', as Evans named it, was completely remodelled at the start of the New Palace period to create a magnificent suite of rooms. These rose three, or even four, storeys in a great cutting in the hillside on the south-east of the palace. Here the 'Grand Staircase' still reaches the level of the central court in a series of majestic flights of balustraded stone steps. At the lowest level are the best preserved of all the 'state' rooms: the 'King's Megaron', with its multiple doorways and surrounding pillared verandah, and the smaller 'Queen's Megaron' with 'en suite' bathroom and lavatory. Four deep shafts were needed to provide light and ventilation to the lower levels, a natural consequence of the great size of this part of the palace, and the height to which it was built.

Everywhere in the palaces, there is evidence of the great skill of the architects and builders responsible for their construction. The soft local stone found near Phaistos and Knossos was carefully dressed into large blocks for the foundation levels, or for stairways and important public areas. At Mallia and Zakros the local stone is much less tractable and there is more use of rubble walls and mud-brick in the construction. Whatever the basic building material, the whole structure was laced with timber posts and beams, to afford strength and flexibility to buildings in a region where earthquakes are frequent. Many of the walls were faced with large sheets of gypsum, in important parts of the palaces, while elsewhere rubble masonry or mud-brick was finished with a lime plaster surface. Elaborate wall painting provided further decoration. Mason's marks, common on the exposed and the concealed surfaces of dressed stone, provide a glimpse of the organization in the quarries. The drains and water courses were also designed to take rain water from the vast roof area and lead it away safely, while fragments of clay pipes suggest a complex system of aqueducts to bring in fresh water.

Around the palaces, and in particular at Knossos, are buildings on a smaller scale which have the same architectural elaboration. The largest of these, the 'Little Palace', where the famous black steatite bull's head rhyton was found, may have been the residence of a palace official. Others, such as the 'Caravanserai' to the south with its spring, bathing pool, and naturalistic wall paintings of birds and vegetation could be private houses while the 'House of the Chancel Screen' with a raised dais situated at one end of the main room beyond a low stone screen may have had a cult function. At Agia Triada, there is a smaller palatial complex, which was perhaps a dependency of Phaistos. Here, too, there are elegant rooms with gypsum benches and wall facings. A little further away on the coast, ashlar buildings at Kommos on the shore mark the site of the port for Phaistos.

The large towns of the Old Palace period were rebuilt and continued to flourish, but in only two cases, Gournia and Palaikastro, has enough excavation taken place to reveal an extensive area. At Palaikastro, in a level coastal plain, the main street had branches

THE GRAND STAIRCASE in the east wing of the palace at Knossos. This majestic staircase once ascended through three storeys. When Evans found it the wooden beams and tapering columns had long since rotted away but patient study and skilled engineers enabled him to restore it to its former grandeur. (The downpipe is modern!)

THE ROYAL ROAD at Knossos may be even older than the palace. It leads from the stepped 'theatral' area north-westwards to the Little Palace and the heart of the Minoan town. The raised walkway down the centre is a standard feature of Minoan planning.

running off at right angles on either side and the street façades were of imposing ashlar blocks. The houses are irregular agglomerations of rooms, and some had colonnaded light wells even though the size of the houses did not warrant them. Gournia, clustering around a small hillock, is less imposing with winding cobbled streets and small two-storey houses. On the summit is the only building to use ashlar masonry, a small 'palace' with a porticoed inner courtyard. At Myrtos on the south coast was a small community which had a similar, but smaller, ashlar building at its centre, with a paved courtyard and verandah, and light well with gypsum bench. These single central buildings suggest a ruler or governor, perhaps appointed by the palace authorities to administer the community and collect the agricultural produce ready for transport to the palace itself.

The 'villa' in the countryside, without an associated settlement, seems to have been an agricultural centre exploiting produce such as wine or oil, in particularly fertile districts, for the benefit of the palace. Vathypetro, to the south of Archanes, provides a good example. A central ashlar building, including a storeroom full of pithoi and installations for pressing olives and grapes, is surrounded by outbuildings with signs of the kind of production necessary to a small self-sufficient economic unit such as a potter's kiln.

Few tombs can be dated to the New Palace period. The 'Temple Tomb' a little to the south of Knossos, was monumentally built in the same style as the palace. This was a two-storey building set into the hillside with a forecourt leading to an outer hall. Beyond this is a rectangular chamber with two ashlar pillars, and a rock-cut chamber lined with gypsum. At Isopata another imposing rock-cut tomb had a sloping entrance passage, a forehall, and a large rectangular inner chamber lined with masonry.

The Linear A script was widely used in Crete, with some discoveries outside the island, as at Agia Eirene on the island of Kea. Nowhere, however, has any quantity of clay tablets been found and no convincing decipherment of their contents has yet been proposed. There are sufficient similarities with signs used in the later Greek Linear B tablets, to show that most of the tablets are administrative records, listing quantities of different commodities such as cereals or wine and animals such as sheep or cattle. Apart from the clay tablets there are other items with longer texts. Some of these are inscribed on stone 'lamps' and seem to be dedications as does the inscription on a gold pin from Apesokari. The longest texts of all, however, are in a more archaic form, related to the 'hieroglyphic' script developed in the Old Palace period. The best known is the 'Phaistos Disc', made of clay, stamped with forty-five different pictographic symbols on both sides to form a spiral text and then fired. In total there are 241 signs divided into sixty-one 'words' by roughly incised lines. Many attempts have been made to translate the

A HOUSE MODEL OF CLAY found at Archanes, south of Knossos, provides useful information about details of Minoan architecture.

inscription but there is not even any agreement on whether to read it from the inside outward or vice versa. A second enigmatic item with a long text is a bronze axe from the Archalochori cave, where the context would suggest a votive inscription or, by analogy with texts from the Near East, a hymn to some divinity. It is hard to believe that so sophisticated a society did not make much wider use of writing on parchment, imported papyrus, or wooden, or even wax tablets such as that recently found in the fourteenth-century Kaş wreck off the south coast of Turkey. Failing any decipherment of written texts, we must turn to the ways in which the Minoans depicted themselves, their interests, and their activities for more information about the people who ruled over and worked for the palace system. The chief source is the wall paintings, although the rings, sealstones, and the carved decoration on stone or ivory objects also help.

Wall paintings were popular, especially at Knossos where the subject-matter was very varied. It included processions, as in the long corridor leading to the central court from the south, where young men clad in loincloths with codpieces carry a variety of vessels. A miniature fresco found in the northern wing of the palace shows a crowd around a small building. This was decorated with the 'horns of consecration' which may originally have indicated a shrine, but became little more than a decorative motif in later Minoan and Mycenaean art. The women wear elaborate dresses with the multiple-tiered skirts so characteristic of the well-dressed Minoan lady. From the 'Queen's Megaron' are fragments showing the head and upper body of a girl with short jacket, bare breasts, and flying hair while equally violent activity is suggested in the miniature 'Toreador' fresco. Here young men and women leap, or prepare to leap, over the horns of a charging bull. The bull motif, so frequent in Minoan art, may be the origin of the legends of the Cretan Bull and the half-human Minotaur. It is seen again in the head of a charging bull, executed over life size in partial relief as part of a scene in a room or verandah above the north entrance. Wall paintings were also used outside the palace at Knossos, as in the House of the Frescos, with its natural scenes of blue-painted monkeys, birds, lilies, crocuses, and myrtle, or in the Caravansarai. Similar scenes of natural life were used at Amnisos, where walls were decorated to look like gardens, or at Agia Triada where a cat can be seen stalking a pheasant. Curiously the other palace sites have produced very little fresco work, and may hardly have used it. At Phaistos, for example, the walls were regularly covered with a plain coloured wash.

Although many of the objects made and scenes painted by Minoan craftsmen are regularly said to have a religious or ritual function (often because no practical explanation can be given) the truth is that little is known about who (or what?) they worshipped, or even how this worship was carried out. We can speculate that, as at Anemospelia, offerings of the produce of the land or the work of the palace craftsmen, were made at altars or on benches in sanctuary buildings. The collections of strange objects, or the unusual architectural arrangements are hardly capable of explanation. Female figures predominate in 'cult scenes' but it is not clear whether these are divinities or worshippers. The peak and cave sanctuaries were less frequented in the New Palace period. The Minoan-

A FINE STONE VASE, one of many from the 'shrine treasury' in the west wing of the palace of Zakros. Minoan craftsmen excelled in the production of elaborate vases, often in the hardest stone, which they ground into shape with emery and great patience.

style shrine of this period is best illustrated at Agia Eirene on the island of Kea, over 150 kilometres away, where half-size and life-size female figures with the Minoan flared skirt and bare breast had been placed in a modest building near the town wall.

The palatial centres were, without doubt, the principal manufacturing centres, controlling all production—whether this took place within the palace or further afield. Pottery must have been one of the most basic needs and small unpainted utilitarian vessels were produced in hundreds of thousands, while the simpler painted types were almost as common. Vases with intricate naturalistic designs were highly prized and the specialized production of the pithoi flourished. A new style developed, using dark, glossy slips to paint on a light coloured surface, in place of the dark surfaces of the Old Palace pottery. At first, the new style was explored with plant motifs but, later, a small proportion was exuberantly decorated with marine creatures such as octopus and cuttlefish, or with seaweed and rockwork. This class, perhaps made entirely at Knossos, includes some of the finest vases made in prehistoric Greece. Bronzeworking must also have been very important for the vessels and tools which were needed in the palaces. Several tablets deal with amounts of bronze, and two sites, Agia Triada and Zakros, had bronze ingots in store when they were destroyed by fire. These ingots had the 'oxhide' form which was one of the acceptable standards throughout the central and eastern Mediterranean. Cloth production may also have taken place on a large scale, as suggested in the later Linear B tablets and in the illustrations, in Egyptian tomb paintings of Cretan tribute bearers carrying cloth.

It was in luxury products that the Minoan craftsmen excelled. Even though there are few tombs of the period and, therefore, few objects intentionally buried, enough have survived the destruction fires and looting, or salvage which followed, for us to have a clear idea of the technical skills and artistic flair of the Cretans. Stone vessels, each the product of many hours of laborious drilling, grinding, and polishing, were made in large numbers. The raw materials for these ranged from locally available limestones, to granite imported from Egypt, lapis lacedaimonius from the Peloponnese, or obsidian from the island of Melos. The craftsmen were not deterred from working hard stones like rock-crystal while softer stone like steatite was used for elaborate figured scenes as on the Harvester vase from Agia Triada. The most common shapes were relatively simple, but some were extraordinarily elaborate. Vases were carved to represent different creatures such as the bull's heads from Knossos and Zakros, or the feline head from the South House at Knossos. On some, even the most intricate carving was not enough, and, as with the rhyton from Zakros showing a peak sanctuary, the carved surface was covered with gold foil.

Delicately carved sealstones were another characteristic product of the palace workshops. Little more than 1 centimetre across, these were chiefly lentil-shaped and decorated with a wide variety of designs: some may show divinities, others pairs of animals in combat. Their function was perhaps equally varied: some served as jewellery, worn at the wrist or as part of a necklace, while others may primarily have provided proof of identity and were frequently used to make impressions on the clay seals and tokens already mentioned; some, with symbolic or religious scenes, may have been worn to protect the wearer from harm or to bring good fortune. The gold rings with bezels 2–3 centimetres across are rarer, but closely related in terms of technique and composition. Although most examples have been found in the mainland, particularly in the Shaft Graves and chamber tombs at Mycenae, enough come from Crete to show that they were part of the palace repertoire. Their size allowed elaborate scenes, such as the group of figures engaged in a dance—perhaps ritual—in the countryside, on a ring from Isopata near Knossos. Others show small buildings which may be shrines. Imported ivory was skilfully carved into a range of different objects both decorative and functional. Miniature figures such as the bull-leaper found at Knossos were made in sections and mortised together, a more economical procedure than carving in the round. A recent find of a standing male figure 50 centimetres high at Palaikastro shows fine detail of muscles and sinews, while the hair and back of the head are made from stone rather than ivory. 'Faience' was also used to make elaborate items such as the 'goddess' figures from the cists below the floor in the cult area to the west of the central court at Knossos. In the same deposit were inlays depicting cockle-shells, argonauts, and figure-of-eight shields, as well as a relief plaque showing a cow suckling its calf. Ivory and faience were used together to decorate a gaming board found in a corridor in the eastern part of the palace.

Minoan civilization was at the height of its prosperity when disaster struck all the palaces, towns, and villas, with the exception of Knossos. Devastating fires brought destruction to the majority of sites and they were abandoned for many years. The cause is still unknown. The eruption of the Thira volcano can now be ruled out since it took place as much as three generations earlier. At Knossos, mainland influence is clear in the following period. Greek was used for the administration, and mainland-style chamber tombs with weapon burials were introduced. Mycenaean pottery replaced Minoan in the islands of the Aegean and in the Near East and Egypt. Mainlanders may have invaded Crete to take advantage of its prosperity. Equally they could have arrived to find the island devastated by earthquakes of even greater violence than usual in one of the most seismically active areas in Europe.

The Buried City at Akrotiri on the Island of Thira, 1600–1525 BC

About three and a half thousand years ago while the Cretan palaces flourished, the volcano, which formed the heart of the small island of Thira in the southern Aegean, resumed activity after a long period of quiescence. First, earthquakes shook the island and forced the inhabitants of a thriving town near the modern village of Akrotiri to flee for safety. A period of calm followed, during which workmen set about temporary repairs. After an interval the volcano erupted violently and rained down fine ash, then pumice on the whole island. The streets and rooms of the damaged buildings were rapidly filled so that many of the houses survive to a height of two or three storeys, often with their internal floors still in place. Soon after, the great chamber created deep below the earth's surface by the expulsion of a such an enormous volume of ash and pumice collapsed and the centre of the island disappeared to leave a vast sea-filled basin. We do not know whether the inhabitants of the town survived, or were caught up in the final cataclysmic convulsion which sent great waves radiating out across the Aegean and triggered earthquakes in the whole surrounding area. The island was not reoccupied for hundreds of years, until the pumice had weathered sufficiently to allow vegetation growth and then cultivation.

This series of events cannot have passed unmarked in the rest of the Aegean. The ash fall has been traced in sea-bed cores stretching far to the south-east, beyond Crete into the eastern Mediterranean. The discovery of ash and pumice in levels much older than the palace destructions at several sites on the north coast of Crete, from Chania to Mochlos, at Myrtos on the south coast, and at Trianda, on Rhodes, shows that there can be no direct connection between the two events. Even so, economic damage must have occurred as the ash seared crops and trees and the waves battered coastal areas and destroyed boats on shore. The ash fall provides an unparalleled opportunity to understand the architecture three-dimensionally, and preserved large sections of wall paintings and durable objects, left where they were abandoned as the inhabitants fled the initial earthquakes with only what they could carry. Valuable items are relatively rare, but thousands of pottery vessels were found as well as bronze tools and sets of lead weights.

The excavation has concentrated on a narrow strip of the town, where walls were exposed by a winter ravine cutting deeply into the layers of pumice. About a dozen houses lie haphazardly on either side of a narrow street, opening at one point into a small triangular 'square'. The larger houses, built with finely squared ashlar blocks, (Xeste 1–4) are more or less free-standing, while others, of rubble masonry, laced with timbers and faced with clay plaster, are built one on to the next as at Palaikastro, in Crete. None has a regular plan and they were all presumably built to fill an existing space, and added to as need demanded. The ground floors were storage and working areas, with the majority of the better rooms on the upper floor, as in the West House. The most consistent feature of the architecture is the arrangement of the entrance, with a window beside it, opening on to a small lobby from which a stone stair leads in two flights to the floor above. The finer houses show the same architectural features as in Crete, such as the multiple doorways of Xeste 3 and 4. It seems likely that the majority of these buildings are private houses, perhaps owned by wealthy merchants. Certainly the abundance of fresco decoration indicates ample resources. One of the best compositions was above the lustral basin in Xeste 3, where young girls dressed in elaborate multiple-tiered skirts and open-fronted bodices, wearing jewellery of gold and lapis lazuli, are seen in the countryside collecting crocus flowers in baskets. The focal point is a seated older woman receiving handfuls of crocus blossoms from a blue-painted monkey. Another painting shows young nude boys whose heads are shaven to leave isolated locks of hair and an older man, equally nude but with a full head of hair. Some scholars suggest that the scenes depict initiation rituals, familiar in anthropological parallels from modern primitive societies, but even so, their function in this position may be no more than decorative. Whatever their significance, a particularly human touch is added by a girl who has injured her foot and sits holding it to ease the pain.

The 'Ship Fresco', from the West House has also prompted much discussion. This is a miniature fresco forming a continuous frieze above the doors and windows of an upper room. It shows several towns, with carefully painted doors, windows, and balconies, set on a more or less continuous shoreline. In the foreground a flotilla of galleys of different sizes moves across a sea filled with fish, dolphins, and even humans. The boats are crewed by paddlers and contain well-dressed passengers travelling 'in state'. At one end of the larger boats is a kind of tent supported on poles—a motif repeated at full size on the walls of the next room. Some see this part of the scene as a military expedition, others as a festival. On shore there are dozens of men and women, spectators looking on, herdsmen with their flocks, warriors with spears and shields at the ready, priests and

THE VIOLENT ERUPTION of the Thira volcano *c.*3,500 years ago covered the prosperous town at Akrotiri (*above*) with several metres of fine ash and pumice—an unparalleled disaster for the inhabitants and a stroke of good fortune for the archaeologist. Houses stand two and three storeys high, and vivid paintings remain on the walls.

THE VOLCANIC ASH at Akrotiri has preserved the contents of many rooms (*below*), such as this storeroom in block B, with clay storage jars set in benches and conical 'rhyta'—here, no more than funnels.

worshippers at a mountain-top shrine. In another section is a winding river, lined with palm trees and papyrus plants, beside which lions and griffins hunt deer and birds fly. We do not know whether this illustrates a specific story, or whether these are no more than genre scenes used for decoration. Perhaps the best parallel for the whole is Homer's description in the *Iliad* of the decoration of the wondrous shield made by Hephaistos for Achilles.

Space does not allow justice to the other paintings at Akrotiri. There are life-size fishermen with their catch, boy boxers sparring with one hand bound with thongs, antelope elegantly drawn with bold simple lines. Swallows swoop and meet among flowering lilies in a fantastic landscape. Blue monkeys cavort among rocks of red and yellow, another plays what seems to be a lyre. Several artists must have been at work in this small area of the town: their styles vary from the minutely detailed to the impressionistic, their figures from wooden to lively. The girls in Xeste 3, in particular, are painted by an artist whose genius and skill was the equal of many more recent masters. Comparison with the fragmentary Cretan paintings is difficult. Many themes are similar, but the Thiran paintings seem much more natural.

The independent character of Thiran culture is also shown by the pottery. The majority was of Cycladic manufacture and style and included typical long-beaked jugs which are often decorated with bird motifs. The proportion of Cretan imports is small and few vases are of mainland origin. Several other flourishing island communities are known in the Aegean from this period, all showing the strength of Cycladic culture. Three towns had defensive walls, Phylakopi on Melos, Agia Eirene on Kea, and Kolonna on Aegina. Their architecture is similar to that of the Cretan towns, with houses of different size and quality set close together in a network of streets and alleys. Fresco decoration and Linear A tablets have been found at Phylakopi and Agia Eirene.

The Shaft Graves at Mycenae and Early Mycenaean Civilization, 1600–1400 BC

Long after Schliemann discovered the Shaft Graves in Grave Circle A, the objects in them seemed so new and barbarous, that they were assumed to represent a foreign culture brought by invaders. They possessed horses and chariots. They had a profusion of weapons unknown in earlier periods, either in the mainland or in Crete. They had beads of Baltic amber as well as gold work, and jewellery whose intricate spiral decoration resembled that of central Europe. The discovery in 1952, with the decipherment of the Linear B tablets, that the Mycenaeans used the Greek language and were thus of Indo-European stock, seemed to show a northern origin beyond dispute.

In the same year, however, excavation at Mycenae itself provided incontrovertible evidence of the native antecedents of Mycenaean culture. A second cemetery, Grave Circle B, was discovered outside the citadel. Here the earliest graves were no different from those used throughout southern Greece in the preceding period. A pit or slab-lined cist was sunk a metre or so into the ground. The floor was prepared with a surface of pebbles and offerings of pottery, tools, or ornaments were made beside the body before the cist was closed with slabs. Later graves, within the circle defined by a rough stone wall, were larger, sunk deeper, and had richer offerings. The latest were deep shafts, large enough for two or three burials. They were constructed with rock ledges or stone walls to support the beams of a wooden roof a metre above the floor. Pebbles were still strewn on the floor, offerings included jewellery of gold and silver, gold cups, stone vases of Cretan manufacture, weapons, and even one electrum face mask. The pottery was a mixture of elaborate 'matt-painted' types with geometric patterns and the first Mycenaean wares with lustrous paint. One had clearly developed from the other, with changes of technique and with new shapes and patterns. Many graves had stone markers, some with carved spiral decoration, others with scenes of chariots. These were graves of chieftains or kings, buried in a cemetery which was clearly pre-Mycenaean in origin. Other parts of southern Greece were equally prosperous, especially Messenia in the south-west Peloponnese. Burials were often grouped together under tumuli, as at Marathon, Voidokoilia, or Argos, which continued in use into the Mycenaean period. Although there is no proof that either Grave Circle at Mycenae was covered with a mound, both illustrate the same principle—a separate burial place for the wealthy and powerful.

Schliemann's Grave Circle A is contemporary with the latest burials in B and continued to receive fresh burials and offerings for another fifty years. Here there were only six

BRONZE WEAPONS from Shaft Grave Circle B outside the walls at Mycenae, *c.*1600 BC, include rapiers and short swords. The rapiers were to prove poorly hafted and soon went out of fashion.

THIS BRONZE DAGGER blade from Shaft Grave Circle A at Mycenae, *c.*1550 BC, is inlaid with gold, silver, and 'niello'. The scene shows men hunting lions with spears and bow and arrow. They are protected by figure-of-eight shields and the 'tower-like' shields described by Homer.

shafts, of which three were larger and deeper than any in the earlier circle, as well as far more lavishly furnished. They contained the bodies of adult men and women, children, and infants. The original appearance of the circle is unknown, since some two hundred years after the last burial the area was landscaped when the citadel wall was extended. The ground level was raised, and the present double circle of slabs placed around the graves below. The original carved stone markers were re-used haphazardly. The whole process must be one of the first examples in Europe of the creation of an 'ancient monument'.

Offerings included five gold masks, gold body and dress ornaments, and ear-rings like those worn by the girls in the Xeste 3 fresco at Akrotiri. A large gold ring found near the shaft graves with other precious items, perhaps robbed from one of them in ancient times, depicts three women with flowers in their hands approaching another seated woman holding poppy-heads in her hand. There were dozens of long bronze rapiers and heavy spears as well as five short daggers inlaid with gold, silver, and black enamel to depict hunting scenes, a river, like that in the Ship Fresco from Akrotiri, with leopards hunting birds, or lions attacking deer. There were gold cups and other vessels, plain and decorated, silver vases including two with elaborate relief decoration showing battle scenes, and others of bronze and lead. Imported items included amber necklaces with pierced 'spacer' beads of the type also known from the British Wessex culture. These, together with the segmented beads of faience, also found in Britain and western Europe, continue to fuel argument about the relative date of the two cultures and the connection, if any, between them. Stone vases from Crete, an ostrich egg rhyton with faience fittings, ultimately from the Near East or north Africa, items of ivory, lapis lazuli, and other luxury materials all show the wealth commanded by those who ruled Mycenae around 1500 BC.

It is hard to explain why this wealth should have been acquired so suddenly, especially at a site like Mycenae, which is neither a port, nor in control of abundant agricultural resources. It is likely that increasing prosperity and the increasing influence of Minoan trade interacted to create a situation in which a few powerful and energetic rulers were able to exploit the circumstances, whether by trade or by military strength, to amass the gold and other items which amazed Schliemann and his contemporaries, and still astonish, today, in the Mycenaean Room of the National Museum in Athens.

A GOLD RING AND A GOLD SEAL from Mycenae illustrate the artistic and technical skill of the Bronze Age engraver *c.*1500 BC. They clearly depict familiar stories, whose nature we can only guess at. Does the oval ring show the enforced separation, for some reason, of a man and a woman or frenzied ritual at a rural sanctuary? Does the rectangular seal show a specific pair of warriors in single combat? The loser wears a boar's tusk helmet and shelters vainly behind a figure-of-eight shield.

Messenia was equally prosperous and a different kind of tomb, the tholos, was developed there by incorporating a burial chamber inside a tumulus. The tholoi at Pylos, Routsi, and Koryphasion were built on level ground of rough masonry with a circular chamber, and massive undressed lintel blocks above the doorway. The vaults were corbelled. Individual offerings, the equal of any from the Shaft Graves at Mycenae, include inlaid daggers with marine scenes, gold cups, amber beads, and bronze weapons.

At first, Mycenaean Greece included the Peloponnese, Attica, Boeotia, and Phocis, and just reached the Thessalian coast. Most settlements are located around defensible hilltops or promontories, with good agricultural land and a water supply which had been used since the Early Bronze Age. Unfortunately, later construction programmes, virtually everywhere, have swept away or concealed early buildings or fortification walls. These spectacular beginnings were the basis for the consolidation and expansion of Mycenaean influence in the next half century. The power of the rulers is now shown by the efforts devoted to their tholos tombs as much as by treasures of gold. These are cut into hillsides with a long entrance passage (dromos) and constructed in better masonry, with particular attention paid to the door jambs, one of the points of structural weakness. The finds illustrate the material wealth of almost every region: from Vapheio near Sparta, gold cups decorated with elaborate scenes of bull-hunting; from Kokla near Argos, silver cups; from the 'Clytemnestra' tholos tomb at Mycenae, ivory-handled mirrors; from Spata in Attica, ivory combs. The wealth of the next level of society below the

ONE OF FOUR identical gold cups from a hoard hidden near Grave Circle A at Mycenae. The handles are decorated with dog's heads. Common imitations of the goblet shape in clay suggest they were made around 1400 BC.

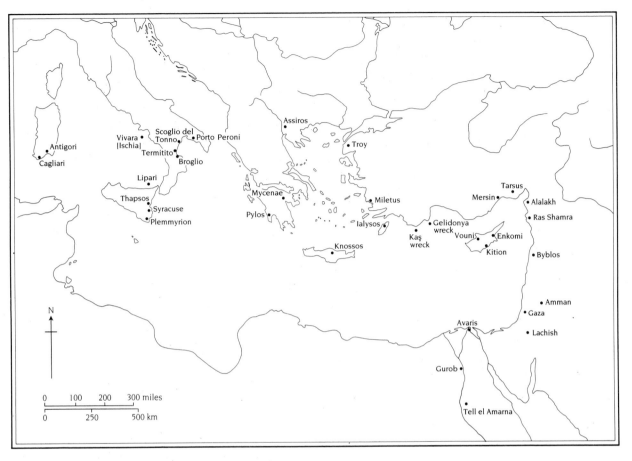

PRINCIPAL SITES illustrating Mycenaean trade and contact in the central and eastern Mediterranean during the fourteenth to thirteenth centuries BC.

rulers is shown by their chamber tombs cut into hillsides wherever the soft limestone allowed. Their sloping dromoi and square or circular chambers, set fully underground, were built for use over several generations, a clear sign of social and economic stability at this period. These tombs cluster in large cemeteries and contain weapons and fine pottery, as well as many items of greater value, such as the gold rings from Mycenae, which often depict scenes of warriors or huntsmen in addition to the 'cult' types used in Crete.

In almost every chamber tomb, as well as in the tholoi and Shaft Graves, are objects which show the close relationship between Mycenaean Greece and Cretan Palace civilization. It is often impossible to decide which were made in Cretan workshops and which in Mycenaean. The cultural and artistic repertoire was clearly a shared one, and the often used criterion that everything stylized must be from the mainland and everything naturalistic from Crete is less than helpful.

The discovery of foundations of an earlier royal residence below the thirteenth-century palace at Tiryns confirms the suspicion that early Mycenaean kings did have palaces and controlled craftsmen as well as warriors. Fragments of wall paintings include a bull-leaping scene, so similar in style and subject-matter to that from Knossos, that direct copying may have taken place during the late fifteenth century. At the very least, skills were transmitted in an unbroken tradition. Only one plausible 'palace' from this period has been excavated, near the Archaic sanctuary of Helen and Menelaios south of Sparta. This was a large two-storey mansion with a central megaron (the Homeric term for a king's hall) with outer porch, anteroom, and main hall, flanked by corridors with smaller rooms on either side. Soon after its construction it was damaged, perhaps because the foundation terrace slipped, leaving little but the foundations and none of its contents.

A CLAY TABLET (*above*) in the Greek Linear B script from Knossos, lists military equipment: a suit of armour, a chariot with wheels, and a single horse—the property of a man called Opilimnios.

THE EARLIEST KNOWN European suit of armour (*left*) was found in a chamber tomb at Dendra in the Argolid. Its cumbersome appearance belies its sophisticated conception. A separate neckpiece and hinged shoulder plates complete the protection afforded by a fitted bronze cuirass with a 'skirt' consisting of three telescoping plates in front and behind. Bronze cheek pieces from a boars' tusk helmet, a pair of greaves, and a single wrist-guard, were also found, which completed the panoply.

The nature of early Mycenaean society is still subject to much discussion. The Shaft Graves and the finds in them are taken to represent the burials of chieftains of a still-fluid tribal society. In contrast, the traces of palatial architecture and the permanence implied by tholos and chamber tombs suggest that the forms and perhaps even the substance of the sophisticated Cretan palatial societies was rapidly adopted (and adapted) after this initial stage. As yet, however, no sealings or inscribed tablets can be attributed to this phase.

Nothing in the mainland marks the destruction of the Cretan palaces, while in Crete, the mainland tradition of weapon burials in chamber tombs appears at Knossos and at Phaistos in the 'warrior graves' of the late fifteenth century. The chamber tomb was now regularly used in Crete for multiple burials in the old Cretan tradition, rather than for a few members of the same family which was the mainland practice. The palace at Knossos seems to have been modified in a minor way at this time to include such features as the 'Throne Room' with its stylized paintings of heraldically opposed griffins—popular in later Mycenaean wall painting but not seen before in Crete. This throne is assumed to be the equivalent of those in the 'megaron' which forms the focus of the later mainland palaces. Elsewhere at Knossos new building was of poor quality. The 'Unexplored Mansion' was left uncompleted and some of its finer rooms given over to a bronzesmith's workshop. The most important change at Knossos is the adoption of the Greek language for the administrative records, Linear B, whose decipherment provides details of the economy of much of Crete. One striking group lists thousands of male sheep, which were the basis of woollen cloth production on a massive scale (if we rule out Evans's interpretation of heroic sacrifices and feasting). Another group of tablets deals with military equipment including chariots and suits of 'armour' thought to be of heavy canvas until the discovery at Dendra in the Argolid, of a complete suit of bronze armour, clumsy at first sight but, in fact, simple to make and flexible in use.

Whether the Mycenaeans ruled Crete from Knossos is debatable, but tholos tombs throughout mainland Greece, especially single ones associated with relatively minor settlements, show that everywhere there were powerful men. Greece is naturally divided into small physical units and it is probable that each was ruled separately, even if, as Homer recounts, all owed a measure of allegiance to an 'Agamemnon'. These local princes commanded not only the large labour force needed to build a tholos, but also the specialist 'architects' who designed them. The Knossos tablets show a hierarchy of land tenure ranging from the king through lower ranks of officials, which reminds us of a feudal society. The thousands of 'workers', often women, seem to be organized in gangs under a foreman who receives their rations, but on the whole this level of society leaves no trace in the archaeological record, apart from the products they laboured to produce. We know nothing about where the bulk of the population lived or even if they were buried with respect.

The date of the destruction of Knossos by the fire that preserved the Linear B archives there is the subject of great dispute. Evans thought it occurred around 1400 BC, soon after the destruction of the other Cretan palaces. The linguistic similarities between the Knossos tablets and those found at Pylos in thirteenth-century contexts are, however, so great that his findings and the accuracy of his records have been questioned and a much later date proposed, much nearer 1200 BC, especially by Palmer. A recent find of a tablet at Chania in western Crete, written in the same hand as a large group from Knossos, which are dated some seventy years earlier on the traditional chronology, serves rather to complicate the problem than to provide a simple solution.

The Mycenaean Palaces and Fortresses, 1400–1200 BC

Following the destruction of the palace of Knossos (*c*.1400 BC) Mycenaean culture became more standardized and its influence and exports can be seen more and more clearly in the eastern and central Mediterranean.

The greatest of the tholos tombs were built in the mid-fourteenth century, but nothing of their original contents survives. The Treasury of Atreus, mentioned by the Greek travel writer Pausanias in the second century AD, is the finest preserved monument of Mycenaean architects and engineers, the product of great skill and immense labour. It is built with the local conglomerate limestone which must be hammer-dressed into shape and finished by grinding. Like the pyramids of Egypt, it was built during the lifetime of a powerful king as a mark of his importance. It may have been intended as a visible monument and funerary temple (which is probably not the case with the majority of tholoi), to judge by the remains of a splendid façade, and the provision for elaborate doors. Like the ruined tholos at Orchomenos, of similar size and splendour, it has a side chamber, for the burial itself, leaving the main chamber free for ceremonies at the time of the funeral, for offerings and perhaps for continuing ritual. The main chamber has a diameter of 14.5 metres and the intact corbelled vault reaches a height of 13.2 metres. Some of the bronze rosettes, which decorated its surface, were still in place early in the nineteenth century. The side chamber is rock cut and roughly finished unlike that at Orchomenos where the ceiling was formed of slabs decorated with complex linked spirals. Two massive slabs of conglomerate limestone cover the entrance passage. The inner one must weigh well over 100 tonnes. The doorway, which is 5.4 metres high, was flanked by half columns with spiralling rosettes of lapis lacedaimonius brought from Krokea near Sparta. Above the doorway, a second pair of similar, but smaller, half columns was set on either side of a decorated panel which concealed the 'relieving triangle'—a triangular space above the whole length of the lintel, which was used by the engineers to transfer the weight of the vault above away from the lintel itself. The dromos, 36 metres long and 6 metres wide, is lined with massive blocks to complete the grandeur of the approach.

THREE OF THE GOLD DEATH MASKS from the Shaft Graves at Mycenae, *c*.1550 BC found by Heinrich Schliemann in 1876. The profusion of gold jewellery, ornaments, and vessels found in these graves provided vivid confirmation of the Homeric description 'Mycenae rich in gold'.

The matching grandeur of the royal palace at Mycenae, occupied by this powerful ruler, can only be imagined since the existing remains are of the buildings which replaced it.

Massive 'Cyclopean' fortification walls at Mycenae, Tiryns, Athens, and many other sites demonstrate the enormous resources of manpower available to Mycenaean rulers, but they are difficult to date. Several stages of construction occurred, and the circuit walls visible today were started in the fourteenth century and repeatedly enlarged. At Mycenae, a major extension in the thirteenth century on the western side enclosed important buildings erected earlier, as well as Grave Circle A, which was 'landscaped' as already described. This extension included the construction of the principal entrance, the 'Lion Gate', with the projecting bastion on the west which enabled defenders to repulse from all sides an enemy attempting to force the gate. The same kind of bastion was built to protect the entrance on the north-east, and the principle was widely used in Mycenaean fortification, as at Midea, Gla, and the Athenian Acropolis where a Mycenaean bastion, which commanded the main approach, underlies the classical temple of Athena Nike. At Tiryns, attackers had to approach up a ramp with their sword arm exposed on the right, and even if they passed the main gate, found themselves in a narrow passage over 6 metres high. The great walls which enclose the lower citadel at Tiryns, the chambers included in their width to provide accommodation or storage, the two groups of chambers forming galleries on the east and south, and the winding stair to the postern gate on the west, were all built late in the century, perhaps not long before the upheavals which brought Palace society to an end. These Cyclopean walls were built from the limestone on which they stand, using the natural planes and fissures in the rocks to prise out polygonal blocks two or three metres across. These were levered into position, to form walls up to 5 metres thick and 7–8 metres in height. The blocks were selected to fit as closely as possible and were locked in place by smaller wedging stones forced into the gaps. This technique of building is used in Mycenaean architecture wherever the local geology is favourable, even for the walls of smaller domestic buildings.

It is questionable how efficient this expenditure of manpower was in terms of defence. Smaller walls would have had the same effect in preventing surprise attack and would have withstood an attack without siege engines. The principal threat to the Mycenaean citadels, apart from internal treachery, was from protracted siege, especially if this deprived the defenders of their water supply. Late in the thirteenth century at least three citadels, Mycenae, Tiryns, and Athens, were provided with vaulted passages leading beyond the walls to a protected water supply. Unfortunately they were vulnerable to

THE PALACE OF MALLIA in northern Crete (*above*), destroyed *c.*1425 BC, lies at the centre of a large town. As in all the Minoan palaces, a maze of rooms surrounds a central court. The eight circular granaries (*lower right*) provided storage for the whole community.

PART OF THE MINIATURE FRIEZE (*below*) from the West House at Akrotiri on the island of Thira, *c.*1550 BC. Soldiers in boars' tusk helmets hold 'tower' shields and spears at the ready, while women fill jars with water and herdsmen drive sheep and goats to a fold. In the foreground, parts of three boats and men, perhaps drowned, in the sea.

THE TREASURY OF ATREUS is the finest of the vaulted 'tholos' tombs which illustrate the architectural skills of Mycenaean engineers. Completed before 1300 BC, its magnificent facade was once decorated with carved half-columns. The inner lintel block must weigh well over 100 tons.

discovery of the source itself and were abandoned not long after, either because they were ineffective, or because the threat, or the will to resist, no longer existed in the changed circumstances of the twelfth century (to be described in the next chapter). The motivation for the scale of the Cyclopean walls was, like the construction of the Treasury of Atreus a generation before, as much the desire of the ruler to impress his peers and rivals as to deter any potential enemy.

Other major engineering works had a more practical application. The shallow Lake Copais seems to have been drained with banks and channels at the same time that the spacious citadel of Gla was constructed on a rocky outcrop above what, without human intervention, was marshland. Within this 200,000 square metre enclosure were regularly planned buildings and ample open space. There is no trace of a conventional settlement inside and it is likely that Gla was built and the lake drained as part of a single plan

THE LION GATE AT
MYCENAE (*left*), completed
around 1250 BC, is the main
entrance to the citadel. Set
above the lintel, the
heraldically opposed lions on
either side of a pillar provide
the most familiar image of
Mycenaean art. This form of
composition was also
frequently used on sealstones
and carved ivories. The
missing heads were held in
place with dowels and their
exact form is the subject of
endless speculation.

THE CITADEL OF TIRYNS
(*below*) from the south-west.
The 'Cyclopean' walls,
typical of Mycenaean
fortresses, once stood up to
eight metres high and often
five metres thick. The stones,
too vast according to the
ancients for mere mortals to
move, were hewn from the
rock on which the fortress
stood.

to bring large areas into cultivation, to administer the new 'estate' and to store the produce within the fortress. In addition the citadel was large enough to give shelter to the flocks which must always have been the most vulnerable of a community's assets. Another project which illustrates the vision of Mycenaean engineers, was the massive earth dam 10 metres high across a ravine 4 kilometres to the east of Tiryns, and the embankments, which directed the stream into a new course, which avoided the citadel and settlement around it and removed the danger of repeated flooding during winter rains. Over 30,000 tonnes of earth were moved so successfully that the stream still follows the diverted channel today. Other public works included the construction of roads and bridges to allow wagons laden with the produce of the area to reach the palaces rather than to enable a Telemachos to drive his chariot from Pylos to Sparta in a single day.

Resources were also lavished on the construction and decoration of palaces, which served as administrative centres on the model established in Crete. The layout of the palaces at Tiryns and at Ano Englianos near Pylos in Messenia, generally identified with the palace of the Homeric hero Nestor, are well preserved. That at Mycenae is harder to understand, since the summit of the acropolis is now so eroded. Tablets, jewellery, and wall paintings in the 'New Kadmeion' at Thebes, substantial buildings at Orchomenos and under modern Volos (presumably Homeric Iolkos), as well as Chania in western Crete, all indicate a network of palatial centres each controlling a large area. Ithaca, alone of the great centres described by Homer, has no site to match its importance in legend.

Mycenaean palaces were much smaller than their Minoan predecessors. The main block at Nestor's Pylos, measuring 54 by 30 metres, would almost fit within the central court at Knossos, and the area of that at Tiryns (excluding the outer, southern courtyard), is only 70 by 60 metres. The focus of the Mycenaean palace was the megaron hall, *c.*12 square metres, with its central hearth and four columns supporting the roof. The base for a throne has been found at Pylos and Tiryns, but at Mycenae the terrace supporting the south-east corner of the megaron slipped into the Chaos ravine below removing any trace of one. At Pylos there are long corridors on either side separating the megaron from other rooms, as already noted at the Spartan Menelaion. Access to the megaron was gained through a columned-porch from a small courtyard, even in the cramped circumstances at Mycenae. At Tiryns the courtyard was surrounded by a wooden-columned portico, and at Pylos a small portico was set to one side. The approach was carefully devised, through a long corridor or up a monumental double flight of steps at Mycenae, or through a columned-entrance from an outer courtyard at Pylos and Tiryns.

All three of these palaces were elaborately frescoed and even the stuccoed floors had painted squares like patterned tiles, with a marbled-effect or designs such as dolphins or octopus. The megaron hearths were repeatedly stuccoed and painted with fresh designs of flames and spirals. Some wall paintings, such as the ladies dressed in multiple-tiered skirts with elaborately coiffured hair, resemble those of Crete 200 years earlier, while warriors wear the short Mycenaean tunic and kilt. Some figures are part of processional scenes, but others engage in activities such as hunting and battle, hardly seen in Crete. At Tiryns there are dogs and huntsmen hunting wild boar, while at Pylos spear-armed warriors wearing greaves and boar's tusk helmets do battle across a river with lightly armed 'savages' clad in ragged skins. Fresco helped to conceal the poor materials of Mycenaean palace buildings. Stone suitable for fine masonry was rare and reserved for special effect or weak points such as door-jambs, while the gypsum so widely used in Crete was not available for facing unless imported. Most walls were rubble built, or used mud-brick, as at Pylos, over a well-laid foundation course. Timber lacing was used, as it had been since the Early Bronze Age, and the builders had no hesitation in raising their work to two or even three storeys. Folding double-doors were normal but Cretan-style light wells were unnecessary in the smaller mainland complexes.

As in Crete, the palaces were administrative centres. Many Linear B tablets were found at Pylos, as well as smaller numbers at Mycenae, Tiryns, Eleusis, Thebes, and Orchomenos, and at Chania and Armeni in Crete. Apart from the administrative accounts of the distribution of rations to different classes of workers, and those which give more information about land holdings, Pylos has tablets relating to a perfume industry and to bronzeworkers. One set of tablets relates to the posting of 'watchers on the coast' in two separate provinces, which has been interpreted as the record of defensive dispositions in the face of an enemy threat, perhaps that which caused the destruction and abandonment of the palace. Others give the names of classical Greek divinities such as Zeus, Athena, and Poseidon, and one small group lists the contents of a temple storeroom.

Provision for the storage of agricultural produce, the basis of the Palace economies, was of particular importance. At Pylos, directly behind the megaron, was an oil storeroom with large pithoi set in benches. Nearby was another oil store, while a separate building to the north held dozens of jars for wine storage. At Tiryns, the great chambers in the thickness of the wall may have served as granaries but nothing remains of their contents. Only at a small fortified site on the northern fringe of the Mycenaean world, Assiros in Central Macedonia, is there tangible evidence for the crops themselves. A destruction fire preserved enormous quantities of charred cereals in a series of storerooms within the regularly planned settlement. The quantity of stored crops represented by the storage jars and other containers is far greater than necessary for the small community, who could have lived within the fortifications, and reflects clearly, in microcosm, the centralized storage of the palaces themselves. At Assiros, the crops found in quantity, wheat and barley, match those listed in quantity on the Pylos tablets, while other basic crops such as lentils, bitter vetch, and grapes are familiar in Mediterranean agriculture.

The tablets also list large quantities of animals, cattle, pigs, sheep, and goats, while care is taken to show whether they were male or female. The bone remains from many sites confirm this pattern, but in addition often show the importance of hunting, per-

AN IVORY PLAQUE found below the temple of Artemis on Delos illustrates a Mycenaean warrior with figure-of-eight shield and boar's tusk helmet. It probably once formed part of a piece of furniture or an elaborately decorated chest.

THE IVORY HEAD of a youth found by the altar in the 'Room with the Fresco' may have been part of a cult image with a wooden body. Carved from a single piece of elephant tusk, it is one of the finest Mycenaean sculptures yet found.

haps as a prestige activity. Even lion bones have now been found at several sites including Tiryns and Kastanas in Macedonia to show that the lion hunts of Mycenaean art were no mere figments of the imagination.

Our knowledge of settlements beyond the palaces is restricted. No town has been excavated on the scale of Gournia or Palaikastro in Crete, although large settlements surrounded Mycenae, Tiryns, and Pylos. Individual houses were substantially built with two storeys. The lower level was devoted to storage, as in the 'House of the Oil Merchant' outside the citadel at Mycenae. This and its immediate neighbours contained valuable objects such as vases of stone and faience and vast numbers of ivory inlays, perhaps from furniture or from a workshop where furniture was assembled. These inlays included heads with boars' tusk helmets, figure-of-eight-shaped shields, dolphins, shells, and tapering columns with elaborate capitals. The importance of this group of houses is emphasized by the discovery in them of Linear B tablets.

The 'Cult-Centre' at Mycenae has produced the clearest evidence for the paraphernalia of religion. A group of buildings, erected in a cramped space to the south of Grave Circle A, housed extraordinary assemblages of objects. The buildings include the 'Temple' with a central platform, benches around the walls, and inner storerooms, and the 'Room with the Fresco', with a central hearth, an altar-like bench below the fresco and an inner room with a bench. In the main room of the Temple, a crudely modelled female clay figure stood on a bench almost out of sight behind a post supporting the roof, while large numbers of male and female clay figures of horrid appearance, with outstretched arms, were found broken in the sealed storerooms behind, together with tightly coiled clay snakes with raised heads and a single elegantly painted female figure. Lying beside the altar in the Room with the Fresco was a superbly carved ivory head of a youth, which had once fitted onto a wooden body. Nearby was a couchant ivory lion with a rectangular socket on the underside, which was probably the arm of a throne. On the lower part of the fresco itself was a female figure facing the altar. She had an elaborate head-dress and held up ears of wheat. Above were two larger figures, one certainly and the other probably female, who faced each other. One carried an upright sword and the other a staff—perhaps a spear shaft or bow. Elsewhere in the room were a clay 'larnax' or bath-tub and a lead vessel which contained a variety of objects including an Egyptian faience plaque with the cartouche of Amenophis III, already 150 years old and probably the relict of some official contact rather than the product of private trade or curiosity. There was also a great mass of domestic pottery vessels. Standing on the bench at the back of the inner storeroom was another small, elegant female figure.

Worship here involved offerings of different kinds, sometimes jewellery which might be placed on the benches or held out in the hands of the cruder figures. The role of the elegant females is not clear, and the only image which might be thought to have a focal position was the ivory-headed youth standing on or beside the altar in the Room with the Fresco. The difficulty of access to these rooms suggests that neither was a public place of worship. Neither the snakes nor the cruder figures are known from other sites, but figurines from Tiryns in the lower citadel and at Phylakopi beside the city wall, confirm the general nature of Mycenaean shrines. However, we have too little information to tell whether the cult was any different from that practised in Crete. Numerous small female figurines, or animals and schematized chariots, are typical of Mycenaean sites and are found in household debris and in tombs. At least some must have had an everyday function, whether as representations of household divinities or as children's playthings.

Few tholoi were built in the thirteenth century, but chamber tombs were still common. The lack of precious objects from this period could indicate either a loss of prosperity, because of the effort devoted to fortification and other public works, or merely a change in fashion. Swords and spears are still relatively frequent gifts in tombs, but the short stout-bladed swords now suggest a change from thrusting with spear and rapier in a relatively static confrontation to a more vigorous conflict at closer quarters. Perhaps the provision of body armour of the kind found at Dendra had forced a change in military tactics. The commonest offerings were pottery vessels, normally small containers for perfumed oil or other precious liquids, decorated in a standardized manner, which suggests cheap mass production. Jewellery, particularly beads of stone, of blue faience, and even of clay or shell, is regular. There are occasional items of gold and sealstones, though many of these are heirlooms. Few graves have objects of the quality of the gold and lapis lazuli jewellery and collection of imported 'antique' cylinder seals found in a workshop in the New Kadmeion at Thebes.

RESTORED FRESCO from the 'Room with the Fresco' at Mycenae. The head of the cloaked figure, the hilt of the sword, and the type of animal behind the lower figure are conjectural. The interpretation of this fresco, the most complete from mainland Greece, poses many problems. Three figures can be seen in a building and the altar built in front of the fresco was decorated to form part of the building. The central figure of the composition is dominant and may be a deity. The other two women are either worshippers or minor deities. The two small male figures, one black, one red, are possibly added 'graffiti'. A real door to the left of the fresco led to another shrine. (Restored drawing by Diana Wardle.)

ONE OF MANY clay 'larnakes' or coffins from a chamber tomb at Tanagra in Boeotia, *c*.1250 BC. Five women tear their hair in a gesture of mourning.

By the beginning of the thirteenth century the area which can be recognized as Mycenaean reached its fullest extent. It included Aetolia, coastal Thessaly and Mt. Olympus, the islands of the central and south-east Aegean as far as Rhodes, and south-west Asia Minor. It is likely that there were settlements on the coast of Chalcidike in Macedonia, but inland Macedonia, like Epirus and Thrace, preserved its own local identity. The north-east Aegean was dominated by Troy, while Crete, though sharing Mycenaean culture, remained distinctly Minoan. Although several sites in southern Italy and Sicily have large quantities of Mycenaean (and in one case Minoan) pottery, there is little trace of other typical aspects of Mycenaean culture, such as chamber tombs or miniature clay figurines, and it remains unlikely that Mycenaean settlement in this area was extensive.

The Influence of Aegean Civilization in the Central and Eastern Mediterranean

Crete, the islands of the Aegean, and the southern Greek mainland are natural intermediaries between the sophisticated Bronze Age societies of the Syro-Palestinian coast and

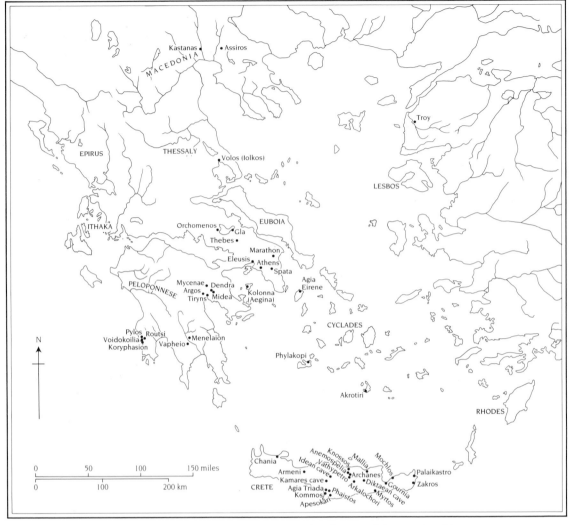

MINOAN CRETE AND MYCENEAN GREECE: location map of sites mentioned in text.

Egypt to the east and Italy and the circum-Alpine regions to the west, where material culture, at least, was not so advanced and literacy did not develop until over a thousand years later than in the Aegean. Once seafarers, whether Aegean islanders or easterners, had learnt the sea routes, winds, and currents in the eastern Mediterranean, there was nothing to prevent the expansion of trade as far as economic and political circumstances allowed. Most of this trade remains invisible to us and it is only with the discovery of Bronze Age shipwrecks off Cape Gelydonia and Ulu Burun near Kaş that we have any picture of how trade was conducted, what the ships were like, and the kind of cargoes they carried. Invisible influences such as the standards of weights and measures and the use of writing and systems of administration must have been equally important. Contact with Egypt was already established by Cretans well before 2000 BC, but it was infrequent and perhaps indirect. The first two-way trade can be seen in the Old Palace period with the import of Egyptian scarabs found in tombs at Archanes, Gournes, and Lebena, for example, and exports of Minoan pottery as far as Aswan, Abydos, and Kahun. The treasure of 153 silver vessels from Tôd in Upper Egypt, which show distinct parallels with Cretan pottery and metalwork, is a hint of trade on an even greater scale.

The importance of Minoan trade by the New Palace period has been dramatically confirmed by the recent discovery in the Nile delta at Tell el Dab'a, the ancient Avaris, of fragments of wall paintings wholly Minoan in style and subject-matter. The excavator, Manfred Bietak, believes them to come from a sanctuary belonging to a group of Minoan traders settled there during the Hyksos period *c.*1550 BC. The scenes include bulls and bull-leapers set against a labyrinth-like background of crossing lines, as well as

A MYCENAEAN 'KRATER' found in a tomb at Enkomi on Cyprus, *c.*1300 BC. These large bowls with their striking decoration of bulls, chariot groups, and other pictorial scenes were especially popular in Cyprus and have even been found in Jordan.

lions and leopards. Such enclaves of merchants are well documented in the clay-tablet archives of Near Eastern Bronze Age communities, but this discovery is the first to show that these enclaves included traders from the Aegean. The number and variety of the items exchanged illustrate the strength of the trade. Fifteenth-century Minoan pottery has been found at many sites in Egypt and Syro-Palestine, while imports to the Aegean area include Egyptian scarabs and Cypriot pottery as well as stone vases from Egypt and Syria.

The raw materials imported by the Cretan Palace workshops included whole tusks of ivory and vast amounts of copper in the standard 'oxhide' ingot form found throughout the eastern Mediterranean. One store of copper ingots was found at Agia Triada, and another at Zakros. Lead isotope analysis of ingots and copper objects shows that some originate from the mines at Laurion in Attica, although the source of most is still to be identified. Only a few items at Akrotiri and an ingot found in Kea are from Cyprus, even though this is the period of the first Cypriot involvement in east Mediterranean trade. One part of tin was required for every nine of copper to make bronze, but its source remains a mystery. There are no obvious ore bodies in the Aegean area and the size of the recently identified deposits in the Taurus mountains near the south coast of Turkey is still uncertain. The nearest large-scale deposits are in Bohemia and Iberia. The need for

ASCENDING A STAIRCASE of copper ingots (*right*), nautical archaeology student Nicolle Hirschfeld removes a Canaanite amphora from the wreck. Ingots and amphorae formed the largest part of the cargo of the late fourteenth century Kaş wreck. (Photograph by Donald A. Frey.)

INGOTS OF COPPER (*below*) in standard 'ox hide' shape were traded throughout the central and eastern Mediterranean. Some have been found in Cretan palace storerooms, in shipwrecks off the south coast of Turkey, and even illustrated as part of the 'tribute' shown in Egyptian tomb paintings.

tin, as much as for copper, may well have been the spur to long-range trade. The silver-rich lead ores of Laurion and Siphnos gave those who controlled them a valuable commodity much in demand in the Near East. Isotope analysis has shown that Laurion silver reached at least as far as Cyprus.

Aegean pottery found in the Aeolian Islands, which were perhaps used as secure bases for trade with the mainland of Italy and Sicily, demonstrates interest in the resources of the central Mediterranean. Baltic amber must have reached Greece from this direction, but there is no sign of activity on the most obvious route, from the head of the Adriatic. Early Mycenaean rapiers and horned swords were exported northward to Albania and the Danube valley, where local imitations occur in Bulgaria and Romania. Minoan and early Mycenaean pottery have also been found at Troy.

The extent of Egyptian contact with the Aegean depended greatly on whether Egypt's rulers took an active interest in what happened beyond their frontiers. In the reign of Tuthmosis III, tombs of officials include 'Keftiu' in the painted files of tribute bearers, carrying Cretan precious metal vases and wearing Cretan codpieces, as in the tomb of Useramon (*c.*1451 BC). A little later, in the tomb of Rekhmire, the codpieces have been overpainted with Mycenaean-type kilts, perhaps a reflection of mainland domination of the Aegean by the late fifteenth century. Amenophis III was another ruler who encouraged foreign contact and several scarabs with his names reached Crete and mainland Greece in the fourteenth century. His was also the name on the faience plaque from the Room with the Fresco at Mycenae, already noted as a sign of official contact. Mycenaean pottery is found at many sites in inland Syro-Palestine as well as in southern Egypt. Most of the vessels are small containers, neatly, but not elaborately, decorated, which reached the eastern Mediterranean because of their contents rather than for their own sake. The contents must have been liquid and precious, for example perfumes or unguents, much sought after in Egypt and the Near East. Mycenaean pottery was also found in the rubbish dumps of the workmen's quarters of the new city founded by Akhenaten at Tell el Amarna, and occupied for only nineteen years. The valuable ointments were perhaps acquired by the rich, and the discarded containers then put to other uses by their servants until broken, rather like glass jars in recent years.

The fourteenth-century Kaş wreck gives a fascinating picture of the mix of cargoes carried at this time, even if we do not know whether it was Levantine, Cypriot, or Aegean. Copper ingots, pithoi packed with Cypriot pottery, and Canaanite amphorae full of terebinth resin were the bulkiest part of the cargo. Many fragments of these amphorae have been found in Crete and Greece. There were also ingots and objects of tin, ingots of glass, and segments of elephant tusk. Some items, including a number of Mycenaean pottery vessels may have belonged to the crew. Other personal items such as a gold scarab of Nefertiti, a Mesopotamian cylinder seal, two Syrian pendants, a Mycenaean and a Syrian sword all show the variety of cultural influences. Most striking of all the finds was a wooden tablet with ivory hinges which was probably coated with wax for writing. The thirteenth-century Gelydonia wreck is less opulent. Its cargo was principally copper ingots and agricultural tools: worn or damaged items indicate a travelling bronzesmith who collected scrap in part exchange for new tools and weapons.

Mycenaean influence in Cyprus steadily increased in the fourteenth and thirteenth centuries, as did the amount of Cypriot copper in the Aegean. Some vases, particularly the large kraters decorated with chariots, bulls, or other boldly painted scenes, were especially favoured by the wealthy. These are often found in Cypriot tombs and one travelled as far as Amman in Jordan before accompanying a burial. At the same time there was a great expansion of Mycenaean trade with southern Italy, Sicily, and Sardinia. Metals are still likely to have been the principal interest, although some of the ingots found in Sardinia are of Cypriot copper. The Aeolian Islands were no longer essential as safe bases and the majority of finds come from sites on the coast such as Scoglio del Tonno near Taranto, Broglio di Trebisacce and Termitito in Calabria. European influences can also be seen in Greece, particularly at the end of the thirteenth century. Mycenaeans started to use the European cut-and-thrust swords and 'Peschiera' daggers, as well as violin-bow fibulae and median wing axes. Short-socketed spearheads were widely used in Greece as well as in central Europe. These links, particularly with the Terramare culture of the Po valley, indicate the increasing strength of Adriatic trade during the last years of Mycenaean palace civilization.

Despite this maritime activity in the central and western Mediterranean, any influence the Mycenaean visitors had on the native peoples is limited and restricted to coastal areas. There is no sign that the pattern of social organization developed in the Aegean was ever transmitted further west, perhaps because the complex economic and social patterns of the Aegean had little of relevance to the pre-urban communities of Europe.

7

The Emergence of Élites: Earlier Bronze Age Europe, 2500–1300 BC

ANDREW SHERRATT

Introduction: Regional Similarities and Contrasts

The second millennium BC saw the emergence of the first urban civilizations on European soil, in the form of the palace-centred states of the Aegean. Unlike the first-millennium civilizations of the Mediterranean, however, these newly complex societies, with their trading links to the cities of the Near East, had no major effect on the societies in their continental hinterland. While aspects of advanced technology and perhaps also symbols of power and military prowess did spread northward among the groups with whom they were in contact, it was not until the crisis of east Mediterranean urban civilization in the thirteenth and twelfth centuries BC that their fortunes were decisively linked.

Nor were their neighbours on the steppes more directly influential in affecting the course of development in temperate Europe. Pastoral societies expanded eastward, reaching as far as central Asia during this time; but they won no more territory in eastern Europe. They did, however, form an important new metallurgical community which influenced eastern European practice, while their skills in horse-rearing, and their new vehicle the chariot, spread through much of Europe as they did through the Near East. Other forms of transport were developed locally: boats, for fishing, trading, and raiding, brought a new element of mobility to the Baltic as they had done somewhat earlier to the Aegean; and much trade took place by dugout canoe along inland waterways. Chariots and boats, along with east Mediterranean symbols of power, were taken up by the kinds of hereditary élites that emerged throughout the Continent and whose artefacts dominate the archaeological record of this period.

While gold (and, to a much lesser extent, silver) objects were made and deposited in élite tombs in many parts of Europe, it was bronze which was much more widely traded and used to manufacture weapons, ornaments, and certain kinds of tools. Copper was now regularly alloyed, and the earlier use of arsenic soon gave way to the regular use of tin. If copper was relatively rare as a naturally occurring material, tin was even rarer; and the circulation of bronze objects in extensive cycles of exchange depended on regular supplies of both metals. Bronzes were buried with the dead and also offered to the gods or supernatural powers whose world probably mirrored many aspects of the world of the living, and some of the legends preserved in the Homeric epics give an echo of the kinds of dynastic struggles which must have characterized societies in many parts of Bronze Age Europe. These 'barbarian' societies (as the inhabitants of the classical world were to regard their northern Iron Age neighbours) measured their success in the quantities of desirable materials and objects available for their disposal, somewhat in the same way that the societies of sub-Saharan Africa traded 'prestige goods' of metal and imported materials at the time of early colonial contact. Bronze seems to have had many of the properties of a material of prime value in a 'protocurrency', not often expressed in standardized units (although examples can be cited), but more like the family silver, which can be used for elegant display and also exchanged for everyday necessities when times are hard. Yet it was frequently also used to purchase fame or the goodwill of the gods, in votive hoards and offerings that have no real equivalent in the more advanced economies to the south.

The other element which distinguishes these groups from their urban neighbours is their architecture, and especially the lack of elaborate, permanent dwellings for an upper stratum of society. While both barbarian and urban societies built showy tombs, the buildings—and even the settlements—of early barbarian Europe were remarkably modest. Large fortified settlements on trade routes appeared in a few areas, notably on the edges of the Carpathian mountains, in a central location with contacts in all directions: east to the steppes, south to the Aegean, north to Scandinavia, and westward via a chain of wealthy élite groups as far as Brittany and the British Isles, where changes in the design of bronze daggers provide an ultimate echo of the styles produced by master metalsmiths in Hungary. Yet even in the defended centres and hill-forts of Hungary and Slovakia, where bronze, amber, and gold objects can be recovered from burnt and abandoned settlements, there was no equivalent to the great halls of third- and second-millennium Troy, still less of Pylos or Mycenae. And in Britain, where gold and amber mark the burials of the wealthiest of the princely lines of Wessex, older forms of ritual centres like Stonehenge still retained their symbolic power.

Slowly, however, the societies of temperate Europe converged towards a common ideal. Bronze became the universal medium of prestige; styles of fighting and warfare spread across the Continent and resulted in common weapon combinations and designs; hospitality was everywhere expressed in carefully made drinking-vessels, often produced from expensive materials; horses and wheeled vehicles were everywhere admired; textiles, amber necklaces, and the metal dress-pins needed to hold loosely woven woollen cloth in position became visible signs of wealth. Technical innovations in bronzecasting were diffused from leading centres of metalworking and widely

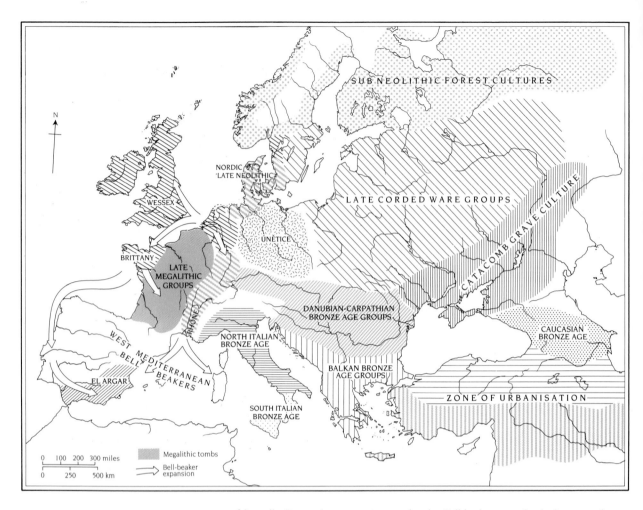

EUROPE IN THE FIRST PART of the earlier Bronze Age, 2500–1800 BC, showing Bell-beaker expansion in the west and the spread of urban civilization to Anatolia and Crete, followed by the emergence of regional bronze-using cultures in central, northern, and western Europe. Links established in the Bell-beaker period remained important.

adopted, so that typological sequences are especially useful in correlating the chronologies of different regions. All these give an impression of uniformity which is in marked contrast to the disparate developments of the Copper Age. It took some centuries, however, before these patterns became more or less universal among the farming communities of Europe. Scandinavia remained largely metal-less, except for occasional imports of bronze axes and daggers that were carefully copied in flint, for more than a millennium after bronze began to circulate in the Aegean, and perhaps 300 years after local copper and nearby tin were combined by the metalsmiths of central Germany, between the copper ores of the Harz mountains and the tin-rich streams of northern Bohemia. Yet very rapidly it then adopted the artefacts and styles of central Europe, participating fully in the long-distance exchanges by which metal supplies were acquired. What did it give in

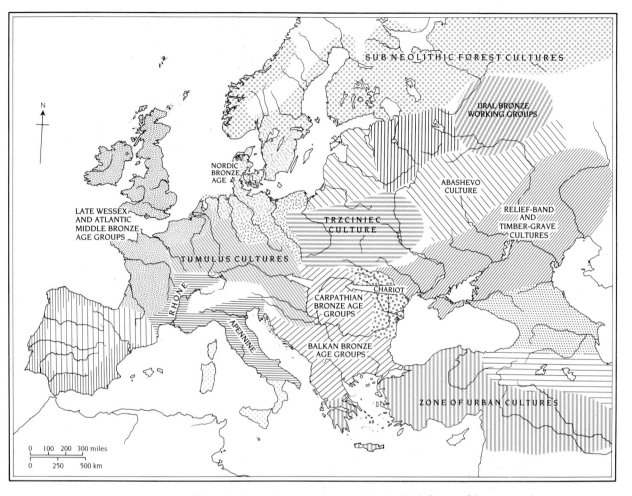

EUROPE IN THE SECOND PART of the earlier Bronze Age, 1800–1300 BC, showing the influence of the steppe region on central Europe and the spread of urban civilization to the Greek mainland. Scandinavia emerged as a bronze-using area, linked southwards first to the Carpathian Basin and then to the area of Tumulus cultures, and ultimately (via Italy) with Mycenae.

exchange? Amber, certainly; hides or coarse wool, perhaps; possibly also furs from animals trapped in northern forests. Whatever the commodity, this was a degree of interregional exchange not attained by earlier forms of economic organization, and not to be greatly exceeded before urban economies appeared in southern temperate Europe in Roman times, or made their belated northern appearance in the early medieval period.

Despite the similarities between the portable artefacts used in different parts of the Continent, there was one major regional contrast in mode of life. Earlier Bronze Age Europe falls into two vast zones, created in the preceding millennia. South of the Carpathians, a zone of often fortified settlements and flat-grave cemeteries with large numbers of burials gives an impression of territorial stability in which possession of land was the object of social strategies. Although votive deposits or 'hoards' were common

SCENE ON A STONE (*right*) from a cist burial under a large tumulus at Bredarör near Kivik in Scania, southern Sweden. The carving is amongst the first datable depictions of a complete chariot from that area, *c*.1300 BC. The construction of these early chariots was very simple — essentially a platform and a draught-pole, with two detachable four-spoke wheels.

BOAT INCISED on a bronze sword (*below*) from Rørby, near Kalundborg, Denmark, *c*.1600 BC. The sword is a distinctive type with a curved end, and the drawing is one of the earliest representations of a boat in the Nordic Bronze Age. It was probably made of skin on a wooden frame with projecting ends. The strokes above the gunwale may represent paddlers.

throughout the period, this zone has notably few rich, monumental burials like the tumuli of northern and western Europe. In this latter zone, by contrast, settlement traces are correspondingly meagre, and the turf-built mounds which provided pasture for the dead suggest a greater emphasis on livestock as sources of wealth. While this may correlate with different densities of population, it does not imply a simple division into 'farmers' and 'pastoralists', for each area practised both farming and herding, perhaps in roughly equal proportions; rather it refers to the social value placed on these activities, and the way social relations were structured around them. It is this contrast which is expressed in the different material record of tombs and settlement forms.

The way of life of Bronze Age communities north of the Carpathians has few analogies in later protohistoric Europe. It was a unique episode, specific to the conditions of its time, in which forests on light soils were rapidly cleared to provide a few years of good crops and a longer period of pasture. With the development of a heavier plough in the first millennium, and the colonization of areas of heavier but agriculturally more productive land, many of these lighter lands were to be abandoned to forest and heathland, where the burial mounds now survive in large numbers. The pattern of earlier Bronze

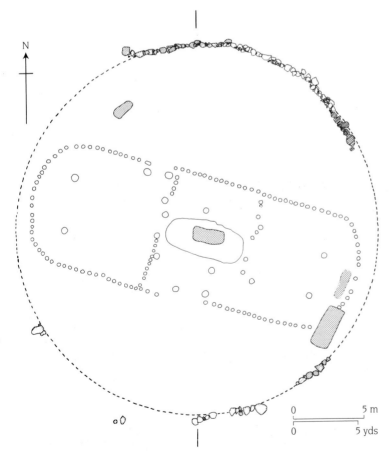

N

PLAN OF A CIRCULAR BURIAL-MOUND from Trappendal, south Jutland, Denmark, *c.* fourteenth century BC. The mound contained burials similar to the well preserved example from Egtved, but is notable because it covers a rare example of a contemporary house, some 24 m long and 9 m wide, divided into three rooms — perhaps the dwelling of the person buried in the mound.

0   5 m

0   5 yds

Age extensive farming in northern Europe came to an end. It was the more intensive pattern of agricultural existence established in south-east Europe that was to provide the basis for future developments. In the later Bronze Age, after the collapse of the first Aegean experiments with urbanism, when Mycenaean Greece reverted to effectively prehistoric conditions in the final centuries of the second millennium, the lands along the middle and lower Danube experienced a surge of growth which carried their pattern of hill-forts and flat-grave cemeteries further into central Europe and out towards the peripheries of the Continent. This period of 'Urnfield' expansion, incorporating new technologies such as sheet-bronzeworking previously developed in urban contexts, is discussed in Chapter 9.

These contrasting models of Bronze Age life had their origins in the differences between north and south which went back to the very beginnings of farming in the Continent, and to the two great blocs into which agricultural Europe had come to be divided during the Copper Age (as described in Chapter 5). In south-east Europe, where village-based farming had first taken root, substantial settlement sites with flat-grave cemeteries continued to form the fixed points of social life; and from the mid-fourth millennium onward their pottery shows the elegant, metal-influenced shapes of the Aegean and Anatolia. Despite the local intrusion into the south-east of tumulus-building groups from the steppes, this stable, sedentary pattern nevertheless persisted through to the Bronze Age. Northern Europe, however, where, during the Neolithic period, domestic settlements had tended to give way to monumental tombs and ceremonial centres, came to experience a rapid devolution from these megaliths and earthwork enclosures. In the Corded Ware period, after 3000 BC, settlement traces became very dispersed, and steppe elements such as cord-impressed pottery and tumuli were adopted and integrated into the fabric of society. Burial monuments still played a prominent role in the organization of the landscape. This alternative pattern of extensive farming and livestock-rearing in northern Europe formed the basis of Bronze Age developments there. It was slower, however, in penetrating into Atlantic Europe, where megalithic, ritual-centred societies lasted longer; and a comparable set of changes in western Europe only came about in this area after *c*.2500 BC, when the spread of Bell-Beakers brought these changes to the West, and it is with this episode that the following account begins. The sections of this chapter are, therefore, not rigidly divided chronologically, but rather follow the series of regional developments which came to affect Bronze Age Europe as a whole.

The Bell-Beaker Phenomenon and its Successors, 2800–1800 BC

As with the Corded Ware pottery of northern Europe, the decorated handleless drinking-cups known as Bell-Beakers stand *pars pro toto* for a whole new way of life in the areas where they appeared, from Scotland to Sicily. Throughout this Atlantic zone, a common set of artefacts made their appearance in the later third millennium: the Bell-Beakers themselves, individual burials in round mounds, and an associated set of weapons and small stone and metal artefacts. These Bell-Beaker tumuli often formed the nuclei for continuing clusters of such barrow-burials in succeeding centuries. Earlier generations of archaeologists imagined the users of these pots as a set of warriors and tinkers, the 'Beaker Folk', who spread out from Spain. While possessing a few elements of truth, this explanation mistakes both the nature and the assumed origin of these groups. Rather than representing a coherent migration of a distinctive people, the Bell-Beaker phenomenon is better seen as the outcome of the kind of processes discussed at the end of Chapter 5: as part of the breakdown of traditional social structures and the emergence of more mobile ways of life that began in northern Europe after 3000 BC. It was the often spectacular intrusion of these new ways of life into the more isolated parts of western Europe that gave this period its distinctive trace in the archaeological record, and the new maritime links that were forged in this process that gave it such an international character.

The name given to this phenomenon comes from the characteristic drinking vessel with its inverted bell-shaped profile, which carries incised decoration in horizontal zones around the body. At first tall and slender, with uniform bands of cord impressions from rim to base, these early 'international' forms developed into a variety of regional types in which wider zones of textile-like ornament were generally deployed across shorter, broader-bellied pots. The similarities between early Bell-Beakers and the Corded Ware drinking-cup are not accidental, for the bell-shaped forms seem to have begun as a regional variant of Corded Ware beakers in the lower Rhine delta, where the main artery of continental north-west Europe reaches the sea. It was contacts by sea that gave these otherwise marginal groups their advantage, and led to their widespread appearance along the Atlantic coasts. Like the Corded Ware vessels, these pots were also typically placed in single male burials, often accompanied by weaponry and covered by a circular mound. They thus represent a diaspora of continental north-west European practices among largely alien populations, carrying the aggressive, individualizing ideology of this area to new parts of Europe. Whereas Corded Ware beakers were usually buried with stone battleaxes, Bell-Beakers are generally found with other weapons: daggers, and archery equipment such as triangular barbed-flint arrowheads and wristguards of fine stone. The first users of Bell-Beakers did not practise metallurgy, and the earliest daggers were made of flint; though they soon came to be cast in copper, and then bronze. This martial image was perhaps completed by leather jerkins and later by woven fabrics, held by a belt with an ornamental bone ring to secure it: such figures are schematically represented on the later statue menhirs of the west Alpine region. Early Bell-Beakers display the cords and thongs that distinguished their Corded Ware predecessors; perhaps the later zoned ornament, too, is significant, for the Greek word *zone* means a belt, and the élite of Greek warriors are still the *evzones*, 'the well-belted ones', while black belts still symbolize prowess in the martial arts. The imagery of third-millennium Europe was replete with such symbols, and Bell-Beaker graves expressed the warrior values appropriate to a more mobile and opportunistic way of life. This pre-

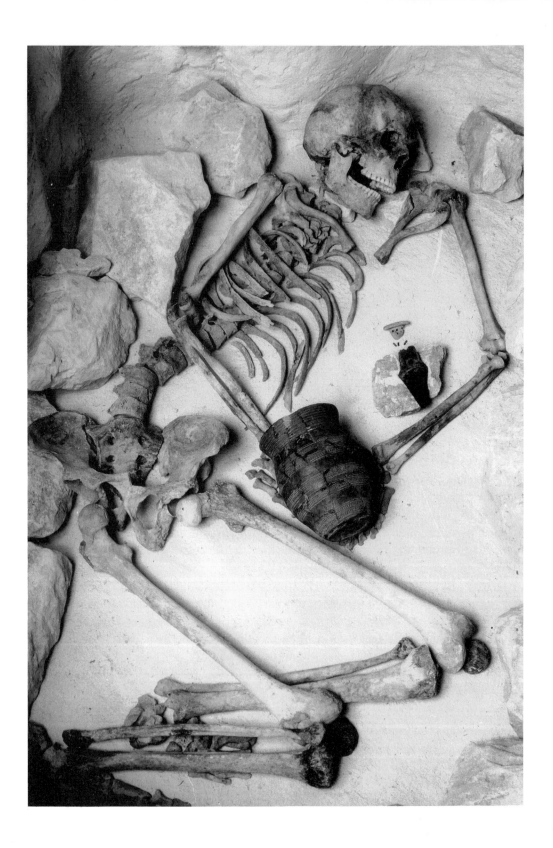

sented indigenous groups both with a challenge to established values, and an opportunity to join a new community with access to exotic items of material culture.

The relatively sudden appearance of Bell-Beakers on the western edge of Europe is thus indicative of the intrusion of a whole range of novel elements which had accumulated in central and northern Europe during the earlier third millennium BC, and which were adopted together (often in a phase of radical upheaval) either by local élites or by small numbers of adventurous outsiders who saw the opportunity to open up hitherto closed, archaic societies and perhaps align themselves with disadvantaged elements of their population. The disruptive character of this process is epitomized in two of these features (both of which were to have an equally dramatic impact some 4000 years later on the New World): alcohol and horses. That beakers were used for something like mead, flavoured with herbs such as meadowsweet or wild fruits, has been demonstrated from pollen grains found in the bottom of such drinking-cups. As with Corded Ware beakers, these vessels suggest individual hospitality rather than the great communal ceremonies at central gathering places which had hitherto dominated the ritual life of western Europe: the dry detail of pottery typology understates the social reality of a clash of cultural values. So, too, with the first appearance of horses in areas such as Spain or the British Isles: the animals were few in number, but their impact must have been a powerful one. Along with these, somewhat later, came metallurgical skills and woollen textiles, which by absorbing dyes could present a more colourful appearance than garments of skin or linen. The extended (rather than crouched) posture in which certain prominent individuals were now to be buried was presumably designed to show off this finery in the grave. Such ostentation on the part of particular individuals (or their heirs!) is symptomatic of the profound change in attitudes which accompanied the spread of Bell-Beakers.

Such a formulation inevitably disguises the great diversity of situations encountered during this process. Not only did it affect the Atlantic sea-ways, linking up regional centres in places such as the Rhineland, Britain, Brittany, and Portugal, it also spread back inland to central Germany and former Czechoslovakia, and along major rivers such as the upper Rhine and Rhône. Throughout this area, a common symbolic system prevailed, centred on the beaker cup and archer's weapon-kit, with decorative elements such as bone belt-fasteners or v-perforated bone buttons for fastening leather jerkins. These were all the products of especially fine craftsmanship, some literally to be capped with gold. These links between local élites were to provide the paths along which superior forms of metal weapons, and other decorative and dress fashions, were to spread: especially from the middle Danube, where the makers of metallic-looking pottery traded from fortified centres along the rivers, and from central Germany, where some of

CROUCHED INHUMATION BURIAL with a Bell-Beaker and bronze dagger from Nett Down, Shrewton, Wiltshire, England; cut into chalk, and covered by a circular burial-mound. The bronze dagger originally had an organic (probably horn) hilt and a bone pommel, and was wrapped in moss inside a piece of cloth. The grave neatly encapsulates the ideal male image of drinking and fighting.

the most advanced techniques of metalworking were being pioneered. Beyond this zone, on the North European Plain and Scandinavia, and eastward to the edges of the steppes, later forms of Corded Ware continued the traditions begun in the early third millennium. In their social organization and settlement patterns, these groups resembled those propagated by the makers of Bell-Beakers, though they largely lacked the new finery made possible through trade and communication by sea and river.

Even within the Atlantic zone, however, the makers of Bell-Beakers experienced a variety of relations with older, established groups, many of whom had their own forms of social complexity. In some areas — usually those marginal to earlier centres of activity — the new way of life took over more or less immediately; in others, it seems to have been actively resisted; while yet other areas merely adopted certain aspects of decorative style. In this diversity of responses it is often hard to distinguish intrusive populations from the spread of the ideology, or simply from the adoption of fashionable motifs and designs. The subtlety of this process is well illustrated in Ireland, where new technologies of copperworking and goldworking now came to flourish, even using Beaker-style motifs on sheet-gold crescentic collars (lunulae), but without taking over Beaker drinking habits and burial forms. Nevertheless it must be remembered that all these new elements of material culture were symptomatic of radical changes in attitudes to social life and material production, and did not simply represent display for its own sake. The adoption of a deliberately ostentatious personal lifestyle, in contrast to the communal emphasis of megaliths and cult-centres, was in itself a major break in cultural traditions and the social structures they supported.

It would be wrong, however, to write the history of this period simply in terms of artefacts: the products of fine craftsmanship were only available to the most successful, and such social success was attained by achievement in the real world of raising and trading livestock. These constraints explain why the centres of new wealth often coincided with, and extended, the areas where earlier groups had achieved prominence. Cleared land suitable for grazing, and so for amassing individual wealth, was itself a valuable commodity in a still heavily forested continent. Hence the continued importance of areas such as Wessex, where this resource was plentiful and extensive. It is notable, therefore, that the Bell-Beaker pattern only took over in this area after a prolonged struggle with older entrenched orthodoxies, represented by the henge monuments described in Chapter 5. The first burials with Bell-Beakers occurred well away from these existing ritual centres, as if these were reflections of incompatible systems of belief and social practice. Only the later forms of Bell-Beaker occur at such ceremonial sites, and indeed were associated with the elaboration and refurbishment of Stonehenge around 2000 BC as a stone circle rather than an earth and timber monument. Similar transformations took place at neighbouring centres such as Avebury, and at the nearby West Kennet long-barrow which was blocked with massive stones as if to emphasize the final assumption of symbolic authority by beaker users. An intrusive ideology had become the new orthodoxy. Soon the individual burials in the beaker tradition became larger and richer, marking the emergence of the 'Wessex culture'—an élite group with international contacts demonstrated by sheet goldwork, amber, and the latest bronze weaponry interred in large tumuli.

A different pattern prevailed in Brittany. Here, the earliest Bell-Beakers also concentrate in the older centres like the Morbihan; but their most plentiful occurrence is as secondary deposits in the older passage graves—often accompanied by small gold ornaments, rather than weapons. Such syncretism was a passing phase, however, and later forms of beaker occur more commonly in newly cleared areas on the edge of this concentration: and it may be that the largest monuments of the Morbihan, the great stone avenues of Carnac and Erdeven, represent a deliberate attempt to revive traditional values in response to this threat, intended to hold the local population to older beliefs. Ultimately, however, farmland proved less valuable than mineral resources: when large barrow-burials comparable to those of Wessex finally appeared (at about the same time as their English counterparts), they were situated in new areas that were better located for metal exploitation and maritime trade—not least with Wessex, to which they supplied fine daggers. Their links at this time also reached out to the Baltic amber routes and the central German metalworking centres, from whom they acquired their designs. Quite different was the contemporary culture of inland France, in areas such as the Paris basin and east-central Brittany, where the later Neolithic pattern centred on *allées couvertes* persisted almost unchanged, with no signs of the new wealth or even echoes of it. Their smaller, scattered patches of cleared land proved less susceptible to the new patterns, and without valuable mineral resources had little attraction for adventurers.

AIR-PHOTOGRAPH OF A GROUP of earlier Bronze Age burial mounds near Stonehenge, Wiltshire, southern England. The linear arrangement is characteristic, and may indicate genealogical relationships within a local ruling family. The group includes both simple mounds and more elaborate forms with ditches and banks. (The rectilinear features are products of modern farming).

In eastern France and Switzerland, yet a further pattern may be discerned, which looks much more like the actual intrusion of small groups along the upper Rhine and Rhône. In the Alpine region, they introduced the new warrior images which stare out from the later statue menhirs, and rearranged earlier stone structures to make individual burial-cists; and they penetrated in small numbers to northern and even central Italy. Significantly, some of their burials there are associated with rare remains of horses— originally acquired by Bell-Beaker groups from communities on the middle Danube. In southern and south-western France, beakers and their associated equipment are also plentiful; and here their imagery and way of life may more easily have converted the extensive farming groups on the dry plateaux of Languedoc and surrounding areas. In Atlantic Iberia, their links may first have been established as traders. The very earliest forms of Bell-Beaker occur as far south as Portugal, indicating an early interest in voyaging to areas accessible by sea; and they soon penetrated to other parts of the peninsula and even nearby parts of north Africa. In Portugal and southern Spain they encountered the already complex and copper-using groups living in elaborate fortified centres, and beakers occur both in settlements such as Vila Nova de São Pedro and Los Millares (significantly, in the former case, in buildings associated with metallurgical activity) and in the later collective tombs. There were no revolutionary consequences to this encounter, however, but rather peaceful relations and the exchange of status symbols. Iberian populations acquired horses, probably some quaint northern recipes for food and drink, and a geometric decorative repertoire that was widely adopted on local pottery shapes such as wide bowls, and spread beyond the area of immediate beaker influence. In return, beaker groups and their successors in Brittany acquired Iberian copper (sometimes specifically in the form of local arrowhead shapes), and rare objects of silver. A comparable penetration of eastern Spain took place from adjacent areas of southern France, bringing other beaker-using groups to the Mediterranean.

It was at this stage that inter-island trading really began in the west Mediterranean, carrying small metal items and other prestige goods, at the same time as trading voyages in the east Mediterranean were bringing Levantine objects to Crete. Ostentatiously fortified centres on the Balearic Islands have yielded mainland objects, and even the bones of horses. Beakers reached Corsica and Sardinia, and even as far as western Sicily, where they were imitated in the local style of painted pottery, just as the inhabitants of eastern Sicily imitated the decorated bone plaques of Troy. The diverse regions of Europe were linked as never before.

The Development of Metallurgy in Central Germany and its Interregional Effects,
2300–1800 BC

Copperworking on a small scale had been introduced to northern Europe by Corded Ware groups, but the northern ores largely lacked the well-developed zone of secondary weathering which gave the southern sources their ease of smelting. Their beaker-using

VOTIVE HOARD of bronze objects from Dieskau, Saalkreis, central Germany, *c.*2000 BC: one of a large number of such deposits from an area adjacent to the rich copper sources of the Harz mountains. It was carefully packed in a pot, and consists of halberd blades, spiral and solid arm-rings, neck-rings, and axes, along with 126 amber beads and 23 spiral bronze ones (not shown).

successors in the later second millennium BC had a somewhat improved technology, and were the first to alloy the copper with Bohemian tin; and the new techniques which had reached the Carpathian basin from metallurgical centres in the Caucasus, via the new steppe connections, provided the basis for the growth of a major indigenous industry. The general interest in objects of display ensured that this development had repercussions both in neighbouring areas and among distant élites.

It was at this point that the classic image of the Bronze Age made its appearance: the great hoards of bronze objects, which are known in such large numbers from this area at the time, and the spectacular burials with gold and bronze objects under massive mounds. Archaeologists name this phenomenon the Únětice culture (a Czech name sometimes Germanized to Aunjetitz, which indicates how it should be pronounced); thereby designating not only the local pottery style but also the wider metallurgical province, within which it set the style in display gear and standards of ostentation. The chief weapon was the dagger. Beaker metallurgists had progressed from simple tanged forms of copper to bronze forms in which the hilt, of organic material (wood, bone,

TRACES OF BRONZE AGE smelting activity in the copper-mining area of the Mitteberg, near Bischofshofen, Salzburg, Austria. The area of the *Salzkammergut* was famous in the Medieval period for its salt and metal sources, and its rich copper pyrite ores were exploited from the earlier Bronze Age onwards to produce large quantities of the metal used for neck-rings (*Ösenringe*).

horn) was attached by rivets. Únětice metallurgists now improved it by the addition of a solid metal hilt, added to the blade by the process known as casting-on. The blade might be further ornamented by punching, or an organic hilt adorned by the addition of metal nails (especially in the western areas of Únětice influence, in Wessex and Brittany). Such a blade might also be used as a pole arm, by attaching it at right angles to the shaft by large rivets, to form a so-called halberd. Spears were not generally used outside the east Mediterranean at this stage, since they were harder to attach securely to the shaft. Axes, too, were made in bronze: both flat axes (used as prestige tools as well as weapons), and shaft-hole axes, that in this region usually had two narrow, balanced blades. Among other tricks of the trade, Únětice metallurgists knew how to encourage the surface enrichment of tin, to produce a blade resembling silver.

Complementing these armaments were metal ornaments, particularly rings. The production of a standardized but roughly shaped neck-ring (termed an *Ösenring* from the flattened and recurved ends) was a speciality of another mining area at this period, located either in the western Carpathians, or more probably in the eastern Alps. These rings, formed by casting a blank and then bending and shaping them by hammering, were widely traded as a standardized commodity, before being alloyed and recast and shaped in final form. Some were moved by canoe along the Danube, but many found their way northward through former Czechoslovakia to central Germany. They are found in hoards of up to 500 or more examples in Moravia, though in smaller numbers further out from their production source. This trade illustrates the way a limited number of commodities circulated—as cast blanks whose prime value was in their metal—even towards rich regions which had their own metal sources. It was not a highly differentiated economic system, and only a limited number of commodities were traded, so that in order to acquire tin or status items like northern furs or amber, metal might be exchanged (presumably at a low equivalence) in an apparently irrational direction. This led to the massive local accumulation of bronze, which was removed from circulation by ritual deposition as votive offerings in finished form. Some analogy to this process is offered by the recent tribes of the Northwest Coast of Canada, whose 'potlatch' ceremony involved the comparable destruction of wealth in the form of copper, and was the principal means by which local leaders competed for prestige. Control of such supplies, concentrated in the hands of a few powerful lineages, enhanced the status of such groups.

Not all Bronze Age votive deposits or hoards had this character. In central Germany, such great hoards are largely restricted to a period around 2000 BC, and then ceased until a new episode began in the Urnfield period of the later Bronze Age, when they contain many more used and recycled pieces, and indicate a rather different pattern of behaviour. South of the Carpathians, votive hoards have a rather more continuous history than this 'boom-and-bust' cycle, and their dedicatory character will become clear from examples to be discussed later. This indicates both the more continuous nature of metal production from the Carpathian sources and the rather different role which such hoards played there. As in certain parts of Bronze Age Denmark, deposition of metal in hoards rather than graves seems to be an alternative means of dedicating wealth. Further west, the tradition of river and bog deposits may have continued practices established during Neolithic times. All this argues a diversity of motives, within a system in which alternative uses of wealth objects (for example, the payment of armies, or more general forms of exchange) were limited, and possession was hedged about with restrictions and prescriptions as to the appropriate uses of material items. What is certain is that the old idea (by analogy with coin-hoards) of wealth hidden in times of insecurity is often inappropriate, as is the idea that such assemblages represent the stock in trade of itinerant merchants and craftsmen. It is important not to build such conceptions into chronological schemes based on 'hoard-horizons', taken to represent periods of warfare or the anticipation of invasion.

The great burial mounds of the period around 2000 BC in central Germany are less enigmatic in their interpretation. Three in particular stand out, by reason of their size, structure, and contents, from their less spectacular contemporaries and flat-grave cemeteries: Leubingen, Helmsdorf, and Łęki Małe in adjacent Poland. The Leubingen and Helmsdorf mounds (the former eight and a half metres high) both enclosed substantial pitched-timber burial-chambers. Their association with metal production is not in doubt: Helmsdorf was discovered in 1906 while building a railway for a modern copper mine, and might be considered as the burial of a successful coppermaster. While Wessex magnates gained their prominence as stock-raisers, superwealth came from direct control of primary commodities. Such nineteenth-century images should not obscure ethnographic reality, however: Leubingen contained a carpenter's tool-kit and a cushion-stone for metalworking, as well as a solid gold ring and gold dress-pins; other tumuli, from The Netherlands to the Volga, have yielded smith's equipment—showing that metallurgy itself was probably an esoteric, élite skill, not to be delegated to an industrial underclass, or even craftsmen-retainers. Manipulation of the mysteries of nature was another mark of power and authority.

Metal industries influenced by Únětice designs and largely supplied by its copper and tin grew up in neighbouring areas of Poland and Germany, but none with the same concentration of wealth. Únětice external relationships, through a chain of intermediaries, were with comparably differentiated societies in areas such as Brittany and Wessex, and with other nodal areas of the old Bell-Beaker network down as far as Switzerland and north Italy. Wessex was supplied by the metal sources of western Britain and Ireland, where an indigenous metallurgical industry (albeit of a relatively simple character) now flourished. Occasional pieces of metalwork from one end of this east–west chain reached the territory of the other, and along it spread other materials including gold, amber, and tin, and no doubt some organic commodities which have since perished, as well as elements of living culture such as sagas, heroic poetry, and myths—all now lost.

Long excluded from this community of equals, Scandinavia—and especially Denmark, with its relatively large and dense population—lived in a retarded Stone Age, exporting amber and importing both Irish axes and Únětice daggers, but without metal sources in its own sphere and without an indigenous industry for reprocessing imported metal on any scale. Even Bell-Beakers had failed to penetrate northern Europe, and the older Corded Ware tradition persisted and developed, giving way to a 'Late Neolithic' otherwise called the Dagger period. During this long phase, from around 2200 to 1800 BC, burials were made in stone cists and men were often accompanied by a flint dagger. Such tombs, unprotected by large mounds, were uncovered in enormous numbers during nineteenth-century AD agricultural improvements, when thousands of these objects found their way into private collections and museums. They are of astonishing quality of craftsmanship, as flintworkers supplied with good material strove to emulate and copy the achievements of central German bronzesmiths. Nevertheless, Scandinavia at this time must be considered as a periphery, exporting valuable primary materials and without the capacity to participate in interregional trade using bulk materials and products of its own workmanship. This situation was soon to be changed, as long-distance north–south exchanges were to begin with the Carpathian basin.

The Rise of Carpathian Metalworking Centres and their Wider Links, 2500–1600 BC

The small groups of tumulus-building steppe intruders who had entered the Carpathian basin in the early third millennium had settled principally on the open, and increasingly saline, low terraces of the extensive flood plain that occupies eastern Hungary, drained (and seasonally partly flooded) by the Tisza river and its tributary the Körös. Competition with indigenous agrarian populations was largely avoided since the use of the light plough had opened up the surrounding terraces and foothills, leaving the plains depopulated. By the mid-third millennium, however, the two groups had merged into a single cultural community in the north-east Carpathian basin, with a mixed economy of agriculture and stock-raising.

The eastward connections remained important, both in the continuing importation of horses in larger numbers from the steppe area, and also because of continuing links with the metalworking centres of the Caucasus. From around 2500 BC, at about the time when Bell-Beakers were appearing in Portugal or Levantine influences were beginning to be felt in the Aegean, the impact of Caucasian metal forms can be detected in east-central Europe. The most striking new form was the metal battleaxe: not the shallow, balanced axe-adze or axe-hammer of the indigenous copperworking tradition, made by casting in a single-piece mould and then forged into shape; but a more effective, deep-bladed type with a shaft hole at the end, made by casting in a two-piece mould. Along with this improved technology for shaping metal objects came the use of arsenic as an additive to improve the casting properties of copper and to give a harder edge. It was these innovations, together with Bohemian tin, that were to give the central German metalsmiths their scope; but the new Carpathian metal industries, centred in Transylvania, were slower to develop (perhaps because the more accessible ores had been exhausted in the Copper Age), and less climactic in their initial effects. They were also initially less innovative, and their principal product was the shaft-hole battleaxe of arsenical copper. A typical form has a projecting shaft tube, and these occasionally occur in hoards of up to thirty examples, for instance at Băniabic (formerly Bányabükk) in

LATE NEOLITHIC FLINT
DAGGER (*right*) from
Denmark, *c.*2000 BC, imitating
an imported bronze type with
solid hilt made in central Germany
(*far right*). Lacking its own metal
deposits, Denmark was dependent
on external supplies, and finished
objects were obtained by exchanging
amber. Craftmanship in flint reached a
peak unequalled before or after, using
advanced techniques of pressure-flaking.

BRONZE SHAFTHOLE AXE, *c.*2000 BC
(*below*), probably for use primarily as a
weapon; found with 30 others at Pakrac,
Slavonia, Croatia. This type was made with a
two-piece mould and clay core for the shaft-
tube, in a technique that spread to Europe
from the Caucasus. Axes rather than daggers
were the preferred weapon in eastern Europe.

Transylvania; similar local variants occur widely in eastern Romania and Bulgaria, and indeed across the steppe area under tumuli in so-called 'catacomb graves' (pits with a side chamber) which succeeded the earlier pit graves in this area. Other forms include the lugged chisel, also known in the Caucasus. These types, and indeed the dominance of the axe as the main weapon of metal, demonstrate the close Caucasian links of this tradition, and distinguish it from the dagger-using style which characterizes this period further west.

The settlements of these groups in the Tisza basin and its margins took the form of nucleated villages or tells: but these differed from their Neolithic predecessors (though occasionally overlying them, as at Herpály) in being surrounded by deep ditches and banks, and in being created within a shorter time span than the earlier, long-occupied, villages. Metalworking took place on some of these sites, to judge by the presence of clay moulds, and certain riverside settlements such as Vučedol on the Danube (near its confluence with the Drava) had more the character of fortresses. With the exception of certain parts of this network, such as the area at the junction of the Tisza and Maros (Mureş) where rich flat-grave cemeteries occur instead, this pattern was to dominate the Bronze Age landscape of the eastern Carpathian basin.

In the western part of Hungary, along the Danube, the flat-grave cemeteries were more typical; and this pattern extended along to the upper Danube, in Austria and Bavaria. These areas were mainly supplied by the copper sources producing ring-ingots (*Ösenringe*), and their metal supplies were carefully eked out in the production of ornaments such as pins, and especially small sheet-ornaments suitable for display as headgear or clothing fasteners and adornments, often with antecedents in bone. Shells (both recent and fossil) were used for necklaces. Another artificial material which supplemented metals for beads was a glass frit (usually miscalled faience), coloured with blue copper carbonate and probably discovered as a result of smelting the more complex ores that were now used as sources of copper. None the less, where metal supplies were more plentiful, these groups produced their own forms of axes or used central German types of daggers. Rivers provided the arteries of this network: the Danube, especially, linked communities along its banks and tributaries, with particular concentrations of wealth at nodal points in the transport system. While agrarian production must have occupied most of the daily lives of these communities, the flows of imported materials were beginning to pick out regions and sites with particular advantages in the distribution network, especially in the canoe-borne traffic along rivers. Besides stock-raising and primary production, here was a third path to wealth. These local advantages were to be further enhanced for one or two locations by the growth of longer-distance trade in metal and other commodities; and the conjunction of these three advantages was to produce spectacular concentrations of riches.

The metallurgical community of which the Carpathian basin—now beginning a larger scale of exploitation of the rich Transylvanian ore bodies—formed a part, had grown to even more massive proportions. During the later third millennium, metal use

DECORATED ANTLER
CHEEK-PIECE to a
bridle bit, *c.*1800 BC,
from a settlement-site
at Százhalombatta,
north-east Hungary.
The holes are for the
attachment of reins and
mouth-piece of leather.
These finely decorated
antler forms are
especially characteristic
of the Carpathian Basin
and the Pontic steppe
region, and were used
for chariot-horses.

and the beginnings of metalworking had spread by way of the steppe tribes to the copper sources of the southern Urals. These supplied not only a local demand, among forest groups increasingly adopting agriculture and living in subterranean rectangular houses, but in the centuries after 2000 BC came to supply an even larger area of the steppe zone. As well as the north Pontic steppes, occupied by the makers of so-called 'multiple-relief band' (*mnogo-valikovaya*) pottery, the area north of the Caspian was marked by new, larger graves which incorporated a timber-built underground chamber (timber graves) that perhaps replicated contemporary houses. Eastward, as far as the Altai mountains, the closely related Andronovo group carried this way of life to the borders of Mongolia, where there were further rich deposits of copper and tin. These new metallurgical centres maintained their connections across the steppes, and their links reached out as far as north China. Types with a hollow socket, formed by casting in a two-piece mould with a suspended core, are a common component of these groups. Throughout the steppe zone the mobility implied by these links sprang from the use of horses, and especially the newly invented chariot: a light, bentwood construction that could easily be pulled by the small horses of the time, which were controlled by a bridle-bit with spiked cheekpieces of antler. At the timber-grave cemetery of Sintashta in the southern Urals, five chariot burials (with the wheels sunk into slots in the floor) have been recovered, with horses buried in the tumulus and exposed as heads and (stuffed?) skins.

In the early centuries of the second millennium, the Carpathian basin benefited from the existence of this vast hinterland to create the most advanced 'barbarian' culture of its time. Combining the metallurgical skills pioneered in central Germany (such as the cast-on hilts) with those of the circum-Pontic network, and their own rich resources in copper and gold, Transylvanian metalsmiths added their own craftsmanship and skill at incised ornament. Living in large fortified communities, and using chariots like their steppe neighbours, their masters (for they surely now employed specialist craftsmen) traded over long distances with surrounding areas of temperate Europe, and soon their influence reached to all parts of the continent: to Denmark, to Italy, to Greece, and in less direct fashion to influence the design of weaponry as far away as the British Isles.

The find, which epitomizes these developments, and gives its name to the period around 1800 BC in this area, is the hoard of Hajdúsámson from the sandy region of north-east Hungary. Discovered in drainage works in 1907, it consisted of a solid-hilted sword placed with its blade pointing due north, across which had been placed twelve shaft-hole battleaxes with their blades to the west. Clearly a votive offering rather than a casual loss or a set of possessions hidden in time of danger, it represented a considerable quantity of wealth. The sword itself and three of the axes were richly decorated with incised C-scrolls and curvilinear ornament, and each one of them is a unique creation rather than a piece of mass production. A comparable sword was found with three battleaxes at Apa, just across the Romanian border. The swords are rather special weapons—magnificent developments of the dagger tradition, in a largely axe-wielding zone: hence the added length! The cast-on hilt is a central-German feature, though the long, ogival blade is a sophisticated local design; the axes are of ultimately Caucasian form, but here in local types with cast-on circular butts that carry the characteristic swirling ornament. What is the origin of this type of decoration?

The answer lies in another class of objects which is also associated with a prestige use, and has a background on the steppes. Various items of decorated antler- and bonework form a set of horse-gear: cheekpieces, strap-junctions, and possibly whip-caps. They are ornamented with compass-work—used to form concentric circles, running waves (*Wellenbandmuster*), or C-scrolls. Simpler forms of this ornament are found on steppe horsegear, where they are associated with use of the chariot. The presence of such vehi-

GROUP OF GOLD CUPS from Co. Bihar, Hungary, *c.*1800 BC. These are the earliest known metal vessels from temperate Europe, and are raised from a single sheet of metal which includes the handle. They carry incised compasswork which is transitional between that on antler objects and the more flowing style of the free-hand curvilinear incision on bronzes.

cles in the Carpathian basin is indicated by clay models of four-spoked wheels. There are some differences of form between the Carpathian and the Ural bridle equipment: bar cheekpieces predominate in the former area, circular, spiked ones in the latter; but there is no doubt that they are closely related and indeed there are hybrid forms in both areas. The Carpathian ones are more richly decorated, however, and the discipline of this compass-work lies behind the curvilinear ornament on metalwork, and even on pottery.

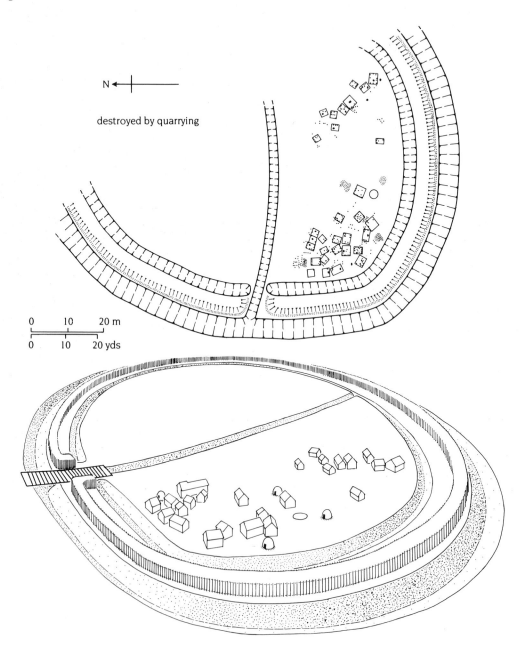

N

destroyed by quarrying

| 0 | 10 | 20 m |
| 0 | 10 | 20 yds |

VIEW OF THE IMPORTANT earlier Bronze Age fortified site (*above*) at Spišsky Štvrtok near Spišska Nová Ves, Slovakia, high in the Carpathians on one of the most important passes leading northwards to the upper Vistula in Poland. The elaborate stone-built fortifications and finds of gold and bronze-work testify to its important position in inter-regional trade.

PLAN AND RECONSTRUCTION (*left*) of the defended hilltop settlement of 'Zámeček' at Nitriansky Hradok, near Nitra, Slovakia, *c.*1800 BC. Half of the site has been destroyed by quarrying, but the remainder has revealed an important Bronze Age centre, surrounded by a timber-framed rampart of a kind which did not become general in Europe before the Iron Age.

Such decoration occurs on solid, cast goldwork, such as the gold arm-ring from Bilje in northern Yugoslavia; and on a splendid set of sheet-gold cups found in Co. Bihar (now split between Hungary and Romania). These are not regular, lathe-finished forms like second millennium examples from the east Mediterranean, where wheel-made pottery was already in use, but testify to the indigenous skills of Carpathian metalsmiths. Rare finds of worked iron, such as a dagger handle from Gánovce in Slovakia, show that metallurgists were now familiar with a wide range of materials. The pottery of this area, too, shows the same swinging curves and elegant designs that distinguish the metalwork, and together these items of material culture are among the most sophisticated products of prehistoric Europe.

The wealth of these communities is reflected in the substantial, and often fortified, settlements of this period. Finds from these sites, and the large hoards of bronze objects which characterize this area, go some way to redressing the absence of spectacularly rich burials—which are often an expression of political insecurity. Instead, the hundreds of tell sites give an impression of a stable and organized existence. At crucial points on trade routes, along rivers and especially on northward routes through the Carpathians (such as Nitriansky Hradok and Spišsky Štvrtok in Slovakia), major fortified sites have the character of hill-forts with box-ramparts not otherwise known before the Iron Age. At one such site, Barca in Slovakia, a destruction level has preserved house contents which included fine bronzes, an amber necklace, and gold beads and hair-ornaments. These finds form part of a wider pattern of long-distance contacts that created a new structure to the temperate European Bronze Age in the middle years of the second millennium.

Long-distance Trade Routes

Whereas the pattern of contacts established in the Bell-Beaker period and developed in the earlier part of the Bronze Age had linked the Atlantic area and central Germany in a broadly east–west pattern, largely excluding Denmark, the new structure emphasized north–south links, from the Baltic to the Danube. Scandinavia changed its role, from being a passive importer and imitator into an active participant in long-distance trade, with a distinctive bronzeworking style of its own. The commodities which circulated over these distances were low in bulk and high in value: amber was one which reaches the archaeological record, and is especially useful for reconstructing the pattern of contacts, but more perishable materials must also have been involved. Two sets of routes can be reconstructed, often coexisting but to some extent in competition, between west Denmark and the Rhine and upper Danube on the one hand, and east Denmark and the Oder and middle Danube on the other.

The trail was pioneered by the north Carpathian area, as it took over from the declining central German region around 1800 BC, and is marked by a scatter of the distinctive forms of curvilinear-decorated axes through the territory of the former group and up to the west Baltic, where a dozen swords of Apa type have been found. If we are not being misled by different conditions of preservation (such as local practices of hoarding and ritual deposition), it looks as if the finest objects were travelling over the longest distance, to reach the hands of powerful local chiefs. This has great importance for social reconstruction, since it implies a network of contacts and even specific alliances stretching right across the North European Plain and bypassing earlier centres of power. As well as swords and battleaxes, which were imitated in a specific local style, spearheads appeared in Scandinavia for the first time. These items, still relatively rare, occur only in hoards; but the élite were also distinguished by burial in circular mounds or tumuli, in a manner that was coming to replace flat-grave cemeteries over a larger part of west-central Europe.

In a more generalized way, the influence of Carpathian bronzeworking industries also affected areas to the west—along the Danube, in the Alpine foreland, up the Rhine to the Atlantic, and also down the Rhône. This can be seen not only in the spread of new forms such as spearheads, but also in the more subtle, ogival outlines of dagger-blades. Soon these, too, gradually lengthened into swords, which took the narrow, thrusting form of dirks or rapiers rather than the broad, slashing form of the axe-wielding areas. Women's appearance, too, was affected by the spread of more elaborate bronze pendants, anklets, and long spiral bracelets; while a distinctive form of wheel-headed pin may indicate that local élites had now acquired that ultimate symbol of prestige, the chariot. Tumulus burial came to be practised over the areas linked by the Rhine and upper Danube, and this increasingly unified area is generally referred to as the territory of the Tumulus cultures (although tumuli were used in the Atlantic area too, in continuation of an unbroken tradition going back to Bell-Beaker times). This west-central European group of cultures rapidly became a competitor with the older-established

HILT OF A BRONZE SWORD from Denmark, *c.*1500 BC. The characteristic octagonal-sectioned hilt, decorated with incised circular and semicircular motifs, is recognizable as an import from the area of the Tumulus cultures and was probably made in the north Alpine region.

NECKLACE OF IMPORTED AMBER from a rich female burial under a tumulus at Upton Lovell, Wiltshire, England, *c.* sixteenth century BC: one of the most richly equipped female burials of the period. It also contained sheet goldwork from clothing, a bronze awl and knife, and pottery vessels. The beads include both simple forms and complex-bored spacer plates.

Carpathian groups in the long-distance trade with the north. A vigorous branch of the tumulus-building culture became established in north-west Germany, centred on the Lüneburger Heide, from whence trade routes pushed up the dry outwash-sands into western Jutland. From here objects such as amber entered into interregional circulation along the new axis of alliances; and south German metal and metalwork reached, and began to influence, Scandinavia. Here the local bronze industries reached a new height, making spiral-decorated weapons and female ornaments (collars, belt-plates) in a distinctive local technique based on skilled casting. The Atlantic areas, such as Britain and Brittany, also benefited from this westward shift of activity; while the Baltic area was increasingly linked by canoe-traffic in the kinds of ships shown on contemporary rock engravings, and which themselves became one of the symbols of élite power.

Meanwhile, in the Carpathian basin, output continued undiminished. While the western parts such as Pannonia and west Slovakia joined the new Tumulus axis, the eastern areas continued to elaborate earlier traditions and to expand production of bronze and gold. There are hints that new sets of long-distance links may have been established southward, from Transylvania along the lower Danube to the Black Sea and thus with the communities of the north Aegean and the growing power of Mycenae. A gold dag-

BURIAL OF A 20-YEAR-OLD WOMAN from a tumulus at Egtved, south Jutland, *c.*1370 BC. The body and a birch-bark drink-container lay on a cowhide and was covered by a coarse woollen blanket. The burial took place in summer, and the woollen clothing consisted of a string skirt and a short-sleeved shirt, with a woven belt and bronze spiked belt-disc.

ger from Perşinari in Romania, found with three gold halberd-blades, seems to show Aegean (or Anatolian) influence in the design of the hilt; and the appearance of lathe-finished gold vessels around the western Black Sea (Vulchitrun, Rădeni, Kryzhovlin) marks the spread of this more advanced technique into temperate Europe, where it was also to be employed in fashioning cups of wood, shale, and amber. The appearance in the Mycenae Shaft Graves of objects (including horsegear) which are decorated with *Wellenband* compass-work might suggest that circum-Pontic horse-training skills were among the less tangible products of these contacts. More concrete evidence of long-distance contacts, this time with the Tumulus area, is provided by amber beads which include a characteristic spacer-plate with complex boring for use in a crescentic necklace, which must have travelled via southern Germany and Italy to arrive in an early Mycenaean royal grave. Thus Mycenae tapped the wealth of its European hinterland, before making its own debut as an Aegean power (see Chapter 6). Signs of continuing northward contacts with the Tumulus area in subsequent centuries (and especially, perhaps, at the height of its power in the fourteenth century) are the appearance of folding stools—a symbol of power in the Mediterranean world—and also perhaps more sophisticated forms of carpentry used in the construction of chariot wheels, as indicated by the earliest metal models (Tøbol and Trundholm). The folding stools are best evidenced in far-off Denmark, where the unique conditions of preservation in coffins made of hollowed-out tree-trunks set under stone cairns in barrows have yielded not only wooden objects but also complete sets of woollen clothing. Although decorated with a variety of devices such as embroidery, the monochrome appearance of these textiles contrasts with the elaborate coloured weaves shown on frescoes from the Bronze Age Aegean; and the disparity in cultural sophistication demonstrates the impact which introduced styles and imported southern pieces would have had on remote northern peoples. Yet the links were too rare and too erratic to produce a fundamental cultural transformation or to build up the kinds of social interdependence which were to characterize the relations between urban societies and their barbarian hinterlands in the first millennium. Bronze Age Europe remained an autonomous domain.

The West Mediterranean World

While the Aegean and Anatolia were increasingly drawn into the international world of the east Mediterranean Bronze Age, with its own economic and political concerns, the west Mediterranean remained part of prehistoric Europe. With the growth of Aegean (and especially Mycenaean) power, Sicily, Italy, and Sardinia were affected more deeply than inland Europe by the growth of maritime trade routes; but southern France, the Balearic Islands, and Iberia were largely untouched until the closing years of the second millennium, when the Mycenaean palaces had been swept away in the changes which brought the Near Eastern Bronze Age world to a close, and a new generation of adventurous traders was to penetrate further than their palace-based predecessors.

OBJECTS FROM GRAVES of the earlier Bronze Age El Argar culture, *c*.2000 BC, Almería, southern Spain. The pots suggest metal prototypes, known from this period in Brittany. Male-associated objects include weapons (daggers, halberd), and female ones include silver bracelets made from local native silver. Fortified hilltop settlements are known from this period.

In southern Spain the Bell-Beaker intervention of the later third millennium was largely absorbed by local Copper Age groups, but the innovations which they introduced, and the long-term degradation of the environment in this arid zone, eroded the stability of communities like Los Millares with its small-scale horticultural base and ritual-centred polity. The new centres, although broadly within the coastal zone of Almería and Valencia, were in a different part and in different sorts of location, which themselves testify to a radical change in the way of life — probably involving a greater element of livestock-rearing, and the use of cisterns for storing water. For the most part they consist of hilltop settlements, some in spectacular positions, defended by thick stone walls and enclosing numbers of rectangular huts layed out in streets. They begin at around 2200 BC. At El Argar, which gives its name to the whole group, large numbers of individual burials were recovered, both in cist graves and at a later phase in large pottery storage-jars or brewing-vats. The burials were accompanied by plentiful grave goods: the men with copper or bronze axes, daggers or halberds, the women with awls and knives and sometimes with silver ornaments, including rings and lobed diadems. The pottery is especially fine, although handmade and often round-based: it includes elegant pedestalled chalices and other drinking vessels in dark micaceous clay, whose appearance somewhat resembles the silver cups known from the same time in Brittany, and were perhaps made here also, though none has been preserved. The wealth of metal, which indicates a comparable economic role for bronze as in the rest of Europe, was nevertheless largely of local origin, in the plentiful polymetallic deposits of that region. The quantities of silver (perhaps largely native rather than a product of cupellation from lead) are unusual in Bronze Age Europe, but probably reflect local sources, and it does not seem to have had any special role in circulation. The bronze metallurgy is rather simple by central European standards, being mostly flat castings of rather basic design; and despite some innovations the tradition lasted throughout the second millennium.

The west Mediterranean islands show the same transition as in Spain: a shift, after the Bell-Beaker period, from temples and burial-sites for communal ritual to individual graves and evidence for fortification. In Malta, for example, the temple of Tarxien was overlain by a cemetery whose individual cremations were accompanied by bronze flat-axes and daggers. In Corsica and Sardinia the megalithic monuments gave way to secular stone constructions for defensive purposes: the *torri* and *nuraghi* which were later, in the thirteenth century and after, to grow to quite complex constructions, as with the *talayots* of the Balearic Islands.

In these areas, the early second millennium was a period of relative isolation. Southern France, on the other hand, was continuously affected by impulses down the Rhône valley from Bell-Beaker times onward, and shows a comparable succession to that in central Europe, through an early Bronze Age with solid-hilted triangular daggers to a local facies of the Tumulus complex. Its history was tied to that of inland Europe. Northern Italy, too, was closely linked to developments further north, and its lakeside settlements form part of a circum-Alpine province. This resemblance is not just one of environment: the increased use of the Alpine passes, and the use of upper valleys as transhumance routes (often marked by concentrations of rock engravings, as at Monte Bego and Val Camonica) led to a greater degree of cultural interchange across the mountains, both with Slovenia (and so to the Carpathian basin) and with Switzerland and the Rhône valley. The bronze industries of Italy thus parallel those of central Europe to a considerable degree, and substantial numbers of imports can be identified which testify to a desire to acquire the latest developments in weaponry and ornaments, and even fortifications such as timber-laced ramparts. Central Italy has more of its own character, however, with substantial sites in the coastal plains and extensive areas of occupation in the Apennines whose material culture is less rich and which may represent an extensive, stock-rearing economy. Nevertheless the lowland sites are known to have participated in trade with the Mycenaean world, so that it cannot be assumed that the area was economically autonomous. Further south, in southern Italy and Sicily, Mycenaean contacts caused substantial changes.

It would be wrong to see this Mycenaean penetration of the central Mediterranean simply in 'colonial' terms, like Europeans reaching America. The organizational disparity was far less stark. The Tyrrhenian Sea, between Sicily, southern Italy, and Sardinia, already supported an indigenous maritime exchange cycle partly centred on the Lipari Islands, where the deep levels on the Lipari acropolis show a succession of large buildings. A localized coastal trading system distributing metals and other materials grew up here during the third millennium, and it is likely that Minoan and Mycenaean traders began by establishing contacts with it. The voyage from Corfu to the Gulf of Taranto is a short one, whence a coastal route to the Strait of Messina gives access to the Aeolian Islands; and some trade may have occurred in this way in the earlier second millennium. By the sixteenth century, when the Mycenae Shaft Graves were in use, it is likely that these contacts provided the route by which materials such as amber reached the Peloponnese. (The Adriatic route did not come into use until the thirteenth century.) During the fifteenth and fourteenth centuries these transactions grew in scale, though they were probably still mediated through something like ports of trade on Lipari and Vivara, a small island off Naples. This west Italian link provided the point at which long-distance European exchange systems met those of the Mediterranean, and Italian metals entered the Mycenaean system. Sicily, too, was involved in this maritime trade, perhaps in local products rather than long-distance commodities, and by the fourteenth century a remarkable palatial building with corridors and suites of rectangular rooms was built at Thapsos near Syracuse in Sicily. While not itself Mycenaean, such a structure could only exist in the context of a complex economy and external exchanges such as those indicated by nearby tomb finds of Mycenaean and Cypriot pottery and metalwork.

Westward along the Mediterranean, therefore, there was a successive decline in complexity—from the international bulk trade of the east Mediterranean, through the contact zone of Italy and the central Mediterranean islands, to the relative isolation of Iberia. The rapidity of this fall-off reflects both the limitations of Bronze Age shipping before the innovations of the late second millennium, and also the centralized nature of trade in the command economies of the Bronze Age east Mediterranean. It was the revolution in this system, and the restructuring of maritime trade from around 1300 onward, that unleashed a further phase of activity with profound implications for later Bronze Age Europe.

Conclusion: On the Edge of the Bronze Age World

The transformation of Europe, which occurred between 2500 and 1300 BC, was cultural and social rather than economic and political. The fundamental changes which accompanied urbanization affected no more than the edge of the Continent, and while the Bronze Age in the Near East saw a succession of states and empires on an increasing scale, Europe retained its autonomy. What did change was the nature of its social organization and how this found material expression. Small, competing dynasties of local chiefs set up complex networks of alliances to secure the material symbols of success. No one area emerged as so different from its neighbours as to restructure the nature of its production or to engage in an unequal trade. No fortresses dominated the landscape and enforced territorial boundaries or asserted territorial control. Certain commodities that were universally valued brought prosperity beyond agricultural wealth to areas which produced them or which occupied a middleman position in their distribution; but this was not achieved by social stratification and the exploitation of dependent labour—rather by participation in an elaborate game of one-upmanship which depended on access to symbolic tokens of success. Even possession of simple items like razors and tweezers could alter bodily appearance so as to enhance social distance. The proximity of urban cultures ensured that new forms of material products (and the means of producing them) could be acquired to keep the game in play: novel eating and drinking habits, clothing, furniture, means of transport, prestige ornaments, and weaponry. Yet European societies did not become dependent on a steady flow of exotic commodities, like the 'barbarian' societies of the Iron Age. They existed on the margins of the Bronze Age world system, altered by its existence yet not forming an active part of it.

German scholars describe the climax of this period as the *Hochbronzezeit*, the 'High Bronze Age' before the changes which affected the whole of the Old World after 1300 BC: the collapse of the palatial experiment in the east Mediterranean and the beginning of the Iron Age there, the surge of bronzeworking activity in Urnfield Europe, the Caucasus, and highland Iran, the beginnings of true nomadism on the steppes. This later European Bronze Age was very different in character from the one which preceded it; and its hill-forts, field systems, flat cemeteries, scrap hoards, and votive finds from rivers combine to suggest a less stable and ordered society, in which territorial struggle was more serious and radical reorganization was necessary.

8

The Collapse of Aegean Civilization at the End of the Late Bronze Age

MERVYN POPHAM

THE years around 1200 BC witnessed a dramatic and profound change in the political map of the east Mediterranean. In Greece the Mycenaean palaces were destroyed, while further afield the two great powers, Egypt and the Hittites, came under severe external attack which led to the rapid decline of Egyptian control and the extinction of the Hittite capital of Bogaz Kuy. Intermediate states in Syria, Palestine, and Cyprus were attacked, and destruction throughout the region was widespread and devastating. The century which followed is one of confusion: in many areas there was emigration and a regrouping of the population, with some regions being left virtually desolate: in other places we find the settlement of 'alien' peoples or the establishment of mixed communities combining different elements of previous cultures with new features. Afterwards, it looked initially as though some stability and a reasonable prosperity might result, but overall this recovery failed, though to varying degrees in different regions.

In Greece there were further attacks, severe depopulation, and a rapid decline into the virtual extinction of its Mycenaean civilization. Aspects of Hittite culture continued for some time in north Syria, but its homeland remained deserted. Much of Palestine was slow to recover, and survival was at a low ebb; exceptionally, settlements in southern Palestine with their new populations entrenched their position. In Cyprus the rebuilt cities and the flowering in arts and crafts, which they witnessed, were destroyed and there followed a rapid recession. Egypt, no longer an imperial power, suffered further external attacks and internal dissensions.

The cause or causes for the collapse of the old Late Bronze Age civilizations are much disputed and may well be multiple. There exists, however, a considerable factual basis of archaeological evidence to which may be added the reasonable assumption that the general uniformity of the picture in the east Mediterranean indicates certain common factors and interconnections of some kind.

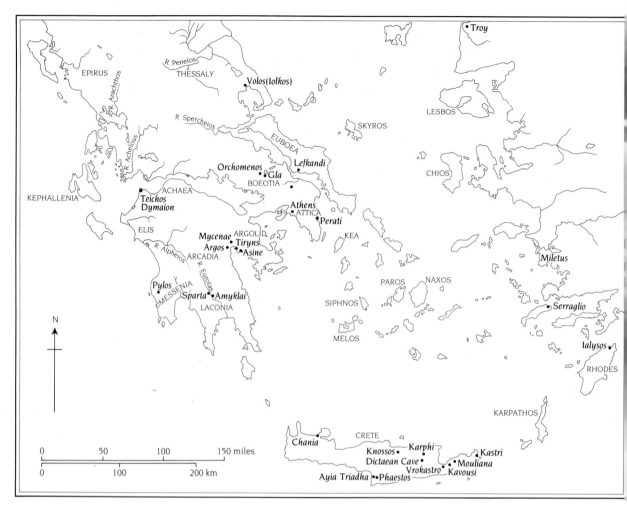

THE MAIN SITES mentioned in the text.

Our main region of interest is Greece, and the Aegean, extending to Crete in the south, and we start with a review of the evidence there.

Preparations for Attack and the Destructions of c.1200 BC

By around 1300 BC the beginning of the Late Helladic IIIB stage, radical changes had taken place in the Mycenaean kingdoms. Their rulers and aristocrats were no longer concerned with constructing magnificent stone-built tombs (tholoi), and, indeed, there is little evidence for the continuance of any rich burials of the kind which had been such a feature of previous centuries. The palaces at Tiryns and Pylos, and probably those, too, at Mycenae and Thebes had already assumed the form which they would essentially retain until their final destruction. In the course of the thirteenth century (the Late Helladic IIIB stage), building resources were largely diverted, both at the main centres and in part elsewhere, to fortifications. At Mycenae and Tiryns the walls were strengthened and enlarged and access built underground to outside springs. Similar measures were undertaken on the Acropolis at Athens where access to its water source was secured by impressive, deep engineering work. In northern Boeotia, the new, fortified settlement of Gla was constructed on a plateau in the Copais basin. Equally indicative of danger from invasion is the building of a wall or fort with bastions at the Isthmus of Corinth, which may have been designed to seal off access to the Peloponnese by land from the north.

THE UNDERGROUND SPRING at Mycenae (*left*), approached by a descending stairway from within the walls.

THE NEAR VERTICAL PASSAGE (*right*) with steps leading to the spring from within the citadel on the Acropolis at Athens.

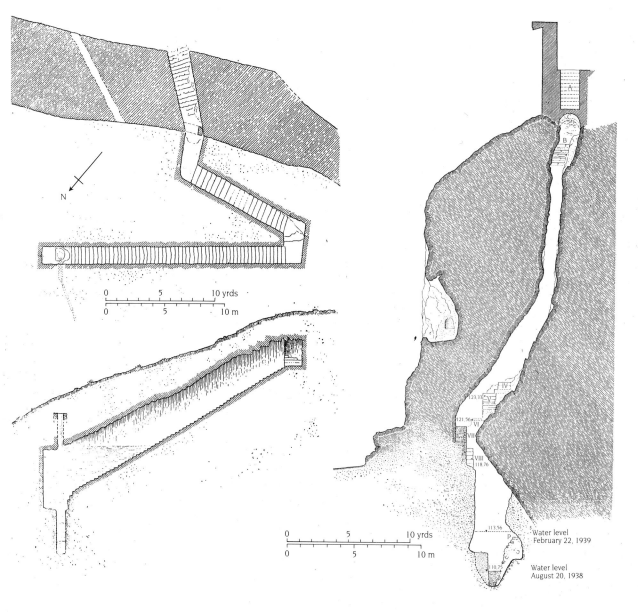

This and other evidence point to a general fear of attack and, even more, to serious preparations for prolonged seige. Reasons for this fear have been variously explained; but two causes appear most probable, aggressive interstate rivalry, or an external threat. The defences at the Isthmus and their disposition suggest preparations for an attack from the north, perhaps coming from beyond Boeotia if, as appears likely, the citadel at Gla was intended as a defensible refuge centre and military outpost. The fortification of the Acropolis at Athens would then be readily explainable since that city lies on the route of any hostile land force making its way to the Peloponnese. But equally, in a country where many of the principal centres lay on or close to the sea, defence against piratical raids also remains a possibility.

The main alternative explanation of interstate conflict is only too likely, given the geography of Greece with its limited pockets of agricultural land and the high population dependent on them at this time. Later Greek history, especially in the fifth and fourth centuries, clearly illustrates how rivalry between neighbouring cities or coalitions of states could arise. It is the concept of a prevailing Mycenaean empire with Mycenae as its centre, derived largely from the Homeric epic of the Trojan War, which has led to this possibility being given less attention than it deserves.

In balancing the probabilities of the various explanations, the limitations of archaeological evidence become apparent and, as is often the case, it may be that the likely answer is revealed more in the aftermath of events rather than in the details of their perceivable course, to which we now turn.

It is clear that some sequence of events is discernible, at least in outline. Destruction at Thebes occurred shortly before the beginning of the thirteenth century when an ivory workshop within the citadel was burnt. This, however, could easily have been a local, even accidental, fire, unless the destruction of the large building at Orchomenos is to be ascribed to the same stage: publication is at present too sketchy to decide.

The deliberate destruction of Pylos and its palace by fire is, however, unequivocal and certainly of major importance. This event, in my view, took place very early in the thirteenth century, and apparently at a time when no major threat had been anticipated, given that the Acropolis was unfortified. If this dating is correct, it could well have led other major centres to begin to look seriously to their own protection and to strengthen their fortifications. The results of attack are later to be seen at Mycenae where buildings just outside its citadel were destroyed as, also, were nearby settlements, including Zygouries and Berbati. This may conventionally be placed at about the mid-century or somewhat later, though precision is not possible. Further strengthening and enlargement of the fortifications of Mycenae, with the possible withdrawal of some industrial activities within its walls, can be viewed as a natural response. Similar preparations were made elsewhere, as we have seen, especially at Tiryns. Despite massive and elaborate defences, these protective measures proved inadequate to meet the major threat when it materialized around the end of the century. The fortresses of Mycenae, Tiryns, and Dendra in the Argolid were overrun and burnt. Destruction was not, however, by any means limited to this region. Evidence for similar catastrophies is apparent elsewhere in the Peloponnese, near Sparta (the Menelaion) and at Nichoria. Further afield, such centres as Thebes and the fortress of Gla in Boeotia were also destroyed; still further north the settlement of Iolkos in Thessaly suffered. Whether these events were more or less contemporary is, and is likely to remain, uncertain. The limitations of archaeological evidence—essentially the pottery at this stage—when uniformity was less strong than before, leaves a leeway of at least a quarter of a century.

The Results of the Destructions

The Greek mainland and the Aegean Islands   The extent, however, of the disasters is not in doubt. Not only major centres suffered but their surrounding territories as well. The few minor settlements, which have been explored archaeologically with few exceptions present the same picture of general destruction. More significant are the results of field surveys which reveal a widespread desertion of the countryside, a picture supported by the cessation of the use of many burial grounds. There were, of course, survivors and, as we shall see, some settlements revived. In particular, the old centres of Mycenae and Tiryns were partially restored and well populated, perhaps following some withdrawal from the open countryside, an explanation which may also account for the increase in burials at Asine, in the south Argolid. Another outcome of considerable relevance is the movement of peoples. Certain regions now show an increase in population, the result, it would appear, of a congregation of refugees from other areas which were presumably under greater threat. The overall situation is very apparent when we compare distribution maps of sites known to have been occupied in the thirteenth century at the time of the Late Helladic IIIB destructions with those afterwards when large areas must have been very sparsely occupied indeed.

To what extent the islands of the Aegean were also affected is far less clear, since very few settlements of this period, as distinct from cemeteries, have been excavated and even fewer adequately published. Two islands, Siphnos and Melos, show concern about fortifications in the thirteenth century. On the latter, the long-lived settlement of Phylakopi suffered some damage but survived. On Paros, trouble of some kind is likely to account for the establishment on a rocky eminence of a fortified settlement away from the central plain soon after 1200 BC. Further westward, our information is again deficient about the Dodecanese and Mycenaean settlements on the coast of Asia Minor. Rhodes sees some contraction in its known sites soon after 1200 BC, but with an increase in burials at the main citadel site of Ialysos. Such a pattern signifies perhaps a retreat into safer locations, though it does not exclude the possibility of the arrival of refugees, some from the mainland and others from nearby islands such as Karpathos, which is now apparently deserted. Serraglio, the main town of Cos, suffered at least partially from destruction by fire, but remained occupied for some time afterwards.

On the opposite shore of Asia Minor, the Mycenaean colony of Miletus was burnt—

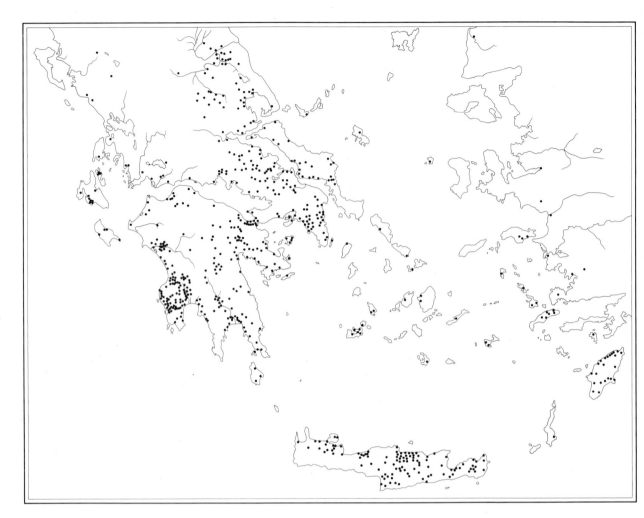

SITES AND CEMETERIES attested in the LH IIIB period.

according to the latest account of the excavators around 1200 BC—an event followed by the building of a massive fortification wall. The evidence is thin but indicates fore-knowledge of danger, followed by attack and disruption, the latter apparent in the seem-ing desertion of several of the islands.

Crete The picture on Crete, to the south, is much clearer and, in certain aspects, resembles that on the mainland—destructions of a few sites, abandonment of many more, with a contraction in the number of known settlements. In this case, there fol-lowed a frequent, though not uniform, retreat to more easily defensible locations. At Palaikastro, for instance, the inhabitants left the long-lived town on the plain by the seashore in favour of the nearby natural acropolis of Kastri, occupied again after a gap of some 800 years.

The situation, however, is more complex than this, a perception perhaps possible because we are now better informed. Even allowing for the individual character of the

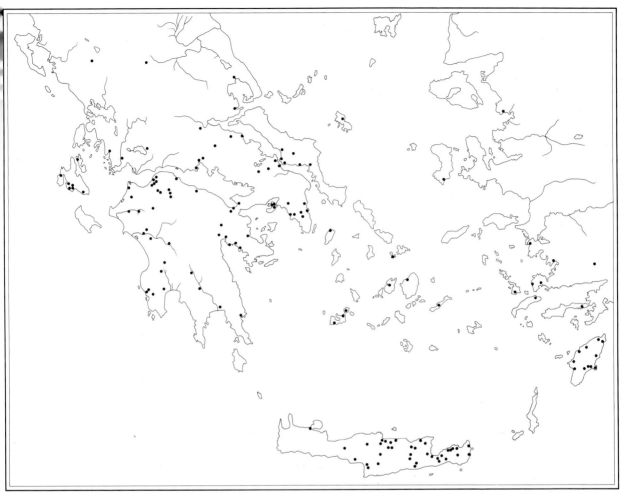

SITES AND CEMETERIES attested in the LH IIIC period, showing the extent of depopulation and dispersal of peoples.

island and its geographical position, this knowledge may perhaps give a better lead towards understanding events and their causes elsewhere, and so is nevertheless worth considering more fully.

Though the island never properly recovered from the severe destructions around 1450 BC and the loss of its empire abroad, yet by the thirteenth century it was again well populated and enjoying a reasonable degree of prosperity. At this time its main centre is likely to have moved from Knossos in the centre to Chania (ancient Kydonia) in the west. Towards the end of the century, after a long stage of isolation, Crete, once again, began to make an impact abroad, with pottery exports as its main indicator. Vases, principally but not exclusively from western Crete, reached Cyprus in some numbers, with a thin but widespread scatter in the Dodecanese and mainland Greece. More surprisingly they were reaching southern Italy and even Sardinia in considerable quantity, and, in this case, the exchange was mutual. On a few Cretan sites, including Chania, there

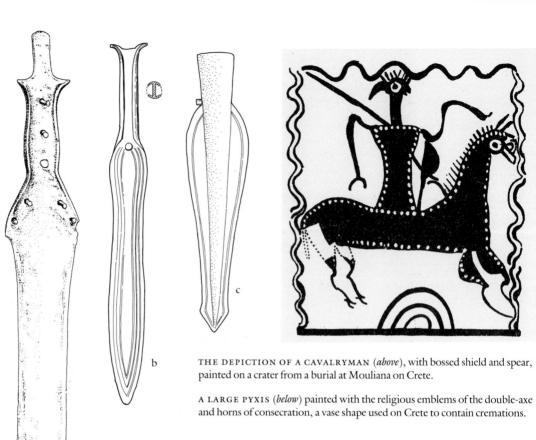

THE DEPICTION OF A CAVALRYMAN (*above*), with bossed shield and spear, painted on a crater from a burial at Mouliana on Crete.

A LARGE PYXIS (*below*) painted with the religious emblems of the double-axe and horns of consecration, a vase shape used on Crete to contain cremations.

(*a*) AN ADVANCED VERSION of a bronze Naue II cut-and-thrust sword from Crete.
(*b*) AN ITALIAN-TYPE BRONZE KNIFE from a burial at Knossos.
(*c*) AN EXAMPLE FROM CRETE of the IIIC short-socketed spearhead.

a

b

c

appeared a small number of clearly alien vases, handmade and of grey ware, principally large jars, bowls, and cups, parallels for which, in shape and fabric, are closest to the pottery of southern Italy. Datable to the same period are a very few bronze imports apparently from the same region, a knife at Knossos and a fibula at Mallia; there could be others in now undatable contexts. Their importance, however, lies mainly in that they are the known forerunners of more which were to arrive after the dislocations and destructions towards the end of the thirteenth century.

The evidence comes largely from the offerings made in the sacred cave at Psychro in the high mountain plateau, not far from the refugee settlement of Karphi, a site with a wide vista of the coastline, but terribly exposed to the winds and to the snows of winter. Among the bronze dedications, which have survived extensive robbing, are thirteen objects with a strong claim to be of Italian or central European types and probable origin, daggers and knives in particular, some fibulae, and a swivel pin. The two hilts among the offerings of swords or daggers are Aegean in shape, as are the spearheads. For European versions of these we must look to three warrior burials of the twelfth-century IIIC stage, at the east of the island in which were placed five Naue II cut-and-thrust swords (not all contemporary) and a new version of the spearhead with a very short cast socket. Additional similar weapons without a definite provenance are very likely to have been found in the same region. To these may be added other innovations in the form of two shield bosses and the occurrence of cremation. One example of this, at Mouliana, had been placed in a large crater on one side of which is depicted the first known Aegean cavalryman of the Bronze Age with a bossed shield and spear. Cremations of the same period elsewhere on Crete were placed in large pyxis-shaped containers, some depicting the old Minoan religious emblems of double axe and 'horns of consecration'.

The Causes of the Destructions and the Near Eastern Evidence

We have strayed beyond the disasters of 1200 BC and well into the succeeding IIIC stage: this was necessary in order to place the earlier Italian and other alien objects on the island into a historical framework. It will, moreover, have wider implications in other regions as we shall see later.

Taken as a whole, the evidence presents a strong case for believing that, even before the destructions and dislocation on Crete, the island was already well known to the Italians, some of whom may even have joined existing settlements, bringing their pots with them. Intensification of these interrelations, with weaponry very much a part, followed. An added complication to the picture is the arrival of a group of Mycenaeans from the mainland, who hitherto appear to have shown little interest in Crete since the early fourteenth century, when their hegemony over the island, centred at Knossos, came to a violent end. Mycenaean pottery and figurines appear at Ayia Triadha—not an acropolis site—followed by the setting up of a shrine there with large votive animal figurines. Religion had long been a major feature in Minoan life and remained so. Just before the

ONE OF THE LARGE CLAY STATUES (*right*) from the shrine at Karphi, wearing the religious emblem of horns of consecration on its head.

A BRONZE STATUETTE (*far right*) from Enkomi in Cyprus of a warrior god wearing a horned helmet and carrying a round shield.

troubles, shrines had been set up in earlier Minoan buildings, in the villa at Mitropolis, in Gournia, and amid the ruins of the palace at Knossos, representing perhaps a call for assistance from the great ones of the past. Those were abandoned around 1200 BC, but the subsequent shrines built at Karphi and elsewhere, with their large religious clay statues, and the renewed interest in cave worship, may reflect a very real need for divine support in continuing times of distress.

Emigration This Mycenaean arrival on Crete is not the only evidence for a diaspora of mainlanders. Mycenaean type pottery, implying at least the presence of Mycenaean potters, is one of the features of the very complicated picture in the Near East following the disruptions there. Thus we find at Tarsus, on Cyprus and in Philistia the almost wholesale adoption of not only Mycenaean decorative motives but vessel shapes as well, which are not in the native tradition. The presence of a Mycenaean element in these areas is hardly to be doubted, but if they were refugees from the troubles at home, as is sometimes maintained, they chose unlikely havens. That they were prisoners of war seems a more likely explanation, or, a theory favoured by some scholars that some Mycenaeans had joined in the attacks in that region.

We have now surveyed the position before and just after the wholesale destructions in Greece and their reflection in the islands. The magnitude of the disaster, its extent, and the resultant depopulation, disruption, and movement of peoples in some regions to more easily defended locations elsewhere require a cause well beyond that of interstate warfare, internal dissension, or a 'systems collapse' within the kingdoms themselves, though these factors may have played some part in hastening events and undermining morale. The success of the attacks against such well-protected centres as Mycenae, Tiryns, Gla, and perhaps Athens, too, where a bronzeworker's hoard remained unrecovered on the Acropolis, points to an efficient military force. Assuming it was not Mycenaean, the insurgents attacked and departed or, if (as I believe) some stayed on, their numbers must have been few, insufficient to populate the regions from which their inhabitants fled or to alter, to any appreciable extent, the basic continuation of the previous culture.

We have, in effect, defined aggressive, well-armed, efficient and ruthless raiders. Obvious candidates for this role are not far to find: an element of that warrior fleet of whose destructive activities there survive written accounts and depictions in the Near East and especially in Egypt. For example, Rameses III had vivid scenes of the land and sea attack on his country engraved on the walls of the Temple at Medinet Habu. The enemy came, we are told, after devastating centres of power further north, but they failed to conquer Egypt. The scene of the sea raid depicts the distinctive armament of the attackers who include a detachment with horned helmets, large round shields; some with swords, others wielding spears. Similarly equipped soldiers had appeared on earlier Egyptian depictions both as part of an attacking force and as mercenaries in the Egyptian army. The names, too, given to some of the contingents of the sea raiders had appeared before, in particular those of the Shardana and Shekelesh, who will concern us most.

The outcome in the Near East is beyond the geographical scope of this chapter. Here it must suffice to say that some of the attacking force stayed on; one element, whom we later know as the Philistines, settled in southern Palestine; others formed an important and probably dominant element in the rebuilding of the main cities of Cyprus, where, exceptionally, there followed a phase of unusual prosperity and a flowering of the arts and crafts in which Mycenaeans and Near Easterners clearly played an important part. It is there, significantly, that the majority of swords and knives with a European ancestry, such as those we have seen on Crete, occur; while the bronze statuette of a war god found at Enkomi is equipped with a horned helmet, round shield, and spear, closely reminiscent of the armament of one contingent of the sea raiders.

Before returning to our proper sphere, the Aegean, two interrelated issues deserve attention since they concern the interpretation of evidence already presented. The first concerns the homeland of two of the contingents of the Sea Raiders, the Shardana and the Shekelesh, with a possible third, the Teresh. These peoples have been thought to be in some way connected with the regions later known as Sardinia, Sikelia (Sicily), and,

more dubiously, with Etruria, either as being the locations in which they eventually settled after the troubles—the more favoured view—or as being their place of origin. If
there is an association, as seems likely at least in the case of Sardinia, then the evidence
on Crete of possible settlers there from the West before the raids, increases the probability of the latter explanation. Crete, moreover, would be a convenient stepping-stone
on the route to the Near East and to Libya where these groups were participants in an
attacking force against Egypt a generation or so before the sea raid. The Shardana, at
least, had been active before this and some had been enlisted as mercenaries in the Egyptian army. This leads to the second issue of whether the same may not have happened on
the Greek mainland, a possibility strongly favoured by Catling in his studies of the
weapons of this period. He suggests that the new, non-Aegean armament was introduced into Greece by mercenaries hired by the Mycenaean kings as a military need in the
time of increasing danger before 1200 BC. If so, as has been seen, they failed to provide
an effective defence.

Until some twenty five years ago most general accounts of the Mycenaean Age concluded with the destruction of the palaces, implying that the Dark Age then closed in on
Greece. Due largely to the masterly survey of the succeeding era by Desborough and in
part to recent excavations we can now see clearly that this was by no means the case.
Indeed, Mycenaean civilization was still to survive for nearly a century, and all was not a
steady and uninterrupted decline. Any account, however, of this stage meets serious
difficulties, not least from the early excavations of Schliemann, when the palaces at
Mycenae and at Tiryns were cleared without any adequate record being kept of the pottery found in these and other buildings. To some extent, therefore, it remains only reasonable conjecture that the destruction of these palaces is ascribed to the events at the
end of the thirteenth century. If so, we can be far from certain that they were not at least
partially reoccupied to house the succeeding rulers, for such there must have been whatever the changes to the social order. There are no written records to assist us on this point
and this alone makes the loss of any palace bureaucracy a likely assumption. Nor, curiously, have we any evidence for a royal residence or ruler's house and, so far, no 'princely'
or 'aristocratic' burials have been found to indicate any clear social distinctions. So, in
these circumstances, it might be better to admit that we are virtually ignorant on this
issue, while wondering whether it was at this stage that the leader became known as a
'basileus' instead of a 'wanax', and whether there was, in fact, some form of interrupted
kingship down to the kings of Argos in the late eighth century, of whose existence we,
again, have some knowledge from written sources.

Furthermore, there is the hindrance that for the more recent and quite extensive excavations at these and other important centres, such as Thebes, Volos, and Teichos
Dymaion to single out but a few, only preliminary accounts have been published, some
quite insufficient to form any firm conclusions.

If, therefore, undue prominence is given here to the site of Xeropolis at Lefkandi in
Euboea, and to the cemetery at Perati on the east coast of Attica, this is not because they

THE DEPICTION AT MEDINET
HABU· (*above*) of the sea attack on
Egypt, defeated by Ramesses III.

PART OF THE SAME SCENE (*left*)
showing details of one of the
attacking ships with its contingent
of warriors equipped with horned
helmets and large circular shields.

may adequately reflect events over a much larger area, but on account of the full excavation of the latter and its detailed publication, and, in the case of Lefkandi, the unusual circumstances that the site is well stratified and suffered little from post-Bronze Age occupation: it is, also, helpful in providing some counterbalance to the great preponderance of evidence from burials.

Certain features of the post-1200 BC era have already been mentioned in order to assess the nature and cause of the upheavals: the considerable resultant depopulation with the virtual abandonment of some regions; the new concentration of peoples in other areas; the probability of some emigration; a feeling of insecurity to be seen in the movement to natural acropolis sites and the congregation towards those already well fortified. Other features touched upon have been the appearance of new types of weaponry with a European, and in some instances a specifically Italian, origin; the presence on some sites before the disasters of a small but significant amount of completely alien handmade vases (and Tiryns should be added to the sites already mentioned) with, again, in certain instances, a specifically Italian connection being most likely; warrior burials and the appearance of cremation.

Some of these aspects will be explored further but, before doing so, it is necessary to set out a chronological sequence, however imprecisely, into which distinctive features or changes can be fitted. Such a sequence was established some forty years ago by Furumark in his great study of Mycenaean pottery, when he proposed three main stages in Late Helladic IIIC which subsequent knowledge has confirmed to be a valid and useful chronological framework. Since then various additional subdivisions or stages have been proposed but it has yet to be seen whether they have sufficient general application to be other than valuable but local refinements. The duration of each of Furumark's three phases is at present little more than intelligent guesswork and they need not concern us here beyond the dates for the beginning and of the end of the IIIC stage as a whole, starting around 1200 BC, though it could well be a little later, and finishing about 1100 in round figures. The divisions, based on pottery styles, may be characterized, with a more general validity as will appear, as a period of stabilization, followed by recovery and innovation, and ending in eventual impoverishment and decline.

Consolidation after the Destructions

For the initial stage, we may turn first to the site of Xeropolis at Lefkandi and, in part, to Euboea more generally. No certain evidence has been found that the settlement suffered in the general 1200 BC destructions, though it must be emphasized in this and other respects that only a very small part of the town has been explored other than superficially. There is, however, reasonable certainty that the whole of the hill site, which was fortified, underwent complete reconstruction at the beginning of the IIIC stage when it received a great increase in its population. The same seems true of other sites in central Euboea. The likely origin for these 'refugees', if such they were, is from across the water

THE EXTENSIVE SEASIDE site of Xeropolis at Lefkandi, Euboea.

in Boeotia. The new settlement survived long enough for relayings of the floors to be made as well as some structural remodelling before it was burnt to the ground, a disaster which, I understand, may be general in the central region of the island. The almost immediate levelling of the ruins and reconstruction with a more regular plan and on a somewhat different orientation suggests that the destroyers came to settle.

The pottery used by these first occupants was traditionally Mycenaean in nearly all respects, a somewhat dull and sparsely decorated continuation of that current in the thirteenth century. Exceptional, however, was the presence in a destruction deposit of a handmade and burnished cup of a type at home in southern Italy. It was not the earliest appearance of this ware, for pottery of a similar fabric is present in the earliest level following the newcomers' arrival. Then, however, the predominant shape was different, a shallower cup with a high arching handle. It occurs in very small quantities; much more popular was its imitation in the local wheel-made tradition. On Xeropolis this version had a very short life but, surprisingly, it occurs at a much later stage at Tiryns, Mycenae, and Korakou in the Argolid. It is probable, then, that the initial 'refugees' in Euboea included aliens: contact may have been maintained by them with their homeland for some time after as indicated by the cup mentioned above and a bronze knife, with a non-Mycenaean stop at the top of the blade, found in the same destruction deposits. It remains to be seen whether there exists evidence in Boeotia that these aliens had already arrived and settled there before 1200 BC.

The burning of Xeropolis after its reconstruction shows that troubles continued in the early stages of the twelfth century. How widespread they were it is impossible to say

A HANDMADE AND BURNISHED CUP of Italian type (*right*) and probable origin, found in the earliest LH IIIC destruction at Xeropolis, Lefkandi.

A LOCAL WHEELMADE CUP (*below*) from Xeropolis, imitating the shape of a handmade Italian-type cup, some examples of which were imported at the site.

given the poor evidence available. It may be, however, that two other sites suffered at roughly the same stage, one on Paros, the other in northern Elis, far distant from each other. Occupation and fortification of Koukounaries on Paros by early IIIC has already been mentioned as a possible example of a refuge settlement. It was burnt not long afterwards though no precise chronological correlation can be made with Lefkandi on account of their very different pottery styles.

Matters may be more favourable in the case of Teichos Dymaion, a fortified acropolis at the entrance to the Gulf of Corinth, opposite Kephallenia. Inadequate publication, to date, presents considerable problems; but it appears to have been destroyed, with so many other sites, in the thirteenth century and may then, as in the nearby Ionian Islands, have received fresh arrivals and have strengthened its fortifications in IIIC. It was subsequently again destroyed, but it is uncertain when this occurred and whether the settlement survived thereafter. The main reason for suggesting that its burning and that at

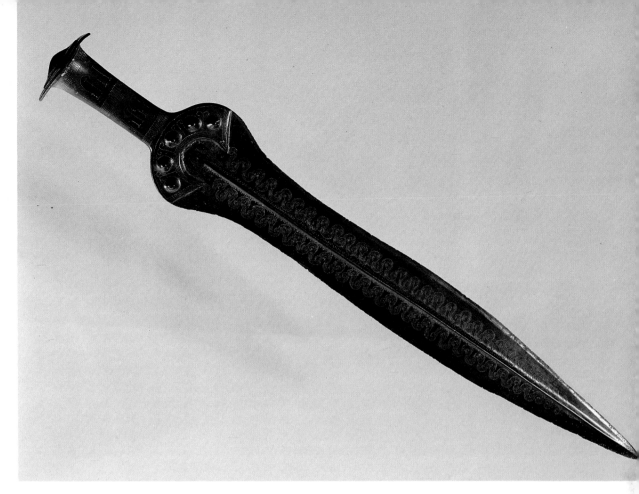

BRONZE SWORD (*above*) from Hajdú-sámson, County Hajdú-Bihar, Hungary, *c.*1800 BC. Found in a sand-pit in 1907, the sword was lying with its point due north, covered by 12 battle-axes lying at right angles across it. Clearly a votive deposit, this cache of weaponry incorporates considerable wealth and craftmanship.

GOLD CUP (*left*), *c.* sixteenth century BC, from Wachtberg-Fritzdorf, near Bonn, Nordrhein-Westfalen, Germany. The biconical cup, 12 cm high, was raised from a single sheet of gold and the handle added as a separate piece, attached by rivets with lozenge-shaped washers. It was probably finished on a lathe to give a regular profile, in the same way as contemporary cups of shale and amber.

Lefkandi might be roughly contemporary rests on use of kylikes, identical in form and decoration, belonging to the destruction levels on both sites. Equally in doubt, unfortunately, is which of the disasters at Teichos Dymaion was responsible for the very unusual state of preservation of the burnt pommel on a knife related to a type recorded in Italy. But whatever the date, its mere existence helps strengthen the opinion of those who hold that the Gulf of Corinth was an important route for the entry of such imported bronzes into Greece.

That weapons with a similar origin continued to circulate in the early stages of IIIC has been seen in the case of Crete. Further evidence comes from the island of Cos where a warrior was buried with a Naue II type sword and short-socketed spear. Another similar spearhead was retrieved from the Serraglio settlement near by. A fibula with incised decoration, also with Italian/European parallels, was deposited in another burial and may feasibly belong to this early stage.

On Rhodes, however, despite the number of tombs which have been excavated, no such weapons of clearly non-Aegean type have so far been found, though a ring-handled knife may be an example. Another kind of European connection, however, may exist there of a non-warlike character: in one tomb were preserved two amber beads of a specific type, named from the shape of those strung on the gold 'wheels' found in a hoard at Tiryns. That object, which is of undoubted European origin, has been dated to an early stage and could, therefore, be roughly contemporary with another Naue II sword of early type in the same hoard. Other amber beads of indeterminate shape were deposited in burials on Cos as well. This occurrence of amber raises wider issues. Amber was, of course, no novelty in Greece but a detailed study of objects of this material found in Greece and on the islands has concluded that the IIIC period witnessed a marked increase in the amount reaching Greece and especially the Ionian Islands; this, with other evidence, it is suggested, points to a route down the Adriatic. At the very least, a fresh supply and demand of this commodity is indicated. It could signify more, the arrival of women wearing such beads who accompanied the foreign warriors of whose presence evidence has already been set out.

Support for such a view may be found in a recent attractive suggestion by Sinclair Hood that nine burials at Saqqara in Egypt, provided with necklaces of amber beads, may be those of the womenfolk who accompanied foreign mercenaries enlisted in the Egyptian army. These burials are part of a cemetery, dated to the XIX Dynasty, consisting of unembalmed inhumations wrapped in rush mats, a type of burial alien to the customary practice of the Egyptians. The amber beads are said to be of shapes found in central Europe and in part in Italy. If the amber beads found in Greece were, in some

THE STEEP-SIDED HILL OF KASTRI (*above*), Palaikastro, in east Crete, occupied in LM IIIC after the abandonment of the town site in the plain below.

PROMINENT ON THE HORIZON is the mountain-peak settlement of Karphi (*below*), a refugee site first occupied in LM IIIC.

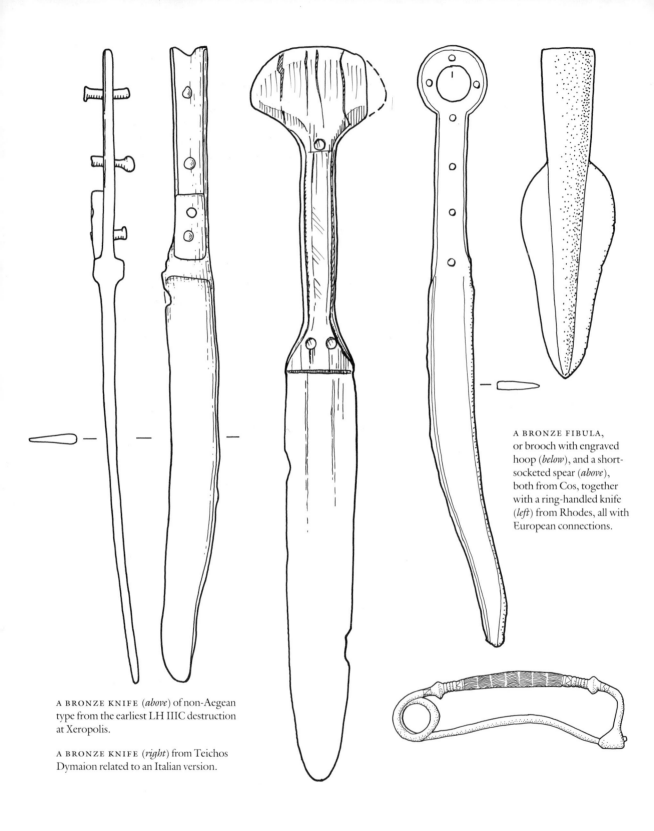

A BRONZE FIBULA,
or brooch with engraved
hoop (*below*), and a short-
socketed spear (*above*),
both from Cos, together
with a ring-handled knife
(*left*) from Rhodes, all with
European connections.

A BRONZE KNIFE (*above*) of non-Aegean
type from the earliest LH IIIC destruction
at Xeropolis.

A BRONZE KNIFE (*right*) from Teichos
Dymaion related to an Italian version.

instances, the possessions of the wives of foreigners, there is no clear impact of their presence in the realms of kitchen furniture and methods of cooking, such as happens much later. Nevertheless it may turn out that the central hearths with their construction of clay laid over a sherd bedding—a feature of the houses and their cooking facilities, at this time, in Xeropolis and apparently at Tiryns also—are such an innovation with non-Mycenaean parallels.

The warrior burials on Cos and Crete, and another not thus far mentioned, on Naxos, belonging to this stage, raise several questions. Are these warriors, with their new types of armament, including, we may add, the greaves attested in Achaea and Athens with non-Aegean features, to be viewed as raiders who have stayed on and settled, perhaps even in some cases have taken over control? Or, are they Mycenaeans and Minoans who have recognized the value of a new and more effective method of fighting and have acquired the accoutrements for it? And, if so, why were the foreign-type weapons eventually to oust those with an Aegean ancestry although they had now been correspondingly modified and would seem to be equally effective? Answers to these questions remain uncertain and even contentious, but the finds themselves indisputably indicate a new phase of militarism.

Before we leave this phase, one other innovation requires attention though its significance eludes any satisfactory explanation: that is the introduction of cremation on a minor scale. It has already been mentioned on Crete; the practice is attested, also, in the Attic cemetery of Perati and in those of Rhodes and Cos, regions with which east Attica had close links. No social connection is apparent nor is its region of origin at all obvious, though the prevailing opinion favours Anatolia where cremation was practised at this and earlier periods. Once introduced, it persisted sporadically in the same regions with perhaps some greater frequency in east and central Crete.

The initial stage of the twelfth century continued, then, to experience some disturbances but they were not serious enough to prevent considerable long-distance interconnections. Cretan and Cypriot objects, for instance, reached Perati as did trinkets from the Near East; Cretan vases, too, were imported into the Dodecanese where they were to have a marked effect on local production.

Recovery

More settled times, however, must be the background to the middle stage of IIIC which follows, a time when freer communications allowed developments in one area to be reflected on others, sometimes far distant, though an underlying strong regionalism nevertheless prevails. Contacts with Cyprus intensify, more apparent in Aegean influences on the island than in the few objects it exported to Perati and elsewhere. Gold and other precious materials remain very sparse and there are few obvious signs of increased wealth. The resurgence over much of the Aegean and its shores is visible more in a widespread revitalization of its artistry, which is preserved only on pottery.

For an example of this apparent feeling of confidence, we may again turn to Xeropolis where partial destruction caused some damage to its rather orderly planned town of this stage. The pottery in the deposits, though largely fragmentary, illustrates the great change which had taken place. One of the more surprising features here, and elsewhere, is the reintroduction of pictorial representations which had largely ossified before the troubles of 1200 BC and had virtually ceased thereafter. The drawing now has a new spirit of vitality embracing a wide range of subjects including birds (evidently a popular theme), animals of different species, mythical creatures, and human activity. Most of the pottery at Xeropolis is tantalizingly fragmentary, but one intact vase, a large alabastron, depicting a central composition of two griffins feeding their young in a nest, accompanied by a range of other animals, demonstrates the fantasy and confident draughtsmanship of the new generation of artists. Clearly they had not encountered lions, for their portrayals resemble bull terriers, but the painting of human beings can be quite accomplished. One fragment depicts a warrior dressed in a fringed-kilt, sword at the waist and wearing greaves, recalling the well-known and presumably contemporary crater from Mycenae with its two files of soldiers, one wearing horned helmets—a feature to which we shall return. Formal patterns, too, embrace a considerable range of designs, especially versions of the so-called 'antithetic streamer' pattern which is now found spread over a wide area: at Mycenae, to a lesser degree on the islands, on Crete, and in Cyprus, where its impact is considerable and provides a sure indication of the long-distance transportation of ideas.

Pottery of these styles spread northward up the sea line between Euboea and the mainland to Volos in Thessaly.

Further south, however, the cemetery at Perati shows little reflection, perhaps largely due to its fondness for stirrup jars as tomb offerings, a container little favoured on Euboea. The inhabitants of Perati clearly looked for their models and imports principally from the Dodecanese, with an imported Cretan vase probably obtained through the same channel. The pottery of the islands, Rhodes and Cos in particular, evolved their own speciality, the stirrup vase with elaborated octopus decoration. On these they placed their wildlife, birds, fish, even hedgehogs, mainly as filling ornaments between the octopus' tentacles. The origin of this style is clearly Crete where the octopus had long been a favoured subject, and its representation elaborated in IIIC. Such versions imported into the Dodecanese were imitated and given yet further decorative embellishments. The tomb offerings in this region, with their emphasis on preferred shapes of vase, especially the stirrup jar, have led to an overemphasis of certain characteristics. It is now apparent from the settlement pottery at Serraglio that there was a wide range of differing decoration, especially on craters, which carry such subjects as those already met at Xeropolis: birds, goats, fish, and the rare, and in this case poorly depicted, humans.

In the Argolid, a somewhat less exuberant style evolved with its main centre at Mycenae, where interest in wildlife is largely restricted to stylized birds. Preference is given to embroidered formal patterns executed in a fastidious manner, the so-called Close Style.

A PYXIS from Xeropolis painted with a frieze of animals which include a sphinx, a deer, and two griffins feeding their young in a nest.

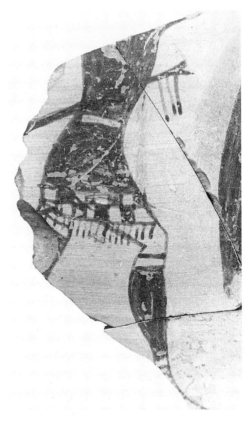

A CRATER FRAGMENT from Xeropolis depicting a grown and baby sphinx, preceded by a woman carrying a jug.

A KILTED WARRIOR with sword painted on a crater fragment from Xeropolis.

VASES FROM LEFKANDI (*a*), Crete (*b*) and (*d*), and Cyprus (*c*), reproduced at various scales, with versions of the antithetic, streamer pattern, showing artistic interrelations between these regions.

Its circulation was much more local though it probably had an effect in Achaia, which also displays a local style of its own.

This emphasis on pottery is due in part, as has been said, to the scarcity of other evidence; there are no surviving ivories, such as in Cyprus, and no examples of its outstanding gold jewellery, or evidence for the continuity found there of a seal-making industry. However restricted a view, the pottery does none the less provide an insight into the climate of the times and, more concretely, demonstrates that conditions were such as to allow a widespread dissemination of artistic developments in an interchange which, otherwise, would have remained largely unsuspected.

Circumstances were, it has been suggested, more settled and some recovery from the earlier devastations achieved. Militarism, however, and warfare remained an underlying feature. In this, grave offerings, our main source of information, may be misleading in containing few weapons. The warrior depictions at Xeropolis, Mycenae, Tiryns, and elsewhere are indications of this state of affairs. The kilted-warrior of Xeropolis resembles in part the file of soldiers on one side of the Mycenae crater. Unfortunately he lacks his head to show whether, like them, he wore a horned helmet or the type with spiky outline, suggestive of helmets of hedgehog pelts, worn by the warriors on the other face of the Mycenae vase, and attested elsewhere—at Tiryns for instance—as the headgear of soldiers armed with spears and, in this case, mounted on a chariot.

A new aspect of war, or rather one attested for the first time, appears on two fragmentary craters of this stage recently found at the coastal site of Livanates in Locris: armed warriors fighting on board ships. To these aspects may be added the updating of weapons, with the arrival of the second generation of Naue II swords found on Crete, in Achaia, and possibly Tiryns, and there are others of uncertain locality.

Finally, there is the evidence for destructions in mid-IIIC: partial at Xeropolis; one perhaps somewhat later within the acropolis of Mycenae, where the Granary was burnt; and another contemporary with it at the small Argolid town of Korakou. How these relate chronologically with the several destructions reported at Tiryns is as yet unclear. In more distant regions, occupation at Phylakopi on Melos and at Serraglio on Cos seemingly ends. On Crete, Kastri at Palaikastro and a reoccupied part of the old palace of Phaistos together with the important town of Chania are abandoned though at what stage or stages is uncertain.

OCTOPUS STIRRUP JARS with their elaborate LC IIIC decoration from the Dodecanese.

Scarcity of settlement evidence, again, hinders an overall assessment of the extent and severity of the troubles during this phase. The damage may as before, have been widespread with repercussions further afield, such as, possibly, the further destructions suffered by the major centres of Cyprus. This time there was to be no recovery even though Mycenaean culture survives for a generation or so. Minoan traditions were maintained mostly on the hilltop, inland settlements where, isolated, they remained little affected; but at the western end of the island, the evidence indicates wholesale abandonment.

Evidence is even less adequate to chart the speed and degree of this decline. It was not immediate by any means as can be seen at Xeropolis where the second IIIC town was in part repaired and, surprisingly, its occupants now buried their dead below the floors of rooms, possibly for protection. No precise contemporary parallel for this practice is known though similar conditions may account for the numerous burials within the walls at Tiryns and the probable bath burial at Mycenae. Xeropolis must have suffered yet further damage since there is some evidence for the construction of a third settlement though its size is quite unknown. By this stage its pottery reflects the period: impoverished in style, restricted in its range of shapes, and technically of poor quality. Desertion rather than further destruction is likely to account for its end. Not long before this happened, vases of identical types and fabric, and presumably exports, reached the island of Kea where worship appears to have continued at a long-lived shrine; then this

FILES OF MARCHING WARRIORS wearing two different types of helmets, painted on the two faces of the well-known Warrior Crater found at Mycenae.

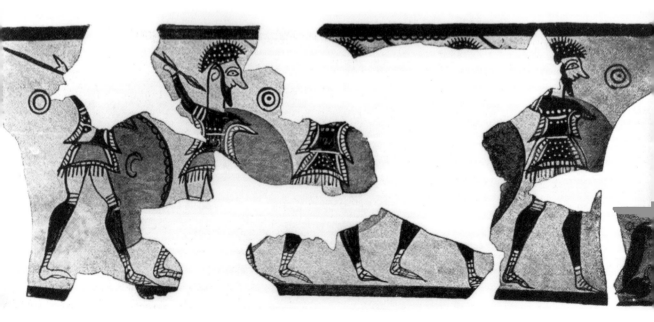

also is abandoned. Emigration is possible to Chios where a roughly contemporary settlement was established, using very similar pottery before it, too, was deserted.

At Perati, burials continue to be made for as long as the occupation of Xeropolis, with which it had some contact, but then cease. The latest use of the old cemeteries on Rhodes is approximately contemporary.

There is scant but certain evidence for occupation at Mycenae with the unique recent discovery not far distant, at Argolid Chania, of a walled tumulus into which had been inserted cremations contained in pots, an innovation highly suggestive of arrivals from elsewhere. Further south, the size of the remaining settlements at Tiryns and Asine is unclear, but is likely to have been greatly diminished; they, like Mycenae, may well have housed small communities without break into the Iron Age. Towards the end, Argolid pottery, too, has become debased and dull, retaining only the simplest of decoration.

How long the cemeteries of Achaia, and more importantly of Kephallenia, continue in use is difficult to gauge, especially in the Ionian Islands which had by then developed a completely regional style of pottery. One of the latest imports from Europe is likely to be a multiple-looped fibula of the same type as one found on Karphi in Crete, a settlement which may have lasted to the end of our period. It is sometimes claimed that the cemeteries of Kephallenia continue even longer, well into the Iron Age, but there is no convincing evidence to support such a view. To the south in Messenia, the contents of a tomb near Pylos attest some continuing occupation in that region, extending probably from late in the second stage of IIIC (its degenerate pictorial crater) until possibly the very end of the period, since some of the vases have already adopted linear motives as decoration, a feature characteristic of Messenian early Iron Age pottery. With these may

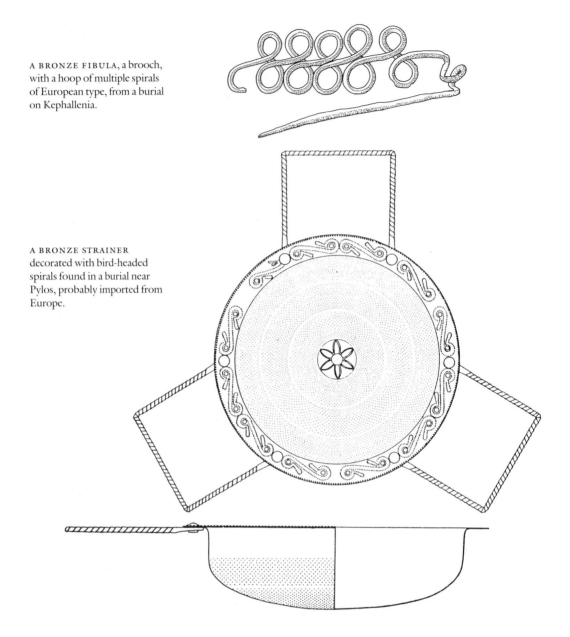

A BRONZE FIBULA, a brooch, with a hoop of multiple spirals of European type, from a burial on Kephallenia.

A BRONZE STRAINER decorated with bird-headed spirals found in a burial near Pylos, probably imported from Europe.

belong a bronze sieve or strainer with torque handles and duck-headed spirals, having firm but late central European connections.

Failure

The cause or causes for the final collapse of the Mycenaean culture are obscure. A drastic drop in population there certainly was, and this condition was to persist well into the succeeding era. Artistic and economic poverty, too, is clear. Yet survival at such a low level is difficult to explain in a country where the staple diet for existence (olives, barley, grapes, fish, and game) is not difficult for small communities to secure. Further disruptions and probable raiding would seem to be required, such as befell, once again, the communities of Cyprus where its period of recovery had been earlier disrupted. This time there was a rapid decline.

We may look to the immediate outcome for some further light on events, though again we are, unfortunately, almost entirely dependent on cemetery evidence. At Lefkandi, burials begin in one of the new Iron Age burial grounds. Though the vases have a basic Mycenaean ancestry, they have no links with the latest IIIC pottery from Xeropolis. Burials, both inhumations and cremations, are housed in stone-built cists and are individual interments, not family tombs as was the general, though not universal, Mycenaean practice. The same is true at Athens and on nearby Salamis from where comes most of the evidence for this stage; the pattern is new burial grounds of cist tombs. A similar picture is given in other parts of Greece, at Mycenae and Tiryns for instance, though the change-over was not uniform throughout. Crete is not affected and continues with multiple burials, a difference which highlights the great change in Greece.

Certain common features permitted Desborough to define what he called a sub-Mycenaean culture over widespread regions of the mainland. But the term is unfortunate in its implication. Continuity with the past is almost entirely confined to the persistence of a very debased version of Mycenaean-type pottery, but even in this sphere undue emphasis has been placed on the decorated vases. If we turn to the standard cooking-pot jug, we see that this is now utterly alien in its handmade and burnished fabric and in its rather sack-like shape. Only settlement evidence, sadly lacking, will show just how radically the kitchen had changed, and, by implication, those working in it. As Desborough rightly stressed, it is not only the new features which are important, but also the loss of the old ones. Gone for instance are the Mycenaean 'buttons', now presumably no longer required because of a change of costume.

On archaeological grounds alone, a case could easily be made for a considerable, even fundamental, change in population, involving the arrival of people of non-Mycenaean origin. Some such change, whatever its degree, is very likely.

The Mycenaean Age has ended. Some continuity from it is certain; most apparent not from artefacts but in the more basic aspects of language and religion (in part at least), and not least in myths and legends of the past, preserved in the continuous, though constantly modified, bardic stories, two of which were to be preserved for us under the name of Homer.

9

Reformation in Barbarian Europe,
1300–600 BC

ANTHONY HARDING

I F the period before 1300 BC in Europe might be dubbed the 'Age of Stonehenge', it is harder to find a label that fits the time after that date and before the advent of the next major changes in economy and society. It is properly called the 'Urnfield period', but this gives little idea of the extent of variability in the various fields of activity. If anything, it was an age of revolutions: industrial, social, military, and religious.

As a period, however, this chunk of time has not attracted the attention it perhaps deserves. There are no great stone monuments to visit, few large burial mounds, or extensive settlements. And yet the period can be regarded as of crucial importance in the formation of historic Europe. The ensuing centuries saw a full return to literacy in the Mediterranean, and its spread to central Europe. Europe emerges into history with many populations already in place, for example the Celts in central and western Europe, or the Illyrians in the western part of the Balkans. Since we have no reason to suppose that they only arrived in those spots shortly before the literary sources recorded them there, they were, in all probability, there through the Late Bronze Age, and perhaps before. What happened in these seven centuries is thus directly ancestral to the earliest recorded history of many of the peoples of Europe.

Europe was prehistoric, that is without written history, throughout these 700 years, but in the south the contacts with the great civilizations of the east Mediterranean provide information that is historical, or almost so. The opening two centuries are marked by a period of turmoil in the east Mediterranean. The great civilizations of Mycenaean Greece and Hittite Anatolia fell, numerous smaller states and individual cities were sacked, and Egypt had to fight major battles on its frontiers to preserve its pre-eminence, which was in any case reduced. Although many of the events of this period are hazy, and the documents that record them ambiguous, there are some reasons for supposing that this was a 'migration period' not dissimilar to the better known one in the early medieval period. Largely because of oblique references in the Egyptian texts, it is thought that a confederation of peoples—to the Egyptians the 'Peoples of the Sea'—were responsible for raids on the cities and states of the Levant and Cyprus, most of which suffered destruction at this time. At much this time, too, objects that are better known in central and northern Europe began to appear in Mediterranean lands, such as northern forms of sword, spearhead, and armour, safety pins, certain ornaments, and even pottery of possible Italian origin. Scholars have been tempted to link the two phenomena—destructions and 'foreign' artefacts—and to suppose that people of northern origin moved southward into Greece and elsewhere at the end of the Bronze Age, but much of this remains highly speculative. It is in any case based on a view of material culture which supposes that artefact styles reflect the ethnic identity of their makers and users; such a supposition is, today, regarded with considerable suspicion.

Whatever the effect on Greece, notable developments occurred widely through the Europe of the Late Bronze Age. The most striking of these is the almost universal change from burying the dead in graves to cremating them and putting their ashes in pits in the ground or in funerary urns. This practice has led to the period being dubbed the 'Urnfield period'—a curious, if suitably descriptive, label. This practice continued through most of the period we are concerned with in this chapter, in most of Europe. Burials, indeed, are among the most visible remains of the period (except in certain areas, of which Britain is one): settlements are rather infrequently found, and only metal artefacts, found with no archaeological context, can rival them numerically. This fact reflects the enormous expansion of the metal industry in this period, both quantitatively and qualitatively. This metallurgy was initially concerned mainly with bronze and to a lesser extent with gold, later increasingly with iron. Metals were not the only materials being exploited, however; true glass, for example, was also used, and stone and wood were still of great importance.

Although it is not possible to isolate events in a historical sense in this period, it is possible to note certain key developments that affected all or part of Europe. A marked trend towards fortification is visible; people created forts on hilltops or stockades on lower ground, starting around 1100 BC. There were also phases of markedly more ostentatious burial in some areas, leading to the deposition of large quantities of grave goods with the dead. In many cases, goods were moved over considerable distances before they reached their final resting-place, evidence of powerful exchange networks. Nowhere is this more likely to have been true than in the exploitation and movement of salt, especially of the salt that was extracted from the mines of the Austrian Alps. It can surely be no coincidence that one of the richest cemeteries of the entire period under review—Hallstatt—lies beside one of these salt mines, and later on other centres, such as the Dürrnberg near Hallein (also in the Salzburg province of Austria), were also found close to salt extraction sites. All of this was accompanied by fluctuations in the natural setting of human settlement and subsistence, and in the response of farmers to new economic and environmental conditions. There is some evidence to suggest change, too, in spiritual life, though such matters are notoriously hard to elucidate from archaeological evidence. From 1300 BC, in fact, we can categorize Europe in terms of a series of revolutions.

AIR VIEW OF THE EXCAVATIONS at Feudvar, Vojvodina, a large mound with occupation stretching from the Early Bronze Age to the La Tène Iron Age. Numerous house plans have been recovered.

Europe in 1300 BC

Europe in 1300 BC was a mosaic of essentially small-scale communities, at different stages of social and economic development. The extent of contact between them is a matter of some debate. Small though the communities undoubtedly were, many aspects of societal development were already in place, notably social divisions that distributed wealth unequally across the community. But daily life for most people in 1300 BC, as in so much of the ancient past, revolved around the tasks of field and workshop. Provision for the dead also had to be made, but preoccupations with the more elaborate forms of ritual and religion were perhaps the preserve of only a few.

The settlement patterns of Europe at the time of the Late Bronze Age revolutions, to be described in this chapter, were modest in scope and scale. Most villages that have been recovered were essentially agricultural in nature, though, of course, some, especially those placed near metal sources, were also involved with industrial activities. Others, such as those in the south of Italy where ships from the east Mediterranean called, existed largely for trade purposes. Over large parts of Europe, from the Aeolian Islands in the south to the moors of Britain in the north (though not in central Europe), small, round houses were the norm, organized into groups that formed hamlets or villages. House plans tell us little about the social organization of the time, since differential status—as known from burial evidence—was not reflected in domestic arrangements. Nor is there much information available on the density of settlements in particular areas. This must largely be due to the difficulty of spotting the sites in question, but even where good information is available, patterns such as that reconstructed for the Linear Pottery area of central Europe are not seen.

The subsistence practices involved in the earlier Bronze Age continued the pattern of the Neolithic and Copper Ages. The principal food sources were the standard domesticates, both plant and animal—though wild foods were also appreciated when available. It is not often realized that as late as 1300 BC large wild animals—wild pig, red deer, even aurochs—were still available in a highly exploited area such as the Hungarian plain. This must indicate that substantial areas of woodland remained, some presumably regenerated after initial clearance, other parts original uncleared forest. But for most people, most of the time, the daily round consisted of tillage and husbandry, utilizing an unvarying range of foodstuffs. In certain areas, notably in the British Isles, there is a remarkable amount of evidence deriving from the physical activities of Bronze Age agriculture, principally in the form of field boundaries. It is less certain, in most instances, what exactly went on in the fields in question, but at least in some of the lowland examples arable exploitation is assured. Such a pattern may legitimately be assumed for most of

POTTERY FROM THE EARLY IRON AGE settlement at Kalakača, on south bank of the Danube in Vojvodina, Serbia. Tenth to eighth centuries BC.

WOVEN CLOTH and a net of twisted fibres from pile-dwelling sites on Lake Zürich, Switzerland.

lowland Europe, even in the absence of specific evidence. The finds of carbonized grain, and the environmental conditions, make it next to certain that this was the configuration that applied.

Industrially, the main activity was metalworking, though potting and carpentry were also very important. Metal extraction from the prolific ore sources of the Alps, Carpathians, and other mountain areas was in harness and thousands of tonnes of copper were being produced. The range of metal goods was constantly increasing, even though the epic proportions achieved in later centuries were not yet in prospect. As well as metal, other materials were produced, such as faience (at this stage little more than a primitive form of glass), and raw materials like amber and jet were worked. This aspect of production is of great importance for an appreciation of the extent of trading networks. In much of earlier Bronze Age Europe, the movement of goods took place only on a local, or at most regional, scale and in modest quantities. There are strong signs, however, that goods did move over long distances when contact with the advanced cultures of the east Mediterranean was involved. Particularly in the case of the Mycenaean world, several classes of object—most notably amber—suggest that long-distance contact was both possible and regularly effected. This situation continued in the ensuing centuries, as we shall see below.

More than these day-to-day activities, however, it was the affairs of spiritual life that attract attention in the earlier Bronze Age. Societies which could produce monuments of the complexity of Stonehenge or Filitosa, and burial sites as extensive as the great barrow cemeteries of southern England, Denmark, or the Pontic steppe, are worthy of interest as social entities as much as they are for technological reasons. These societies must have possessed an organizational system and structure of authority, and it is commonly supposed that the richer graves (and such graves are on occasion exceedingly well provided for) were those of chieftains and other group leaders. This situation did not prevail equally over all of the Continent, however. In most of central Europe, graves were in 'flat' cemeteries (i.e. not under barrows), and the degree of differentiation between them is much more slight. But in most areas the funeral rite was that of inhumation. Cremation of the dead, though not unknown, was rather uncommon except in a few regions, such as the Hungarian plain. It has often been supposed that these differences in the treatment of the dead relate to ethnic differences, but at present no clear picture of the racial make-up of Europe in the earlier part of the Bronze Age is possible. The spread of technological innovations, such as the wheel and horse-riding, that took place through the Old World in the third and second millennia BC is commonly supposed to have been connected with the movement of Indo-Europeans (i.e. peoples speaking Indo-European languages)—as is demonstrable for Greece, Anatolia, and some other parts of the Near East.

The Late Bronze Age Industrial Revolution

What was special about the Late Bronze Age that meant such a difference in industrial production compared with the immediately preceding centuries? The differences lie both in the scale of the operation and in the technological advances that took place. In these terms 1300 was not a firm dividing line, but in general what followed after that date was more advanced technologically than what came before it. In fact there was a continuous process of technological change in action, and it would be wrong to try to freeze the clock at 1300 rather than another date. We can examine these processes in the cases of metallurgy, both of bronze and of iron, and of other industrial processes.

Metallurgy Metallurgy was far from being a new skill at the time of the onset of the Late Bronze Age, but the explosion, quantitatively and qualitatively, of metallurgical activity at this time means that the word 'revolution' is an apt one to describe the situation. A startling surge in metallurgical production can be detected, principally from the amounts of metal actually recovered from the ground (for the implications of this see below, p. 314). Coupled with this was a large increase in the range of techniques used, including some which enabled the smith to exercise much greater control over his medium in both technological and artistic terms.

From 1300 BC for several hundred years, the most important metallurgical processes were those involving copper and tin, alloyed to make bronze. After 1000 BC, iron increasingly became dominant. Gold was also worked, in some quantity in certain areas such as Scandinavia and Ireland. Other metals, notably lead, were used, but sparingly at this stage. At this time, and through the ensuing seven centuries, the need for metals must have determined much of the industrial activity of the Bronze Age world, and the systematic exploitation of copper ore sources—Alpine, Carpathian, Balkan, Irish, as well as numerous smaller deposits—plainly continued from the immediately preceding period (cf. chapter 7). In fact, relatively little is known about the Late Bronze Age operation of the main mining areas, though it is assumed that the same methods—fire-setting and tunnelling in adits—continued. Whereas in the earlier period characteristic ingots in the form of neck-rings were apparently the main means of disseminating the metal (cf. chapter 7), in the later period ingots were of the plano-convex type, flat on top and curved underneath, reflecting the way in which they formed at the base of bowl-shaped furnaces. It is also more difficult than hitherto to trace the passage of metal objects through constituent analysis, since the utilization of so many sources, and the mixing of the metal stock, renders the most commonly used method, spectrographic emission, unworkable, and the more promising lead isotope method has not yet been able to tackle the question of metal provenancing outside the Mediterranean area. Even there, where the metals trade as seen in the movement of ingots of characteristic 'ox-hide' form (cf. chapter 6) is well studied, the bulk of the available analyses indicate that it was the east Mediterranean ore sources and not those in the west, such as in Etruria or Sardinia, which were providing the Mediterranean world with its raw materials.

The source of the tin used for the manufacture of bronze in this period is no better known than in the preceding one, but the candidates—Cornwall, Brittany, the Ore mountains of Germany and former Czechoslovakia, certain parts of Spain and Italy—remain the same. In the Mediterranean context all the indications are that tin was obtained from the East (perhaps Afghanistan) rather than the West, but for central, northern, and western Europe it is these more local sources which must have been exploited. It is even harder to pin tin down to its point of origin than it is copper, but the limited distribution of tin sources means that in each context there are only a few possibilities for the origin of the metal.

In the case of gold, the Irish and Carpathian sources probably continued to supply smiths and their customers with surprising quantities of the precious metal. Especially in Ireland and north Germany and Scandinavia, large numbers of high-quality gold objects (mainly ornaments, but also vessels and other objects) occur. The release of such a large amount of a material which to all appearances was as highly valued then as it is now must have had a striking effect on the economy of the time, not only as a whole (in that new elements of value were continually being introduced into the system), but also in terms of personal wealth distribution and the ability to exhibit status.

Once the raw materials had been obtained, the smith had to turn them into objects that his customers required. In this area, too, new skills were brought to bear. Whereas up till now objects were mostly cast using two-piece moulds, of metal or stone, now multiple-piece moulds began to be used, as well as an increasing reliance on the lost-wax

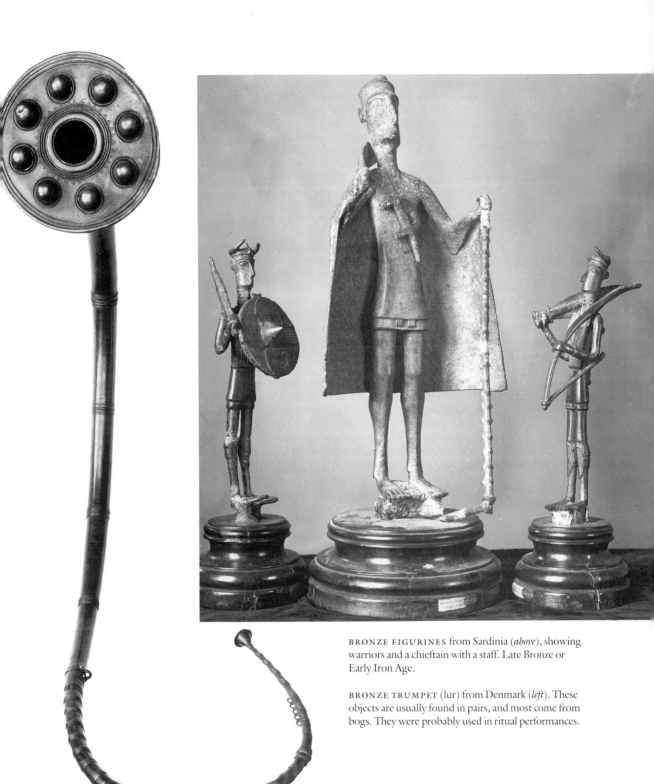

BRONZE FIGURINES from Sardinia (*above*), showing warriors and a chieftain with a staff. Late Bronze or Early Iron Age.

BRONZE TRUMPET (lur) from Denmark (*left*). These objects are usually found in pairs, and most come from bogs. They were probably used in ritual performances.

BRONZE CUIRASS (body armour) from Marmesse, Haute Marne, France. Late Bronze Age. Such sheet bronze objects were much more effective visually than functionally; it has been shown experimentally that sword blows can readily pierce such armour.

(*cire perdue*) method. Fine examples of the former are the horns of Ireland and the *lurer* of Denmark, magnificent bronze musical instruments (cf. below, p. 325); of the latter, the finely made figurines of Sardinia or Sweden. Use of the lost wax method meant that very fine details could be modelled, the bronze faithfully retaining the impressions originally carved on the wax and then preserved on the negative of the outer mould surface. Such a magnificent *tour de force* as the Trundholm sun chariot illustrates well both the technical mastery which the smith had over his medium and the refined appreciation of line and proportion which he brought to bear on what is basically a mundane subject. It is above all the spread of new mould technology that made this technically achievable.

With the increase in quantities of metal objects that came about in the Late Bronze Age, the main material for the moulds used for the castings changed to clay, or perhaps sand with a small admixture of clay, a material which does not often survive the conditions of burial that have prevailed over the last 3000 years; hence, the appearance of too few moulds for the vast number of bronze objects. Such moulds were used once only, since they were broken in the process of extracting the casting. But a number of large collections of clay moulds, such as at Rathgall, Co. Wicklow, Ireland, or Dainton, Devon, England, show what must frequently have happened. There fragments of moulds for a wide variety of objects were found, testimony to on-site metallurgy (a phenomenon found only infrequently). The Dainton finds included crucibles and moulds for swords, spearheads, and ferrules (spear-shaft fittings), while the Rathgall material included moulds for swords, spears, and socketed-bowls, as well as for gold objects. It was not only mould casting that constituted the Late Bronze Age metallurgical revolution. One of the most popular techniques to be adopted during the middle part of the Bronze Age and widely practised thereafter was the use of sheet metalworking. This was usually forged, that is beaten into shape from cast bars of bronze, and joined by riveting or over-casting. Sheet bronze was used for a great variety of objects: armour (cuirass, greaves, helmet, shield), vessels, vehicles and their fittings, and other smaller ornamental objects.

What was the economic and social framework within which this metallurgical activity functioned? The products of the smith were only one aspect of industry in the Late Bronze Age, but they must have been a very important one. We have no means of knowing how many smiths functioned in a given society, or the ratio of smiths to other work-

PART OF THE GREAT HOARD of bronze objects from Isleham, Cambridgeshire. The picture shows a complete sword and fragments of others, a chape (lower part of a scabbard), spearhead, palstave, socketed axe, knife, cauldron handle, and various ornamental pieces probably connected with horse harness. Late Bronze Age.

ers, but historical and ethnographic parallels suggest that smiths were relatively few in number and important out of proportion to their numerical strength. Much of what we know of Bronze Age metallurgy comes from the finds of bronze hoards, usually of tools but sometimes of weapons or other objects, which were left in holes in the ground, presumably intended for later recovery. Many of these hoards consist of broken objects intended for remelting, and sometimes contain metalworking tools. Since they are usually very heavy—too heavy to have been carried around—it is a reasonable assumption that smiths buried their stock in hiding-places known only to them at various points on their rounds, intending to return on later visits to recover it. The fact that they did not do so may bespeak troubled times and a high mortality among smiths: it is hard to believe that the so-called founder's hoards were intentionally lost to the ground. This is a different situation from the hoards of perfect, undamaged objects to which we will return below. In their case, the deposition seems to have been intentional, though the motives are obscure.

Increasingly during the later stages of the Bronze Age, iron came into daily use. The sources of iron are much more numerous and evenly distributed across Europe than those of copper or gold, and many communities, which hitherto had had no indigenous supplies of the raw materials necessary for tools, now found themselves with easy access to large-scale sources of iron. Low-lying regions, where iron occurs in carbonate ores in association with clays and sands, or moorland and peat regions where 'bog iron' occurs, were particularly favoured as against the preceding period. The change to iron only became numerically significant in ensuing centuries in central and northern Europe, but in the south a wide range of objects could be made in iron (axes, swords, spearheads), as shown from the finds in tombs in the Illyrian areas (Albania, Yugoslavia) or in Italy. The use of iron has implications, too, for pyrotechnology: the reduction of iron ore only becomes possible when minimum temperatures of 1100 °C are achieved; this could only be brought about in enclosed clay-lined shaft and bowl furnaces, driven by bellows, with a strongly reducing atmosphere to drive the oxygen out of the oxide ore. Such temperatures were achieved by bronzesmiths (the melting point of copper is 1083 °C), and early iron metallurgy probably used the methods and equipment of bronzeworking.

Glass Beads of primitive glass (so-called 'faience', actually a glass-like substance fired to a rather low temperature) had been known since the Early Bronze Age, but it was only rarely that the higher firing temperature necessary for the formation of true glass was achieved. When this did happen, practically the only objects created were beads, though in Egypt and the Near East elaborate objects such as vessels and various ornaments were being produced. The discovery of partially and fully formed glass beads, crucibles with glass adhering, and partly fused glass raw materials at Frattesina in the Po valley in northern Italy is of great importance, the more so as the analytical composition of the glass demonstrates that the material is of a local composition type and not brought in by Near Eastern traders. The Kaş shipwreck (see Chapter 6) also contained glass ingots, so that movement of glass is now a well-established phenomenon in the Bronze Age. Production in the barbarian world was on a small scale. True, certain more highly decorated forms were created, as the eye beads and those with twists of different colours (such as the 'Pile dwelling beads' of Switzerland) demonstrate. Such beads were quite numerous, and probably produced in a number of different centres, but really it is the small scale of the enterprise that strikes one, especially when compared to the level of production that had been sustained in the world of the east Mediterranean. Nevertheless, the adoption of the technique throughout Europe is significant in that it illustrates well the manner in which technology transfer apparently occurred with ease in a period which can be seen as truly international in its linkages and leanings.

The Agricultural Revolution

At first sight, changes in subsistence practice in Europe after 1300 BC might not appear particularly dramatic. In all temperate zones where the information is of any quality, it appears that mixed farming continued as the principal subsistence mode, as it had been for millennia up till this point. A broad mix of plant and animal foods were exploited both before and after this date, with little sign that any marked 'revolution' had occurred. Yet highly significant changes were there, even though some of them were of a subtle nature.

In terms of crops grown, various kinds of wheat and barley were the most popular by far. Several legumes were also popular, notably lentils, peas, and—making an appearance for the first time on a large scale—broad or Celtic beans. But this is far from being the whole story. Among the grain crops, we see the regular appearance of millet (*Panicum miliaceum*) in continental Europe, and in the north-west and Britain the first evidence for rye. Another innovation is the widespread and regular use of oil-bearing plants, such as flax, poppy, and gold-of-pleasure (false flax, *Camelina sativa*). Taken together with the Celtic beans, the overall impression is of a marked shift in cultivation preferences from about 1300 BC. This is not to say that the basic staples changed; they did not, but they were supplemented by a far wider range of support crops than had been the case hitherto. What is the reason for this remarkable change? We do not know for certain, a number of features stand out. Millet as a crop is noteworthy because of its short growth time from sowing to maturity, and its ability to withstand harsh climatic conditions, notably drought. It has been known in many historical and ethnographic situations in Europe, and from the Roman period achieved pre-eminence as the grain crop most popular with the poorer classes, who used it not only for an unleavened bread, but also for fermented drinks and porridges. Its appearance in Macedonia in the Late Bronze Age, in northern Italy in the Middle Bronze Age, and in central and northern Europe from the earliest part of the Iron Age, seems to document an early interest that was to become a major part of life support by the early medieval period. The situation is similar with the other plants mentioned. Celtic beans are both prolific and easy to grow, serving as nitrogen fixers in the soil, and capable of reaching maturity in a wide

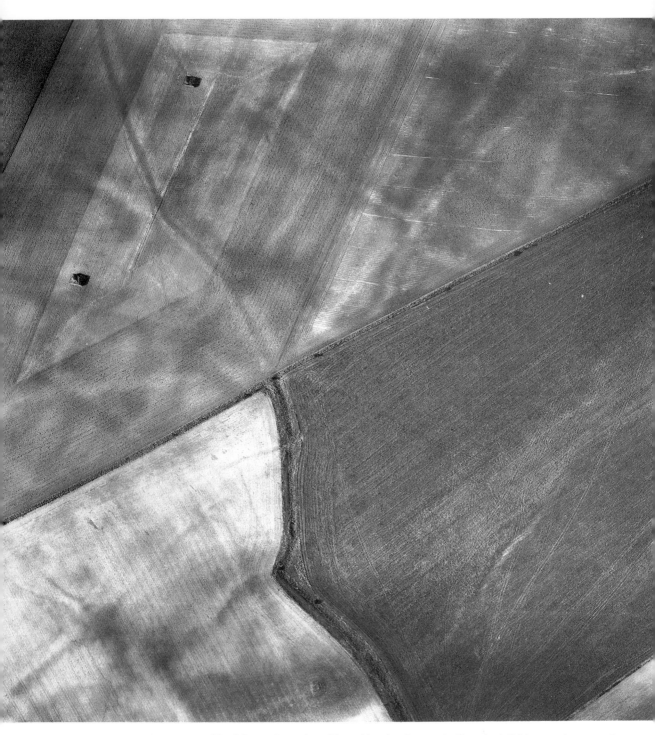

AIR PHOTOGRAPH of Knoll Down, Damerham, Hampshire, showing a major linear land division running across the countryside and visible both as an upstanding earthwork (*lower half of picture*) and as a ploughed-out cropmark. It lies on a different orientation to the grid pattern of 'Celtic' fields visible in the upper half of the picture.

variety of weather regimes including cool, moist conditions. The oil plants are perhaps more problematical, but their high protein content would have rendered them highly nutritious and they are in themselves tasty: a loaf of bread with seeds of *Camelina sativa* sprinkled on the top comes from the Early Iron Age site of Aggtelek in Hungary.

Changes in the exploitation of animals were less rapid and obvious, but present none the less. It is often forgotten that domestic animals were by no means the only ones present or the only ones of interest, and that large wild animals were also available. Records of aurochs (wild cattle) and wild pig of exceptional size come from excavations both in Hungary and the North European Plain, quite apart from red deer and a wide range of small mammals, fish, and birds which would be caught on an opportunistic basis. Few sites provide enough detailed evidence for a systematic picture to be built up, but Bovenkarspel in the The Netherlands shows a massive preponderance of cattle in the bone record, with the systematic herding of animals according to age and sex. Elsewhere, along Mediterranean shores for example, sites might specialize in sheep or goat-keeping, and pigs were frequently the most numerous animal in the temperate zone: in Hallstatt period Poland, for example. Horses were also present, of course, though never as a main food source; their usefulness as draught animals and for riding, appreciated since before 2000 BC, took on a new aspect during the early centuries of the first millennium as items of horse harness in bronze and iron begin to appear in graves over a wide tract of eastern Europe. Much has been written about the significance of these finds in ethnic terms (cf. below, p. 334); the widespread presence of horses that is attested perhaps indicates the start of the appreciation of the horse as a noble animal fit to accompany the warrior into battle.

One should not forget the smaller, but no less useful creatures that served man's needs: in an age before sugar, all sweetening would have been done by means of honey. It is surprising that so little evidence of this most useful substance survives, but an object interpreted as a beehive from a site in Berlin perhaps indicates something of what was once present. We can reconstruct even less of useful bacterial agents like yoghurt, which in many societies turn milk into a more solid and enjoyable foodstuff, but no doubt they were present too.

Of course crops and animals required space: space in the landscape, by means of fields, farms, and estates. Fields were no doubt present everywhere, but it is only in the north and west that they have been recovered in significant numbers. Partly this may be a reflection of the priorities of fieldwork, partly a factor of preservation; it surely cannot reflect the true prehistoric situation. Wherever arable crops and animals were reared, partitioning between activities would have been necessary, and protection afforded to the new progeny. Such dating of evidence as there is suggests that the main phase of field creation took place in the earlier half of the Bronze Age. This was by no means the end of the story, however. During the centuries after 1300, a remarkable series of modifications were introduced in at least some of these cases. Where hitherto a system of small fields had existed, now long boundary ditches and banks drove straight through them, dividing the landscape into important chunks that have aptly been named ranches or estates. A major dyke such as Bokerley Dyke on the borders of Hampshire, Wiltshire, and Dorset, for example, has been subjected to intensive study and its Roman and early medieval final form shown to draw on Middle Bronze Age origins. In similar ways, the Wessex hillforts are tied-in to their surrounding countryside by extensive systems of fields and linear boundaries. It is hard to find comparable evidence from continental sites, where the field boundaries tend to be on a smaller scale, and often much later in date. That such boundaries do exist in certain Mediterranean locations, however, is known from survey work such as that undertaken on the Neothermal Dalmatia project in coastal Croatia.

The Spiritual Revolution

The most noticeable change occurring at around 1300 BC in Europe was not in the sphere of technology or subsistence: it was in the attitude to death and burial. Up till now, most parts of Europe had inhumed their dead, either in simple pits or stone-lined

AIR PHOTOGRAPH of a Late Bronze Age urnfield in excavation: the site at Ingolstadt-Zuchering, Bavaria. The circular ditches enclose the urn burials themselves; the rectangular feature is later in date.

SHIP SETTING from Boge parish on Gotland, Sweden: numerous such ship-shaped settings of stone were created in the later prehistory of Scandinavia, especially on the island of Gotland. The stones are graded in height towards stern and prow. Where excavated they usually contain burials.

boxes cut into the ground surface, or under heaped-up mounds of earth (barrows or tumuli). At around 1300, this practice changed dramatically: the dead were from now on usually cremated, and the ashes collected and placed in urns. These urn burials were then put in defined cemetery areas, hence the name applied to the phenomenon: Urnfields. It is this name that is usually applied to the period as a whole, and it is usual to refer to the Urnfield culture (or cultures) as characterizing the span of time from about 1300 to 700. Even then, as we shall see, many of the same burial rites continued, although officially we are in the ensuing Hallstatt Iron Age.

It would be wrong to imagine, though, that there was uniformity in burial practice over the whole of Europe either before 1300 or after it. Some people were cremated in the Early and Middle Bronze Age; parts of Hungary did this on a regular basis; in other areas, such as Britain, it happened more sporadically and perhaps reflects distinctions in life that were repeated in death. There was thus a background for the adoption of cremation on such a wide scale in the Urnfield period, though the processes by which one turned into the other remain obscure. Similarly, not all individuals in the Urnfield period were cremated; in some locations none were, in others there was a mixture of the two rites. If one looks at a large published cemetery such as Przeczyce in southern Poland, for example, one finds that out of the 874 burials that took place in the cemetery, 132 were cremations and 727 inhumations. It might be tempting to think that this could be correlated with grave goods and thus provide an indication of the status or identity of the individuals buried in particular ways, but in fact there is no regular association with types of grave goods; the cemetery is, in any case, very poorly provided with goods (the normal situation), and the provision of a few pots and bronze buttons can hardly be taken as indicating a significant degree of wealth.

The curious attitude to the rite performed can perhaps be gauged from the Nordic area, where, at a time equivalent to the start of the Urnfield period, the numbers of cremations dramatically increased, and the apparent need to maintain the favoured rite even went to the extent of putting cremated remains into large grave pits big enough to accommodate an inhumation! Sometimes, too, graves of special form, a boat-shaped setting of stones, were provided: cremations were also put into these. In parts of central and northern Europe small mounds or barrows could be erected over the cremated remains, providing a clearly visible marker for future generations and perhaps suggesting that the deceased was an important ancestor to be remembered by generations to come. This attitude finds its most impressive expression in the large mounds that occur sporadically across the Urnfield world: in Slovakia (Očkov), early in the period, in north Germany (Seddin), and in Sweden (near Uppsala) later on. One of these, the 'King's Grave' at Seddin near Pritzwalk in Brandenburg (north-east Germany), consisted of a stone corbel-vaulted chamber with an enormous mound, around 130 metres across and still 8 metres high, erected on top. Such vaulting, effectively unknown in barbarian Europe since the days of Neolithic chambered-tombs, taken together with the richness of the grave goods (sword, spearhead, hanging-bowl, razor, knife, tweezers, rings, axes, and vessels of bronze and pottery), vividly illustrates the ability of a very small number of people to acquire possessions and status obligations from local populations. It also provides a striking demonstration that such displays of wealth could, on occasion, be indulged in, for as a rule Urnfield graves were poorly provided for. We know of the swords, weaponry, armour, fine metal vessels, ornaments in metal or glass, and other objects which were being turned out at this time, yet they were almost never placed in graves. Why not?

The change to cremation is usually regarded as one of the most significant aspects of the later prehistoric period, in that it bespeaks a marked change in attitude to death and the afterlife. Perhaps the practice of inhuming implies a belief that the wholeness of the body is somehow important to the persona of the deceased in his or her 'existence' after death. Cremation, on the other hand, indicates that the body itself is valueless, prone to decay, and but a feeble and intransient vehicle for higher things—emotions, reflective thought, spiritual conceptions. The continuance of these abstract notions depends not on the body but on the recalling of them through recitation and repetition in the honouring of ancestors. The radical change of burial rite involved thus probably reflects a very marked reorientation of beliefs in Bronze Age societies. This may have had more to do with attitudes to the living than to anything one may term 'religion'. The way in which the dead were rarely provided with their possessions in life, or marked out in other ways, reinforces the view that memories of the dead and their achievements, not their physical presence, was what interested people in the Urnfield world.

It should not be concluded from this, however, that religion played no part in the lives of the inhabitants of Late Bronze Age Europe. Far from it: a broad range of sites and objects shows us that spiritual life was extremely important. To begin with, a number of signs or symbols were used again and again, and are found widely from one end of Europe to the other. The bird, for instance, assumed an importance that it had not had since the Neolithic, and then in a very different form. Clay and bronze bird figurines are commonly found, either self-standing objects (and therefore possibly connected with cult activity in shrines) or attached to large-scale pieces like wagons and cauldrons. Birds also appear as decorative motifs on bronzework and pottery, and clearly possessed a

RITUAL POURING VESSEL (rhyton) from the Villanovan cemetery at Bologna.

significance in belief systems even though we do not know exactly what it was. Sometimes water birds (ducks?) are shown drawing boats or wagons: a good example is the famous chariot from Dupljaja (near Belgrade). Here three birds are depicted, two in front flanking a central spoked wheel, one behind rising from the body of the vehicle. A figurine, apparently female but with bird-like head, having a bell-shaped skirt and incised decoration to show the bodily features, stands in the chariot, which is supported by two more four-spoked wheels. In other cases the bird designs are often shown only schematically, merely eye and beak clearly discernible; a sure sign that the original idea was of importance, since the viewer was able to put together the significance of the picture from only a notional sketch of the original.

Such symbols are but one part of the evidence for religious and ritual activity in Urnfield and early Hallstatt Europe. Cult activities had to have a location, and some of

BRONZE CULT CART from Eiche (*above, left*), eastern Germany, showing schematic birds on a vehicle frame with two four-spoked wheels. Birds such as these are a standard element in the Late Bronze Age repertoire of symbols.

RECONSTRUCTION (*below, left*) of the ritual wooden construction at Bargeroosterveld, Drenthe, Holland.

PLACED DEPOSITS of two male skeletons (*below*), within the inner ditch on the Middle Bronze Age fortified site at Velim, Bohemia. The site contained many such placed deposits of human and animal bone, pottery, and gold finds.

these—though not all, for no doubt open-air sites such as groves and hilltops played a role—are known. A remarkable wooden structure found in the peatlands of Drenthe at Bargeroosterveld consisted of a ring of small stones surrounding two flat sleeper-beams on which stood four posts: two of round section, two square. Pointed horn-like wooden terminal pieces probably ornamented the corners of this construction, which had been deliberately dismantled. A ritual construction of quite different type was found at St Moritz in the Engadin (eastern Switzerland). Here a rectangular setting of planks enclosed two cylinders of larch-wood, the whole surrounded by a further enclosure of poles laid across one another and jointed at the corners. In the barrels were found two swords and the fragment of a third, a dagger and a pin. It should also not be forgotten that Stonehenge, although the creation of earlier ages, continued not merely visible but actively in use: pottery of the local later Bronze and Iron Ages types was found in the Y and Z holes that surround the central constructions, and radiocarbon dates obtained from material in the Avenue ditches at their southern extension near the River Avon indicate a Late Bronze Age construction. Such continuing activity on ritual sites of an earlier age is usually very hard to document, and it is a moot point whether continuity of rite is thereby attested. This aspect of Bronze Age life, at any rate, appears not to have undergone a revolution.

There is another aspect of ritual life, in all probability emanating from the period under review (at least in part), and that is the practice of carving rock surfaces with engravings depicting figures (human and animal), boats, and a variety of symbols. These scenes are best known from southern Scandinavia (especially Sweden), but two areas of the Alps also have them in great numbers: the Val Camonica north of Brescia, and the area centred on Monte Bego on the French–Italian border near Bordighera. The dating of the Alpine engravings is hard to establish, and in any case varied, with some plainly emanating from a period earlier than 1300, others later than 600 BC. Much of the Scandinavian art, on the other hand, may well fall between those two dates, though here, too, dating is extremely difficult and usually determined by an analysis of the objects being depicted. In a few cases proximity to burials is suggestive, though hardly conclusive. Such a case occurs at Simris on the south-east coast of Scania (southern Sweden), where a large cemetery that spanned the Late Bronze Age and Early Iron Age lies close to engraved rock faces. While this gives no certainty that the two go together, at the very least it suggests that the area was one of continuing importance for ritual activities.

The art on these glacially polished, gently inclined rock faces consists of a very restricted range of motifs, repeated *ad nauseam*. Ships represent the single most common motif, and these occur not only near the sea, but in situations that are today well inland. Animals, especially bovids and deer, are also frequent, with ploughing scenes and other pictures that may be presumed to emanate from daily life putting in regular appearances. But it is the scenes involving humans that are most intriguing. These are much less common than ships or animals, but where they do appear they are shown in the act of carrying out what seem to be ritual dances or other performances, often with

GOLD GORGET (collar) from Shannongrove, Co. Limerick, Ireland (*above*). The terminals are decorated with concentric ribs and repoussé dots, and the main collar with bands of short parallel repoussé lines. The terminals are fastened to the collar itself with thin twisted wire.

GOLD CONE FROM AVANTON, Vienne, France (*left*), decorated with repoussé bosses and concentric circles, arranged in rows. Middle Bronze Age.

ROCK ART from western Sweden (*above*): a boat with two axe-wielding warriors in it, from Fossum, Bohuslän. The board has raised prow and the row of vertical dashes above the gunwales may represent the crew. The figures, which are phallic and wear swords at the waist, are probably taking part in a ritual contest or dance.

BEADS OF GLASS, AMBER, AND METAL (*below*) from Zürich-Wollishofen, Estavayer-le-Lac (Fribourg), Concise (Vaud), and Auvernier (Neuchâtel). All emanate from settlement sites of the Late Bronze Age.

arms raised, on occasion carrying lures or axes (infrequently bows), and invariably phallic; women and children (clearly identifiable as such) are seldom depicted. It is usually unclear to what extent the various figures are meant to be viewed as part of a compositional whole, that is, a scene: sometimes it is tempting to believe that a panel was intentionally created, but this remains pure supposition. Such scenes would, if detectable, be of a genre nature and not the actual representation of a single real event—though we can hardly doubt that the ceremonials depicted really did occur.

An exception to this is formed by the remarkable panels on the slabs that line the chamber of the tomb at Bredarör, Kivik, also Scania. These slabs, now unfortunately much damaged and partly lost, give the appearance of a funeral procession celebrating the last rites for the deceased who was buried in the tomb (nothing is known of the burial in question). The figures shown include ships, animals, battleaxes, four-arm crosses in circles, wavy lines, and, on the final two slabs, processions of mourners (including lure-blowers and drummers) with a chariot and a sign thought by some to represent the open grave. This curious set of depictions recalls, in its feel and subject-matter, the comparable scenes in Greek Geometric art. Perhaps the nearest we may come to it in Bronze Age terms is with the engraved stelae (grave markers) found in Spain. These commonly depict warriors, drawn as stick-men, but armed with sword, spear, shield, and horned-helmet. Much more attention is paid to the weaponry than to the figure himself; it was the martial nature of the deceased that was being stressed, not his physical side, but the fact that the slabs were decorated at all indicates an interest in perpetuating his name and depicting him in his most important light, equipped as a warrior.

Trade and Transport

The world of the Late Bronze Age and Early Iron Age was economically not complex, but it exploited the possibilities of contact through trade and exchange to a high degree. Coinage had, of course, not yet been invented, and there are no certain examples of 'value tokens' (objects of little or no intrinsic worth that served as a medium of exchange), though certain classes of artefact have been suggested for that role. A series of socketed-axes found in Brittany has too high a lead content to have served effectively as carpentry tools and may simply have operated as barter tokens. Nor can we certainly reconstruct markets, even though something rather like them had existed in some Near Eastern cities for centuries prior to 1300 BC. The economy was, to use the terminology adopted by the 'substantivist' school of Karl Polanyi, 'embedded' in social relations, so that economic activity invariably took place within a social context and was endowed with social meaning. This is not to deny, of course, that exchange had the effect of moving goods between partners for whom it was desirable from the point of view of obtaining the commodity in question; indeed, most such exchanges must have aimed at this goal. But it lacked a formalized location for exchange, and there is no evidence that it operated on anything other than a rather local level. Most Late Bronze Age groups were small in scale and based on the normal subsistence activities; it would be wrong to imagine that large quantities of foodstuffs, for instance, were transported around Europe at this stage.

Nevertheless, exchanges did occur, and apparently over long distances, to judge from a number of shipwrecks emanating from this period. While the Cape Gelidonya wreck, off the south coast of Turkey, comes from the period of the death throes of the east Mediterranean Bronze Age city-states, the Huelva and Cap d'Agde wrecks fall squarely within our period, and two wrecks off the south coast of England also lie close in time. The hoard of material from Huelva, found in the estuary of the River Odiel and probably, therefore, from a wreck, includes swords of a characteristic type with narrowing blade tip ('carp's tongue') that are distributed along Atlantic coasts as far north as Britain, along with much other material, both weaponry and ornaments, that indicates its connections over a wide field. The Cap d'Agde find, on the south coast east of Narbonne, contained material typical of the local 'Launacian' bronze industry, dating to the very end of the Bronze Age, around 700 BC. The evidence from these finds is similar to that from the hoards of Langdon Bay and Salcombe, which contained substantial numbers of metal objects of French types, whether intended for import into Britain or merely driven off course is not known. The fact that large quantities of metal were shipped around demonstrates, for us, that the mechanisms of transport were present even where the precise aim is not clear. It is thus not surprising to find that a type like the Rosnoen sword (an early form with simple riveted tang) is distributed from Britain to former Czechoslovakia; or that the standard 'flange-hilted' sword occurs throughout the whole of Europe from Sweden to Greece.

Bronzes, and in particular weaponry, were one of the goods transported for exchange in Bronze Age Europe, but, of course, there were other materials involved. One of the most remarkable phenomena in prehistoric exchange is that involving salt from the mines and evaporation sites of the Austrian Alps, notably at the site of Hallstatt itself and later at neighbouring centres such as Hallein (both words are etymologically connected with Greek 'hals', salt, and comparable words in other Indo-European languages). At Hallstatt, a Late Bronze Age exploitation of the salt-bearing strata continued on into the Iron Age, apparently without a significant break in occupation. Considerable numbers of graves of the Late Bronze and Early Iron Ages are known from the nearby cemetery. Although there is no direct evidence for the routes that the resulting cakes of salt took, the appearance of objects derived from both north and south of the Alps shows some of the likely recipients of this valuable commodity. Those in control of the salt sources must have derived large profits from the business, to judge from the wealth of their graves. Presumably they did not do the actual mining themselves, which must have been dangerous and unpleasant work; the techniques were similar to those used since the Early Bronze Age for copper extraction.

There is some evidence, too, for the movement of glass and glass products. The Ulu

Burun ship carried cakes of blue glass, so that where glass of Near Eastern compositional type (high magnesium) is found in Europe, there is at least a chance that the raw glass materials, in ingot form, came by sea from the East. This is a different type from that being made at Frattesina (above, p. 314); finds of this type are found widely distributed in the Late Bronze Age world. Another material imported from afar was amber. From at least the sixteenth century BC amber was moved from northern Europe to Greece, but after 1300 the areas in receipt of the 'gold of the north' increased in number and diversity. While Greece continued to receive a certain amount down to and probably beyond 1100, the centre of gravity of the exchange shifted to the west and north, especially to Italy and Yugoslavia, where it became common to decorate fibulae (safety pins) with beads of amber and glass.

These exchanges imply, of course, the technical means with which to carry them out, to transport the materials from source and the finished products from workshop to customer. We have already had occasion to refer to ships, but little is known of the form of the ships in question. The only regular source of illustrations comes from the rock art of Scandinavia, where boats are usually shown as high-prowed, shallow-draught vessels without sails, apparently propelled by a bank of oars. Such boats were used for sailing up the creeks and across the narrow strips of water along the Swedish archipelago, and do not necessarily relate to the boats that were used for undertaking longer sea voyages. Rare depictions of sailed vessels may represent such boats, but it is only in the east Mediterranean that they appear at all regularly. This must not obscure the fact, however, that long sea voyages were patently undertaken in the Mediterranean both before and after 1300, as the diplomatic and economic archives of Egypt, Anatolia, and the Levantine cities clearly show.

Travel by land was also important; more so in areas away from coasts. Knowledge of

MODEL BOAT FROM CAERGWRLE, Clywd, Wales, made of wood with gold foil decoration. The wavy lines at the bottom probably represent the water, the upright dashes may indicate the structure of the boat.

this is confined to those areas where the remains of ancient tracks or artificial paths were created, for example through wet, boggy land, as in Lower Saxony, Holland, and parts of Britain and Ireland. In the Somerset Levels, a major phase of track-building was undertaken early in the first millennium BC, perhaps responding to a period of higher rainfall when water-tables rose and more ground became wet. Trackways such as those on Tinney's Ground were built of brushwood pegged in place, and supplemented by additional planking where the ground was particularly damp. In a remarkable instance from Lower Saxony, two trackways 40 kilometres apart were both built in 713 BC from the same trees: this must indicate some form of centralized planning and organization of the trackway construction. In dry areas, it is much more difficult to reconstruct the paths of ancient routeways, and it becomes largely a matter of supposition based on the known position of important sites. It may well be, for example, that the ridgeway route that connected Iron Age forts along the line of the Berkshire Downs existed already in the Bronze Age: the fort at Rams Hill was preceded by a Bronze Age enclosure, and the same may well have been true for other sites.

The vehicles that ran along these routes are known both from depictions in rock art, and from the finding of bronze fittings and wheels belonging to them. Some of these wheels, such as the magnificent examples from Stade in Lower Saxony or Coulon in Deux-Sèvres, probably belonged to great ceremonial wagons, used in important parades such as at burials or other ritual occasions. The small clay model of a three-wheeler from Dupljaja, already alluded to for its ritual symbolism (above, p. 323), was probably of this nature, while wheeled-cauldrons, such as those from Peckatel (Mecklenburg) or Skallerup (Jutland), can only have served in cult activities. They may none the less show the kind of construction that was in use for more everyday activities. In farmyard and field, however, the construction of carts probably changed little over centuries and millennia: solid wooden wheels, some with crescentic or other openings, or cross-bar wheels, are known from bog finds, and must represent the slow-moving wagons and carts that had been built at least since the end of the Neolithic to bring produce in and take manure out. Such vehicles, drawn by oxen or horses, would have been the kind familiar to most denizens of the Bronze Age world, for whom elaborate bronze-fitted carts can only have been seen rarely, at the ceremonies depicted in the art of Tanum, Frännarp, or Naquane.

Warfare

Although many, perhaps most, people in the Urnfield world probably lived lives of rural peace, punctuated only by the seasonal demands of the agricultural year and the associ-

BRUSHWOOD TRACK, Tinney's Ground, Somerset (*above*), *c.*1200 BC; one of a number of excavated trackways that crossed the wet ground of the Somerset Levels in the Neolithic and Bronze Ages.

FLAG FEN, PETERBOROUGH (*below*): general view of the post alignment with horizontal timbers at an early stage in the excavations by the Fenland Archaeological Trust.

SPEAR AND CEREMONIAL AXE (*left*) from Krottenthal, district Dingolfing-Landau, Lower Bavaria. Late Bronze Age, around 1000 BC.

HELMETS OF SHEET BRONZE (*below, left*) from Viksø, northern Zealand, Denmark. These two magnificent horned helmets were found in a peat bog in 1942. Raised bosses and ridges represent eyes and eyebrows, and cast-on pieces form a ridge across the head from back to front, terminating in a beak.

AIR PHOTOGRAPH of the hillfort at Moel y Gaer (*below, right*), Denbighshire, showing double and triple lines of defences and two entrances.

ated obligations of cult and ceremony, some engaged in activities of a distinctly more warlike nature. From the scale of the operation (as far as we can reconstruct it from rock art and depositions of weaponry) it would appear that individual or small-group conflict was the order of the day, not the manœuvres of massed armies. The rock art depicts many scenes of men with upraised weapons, but they are usually shown as individuals, and not usually in situations of conflict except in the later panels of the Val Camonica—some of which may, however, be later than 600 BC. Yet the site and artefact record of the later Bronze Age leaves a strong impression of a society for whom warfare was an important element, frequently undertaken. This is seen above all in the abundance of weaponry that has survived. Swords, daggers, spearheads, arrowheads, and armour show us the repertoire of offensive and defensive materials available to the Urnfield warrior, and the grave stelae of Iberia and statue menhirs of Corsica show us something of the importance attached to the warrior's appearance.

The sword, for instance, which had been developed in the east Alpine area in the Middle Bronze Age, assumed a variety of forms whose rather rapid pace of change probably reflects the need constantly to update equipment if military success is to be maintained. It was at once a functional implement (as shown by the degree of wear and resharpening

on some pieces) and an object important for display purposes. The hilts were usually of organic materials such as bone, and were capped by a bronze pommel, but sometimes they were made in bronze cast over the blade heel and elaborately decorated. In such cases it is frequently evident that suitability for use in action has been sacrificed to appearance: wherever one can accurately assess the relative merits of the two hafting methods, it is the attached organic hilt-plates which come out best. The fact that both types coexisted probably indicates that the division between functional efficiency and striking appearance was intended and maintained.

Armour (shield, helmet, cuirass, greaves) played an increasing role in the mechanisms of Bronze Age warfare, but archaeologically it is those pieces that were made in metal that survive, and these were not the ones that were functionally most effective. It has been shown experimentally, for instance, that shields of sheet bronze can be cut by a slashing blow from a sword, whereas those of leather or wood are much tougher. Added to the difficulty of moving freely in sheet-metal armour, it is much more likely that leather was the normal material and that these metal pieces were for display—either in warlike ceremonies, or intended to strike fear into the hearts of opponents at the mere sight, much as happened with Homer's heroes in the *Iliad*.

The Urnfield period was also a time when groups systematically began to protect themselves against the effects of warfare by adding ramparts and ditches to their sites, thus creating forts. These forts are best known in hilly areas, but they occur, too, in low-land parts. While the sequence of fortifications has been best studied in the Lausitz area of eastern Germany (around Cottbus near the Polish border), the phenomenon was widespread, and examples of such Bronze Age forts are known from most areas of continental Europe, and from Britain. While the initial stages of such enclosure often consisted of little more than the addition of a timber palisade, later on this developed into an elaborate series of wooden frames supplemented by stone facings, rubble infill, and sloping revetment bank. It can be shown in other parts, for instance in south-west Germany, that the forts have an almost territorial distribution, appearing along the sides of river valleys at roughly equal intervals (10–15 kilometres), and presumably serving as refuges for the land in the immediate vicinity. It is also striking how, in spite of these precautions, almost all forts were in fact rapidly destroyed. The majority have pottery finds of only one phase and were never reoccupied. While the chronology of these phases is still rather imprecise, we do now know (as a result of the developments in dendrochronology, referred to earlier) the time brackets involved, and these rarely exceed one hundred years. The same situation may be seen at the great stockades of Poland, where sites such as Biskupin or Sobiejuchy went through two or three phases of devel-

THE CENTRAL TOWER and adjoining fortified courtyards of the Nuraghe Oes (*above*), district of Torralba, Sardinia. *Right*: the vaulted interior of the nuraghe 'Is Paras', district of Isili, Sardinia.

THE TUMBLED STONE of the outer rampart at Velim, Bohemia (*far right*). Finds from the destruction debris indicate a date at the start of the Late Bronze Age.

THE RECONSTRUCTED GATEWAY in the Early Iron Age stockade at Biskupin, central Poland. The site belongs to the Lausitz culture, and is one of a number constructed in this part of Poland at this time.

opment in rapid succession, catastrophic destructions bringing about the end of sites that had been created through major investment of time and energy.

Finally, we should not forget the role of the cavalry in Urnfield and early Iron Age warfare. Since the adoption of the horse to pull chariots (and later for riding) in large parts of Europe after 2000 BC, its versatility and power had been increasingly appreciated. A series of bridle fittings in bone and antler in the first half of the second millennium was increasingly supplemented by metal pieces, both the bits themselves and, much more common, the cheekpieces to which the bit and the rest of the bridle were attached. An increasing use of horses, in ceremony and perhaps also in warfare, can be seen, but the really dramatic change occurred after about 800 BC, when graves containing horse-riding equipment began to appear over a wide area of eastern and central Europe. Their interpretation as 'Thraco-Cimmerian' reflects the traditions recorded by Herodotus of a movement of peoples from the steppelands to the east, westward into Europe at a time that preceded the Scythian settlements. These latter are supposedly represented at cemeteries such as Szentes-Vekerzug in south-eastern Hungary, with iron bridles and bits, dating after 600 BC; the typologically earlier forms, made of bronze, go back at least to 1000 BC, and antler versions of the same objects had been in use since the Early Bronze Age.

Epilogue: Europe in 600 BC

By 600, Europe lay on the threshold of written history, and writers like Herodotus were soon to record events in Greece and in some cases their interactions with the 'barbarian' tribes to the north. The scale of north–south connections after 600—which was vastly greater than anything we can document before that date—indicates how successfully the formation processes of the Urnfield period laid the foundations for the next major phase of development. Part of this was no doubt the result of developments south of the Alps, as Greece and Italy experienced the phenomena of colonization, political evolution, and trade expansion that played key roles in the emergence of state societies in those areas. But events had been on the move in the north as well, and the scale of the societies that emerged was significantly larger than anything seen before that time. Both the size and the elaboration of the Heuneburg, for example, mark a major advance on the Urnfield pattern (cf. pp. 332).

The widespread appearance of iron also played its part. As we have seen above, the increasing quantities of iron that are found in Europe through the first millennium suggest a marked movement away from reliance on traditional materials and towards those whose supply was easier to assure, whose sources were much more widespread, and whose products were preferable in terms of hardness and sharpness. By 600, iron was the standard material for tools and weapons, though the highest quality art products were still made in bronze. Skill in iron metallurgy was important, though it was only one of a number of skills developed over the previous few hundred years that came to full fruition in the development of the major social, political, and artistic achievements that form the subject of the next chapter.

10

Iron Age Societies in Western Europe and Beyond, 800–140 BC

BARRY CUNLIFFE

The Birth of the Graeco-Roman World, 800–400 BC

EUROPE at the height of Mycenaean power in the fourteenth and thirteenth centuries BC presented a foretaste of what was to come. To judge by the distribution of Mycenaean pottery in Italy and southern Spain, Aegean ships were venturing into the Adriatic and the west Mediterranean on a regular basis to satisfy the demand of the Mycenaean polities for raw materials. Further afield in the fringes of barbarian Europe the local élites which emerged owed much of their, albeit unstable, equilibrium to their abilities to control the throughput of goods to the consumer markets of the Aegean. In the same way that the brief flowering of Mycenaean society was a foretaste of Greek, and later Graeco-Roman, civilization, so were the trading systems of the Mycenaeans and the responses of the barbarian tribes of the periphery to presage developments five centuries or more hence. It is almost as if the Mycenaean system was a trial run for the fully fledged Graeco-Roman world.

To understand what was happening in Europe beyond the precocious Mediterranean fringes it is essential to look first to the Mediterranean itself, since from the eighth century BC onward the fortunes of the two worlds were inextricably bound together. The story of the Mediterranean in the four centuries from 800 to 400 BC opens with trading rivalries between the Greeks and the Phoenicians and closes as the two successor powers, the Romans and the Carthaginians, square up for military confrontation. The intricacies and sub-plots are many and fascinating—here we can tease out only a few of the major themes.

By 800 BC the city-states of the Greek mainland and the Aegean coasts of Asia Minor were beginning to emerge from obscurity. As populations consolidated at focal locations so social systems became more complex, and with urbanization came a range of problems, in particular social stress exacerbated by rapid increases in population and the inability of the productive sub-systems to maintain food supplies over extended periods of shortage. Together these problems were relieved by substantial bodies of population leaving the home base and setting up colonies. While the Greeks distinguished *apoikiai*—settlements away from home—from *emporia*—trading posts—the differences cannot have been great and whatever the motives for the original settlements, the siphoning off of surplus population and the desire to create trading enclaves on the fringes of regions of high production, be it the corn lands of the Pontic steppe (pp. 384-9) or metal-rich Etruria, must soon have become blurred.

The two centuries from 800 to 600 saw the opening up of the western Mediterranean to the Greek world. According to Greek tradition the earliest colonial movements were initiated by Euboeans from Eretria and Chalcis, and from the archaeological evidence it is clear that intensive trade was already underway by *c.*770. One of the earliest of the colonial settlements so far discovered was established at Pithekoussai on the island of Ischia at the northern extremity of the Bay of Naples, admirably chosen to be in direct and easy contact with the highly productive region of Etruria to the north and with the island of Elba whence came a range of metals, especially high-quality iron. The island location was evidently judged well placed, for within a few years the Chalcidians established a new settlement on the adjacent mainland at Cumae.

The journey from Greece to these outposts in the wilds of the western Mediterranean was long, but the land-hugging style of early navigation and the provision of safe and well-tried anchorages around the coasts of Italy and Sicily made the voyaging less precarious. As the intensity of trading increased so many of these havens became established settlements. Naxos, just south of Taormina on the east coast of Sicily was, traditionally, founded in 734, the next year the Corinthians chose to establish a colony at Syracuse 80 kilometres to the south. Others followed in rapid succession until, by about 650, Sicily and southern Italy had become an extension of Greece itself—not for nothing was it known as Magna Graecia.

To begin with, trade with the Etruscans satisfied the metal demands of the home markets of the Greek mainland, but in the middle of the seventh century a new group of explorers appear on the map—the Phocaeans—from the town of Phocaea on the Aegean coast of Asia Minor. Herodotus tells us that they 'were the first of the Greeks to make long voyages and it was they who opened up the region of the Adriatic, Etruria and Spain, and Tartessos'. They sailed, he said, not in merchant ships but in *pentekonters*—fifty-oared war galleys—a reminder that exploration was much the same then as it was 2000 years later when Vasco da Gama used his fire power to establish Portuguese supremacy in India. The account makes it clear that the mineral resources of the pyrite belt of south-eastern Spain was the main attraction. These resources were controlled by the Tartessians occupying the territory around the lower reaches of the Guadalete, Guadalquivir, and Tinto rivers. Herodotus goes on to say that so well disposed were the Tartessians to the Phocaeans that when the latter came under increasing pressure in their homeland from the Persians, the Tartessian king invited them to migrate *en masse* to his kingdom—an offer which they declined, accepting instead money to build a defensive wall.

In all probability the route which the Phocaean sailors used led northward, from the Bay of Naples to Corsica and then to the coast of France, thence along the Mediterranean coast of Spain, through the Pillars of Hercules (Straits of Gibraltar) to the Tartessian ports of the Atlantic. Like all mariners they would have chosen havens along the route to take on food and water, in this way establishing close relations with a number of native communities. Gradually the best-placed havens would have developed the functions of ports-of-trade and eventually the more favoured sites would have received their first permanent colonists. Massalia (Marseilles), close to the mouth of the Rhône, became a colony in 600 BC, Emporion (Ampurias) soon after, and Alalia, on the east coast of Corsica, by about 560 BC: daughter colonies developed later to fill the spaces in between. Thus by the middle of the sixth century the Phocaeans had firmly established themselves as masters of the northern waters of the west Mediterranean, gradually taking over what had been an Etruscan preserve. In this way the barbarian communities of western Europe found themselves in close contact for the first time with the city-states of Greece.

In parallel with the Greek expansion, the Phoenicians, a Semitic people from the coastal cities of the Levant (now Lebanon), were establishing direct trading links with the coasts of north Africa and southern Spain. They too, it appears, were attracted by the mineral resources of Tartessos. Traditionally they are supposed to have set up a port-of-trade at Gardes (Cádiz), then an island on the southern flank of the Tartessian kingdom, about 1200 BC—a date archaeologically unproven. The earliest occupation, so far discovered, dates back only to the eighth century. Certainly by 800 BC Phoenician trade had intensified, the motive force behind it probably being the Assyrian demand for silver. The Phoenicians, by virtue of the coastal location of their home cities, were the natural middlemen occupying the interface between the productive Mediterranean and the consuming empires of the Near East.

Herodotus gives a detailed picture of the nature of the exchanges between the Phoenician traders and the Tartessians. 'After importing to that place oil and other small wares of maritime commerce', he says, 'they obtained for their return cargo so great a quantity of silver that they were no longer able to keep or receive it, but were forced when sailing away from those ports to make of silver not only all other articles which they used but also all of their anchors'—a gross exaggeration, no doubt, but sufficient to imply that the silver exports may have been prodigious. In all probability Tartessian silver ended up as Assyrian coinage.

The Phoenicians traded more widely than with Tartessos alone. Their presence has been traced well down the Atlantic coast of north Africa, and within the Mediterranean a succession of small ports are known at regular intervals along the southern coast of Spain. From here the productive hinterland of the inter-mountain plateaux of the Sierra Nevada, and the Guadalquivir valley beyond, could be tapped. Phoenician settlements were also established along the route used by the traders across the length of the Mediterranean, but were most numerous around the Tunisian coast. The earliest was at

Utica, but it was soon eclipsed by Carthage which began to flourish in the seventh century. Elsewhere along the route ports were established in western Sicily, along the south and west coasts of Sardinia, and on the Balearic Islands. In other words, while the Greeks controlled the northern part of the west Mediterranean the Phoenicians were in command of the southern. This does not mean that the two spheres were exclusive: on the contrary there is much evidence for interaction. Quantities of Greek products have been found in early layers at Carthage and it is highly likely that Phoenician merchants picked up Greek oil and other commodities in Sicilian or Italian ports which they then transhipped to their trading partners in the West.

The middle of the sixth century saw a significant change in the political structure of the west Mediterranean. In 573 the Babylonians overran the Phoenician cities of the Levantine coast severely dislocating long-established trading systems. The west Mediterranean was now severed from the east and from now on Carthage rather than the old mother cities of Tyre and Sidon became the principal focus for the Phoenician traders in the west. Not long after, in 544, the Persians, who were annexing the cities of Asia Minor, besieged the town of Phocaea. The population fled *en masse* to the west with the intention of settling at their colony of Alalia on Corsica. Such a massive Greek presence was seen as a serious economic threat by the Etruscans, who were at this time still trading widely in the northern reaches of the west Mediterranean. An alliance was struck by them with the Carthaginians and a sea battle ensued off the coast near Alalia in *c.*537. Although the Greeks won, it was a close-run encounter and the settlers decided to move from Corsica, out of the Etruscan ambit, to found a more secure colony at Elea (Velia) in southern Italy.

The incident is a reminder that the western Mediterranean was beginning to be too small a place to satisfy the growing economic ambitions of the Greeks, Etruscans, and Carthaginians. Alalia was the first significant conflict in the long period of increasing tension, which culminated in the outbreak of the First Punic War in 264.

The Battle of Alalia did not mean that the Etruscans retained the northern sea-ways for themselves: indeed it is about this time that the Greek city of Massalia begins to develop rapidly dominating the trading routes to barbarian Gaul and beyond. One reason for this sudden growth may have been that, following Alalia, the Carthaginians effectively took control of the southern Spanish ports and prevented the Greeks from obtaining access, not only to the mineral wealth of Tartessos but also to the Atlantic trading systems beyond where much of the tin for the Greek market was obtained. By developing Massalia and the other ports of southern Gaul, the Greek settlers could take direct control of two major trade routes through barbarian Europe: the Rhône-Saône valley leading to the north and the Carcassonne Gap — Garonne-Gironde route giving access to the Atlantic sea route and thus the invaluable sources of tin in Galicia, Armorica, and Cornwall. One consequence of the Carthaginian monopoly of the Straits of Gibraltar, therefore, was a stronger and more determined Greek presence in southern Gaul, which in turn led to a gradual ousting of Etruscan interests.

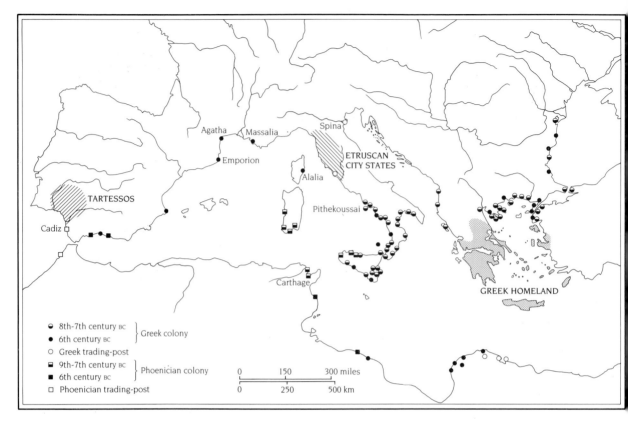

THE MEDITERRANEAN at the time of Greek and Phoenician colonization. The development of the Etruscan cities and of Tartessos was influenced by the culture of the east Mediterranean traders and travellers.

The effects on Etruria can be readily detected. The old coastal towns begin to decline and a new system of trade routes develops northward through the Apennines. Towards the end of the sixth century towns, like Marzabotto and Felsinia (Bononia), were founded on the northern side of the Apennines overlooking the rich Po valley. This reorientation provided the Etruscans with direct access to two new markets, the one leading through the Alpine passes to the barbarian north, the other, via the coastal towns of Spina and Adria, to the Adriatic and thus direct to the markets of Greece without having to go via the avaricious middlemen of Magna Graecia. On present evidence, Spina seems to have been founded about 520, with Adria perhaps a little earlier. These economic readjustments were to set the Etruscans in good stead for nearly a century. Meanwhile, in the western Mediterranean, freedom of movement was gradually denied to them culminating, in 474, in a great sea battle with the forces of Magna Graecia off Cumae where the Etruscan fleet was soundly beaten.

Standing back from the detail it is possible to detect a phase of unrestricted trade in the period 800–600, followed by a phase of conflict, competition, and intensification in the period 600–450. During the first, a wide swath of the European coast, from Italy to Portugal, came into contact with Greek, Etruscan, and Phoenician culture; during the second there was an intensification of Phoenician/Carthaginian influence focusing on southern Iberia, while to the north the Greeks began to dominate the southern shores of Gaul as the Etruscan sphere refocused itself on the Adriatic and the eastern Alps. All these shifts and readjustments are, as we will see, to have a dramatic effect on the communities of the European hinterland.

The Barbarian Periphery, 600–450 BC

The trading ports established around the shores of the Mediterranean provided a stimulus to development in barbarian Europe. Different local communities reacted in different ways, but in each case the pattern was similar—Mediterranean goods were avidly sought, the most valuable being acquired by the aristocracy and used to demonstrate their exalted status: while goods of lesser value were passed down by the élite to those of lower status in cycles of gift exchange. At the same time there came the desire to emulate the exotic, by having local craftsmen copy imported luxury items and by adopting aspects of alien behaviour.

In southern Spain it is possible to see these processes at work particularly clearly as the Tartessians and their neighbours developed close trading links with the Phoenicians and Greeks. The quantity of the imports was enormous. In one excavation in Huelva (almost certainly the site of ancient Tartessos) a single trench 6 by 4 metres produced sherds from 1400 Greek pots drawn from a number of centres in the east Mediterranean including Athens and the islands of Chios and Samos. The earliest date to the second half of the seventh century but the majority were of the sixth century. If the density of material from this single excavation was consistent throughout the occupied area it must imply that many hundreds of shiploads of goods entered the port.

On the outskirts of the settlement, at La Joya, lay a cemetery where some of the local Tartessian élite were buried in the seventh century. In one, tomb 17, the dead noble was provided with a chariot of walnut wood decorated with bronze and accompanied by an ivory box, and a set of ritual bronze vessels comprising a jug, a dish, and an incense burner. These items were evidently made by local craftsmen, but the beliefs implied by the grave furniture seem to have been adopted from the east Mediterranean. Elsewhere in Tartessian territory rich burials are rare, but around the northern periphery of the kingdom a number have been found. One group, at Carmona, were provided with finely carved ivories. Another find, at Alisada, comprised an astonishing range of gold jewellery, much of it locally made but incorporating a Syrian amethyst seal and an Egyptian ear-ring. These rich burials probably represent the wealth of local élites who, by controlling the flow of commodities through their territories to the coastal ports, were able to grow rich.

The importation of Greek and Phoenician ceramics through the main ports of Cádiz and Huelva and the smaller coastal stations along the southern Spanish shore led to dramatic changes in local production. In place of dull grey wares there was a rapid acceptance of lighter ochre-coloured fabrics painted with red and black geometric patterns. This was all part of what has been called the orientalizing phase, dating to *c.*750–550, and with it came the equally rapid development of urban sites throughout the length of the Guadalquivir valley. By the sixth century quite substantial towns were in existence with encircling defensive walls, and not long after, at sites like Porcuna, the first manifestations of Iberian art appear in startlingly sophisticated compositions of statuary, blatantly native in details of armour and clothing but with their east Mediterranean inspiration still clearly displayed. This dramatic series of developments in the Guadalquivir valley may be due to the reorientation of trade networks, for it was at this time that the Phoenician ports along the southern Spanish coast were at their most active. The implications would seem to be that direct contact was now being established from the Mediterranean coast northward with the communities controlling the rich resources of the valley and the silver-producing region of the Sierra Morena beyond. There is some evidence to suggest that at about this time the pace of change in the Tartessian territory to the west

THE SO-CALLED 'LIONESS OF SAGUNTO', actually a bull. A masterpiece of Iberian sculpture from a sanctuary or tomb probably dating to the fourth century BC. From Sagunto, Valencia, Spain. Height 0.8 m.

LIMESTONE BULL FROM OSUNA, Andalucia, Spain. A typical Iberian carving of the fourth or third century BC probably from a religious context. Height 0.65 m.

THE DAMA OF EL CERRO DE LOS SANTOS, Albacete, Spain (*left*). Probably a priestess officiating in a religious ceremony. The limestone was originally painted. The dress and stance is typical of Iberian sculpture of the fourth and third
centuries BC. Height 1.35 m.

MONUMENTAL STATUE OF AN IBERIAN WARRIOR (*right*). One element of a large and complex monument, possibly
a funerary sculpture. From Porcuna, Andalucia, Spain. Fifth or fourth century. Though the armour is Iberian the artistic
inspiration is Greek.

slowed, possibly because the eastern Mediterranean traders now preferred to use the
more direct route rather than venture into the Atlantic to trade through the Tartessian
middlemen.

A further shift of focus is apparent as the sixth century proceeds. Judging by the distribution of Greek pottery imports, the ports of south-eastern Spain became major
points of entry, a development which may be linked to the rising importance of Ibiza as
a Phoenician centre after *c*.550. Why this change should have taken place is not entirely
clear, but the development of the silver mines near Cartagena may have provided one of
the attractions. From the south-east coast the traditionally exploited resources of the
Guadalquivir could still have been reached via the Segura valley. The result of all this was
that by the fifth century the entire coastal zone of Mediterranean Spain had developed a

vibrant urban-based society with a highly distinctive art and writing, underpinned by a complex military structure. The Iberians, as they are now called, emerged from indigenous roots, their cultural development quickened and enhanced by the energies generated by three centuries of intense interaction with east Mediterranean entrepreneurs.

Further north mountain ranges like the Alpes-Maritimes and the Cévennes formed a significant barrier between the Mediterranean zone and temperate Europe, but the valleys of the Rhône and Saône provided a single easy route of access to a wide region stretching from Burgundy to southern Germany. This west Hallstatt zone occupied a focal position in Europe since it spanned the upper courses of the Seine, Saône, Rhine, and Danube and thus commanded direct access to much of the rest of the Continent north of the Alps. It is hardly surprising, therefore, that when, in the latter part of the sixth century, Greek-led trade intensified through Massalia, the élites of this northern zone were able to command and control the exotic Mediterranean products sent north as trade goods. The flow of goods had started earlier involving prestige equipment for the wine-drinking ritual of the Greek symposium such as the 'Rhodian' flagons found at Vilsingen and Kappel, manufactured towards the end of the seventh century, and the *hydria* from Grächwil made in southern Italy in the early sixth century, but after the middle of the sixth century trade intensified. Large items of considerable value, such as the

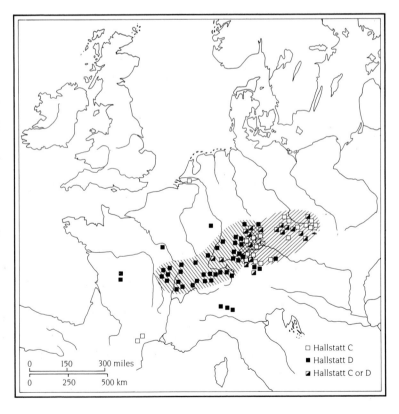

IN THE HEART of barbarian Europe the Iron Age élite developed a distinctive burial rite which involved interring the body with the funerary vehicle which carried the deceased to the grave. The earliest of these burials (Hallstatt C, *c.*720–600 BC) stretched from Germany to former Czechoslovakia. Later in the Hallstatt D period (*c.*600–480) the centre of power moved westwards.

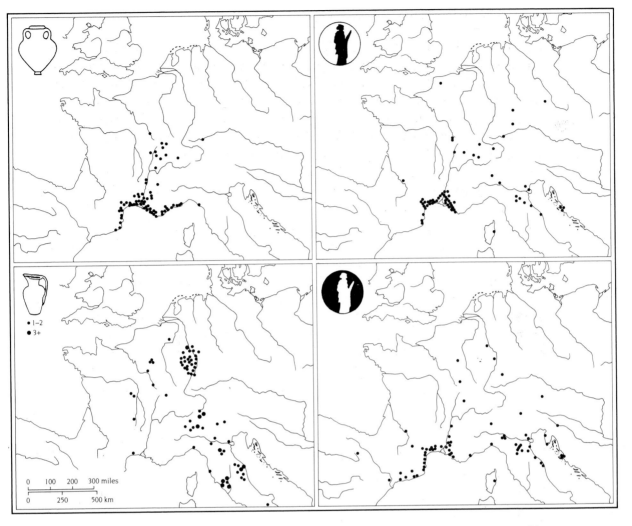

COMMODITIES ASSOCIATED WITH WINE DRINKING were transported from the Mediterranean to the courts of the Iron Age nobility of west central Europe. The upper maps show the distribution of Massaliot wine amphorae and of Greek Black figured wares dated to roughly 560–500 BC; the lower maps show finds of Etruscan jugs and Greek Red figured pottery (*c*.500–450 BC).

man-height bronze crater from Vix, continued to be imported along with a range of goods of lesser value including Attic pottery, first black-figured and later red-figured, and Massaliot amphorae filled, no doubt, with local wine from Provence.

The mechanisms by which the trade was articulated remain obscure, nor can we be sure what local products were given in return. Gold is one possibility, so, too, are hides, furs, and foodstuffs, like the smoked hams for which the region was famed a few centuries later. Another product essential to the Mediterranean economy, and featuring frequently in later commercial transactions, were slaves. The native élites maintained full control of these exchanges and used their acquisitions as symbols of their exalted status.

THE HILLFORT OF THE HEUNEBURG, in southern Germany, overlooks the river Danube. The hill was redefended at the end of the sixth century with a mudbrick wall built on stone foundations—a technique common in the Greek world but totally alien in a temperate European climate. It marks a brief phase when the resident élite embraced Greek aspects of Greek culture.

In life there would have been lavish feasting and cycles of gift exchange between paramount chieftains and their subordinates, and in death the lineage demonstrated its social prestige by burying costly sets of wine-drinking equipment and other exotic gear with its dead. Conspicuous consumption on this level created shortages and demands which provided an added spur to trade: all the time the Mediterranean entrepreneurs were able and willing to feed the system, the equilibrium, albeit unstable, was maintained.

The archaeological manifestations of this 'prestige goods economy' were dramatic. A number of hilltop locations developed as defended residences for the nobility. At Mont Lassois in Burgundy, Heuneburg in southern Germany, and Châtillon-sur-Glâne in Switzerland quantities of Mediterranean luxury goods have been found, while the Heuneburg was at this time defended by a remarkable wall built of mud-brick on dry-stone footings, enlivened by forward-projecting rectangular bastions. The technique, common enough in the Greek world, was totally alien to temperate Europe where winter rains would soon have wrought havoc. It is, none the less, a striking example of how avidly the barbarian élite espoused what they understood to be the accoutrements of Mediterranean culture.

In their burials, too, the élite demonstrated their command of Mediterranean behaviour by providing themselves with an array of luxury goods. At Vix, near Mont Lassois, the body was accompanied by a complete set of wine-drinking equipment ranging from the crater for mixing the wine to the cups for drinking, while at Hochdorf, a large cauldron of Mediterranean origin contained mead, which was drunk from locally made gold-encrusted drinking horns. Elsewhere flagons and Attic cups are frequently found. High-status graves could also be distinguished by the quantity of gold employed and by the presence of elaborately decorated funerary carts, that at Hochdorf being extensively covered in iron sheeting, a work of no utility but expressive of the lineage's ability to command almost unlimited labour.

The leading households of the west Hallstatt zone were linked together in cycles of competitive exchange and there is evidence to show that their fortunes relative to each other varied over time. One cause of change would have been variation in the flow of prestige goods resulting from political reorientations in the Mediterranean. Minor changes are difficult to distinguish archaeologically, but a major dislocation followed from the reordering of the Etruscan trade network after the battle of Alalia (above,

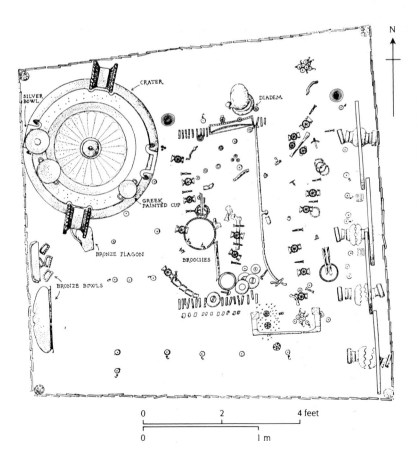

THE BURIAL OF A BARBARIAN ARISTOCRAT was found in a burial pit beneath a large barrow at Vix, Chatillon-sur-Seine, France. Beside the body and its personal equipment, the dismantled funeral cart was found as well as imported Mediterranean vessels used in wine-drinking rituals. The burial dates to the end of the sixth century BC.

THE HUGE BRONZE KRATER used for mixing wine found in the burial chamber at Vix was probably made in a Greek workshop in southern Italy at the end of the sixth century. It would have been dismantled for transportation by sea and up the river Rhône before being reassembled possibly in the nearby princely stronghold at Mont Lassois. The krater is 1.64 m in height.

THE PRINCELY HILLTOP SETTLEMENT at Mont Lassois was surrounded by rich aristocratic burials of which Vix is, so far, the most spectacular. Not far away was another rich grave containing a griffin-headed cauldron standing on a tripod. The item was of Greek manufacture and like the Vix krater must have been transported up the Rhône by boat in the later part of the sixth century BC.

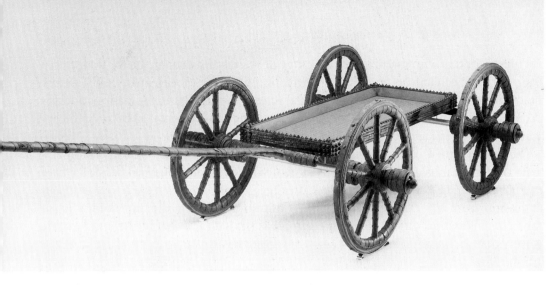

THE BURIAL OF A CHIEFTAIN was found in a wooden chamber beneath a large barrow at Hochdorf in Germany. The body had been taken to the grave in a funerary vehicle built of wood but covered in iron sheeting.

p. 339). This manifests itself most clearly in the distribution of beaked flagons manufactured in Etruscan workshops at Vulci and neighbouring towns in the century or so after 525. These flagons are found scattered along routes through the Apennines, across the Po valley, and following the passes leading northward through the Alps. Beyond there is a dense cluster from a group of élite burials in the middle Rhine–Moselle region with a smaller concentration in the Marne region of northern France. The simplest interpretation of this pattern is that the Etruscan traders, excluded from access to the rich pickings of northern Europe via the Rhône corridor, because of the monopoly the Massaliots now held, developed a new access of their own, outflanking the west Hallstatt zone and establishing direct contacts with the communities of the northern periphery—the Marne–Moselle zone. One of the attractions of this area may well have been the high-quality iron ore available in the Hunsrück-Eifel region.

The effects of this contact on the Marne–Moselle zone were dramatic. Previously it had begun to develop the characteristics of a widely dispersed warrior aristocracy, its warlike nature quite possibly resulting from the fact that the region had procured slaves to exchange with the west Hallstatt élite who transhipped them to the Mediterranean. Newly established contact with the Mediterranean, via the Etruscan network, introduced prestige goods direct to the area for the first time, allowing the prominent warriors to become an élite by manipulating luxury goods. Such men were buried in rich tombs like those at Weiskirchen and Schwarzenbach in the Saarland, and La Gorge-Meillet and Somme Bionne in the Marne.

The Etruscan contact with the Marne–Moselle region is most vividly demonstrated by the distribution of imported beaked flagons, but it is also manifest in more subtle ways. The new élite adopted the two-wheeled chariot in their burial ritual, a fashion learnt from the Etruscans. There also came into existence schools of immensely inventive metalworkers who manufactured a range of vessels and ornaments for their aristocratic patrons, relying on an eclectic repertoire of artistic motifs, many only slightly removed from Etruscan originals. What they created in this short, brilliant period was an entirely new art style—known as Celtic or La Tène art—destined to become the first truly Pan-European art style of the Continent.

The sudden emergence of this new élite in the early fifth century had a destabilizing effect on the established west Hallstatt system which rapidly collapsed, whether from internal instability, because its supply of prestige goods had diminished, or because of aggression from the northern periphery is not entirely clear: the chronology is too imprecise, allowing a variety of interpretations. What is clear is that by the middle of the fifth century the west Hallstatt prestige-goods economy was at an end and in the Marne and the Moselle the warrior élites were vigorous and fast developing. The energies of these regions were soon to be felt far and wide (below, pp. 358-69).

The head of the Adriatic provided another convenient interface between the Mediterranean world and temperate Europe. From the plain of Venezia comparatively easy routes were available through the Julian Alps to the hilly country of Slovenia and thence eastward via the Drava and Sava to the plains of the upper Danube or northward along the edge of the eastern Alps crossing the Danube near Bratislava to the valley of the Morava and the North European Plain beyond. The focal position of Slovenia, lying as it does between the Alps and the mountain ranges of the Balkans, was crucial and it was here from the eighth to the fifth centuries that a distinct grouping of communities emerged based on large fortified settlements like Magdalenska Gora, Vače, and Stična with huge cemeteries spread out below them. The overriding impression, given by the archaeological evidence from these sites, is of stability and continuity over nearly four centuries.

It is impossible to be sure what products were passing through Slovenia, but amber from the Baltic coasts is likely to have bulked large. Locally there were high-grade iron ores with ample evidence of iron extraction and working: another specialist production was glass which was usually made into multicoloured beads. Given the crucial location and productivity of the area, one might have expected an élite to emerge creating a demand for Mediterranean luxuries on the model of the west Hallstatt zone, but this was not so. There is evidence of an aristocracy, in the form of rich burials often furnished with sheet bronze body armour and accompanied by decorated situlae, but imported luxuries are rare and the extremes of wealth evident in the West are not found here. Clearly the social system was quite different.

The most likely explanation is that the entrepreneurial energy which the eastern Mediterranean traders showed in Spain and southern France and which the Etruscans used to exploit the mid-Alpine passes was, for some reason, not focused on the east Alpine region. The trading ports at Spina and Adria were concerned to exploit the Po valley and routes to the north-west. It may simply be that the commodities reaching the Adriatic from the north-east were far less in demand. If so, they would have passed through Slovenia by means of traditional methods of exchange embedded in the social system, leaving it largely unperverted by the avaricious commercialism of the Mediterranean.

Beyond the Fringe, 600–450 BC

Beyond the irregular zone of territory, stretching from Portugal to Croatia, which was directly influenced by the Greek, Phoenician, and Etruscan worlds, lay a vast swath of the European continent. Geomorphologically and climatically the landscape, and, therefore, its resource potential, varied and this in turn conditioned a bewildering variety of cultural responses. At the expense of oversimplification we may divide the region into three broad zones: a temperate zone stretching from southern Britain and northern France to Slovakia; a northern zone including Holland, northern Germany, Poland, and Scandinavia; and an Atlantic zone extending from Portugal to north-western Scotland. Needless to say, within each there is considerable variety not only in culture but also in the quality of the evidence available.

Within the temperate zone a surprising number of the disparate communities invested a tithe of their energies in the creation and maintenance of hill-forts and related structures. In many of these areas, for example southern Britain and southern Germany, hill-forts began to develop in the Late Bronze Age and were well underway in the seventh century, but the sixth and early fifth centuries saw the phenomenon at its height. Clearly, these structures, usually between 1 and 6 hectares in extent, required communal effort organized under some kind of coercive power, and their very existence demonstrates a degree of centralization both of power and of the socio-economic systems which bound the community together. But it would be wrong to assume that the existence of hill-forts in different parts of the zone implies closely similar social structures.

Given the potential interest of the phenomena, excavation has been surprisingly slight. In southern Britain, where several forts of this period have been excavated, some on quite a large scale, it is clear that many were occupied by substantial communities. At Danebury the circular timber-built houses were concentrated around the periphery of the site just behind the rampart and along metalled roads in the southern part of the enclosure. Elsewhere areas were set aside for the storage of grain in timber store buildings and in pits. In some parts of the country, especially in the central-south, large numbers of hill-forts were built in the sixth and fifth centuries, but after about 400 BC the majority were abandoned with only a few continuing in use and rising to positions of dominance. Many of these 'developed hill-forts' as they are called continued in occupation into the first century BC. In this region, therefore, it seems that the social systems, which encouraged the construction of the early forts persisted, though in a developing form, for 500 years or so.

In northern France and southern Belgium, the density of forts is somewhat less and few have been excavated, but those which have been sampled on a sufficient scale, for

352 <i>Iron Age Societies in Western Europe</i>

example Fort Harrouard in France and Buzenol, Kemmelberg, and Hastedon in Belgium all seem to have been abandoned by about 400–350 BC. A little further to the east, however, in Luxembourg, two forts, Otzenhausen and Altburg, were intensively used in the period after 400. Here, perhaps, we are seeing a localized development of the hillfort phenomenon comparable to that in southern Britain. The zone of hill-forts continues through central Germany into former Czechoslovakia. At Smolenice, in south-west Slovakia, excavation has exposed a sixth-century fortification which differs little in basic size, location, and underlying economy to that of a typical fort in the Welsh Marches.

The idea of communal fortification was also well developed in Poland where the majority of the forts, dating to the seventh to fifth centuries, are found in Great Poland and Silesia. Not all are on hills and some are to be found on islands in lakes. The most famous is Biskupin, near Bydogszcz where excavations undertaken between 1938 and 1949 exposed much of the plan of an island settlement surrounded by a substantial timber rampart. The entire area within the defences was taken up with thirteen parallel rows of houses packed closely together with corduroy timber roads between, joining a ring road which encircles the complex within the rampart. The house rows are comprised of between three and ten individual houses aligned together in terrace fashion under a single gable roof. The entire layout of this remarkable settlement is redolent of communal order maintained under a strong coercive power though there was no evidence within of significant social differentiation. Assuming that all 105 houses were in use at the same time and that each accommodated a single family, the resident population is likely to have been 400–500.

For all its variety, it is tempting to see, in this hill-fort zone of temperate Europe, a broadly similar underlying level of social and economic organization, the forts representing a concentration of population, and services maintained, presumably, by the authority of a local leader. The processes inherent in this development were rooted in the Late Bronze Age (chapter 9) but there is clear evidence of intensification in the sixth and fifth centuries. The very act of fortification, and the fact that a significant number of the sites from Britain to Poland bear evidence of attack is sufficient to suggest an underlying current of aggression occasionally breaking into open warfare. What the causes of tension were it is difficult to say, but a general climatic deterioration combined with an increase of population may have been sufficient to cause social instability over a wide area. The tensions created by the competing élites in the west Hallstatt zone and the Marne–Moselle region to the south may also have been an ancillary factor, more particularly so if the acquisition of slaves by raiding, ultimately for the Mediterranean market, formed a significant part of the exchange process between the two zones.

The economic systems underpinning the various communities of this hill-fort zone varied considerably with the resource potentials of the different regions, but the very permanence of the fortifications and the long-lived nature of the settlements associated with them suggest an emphasis on the ownership and exploitation of the land. The considerable storage capacity evident in the hill-forts of southern Britain at this time amply demonstrates that here, at least, the acquisition and storage of food surpluses was an important underlying motivation, though to what extent this reflected an organized system of regional redistribution or simply a hedge against periodic shortages it is difficult to say. One thing, however, is clear—throughout the region imported luxury goods played no significant part in the economy: the forts were essentially the centres of regional systems which were largely self-sufficient. Only in essential commodities such as iron, bronze, stone, and minor luxuries like glass, amber, and coral did interregional exchange take place, no doubt, in systems of gift exchange embedded in social interactions.

Only rarely within this zone are rich burials encountered, but occasionally élites can be recognized as, for example, at Court-St-Étienne in the Haine region of Belgium where, in a long-lived cemetery spanning the eighth to fifth centuries, rich warrior burials were interred from time to time. Regional élites of this kind are to be expected where the command of materials or routes enabled wealth to accumulate.

Beyond the hill-fort zone to the north, stretching from the Rhine mouth to the Vistula across the North European Plain and northward across Denmark and southern Sweden, lies a vast expanse of territory characterized by villages which shifted focus from generation to generation within defined territories. This village economy is a remarkably persistent phenomenon which had its origins in the Neolithic period and was still observable in Viking times. Throughout the three millennia or so, technological changes and modifications to agricultural regimes can be detected, but what impresses is the sheer magnitude of social continuity within the region. Even the proximity of the Roman world in the first four centuries AD created surprisingly little dislocation (p. 444).

In the middle of the first millennium BC the typical village consisted of a group of long houses and ancillary store buildings with each complex representing a family unit: seldom was there any significant social differentiation between them, but regional and chronological variations occur in the vernacular architecture. In the sixth-century settlement at Haps in The Netherlands the ridges of the roofs were supported on centrally placed rows of timbers, the lateral thrust being taken by stout wall posts, whereas in the fifth-century settlement at Grøntoft in Jutland a three-aisled construction was adopted. One recurring characteristic throughout the region is the division of the house into two parts by a central cross-passage running between opposing doorways. One of the sectors, usually the smaller, was set aside as a communal living space with a centrally placed hearth, the other was usually used for stalling cattle. This division is particularly clear in villages like Grøntoft where the aisles of the byre end were divided into individual stalls, some of the larger houses having provision for between ten and twenty beasts. Cattle clearly played an important part in the economy, but by no means to the exclusion of grain production, since field systems became common in many regions in the later first millennium and wooden ards have been found from time to time preserved in bogs.

The village economy of the North European Plain presents the most stable social and economic system evident in the whole of Europe in the first millennium. Isolated from the disruptive effects of the developing consumer markets of the Mediterranean and constrained by the rigours of the landscape in which they worked, the peasant communities had little incentive to embrace innovation or to aspire to status through the manipulation of luxury goods until Roman trading networks of the first and second centuries began to introduce a destabilizing note.

If the communities of the North European Plain lived in a world where social mobility was at a minimum, the communities of the Atlantic sea-ways were locked into a system of busy movement. The whole of the Atlantic front of Europe, from the Shetland Islands in the north to the harbours of Tartessos and Cádiz in the south, was bound in a series of interlocking systems of trade and exchange based on easy access by sea. The motive for these movements is not difficult to understand, for the Atlantic zone was metal-rich. The pyrite zone of western Iberia produced silver, copper, and iron, while Galicia, in the north-west corner of the peninsula, was one of the principal sources of tin in the ancient world, and gold was to be had in the Cantabrian mountains. The old hard rocks of the Armorican peninsula were another potential source of tin with lesser quantities of silver and copper, while the Cornish peninsula was renowned in the ancient world for its tin. The fringes of the granite moors of Devon and Cornwall also produced copper, silver, and smaller quantities of gold. Copper and gold were also to be had in Wales and in southern Ireland. Inevitably these riches were exploited by the local communities and transported over very considerable distances by down-the-line exchange from one local system to the next.

The Atlantic exchange network had been long established by the sixth century BC and its extent is amply demonstrated by the discovery of Irish bronze spearheads from what is presumably a seventh-century shipwreck in the estuary near Huelva—the port of Tartessos. Throughout the Atlantic zone the distributions of artefacts reflect more localized exchange networks within the greater system. In the sixth century, for example, vast quantities of high-lead bronze were being turned into axe-shaped ingots in Brittany and distributed thence to northern and western France and central-southern Britain at the very moment when the bulk exchange of bronze was coming to an end. But while copper and gold were undoubtedly significant exports, it was tin which captured the notice of classical authors. The late-Roman poet Avienus, in his poem *Ora Maritima* incorporates tantalizing scraps of information gleaned from an ancient account of the Atlantic sea-ways, known as the Massaliote Periplus, which is believed to date to the sixth century BC. This sailor's manual described the journeyings of the Tartessians and Carthaginians from the southern ports of Iberia northward to Brittany, Ireland, and Britain in search of high-value trade goods. How frequent these long-distance missions were it is difficult to say, but some time later, about 330, we learn of the journeyings of a Greek merchant-explorer, Pytheas, who sailed northward, via Brittany to explore the northern waters around Britain. By this time a regular trade route had been established for Cornish and Breton tin to be brought from the Bay of Biscay, via the Garonne and the Carcassonne Gap to the Aude and thence to the Mediterranean and Massalia thus cutting out the long and treacherous sea route around the Iberian peninsula and through waters controlled by the Carthaginians.

Given the extent of the exchange networks, it is highly likely that ports-of-trade were established on suitable harbours and estuaries where exchanges could take place. In one famous account Pliny describes the British island of Ictis, joined to land at low tide, where the natives brought ingots of tin for exchange. The location of Ictis is not known, but a plausible case could be made for the promontory of Mount Batten in Plymouth Sound. Here plentiful evidence of a trading base flourishing in the eighth to third centuries has been found.

The communities of the Atlantic zone varied considerably in their social and economic structures. In Galicia the existence of many large hill-forts (*castros*) suggests a degree of complexity and centralization in the social system. But further north, in Brittany, Cornwall, Wales, and Ireland, the basis of the settlement pattern was the small defended homestead, called variously rounds or raths, and representing the single family unit. Throughout the second half of the first millennium some developed characteristics of elaboration and size, indicating enhanced status and élite trinkets like glass beads and bracelets, are found in them, but the economic basis was probably more the exploitation of food resources and the herding of cattle than the manipulation of trade goods. For all the documentary evidence of Atlantic exchange systems, luxury goods from the Mediterranean are notoriously rare.

The Fight for Supremacy in the Mediterranean, 450–140 BC

In the centuries before 450, the struggle for the control of trade routes in the western Mediterranean had engaged the Phoenicians and Carthaginians on the one hand and the Greeks on the other, with the Etruscans being squeezed between, and something of an unstable equilibrium had been reached with distinct spheres of influence established and agreed by treaty. But now a new and disruptive force was beginning to appear as the city of Rome threw off Etruscan domination and began to exercise its territorial ambitions—ambitions which were to culminate in the acquisition of a vast empire.

Throughout the fifth century, Rome was extending its sway over the cities of central-western Italy, the Latin towns to the south and the cities of southern Etruria to the north. The phase of expansion culminated in the siege and eventual capture of Veii (traditionally 405–396), which opened the way to the north. But the Celtic migrations (below, p. 358-69) caused a temporary halt. However, by the middle of the fourth century, after a non-aggression treaty had been concluded with Carthage in 348, Rome began once more on its acquisitive advance south, fighting sporadic wars with the Samnites, who managed to stir up anti-Roman feeling among many of the towns already under Roman control, using Celtic mercenaries to good effect. The great anti-Roman coalition met the Roman army, in 295, at Sentinum in Umbria. Rome triumphed and

ETRUSCAN FUNERARY STELE from Bologna, Italy, dating to the fifth century BC. The lower scene shows a mounted Etruscan warrior attacking a Gaul.

STATUE-MENHIR FROM FILITOSA, Corsica (*left*). The stone is anthropomorphic, with sword and dagger (in sheath) clearly visible; around the neck is some kind of ring or necklace. Such a standing stone clearly represents a warrior, and may have been erected on the death of a notable fighter or chieftain.

FUNERARY STELA FROM MAGACELA, Badajoz, Spain (*right*). The stone illustrates schematically a warrior, complete with shield (*at bottom*), horned helmet, dagger, spear, and oval mirror, probably seventh century BC.

HOARD OF GOLD TORCS AND BRACELETS found at Ersfeld, Switzerland (*left*). Late fifth or early fourth century BC.

WOODEN BUCKET (*right*) with copper alloy covering plates and fittings from a grave of the late first century BC at Aylesford, Kent, England.

within five years was master of a huge swath of territory across the centre of the Italian peninsula, from the Tyrrhenian Sea to the Adriatic.

By this time the Greek cities of southern Italy were in a state of economic and social decline, attacked by hostile natives and racked by political intrigue. Inevitably Rome was drawn in and when, in 264, the Greek cities of Sicily found themselves in conflict with their Carthaginian neighbours, Rome intervened on the side of the Greeks instigating the first of the three Punic Wars. The victory did not come easy for Rome, but in 241 the Carthaginians capitulated: Rome had benefited more, perhaps, than it realized, for in the brief span of fifteen years it had learnt the value of a navy. As part of the disengagement terms Carthage undertook to prevent its own ships entering Roman waters and agreed to give up all claims to Sicily, as well as paying a huge indemnity. Taking advantage of its rival's weakness Rome then proceeded to annex Sardinia and Corsica.

Thus within a generation Rome had successfully taken control of a significant part of what had, for nearly five centuries, been within the economic orbit of the Phoenicians and their successor Carthaginians. One of the main results of this was that Carthage had to look elsewhere to strengthen its faltering economy: it chose Spain and in 237 Hamilcar Barca, the head of one of the principal aristocratic Carthaginian families, set sail for Iberia to establish Carthaginian control over the productive south. Unlike his predecessors, who went to trade, he set out to conquer, founding at the outset the port city of New Carthage (Cartagena).

By this stage Rome was being drawn into the political events of the French and Spanish littoral by the old Greek cities now economically unstable and fearful of Carthaginian expansion northward along the coast. As Rome extended its protective influence, so Carthage advanced until inevitably, in 218 BC, the two giants clashed and the Second Punic War erupted. The war was of crucial significance for the course of European history and was a close-run affair. The conflict rapidly spread. Fighting took place in Spain and Italy and it was only after the brilliant stroke of invading Africa in 204 that the Roman commander Scipio Africanus was able to bring Hannibal and his forces to a final defeat at Zama in the hills of Tunisia in 202. As a result Rome now found itself in control of a substantial part of southern Iberia.

Carthage was seriously weakened, but still a potential threat. Moreover, the covetous eyes of the Roman aristocracy had turned to the productive lushness of Tunisia. When the Elder Cato threw ripe Carthaginian figs before his fellow senators with the cry of 'Carthage must be destroyed' he was reminding them not only of the proximity of their commercial rival but also of its rich agricultural lands. The temptation was too great and in a brief campaign lasting from 149 to 146 Carthage was destroyed and its territory annexed.

The subjugation of Carthage ran parallel with Rome's early involvement in Greece and the Balkans. It began in 229 when war was declared on the Queen of Illyria whose subjects had been attacking Roman merchant shipping in the Adriatic. The Illyrians presented little problem, but the war led inevitably to a long drawn out conflict with the

Macedonians. By 190 Macedonia was subdued and forty years later, following an uprising, it became a regular province. All this while the remnants of Greece, known as the Achaean League, remained notionally self-governing. But in 146 an ill-considered revolt broke out and the Roman armies moved in: the great maritime city of Corinth was taken and sacked. Thus in one single year, 146, within the space of a few months, Rome's two powerful maritime rivals, Corinth and Carthage, had been destroyed and Rome became inheritor of their trading empires. By accident, fate, and design Rome had become an Imperial power. Some years later Virgil could write in the *Aeneid* 'Remember, Rome, that it is for you to rule the nations. | This shall be your task: to impose the ways of peace, | to spare the vanquished and to take the proud by war.' The average Roman would have seen nothing exceptional or arrogant in such a statement.

Thus the three centuries from 450 to 140 saw the Mediterranean change from being an ocean of competing polities composed largely of city states trading, some in harmony and some in competition, to becoming the virtual monopoly of a single megastate. But even by the end of this period the Roman sphere of influence was still essentially Mediterranean. It had not yet begun to turn its attentions to the barbarian European periphery.

One effect of the Roman expansion was to create in the west Mediterranean a state of virtually continuous warfare totally disrupting the trading systems which had flourished in the sixth and early fifth centuries: on the one hand this lessened the direct effect of Mediterranean systems on the barbarian north, but on the other, the collapse of the trading network exacerbated the changes which were already underway particularly in the Marne–Moselle region to which we must now return.

The Celtic Migrations, 450–200 BC

We have already seen that by the middle of the fifth century the prestige-goods economy of the west Hallstatt province had broken down partly because the flow of luxury commodities needed to fuel its cycles of competitive exchange had dried up and partly because of the rise of new élites to the north with expectations and demands of their own. This northern periphery was able to maintain itself for some while by relying on native craftsmen to produce luxury goods like the many masterpieces of Celtic art found in élite tombs in the latter part of the fifth century. Nevertheless, other factors such as a rapid population increase, evident in the growth in the number of cemeteries, rocked the already unstable social equilibrium. Taken together these factors caused a major systems collapse which resulted in a phase of widespread migration.

Classical writers were only too well aware of this phenomenon and sought to explain it. The Elder Pliny was convinced that it was the attraction of southern luxuries such as figs, grapes, oil, and wine which had encouraged the marauding masses to flow southward into Italy and Greece. Pompeius Trogus put forward a different reason. The Gauls (used in the same general way as 'Celts'), he said, had outgrown their land: population

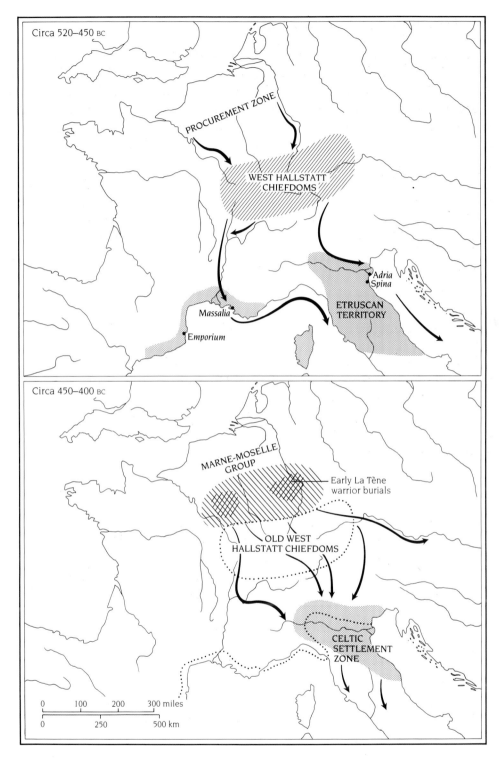

Circa 520–450 BC

PROCUREMENT ZONE

WEST HALLSTATT
CHIEFDOMS

Adria
Spina

Massalia

Emporium

ETRUSCAN
TERRITORY

Circa 450–400 BC

MARNE-MOSELLE
GROUP

Early La Tène
warrior burials

OLD WEST
HALLSTATT CHIEFDOMS

CELTIC
SETTLEMENT
ZONE

| 0 | 100 | 200 | 300 miles |
| 0 | | 250 | 500 km |

IN THE LATE SIXTH and early fifth centuries BC the West Hallstatt chieftains benefited from trade with the Mediterranean, first via Massalia and later through the ports at the head of the Adriatic. Later in the fifth century the system collapsed and warriors from the Marne-Moselle region began a series of far-flung migrations.

THE FAMOUS STATUE of the Dying Gaul in the Museo Capitolino in Rome is a Roman copy in marble of a bronze original erected by Attalos I at Pergamon to celebrate his victory over Gauls who lived in the centre of Anatolia and raided the Hellenistic cities of the Aegean coast. The Gaul fought naked but for his torc.

pressures caused social stress which became so serious that 300,000 men set off to seek new lands. Livy expanded on the same theme. The most powerful of the Gauls were the Bituriges, who were ruled by King Ambigatus. They grew rich on corn and the population increased to such an extent that the maintenance of order was difficult. The king, wishing 'to relieve his kingdom of the burdensome throng' chose two kinsmen, Bellovesus and Segovesus, and charged each young man with the task of leading a mass migration. Segovesus rode east in the direction of the Hercynian hills while Bellovesus led his followers southward to Italy. In general, then, the classical sources, written several centuries after the event, are by no means at odds with the archaeological evidence in suggesting that population growth and the threatened breakdown of the social system led to migration. The direction of that migration is shown by the distribution of cemeteries of the later fifth and early fourth centuries to extend southward down into the Po valley and eastward along the Danube into Hungary, with some early groups crossing the great Hungarian plains and settling in Transylvania, in the heart of what is now Romania.

At home in the Marne–Moselle region élite burials continued for a time at Somme-Bionne, Reinheim, and Waldalgesheim, but the number of cemeteries is far fewer suggesting that it was from this region that the initial migrations emanated. We have already seen that before the migrations the Marne–Moselle region supported a warrior society. Young men were invariably accompanied in the grave by their spears and sword and probably by their shields, though these were largely made of wood and leather and leave little trace. The more wealthy could acquire bronze helmets and the paramount chieftains had fast two-wheeled chariots which could have been used in warfare. It was these warriors who, in their tens of thousands, made their way across Europe seeking new lands and plunder.

Over the next four hundred years or so the communities of the Mediterranean gained firsthand knowledge of these northern peoples whom they classed together as 'Gauls' or 'Celts'. They encountered them first as barbarian invaders, later as mercenaries, and finally as populations to be overrun and governed. Many broadly contemporary accounts of the Celts exist, and especially of their mode of warfare. They are anecdotal rather than anthropological, but sufficient to allow us to build up a generalized picture of Celtic society at the time of the migrations.

There seems, from an early stage, to have been a significant division between the warrior class, free of the ties imposed by working the land, and that sector of the population—the elderly, the women and children, and the unfree—who remained at home to tend crops and husband animals. Among the free warriors, the focal point of the system for maintaining social order was the feast. As described by the writer Athenaeus, banquet arrangements were rigorously regulated:

When several dine together, they sit in a circle; but the mightiest among them, distinguished above the others for skill in war or family connections, or wealth, sits in the middle like a chorus-leader. Beside him is the host and next on either side the others according to their respective ranks. Men-at-arms, carrying oblong shields stand close behind them while their bodyguards, seated in a circle directly opposite share in the feast like their master.

The feast was the occasion when rank was proclaimed and accepted. One of the procedures for doing this was the serving of the hero's portion. 'And in former times, when the hindquarters [of the roasted animal] were served up, the bravest hero took the thigh piece, and if another man claimed it they stood up and fought in single battle to the death' (Strabo). The host, or his carver, would have served each according to his perceived status, providing any member of the company who felt undervalued with the opportunity of entering into a public dispute, which could end in combat. Whatever the outcome, it was legitimized by the fact that the assembled company were the witnesses.

The assembly also provided the occasion when aspiring leaders could propose a raid on neighbouring communities. The status of the individual would be measured by the number who signified their willingness to follow him. If the raid was successful and the spoils sufficiently rewarding then his following the next time was likely to increase.

Raiding neighbours provided a mechanism for maintaining and reproducing hierarchies within the social group: it also allowed the tribe to reassert its identity by continuously redefining its territory. Warfare was, therefore, endemic: it was an essential part of the social system. As Strabo said 'the whole race is madly fond of war, high-spirited, and quick to battle, but otherwise straightforward and not of evil character.'

Classic Celtic warfare, before methods altered to suit conflicts with the Mediterranean armies, involved the opposing forces drawing up and facing each other across the battlefield. The heroes would then come forward in their vehicles or on foot and would shout boastful abuse at their opponents. Then single combat, in full view of both forces, would be enacted. At the end a more widespread mêlée might break out or the hordes might disperse. Warfare of this kind had a strong symbolic character: it was in stark contrast to the warfare of conquest practised by the Mediterranean states. Finally, what of the warriors themselves?

Almost all of the Gauls are of tall stature, fair and ruddy, terrible for the fierceness of their eyes, fond of quarrelling and of overbearing insolence. (Ammianus)

THE HELMET OF AN IRON AGE WARRIOR from a cemetery of the early third century BC at Çiumeşti, Romania. Helmets with animals, horns, and birds on the crests are mentioned by classical writers. The raven is a bird of ill-omen who would have inspired fear in an opponent.

On whatever pretext you stir them up, you will have them ready to face danger, even if they have nothing on their side but their own strength and courage. (Strabo)

To the frankness and high-spiritedness of their temperament must be added the traits of childish boastfulness and love of decoration. They wear ornaments of gold, torques on their necks and bracelets on their arms and wrists, while people of high rank wear dyed garments besprinkled with gold. It is this variety which makes them unbearable in victory and so completely downcast in defeat. (Strabo)

The picture which emerges of the Celts and their society is of a restless exuberance loosely contained within a social system based on warrior prowess. Raiding and warfare were the essential mechanisms by which society maintained and reproduced itself. This kind of system is readily identifiable in the warrior burials of the Marne–Moselle zone in the fifth century. Also, it was a recurring theme in the next four centuries as warrior aristocracies spread throughout much of temperate Europe and began to interact with the Mediterranean states. It is at this point that we pass from prehistory to protohistory.

The Celtic penetration of the Po valley and of the Italian peninsula is well attested both historically and archaeologically. Livy distinguishes two distinct phases, the first around 600 BC, the second 200 years later. The validity of this first immigration has been doubted, but there is an increasing body of archaeological evidence to suggest that some northern communities may have moved through the Alpine passes to settle in the foothills around the Lombard lakes during the sixth and fifth centuries. Vehicle burials in Hallstatt style are known at the cemeteries of Ca'Morta and Sesto Calende, while further south at San Martino, near Ravenna, and Casola Valsenio, near Bologna, artefacts of north European type have been identified in cemeteries of fifth-century date.

These early penetrations paved the way for the main thrust which came at the end of the fifth century when successive waves of northern tribes moved south. The Insubres attacked and captured the city of Melpum (Milan), the Cenomani settled around Brescia and Verona, the Lepontii chose the region of Lake Maggiore, while the Libici and Salluvii settled on the banks of the Ticina. Slightly later the Boii and Lingones passed through this northern settled area to take over land south of the Po. One of the last tribes to arrive, the Senones, moved even further south into Umbria and the Adriatic coastal zone. The settlement was accomplished by force. A stela from Bologna, depicting a battle scene between Etruscans and Celts, and a layer of destruction debris blanketing the Etruscan town of Marzabotto on the north slope of the Apennines bear witness.

This phase of the migration was essentially a folk movement of entire families come to settle the rich lands of the valley. Polybius, writing some time after the event, describes the fertile fields of the Celts producing wheat, barley, millet, and vines, and roamed by pigs. Little is known of the settlements archaeologically, but judging from the large number of cemeteries, all of comparatively limited size, it seems likely that the population lived in small scattered settlements. Native burial rites were retained, the warriors being accompanied by their swords, spears, and helmets, though some had now adopted Etruscan body armour as well.

The settlement of the Po valley marked a first stage, the Apennines providing a significant barrier to further expansion. Meanwhile, further south, the Romans were moving against their Etruscan neighbours acquiring control of the cities of Veii, Falerii, and Volsinii. By about 390 Roman territory had extended north to the Ciminian Forest. It was precisely at this time that Celtic war bands broke through the Apennine barrier and fell upon the cities of the south. Diodorus says that they were war bands raiding from the territory settled by the Senones, but Polybius believed them to be a new wave of tribesmen from beyond the Alps. Such was their energy that within a few days they were advancing on Rome itself.

The terror in the city is summed up by the speech which Livy ascribes to the Roman consul M. Popillius Laenas, 'You are not facing a Latin or a Sabine foe who will become your ally when you have beaten him: we have drawn our swords against wild beasts whose blood we must shed or spill our own.' At Allia, on the left bank of the Tiber, the last Roman defences broke, leaving the city open to the Celtic hordes. The trauma of this event was thereafter rooted deep in the Roman soul and was later recalled on more than one occasion as we shall see. Much of Rome was burnt and pillaged though the Capital held out for seven months before the Celtic warriors moved off. For the next sixty years Celtic raiding parties were active on the Italian peninsula. Some may have come from their home bases north of the Apennines for a season's raiding, returning home with their plunder, others served as mercenaries in the employ of southern tyrants, but by the 330s raiding had all but ceased and in 332–331 Rome concluded a treaty with the Senones.

The third century was a time of retreat when gradually Rome extended its power northward to encompass the entire Po valley. The first major confrontation came *c*.295 at Sentinum when the Insubres and Boii called for help from their kinsmen to the north, and after the battle of Telamon, in 225, large Celtic-settled territories were annexed by Rome. Polybius' account of the event is worth recalling:

The Insubres and Boii wore their trousers and light cloaks but the Gaesatae had discarded their garments owing to their proud confidence in themselves and stood naked with nothing but their arms, in front of the whole array. . . . The Romans . . . were terrified by the fine order of the Celtic host and the dreadful din, for there were innumerable hornblowers and trumpeters and, as the whole army were shouting their war-cries at the same time, there was such a tumult of sound that it seemed that not only the trumpeters and the soldiers but all the country round had got a voice and caught up the cry. Very terrifying, too, were the appearance and gestures of the naked warriors in front, all in the prime of life and firmly built men, and all in the leading companies richly adorned with gold torques and armlets.

But Roman might and order prevailed against Celtic flamboyance and impetuosity, and the Celtic troops were routed. After two further campaigns in 197 and 196 the Latin settlement of the Po valley began. The Boii rebelled, but were finally overcome in a bat-

STATUE OF A GAULISH WARRIOR
from Vachères, Basses-Alpes, France,
dating to the late first century BC. He
wears a mail tunic with sword slung at the
right side.

tle fought at Bologna. Their losses were heavy and much of their land was appropriated:
as a result the remnant of the tribe set off once more retracing the steps of their ancestors
through the Alps to settle in Bohemia in which name their presence is remembered.

The easterly migration of the Celts can equally well be traced in the archaeological
record and in the works of the classical historians. The initial movement seems to have
spread along the Danube, fanning out into Transdanubia (eastern Hungary) in the late
fifth and early fourth centuries, and substantial settlements were established within the
arc of the Carpathians and the Transylvanian Alps by the early fourth century. It was
probably from their homeland in Transdanubia that the raids southward into Illyria
began to be mounted after about 360, causing a dislocation among the local tribes. In
310 there was panic among the Illyrians as the raids intensified, and between 300 and 280
attacks spread into Bulgaria passing through the Iron Gates gorge into the lower

PANEL FROM A SILVER CAULDRON found in a bog at Gunderstrup, Denmark (*above*). It was probably made by Thracian craftsmen for a Celtic patron in the middle Danube region in the third or second century BC. The soldiers wear 'Celtic' armour and the three at the right blow carnexes (war trumpets). How it got to Denmark remains unclear.

ROMAN DENARIUS (*left*) minted in *c.*48 BC depicting a barbarian war chariot of the kind Caesar described following his incursions into Britain in 55 and 54 BC.

Danube valley and the plain of Wallachia. Throughout this time the momentum was building and finally, in 279, a vast force poured into Macedonia bent on plunder and settlement. It was organized as three separate armies: Bolgius led a force via the Aoüs Pass, but later moved off into Serbia to found a kingdom, Cerethrius took his followers into Thrace, while Brennus moved first to Paeonia and then, with his army of 30,000, advanced through Thrace and, by the Pass of Thermopylae, deep into Greece to Delphi, attracted, no doubt, by reports of the great wealth stored in the protection of Apollo's shrine. The campaign was a failure, not least because of the severe winter weather encountered, and the tattered remnants of the Celtic host were forced to fall back to Macedonia. A substantial part of the population travelled northward to the Danube valley where they swelled the Celtic population already present. The combined population became known as the Scordisci, with their major *oppidum* (town) at Singidunum (Belgrade).

Another part of the original force made up of three tribes, the Tolistoagii, the Trocini, and the Tectosages, moved eastward by various routes into Anatolia eventually settling in northern Phrygia from where, over the next few years, they conducted seasonal raids against the cities of the Aegean coast of Asia Minor. The origins of the tribes were remembered nearly three hundred years later in their name—their descendants were the Galatians to whom St Paul wrote in such chiding terms.

Our picture of the Celtic migrations is only partially understood and is, of necessity, incomplete, but in the period from 450 to 200 a remarkable cultural similarity can be traced across the face of Europe from Pas de Calais to Transylvania and from the Po valley to southern Poland. This La Tène culture, as it is called, is the culture of Celtic speakers. To what extent it was spread by migrating populations or simply by processes of acculturation it is impossible to say, but no one can doubt that the physical mobility of people played a large part. That it was a time of turbulence is vividly captured in the art of the period—Celtic art—redolent of the tensions, opposition, and sheer vibrant energy of the people. The persistence of warrior burials throughout the entire zone is a further reminder of the prevailing social system.

Much of this great swath of temperate Europe was densely settled by communities living in farmsteads or in larger village agglomerations, and farming the land around. Raw materials seem to have been exchanged from community to community within the normal processes of social intercourse. There is no evidence of intensive long-distance trade, but many of the villages show signs of increasing craft specialization. Thus, by the time the flood of migration was receding, and a degree of social stability was beginning to emerge in barbarian Europe, Rome's first phase of conquest in establishing command of the Mediterranean was nearing an end. The scene was now set for the two worlds to establish, once again, a new, dynamic relationship.

Finally, we must consider to what extent the west and north of Europe can be said to have been part of the Pan-European Celtic (or La Tène) culture. There were no historically recorded westerly migrations nor does the archaeological evidence suggest a close similarity between the culture of the western communities and that of the central La Tène zone: indeed a strong continuity seems to have been the rule with La Tène artefacts and art styles absorbed into the local system and often modified by local craftsmen. In Aquitania, for example, a group of distinctive gold torcs were made utilizing the motifs of Celtic art in their decoration, but in an original manner which totally lacked the elegance of pure Celtic forms. Further north, the culture of Brittany retained its highly individual character while at the same time adapting Celtic designs, probably learned from metalwork, to suit their sophisticated range of locally made pottery. Armorican pottery together with other elements such as underground chambers (fogous) probably used for storage, and a range of carefully finished stone stelae serve to distinguish the culture, and thus society, of Brittany sharply from the rest of France. Further north, in central-southern Britain, the hill-fort phenomenon so evident in the sixth century continued and intensified, the developed hill-forts playing an increasingly important role in ordering the redistribution systems in society. An even greater emphasis on defence is indicative of escalating aggression. But overlying this insular continuity was a range of La Tène metalwork imported from the Continent in sufficient quantity to inspire local craftsmen to develop their own skilled and highly articulate versions.

In this western fringe of Europe the continuity of indigenous traditions is far more impressive than similarity with Pan-European La Tène culture. The conclusion must be that the folk movements which affected so much of Europe left this peripheral zone largely unscathed. This is not to imply that the region received no migrant groups. A number of vehicle burials found in Yorkshire, which belong to the locally named Arras culture, have very close similarities to those of the Seine valley and northern France. This has suggested to many that the burials reflect an immigrant élite, an observation which gains further support from the similarity of the tribal name, Parisii, and that of the Parisi in the Seine valley. The alternative view, that the élite was indigenous and was simply adopting a 'foreign' burial mode to distinguish itself cannot, however, be ruled out.

POTTERY VESSEL of the fourth or third century BC from Saint Pol De-Léon in Brittany. The La Tène-style decoration is closely similar to motifs used on fine metalwork.

BRONZE SHIELD-BOSS from the river Thames at Wandsworth. The repoussé decoration resolves itself into two birds.

Items of La Tène metalwork spread northward across the North European Plain and into Poland, but the true northern limit of La Tène culture lay roughly on the line from south of the Rhine mouth, across southern Germany to the Sudeten mountains of former Czechoslovakia, to the Carpathians. To the north, the villagers of the North European Plain continued to tend their herds and raise their crops much as their ancestors had done for over a thousand years, untouched by the momentous events which were being played out to the south. To the Roman writers a little later, these disparate communities could be lumped together under the general name of Germans—a name which was soon to feature large in Roman history.

The Unstable Equilibrium, 200–140 BC

When, in 206, the Roman army took the port city of Cádiz they became masters of the Carthaginian-held territories of southern Iberia, but the native tribes of the remainder of the peninsula were far from cowed. Roman exploitation of their newly won territory was rapid: colonial towns were founded at Italica, near Seville, in 206, and further up the Guadalquivir valley at Córdoba in 179. Within the decade following the fall of Cádiz, 59,000 kilograms of silver and over 1800 kilograms of gold had been shipped to Rome. In the silver mines near Cartagena 40,000 slaves were said to have worked. Rome now controlled the richest part of the peninsula—not only the silver mines of Cartagena, but also the gold and silver resources of the Sierra Morena, behind Córdoba, and the copper and silver deposits of the Rio Tinto region. Of no lesser importance were the immensely fertile lands of the Guadalquivir valley producing olives, wine, and corn in abundance. The Spanish adventure brought home to Rome more forcefully than ever before the rewards of colonization.

The native tribes of Iberia did not take kindly to Roman exploitation and in 197 the Turdentani of the Guadalquivir region rebelled to be joined in 194 by the Lusitanians occupying the south-west region of the peninsula. Resistance to Roman advance continued in a desultory way until 154 when a full-scale rebellion broke out, the Lusitanians of the west this time allying themselves with the Celtiberi, a confederation of tribes occupying the central areas of Spain. The successes of the rebellion were largely due to the charismatic nature of their leader Viriathus. When he was murdered in 138 opposition fragmented, with the result that much of what is now Portugal passed to the Romans. The Celtiberi continued the struggle for a few years, but were finally brought to their knees in 133 when their last stronghold, the fortress of Numantia in the north between the upper reaches of the Douro and the Ebro, was taken after a long siege by the Roman commander Scipio Aemilianus.

In the seventy years or so it had taken the Roman armies to acquire a firm hold on much of Iberia, the value of the peninsula's resources was making itself felt on the Roman economy. In the first century AD Pliny could write:

Spain outdoes the Gallic provinces in her spartum and her specular stone, the products of her desert tracts, in her pigments that add to our luxury, in the ardour displayed by her people in laborious employments, in the perfect training of her slaves, in the robustness of body of her men and their general resoluteness of character.

The emphasis is interesting—while raw materials were welcome and necessary to the Roman economy, manpower at all levels was now an urgent necessity. Edward Gibbon, taking a characteristically shrewd long look at history, remarked that Spain was to Rome as Peru and Mexico were to the Old World.

Rome's general dislike of long sea journeys meant that the land route from Italy to Spain, through southern Gaul, became increasingly used as the Roman hold on the peninsula intensified. In the wake of the army came the traders—entrepreneurs from Italy intent on exploiting the markets of southern Gaul. Their activities are vividly demonstrated by the flood of Roman imported goods which came increasingly to be found in the occupation levels of the developing southern towns after the end of the third century. Gradually, then, throughout the second century Roman interests, both military and commercial, came to be bound up in the fortunes of this southern Gaulish coastal strip. But parts of the route were far from safe. The Ligurian hill tribes were a constant menace. In 189 a governor and his entourage *en route* to Spain were ambushed: he died soon after and fifteen years later another governor was killed, probably in similar circumstances. Added to the problems were the activities of Ligurian pirates preying on coastal shipping. Matters got increasingly worse until, in 154, the Greek cities of Nicaea and Antipolis came under imminent threat from the hill tribes. To help alleviate the danger the Massaliots appealed to Rome for military assistance. The intervention which followed successfully destroyed the power of the two neighbouring tribes, whose territory was now made over to Massalia, but it required the Roman army to overwinter in the region.

The continuing threat from hostile hill tribes presented a danger not only to Rome's military supply lines to Spain and Rome's allies among the coastal cities but also it threatened the increasingly lucrative markets of southern Gaul, which the Italian entrepreneurs were beginning to exploit with much success. In the end, to safeguard Roman interests there was nothing for it but for the entire region to be annexed. Thus it was that, by 120, the province of Gallia Transalpina had begun to take shape.

While Rome's interests were beginning to involve it increasingly in native affairs at the western end of the Alps, a rather different situation was developing at the eastern end. In Carinthia (part of Austria) the local Celtic communities, who occupied the area from the third century, had developed a strong centralized political system which soon became known as the kingdom of Noricum. The economic strength of the region lay in its command of metal resources, particularly copper and high quality iron ore and of its copious salt deposits. The Roman advance into the Po valley and the founding of colonies in the region (at Bologna in 189, at Modena in 183, and at Aquileia, near Trieste, between 183 and 181) brought the Roman world into direct contact with the east Alpine Celts for the first time. One band had moved south into the territory of Aquileia and had begun to build an *oppidum*. This was stopped by the Roman army and the Celtic intruders were sent back to their homeland beyond the Alps accompanied by an embassy of Roman senators to explain the situation and establish friendly relations with the kingdom. The mission was a diplomatic success and the two states remained in harmony for decades.

Rome's initial interests were military—a strong friendly state in the eastern Alps formed a useful buffer against outside threat and allowed Rome security to expand into Istria and Liguria, but it was not long before the economic potential of the situation began to be recognized. In the 160s Roman merchants began to trade with Noricum using the native *oppidum* of Magdalensburg as the main port for exchange, and a little later the discovery of a rich deposit of gold led to a gold-rush. Tension ensued and the Italian gold-hunters were expelled, but the incident did little to sour the diplomatic and economic ties between the two states.

By the middle of the first century BC the nascent Roman Empire was fast becoming aware of the enormous potential of barbarian Europe. The central and western Mediterranean were largely secure and Spain was well on the way to incorporation in the Roman system. Meanwhile at the two ancient interfaces between the Mediterranean and temperate Europe—southern Gaul and the head of the Adriatic—new and lucrative markets were being established. The economic and political crisis which was to grip Italy in the ensuing century was to create needs which could only be met by massive expansion leading eventually to the absorption of much of the Continent within the imperial boundaries.

11

Thracians, Scythians, and Dacians,
800 BC–AD 300

TIMOTHY TAYLOR

Writers and Diggers

IF we search for the origins of the Dacians, the creators of an extraordinary non-literate state, with its spiritual centre at the circular sanctuary of Sarmizegethusa, protected by the curving bastions of the Carpathian arc, we must look to their precursors, the Thracians of the Danubian plain and, with Milton's Satan, our eye must carry further, searching land 'over Pontus, and the Pool Maeotis, up beyond the river Ob' (*Paradise Lost*). The prehistoric peoples of this vast swath—Scythia, the meridian of the grassland steppe, extending unbroken from Wallachia to south Siberia—might indeed please the Devil, for, according to Greek writers like Herodotus, here were werewolves, warrior women with excized breasts, cannibals, transvestite shamans, and head-hunters who drank from skulls, all living in a state of constant warfare. Royal burial mounds were encircled by stuffed retainers who were mounted—in a manner most offensive to English sensibilities—on horses that had been similarly treated. Astonishingly, modern archaeological discoveries for the most part corroborate Herodotus' description. Of course, the understanding of the past gained through archaeology is broadly different in nature to understanding derived from historical texts. Having both sorts of evidence is a boon and a challenge.

The steppe and its transitional zones incorporate parts of many modern countries. The quality of the archaeology that has been carried out in Hungary, Bulgaria, Romania, Moldavia, the Ukraine, southern Russia, Georgia, and regions further east varies, but the quantity of material is very great. Coupled with the often acute observations of the classical authors, we should be able to reconstruct a richly detailed, broad, and reliable picture of many aspects of iron-using societies at the time of the Greek colonization of the Pontic (Black Sea) littoral.

Because of the existence in some but not all societies of historical writing during the first millennium BC, the period has often been termed 'protohistoric' instead of prehistoric. Herodotus of Halicarnassus, who produced his famous *History* in the mid-fifth century BC, is the most informative of the surviving classical authors in terms of his

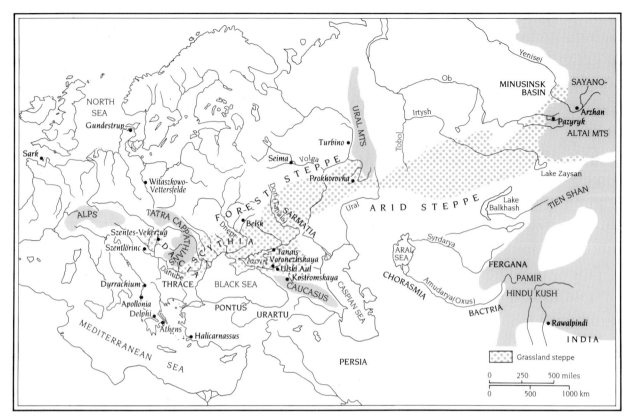

THRACE, SCYTHIA AND DACIA in pan-Eurasiatic context (the Ural mountains and Ural river mark the conventional eastern boundary of Europe).

descriptions of non-literate societies, but there has been considerable disagreement over the trustworthiness of his account. Many scholars have, with Thucydides, cast Herodotus in the role of 'Father of Lies' or, with greater sophistication, characterized his stories, in the light of literary critical theory, primarily as manifestations of the Greek mind and Greek categories, rather than reflections on an objective reality which are still useful today; the classicist François Hartog has argued most eloquently for such a reading in relation to Herodotus' Scythians, whom he terms 'Les Scythes Imaginaires'.

Most archaeologists have read Herodotus with far less sensitivity. The chronicle of historical peoples and events has tyrannized protohistoric archaeology. Archaeological cultures and culture-groups have been uncritically identified with peoples described in the ancient texts, such as the Thracians, the Dacians, and the Scythians (whereas the results of excavation have not been allowed to challenge the overall conceptual framework provided by the texts). In south-east European and Soviet scholarship there has been a strong tendency to use partial and simplistic readings to justify particular lines of interpretation and to link often quite small archaeologically recognized material–cultural groups with names that occur only once or twice in Herodotus' text. For both Eastern and Western scholars the description of political and military events has been

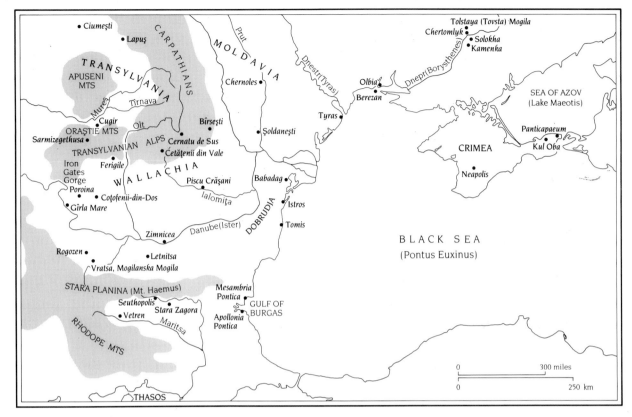

THE CARPATHO-BALKAN AND NORTH PONTIC REGIONS.

considered Herodotus' most important contribution to the history of the region. However, it is when we turn to social questions that Herodotus can help us most. For it is questions of gender, of inheritance, of family and kinship structure, of specific religious beliefs, and of ethnic identity, that archaeology unaided finds most difficult to answer. Used carefully, his information is invaluable.

In south-east Europe, the prehistoric period draws to a close around 500 BC, but the prehistoric cultures of this time grade into the similarly non-literate 'barbarian' peoples of Europe (so called by the Greeks because of the babble of their strange tongues). There are two differences between these social groupings, one conceptual and one geopolitical. The conceptual difference is that, for barbarian Europe we can name names, and talk of *peoples* rather than the *cultures* of prehistoric Europe. The geopolitical difference is that from this time onward, the non-literate peoples of Europe were involved in broadly asymmetrical, and increasingly intensive, 'core-periphery' relationships with the powers of the urban civilizations. These civilizations, particularly those of Persia, Greece, and Rome, had a qualitatively different sort of social organization—the state. The key factors in this were probably literacy and coinage. These allowed the development of sophisticated accounting and credit facilities, and the elaboration of law codes with respect to property and inheritance, and provided the logistical basis for professional armies with good communication systems.

Conventionally defined, the period from 800 BC to AD 300 straddles the prehistoric and historical periods. For the earlier part of the first millennium BC we must rely principally on archaeological data. For the later centuries, a number of texts are available, ranging from the early poetry of Hesiod and Homer, through the great fifth-century BC writing of Herodotus, Thucydides, and the Hippocratic corpus (hereafter 'Hippocrates'), to the Hellenistic, Roman, and early medieval historians, commentators, and copyists.

Both physical anthropological and linguistic data are also available. The Eurasian steppe is the zone in which the Caucasoid and Mongoloid physical types are supposed to meet, and there were many localized physical differences between steppe populations. Some of these differences may have been the result of culture rather than breeding. Hippocrates describes some steppe populations as 'Longheads': 'As soon as a child is born they remodel its head with their hands, while it is still soft and the body tender, and force it to increase in length by applying bandages and suitable appliances' (such an elongated head later became *de rigueur* among the Huns). Herodotus describes the inhabitants of the town of Gelonus as having remarkably blue eyes and red hair—presumably both purely genetic features. Without accurate control over all the factors involved, the identification of genetic differences between populations by measuring skulls is fraught with difficulties; nevertheless, convincing identifications of new or intrusive population groups in particular regions from archaeological material, arguing on the basis of cultural and/or genetic dissimilarity, can be made.

The problem of what languages the steppe groups spoke is thorny. All that survives are some proper names and a handful of other words. Iranian and Thracian languages were certainly spoken, but probably coexisted with languages that belonged to other, smaller language groups. Language provides a focus for ethnicity, and can be a barrier to culture contact or not, according to inclination. When Herodotus' Scythian men meet the Amazons, 'The men could not learn the women's language, but the women learned the speech of the men'; and, in relation to a bald-headed people whom we can locate just on the European side of the Urals, Herodotus says 'the Scythians who come to these people transact their business through seven interpreters and in seven languages'—a poetic formulation perhaps, but this is the region of the archaeologically defined Permian people, who probably spoke a non-Indo-European, Finno-Ugrian, language, very different from that spoken by Scythians. The various other peoples Herodotus mentions to the north of the grasslands must have included the ancestors of Slavic- and Baltic-language speakers too.

Philologists of the nineteenth century believed the Thracians to have been the originators of the Indo-European language. This view no longer makes sense, in either factual or conceptual terms. The arguments concerning Indo-European language and people are as complex as they are controversial. All we can say, on the basis of place-name and other evidence, is that there was at least one major and distinctive Indo-European language (perhaps divided into two principal dialects: 'Thraco-Moesian' and 'Thraco-Illyrian') spoken in Thrace in the first millennium BC. Nevertheless, working on the basis of attenuated lines of linguistic reasoning, eastern European scholars have used the term Thracian to describe archaeological cultures that date to the third millennium BC, and even earlier—long before there is any support for such firm identification.

New Metal, New Style

The term Iron Age is, confusingly, used differently by different groups of scholars. It can be used in a chronological, and/or social, and/or technological sense. The date of the transition from 'Bronze Age' to 'Iron Age' is therefore a matter of convention and disagreement. In Europe it can be said to have occurred earliest in Greece, as iron began to replace bronze for basic tools by around 1000 BC. In central and eastern Europe, iron came into full use three centuries later, and roughly coincided with the Greek colonization of coastal regions and the development of a trade in luxury goods for slaves with the peoples of the interior. Thus, for south-east Europe, the Iron Age designates a period from around 700 BC until the Roman expansion in the first centuries BC and AD. It marks a major social reorientation that takes place in parallel with developments elsewhere in Europe (see Chapter 10).

To understand what the change entailed we must first look at the archaeological evidence for the sorts of societies that existed on the eve of the Greek colonization of the Thracian and Scythian coasts. As we have seen in Chapter 7, among the Bronze Age societies of south-east Europe there were traders in touch with both northern Europe and the Aegean. Most communities had to trade over long distances for the tin they needed for making bronze. This was true for the whole of south-east Europe, which, apart from some smallish deposits in eastern Yugoslavia, had no tin of its own and had to obtain it from either Bohemia, Turkey, or the Urals. By the middle of the second millennium BC, a new metal had been discovered—iron—that needed no alloying and was locally available in many parts of Europe.

Iron seems to have been produced unintentionally at first, during the smelting of some sorts of copper ore that had a naturally high iron content. Production of iron, in both the northern Carpathians (the Tatra mountains of Slovakia) and the Caucasus mountains of Georgia, seems to have begun around 1700 BC, towards the end of a period of remarkable innovation in metallurgy that is observable across a broad band of Eurasia. The early second-millennium BC Seima-Turbino phenomenon—rich burials of exotic appearance that are found among local graves in forest-steppe cemeteries widely separated from one another—may well indicate the emergence of a mobile military élite. These burials contain artefacts that display innovative metalworking techniques, and they precede the appearance of specialized bronzeworking all along the border with the grassland to the south and the subsequent large-scale interconnection of horse and chariot using élites throughout the steppe proper (the Andronovo culture). Thus, although the discovery of iron may have been independent to east and west of the Black Sea, the focus on the development of new weapon types and the extension of interregional contacts created conditions in which a direct transfer of information between the Caucasus and the Carpathians about the new metal was possible.

On the basis of present (certainly imperfect) evidence, iron was used infrequently before 1100 BC (for example, on the Suciu de Sus culture site of Lapuş; eastern European archaeologists conventionally date the beginning of the Iron Age to this time). Thereafter, until around 750 BC (the end of the 'Hallstatt B' period), its manufacture seems to have been greater, though always fluctuating in line with fluctuations in the production of bronze and never put to any very novel use: iron objects were usually copies of the far commoner bronze ones. From around 750 BC, we may observe a sudden increase in iron, connected with the exploitation of new ore sources, and the development of new, specifically ferrous, artefact types.

From a social point of view, we may detect a deep conservatism in this thousand-year prologue to wholehearted iron use. Bronzesmiths probably operated via ties of clientage. Their overlords were the hereditary controllers of the tin supplies. For iron to establish itself, not only did a predominantly alloying and casting technology have to be replaced by a forging one, but society had to undergo a fundamental reorientation. In this reorientation, termed 'detribalization' by David Clarke, manufacturing—and thus social—control was lost by the old order, artisans became less tied to particular tribal groups or lineages, and status became something that was more often achieved than ascribed.

If we look at general trends we can see, between 1100 and 100 BC, a gradual decrease, first in regional differences in types of pottery decoration and then in any kind of pottery decoration at all. By the eighth century BC, rather uniform kinds of decorated pottery were in use over an area extending from the lower Danube plain into parts of Yugoslavia and Transylvania. This pottery has been discovered on lowland farming settlements that are collectively defined as the Basarabi culture. A similar homogenization of pottery types over a wide area also occurred in Moldavia and the Ukrainian forest steppe—the so-called Golygrady (or Holihrady) and Şoldaneşti Thracian cultures—and further east in the shape of the Chernoles culture.

These large pottery 'cultures' replaced the very varied and attractive local potteries of the Late Bronze Age (as manifested, for example, at Gîrla Mare, see Chapter 9), and have been taken as indicative of the emergence of larger social formations. Yet there is no real evidence to support such a view. There is much settlement continuity with preceding periods, and settlements are of similar type: mainly open, with the occasional strategically positioned defended site (such as Babadag in the Dobrudja or Cernatu de Sus in the Carpathians). Until the middle of the eighth century BC there is no evidence for outstanding, competitive ostentation in burials; cremation and inhumation cemeteries show little differentiation between individual burials. Such observations are consistent

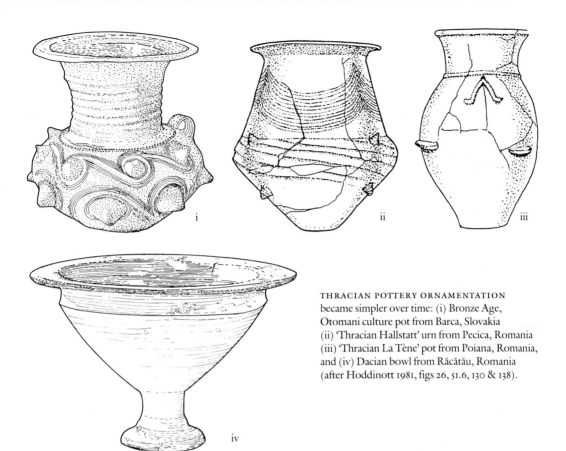

THRACIAN POTTERY ORNAMENTATION became simpler over time: (i) Bronze Age, Otomani culture pot from Barca, Slovakia (ii) 'Thracian Hallstatt' urn from Pecica, Romania (iii) 'Thracian La Tène' pot from Poiana, Romania, and (iv) Dacian bowl from Răcătău, Romania (after Hoddinott 1981, figs 26, 51.6, 130 & 138).

with the idea of stable, sedentary, small-scale chiefdoms, in which status was inherited and did not need to be trumpeted.

It may, therefore, be that the Basarabi culture marks the beginning of a slow trend away from marking ethnic differences through the distinctive decorative schemes of locally produced and relatively immobile pottery. This would correlate with the expectation that, as various forms of pastoralism developed in the region and new groups moved into it, the locus of ethnic identity shifted to the human body and its fashion accessories. Certainly there was a dramatic change in material culture at about this time. Not only did metal traditions alter, with iron prevailing over bronze for common tools and weapons, but new sorts of settlements were built and burial sites and rites became more varied. These things mark the start of the Iron Age proper. While sedentary farming communities continued to live on the plains, their settlements became more defensive, and out on the steppe we can discern a new mobile, nomadic pastoralist component.

Horsemasters and Shepherds

The north Pontic steppe is bordered to the north by forest steppe, followed by deciduous woodland, then coniferous taiga, then, before the Arctic Ocean, treeless tundra. To the south, the steppe grades into semi-desert with artemisia bushes predominating, or is bordered by mountains or seas. In the west it is interrupted by the Carpathian mountains and the Danubian Iron Gates gorge, but continues again for a short stretch as the Hungarian *puszta*. The precise vegetational zonation has varied over time, shifting north or south as climate changed. Towards the end of the ninth century BC there was a significant environmental change, as the sub-Atlantic phase replaced the sub-Boreal and the climate of the steppe became rapidly colder and dryer. This event coincided with the sudden appearance on the borders of both China and the Near Eastern states of nomadic pastoralists from central Asia. Just as today, the prehistoric steppe economy was based on a network of sources of water, unevenly distributed over a vast area, and involved a seasonal pastoral movement over a range of about 2000 kilometres. Such a system is inelastic: pressure at any one point can result in the progressive displacement of populations across the whole of the Eurasian steppe belt. Pressure on pasture can also arise from internal climatic–demographic imbalances, and cyclical climatic–environmental patterns have probably caused regular demographic crises since the inception of steppe pastoralism in the fourth millennium BC. In such crises, after generations of good seasons, an enlarged population of humans and animals has to face drought and the onset of a period of poorer conditions.

The main pressure point has always been the Mongolian steppe—an island of wonderful pasture surrounded by desert and taiga. In the second half of the eighth century BC, the pastoralists in Mongolia (the Hiung-Nu or Hsiung-Nu, often identified with the Huns of later history: see below p. 402 and Chapter 13), lacking water for their flocks and herds, impinged upon China. They were repulsed by the Chou emperor Suan and a domino effect was set in motion, extending back across the Mongolian, Kazakh, and Black Sea, steppelands. From contemporary Near Eastern letters and records, and later Greek narratives, we learn that a group known as the Massagetae moved into the area around the Aral Sea, displacing the Scythians who, in turn, displaced the Cimmerians and precipitated the latter into a collision course with both the kingdom of Assyria, south of the Caucasus mountains, and the Thracian tribes of Moldavia on the flanks of the Carpathians. In another version of the story, the Arimaspians dislodged the Issedones who, in turn, shunted the Scythians into the Cimmerians. The names are different, but the structure is the same.

From the texts we can learn only of those events in which the élite among the pastoralists was involved and which affected the literate world: sometime between 681 and 668 BC, the Assyrian king Assarhaddon defeated the 'Gimmerai' (Cimmerians, the Biblical 'Gomer') under their king Teushpa; around 674 BC, the king of the 'Aš-ku-za' (or 'Ishkuza'—Scythians), Bartatua, married an Assyrian princess and, some thirty or forty years later, these same people destroyed the kingdom of Urartu in eastern Anatolia and took control of the kingdom of Media in northern Iran—possibly in alliance with the Assyrians. Around 610 BC, the nomads, then in alliance with Medes, conquered the Assyrian capital of Nineveh, but afterwards the Medes expelled them back north of the

Caucasus; the Medes were then brought under the hegemony of Achaemenid Persia. From around 520 BC, the 'Saka tigrakhauda' ('pointed-hat Scythians' in Persian) became an increasing threat to the new empire; Darius I's expedition against them in about 513 BC—following them into Europe, through Thrace, and into the steppe—gave Herodotus his pretext for the long account of Scythian origins and customs that he, uniquely, provides for us.

What was a pastoralist élite? Although the nomads in question had probably begun life as relatively small, lineage-based, tribal groups, managing their flocks and herds in the vast expanses of central Asia, it was never possible for them to be fully nomadic—to move wherever they wished. They had always been tied into a network of supply and demand with adjacent communities of the forests and mountains, who provided them with metals and wood, as they in turn provided horses, milk products, and other livestock. A certain amount of agriculture was practised in the sheltered river valleys, and pastoral communities participated in it. But the combative advantages conferred by being able to ride a horse meant that there was a tendency for specialized martial groups to emerge who, while managing their own flocks, could obtain the other materials they needed from sedentary populations whom they 'protected' from attack by other martial groups. For the Cimmerians and the Scythians of the fifth century BC, both Hippocrates and Herodotus make a clear distinction between the 'nobles' who owned and rode horses, and the poorer 'commonality' who did not. The essential coherence of these mounted groups was ensured by a charismatic leader who planned strategy and divided spoils, and not by any strongly kin-based system of traditional obligation. Herodotus' understanding of the name Scythian was that it was a version of the personal name of a king (given in two variant but Graecized forms as Colaxaïs and Skoloti).

An invasion of the Caucasus by mounted warriors can be documented archaeologically as the Srubnaya-Khvalynsk culture, often identified with the Scythians. In some cemeteries in Nagorno-Karabakh there was a sudden shift in the relative wealth of burials after 700 BC, with the appearance of rich warrior burials containing bodies of a different physical type to those whose bodies were sacrificially placed in with them. The weaponry found in these graves underlines the developing military capacity and predatory predelictions of the nomads as they adopted Caucasian weapon types: typically, each warrior was armed with a composite reflex bow and armour-piercing bronze three-barbed (trilobate) arrowheads (modern experiments suggest a projectile velocity of around 50 metres per second, only slightly less than that of a crossbow bolt), iron 'akinakes' sword, and massive iron spears.

It may also have been in the Caucasus that the 'Animal style' in art took shape (*see colour plate facing p. 420*). The central Asian nomads had always lived close to their animals and carved pictures of those they herded and hunted on standing stones. But it was not until contact with Near Eastern metalworking traditions was established that a really innovative style (including composite animals like winged lion-griffins) emerged for decorating bridle appliqués, shield and sheath covers, and jewellery.

A GOLD BELT PLAQUE with turquoise insets; Siberian collection of Peter the Great; possibly third century BC. A yak bites the tail of a feline (perhaps a snow leopard) which in turn mauls an eagle that is attacking the yak.

Thus, proximity to urban civilization further stimulated the specialized development of martial nomadic élite groups. The wealth of booty that could be obtained from a sacked town was far in excess of the humble rewards of raiding a farming village on the river Ob. Even so, eastern and central Europe were also fair game, judging from the number of burial mounds in which new, distinctive steppe-type grave goods—paired horses and chariots, animal style appliqués, 'akinakes' swords, and trilobate arrow-heads—have been discovered. At the barrow cemetery of Szentlörinc on the Hungarian plain the skeletons were of eastern, Pontic-Taurid, type. It seems that the Scythian-type riders of this group (archaeologically termed the Vekerzug group), like the Huns and Mongols who came after them, were attracted by this island of steppe on the middle course of the Danube.

Scythian-type material has been found elsewhere too, notably in the Mureş-Tîrnave group of burials in central Transylvania, and in the famous decorated gold armour which came to light at Witaszkowo (once Vettersfelde) in Poland. The term 'Scythian-type' is used because there are subtle differences in the manufacture of artefacts (such as the swords) found in burials on the south Russian steppe (Scythia proper) and these central European examples. Argument has raged as to whether those interred were 'real Scythians'. However, we have no way of knowing what these people called themselves, or what the classical authors really knew of them (Herodotus speaks of the gold-loving Agathyrsae in this region, but cannot decide whether they should be considered Thracian or Scythian, and of the Sigynnae with their pony traps, who were apparently neither). Further, we should expect the equipment of an intrusive élite of Scythian type to vary with local conditions because they would have relied on local expertise—willingly given or not—to harness their horses afresh and replace their broken weaponry. Finally, animal bone studies show that Scythian riding horses were being traded into Europe (to the head of the Adriatic) by middlemen at this time; the availability of steppe equipment may have encouraged the local emergence of mounted martial élites in particular areas.

The use of iron seems to have been stimulated by the arrival of the steppe groups. They must have disrupted the vested interests that maintained the tin supply, at the same time as they glamorized the new technology that they used to such effect.

New iron sources were discovered in the Transylvanian Alps as upland areas were deforested to create summer grazing for a new, more intensive, regime of indigenous transhumant pastoralism. The cultural group involved in this clearance and prospection (the Ferigile-Bîrseşti group) appears to have shared features of both the old local mixed-farming societies and the new élites. In the cremation burial ground of Ferigile, situated in the southern Carpathian piedmont on an access route to mountain pastures, over 150 warrior-type burials were excavated. Finds included pottery similar to local lowland Basarabi type, offerings of sheep, goat, and other animals, iron horsebits, spears, and an akinakes sword copied from steppe types. Status seems to have been ascribed—at least in death—as nearly all of the cremations turned out to be those of children who could not have wielded the weapons that they were buried with.

Thus, a number of different patterns of subsistence and exploitation existed at one and the same time around the borders of the steppe. Did the people responsible for these patterns coexist peacefully or were they typically in conflict? Were they divided along predominantly economic, or predominantly linguistic, or even predominantly racial lines? In modern Britain, hill farmers, dairy farmers, and cereal farmers may have their differences, but they normally think of themselves as belonging to the same society; in terms of material life, however, their cultures are different—constrained by different requirements and a different range of locally available resources, and their relationships with one another are function-specific and diffuse ('monoplex'). In contrast, it is usual to think of pre-modern, non-urban societies as having natural 'solidarity'—with people involved in closely interwoven ('multiplex') relationships and sharing a clear tribal or national identity. But the Iron Age process of detribalization meant that, though ethnic identity remained strong, or even became stronger, many social relations became monoplex. This was so because the territories of specific peoples became less and less exclusive as economies became more specialized and competitive. This led to conflicts over resources: for southern Thrace, Xenophon records first hand a night-time cattle raid by 'mountain Thracians' on a palisaded lowland Thracian agro-pastoralist village.

The presence of intrusive, militarily superior mounted élites created niches for specialized, 'service' people, such as itinerant blacksmiths, gold-panners, and interpreters. This form of society was prefigured in third-millennium BC Anatolia and, perhaps, in the European Bronze Age at the time of the Otomani culture; re-emerging from around 700 BC, it was set to become yet more complex and specialized, as first slaving and then money were introduced, along with Greek wine and oil.

The Greeks Come and See

When the first Greek ships pushed against the current through the Hellespont into the Black Sea, hopped up the coast finding anchorage in natural harbours, and gingerly poked their noses into the mosquito-infested mouths of the Ister (Danube), Tyras (Dnestr), and Borysthenes (Dnepr), they were following in the wake of the Mycenaeans. But did they know it? The answer is probably yes, to the extent that some knowledge of Black Sea navigation had come down to them orally, later formalized in writing in navigators' coastal geographies. We may thus think in terms of Braudel's *longue durée*: the establishment of Greek colonies around the Black Sea was a return to and a resumption of relations with a hinterland in which, also, the memory of an earlier occasion was preserved.

In the *Iliad* a tract of land north of the Aegean Sea is described as 'Thrace, that fertile country, billowy grassland, nourisher of flocks'. Homer's poem, written down around 700 BC, is often considered to have drawn on memories and surviving traditions of the Bronze Age—the Heroic Age of the Mycenaeans (see above Chapter 8). Where was Homer's Thrace? It is clear only that it lay on the European side of the Hellespont and included a mountain region. In Book 9, Nestor addresses Agamemnon, saying 'your huts are full of wine brought over daily in our ships from Thrace across the wide sea' (the Aegean) and in Book 14 Hera glides 'above the snowy-crested hills of Thracian horsemen'. Broadly speaking, the earlier Greek authors understood Thrace to be the country beyond Macedonia, with both an Aegean and a Black Sea coast, including Mount Haemus (the Stara Planina range of the Balkans). Beyond Haemus things grew less certain. To the north, across the Danube, was a plain considered to be part of Scythia, but later authors located Thracian tribes there, and it was to the north of the Danube, in the Carpathian mountains and beyond, that the Dacians—a people generally considered to have been Thracian in language and culture—later emerged.

Who were Homer's Thracians? First, they were people from Thrace. They spoke a language which Homer implies was intelligible to the Trojans who appear in the narrative as their confrères. A connection seems to have existed between Anatolia and Thrace:

SILVER-GILT DECORATIONS for a horse's bridle, fourth century BC, Letnitsa, Bulgaria, showing topknotted Thracians as mentioned in Homer's *Iliad* (4.531): (*above*) topknotted hunter on horseback and (*left*) topknotted male (perhaps the same person) in a scene often described as a *hierogamy* or sacred marriage.

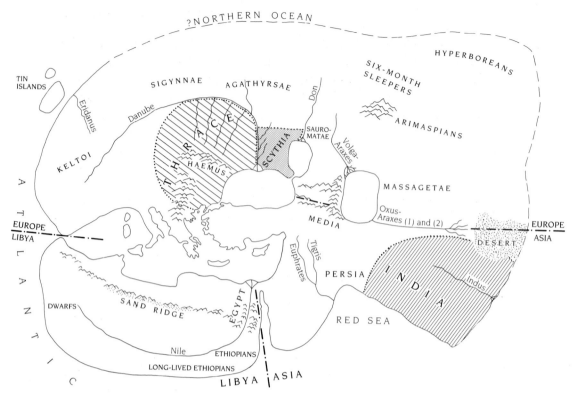

THE WORLD according to Herodotus, whose belief in geographical symmetry caused him to place the mouth of the Danube due north of the Nile delta, effectively enlarging Thrace to Indian proportions and reducing Scythia, which was thought of as 'square'.

archaeologically, Phrygians in Asia appear similar to Thracians in Europe; in Homer, Rhesus the Thracian and Hippocoön the Trojan were kinsmen; Trojan Iphidamus was fostered in Thrace and was on the verge of becoming, through marriage, a kinsman to Cisseus, who lived there. The bride-price which Iphidamus was in the process of paying was partly in Thracian sheep and goats. Homer's Thracians were noble male warriors. The Trojan connection was probably not part of an 'ethnic continuum' at all levels of society, but an inter-élite phenomenon.

Herodotus thought that the Thracians constituted the 'most numerous nation after the Indians'—a formula adopted by many modern 'Thracologists'. His opinion was based on a geographical misunderstanding that made Thrace much larger than it actually was, along with a numerical appraisal of the overall number of different 'peoples' who lived there—as Thrace was closer to Greece than Scythia, the Greeks could name many more local 'tribes'—some, no doubt, no more than single villages.

The motives and timing of the earliest Greek settlements on the coasts of Thrace and Scythia are the subject of much discussion. 'Population pressure' in the Greek homelands has often been cited as a cause. However, the emergence of well-organized colonies, evenly spaced for easy staging of voyages, situated at points of strategic access to the barbarian hinterland indicate—along with the Greek luxuries that found their way into the interior—that trade soon became of central importance.

The first Greek colony on the southern, Aegean shore of Thrace—Abdera—was founded in 654 BC, but the timing of the colonization of the Pontic coast is less certain. Istros, near the mouth of the Danube, seems to have been the earliest formally established colony; available archaeological evidence from the site dates its earliest surviving levels to 630 BC. However, the historians Eusebius and pseudo-Scymnus give dates for

A COMPARISON OF SETTLEMENT LAYOUTS and sizes: (*i*) Greek colony of Istros, south of the Danube delta, Romania, (*ii*) Ramparts at Belsk, in the forest-steppe region of Ukraine, (*iii*) Thracian walled centre, Bulgaria, identified as Seuthopolis, a dynastic seat, and (*iv*) the fortress and temple precinct of Grădiştea Muncelului, Romania, identified as Dacian Sarmizegethusa.

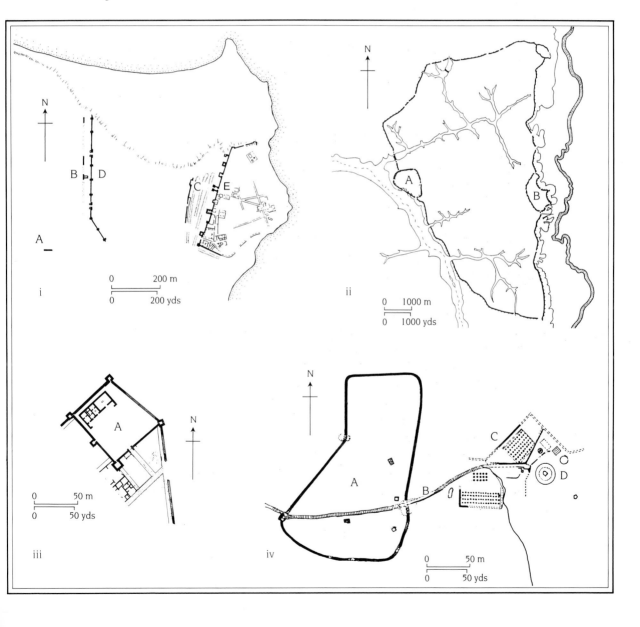

its foundation that bracket the archaeological determination: 656 BC and *c*.600 BC respectively. Chronological uncertainty is increased by other textual evidence that suggests that a revitalization of Aegean knowledge about the Black Sea began well before even Eusebius' foundation date. Hesiod talks of 'mare-milking Scythians' in his *Theogony*, dated to *c*.700 BC, almost a century earlier than the more detailed geographical information on the northern Black Sea coasts preserved in the text of Hecataeus.

An explanation of these apparent discrepancies is that the Greek colonies took time to develop. It has been suggested that initial settlements were in naturally defensible positions which may not have had the most conveniently situated harbours, trade routes to the interior, or adequate space for town planning and expansion. The archaeologically identified colonies are in accessible locations that may have been adopted only after relations with the warlike natives had become well established.

If a search for new materials and markets, rather than an escape from overpopulation, initiated the phenomenon, it may even be that the earliest contact was seasonal, with Greeks travelling up the coast once a year to trade with those who had come from the interior to meet them. It is significant that, by the fifth century BC, Herodotus can record the existence of a group of Scythians 'who sow corn for sale and not for their personal food'; the large-scale restructuring of agrarian production that this implies must have been the result of a considerable period of interaction.

The permanent colonial sites were well situated to conduct trade with the interior: Apollonia Pontica and Mesambria Pontica on either side of the Gulf of Burgas with easy access to the Thracian Plain; Tomis and Istros on the Dobrudjan coast, a short portage away from the lower Danube on its final northern bend before the swampy and inhospitable delta; Tyras on the Dnestr; Berezan and Olbia on the Dnepr; and Panticapaeum on the Kerch strait, controlling the traffic out of Maeotis (the Sea of Azov) and thus the Donets and Don rivers (Tanais was later founded at the Don mouth). We know something about the extent of trade from the Greek wine amphorae and Greek-made silver drinking sets found in steppe burials, for which, as we know from inscriptions and literary sources, the Greeks (and Athens in particular) received slaves and corn.

But at first there were few rich burials on the steppe. The nomads appear to have operated in the forest-steppe zone, forming a tripartite relationship between themselves, the forest-steppe agro-pastoral indigenes, and the Greek coastal and river traders. By the mid-sixth century BC, many defended sites had been built in this zone, and Greek imports reached them in profusion. Among the largest of the known surviving sites is Belsk, on the Vorskla tributary of the Dnepr. Founded at the end of the seventh century

THE IRON AGE HILLFORT of Danebury, Hampshire, England (*above*). First fortified in the sixth century BC and used continuously until the first century BC. The road snakes through the complex earthworks of the main entrance to the excavation in progress in the interior (*see chapter 10*).

THE GRAVE GOODS from the élite burial at Goeblingen-Nospelt (Grave B), Luxembourg (*below*). Late first century BC. The amphorae were used to transport Roman wine (*see chapter 10*).

BC, it consists of an east and a west fort set in an enclosing rampart 33 kilometres in length (equal to the Boulevard Périphérique that encircles modern Paris); the west fort alone, covering 72 hectares (the size of a largish western European *oppidum*, is considered to represent eleven-million-days' work; over a thousand burial mounds lie outside it. The whole thing dwarfs any known contemporary settlement anywhere in the world.

Belsk has been identified by some as the wood-ramparted town of Gelonus, with its mixed Graeco-Scythian and Scythian populations of Geloni and Budini mentioned briefly by Herodotus. But, although he probably had in mind one of these forest-steppe centres, we cannot with any certainty say which. Archaeologically, Belsk is impossible to excavate in full. Crafts such as the casting of trilobate arrowheads, potting, and iron forging were carried on. The central enclosure housed granaries, along with at least eleven separate settlements. We may envisage a seasonal meeting of pastoral groups with their flocks and agricultural groups with their cash crops, converging to barter and bet, play games, and form marriage alliances.

Scythian and Thracian Society

Neither classical sources nor modern archaeology can provide a full understanding of the complexity of Scythian and Thracian ethnicity. Geographically intermediate and marginal groups were of uncertain status for Herodotus, as indeed they are for archaeologists. It is most unlikely that the material–culture groupings that archaeology recognizes accord neatly with the ethnic and social groupings that the classical authors recognized. Scythia denoted a tract of land for the Greeks. Scythian was a broad socio-economic designation, equivalent to the similarly broad term Saka, used by the Persians to denote the steppe nomads. Herodotus, however, made a sustained attempt to define a number of different types of Scythians, Thracians, and others, on the basis of name, language, customs, and appearance. From his discussion of kinship, we learn that inter-marriage took place between Thracians and Scythians, and that their élites—rather in the manner of the royal families of Europe—had an international familial network.

Of the Thracians generally, Herodotus says 'idleness is most noble and being a worker of the land most dishonourable. Noblest of all is living from war and plunder'. He says that they worship only Ares, Dionysus, and Artemis, 'but their kings, in contrast to the people generally . . . swear by no other deity but Hermes, and claim descent from him'. Mythologically speaking, Hermes is a wanderer god. Thus, although the Thracian élite were probably not nomadic or semi-nomadic in the way that the Scythians were, they may have been ethnically distinct from local, small-scale agrarian societies in Thrace.

We can see from their burials and from their art that they were horse-owners, and that there was a clear social hierarchy. In Bulgaria, there are roughly twenty thousand fourth-

THE ROGOZEN HOARD, Bulgaria, buried *c.*300 BC, during the Celtic raids. It shows Greek, Persian, Celtic, and Indian influence (the latter perhaps via returning veterans of Alexander's campaign on the Indus). At 19.91 kg, the 165 vessels total less than a talent in silver, but weigh exactly 3600 Persian *sigloi*.

and fifth-century BC barrows, each of which must have involved a community in many days of work. Although most have been robbed, few have been obliterated, so that we can estimate that around three thousand per generation were built during a period when the Thracian population south of the Danube, judging by the number of villages and fortresses as well as historical records, must usually have been in the hundreds of thousands. Whoever the majority were, their dead were disposed of in a different fashion, probably in flat, cremation cemeteries of the sort that have occasionally been excavated (they leave little surface trace and, unlike the barrows, are easily destroyed by agriculture). In southern Bulgaria, some communities may have exposed the dead in rock-cut niches on mountainsides.

The classical accounts, when combined with archaeological data, allow us to put forward a model for understanding the overall ethnic structure for the fifth-century BC inhabitants of Thrace and Scythia. In this model, the mobile élites are 'laterally' constituted ethnic groups, eligibility for which, for men, was broadly conditional on having obtained warrior status through experience (although wealth helped, and could clearly be inherited). Such élites formed the dominant political and military formations in particular areas and their names are the names picked up by the classical authors. Subordinate groups were either 'vertically' constituted ethnic groups or tribes, into which one was born and within which status was enhanced through developing relations of kinship

PEOPLES AND TRIBES described by Herodotus, mapped in terms of geographical and social space. The two largest boxes represent the main Thracian and Scythian tribes respectively. The Agathyrsae in Transylvania are indeterminate 'Thraco-Scythians'; the Sigynnae in the lower Danube basin are neither Thracian nor Scythian. The Tauri are in the Crimea; the Argippaei are in the Ural foothills.

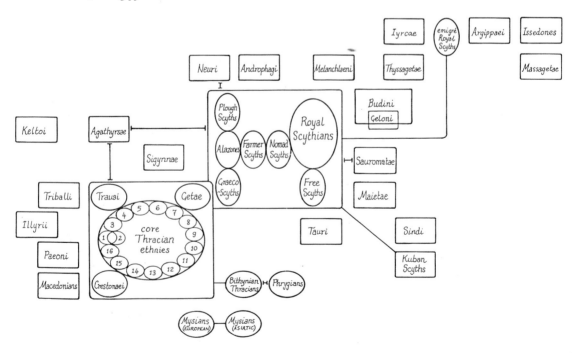

between lineages, or they were 'service' ethnic groups, with a strong 'professional' or 'guild' identity and little internal stratification.

Herodotus gives detailed information on the forms of alliance and dispute settlement; the simplest form of the latter seems to have been the duel. One of the more specialized craft workshops discovered at Belsk produced drinking cups made from human skulls—reminding us of his report that the Scythians sawed off the skulls of their worst enemies to drink from, gilding the insides when they could afford it: 'They do this, too, in the case of kinsmen with whom they have had differences and whom they have finally conquered in combat in the king's presence.' Complex disputes and decisions seem to have been tackled by a specialized class of transvestite diviners (or shamans: discussed further below).

Thracian and Scythian women seem to have been politically subordinate to men (although see below concerning 'Amazons'). We can, therefore, view élite marriages principally as creating or reinforcing links between males. But a more direct method may be alluded to by Herodotus when he talks of the way in which the Scythians made sworn agreements, filling a bowl with wine and the mixed blood of the contracting parties, who then drank from it—in a manner similar to the important institution of *anda* (blood brotherhood), documented for a later period on the steppe among the Mongols (*see colour plate facing p. 420*).

By the fifth century BC, there seems to have been considerable institutional complexity in the Scythian world. Herodotus speaks of 'administrative districts' and of the royal Scythians who seem to have been the overall top dogs. He provides a dramatic and highly detailed description of the burial of a royal Scythian king, the essence of which is that the stuffed and waxed body of the deceased was processed round the territories of 'subject nations'. The king was then buried with the bodies of his strangled court and covered with a great mound; a year later, fifty of his entourage, with their horses, were strangled, stuffed, and mounted in a great circle around the burial. The relatives purified themselves after the funeral rites by inhaling the vapour of cannabis seed, thrown on to hot stones, in small, tripod-supported hemp tents.

This description tallies well with what has survived in the ground in the lower Dnepr basin, where the greatest surviving concentration of rich fifth- and fourth-century BC burial mounds is located. But these kurgan mounds were not simple piles of earth. Careful excavation has revealed that they were originally quite steep and conical, with layers of supercompacted earthen 'armour' to repel robbers, and layers of inverted grass turfs. Symbolically, perhaps, the structure represented an allotment of steppe for the afterlife. The robbed sixth-century BC burial mound of Ulski Aul in the northern Caucasus, partially excavated by Veselovsky in 1898, contained the skeletons of 360 horses, lying in groups of eighteen where they had been tethered to posts driven into the floor of the main grave chamber. Many more (Veselovsky gave up counting!) were found in other arrangements in a layer one-third of the way up in the burial mound, along with mass sacrifices of donkeys, sheep, and cattle. This higher layer probably represents a second

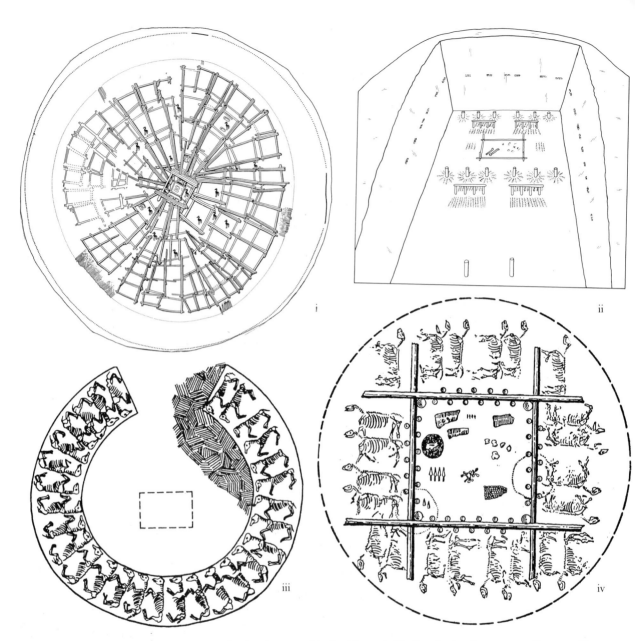

THE EXCAVATED LAYOUTS of various kurgans of the Scythian period in Eurasia, showing patterns of horse sacrifice around the central human burial: (*i*) Arzhan, south Siberia, (*ii*) Ulski Aul, Kurgan I, northern Caucasus, (*iii*) Voronezhskaya kurgan, northern Caucasus, (*iv*) Kostromskaya Kurgan, northern Caucasus.

phase of funeral ritual, possibly completed a year after the main burial, as Herodotus reports. In the Tolstaya Mogila (the 'Fat Barrow') on the lower Dnepr, a man, a woman, and a child were buried sequentially, with perhaps only a year elapsing between each funeral; their various attendants appear to have been killed on the spot, one left guarding a passageway, two lads holding the horses, male and female 'minders' for the child.

Herodotus' account is even more strikingly supported by discoveries made in the cemetery of Pazyryk, thousands of miles from the Black Sea, in the Altai mountains of south Siberia. There, permafrost freeze-dried the burials of rich nomads, preserving most of the organic remains. The skin was still intact on the bodies when they were excavated in the 1950s, showing tattoos and the careful taxidermy Herodotus talks of—indeed, the bodies were stuffed with many of the herbs he lists. Muscle areas had been removed from under the skin, perhaps for some reason connected with ritual cannibalism (Herodotus records that the Issedones practised something of this sort). In a corner of one grave chamber was a fur bag containing cannabis seed, a censer filled with stones, and the hexapod frame of an inhalation tent.

Acculturation and Difference

The Pazyryk kurgans demonstrate the vast network of contacts in which the steppe peoples were involved. Grave goods included furs from the Arctic taiga, combined in one case with local gold to provide an elaborate edging for an imported Persian carpet with

TATTOOED ARM of a warrior from a kurgan burial at Pazyryk, in the Altai mountains of south Siberia; fourth century BC. There is a large wound on the upper arm. After death, muscles were removed and the corpse was embalmed with herbs; stitching from this procedure is visible. Among the animals depicted is a griffin-headed elk with floral antler tines.

lions on it; cheetah fur and coriander from the Near East; a Caucasian bronze helmet; a Chinese mirror; and an embroidered wedding silk—revamped into a taselled saddle-cloth. We see here something of the centrality of the steppe, along with something of the nomads' lack of reverence towards the finer products of literate 'civilization'. A memorable moment in Herodotus' account of Darius' abortive expedition against the Scythians is when the nomad cavalry, who for weeks had refused pitched battle with the massive Persian infantry, ranged themselves as if to charge, but then 'a hare ran between the two sides, and every Scythian who saw it pursued the hare' prompting Darius remark 'These people despise us utterly'.

Actually, the nomadic élites rapidly found themselves suffering from the ills of 'acculturation'. Although the almost total dependence of Athens on imported Black Sea grain after 400 BC made many of the Scythians very rich, the elaborate and ostentatious Greek-made gold and silver drinking sets that they buried their dead with indicate the enthusiastic adoption of wine. Added to their cannabis, the possibilities for developed forms of dissipation must have been great. Herodotus tells us that, despite the fact that they did not like Greek ways and two of their number—Anacharsis and, later, Scylas—were put to death for adopting Greek manners, they did not water their wine and were consequently often drunk. The transformation of old ways was probably inevitable (as it was, later, for the American Indians, in the face of white men and whisky). Under Ateas, they became almost sedentary. It has been claimed by some that their élite took to dwelling in comfortable Greek-style stone-built houses on the acropolis of the town of Kamenka on the lower Dnepr, but the archaeological evidence for this is uncertain. What is certain is that Ateus was badly defeated by Philip II of Macedon in 339 BC in Thrace, and by the third century BC the area of Scythian overlordship had dwindled and was focused on a fixed city-capital at Neapolis in the Crimea. Out on the steppe, a new martial élite with more advanced weaponry, the Sarmatians, replaced them.

In fact, by the time that Herodotus travelled to the Black Sea, the Scythians were already different from those who had taunted Darius. Although still termed Scythians by the Greeks, archaeologically we can recognize the arrival of a new wave of central Asian nomads in the middle of the fifth century BC. Herodotus' ethnography of Scythia, therefore, consists of observations on societies that were in the process of rapid transformation, in which power relations between and within ethnic groups were changing, along with the definition of the ethnic groups themselves. Power relations between men and women also appear to have been changing.

Following Engels, many sociologists have considered pastoral nomadism to mark a new phase in the development of women's oppression by men. This seems to be contradicted, at least in part, by the archaeological and literary evidence which we have for Scythia. The sociologist Maria Mies writes 'It is most probably correct to say that the martial pastoral nomads were the fathers of all dominance relations, particularly that of men over women', because 'the "productive" forces of the hunters could be fully released only at the stage when pastoral nomads, who domesticated cattle and women, invaded agricultural communities . . . For pastoral nomads, women were no longer very important as producers or gatherers of foods . . . they were needed as breeders of children, particularly of sons. Their productivity was now reduced to their "fertility" to be appropriated and controlled by men.' This is not obvious in Scythia, where gender categories appear to have been markedly different from those that operated in the Greek world. The most famous example are the Amazons, who, in Greek and Roman mythology, were a nation of warrior women whose most striking custom was to arrest the development of their right breast in order to throw spears and shoot with the bow more freely (*a-mazos* meaning 'without a breast' in Greek). Amazons are depicted in Greek sculpture and painting with the right side of the chest draped to cover this missing breast.

According to Herodotus, the Scythian word for Amazons was *Oiorpata*, meaning 'man-slayers'; they were a group of women warriors among, or fissioned off from, the Sauromatians. In Herodotus' explicitly mythic account of their origin, he says that when the women of this tribe were invited home by young Scythian men, they remonstrated that 'We cannot live with your women. For we and they have not the same customs. We shoot the bow and the javelin and ride horses, but, for "women's tasks" we know them not.' It is not clear to what extent the warrior role was acceptable for women outside the Scythian world. Herodotus himself was familiar with Artemisia of Halicarnassus as a warrior and war leader and he records that some Amyrgian Scythians were once led into battle by 'Atossa, daughter of Cyrus', mother of Masistes by Darius. But the impression is that these women were exceptional, and that (perhaps) only steppe nomads would be prepared to fight under a woman as a matter of course.

Although often the subject of scepticism, the existence of women warriors in the steppes is archaeologically supportable. Excavators have not always paid proper attention to physical anthropological features as indices of sex. Most Scythian graves have been ascribed 'male' or 'female' on the basis of preconceived notions of the appropriateness of particular grave goods (for example, weapons for men, mirrors for women); nothing could be more unfortunate than this sort of a priori ascription in the case of the steppe groups. Exceptionally, mid-nineteenth-century excavations on the Terek river in the Caucasus uncovered and recognized the skeleton of a woman with armour, arrowheads, a discus of slate, and an iron knife, and a series of graves near Aul Stepan Zminda appear to have been of mounted female warriors (although later than the Scythian period in date). More recently, Renate Rolle's excavations around the Scythian 'royal' kurgan of Chertomlyk (1981–6) have identified four from among fifty warrior graves as skeletally female: one was buried with an arrowhead embedded in her back, another had a massive iron shield, and a third was buried with a young child. About forty such burials are now known in the Scythian region, west of the Don; east of the Don, in Herodotus' Sauromatia, a full twenty per cent of investigated fifth- and fourth-century BC buried warriors turn out to have been women. Hippocrates tells us that the Sauromatian women 'do not lay aside their virginity until they have killed three of their ene-

VASE FROM THE KUL OBA KURGAN, Crimea; made of electrum (gold-silver alloy); fourth century BC; height 12.5 cm. Low reliefs show Scythian warriors in scenes which may have mythological significance. Here a man's shin is being bandaged; embroidered trousers/gaiters are depicted, along with composite reflex bows.

mies' and do not ride after they have taken a husband 'unless compelled to do so by a general expedition'.

This evidence for women's activities does not constitute evidence that women in Scythian society operated on an equal footing with men in all social spheres. The proportion of 'Amazon' burials is low, and they occur alongside more obviously 'feminine' burials—some sacrificed in the tombs of powerful men (a reverse case has not been documented). The surviving symbolism of Scythian riding is strongly male: the 'penis-and-hoof' type of bridle cheekpiece—named for its explicitly shaped terminal—was popular, and in art it is stallions that are depicted as the usual mount.

However, it may be that women had enjoyed higher status, or perhaps some sort of parity, before Greek contact. The accepted explanation for the emergence of female warriors and hunters in the recent ethnography of the North American Indian tribes indicates how such a phenomenon might have been part of core-periphery economics: as European fur traders moved west in Canada, native men, who until that time had been no more than the economic and socio-political equals of women, were able to become disproportionately rich through fur trapping (a male-gender pursuit); in an attempt to compensate for an increasing lack of authority, women began to switch from 'female' to 'male' gender-typed activities. Something of this sort may have happened in Scythia: for Herodotus, among the remote forest-steppe pastoral Issedones 'men and women have equal power'—perhaps a vestige of a situation that had formerly been more general. Certainly, archaeologically, both female weapon burials and secondary female sacrifices in male burials appear to be late, Iron Age phenomena.

The gender-crossing counterpart to Amazons were Enarees whom Herodotus calls 'androgynes'. The word is probably related to Sanskrit *nara* (man), which would give it the meaning 'without manhood'. Herodotus says that these men suffer from the 'female sickness', Hippocrates that:

The men have no great desire for intercourse . . . the constant jolting of their horses unfits them for it . . . the great majority among the Scythians become impotent, do women's work, live like women and converse accordingly . . . they put on women's clothes, holding that they have lost their manhood . . . This affliction affects the rich Scythians because of their riding . . . the poor, who do not ride, suffer less . . . the Scythians are the most impotent of men, for the reasons I have given, and also because they wear trousers and spend most of their time on their horses, so that they do not handle the parts, but owing to cold and fatigue forget about sexual passion.

Hippocrates' explanations are plausible in terms of modern medical knowledge: jolting can cause traumatic and irreversible damage to the testes, while trousers—probably an equestrian invention—raise their temperature and can cause infertility. However, it may be that the Scythians displayed a suite of symptoms, and that no simple exegesis of these texts is possible. Herodotus' 'female sickness' could suggest bleeding, and, therefore, be associated with other cavalry afflictions, such as piles and fistulae (both known and treated in knights returning from the Hundred Years War (1337–1453) by the English surgeon John Arderne).

Another part of any explanation must take into account the role of these people as soothsayers: according to Herodotus, 'the Enarees, who are androgynes . . . practise divination with the bark of the lime tree. When they split the bark in three, the prophet makes his prophecy, braiding and unbraiding the bark with his fingers.' Hippocrates says that 'the natives ascribe the cause of [the] symptom to a goddess and therefore they respect and worship such persons'. Bearing these things in mind, a psychological explanation might be suggested, in which radical division of wagon-bound motherhood on the one hand, and, on the other, the formation of the mounted raiding parties, on campaign for many years at a time (twenty-eight years in the case of Media: see above, p. 380) forced a stressful choice on children, as well as leaving no place for men who—because of a variety of afflictions—could no longer ride to war. Herodotus tells us that it was considered utterly shameful for a man not to die in battle; 'changing' sex and becoming a shaman may have provided an acceptable psychological compromise. Such shamanism has been well documented among recent Siberian pastoralists.

Although so far not recognized in burials, figures who may have corresponded to the Enarees are represented in art: on the fourth-century BC silver-gilt Poroina 'rhyton' (a kind of drinking horn) from near the Danubian Iron Gates in Romania, and on the second-century BC Gundestrup cauldron (discussed in more detail below).

In Thrace, burial and literary evidence suggests a more subordinate position for women at all stages of life. Herodotus writes of one group of Thracian polygamists where, on a husband's death, the wives are judged by his friends. The winner 'so honoured, is greatly praised by men and women and then slaughtered at his tomb by her closest kinsfolk' and buried alongside; the remaining wives are shamed by this. Archaeological discoveries made in the fourth-century BC Mogilanska burial mound at Vratsa in north-west Bulgaria are congruent with this description: a rich central male burial was accompanied by a richly attired woman who had been stabbed through the ribs with an iron knife.

Peoples in Collision

Bride-price rather than dowry was the norm among most of the Thracians according to Herodotus, who also tells us that 'they sell their children for export'. Thucydides commented that 'one can accomplish nothing among the Thracians without giving gifts'. Archaeologically we can see that, as with the Scythians, the Thracians had, by the start of the fifth century BC, been drawn into trade with the money-based economies of Greece and Persia, and so were also undergoing rapid social change. A 'prestige-goods economy' developed, in which exotic luxuries from the colonies and beyond were acquired and used in the trappings of particular social statuses, thus fuelling social competition. This then intensified trade, boosted small-scale warring to endemic levels, and opened the way for the establishment of state-like organizations with their own coinages.

A significant catalyst was Darius I's military expedition against Scythia, which was launched from Thrace, involved Thracian mercenaries, and introduced Thracian élites to the Achaemenid Persian banqueting style with its gold and silver drinking sets. Persian records speak of the maintenance of a tributary administrative district, the Satrapy of Skudra, in the thirty years following the abortive campaign (*c*.513–480 BC); whether or not this was so, Persian-style systems of tribute and something of the Persian ideology of kingship seem to have been subsequently adopted.

In the fifth and fourth centuries BC, Achaemenid metalworking styles directly stimulated the development of Thracian prestige silversmithing. The local use of silver
coinage became widespread, and it seems that local exploitation of silver deposits began
at this time in Thrace, side by side with imports of silver from the Athenian mines at Lau-
rium. Silver vessels were apparently made in weight units of round numbers of coin,
either to a Persian or a Thraco-Macedonian standard.

Many wine-drinking sets of the fourth century bear the name 'Kotys', often followed
by what appear to be place-names. These inscriptions, in the Greek alphabet, are generally thought to relate to the Kotys who became king of the Odrysae around 384 BC. The
Odrysae had become powerful in central Thrace after the Persian withdrawal by virtue
of their close political and military links with Athens. One explanation for the inscriptions is that Kotys may have progressed around his dominions, holding court like an
English medieval king and receiving gifts bearing both his name and that of the place of
manufacture. He was assassinated in 359 BC by Macedonian sympathizers.

The Macedonian expansion into Thrace under Philip was continued by Alexander,
who moved north of the Danube to suppress the Getae. At the river crossing he met
some Celts, who professed to him their—now famous—fear of the sky falling on their
heads. The following year (334 BC), Alexander left, with his Thracian mercenaries, for
Persia, India, and an early death. As Macedonian power waned, the Odrysians re-
emerged under Seuthes III, who minted his own coins. Archaeological and epigraphic
data show that Seuthes' capital, Seuthopolis, had a fortified tower, or *tyrsis*, within its
walls and a sanctuary of which he himself was high priest. The central, walled part of the
city was modelled along Greek lines, probably by a Greek-trained architect, and maintained via tribute payments from subject peoples and the Greek colonies—400 talents
in gold and silver in one particular year, according to the Greek mine-owner and historian, Thucydides (one tonne in silver, as 1 talent equals about 25 kilograms; *see colour plate
facing p. 389*). Here, in southern Thrace, the initial clear distinction between immigrant
Greek colonies and native interior was already giving way to cosmopolitan pressures.
Recent excavations led by M. Domaradski at the Thracian urban and industrial site of
Vetren, on the upper Maritsa, *c*.200 kilometres inland from the Aegean, have documented the presence, by the mid-fourth century BC, of Greek merchants operating
under special legal protection, and of a possible two-way trade in wine.

Further north by this time, trade within the lower Danube riverine network had
become well established, though—on current evidence—populations seem to have
remained spatially segregated to a greater degree. There was a zone of Graecized settlement and burial on the coastal strip just inland from the Greek colonies. This zone was
involved in the portage of goods across to the Danube's main course. The settlement of
Zimnicea, around 300 kilometres from the Black Sea on the Danube's left bank, has
yielded artefacts of Odrysian, Getic, and Scythian type, along with the remains of hundreds of Greek wine amphorae that began to arrive about 430 BC. Amphorae have also
been found between the Danube and the Carpathians, at sites like Piscu Crăşani on the

GUNDESTRUP, DENMARK, second-century BC silver cauldron: detail of inner plate showing a horned figure, often identified with the Celtic god Cernunnos. The figure may reflect the shamanic use of tantric yoga in Dacia and Sarmatia; figures in the similar poses are known from this time in Moldavia and the Don basin.

river Ialomiţa, and at the mouths of the mountain passes, at sites like Cetăţenii din Vale, where the extraordinary numbers of broken amphorae, coupled with their almost total absence further on, suggest that wine was transferred to skins at such points, to facilitate the rough passage over into Transylvania.

The élite among the Getae were buried with silver and gold armour and drinking sets decorated with scenes which appear to relate to the 'royal hunt'—another Persian kingly theme. Scythian Animal-style, Greek, and Persian motifs and conventions are all adapted in this eclectic and distinctive style. Architecture seems to have been inspired by urban models here too: excavations by V. Zirra at Coţofenii-din-Dos, west of Zimnicea, on the Olt tributary, have uncovered a massive mud-brick rampart with regularly spaced towers forming one side of an otherwise unexceptional promontory fort (cf. the Heuneburg, Chapter 10).

Herodotus tells two stories about Getic religion, which he thinks are neither mutually contradictory nor quite believable. He says that the Getae thought of themselves as immortal and were monotheistic, believing in a divine being called Salmoxis or Gebeleizis, to whom they went when they died. They asked worldly things of Salmoxis via a messenger, who was 'sent' by being impaled on their spearpoints. Greek colonists told Herodotus a different story about Salmoxis, namely, that he was a rich former slave who returned to teach a philosophy of immortality—enjoyed after death in a pleasant place. While teaching he secretly constructed an underground dwelling into which he vanished, and was thought dead. He returned after three years, proving his immortality to his credulous audience. The logic of the second story is flawed. If the Getae knew nothing of the underground chamber, why did they believe that Salmoxis had died, when he might simply have gone back to foreign parts? Archaeological evidence from a barrow cemetery near Sveshtari, in north-east Bulgaria, suggests an interesting possibility. Recent excavations show a barrow in which a sliding wooden door had led into and out of the central grave chamber. The stone grooves it had run in are very smooth and indicate regular use. Such a structure is clearly suitable for a ritual of death-and-return, and might well be related to the sort of 'chthonic', underworld-related religion that the Greeks believed existed in Thrace (the birthplace of Orpheus).

The Celts were well established in the lower Danube region when Alexander met them. They had begun to move eastward into Transylvania in the early fourth century BC and continued, pressing down into southern Thrace and Greece, during the third century BC; they sacked Seuthopolis (281 BC) and Delphi (279 BC), after which they established the kingdom of Tylis somewhere in Thrace. North-eastward, Celtic groups crossed the Prut and Dnestr, exploiting the power vacuum left by the decline of Scythian power.

The local Thracians seem to have buried as many of their valuables as they could in the face of the onslaughts, first of Macedonians, then of Celts—many hoards of decorated fourth-century BC silverwork have been, and continue to be, found throughout north-west and north-central Bulgaria. One of the few surviving pieces of the silversmith's art made in the disrupted Celtic period in this region is the Gundestrup cauldron. The puzzle of this cauldron, found in Jutland, in many ways encapsulates the whole problem of our understanding of Thracian, Dacian, and Scythian society. Put simply, these societies were not tightly bounded. On the one hand, they existed within a developing world system with many shared elements and a long time-scale, and, on the other hand, they were composed of a plethora of small, local, short-lived cultural groupings within which these elements were given meaning.

The techniques by which the elaborately decorated cauldron was made, sometime in the first half of the second century BC, were typically Thracian. Some of the figures on it, such as a warrior wearing a bird-crested helmet like that found in the Transylvanian Celtic grave of Ciumeşti, look Celtic. Others derive from Greek and Iranian mythology—the dolphin-rider and the bull-slayer. Yet others come from India and include types of the goddesses Sri-Lakshmi and Hariti, the Chakravartin or 'universal ruler', and a horned-figure in a tantric yogic pose. The latter, presented as androgynous in terms of the cauldron's pictorial grammar, holds a snake and a torc, and wears horns—symbols that may well denote power over male, female, and animal domains respectively. Tantric yoga contributed to the development of steppe shamanism, and involves gaining dominion over creation through drug and alcohol use, and channelling sexual energy via special postures; Buddhist and Jainist tradition diverged from it by becoming celibate, ascetic, and literate. Thematically the cauldron fits into a longer history of Eastern influence along the steppe axis. Before 300 BC this came particularly from Iran, Siberia, and China and afterwards more from Indo-Scythia and India (versions of Indian goddesses appear in Sarmatian silverwork and in the middle Uralic 'Permian' Animal style, from whence they reached Finland). The cauldron was probably carried north as booty by raiding Germans—possibly the ferocious Cimbri who finally settled in that part of Jutland (Himmerland), which preserved both their name and the cauldron.

The presence of pictures of Indian elephants and gods in Atlantic and Scandinavian Europe, along with Chinese silk (found also in a grave at Panticapaeum on the Black Sea), should alert us to the fact that northern Eurasia, beyond the various imperial frontiers, was far more interconnected in the period from 300 BC to AD 300 than is commonly believed. On the steppe, the Scythians had, by 200 BC, been replaced as the dominant élite by the Sarmatians. The Sarmatians were confused by most classical authors with Herodotus' Sauromatians but, although the words may be variants of the same name, the archaeological cultures that can be associated with them are not. The first Sarmatians are usually identified archaeologically as the Prokhorovka culture, which moved from the southern Urals into the lower Volga region, and then into the north Pontic steppe, during the fourth and third centuries BC. During this movement the Sarmatians seem to have grown and fissioned into several groups—the Alani (or Alans), Aorsi, Roxolani, and Iazyges. How the archaeological culture groups of the period from the first century BC to the fourth century AD correlate with these ethnic categories is unclear (both the Susly and Chernyakov cultures seem to have been Sarmatian, and burials on the Mureş and Tisza rivers in Romania and in Hungary may be those of Iazyges or Roxolani). To some extent the westward expansion of the Sarmatians may have been precipitated by events in the east. Around 176 BC, according to the Chinese historian Ssu-ma Ch'ien, the Huns defeated the Yüeh-chi (or Tocharians); and in the first century BC they expanded into the southern Ural and Volga region.

SILVER HORSE-HARNESS *phalerae* were widely popular in the second and first centuries BC. These are from (*i*) Indo-Scythia, bought in Rawalpindi, (*ii*) a Sarmatian grave on the Don, south Russia, (*iii*) the Thracian grave at Stara Zagora, Bulgaria, (*iv*) a hoard found on Sark in the English Channel (now lost), and (*v*) Gundestrup, Denmark (used to patch a hole in the bottom of the Gundestrup cauldron).

i

ii

iii

iv

v

TEMPLE PRECINCT, Grădiştea Muncelului, Romania. Laid out on an artificial terrace high in the Orăştie mountains, several of the structures seem to have had astronomical/calendrical significance. Identified as Dacian Sarmizegethusa, the site is surrounded by a network of fortresses and temples.

The Dacian State and its Aftermath

Some measure of historically respectable order was reimposed in south-east Europe by the second-century BC Roman conquest of Macedonia in the south and the emergence, in the first century BC, of the Dacian state in the north. The Transylvanian Celts (the Boii and Helvetii) were defeated by Burebista in 60 BC and forced westward (later to become involved in the destruction of Manching, see Chapter 10). Burebista seems to have consolidated his power in 62 BC in alliance with Deceneus, a priest (our chief source is Jordanes in the sixth century AD, who preserves parts of several earlier authors — in this case Dio Chrysostom). The Burebista–Deceneus double act brought together four or five smaller groups, including the Getae, the Daci, and the Buri, and created an intermontane state powerful enough to threaten Rome.

In the Dacian state, social stratification was not primarily kinship-based as in the earlier tribal chiefdoms, but related to centralized economic and, especially, religious power. Criton in his *Getica* wrote that 'The Getic kings impose fear of the gods and concord on their subjects by cunning and magic, and enjoy high status.' The idea of a co-ruling priest and king (the latter being nevertheless ultimately more powerful) may con- nect to the Enaree–king relationship of the Scythians (which, as druid-king or chakravartin-yogin seems to have formed part of a common northern Eurasian pattern at this time). A special class of Dacians—plausibly of priestly status—are described as *kapnobatai* or 'smoke walkers', a name which may indicate use of cannabis (which was widely grown in Thrace). Dacian priests were vegetarian and celibate. The religion may have arisen entirely out of local roots. The immortalizing monotheism of Salmoxis may have been one precursor, while hilltop sanctuaries like the Dacian ones were prefigured in the fourth century BC in the Rhodope mountains of southern Thrace. But there were many potential external influences at this time too—Buddhism, Judaism, which had just reached the Bosporan kingdom in the Crimea, and Egyptian cults in the Hellenistic cities of southern Thrace. Whatever the precise form of the Dacian religion, it was clearly powerfully threatening to the Roman conquerors, who systematically razed the temples to the ground, leaving only the column bases.

Dacian burials are not easy to identify. Apart from a lone warrior burial with rich grave goods discovered at Cugir, they seem to survive archaeologically as 'ustrina' cremation sites—barrel-shaped pits containing human bones, around fifteen of which have been identified on settlements. Such evidence is congruent with a new form of religious rit- ual (comparable in some ways with Zoroastrian practice in contemporary Chorasmia, adjacent to Buddhist Bactria, which involved exposing bodies and removing the bones to ossuaries). The absence of any burial evidence that could associate objects with par- ticular individuals means that we can say virtually nothing, archaeologically speaking, about the relative statuses of men and women in Dacian society. The classical authors and the representations on Trajan's column both suggest a male-dominated military and religious leadership.

Although the Dacian state developed a state religion, monumental architecture, cen- tral storage facilities, currency, and control of a vast and diverse territory, it did not have either recognizable cities or writing—both features that we might expect to have accompanied the development of such centralized authority. Writing was available to the Dacians (it had begun to spread into Thrace in the fifth century BC in the form of inscriptions on metalwork, see above p. 399); that they chose not to adopt it for com- munication or accounting suggests that they had adequate methods of their own (as had the Mongols over a thousand years later).

How the internal economy of the Dacian state functioned is at present unclear, but a central ideology was clearly important. The Burebista–Deceneus leadership demanded abstinence and caused the vineyards to be dug up. Lowland grain was concentrated in storage pits in the upland fortresses, themselves linked at higher altitude to the special- ized upland pastoral economy that had first begun to take shape at the time of the Feri- gile-Bîrseşti culture (see above p. 383). It may well be that the Dacian state *was* in fact urban at its upland centre, albeit in a diffuse way, for a high density of fortresses and sanctuaries have been recorded around Sarmizegethusa in the Orăştie mountains, connected to a network of hilltop droveways (or *plaiuri*), and to open settlements and small single-hut terraces on the slopes between. In AD 106 the Romans destroyed this complex and claimed that they looted, in a single hoard, 165,000 tonnes of gold and 300,000 tonnes of silver. Although this amount is perhaps credible in terms of the massive Dacian exploitation of precious metals in the Apuseni mountains (along with trade payments and tributes from abroad), its existence in one spot would suggest that there was central control of circulation.

The external economics of the Dacian state are puzzling. Polybius, writing in the second century BC, records three staple Black Sea exports: cattle, slaves, and grain, for which other grain, olive oil, and wine were imported. As we have seen, much of this reached Transylvania via riverine trading posts such as Piscu Crăşani. But, at the time that Burebista came to power, Piscu Crăşani had been abandoned, and the Dacian king attacked and partly destroyed the Black Sea colonies of Olbia, Tyras, and Histria. This suggests, first, an attempt to curtail the power of the colonies along with that of the Sarmatian lords who were their principal trade partners; the newly dry Dacia needed no wine, but it did need Danubian and north Pontic grain (as well as military security). Second, the truncation of the Black Sea trade network suggests that Dacia's main economic connections must already have lain in another direction. Coin hoards indicate that the

TRAJAN'S COLUMN, the Forum, Rome. Paid for with booty from the Dacian Wars, part of which is shown in this scene, overflowing from the panniers of three pack-horses.

link was southward, from the middle Danubian lands (recently acquired from the Scordisci) to the Dalmatian coast and the colonies of Apollonia and Dyrrhachium, just across the Adriatic from Rome. Slaves would seem to have been the most likely export in this direction, and were paid for with coin—silver tetradrachms struck in these towns.

The Dacian state seems to have operated an internal cash economy. Over ninety coin hoards are known dating from the period 130 to 31 BC, containing over 25,000 Roman Republican denarii along with locally minted copies of them. Apart from coinages, the Dacians seem to have imported virtually nothing made of durable material. They had the spending power to import all manner of luxuries but, on available evidence at least, it seems that they were both culturally isolationist and militarily expansionist, while allowing a certain amount of profitable 'through' trade. Sarmatian graves of the first centuries BC and AD are often found to contain Italic bronzes that arrived via the Dacian–Adriatic trade route.

Burebista seems to have been a military leader of equal stature to Caesar, Ariovistus (see Chapter 10), or Mithridates Eupator (King of Pontus). Caesar planned to attack him, but in 44 BC both leaders were assassinated. We have little clear knowledge of events in Dacia for the subsequent hundred years or so. The state seems to have broken up into its constituent parts to re-emerge, quite suddenly, under a new king, Decebalus, in the later first century AD. Only the period of the Roman campaign against Decebalus' Dacia is known in any detail, but it does not enlighten us very much further as to the social make-up, religion, or economy of this major power. Between AD 105 and 107 the war was won and the Roman province of Dacia established.

The ethnic interrelations of the second and third centuries AD in south-east Europe, and the correlations between archaeology and history, are muddled and, therefore, perhaps seem more complex. The destruction of the Dacian state correlates with a sudden increase in the wealth and social differentiation of Sarmatian burials, and an expansion by the Sarmatians into the forest-steppe zone. Dacians continued to live outside the Roman empire, in the northern Carpathians and Moldavia, archaeologically associated with a group called the Carpi—notable for their rich burial of children (recalling the sixth-century BC children's cemetery at Ferigile). After AD 117, Rome exercised only nominal control over the steppe parts of the lower Danube basin, losing it entirely in AD 275, as the Alamanni, Goths, Vandals, and others bore down on the Empire and the nearly spent force of the Sarmatians. In AD 293, Diocletian created a separate province of Scythia in the coastal strip of Dobrudja still under Roman control, integrated into the Diocese of Thrace and the Prefecture of the East. But, very soon, this new province became part of a very different world—Gothia (see Chapter 13).

Ethnic Legacy

Many of the elements of the modern social ferment in south-east Europe and south Russia were brought together during the period that we have reviewed. Although it is clear that, from the time of the Mesolithic to Neolithic transition (if not earlier), different peoples had coexisted in Europe, the variety and intensity of the interactions during the south-east European Iron Age allow us to speak of the emergence of polyethnicity. The Greek colonization further complicated the dynamic socio-economic picture. (The ostensible descendants—still Greek-speaking and of distinct physical type—of the Greek colonizers of the seventh century BC, the Pontic Greeks, are only recently, having suffered deportation to central Asia under Stalin, slowly returning, not to the Black Sea coasts, but to Greece.)

In Thrace and Scythia, the interactions of interest groups became intense, multi-faceted, and mutable. In an urban environment one might have expected to see an easy-going cosmopolitanism emerge, in which people's differences were elided (in Halicarnassus, where both a *lingua franca* and common law codes were necessary, something of this sort had already happened). But on the steppe, with its possibilities of almost unrestrained movement for some groups, seasonal transhumance for others, and vulnerable sedentism in the river valleys and high places for yet others, individual needs for identity became of paramount importance. Ethnicity became strongly marked and was densely encoded in artefacts that were worn and carried rather than in domestic pottery which was not.

Some groups' identities, like that of the Greeks of the Black Sea, were durable; other groups, such as the martial steppe élites, seem to have changed so fast that the resolution provided by the traditional methods of text compilation represented in the ethnographies of the classical authors cannot hold them in focus. The steppe nomadic formations were inherently unstable, and their ethnic names changed almost with the speed at which individual leaders came and went. Yet—as we have already noted in relation to the Mongol custom of *anda*—there appears to have been great continuity in their customs through time. For a Pathan ruler's burial that took place in the early 1980s, permission had to be sought from the urban authorities to process the king's body in a wagon around his subjects' territory, crossing over the border of Pakistan and Afghanistan, in a manner so reminiscent of Herodotus' account that we might argue that Scythians and Pathans are manifestations of one and the same type of society, contiguous with the steppe and stretching back into deep prehistory. Modern geopolitical boundaries do not accord with the real distributions of the peoples of Europe. They cannot. They have been imposed by the sedentary, the urban, and the literate on the pastoralists, the nomads, and the travellers. The latter find that they now need to ask permission to camp, to drive their flocks from A to B, to gather firewood and catch hares. The scales of power have tipped.

The breaking of the successive waves of nomadic élites against the Carpathian mountains has left its mark in terms of the extraordinary ethnic complexity and fascinating spiritual life of that region. Thus, when we speak of ethnic identity, we may have to reflect first on the many sorts of identity that exist. The history of south-east Europe has been a merging nexus of names and professions, genes and inheritances, in which the

PRESENT-DAY PASTORALISTS in Romania move along upland droveways or *plaiuri*. They sleep in structures called *stíne*, where they process sheep milk into cheese.

tracing of a single line of national ancestry is impossible except as an act of mythic ethnic identification. The prehistory of Bulgaria has often been written in terms of a single, ethnically homogenous people—the Thracians—while north of the Danube, in Romania, by way of national contrast and long guided by Ceauşescu's heavy hand, prehistorians have described the spiritual odyssey of a different, but similarly unitary, group of Thracians—the Geto-Dacians, ancestors of the modern Romanians. Yet neither nation has today, nor had in the past, a homogeneous ethnic make-up. 'In the population of Transylvania there are four distinct nationalities: Saxons in the south; and mixed with these the Wallachs, who are the descendants of the Dacians; Magyars in the west; and Szekelys in the east and north. I am going among the latter, who claim to be descended from Attila and the Huns', Jonathan Harker writes in his journal (Bram Stoker, *Dracula*). In fact, in present-day Romania at least twelve major ethnic groups of diverse cultural background survive cheek by jowl. They include, of course, the service groups of gold-panners and tinkers—inheritors of the Thracian metalworking tradition—the Sigeuners

(Kalderash and other 'Gypsies') with their Indian ragas, their midwifery, their divination, and their horse-trading.

It is the changing relationships between people and peoples, not their ethnic names, that cause new forms of society to come into existence. An echo of the intense interactions—economic, political, and (perhaps pre-eminently) religious and spiritual—that took place in Thrace, Dacia, and Scythia during the Iron Age is preserved in the folk traditions of Transylvania, so that 'every known superstition in the world is gathered into the horseshoe of the Carpathians, as if it were the centre of some sort of imaginative whirlpool'.

12

The Impact of Rome on Barbarian Society,
140 BC–AD 300

BARRY CUNLIFFE

From Republic to Empire: The Beginning, 140–60 BC

IF the year 146, when the two great maritime cities of Carthage and Corinth were both destroyed by Roman arms, was a major threshold in Rome's inexorable progression towards imperial domination of the ancient world, then 133 marked another watershed, for within the span of a few months, three momentous events occurred: in the West, Iberian resistance was overcome at the siege of Numantia; in the East, Rome was bequeathed much of Asia Minor in the will of Attalus III, while at home Tiberius Gracchus, recently returned from military duty in Spain, was elected tribune of the people. The formal acquisition of major new territories at opposite ends of the Mediterranean created new balances and new tensions within the Roman state while the election of Gracchus brought to power a man intent on halting the economic and social decay which had already taken grip of the heart of the Empire.

To understand Rome's problems at this time, and, therefore, her developing attitude to empire, something must be said of the social progress underway in the peninsula. In many ways early Roman society was not unlike that of the Celts in that the social hierarchy maintained itself by acts of military valour which were legitimized in the eyes of the population by the ceremony of the military triumph. Warfare, therefore, was endemic because the social system required areas of conflict in order to reproduce itself. Thus from the fifth century military campaigns became common and after the middle of the third century Rome was almost constantly at war around its ever increasing periphery. Such a system was possible, economically, because the land of Italy was comparatively productive and the type of peasant agriculture practised at first was a sufficer economy— that is, the individual farmer produced only what he needed to maintain his family and pay state taxes. This meant that there existed in the Roman countryside a vast pool of underused labour from which the armies, commanded by the élite, could be drawn.

In the early years of the Republic commanders were chosen annually by lot (to prevent the concentration of power in the hands of any one man) and the peasants were required to provide military service. The system had the potential for creating an equilibrium: so long as the appropriate level of warfare was maintained the surplus energies of the population could be put to productive use, while at the same time population levels could be kept in check through slaughter on the battlefield. Once, however, Rome began to engage in massive campaigns of overseas aggression the balance began to shift.

The prolonged absence of the male peasantry caused increasing destabilization in the countryside. On the one hand smallholdings were unable to be maintained while on the other the seasonal surplus of agricultural labour, upon which the larger estates depended, began to dry up. In addition to this the longer a man was away serving in the army the more disinclined he was to return to a peasant existence on the land. The results of all this were that there was a steady movement of labour from the land to the cities, smallholdings were abandoned or were absorbed in the larger estates and these large enterprises had to rely increasingly on slave labour to maintain productivity. Thus slaves, one of the by-products of war, became the prime source of the manpower required to fuel the Roman agricultural economy. In the cities the urban poor grew into an increasingly volatile mob while in the countryside the vast estates of the élite gobbled up the smallholdings, reducing the size of the free peasantry class from which the army was recruited. As peripheral wars increased and floods of time-expired soldiers with expectations returned to Italy, the social crisis deepened. This was the situation with which Tiberius Gracchus began to grapple in 133.

Gracchus' land reforms, which required state lands, now concentrated in the hands of the élite, to be redistributed among smallholders, met with violent opposition from the conservative faction. Gracchus was assassinated, but the problem remained. It was left to his brother, Gaius, to propose a new solution—the creation of citizen colonies in distant parts of Italy and in newly acquired territories overseas. After initial opposition the programme gained momentum. Between 80 and 8 BC about half of the free male population in Italy were resettled in towns and farms in Italy and the provinces, and between 45 and 8 BC a hundred new colonies were established overseas. The resettlement not only relieved social pressures at home but it provided, at strategic points around the expanding frontier, enclaves of trained military men who, through their desire to hold on to their parcels of land, formed a protective shield around Italy.

Meanwhile in the Italian countryside the large estates continued to flourish. Land was a major focus for investment among the aristocracy and as vast fortunes continued to be made in the provinces so more land was bought up to be managed for profit. Italy, according to Varro and Columella, became one vast orchard, and literary tracts on estate management proliferated. All advised on the use of slaves. A slave might be costly, but he could be made to work hard and had no legal rights. Moreover, slaves, properly managed, could be encouraged to breed to the profit of their masters. The growth of estates brought with it, therefore, a dramatic increase in the number of slaves: by the middle of the first century BC more than a million were employed in agricultural work alone in Italy. These developments created a momentum of their own. The inflow of capital for investment led to the increase in number and size of large estates and this in turn created

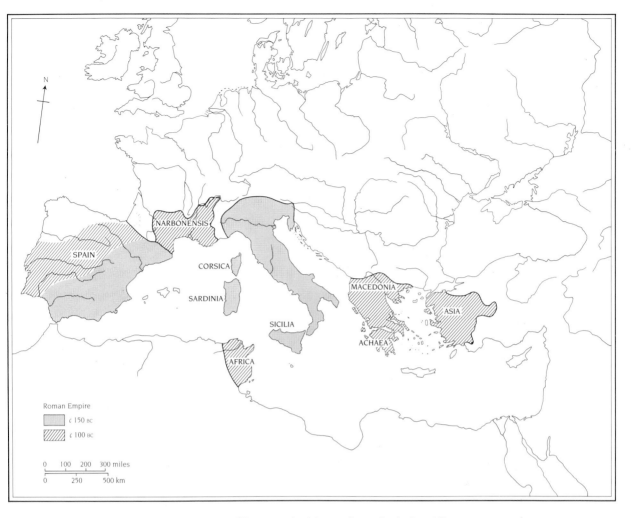

THE BEGINNING of Roman territorial expansion under the Republic.

an escalating demand for slave labour. At the same time, however, to capitalize on their investments, the estate-owners had to produce an agricultural surplus as cheaply as possible and market it for the maximum profit.

Most classical writers, concerning themselves with these matters, believed the most profitable crop to be vines. Wine production, said Pliny, could produce a greater return than even trade with the Far East. This might be true but it depended on finding a suitable market for the wine, and the Italian market was far too small. Inevitably, therefore, the producers began to look overseas and where better than to barbarian Europe where the Celtic passion for wine was legendary:

They are exceedingly fond of wine and sate themselves with unmixed wine imported by merchants; their desire makes them drink it greedily and when they become drunk they fall into a stupor or into a maniacal disposition. And therefore many Italian merchants with their usual love of cash look on the Gallic craving for wine as their treasure. They transport the wine by boat on the navigable rivers and by wagon through the plains and receive in return for it an incredibly high price, for one amphora of wine they get in return a slave—a servant in return for a drink. (Diodorus Siculus)

Thus it was that from the beginning of the second century Italian entrepreneurs began to tranship surplus wine in increasing quantity to the ports of southern Gaul: after the annexation of the territory in the 120s the flow increased to a torrent.

Sufficient will have been said to show that the dynamics which governed the social and economic systems of Roman Italy had a powerful trajectory which was bound, eventually, to spill over into the Mediterranean and through the mountain barriers into barbarian Europe. By the end of the first century BC warfare had become a dominant part of life: it caused problems, but created the opportunities to overcome them. The conquest of new territory provided what the Roman core most needed to maintain itself—wealth, raw materials, and manpower in the form of slaves. But of no less importance, the newly won provinces were a convenient dumping ground for the unwanted surpluses sloughed off from the core—the wine of Italian estates and the veterans from campaigns who, in Italy, would be a serious destabilizing influence. Thus the Roman Mediterranean core came increasingly to rely on the barbarian periphery, and once that periphery had been absorbed there was always another behind it—until the oceans, the deserts, and the forests were reached.

We have considered so far systems rather than individuals because until the middle of the second century the systems largely contained the individuals. After 131, however, during the period of revolution which changed the Republic into the Empire, the aspirations of great men shattered old constraints and became a significant motivating force in a phase of expansion which was to last until the death of Trajan in AD 117.

Barbarian Europe, 140–60 BC

While the Roman state was going through a phase of social stress and economic readjustment, significant changes were taking place in Europe beyond direct Roman control. We can most conveniently begin in southern Gaul where Rome had already begun to establish a firm interest (above, p. 370). By 140 it had become clear that sooner or later the coastal strip would have to pass into Roman hands. The moment came in 125 when the city of Massalia sought the assistance of Rome in countering the aggressive intentions of a neighbouring tribe, the Saluvii, who were being encouraged to raid the coast by the Arverni, a powerful confederation occupying the Massif Central. As the Roman armies moved in, the magnitude of the problem became apparent and it was only after five seasons of active campaigning that the region was brought under some semblance of order and not until a major battle had been fought by a Roman army of 30,000

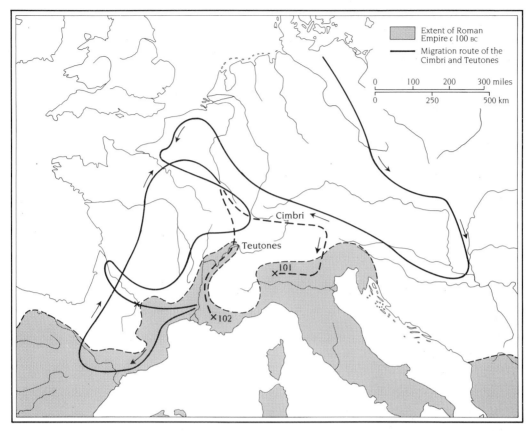

THE MOVEMENT of a hoard of northern tribesmen—the Cimbri and the Teutones—through western Europe and into Roman-held territories at the end of the second century BC and the failure, at first, of Roman armies to contain them caused fear and panic in Italy until they were finally defeated in 102 and 101 BC by the general Marius.

against a combined force of Arverni and Allobroges numbering some 200,000. The battle, which took place at the confluence of the Isère and Rhône, showed that Roman interests had now extended inland 200 kilometres along the Rhône valley.

By 120 the situation was stable and the Romans had begun to create an infrastructure of roads and towns. The establishment of a citizen colony at Narbo Martius (Narbonne) in about 118 BC, was a significant move, heralding a new interest in the West. Narbo was a Mediterranean port close to the mouth of the River Aude which offered a natural route way west, via the Carcassonne Gap, to the native town of Tolosa (Toulouse) occupying a key position on the River Garonne, which led to the Atlantic. This route had, for centuries, been used to bring tin from Brittany and Britain to the Mediterranean. The foundation of Narbo was an overt sign of Rome's intention to take over control of the trade and it was only a few years later that the army was used to subdue Tolosa and thus acquire direct access to the Garonne. The adventures in southern Gaul had, within the space of a decade, given Rome complete command of the two essential routes to western Europe—the Aude-Garonne and the Rhône.

STONE FIGURE OF A GOD from Euffigneix, Haute Marne, France (*left*). The figure has a torc around his neck. The boar depicted on the body may be an attribute of this particular deity or a sign of strength. Height 0.26 m.

WOODEN FIGURES from the Sanctuary of Sequana at the source of the Seine in Burgundy (*right*). The figures were placed around the spring by those seeking divine intervention in their affairs. Late first century BC.

Meanwhile a situation was developing in the far north which was soon to strike fear into the hearts of all Romans. Sometime about 120 a confederacy of northern tribes from Jutland and the North Sea coast, led by the Cimbri and the Teutones decided to migrate south. They first moved through Moravia and Hungary to the middle Danube where they attacked the Celtic Scordisci causing the Scordisci to move south into Macedonia and west along the Sava. Then, in 113, the Cimbri and Teutones turned westward and attacked the kingdom of Noricum which had by this time established a close, and profitable, relationship with Rome. A Roman army moved in but was disastrously defeated. With a vast ferocious Germanic horde within a few days' march of Italy many

Romans would have remembered stories of the terror of the Celtic attack on Rome less than three centuries before. However, for some unaccountable reason, the barbarian horde decided to leave Italy untouched and move westward into Gaul. A few years later we find them rampaging through the western part of the province of Transalpina, on three separate occasions, 109, 107, and 105, inflicting disastrous defeats on Roman armies sent to intercept them. After the third defeat at Arausio on the Rhône in 105 a new wave of terror gripped Italy. In the event Rome met the challenge. Marius, with a newly modernized army confronted the Teutones near Aquae Sextiae (Aix-en-Provence) in 102 and defeated them. In the next year the Cimbri were decimated at Vercellae in the Po valley and the citizens of Italy could breathe again.

It is difficult to overestimate the effects of these traumatic years on the Roman psyche. A deep fear of northern barbarians had existed since the Celtic migrations of the fourth century BC and once more it had become a frightening reality. Henceforth an aspiring commander need only call up the spectre of further horrors from the north to be voted all the powers he needed to deal with them by an over-anxious population. Julius Caesar, as we shall see, turned this fear to good measure.

While the German hordes came and went Roman trade with Gaul continued unabated. Fleets of merchant ships put into the harbours of southern Gaul and their car-

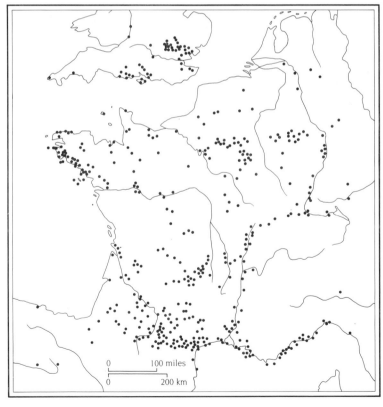

THE DISTRIBUTION of Italian wine amphorae, of the types used to transport wine in the late second and first centuries BC, stresses the importance of the river routes and the Atlantic sea-ways and also the extent to which Roman luxury goods penetrated barbarian lands.

BRONZE FIGURE of a Gaulish deity from Bouray, Seine-et-Oise, France. The date is uncertain but the piece may have been made in the early years of the Roman occupation.

goes of wine amphorae were transhipped to river barges and taken deep into the interior. At some locations like Tolosa and Chalon-sur-Saône wine was decanted into barrels or skins for transport further inland, the dead amphorae being smashed in enormous numbers at Tolosa or simply dumped in the river as at Chalon. Some amphorae were taken overland by Roman entrepreneurs to native *oppida* like Montmerlhe, Essalois, Joeuvres, and Bibracte where they were exchanged with the local aristocracy for slaves and other commodities. Roman merchants may well have been resident in these *oppida*. This is certainly the case at Chalon (*Cabillonum*) where Caesar mentions their presence as settlers in 52 BC. From these major *oppida* in Gaulish territory amphorae were probably distributed through native exchange networks to the settlements where the wine was consumed.

Judging by the distribution of first-century BC wine amphorae in Gaul, the major rivers were the main lines of transport used—a point confirmed by Strabo. The Aude-Garonne route seems to have been especially important partly because it provided access to the mineral deposits of the Montagne Noire and Pyrenees and partly because it led to the Atlantic sea routes. The movement of wine northward in the early first century BC is well documented by the dense concentrations of amphorae in Brittany, especially along the coasts of Morbihan and Finistère and at Hengistbury Head on the Solent coast in central-southern Britain, and its immediate hinterland. Indeed sufficient evidence now exists to suggest that the main route led up the coast of western France to Quiberon Bay where the cargoes were offloaded, some to be taken by local Venetic ships westward round the Breton coast, others to take the cross peninsula route along the rivers Vilaine and Rance to reach the north Breton coast at Alet where a promontory, quite probably defended, served as a major port-of-trade in the first century. From here the ships of the Coriosolites sailed northward, via Guernsey, to Hengistbury which at this time had developed as a major entrepôt. At Hengistbury there is ample evidence to show that metals, including iron, copper, silver, and gold, were being accumulated together with corn and probably cattle ready for export. Imports attested at the port include wine, coloured glass, figs, and whatever commodities were brought from Brittany in Breton-made pottery. Caesar had some, incomplete, inkling of this trading system when he wrote of the maritime and commercial strength of the Veneti.

In the sixty years or so between the foundation of the province of Transalpina and Caesar's conquest of Gaul, the tribes of France, particularly those bordering on the

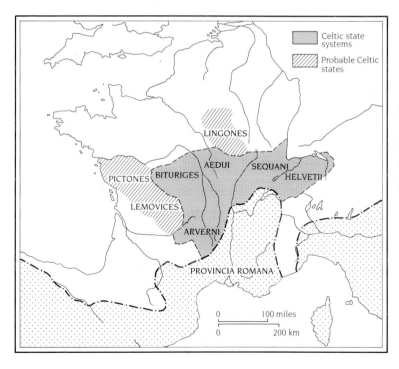

THE ROMAN PRESENCE in southern Gaul (Provincia Romana) in the late second and early first century BC influenced the socio-political development of the native states immediately beyond the frontier.

province, came under increasing Roman influence and it is possible to detect certain changes coming about in their social systems. This is most clearly displayed among the Helvetii of Switzerland. By 58 BC they had dispensed with kingship and were now ruled by elected magistrates, but the system was precarious and one member of the élite, Orgetorix, was accused of plotting to seize royal power. He was imprisoned and had he been found to be guilty would have been burned to death, but it seems that he chose to commit suicide instead. Among the Aedui at this time the magistracy was more firmly established. The chief magistrate, the Vergobretos, wielded very considerable power, but was controlled by the fact that his was an annual appointment and during his tenure he was forbidden to leave the tribal territory. Moreover, no other member of his family could hold the office or even be elected to the Senate during his lifetime. Clearly, these strict rules existed to prevent any one family from becoming powerful and to make it impossible for the magistrate to lead raiding parties, in traditional Celtic style, to enhance his prestige and create a powerful, and thus dangerous, military entourage. All this was in marked contrast to the social systems at work in the third and second centuries BC (above, pp. 358-69). It is tempting to believe that the changes were, in part at least, due to Roman encouragement. It would have been very much in Rome's interests for the frontier zone to be occupied by communities with stable governments rather than to have to confront a system based on warrior prestige and raiding.

The effects of the burgeoning Roman Empire—still essentially a Mediterranean power—on temperate Europe began to intensify after the middle of the second century as Rome's need for raw materials grew. Parallel with this, it is possible to trace, over a very considerable area, the emergence of large defended settlements generally known as *oppida*—the word Caesar applied to settlements of this type which he encountered in France. The distribution of *oppida* spans much of temperate Europe from western France to Serbia and from the Alps to the Sudeten mountains of former Czechoslovakia. Where large-scale excavations have taken place, as for example at Manching in southern Germany, it is possible to show that the areas within the defences were usually densely built up with regularly laid out timber buildings aligned along straight, ordered streets. There is also evidence to show that a wide range of craft skills were being practised and that the output of certain commodities such as wheel-turned pottery, glass beads and bracelets, and ironwork of every kind, was on an industrial scale. *Oppida* were also centres where coins were minted. Given the size of the communities represented, and the sheer intensity of production, it is difficult to resist the temptation of regarding *oppida* as the first urban centres of barbarian Europe: at the very least it can be said that many of them display a significant array of urban characteristics.

The fact that this 'urban' phenomenon can be recognized across Europe, beginning in the second half of the second century BC, might suggest that it was a direct result of the intensification of trade brought about by Roman consumer demands. But, while this probably was a contributory cause, it would be wrong to overemphasize the significance of Rome in a direct causative relationship. There are indications of increasing industri-

GOLD APPLIQUÉ (*left*) from the Kul Oba Kurgan, Crimea, fourth century BC. It may represent Scythians drinking wine and blood to seal a pact. The vaulted stone grave chamber, 6 km inland from the Greek colony of Panticapaeum, held wine-drinking equipment that reflects the influence of Greek values (*see ch. 11*).

SHEET GOLD SHIELD BOSS (*below*) in the form of a stag from the Kostromskaya Kurgan, northern Caucasus; early sixth century BC; 31 cm long; eye inset with amber. Is the stag at rest or in flight? Such deliberate ambiguity in the depiction of movement is a feature of the finest Animal Style art (*see ch. 11*).

alization among the villages of temperate Europe in the early second century, and the gradual coalescence of the smaller migrating tribal groups into more stable political configurations suggests that progress towards urban-based economies, organized under the legitimizing power of kings or major chieftains, was already underway before Roman trade with the north had begun to intensify. It is safer, therefore, to see the emergence of *oppida* as a temperate European phenomenon having indigenous origins, but quickened in its later stages by the increasing demands of the Roman world for raw materials.

The Decade of Conquest and Dislocation, 60–50 BC

By the 60s of the first century BC certain instabilities can be recognized in barbarian Europe. In the East the Dacians were devastating territory held by the Boii in Hungary (see Chapter 11), while in the West tribes from beyond the Rhine—who are referred to as German by Caesar—were beginning to show signs once more of putting pressure on their southern neighbours. There were also squabbles breaking out between the tribes bordering the province. The Aedui, Caesar tells us, who had long enjoyed the prestige of having many satellite tribes pay homage to them, were now in conflict with their neighbours, the Sequani. The Sequani proceeded to win over the allegiance of many of the Aeduan dependencies reducing the Aedui themselves to such a state of subservience that they were forced to surrender the sons of their chiefs as hostages. Eventually, in 61 BC, one of the nobles was sent to Rome to ask, unsuccessfully as it turned out, for help. To add to their problems, three years later a Germanic tribe led by Ariovistus began making threatening noises. At the same time the Helvetii of Switzerland, having decided that they had outgrown their territory made up their minds to migrate to western France on a route which would have taken them through Aeduan territory. It is difficult to be sure to what extent these tensions were normal in the Celtic world or whether they constituted an exceptional crisis, since we owe our detailed knowledge of them to Julius Caesar whose personal interests they were made to serve.

Caesar was at a crucial stage in his career. He desperately needed to create for himself a situation in which his military skills could be displayed and the resulting triumphs would follow. Only in this way could he hope to survive the conservative oligarchy of Rome who hated and feared him. In Gaul he saw his opportunity and in 59 BC steered a special law through the Senate to give him a five-year command in Cisalpine Gaul and Illyricum—a command which he was subsequently able to extend by a further five years. Thus empowered he was able to raise and maintain a large fighting force owing its alle-

THE SANCTUARIES (*above*) in the Dacian stronghold and capital of Sarmizegethusa in the Orăştie Mountains of Romania. The large circular structure is thought to have served as a calendar.

THE GAULISH OPPIDUM of Alesia (*below*) where the war leader Vercingetorix took refuge from Caesar's legions in 52 BC. His eventual capitulation, after a long siege, marked the end of the co-ordinated Gaulish rebellion against Caesar.

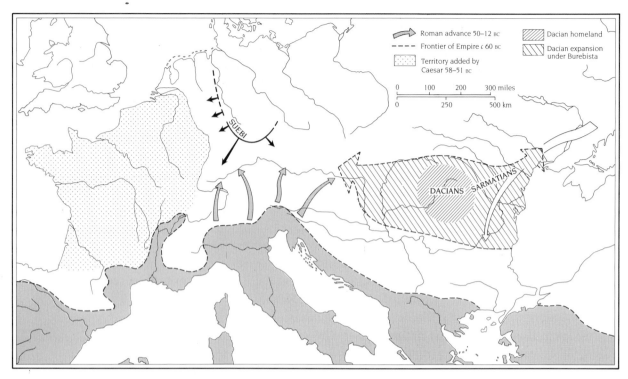

IN THE MIDDLE of the first century BC Germanic tribes were pushing south at the time when the Dacian leader, Burebista, was expanding his authority westwards. It was at this crucial moment that Caesar decided to invade and annex Gaul up to the line of the Rhine to counter, he claimed, the southward advance of Germanic peoples. Within the next decades Rome expanded through the Alps to the Upper Danube.

giance firmly to him. One of the arguments he used to make his case was that the German barbarians were beginning to threaten allied states. Either, he said, Gaul would become Roman or it would be overrun by Germans. The threat of a German attack on Italy, less than fifty years after the Cimbri and Teutones had come so close, was a frightening prospect for the Roman population: Caesar was given his command.

The conquest of Gaul began in 58 BC and was completed in 51 BC, although it was necessary in subsequent years to mount several tidying up operations before the huge territory, stretching from the Mediterranean to the Rhine, could be regarded as fully subdued. Caesar's campaigns were conducted at lightning speed. In 58 he successfully drove back Ariovistus and forced the Helvetii to return home. The next three years were spent dealing with the tribes of the northern periphery from Brittany to the Rhine, culminating in 55 BC with two symbolic crossings—of the Channel into Britain and of the Rhine into Germany. After such a feat of daring Rome could hardly fail to renew his commission. The next year was spent consolidating his power over Belgic tribes and making a more considered exploration of Britain, and in 53 BC, he was intent on extending his foothold across the Rhine. Thus far, much of the army's effort had been spent dealing with the tribes of Belgica between the Seine and the Rhine—the rest of France, apart from a sharp campaign against the rebelling Breton tribes, was left untouched. In 53, however, unrest broke out among the Senones and Carnutes south of the Seine and in 52 much of the centre of France was in open revolt, the rebelling tribes being united for a brief period under the charismatic leadership of Vercingetorix. The situation was serious for Caesar, but Roman might prevailed once more over Celtic enthusiasm. The episode culminated in Gaulish capitulation after a long drawn-out siege at Alesia where Vercingetorix had rather unwisely allowed himself to be bottled up. It remained, in the following year, for Caesar simply to mop up pockets of resistance before he could claim that 'the whole of Gaul was now conquered'.

The conquest of Gaul was, by any standards, a remarkable achievement: in a mere eight years a vast territory had been brought under Roman domination, and in the course of conquest Celtic society had been devastated. A few examples will suffice to indicate the scale of the dislocation. In dealing with the rebellious Veneti in 56 BC Caesar put all the elders to death and sold the rest as slaves. His attitudes to the Nervii in northern Belgica were more lenient. After a fierce and bloody battle only 500 men survived of the original force of 60,000 and the Council of 600 had been reduced to three. But to prevent the tribe from being entirely wiped out Caesar encouraged everyone who could be found, especially the old men, women, and children who had fled to the safety of the forests and marshes, to return to their *oppidum*, and issued orders that the neighbouring tribes should not attack them in their weakness. The Aduatuci were less favoured: their *oppidum* was besieged and taken. About 4000 were killed in the assault, and of the rest, some 53,000, Caesar says that he 'sold all I found inside by auction in one

JULIUS CAESAR changed the face of Europe by his conquests in Spain, Africa, and Gaul. His desire to conquer added huge territories to the emerging Roman Empire.

THE CLIFF-CASTLE OF
LOSTMARC'H on the coast of
Brittany (*above*). It was to
fortifications of this kind that the
Breton population fled when
Caesar attacked in 56 BC.

THIS COIN (*left*), issued in 48
BC, shows Gallic battle
equipment: two crossed
trumpets, an oval, and a round
shield.

lot'. The Carnutes were even more harshly treated because they had slaughtered the Roman traders who lived among them. Their *oppidum*, at Cenabum, was besieged, and when it fell the Roman soldiers were encouraged to take vengeance on the entire population: all but 800 of the 40,000 men, women, and children were cut down. The occupants of the besieged town of Uxellodunum were marginally more fortunate—those who had carried weapons against the Romans were assembled and their hands were cut off.

The eight-year war had been disastrous for many of the Celtic tribes of Gaul. It would have taken several generations for the psychological wounds to heal and for the shattered economy to recover, which may be one reason why Roman interference in Gaulish affairs remained slight until Augustus began a full-scale reorganization in 27 BC.

Expansion to the Rhine and Danube Frontier, 51 BC–AD 14

Caesar's activities had brought Europe, west of the Rhine, under Roman control, but elsewhere Rome's hold on the European continent was slight. The Po valley, the Illyrian coast, and Macedonia and Greece were under Roman authority, but this was still only the Mediterranean fringe bounded by the Alps and the mountain ranges of the Balkans: temperate Europe beyond remained free. By the end of the reign of Augustus in AD 14 the frontiers had been extended far inland to the river Danube leaving only Thrace with the nominal freedom of client kingdom status.

We have already seen that Rome had developed close diplomatic and trading links with the kingdom of Noricum in the eastern Alps by the middle of the second century BC (above, p. 371). Rome's policy was not to interfere in native affairs nor to supply military aid. Admittedly there was a brief intervention in 113 BC at the time of the Cimbric War but it was unauthorized and when the Tigurini moved into south-west Noricum in 102 and the Boii besieged Noreia in 60, Rome remained aloof.

The economy of Noricum flourished in the first century BC, based on intensive agricultural production, on the extraction and working of iron, and on trade. Commercial

SILVER TETRADRACHM of the Kroisbacher Type attributed to Burgenland (Austria). Obv.: Beardless head right wearing pearl diadem in three rows. Rev.: Horse galloping left, with head and neck of rider on back. Second century BC.

LA TURBIE on the Mediterranean coast of France in the Côte d'Azur 26 km east of Nice. Erected in 6 BC to commemorate the triumphs of Augustus over the forty four Alpine tribes. It symbolizes the pacification of Gaul.

relations with neighbouring Celtic tribes were important and by about 70 a locally produced coinage was beginning to appear in southern Noricum to facilitate internal and external transactions. There is ample evidence of trade with Pannonia in the East and Gaul in the West, but of far greater importance to the native economy was the intensifying commercial intercourse with Rome. The principal route from the south led from Aquileia, via the Tagliamento valley to the heart of Noricum. It was adjacent to this road, at Magdalensberg, that an important trading centre developed. The Magdalensberg complex consists of two elements, a native *oppidum* on the summit of the mountain and a Roman trading colony below. The *oppidum* was the principal administrative centre of the kingdom and the residence of the royal family, and as such provided a natural focus for Roman merchants. The Roman colony developed on a south-facing terrace below the *oppidum*. The earliest buildings were of timber and can be dated to *c*.100 BC but by *c*.30 BC the traders' houses were built in stone and were decorated with murals depicting classical mythological scenes painted by immigrant Roman artists. The focus of the colony was a large open forum where the commercial transactions would have been carried out. The Roman merchants who lived and worked here were representatives of the great business houses, mainly from Aquileia, and like all traders in foreign lands they surrounded themselves with the outward and visible signs of their own culture. The scale of the trade with Rome was considerable and acted as a spur to local production; it also introduced the Roman lifestyle to the natives who, over the decades, increasingly embraced Roman luxuries and Roman manners.

The future of Noricum and of the entire region north and east of the Alps was bound up with the ambitions of the leaders of Rome. Caesar had used his opportunities and successes in Gaul to challenge the Roman state and on the Ides of March, 44 BC, paid for his ambition with his life. The years of virtual anarchy which followed ended in the Battle of Actium which saw Octavian triumph. Four years later, in 27 BC, Octavian, now known as Augustus, was established as head of the Roman state. It took a decade for the new order to consolidate its power at home and in the provinces, but by 17 BC the emperor could begin to look northward and eastward to extend his frontiers in Gaul and Germany and the Alpine and Danubian lands.

The first major gains were made in 15 BC by Drusus and Tiberius. The Raeti and Vindelici of the Alpine region were conquered, as were the Scordisci in the middle Danube, and it was probably at this time that Noricum was annexed. In the next year the subjugation of Dalmatia and Pannonia began, but was not completed until a major thrust in 12–9 BC. Noricum had posed no real threat but now that it was imperial policy to extend the frontier northward to the Rhine–Danube line, the enclave could hardly be left as a potential haven for dissidents, and so it was that in place of the colony of Roman traders came the Roman army. The only significant effect was that Magdalensberg became even more affluent: annexation was only really the final act of a process which had started nearly two centuries before when the first tentative trading links had been established with Rome.

Beyond the Rhine, 55 BC–AD 16

To Rome the River Rhine presented a significant divide. It provided a highly serviceable frontier line—though in the minds of some this was to be only a temporary solution—and it served to mark an ethnic divide between the Celts to the south and the Germans to the north. This, at least, was the view Caesar chose to present, though in reality the situation was far more fluid. In the middle of the first century BC the tribes on both sides of the river were very mixed and it is unlikely that rigid ethnic differences could be recognized, but the creation of a frontier along the river prevented further tribal movement. This meant that the Germanic tribes of the north, in their sporadic movements south, would have little choice but to concentrate on the north side of the river in lands previously occupied by tribes of more mixed origin. Thus the Roman presence was itself a significant factor in intensifying the ethnic differences along the river line.

Something of the nature of Germanic society can be glimpsed through the works of Caesar, completed in 51 BC, and of Tacitus written a century and a half later. Neither provides a systematic account, but both attempt to paint an anecdotal picture of a generalized German way of life to amuse and surprise their readers. Caesar suggests that agriculture was not particularly advanced. Land was held by the tribe and allocated to the individual clans in a system which required an annual redistribution. In this way wealth, derived from constant access to a particularly fertile tract, could be prevented from building up in the hands of any single group. Status could, however, be acquired by acts of bravery and leadership in the pursuance of raiding. 'The Germans', says Caesar, 'claim that it is good training for young men and stops them becoming lazy.' Raids were announced by the chiefs at public assemblies and all those who, in the excitement of the moment, proclaimed their willingness to follow were expected to present themselves when the force was ready to leave, otherwise they were derided by the tribe and lost all prestige. Power at this time, as in classic Celtic society, lay with the élite and was measured by the size of their entourage and their ability to bestow patronage. It was they who formed the tribal council. Only in times of exceptional warfare would members of the aristocracy be elected to lead the confederate army.

ROMAN RELIEF from Cabrières d'Aygnes, France, showing wine barrels being transported by barge along one of the rivers of Gaul.

By the time that Tacitus was writing, a century and a half later, the social system had changed, at least among the tribes closest to the frontier. Arable land was now distributed in accordance with social status. Two types of leader were recognized, the *rex* elected for life from among a small group of aristocratic households comprising the royal class, and the *dux* appointed on the basis of military valour to lead the army in times of stress. Councils of the élite were held regularly as were general assemblies of warriors who met to debate issues submitted to them: it seems they were unable to initiate action of their own. This dual system had evidently evolved to maintain some semblance of social equilibrium. But one major destabilizing feature existed in Germanic society as it did in classical Celtic—the ability of an individual to attract a loyal retinue. The point was neatly summed up by Tacitus:

The chiefs fight for victory, the followers for their chief. Many noble youths, if the land of their birth is stagnating in a long period of peace or inactivity, deliberately seek out other tribes which have some war on their hands. For the Germans have no taste for peace; renown is more easily won among perils and a large body of retainers cannot be kept together except by means of violence and war.

He goes on to say that the boldest warriors prefer warfare to agriculture, they 'have no regular employment, the care of house, home, and fields being left to the women, old men, and weaklings of the family'. Germanic society, then, was very much like Celtic society 500 years before: its system of prestige relied on the maintenance of conflict and this inevitably created perpetual instability.

Caesar's crossings of the Rhine in 55 and 53 BC were not serious attempts at conquest, nor was a brief campaign mounted in 38 BC by Agrippa. Throughout this time the Romans were content to develop the river as a frontier line while the affairs of the Empire were put into order by Augustus and his administrators. By 15 BC the situation within the Empire was sufficiently stable to enable the conquest of the Alps to be put in hand and by 12 BC, with the Alps now under control and the north-western corner of Iberia sufficiently subdued to allow troop withdrawals from Spain and Aquitania, the new forward policy across the Rhine could begin.

It seems that Augustus' intention was to make the Elbe–Vltava–Danube the permanent frontier of the Empire, but he seriously misjudged the strength of German resistance. It had been comparatively easy for Caesar to overrun Gaul because the Gauls had become a settled people with a well-developed agricultural base and many tribes were now politically and economically centred on permanent *oppida*. Moreover, Gaulish society had been softened by the enervating effects of luxury goods from the Mediterranean. The Germans were totally different: mobility and warfare were the keynote, there were no *oppida*, and few southern luxuries had penetrated the area by this time. It is one thing to destroy a tribe by besieging its *oppidum*, quite another when its armies simply shrink into the protection of vast unchartered forests.

To begin with, the advance does not seem to have gone too badly for Rome. Annual campaigns from 12 to 7 BC and another in AD 4–5 brought a sufficient degree of control over the area from the Rhine to the Elbe for attention to turn to the conquest of Bohemia—the crucial link between the frontier zones planned for the Elbe and the Danube. Command of Bohemia would also provide the Roman entrepreneurs with a major trading axis leading to the North European Plain and the Baltic, whence came a range of desirable products. At the crucial moment, however, a serious rebellion broke out in Illyricum requiring urgent attention: while the main weight of Roman military effort was tied up in dealing with the situation, the German tribes took the opportunity to reorganize. Arminius, a member of the German élite, who had served as a cavalry officer in the Roman army, was elected war leader with startling effect. Three Roman legions were annihilated in the depths of the Teutenburg Forest and Roman forces were all but driven from German soil. It was a devastating reversal for Rome. The next year, AD 10, the Rhine frontier was strengthened in preparation for a new campaign to regain the German holdings, and in subsequent years there were some notable Roman successes but the Emperor Tiberius, who knew Germany well having fought there himself, eventually conceded that the country was ungovernable. After the final campaign of AD 16, he withdrew Roman troops to the Rhine, thus bringing to an end twenty-eight years of fruitless endeavour.

There is, however, a revealing epilogue. Arminius, as we have seen, was elected war leader by his tribe, the Cherusci, to lead the military revolt against Rome. Success no doubt increased his prestige and thus his retinue, but he was not universally accepted even among his own lineage. His father-in-law, Segestes, and his uncle, Inguiomerus, were both opposed to his policies and were able to galvanize their own, not inconsiderable, retinues against him. Such was the power of the individual aristocrat in German society that personal ambitions and antipathies could overshadow national need. Indeed one wonders if concepts of German national identity were more a construct of Roman historians than a reality. In AD 19, after fighting Romans for twelve years, Arminius lurched towards tyranny. According to Tacitus, the Roman evacuation of Germany and the fall of the pro-Roman king of Bohemia, Maroboduus, persuaded him to make a bid for kingship, but this was anathema to those who believed in traditional values. Conflict broke out and finally 'Arminius succumbed to treachery from his relations'. This incident is a fascinating reminder of the similarities between German society in the early first century AD and the situation in Celtic Gaul nearly eighty years earlier when Orgetorix of the Helvetii aspired to kingship, but was restrained by his people and chose to end his own life (above, p. 420).

The Expanding Empire: Britain and Dacia, 60 BC–AD 130

The Channel separating Britain from the Continent may have been a psychological barrier to Roman expansion, but to those living on its fringes it was a major axis of communication. For centuries people had crossed the waters to exchange commodities with

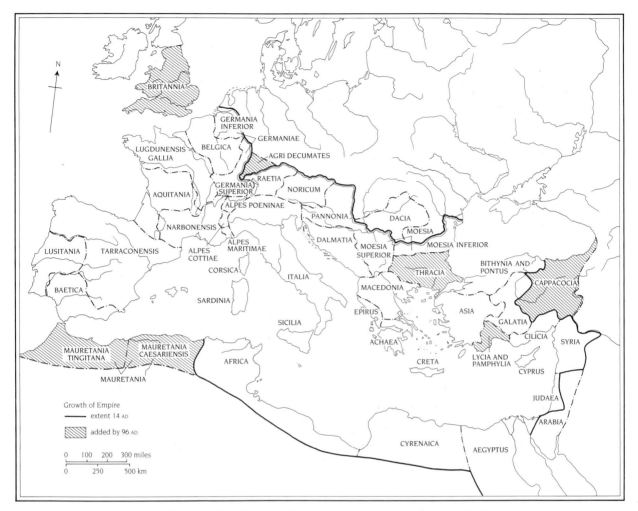

THE ROMAN EXPANSION in Europe was largely complete by AD 14, though a few territories were added during the rest of the first century. Dacia and Arabia were incorporated early in the second century.

each other. In the middle of the first millennium the tin supplies of Cornwall had attracted the attention of Mediterranean traders and soon after the southern French coast was absorbed by the Romans, the ancient Atlantic trade routes were invigorated by demands for slaves and a range of raw materials in return for which large quantities of wine and a variety of trinkets were exchanged. By the middle of the first century BC a regular trade route had been established between St Servan on the northern coast of Brittany and Hengistbury Head on the Solent shore (above, p. 419).

Caesar's conquest of Gaul and his brief expeditions to eastern Britain in 55 and 54 BC brought about a total reorganization of traditional trading patterns. Roman Gaul was now only a few miles away across the Channel and as road communications improved throughout Gaul so the long, dangerous sea routes along the Atlantic fell into disuse. It

was far more convenient for traders to use the short crossing to Gesoriacum (Boulogne) and thence by road to Chalon-sur-Saône and down the rivers to the Mediterranean than to brave the Bay of Biscay. Another factor is worth considering. During his campaigns in Britain Caesar had established treaty relations with certain tribes in the East, especially the Trinovantes who occupied the coastal zone north of the Thames. It may be that, to ensure their continued friendship to Rome, he allowed them some monopoly over cross-Channel trade. In any event the results of the political reorderings of Caesar's time are clearly evident in Britain: Atlantic trade decreased rapidly, and in parallel a vigorous system of exchanges developed between the coasts of Belgica and the British coasts of eastern Britain north of the Thames.

In the ninety years or so between the campaigns of Caesar and the invasion of Claudius in AD 43 the tribal lands of the Trinovantes and Catuvellauni, stretching from the Essex coast to the Chilterns, grew rich on the proceeds of cross-Channel trade. Commodities from the west and north of the country had to pass through these territories *en route* to Gaul. In consequence, the élite who controlled the throughput acquired wealth and enhanced their status through commanding prestige goods such as Roman wine and the cups and jugs necessary to dispense it with appropriate ceremony. As the system of exchange became established, so the range of imported commodities increased to include further exotics like olive oil and fish sauce. The effect of all this was that by the time of the Claudian invasion a substantial part of the south-east of the island had become thoroughly inured to Roman luxuries. Thus, when Claudius was looking for a territory to conquer to enhance his prestige, Britain must have seemed ripe for picking.

The initial stages of the invasion went well for the Romans. The military thrust along the south side of the Thames estuary and through Catuvellaunian and Trinovantian territory was quickly achieved and the consolidation was facilitated by the establishment of two client kingdoms, the Iceni in the north and the Atrebates in the south. Within two or three years a military zone linked by the Fosseway had been created across the territories of the Durotriges, Dobunni, and Corieltauvi forming a barrier between the civilized south-east and the still barbarian north and west. It seems that Claudius and his advisers had determined to occupy only the agriculturally productive south-east. Trading bases soon grew up on the fringe of the military zone. South Ferriby on the Humber estuary and its transriverine partner at North Ferriby facilitated the movement of goods to and from the north, while settlements such as that at Worcester articulated with the communities of the Welsh borderland and the wilder mountains beyond.

The native élite who embraced Rome quickly benefited from the occupation. Along the south coast a number of surprisingly rich Roman villas were in existence by the reign of Nero, all lavishly decorated in high Roman style. One of these at Fishbourne may well have belonged to the local client king, Tiberius Claudius Cogidubnus, who, Tacitus

A ROMAN CAVALRYMAN triumphant over four native warriors one of whom is beheaded. Stone relief on a distance slab found at Bridgeness on the Antonine Wall which was built across Scotland in the second century AD.

says, remained faithful to Rome and was rewarded with additional lands. Urbanization was rapidly underway in the south-east by this time. A *colonia* had been established at Camulodunum (Colchester), Verulamium (St Albans) was probably a *municipium*, London was a seething mass of traders and administrators, and the smaller regional capitals of Calleva (Silchester) and Noviomagus (Chichester) were fast providing themselves with the trappings of Roman city life.

The hostility of the Welsh tribes, rebellion among the Iceni, and political instability in the north soon showed that the Claudian policy of limiting the province to the south-east was too costly to maintain and in about AD 70 the decision was taken to complete the conquest of the entire island—a policy which culminated in a rapid thrust into Scotland, under the generalship of Agricola, ending in the battle of Mons Graupius in AD 84 at which the native resistance was smashed.

While all this was going on in the north a deliberate policy of Romanization was being practised in the more civilized south. Tacitus' cynical words are worth quoting:

To induce a people, hitherto scattered, uncivilized and therefore prone to fight, to grow pleasurably inured to peace and ease, Agricola gave private encouragement and official assistance to the building of temples, public squares, and private mansions . . . competition to gain honour from him was as effective as compulsion. Furthermore he trained the sons of the chiefs in the liberal arts. . . . The result was that in place of distaste for the Latin language came a passion to command it. In the same way our national dress came into favour and the toga was everywhere to be seen. And so the Britons were gradually led on to the amenities that make vice agreeable—arcades, baths, and sumptuous banquets. They spoke of such novelties as 'civilization' when really they were only a feature of their enslavement.

BRITANNIA SEATED. This symbol of the subdued province was a favourite emblem on the reverse of coins of the second century emperors.

TRAJAN'S CAMPAIGNS north of the Danube into Dacia (Romania) were bitterly contested. Here, on Trajan's Column, Dacians are shown attacking a Roman garrison. Dacia finally succumbed to Rome in AD 106 but remained a Roman province for only 170 years.

In that single passage Tacitus sums up the ethos of Roman conquest and imperialism.

Claudius was also active in the East. Thrace, which had long been a client kingdom, was finally annexed to Rome in 46 BC in an attempt to bring a somewhat ill-organized and unstable part of the world into firmer Roman control. The Danube produced a sensible frontier, but the tribes to the north were by this time beginning to pose an increasing threat.

The principal focus of opposition was the Dacians—a broad confederacy of people occupying the uplands of Transylvania in the protection of the enclosing mountain ranges of the Carpathians and Transylvanian Alps. They had first come to prominence under Burebista, who, in 60 BC, led a force of 200,000 warriors westward against the Celtic tribes settled in Hungary and along the Danube into former Czechoslovakia. Then followed an expansion eastward engulfing the rich lands of the lower Danube and threatening the ancient cities of the Black Sea shore. Burebista's empire came to nothing. In the late 40s BC he was assassinated and the outlying conquests were soon lost as the core of the state fragmented between rival factions, but it was a warning to Rome of the potential threat that this unconquered region could pose under a powerful leader.

The Danube frontier was formalized throughout its length during the reign of Augustus, and a regular pattern of trade developed with the tribes to the north. During this time vast quantities of Roman silver, in the form of denarii, flowed north in exchange, no doubt, for slaves and furs. Mediterranean wine, oil, and other luxury prod-

i   ii

ucts were also carried northward. During this time also, the Dacian state developed apace. Craftsmen skilled in the production of silverware were creating a range of goods for the élite, high-quality wheel-made pottery was in regular use and Greek and Latin script were employed for various forms of record-keeping. In the heart of Dacian territory, in the Orǎştie mountains, the *oppidum* of Sarmizegethusa provided a focus for the state. Here, surrounded by stone-built defences owing much in technique to Greek military architecture, a large population lived and worked safe in the knowledge that the approaches to their city were protected by a series of strategically placed forts. At Sarmizegethusa a sophisticated sanctuary had been constructed, its stone and wooden pillars representing days, seasons, and years so arranged that the year was divided into twelve months, each of thirty days with five weeks of six days in each month.

(*i*) A NOBLE DACIAN captured by Roman soldiers during Trajan's campaigns in Dacia (Romania) in the early second century AD. From Trajan's Column in Rome.

(*ii*) DACIAN CAPTIVES, taken during Trajan's campaigns, here shown on the Tropaeum at Adamklissi, in Romania, set up to commemorate Trajan's battles.

(*iii*) A ROMAN SOLDIER attacking a Dacian. Shown on the Tropaeum at Adamklissi.

By the end of the first century AD the Dacian state had had a long relationship with the Graeco-Roman world, not all of it on friendly terms. For all their acceptance of Mediterranean culture the Dacians were still a warlike people prepared to mount raids on their southern neighbours. In fighting they were a formidable foe with their own distinctive weapons. They protected themselves with large oval-shaped shields of wood or hide edged with metal and sometimes covered with plates of iron. These shields like those of the Celts, from whom they were in part descended, were usually elaborately decorated with emblems to ward off evil and possibly to proclaim lineage. The common weapons were arrows, spears, and swords, but they possessed two local models of cutting weapons, the curved dagger or *sica* and the heavy curved sabre (*falas*) used in close hand-to-hand fighting.

In the early 80s the kingdom passed into the hands of an able young aristocrat Decebalus who soon welded the disparate factions into a formidable fighting force: in AD 85 he crossed the Danube, defeated and killed the Roman governor, and rampaged through the province of Moesia. The initial Roman response was to invade Dacia. The fighting went badly for them at first, but eventually Decebalus sued for peace on what, for the Dacians, were reasonable terms which included an annual subsidy from Rome and the loan of some Roman engineers.

An uneasy peace was maintained for another decade or so while Decebalus consolidated his position at home, but the elevation of Trajan as emperor in AD 98 brought matters quickly to a head. Dacia was perceived to be a threat to the security of Rome—a view based partly on military considerations, but influenced, no doubt, by the vast amount of wealth which the Dacian state was known to possess. In AD 101 Trajan moved against Dacia. Details of the war are obscure, but the first year's campaigning was not decisive. The next year, however, Decebalus sued for peace and as part of the terms, agreed to give up the western region of his kingdom at the same time accepting a Roman garrison at his capital, Sarmizegethusa. Once peace had been established Decebalus began rearming and by AD 105 was strong enough to become the aggressor. The commander of the Roman camp was taken hostage and the Dacians swept down on the province of Moesia. Trajan's response was limited to relieving the province, but the next year he was ready to take the initiative. The Roman army marched on Sarmizegethusa and besieged the capital. Decebalus fled and eventually committed suicide while the nobles drank poison. In the wake of the disaster a large part of the population migrated eastward leaving a depleted land to the Romans.

Dacia thereupon became Rome's first and only transdanubian province. A *colonia*—Ulpia Traiana—was founded not far from the old capital and the growth of other towns was encouraged. The rich deposits of silver, gold, and salt were rapidly and thoroughly exploited, but Dacia was and remained an awkward excrescence on the edge of the Empire with no natural boundaries save those created by its encircling enemies. In the face of these problems it is surprising that Rome retained its hold for so long, but finally, after a brief 150 years as a province, Dacia was abandoned. In all probability it was the

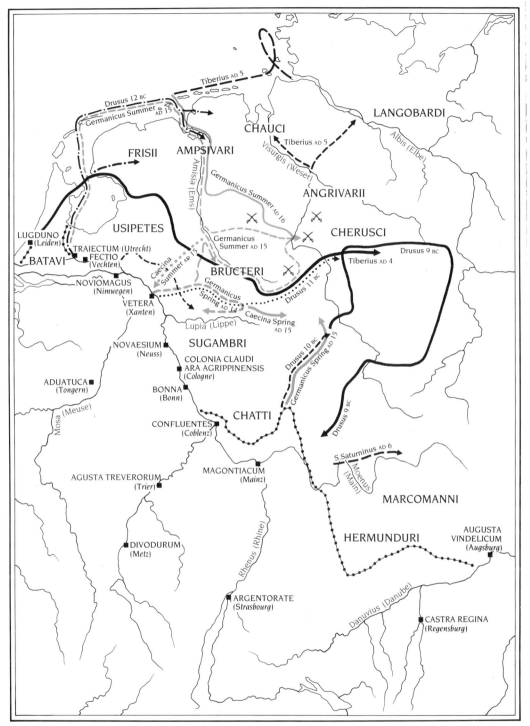

CAESAR HAD REACHED the Rhine and regarded it as a convenient boundary to his Gaulish conquests. Under Augustus and again under Tiberius attempts were made to conquer Germany but were finally abandoned after AD 16.

mobile nature of these east European populations that made it so difficult for Rome to maintain its hold.

Beyond the Bounds of Empire

The Roman Empire was in need of a continuous supply of raw materials and manpower. As its frontiers continued to expand so valuable sources of metals and other commodities were brought within its boundaries, but many luxuries lay in barbarian lands out of direct reach: amber and furs from the Baltic shores and the far north; silks and spices from the East; and gold from beyond the Sahara. Such things could only be acquired by trade. But Rome's greatest dependence on the barbarian periphery lay in its need for slaves to provide the energy needed to keep the Roman system working. The scale of the slave trade was enormous. Cassius Dio records that during the early Empire about a quarter of a million slaves changed hands on the open market annually, and since these were the ones recorded for tax purposes we can be sure that the actual number of deals was much greater. It is estimated that in Italy alone at the end of the first century BC two million of the total population of six million were slaves. To maintain this pool, given a wastage rate of about 7 per cent per annum, it would have required 140,000 new slaves to have come on to the market annually. Thus, Strabo's casual aside that in the slave market at Delos it was not unusual for 10,000 slaves to find a buyer daily, need by no means be an exaggeration.

The means by which the stocks were replenished were varied. Piracy provided a constant flow, while the authorities allowed it to last, and warfare was a highly effective producer. If we remember that in one campaign alone, against the Aduatuci, Caesar sold 53,000 captives into slavery, then his eight years of campaigning must have provided for much of the Empire's need. But as large-scale wars of conquest began to die out in the early second century the principal sources of slaves passed from direct Roman control and the need had to be met by barbarian middlemen working beyond the frontiers.

To maintain a degree of stability and control among the neighbouring barbarian tribes the Romans developed a series of procedures. The native élite could simply be bought off with gifts of luxury goods or money, they could be afforded special monopolies and protection, and in some cases their youth could be 'fostered' in the emperor's household and returned in due course to their tribes, more Roman in their manners than true-born Romans. All these methods were tried and tested and stood Rome in good stead.

The actual processes of trade and exchange are not particularly well understood, but the classical writers provide a range of anecdotal information which throws some light on the systems at work. The Suebi had a reputation of being a warlike tribe during the time of Caesar, but they were perfectly prepared to admit traders to their country 'so that they will have purchasers for their booty rather than because they want to import anything'. This may be a reference to their abhorrence of wine, which they considered made

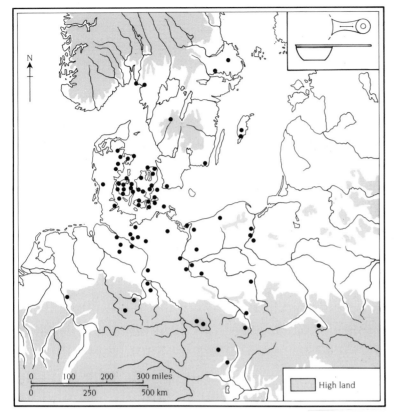

ROMAN BRONZE PATERAE
found in barbarian northern
Europe north of the frontier,
and other luxury items were
acquired by natives as the
result of organized trade, by
raiding or as diplomatic
gifts.

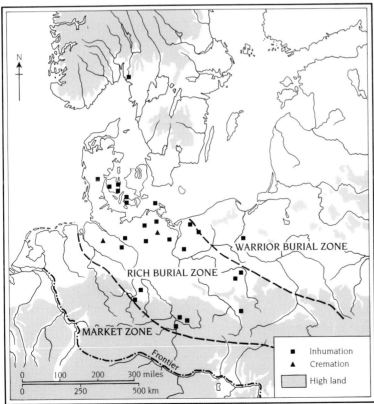

BARBARIAN NORTHERN
EUROPE can be divided into
three broad zones: a market
zone closest to the frontier
where Roman goods were
acquired by direct
marketing; a rich burial zone
where the élite displayed
their prestige by burying
luxury Roman goods with
their dead; and a warrior
zone where Roman
commodities were much
rarer and society was
unstable.

men 'effeminate and incapable of enduring hardships'. That parties of Roman traders were resident in Germany is not in doubt. In the court of Maroboduus, leader of the Marcomanni at this time settled in Bohemia, his opponents in AD 18 found 'businessmen and camp followers from the Roman province [who] had been induced first by a trade agreement and then by hopes of making more money, to migrate from their various homes to enemy territory. Finally they had forgotten their own country'. These men were evidently content to settle where there were rich pickings to be had: others were more adventurous like the Roman knight, who, during the reign of Nero, explored Germany and the Baltic region searching for beasts for gladiatorial shows. He came upon trading ports (*commercia*) and was able to acquire considerable quantities of amber which he transported back to Rome. Nor were the traders always moving one way. Tacitus mentions the Hermunduri who were 'the only Germans who trade with us, not merely on the river bank but far within our borders. . . . They come over where they will and without a guard set over them'. From these few recorded examples it is possible to gauge something of the methods by which goods changed hands in the first centuries BC and AD.

A wide range of Roman commodities was used to trade with the Germans. Judging from the distribution maps of artefacts in Free Germany, coins were the most desirable item in the zone stretching for 200 kilometres or so from the frontier. This is confirmed by Tacitus who says, 'The Germans nearest us value gold and silver for their use in trade, and recognize and prefer certain types of Roman coins . . . they like coins that are old and familiar, *denarii* with the notched edge and the type of two-horse chariot . . . they try to get silver in preference to gold . . . they find plenty of silver change more serviceable in buying cheap and common goods.' The accuracy of this statement is shown by the numerous coin hoards: even those deposited in the second century contained an unusually high percentage of early issues dating to before Nero's currency reforms of AD 64. The reference to their preference for small denomination coinage is particularly interesting since it shows that a market economy was being practised by the frontier tribes by the end of the first century AD. These were the tribes with whom Rome had developed friendly relations and with whom regular trade was taking place in the many market centres which grew up on both sides of the river.

Deeper into barbarian territory a limited range of Roman luxury goods was being carried: most common were the sets of metal vessels concerned with the wine-drinking ritual, buckets, *situlae*, jugs, and *paterae*. Many hundreds have been found in a wide arc stretching from Poland in the east to Sweden and Norway in the north. Within this zone were a number of rich burials in which sets of luxury goods were buried. The general type is named after the Polish site of Lübsow where five such burials were found. One of the most spectacular finds comes from Hoby on the Danish island of Lolland dating to the beginning of the first century AD. Here the dead man had been interred in a wooden coffin accompanied by everything he needed to enjoy a feast in the afterworld—joints of pork and a drinking set comprising a bronze *situla*, a jug and a *patera*, a silver ladle, two silver cups on a bronze tray, and two bronze-mounted drinking horns. His personal equipment included brooches of bronze, silver, and gold, gold rings, belt fittings, and a knife. Evidently the Hoby burial was that of a member of the local élite, who, by virtue of his rank, was able to acquire a set of the most costly Roman luxuries which his lineage group buried with him to proclaim their status. The Lübsow burials seem to represent the kind of prestige-goods economy which was being practised by the west Hallstatt chieftains in the sixth to fifth centuries BC (Chapter 10), and by the élite of eastern Britain and Belgica in the first century BC and early first century AD (p. 433).

The distribution of these burials, in a wide zone well in advance of the frontier and buffered from the frontier by the market economy zone, strongly suggests that the more 'archaic' form of prestige-goods economy practised here may reflect the function of the local élite in facilitating the flow of goods to the Roman world from the Baltic region beyond. In other words they served as middlemen and grew rich on the proceeds.

To the north-east of this élite burial zone, stretching from northern Poland to the Gulf of Finland, a rather different type of social system can be detected at this time. Two cultural groups have been identified: the Oksywie culture of the lower Vistula region and the Bay of Danzig, and the Przeworsk culture of the Vistula-Oder region. These groups are known largely from their burials, which are characteristically those of warriors. The majority were provided in death with their swords, shields, and spurs, but a few, of higher status, were accompanied by silver or gold fibulae. This warrior society may well have been instrumental in acquiring, through raid and warfare, the captives who were driven south to the Roman frontier to be sold as slaves.

The system of socio-economic zones outlined above remained in force throughout the first and the first half of the second centuries AD. It began to disintegrate in the second half of the second century as population pressures and folk movements began to build up deep in Germany, putting pressure on the tribes of the frontier region which, in turn, threatened the stability of the Empire. The pressures emanated, in part, from the warrior-burial zone where the instability of the social system, exacerbated by an increase in population, may have encouraged the tribes to migrate southward. The territory occupied by the warrior burials roughly coincides with the area from which the Burgundians and Vandals were thought to have emerged.

The first recorded indications of the growing problem came in AD 162 when a frontier tribe, the Chatti, attempted to migrate south into Roman territory. A few years later the Langobardi and Marcomanni crossed the Danube into transdanubian Hungary to be followed by an even more massive movement of Marcomanni, Quadi, and Iazyges in AD 167, who managed to reach the head of the Adriatic and besiege Aquileia. These events, and the Marcomannic War fought by Rome between 166 and 180 AD, in an attempt to stem the flow, mark the beginning of a wave of migrations which were, within three centuries, to destroy the Empire (Chapter 13).

We have already seen that the settlement pattern of the North European Plain exhibited a remarkable continuity throughout the first millennium BC and well into the first

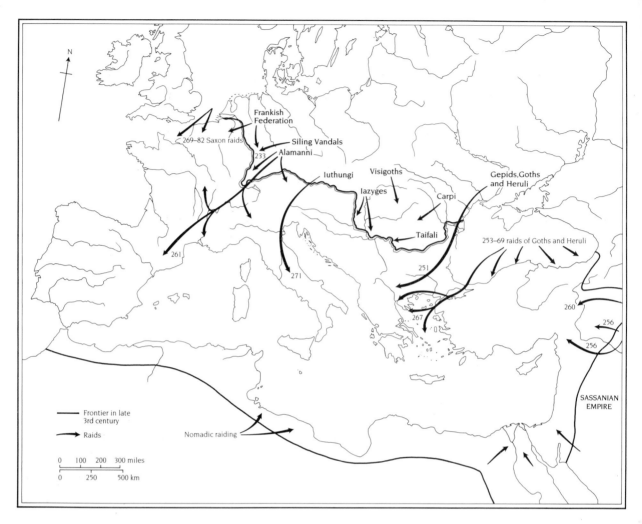

THIRD-CENTURY ATTACKS on the Roman world from north of the Rhine–Danube frontier were at their most intense between 250 and 280 AD.

millennium AD (p. 353). In the North Sea zone, from Holland to Denmark, it is possible to recognize the effects of the nearness of Rome on the developing settlement system. Proximity to the North Sea will have ensured that contact was easily maintained with traders from the south irrespective of the dislocating effects of folk movements further inland. The intensity of this trade is most clearly demonstrated by the large numbers of trinkets and pottery, like Samian Ware, which finds its way into the villages of the coastal zone from the first to the third centuries AD. Reviewing the settlements themselves, two trends can be recognized: intensification in production and hierarchization. Before the period of Roman contact the economy seems to have been based on self-sufficient production, with little need to indulge in complex patterns of long-distance trade. No attempt was made to produce large surpluses and, in consequence, wealth and prestige based on the monopoly of production is not to be recognized in the archaeological record. The development of a Roman-inspired market, however, giving added value to certain local commodities and providing a range of lower value exotics in exchange, provided motivation for social and economic change.

Most noticeable is an increasing emphasis on local specialized production. At the village of Flögeln, in lower Saxony, the number of workshops began to increase, especially from early in the third century AD, and there is evidence that metalworking and probably tanning were being undertaken on an enhanced scale. Further north at Drengsted in Jutland, iron production, far in excess of the needs of the local community, took place, and in the village of Dankirke near by, stocks of luxury goods, including glass items together with lead scale weights, indicate an increased level of local trading. In parallel with this intensification of production, it is possible to distinguish a significant size difference emerging in the farmsteads. At Feddersen Wierde, near Bremerhaven, for example, from the second century onward a single establishment stands out from the rest in terms of its size and central position, its status further demonstrated by the concentration of Roman imports—bronze vessels, beads, and Samian Ware—which cluster within it. Here presumably was the homestead of the village headman.

Increase in the level of production implies the development of a more complex system of exchange than had hitherto been practised. Given the general paucity of raw materials in the North Sea zone and the lack of scope for much significant rise in agrarian productivity, the most likely area of intensification was in cattle rearing and there is some evidence, in the form of an extension in byre provisions, that this was indeed the case. The proximity of the Roman frontier army with its enormous demands for leather, tents, armour, boots, saddles, and horsegear, must have created a ready market. Although the equation, Roman demand for leather—intensification of cattle rearing—development of a market—increase in production, is rather oversimple as an explanation, it does highlight one factor involved in the dynamics of economic change observable in the North Sea zone at this time. By the third century the North Sea trade routes were coming increasingly to suffer from pirate attacks which must have seriously dislocated the long-established exchange systems. It is a distinct possibility that the rapid diminution in the volume of trade goods reaching the North Sea zone was a significant factor in destabilizing the socio-economic system of the regions, and this may have contributed to the disrupting migrations which characterized the North Sea littoral in the fifth century.

Finally, we must turn to the western extremity of the Roman world—to the British Isles. The campaigns of Julius Agricola had brought the whole of Britain as far north as the foothills of the Grampians under Roman authority by AD 84. The last great battle fought at Mons Graupius against a British force led by Calgacus was a one-sided affair. The Britons were archaically armed: chariots were still in use, a technique which had been abandoned in Gaul for almost 200 years, and their long swords with blunted tips were of little value in close hand-to-hand fighting with Roman troops armed with short stabbing swords. The engagement soon turned into a rout with 10,000 Britons killed against only 360 Romans (or so Tacitus would have us believe). But Scotland was not held for long, and by the beginning of the second century the frontier line had been established across the Tyne-Solway isthmus—later to be known as Hadrian's Wall—and for the rest of the occupation it fluctuated between here and a forward position along the Clyde and Firth of Forth line.

Within and beyond this broad frontier region the local tribes continued to develop, little influenced by Rome. Free Scotland had such limited productive capacity that what little trade did develop was at a comparatively low level though some of the old hill-forts served as tribal centres where production and exchange were focused. The communities of the west and north, up to the Shetland Isles, remained dispersed in their isolated settlements occupying locations used for centuries, using and sometimes modifying existing structures. It was these disparate tribes of the north who came together in a loose federation called Picts—the 'painted ones'—a reference to the long-established tradition of decorating the body. From the third century the Picts became an increasing threat to Britain and played a part in the eventual destruction of Roman rule in the island.

In AD 82 Agricola stood on the west coast of Scotland looking across to Ireland. 'I have often heard Agricola say', wrote Tacitus, 'that Ireland could be invaded and conquered with one legion and a few auxiliaries. It would be an advantage, especially with the pacification of Britain, if Roman arms were everywhere to be seen and independence swept from the map.' In the event nothing was done and Ireland remained the only part of the Celtic world to be free of the Roman yoke. Some entrepreneurs crossed the Irish Sea to the harbours of Dublin Bay and Cork carrying bags of trinkets, some flashy Samian pottery and a few bronze vessels, in return for which they acquired slaves, hides, and the famous Irish hunting dogs, but their impact seems to have been slight. Defended homesteads, so characteristic of the Atlantic zone, continued to be built, the rich oral tradition continued to be proclaimed, and ancient law codes continued to constrain the behaviour of the people. Thus it was that Celtic society managed to survive little changed throughout the Roman interlude.

13

Barbarian Europe, AD 300–700

MALCOLM TODD

TH E peoples of northern Europe had been far from isolated from the Mediterranean empire of Rome during the first centuries of the Christian era. Although from the eighteenth century onward scholars have tended to treat the Roman world and its barbarian neighbours as separate blocs of territory and population, the interrelationships between them were much closer than the surviving literary record reveals, and had resonance in a number of fields: military, political, diplomatic, economic, commercial, and, to an extent, cultural and social. The barbarian world, which stretched from the North Sea to the western steppes and from Scandinavia to the Rhine and Danube, was a world of extreme variety, in population, economy, and cultural expression. That variety is inadequately reflected in the written accounts we have and is still in process of revelation by archaeological studies. The divide between Roman and barbarian is not the only divide which modern scholarship has created in the protohistory of Europe. There is the equally false distinction between the more or less settled barbarian societies which coexisted with the Roman Empire and the migrant tribes which swept into that Empire from the late fourth century to the late sixth, there to create structures of power that were recognizably barbarian, though resting on Roman foundations. The great migrations were certainly events which transformed Europe, but they were not triggered by some sudden change in circumstances, some new irruption of peoples. Rather, their origins lay much further back in the complex network of relations which bound many of the barbarian peoples to the great power centred on the Mediterranean. To understand those relations is to begin to grasp what the migrations truly were. A point of departure is offered at the time when Roman power was at its peak.

Towards Migration

The later second century AD was a period of considerable turbulence in central and eastern Europe. The movement of peoples southward towards the Danube and the Black Sea affected wide areas and brought a number of tribes into direct conflict with Roman frontier armies, notably on the middle Danube. A long series of wars, commonly called the Marcomannic Wars—though the Quadi were also heavily involved—was fought

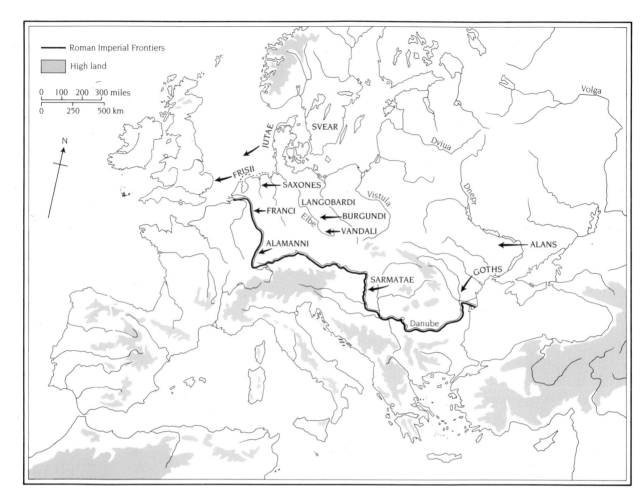

BARBARIAN EUROPE *c*.AD 300.

out between Rome and groups north of the Danube between 166 and 180, Rome's authority being eventually upheld, somewhat precariously, by a combination of military force and diplomacy. Although the northern frontier of the Empire was restored on the middle Danube and strengthened by new military dispositions, the aftermath of the Marcomannic Wars soon revealed the beginning of a shift in military power and ambition to the barbarian peoples beyond the Rhine and Danube. A generation after the end of those conflicts, there are signs of a major realignment of peoples across central Europe and the emergence of new and aggressive confederacies close to the Roman frontiers. The Alamanni are first mentioned in a historical source in 213, when they were driven out of Upper Germany and Raetia by Caracalla. Twenty years later they again broke into the frontier provinces and caused widespread damage. In 260, they, and no doubt other barbarian groups, brought about the abandonment of the Roman frontier system which ran from the Rhine to the Danube. The very name of the Alamanni, 'all men', 'everybody', indicates a confederate origin, and we might guess that it came into being as a loosely linked nexus of war bands under several leaders. The main territorial seat of the Alamanni lay between the upper Elbe and the Roman frontier, where the Suebi and Semnones had earlier held sway. They were later to push forward into the wedge of territory behind the old frontier and on towards the Black Forest and the northern Alps.

East of the lower Rhine, the Franks, although first noted in our sources after 250, probably emerged as a distinct grouping early in the third century. They, too, may have originated in aggressive war bands under several leaders, emboldened to attack the Roman provinces by signs of a loosening Roman grip on the frontiers. There is no indi-

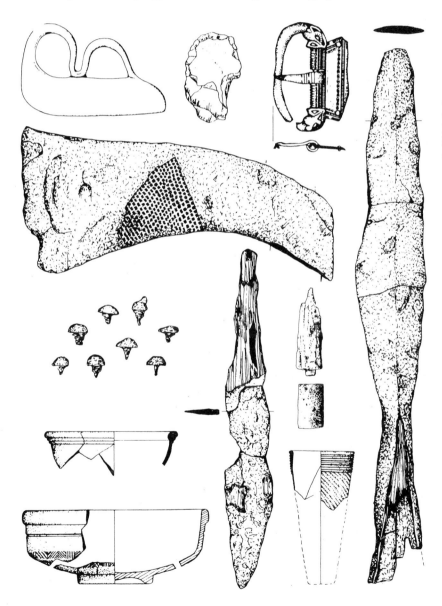

GRAVE OF A GERMANIC WARRIOR, probably in Roman service, at Vireux-Molhain, France: early fifth century AD.

cation of central political control at this early date. The later Franks had rather hazy notions of their own ethnogenesis and the process of unification was slow and relatively undramatic. It was as raiders by sea as well by land that the Franks were known in the third century, like their northern neighbours the Saxons and Frisians, at this same time raising their ambitions beyond the northern coastlands. The archaeological record has little to say about the Franks in the third and fourth centuries, even though there is clear historical evidence for the settlement of Frankish groups west of the lower Rhine under Roman supervision in the late third century. Late in the fourth century, however, a striking series of warrior graves, often richly furnished with fine weaponry, personal ornaments, glass and pottery vessels of some quality, is found between the Rhine and the Seine, in some cases in cemeteries associated with Roman towns and forts, in others in rural locations. These burials frequently include objects which were produced east of the Rhine, and the mere fact that they are manifestly burials of warriors is a further pointer to an origin in the barbarian world for their occupants. Female burials are also represented in these Germanic graves, so that family or kin groups were evidently being introduced to northern Gaul from across the Rhine in the late fourth and early fifth centuries. Until recently, settlements that might be linked to this process have been elusive. But a German settlement of about AD 400 has now been identified at Neerharen-Rekem, near Maastricht in the valley of the Meuse, close to an abandoned villa. Some of the warrior cemeteries are associated with hilltop strongholds in eastern France and Belgium, such as Furfooz and Vireux-Molhain. These localized garrisons perhaps played a part in the protection of late Roman estates and other territories in the disturbed decades about 400.

In eastern Europe, too, there were movements of population and shifts in the political geography of the Germanic peoples and their nomad and semi-nomad neighbours. From late in the second century, contacts had been developing between the population of the Vistula basin and the mixed peoples of the Black Sea hinterland and the steppe fringes. A major migration of people to the south-east probably did not occur, but it is clear that war bands did enter the Black Sea littoral, there gathering allies and resources which were to enable them to attack the eastern Roman world. These new groups were referred to by Roman writers as 'Goths', a term which embraced a wide range of ethnic elements and which bestows a spurious air of unity upon a heterogeneous congeries of tribes, war bands, and other groups. The power base which arose north of the Black Sea in the third century was thus culturally extremely mixed, bringing together various nomadic peoples, eastern Germans, and the populations based in and around the old Greek and Roman cities of the Black Sea shore. In such circumstances, we need not look for any distinctively 'Gothic' culture, for it did not exist. The military threat posed to Asia Minor and the Balkans by this emergent power, however, was real enough. From 238 onward, Gothic armies harried the lower Danube lands with considerable success. Under the resourceful leadership of their king Kniva, they won a resounding victory over a Roman army at Abrittus in 251, killing the Roman emperor and extracting huge

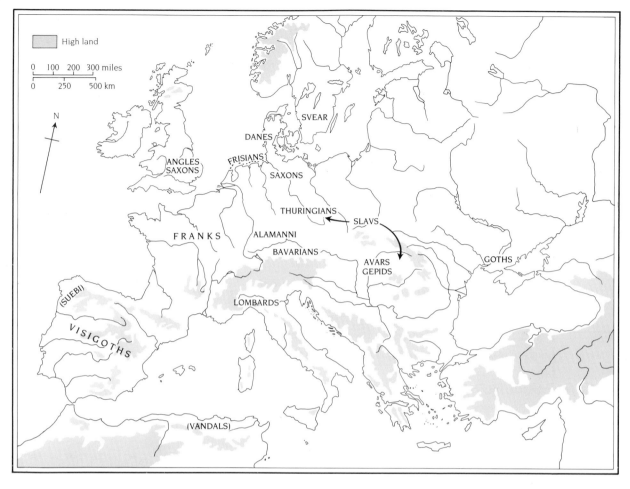

BARBARIAN EUROPE *c*.AD 600.

payments of money from his successor. Later, the range of Gothic assaults was widened to include Asia Minor, which had known no major warfare for centuries, and the Aegean. These attacks were necessarily mounted from fleets, a new departure for barbarian raiders, and the resulting devastation was widespread. An invasion of Greece by several Gothic forces in 257 marked the high point of their success at this period. It was beaten off eventually and thereafter the series of invasions ended quite suddenly. Relations between the Goths and Rome were given stability by a treaty of 332, which provided annual payments to the barbarians in return for manpower and permitted the resumption of trade across the Danube. Money, manpower, military service, commerce: the Goths as federates of the Empire had arrived.

   The archaeologically defined cultures of south-eastern Europe present enormous problems to those who seek to identify distinct peoples with them. This was a region which experienced considerable shifts of population in the later Roman Iron Age, leading to a nexus of cultures bewildering in its complexity. It was also a region in which several peoples were highly mobile in the pursuit of their normal economic activities: by no means all of these nomads and semi-nomads lived on the western steppes. Study of the peoples of this huge territory between the Don and the Danube has not yet advanced very far and what has been done has been bedevilled by nationalist interpretation since the nineteenth century. The most extensive archaeological culture here is that called the Przeworsk culture, which had its origins in the first century BC and flourished until the fifth century AD over an immense tract from the upper Dnestr valley to the Tisza river in Hungary and northward to the valleys of the Oder and Vistula. This was an irregular mosaic of local cultures which bore the impress of many influences, from the German peoples, the Celts of the middle Danube basin, the steppe dwellers, and others. Some have sought the ancestors of the Slavs among the eastern bearers of the Przeworsk culture, far from convincingly. Settlements have rarely been examined in these territories: cemeteries provide most of the material evidence at our disposal. Warrior graves are frequent, many of them containing horsegear. There are a small number of very richly furnished graves, but the vast majority of the dead were modestly provided for. The cultural unity of Przeworsk came to a sudden end in the early fifth century, probably as a result of major shifts southward and westward following the advent of the Huns and the diaspora of the Goths.

In the meantime, an extensive culture had risen to prominence between the Danube and the Dnepr, the Cjernjakhov culture, named after a cemetery site near Kiev. Originating in the second century and with its roots among the Scythian and Sarmatian population of western Russia, this complex reached its peak in the fourth century, by which time it had extended southward to the Danube, possibly through the agency of the Goths and their associates. Cjernjakhov was a remarkably dynamic and innovative culture, characterized by fine, polished pottery, metalwork of high quality, and excellent iron equipment. There is still intense debate over the bearers of this culture. The broad valleys of the Ukraine were probably its birthplace, but its extension to the south-west implies a spread to German and Dacian populations. This stable culture was shattered late in the fourth century, probably by the same sequence of events that brought the Przeworsk complex to an end.

Settlement, Culture, and War

The settlements and settlement patterns of barbarian Europe are much more fully recorded in some regions than in others. By and large, more is known on the subject in western and northern Europe than in the East, where extensive excavation has so far been rare. The most informative regions are northern Germany, Holland, and Scandinavia, both for the Roman Iron Age and the migration period. After the major migrations, settlement within the former Roman provinces is patchily recorded in Italy, Spain, and the Balkans. The picture is becoming clearer in the Rhine and Danube lands,

GILDED SILVER PLAQUE (*left*) showing a member of the Thracian aristocracy in full body armour. Fourth century BC. From the Letnitsa treasure, Bulgaria.

PART OF THE GRAVE GOODS (*below*) from the native burial at Hoby on the island of Lolland, Denmark. The silver cups were made by a Greek craftsman and were transported northwards from the Roman province either as a diplomatic gift or as plunder in the early first century AD to end up in the grave of a member of the native élite.

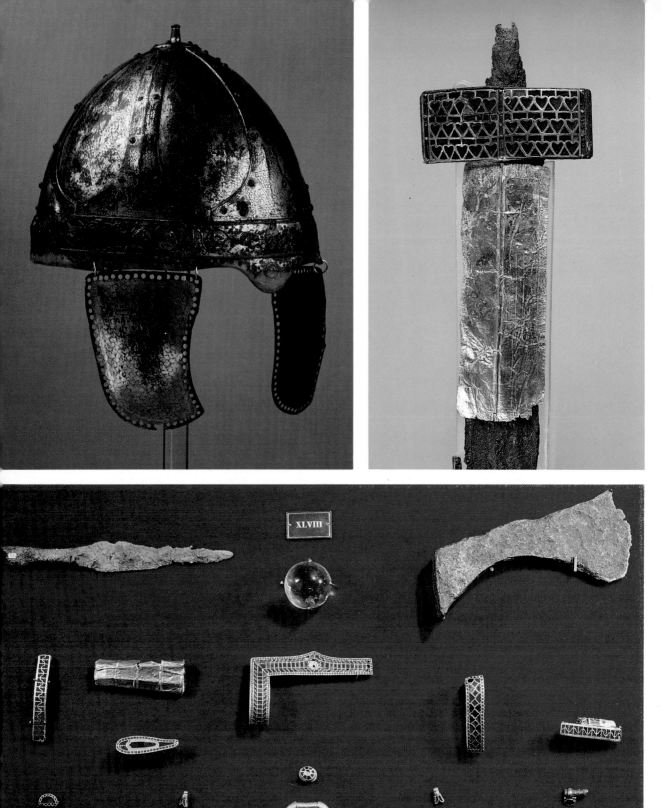

XLVIII

France and Britain, but there is still much to learn. Before the migrations, the barbarian peoples had not developed urban forms of settlement, nor made significant progress in that direction. Societies remained tribal and familiar in their structure. The centralizing functions of economy and administration were inchoate and inconstant, not permitting the emergence of stable urban centres. This situation did not rapidly change when the formation of early states began. Major strongholds or hill-forts, such as had existed in Europe in the first millennium BC, were far from common in the barbarian world of the early first millennium AD. Those that did exist appear to have been strongholds of strictly local power, not central places with wider connections (below, p. 470).

This does not mean that large community settlements did not exist. Large-scale excavation in the north has revealed the existence of large and orderly settlements from the mid-first millennium BC onward. Those of the Roman Iron Age frequently show steady growth from modest homesteads. This is true of Wijster, which began as a single steading in the first century BC, but which had grown into a substantial village by the third century, regularly planned about a grid of lanes marked by timber fences. It continued its growth for another century and then came to a fairly sudden end in the early migration period. A community of the size of Wijster at its peak (it may have housed two hundred in the fourth century) can only have been the product of a stable social structure, probably under the direction of a local chieftain. Some such structure is also in evidence at the coastal site of Feddersen Wierde, a settlement which, in its sequence of phases, occupied a growing mound near the Weser estuary from the first century BC to the fifth century AD. This, too, was an ordered site, its houses radiating from a focal point. Already by the second century, one dwelling near the southern edge was marked off from the rest by an enclosing fence; in the compound thus formed, craftsmen were at work in a variety of materials. This is reasonably seen as the quarters of a local lord, holding sway over the community and a group of dependent craftsmen. Not the least interesting fact about Feddersen Wierde is that this internal arrangement was maintained for over two centuries.

Substantial settlements are also attested in Jutland in the fourth and fifth centuries, often emerging after a long process of development. At Vorbasse, a series of longhouses lay to either side of an axial street, each dwelling set within its own fenced enclosure. This settlement represents only one phase of occupation within a limited area, the main focus of settlement shifting over centuries from the earlier Iron Age to the Viking period. This phenomenon of settlement shift is now well attested in Denmark, in Holland, and in Anglo-Saxon England. Precisely what lay behind it is not yet clear, but it

HELMET (Spangenhelm) from the grave of a noble Frankish warrior, found at Krefeld-Gellep, Germany: *c.* AD 600 (*above, left*).

HILT-GUARD and upper blade of an east Germanic sword from Altlussheim, Germany: mid-fifth century (*above, right*).

THE SURVIVING CONTENTS of the grave of Childeric found at Tournai, Belgium: AD 481 (*left*).

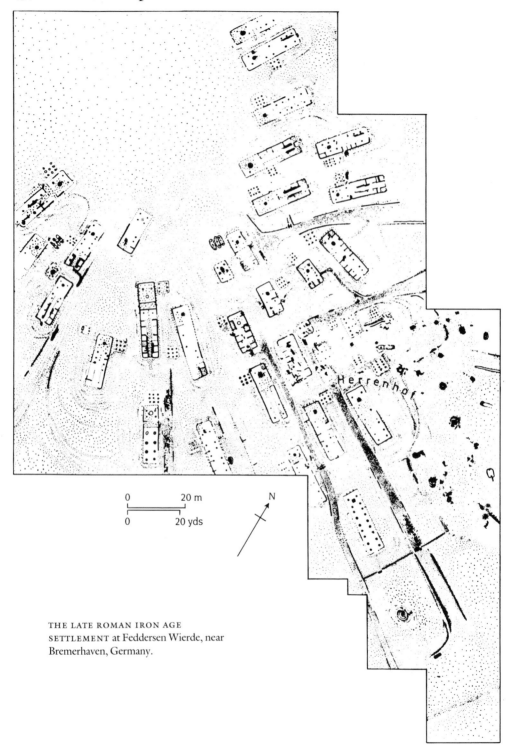

0 ___ 20 m

0 ___ 20 yds

N

Herrenhof

THE LATE ROMAN IRON AGE
SETTLEMENT at Feddersen Wierde, near
Bremerhaven, Germany.

may be related to the need to maintain the fertility of agricultural land which was under intensive use. The nucleated village was by no means the only form of settlement in the north. Smaller groups of steadings are known, as at Flögeln, as are single farms. A dispersed pattern of farmsteads appears in certain areas, for instance in southern Sweden, where the scattered community of Vallhagar provides a type-site for migration-period Scandinavia. Sweden and the Baltic islands of Gotland and Öland also reveal a large number of small fortified sites from the early migration period, of which Eketorps Borg is the most fully examined. These are as yet without analogies further south.

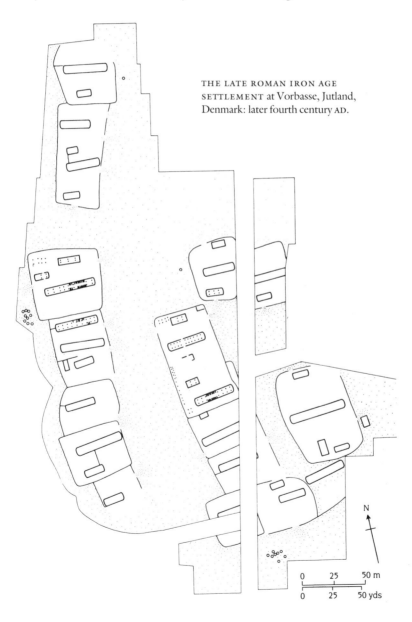

THE LATE ROMAN IRON AGE SETTLEMENT at Vorbasse, Jutland, Denmark: later fourth century AD.

N

| 0 | 25 | 50 m |
| 0 | 25 | 50 yds |

The agricultural economy of the peoples of northern Europe was based on mixed farming, but animal husbandry was a dominant feature of most of the regions for which reliable information exists. As Tacitus said of the early Germans: 'their wealth resides in flocks and herds'. The fact is abundantly clear from the remains of animals found on settlements and from the animal stalling which is an integral feature of the European longhouse. Almost everywhere in the north, cattle were the most important domestic animal, producing meat and milk and serving as draught animals. Pigs, sheep, and goats came next in order, in varying proportions in different areas. Horses were generally the least common of the large animals. The northern breeds of most animals were very little influenced by cross-breeding from elsewhere, with the inevitable result that individual animals were smaller than those of southern Europe. Cattle were often little more than a metre high at the shoulder, horses barely 1.5 metres. Pigs were tiny, though sheep and goats were closer in size to those of the Roman world. Domestic dogs were kept for herding and for guarding the home. Curiously, hunting played a very minor part in the supply of meat, despite the fact that wild animals might have offered much, especially the aurochs, roe and red deer, and wild boar. Coastal communities engaged in fishing and catching seals, but on few sites do these activities seem to have been central. Above all else, the barbarian peoples were farmers and their exploitation of the resources of the land was more than adequately efficient.

The crops grown in the north are well known from seed remains from settlements, from stomach contents of human corpses preserved in peat-bogs, and from pollen spectra. Barley remained the most important grain into the early medieval period, being used for making beer as well as providing food. Several forms of wheat were cultivated from the Neolithic to the Middle Ages, especially einkorn and emmer. Oats, millet, and rye were widely distributed, as was flax, grown for the oil contained in its seeds and for its fibres, which could be used to make linen. Cultivated vegetables included beans and peas, to which could have been added various wild plants, including celery, spinach, lettuce, radishes, and brassicas. Woad was also collected for use in dyeing textiles. Potentially, large tracts of barbarian Europe were productive land, far removed from the forested wastes of some classical and early medieval writers. But famine and hardship could occur, especially in the eastern regions where winters were often severe.

Craftsmanship

Great advances were registered in the techniques and designs used by craftsmen over much of barbarian Europe from the third century onward. In no medium is this more evident than in the precious metals. A greatly increased supply of both gold and silver was available, mainly in the form of Roman coinage and other objects, and chieftainly patrons were eager to demonstrate their growing wealth and prestige in fine ornaments and weaponry. Technically, working in gold and silver was transformed by the more confident use of filigree ornament, of inlays, and encrustation of semiprecious stones,

GOLD CAGE-CUP from the great treasure found at Pietroasa, Romania: first half of the fifth century.

especially garnet. The results are evident in richly furnished graves from the late third century onward, at Hassleben and Zakrow in central Europe, in the dazzling array of jewellery found in graves and hoards on the Danube in the fifth century, and later in the brilliant achievements of metalsmiths in Ostrogothic Italy, Frankish Gaul, Scandinavia, and Anglo-Saxon England. The development of a polychrome style of ornament, in which semiprecious stones were combined with gold, is the most distinctive single feature of fine craftsmanship from the third to the fifth centuries. This has long been seen as one result of the westward movement of the Goths, carrying with them a style which had its origins among the steppe peoples. Although some elements of the new designs did originate far to the East, in Iran as well as south Russia, their full artistic flowering seems now to have been due to craftsmen at work on the middle and lower Danube early in the fifth century. The splendidly furnished burials at Apahida and the astounding hoard of vessels and jewellery from Pietroasa, both in Romania, are the finest displays of the skill of metalworkers, and the wealth of their masters, yet known from early migration-period Europe. What was achieved here was soon to be emulated in other parts of Europe, as is seen in Childeric's grave, at Krefeld-Gellep, at Domagnano, and at Sutton Hoo. As in so much else in barbarian Europe, contributions to this astonishing achievement came from several quarters, not least from the world of eastern Rome.

The barbarian peoples remained largely illiterate until after the migration period. And yet as early as the early fourth century there was the almost superhuman achievement of a translation of the Bible into Gothic by Ulfila, bishop of the Goths north of the Danube, who had to invent an alphabet for the purpose. Ulfila was a Goth who included

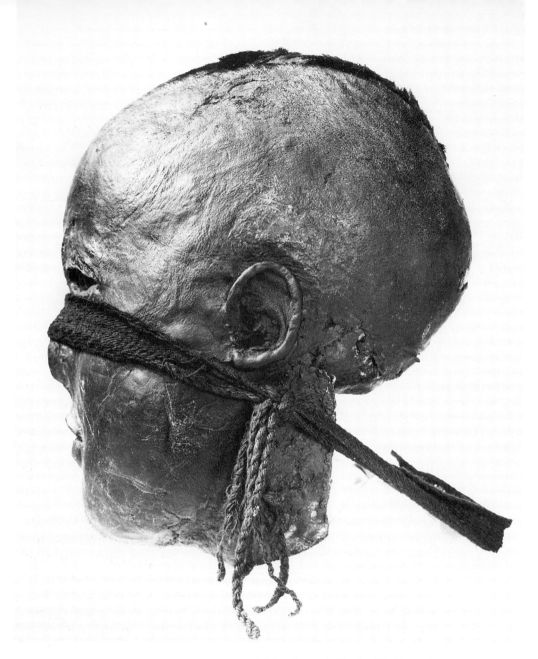

HEAD OF TEENAGE GIRL FROM A PEAT-BOG at Windeby, Denmark. Her head had been shaven and a blindfold placed around her eyes.

among his forebears a Christian prisoner carried off from Asia Minor in a third-century raid. Other attempts at rendering Germanic languages into writing at so early a date are not recorded. There was, however, a system of communication using signs which had developed from at least the second century onward, though for relatively specialized uses. These signs—known as runes since the seventeenth century—in their early forms represent single names or words and appear most commonly on weapons or ornaments.

Several appear to name a particular weapon or to express its power. Others seem to be dedications to deities or imprecations upon enemies. There was probably also a connection with divination and reading the will of the gods. The origins of runes are still not wholly certain. Twenty-four characters are included in the early runic futhark or alphabet. Four of these may be linked to Latin letters, while nine of the signs resemble letters in the north Italic scripts current in the north Alpine regions down to at least the first century AD. Runes may be partly derived from this source, but other influences played a role and these have not yet been convincingly defined. Not until later in the migration period do runic inscriptions appear which are other than telegraphic. It was in the western Baltic lands that this development gained most headway, continuing into the Viking and medieval periods. In other Germanic territories, runes made more sporadic appearances, mainly in the spheres of cult and magic.

The personae and spheres of influence of the northern gods are sketchily recorded for us. As in most primitive societies, deities of fertility, death, and war wielded most power. While their identities are shadowy, there are striking remains of cult observance in the form of votive deposits in pools and peatbogs, most notably in Denmark and northern Germany. Three large deposits came to light in the nineteenth century, at Thorsbjerg, Vimose, and Nydam, and were well studied by Conrad Engelhardt. Others have been more recently recorded at Illerup and Ejsbøl in Denmark and at Skedemosse on Öland, with important clarification of their history and significance. The great deposits of the later Roman Iron Age are dominated by weapons and other war equipment; swords (mainly if not exclusively Roman), spears, javelins, shields, and shield parts, knives, belts, and horsegear. Fine garments and ornaments are represented at Thorsbjerg, brooches and Roman coins at most of the deposits, and even three entire ships at Nydam. The theme of war and the dedication of captured equipment is also to the fore at Ejsbøl and Illerup. At Ejsbøl, the weaponry of a force of about sixty warriors seems to have been thrown into a peatbog at one time, probably in the late fourth century. Animal and human sacrifice is also attested in some of these deposits. At Skedemosse, the horse was a frequent victim of sacrifice, perhaps to a sky god whose symbol this was. At certain sites, including Thorsbjerg, deposits were made over several centuries, those with warlike associations beginning in the third century. In other cases, there were single episodes of deposition, perhaps after signal victories, as at Illerup and Ejsbøl. The deposits of war equipment continued into the fifth century and then came to an end, perhaps because the military *Schwerpunkt* no longer lay in northern Europe.

The objects consigned to the peatbogs are an invaluable source of information on the weapons and war gear used by the northern peoples, to be added to the evidence from graves and sculpted reliefs. Swords were plainly becoming more widespread by the fourth century, most of them of Roman origin and of high quality. The bow and arrow were increasingly significant, but the main weapon for fighting at a distance remained the javelin, often the barbed *ango*. The throwing-axe was becoming more common, an effective weapon against well-armoured opponents. But body armour remained very rare among all the barbarian peoples. Only leading warriors acquired helmets, and covering for the body seems to have been virtually unknown before the late fourth century. For long thereafter most warriors went into battle as poorly protected as their ancestors of centuries before. The use of cavalry formations increased among some peoples, particularly those of eastern Europe, who were in contact with the Sarmatians, Alans, and Huns. Gothic cavalry made a decisive intervention at the battle of Adrianople in 378 and were later a significant force in the invasions of Italy. But barbarian armies were still largely infantry armies, relatively lightly armed and depending for their effectiveness on traditional valour and physical strength. Tactics remained elementary, the surprise attack from concealed positions still being the staple ploy. Assaults on walled cities and other strongholds were generally avoided as exercises likely to be unproductive and requiring expertise in operating siege machinery, which was rarely available. Nevertheless, barbarian armies could, and did, win successes against Roman forces. Indeed the division between Roman and barbarian in this sphere became increasingly difficult to draw. From the mid-fourth century onward, most military engagements were between barbarians from outside the Empire on one side and barbarians in Roman service on the other.

Military service in the armies of Roman emperors offered an ever more attractive outlet for the warlike qualities of the barbarians; from the third century onward barbarian troops were an important element of the Roman forces. By the late fourth century they almost certainly made up the great bulk of the Imperial army, partly reflecting a shortage of manpower within the Empire, partly the high regard in which their fighting qualities were held. For ambitious barbarians, service with Rome could provide both wealth and status far beyond anything to be hoped for among their own people. The creation of a mobile army by Constantine gave a major impetus to the recruitment of Germans in particular. His new force was probably largely drawn from barbarian ranks and many of its officers came from the same source. Alamanni were prominent in the higher commands during the first half of the fourth century; Franks and others came to the fore later. Among the latter was Silvanus, who served as *magister militum* in Gaul in the 350s, a man who seemed to a Roman observer to be 'dedicated to the Empire', but who was to proclaim himself emperor to protect himself against intrigue, only to be murdered shortly afterwards by his own soldiers. In the late fourth and early fifth centuries, many of the most senior military commands were held by Germans, especially in the West. Their power could be as great, or greater, than that of the emperors they supposedly served.

The Goths: From the Balkans to Italy and Spain

After the treaty of 332, the Goths who lay close to the lower Danube maintained a federate relationship with the Roman state, not always easily or reliably, but more or less adequately. By now these barbarians were commonly referred to as Visigoths, by way of distinction from their brethren to the East, the Ostrogoths. In the Goths' own tradition, this division was traced back to an incident during the migration from the Vistula basin, when the breaking of a bridge across a river separated the two people for ever. In actuality, the two blocs had probably developed separate identities after settlement on the plains behind the Black Sea. Relatively little is known of both Gothic powers before the 370s. Both were in contact with the western steppe peoples and had intermingled with them to some degree. Both seem to have been fairly stable powers, occupying productive land and maintaining contacts with others around the Black Sea coasts. This relatively secure world was rudely shattered shortly after 370. The rapid thrust westward of the steppe nomads known to Greeks and Romans as the Huns seems to have taken both the barbarian and Mediterranean worlds utterly by surprise. The invaders overran the Ostrogoths with terrifying speed and made them their subjects for the next eighty years. The Visigoths and their neighbours were now exposed to the raw power of the new masters of the western steppes. Late in 376, large numbers of Goths begged to be allowed to cross the Danube and settle in the northern Balkans. Once there, they found that their conditions of life were scarcely better than if they had stayed to endure the domination of the Huns. After two years of bitter deprivation, the Visigoths and their allies inflicted a crushing defeat on a Roman army at Adrianople and killed the emperor Valens. There was further confused fighting before the Visigoths were formally settled as federates within Moesia, the first barbarian people to be so established within the Empire, under a treaty of 382. Their travails, however, were only beginning. They were not given adequate land on which to settle in the Balkans and their eyes, therefore, turned westward towards northern Italy. Under their leader Alaric, an effective but not brilliant commander, they threatened the heart of the old Empire from their northern base in the first decade of the fifth century. Held at bay by Stilicho until his removal in 408, the army of Alaric eventually took possession of Rome in August 410, an event which shocked contemporaries but had few repercussions of any moment. Alaric's attention quickly turned to the wealth of Africa, but while preparing an invasion across the Mediterranean he suddenly died. The Visigoths still had no permanent home within the Empire. Their new leader Athaulf maintained the north Italian base for a time, and after his murder the mass of his people were settled in Aquitaine in 418, again under the terms of a treaty. This was to remain the territory of the Visigoths, with its centre at Toulouse, for about a century. Politically and culturally, the kingdom of the Goths in Aquitaine played a relatively subdued role in the tumultuous events of the fifth century, its principal contribution being a major part in the defeat of the Hun invaders of Gaul in 451. Parts of northern Spain were also in Visigothic control and the attractions of wider settlement in the peninsula grew as the power of the Franks steadily mounted to the north.

The Visigothic kingdom in Aquitaine is one of the least-known powers of early Germanic Europe. The archaeology of cemeteries, a prime source of information for most peoples of the period, makes little showing among the Visigoths, as it was not their custom to surround their dead with many goods for the afterlife. In consequence, it is not even clear where the main body of the Visigoths was settled in 418. Their kings used Toulouse as their capital and this should mean that the upper Garonne, an area of substantial late Roman villa estates, received numbers of the federates. The wide plains of Poitou and the Saintonge offered another fertile tract, but no evidence for Visigoths has been found there so far. Whatever their material culture when they arrived in Aquitaine, they seem to have quickly divested themselves of it and adapted themselves to what remained of Gallo-Roman cultural identity. The fact that they were now isolated from other Germanic groups may have further inhibited the growth of any clear cultural image. The internal history of the kingdom is similarly poorly known. During the long reign of the first king in Aquitaine, Theoderic I, the terms of the *foedus* were generally observed. In 451, the core of the army which faced the Huns on the Catalaunian plain was formed by Visigoths. Theoderic himself lost his life in that great conflict. His son, another Theoderic, remained an ally of Rome, but his kingdom was soon to come under increasing pressure from the rise of Frankish power. Already before the defeat at Frankish hands in the battle at Vouillé in 507, Visigothic eyes were turning southward to Spain.

The two most Roman kingdoms established by barbarians were those of Goths: the Ostrogoths in Italy and the Visigoths in Spain. The Ostrogoths, released from long subjection to the Huns, invaded Italy in 488, led by the greatest of barbarian statesmen, Theoderic. He had spent much of his youth as a hostage at Constantinople, had acquired a Roman education, and was well versed in Roman statecraft, without losing his native taste for war. The kingdom which he founded in northern Italy, based on several of the old cities, remained a stable power during his long lifetime, but was unable to withstand the resurgent Byzantines after his death. The success of Theoderic's kingdom was largely due to the king himself. While preserving those elements of Roman hierarchy and administration which could serve his purposes, Theoderic remained a Germanic king and commander, but one with exceptional breadth of vision and diplomatic skill. He governed his Goths through *comites Gothorum* and employed German military commanders. But he also appointed Romans to high posts at court, notably Cassiodorus from southern Italy, whose correspondence is so revealing a source for Theoderic's Italy. The weakness of the Ostrogothic kingdom was the Ostrogothic people themselves. They seem not to have responded to the role in which their king cast them. Their main centre of settlement remained in northern Italy, very little Ostrogothic material being found south of the northern Apennines. Despite the security from external attack enjoyed by Italy for nearly half a century after 488, the Gothic hold on the north failed to develop a cohesiveness which would survive Theoderic. After the king's death in 526, Italy again lay exposed to external powers.

The longest-lived Germanic kingdom, on what had been Roman soil, was that of the Visigoths in Spain. The Visigothic hold on northern Spain was consolidated and enlarged from the late fifth century onward and they quickly dominated most of the Iberian peninsula. Early on, they were greatly assisted by Theoderic, but by 530 the independence of the kingdom in Spain was assured. It was to survive until the Arab invasion of 711. Visigothic Spain, although somewhat inward-looking, was a remarkably successful amalgam of Roman and Germanic elements. The wealth of Spain lay predominantly in the south, and from the mid-sixth century the kingdom was ruled from Toledo, oddly, close to the southern limits of Germanic settlement as revealed by archaeological finds. Most of Spain was ruled from here, but for the north-west corner where the Suevi were in occupation until the 580s, and a narrow strip on the south-east coast, seized by the Byzantines in the mid-sixth century. The material culture of Visigothic Spain owed much to the late Roman provinces and to Byzantium. Specifically 'Gothic' material in Spain, whatever that could have meant by the sixth century, is scarce and far from impressive in quality. The kingdom reached its height under Leovigild and his successors in the later decades of the century. It then enjoyed an intellectual life unmatched in any barbarian state. Even so characteristically late Roman a scholar as Isidore of Seville could work comfortably inside it. If it stagnated during the later seventh century, it was by no means moribund when the Arabs crossed the Straits of Gibraltar in 711. But in the face of its vigorous invaders, it collapsed with astonishing speed.

The Franks: From Gaul to France

The rise of Frankish power in northern Gaul is not clearly mirrored in the archaeology of the region. Historical sources relate that much of the Rhineland, the valleys of the Meuse and Moselle, and the broad plains of Belgium were under the domination of the Franks by the middle of the fifth century, and yet the presence of substantial numbers of barbarians is not evident in the archaeological record. Only in the second half of the century do Frankish cemeteries appear in numbers in these areas, the grave goods marking a decisive break with the late Roman past. The colonization of the land seems to have been relatively slow, perhaps spreading out from a number of enclaves which were originally quite small. One of these lay on the lower Rhine, the settlement of Salian ('salty') Franks which had its origins in the fourth century. Another lay in the Meuse and Moselle valleys, a third in southern Belgium with its centre at the small Roman town of Tournai. Later, the area around Reims attracted settlement from several Frankish groups. No centralized authority emerged until the late fifth century when Clovis welded these scattered chiefdoms together into a strong kingdom and expanded its territorial hold over most of northern Gaul from the Rhine to the Loire. By the early years of the sixth century, Clovis had campaigned against the Thuringians and Alamanni east of the Rhine, the Burgundians in eastern Gaul and, above all, had won his victory against the Visigoths at Vouillé. When Clovis died in 511, honoured by the emperor in Byzantium and by Theoderic in Italy, the Franks were the masters of Gaul and would remain so.

Royal burials and other richly adorned graves have played a vital role in the archaeological definition of the Franks. The earliest royal burial in date was also the first to be discovered. The grave of Childeric, who died in 481/2, was found at Tournai in 1653 and

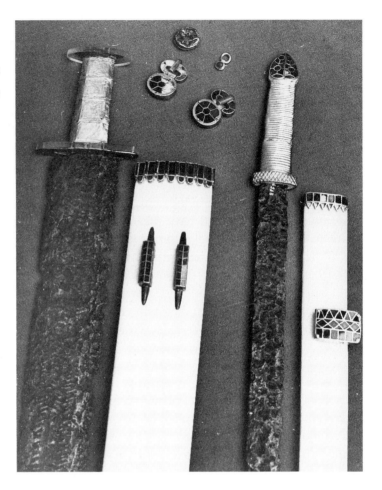

SWORD, LONG KNIFE and their scabbards, and belt-fittings from a richly furnished grave found at Pouan, Aube, France: second half of the fifth century AD.

its contents published not long afterwards. The king, the father of Clovis, was surrounded in death by a treasury of gold, silver, and garnet, including two great swords with garnet-inlaid scabbards, gold belt-buckles, a gold torc, a crossbow brooch of a kind worn by late Roman officers, a hundred gold coins and twice as many of silver, and a richly brocaded cloak on to which there had been sown three hundred gold bees. The grave provides us with an unrivalled view of late fifth-century craftsmanship in metal and precious stones. Just as compelling are the imperial echoes which resound around the grave of Childeric, although he and his son were kings of the very barbarians who would succeed to the power of Rome in the West.

Childeric was a pagan, and the context of his burial is not securely defined. But Clovis was baptized a Christian and from his time onward Frankish kings, their families, and many of their nobles sought burial in or close to churches. Under a small basilica at St Denis near Paris lay the grave of a noblewoman who had died in her forties. She lay in her stone sarcophagus clad in magnificent garments, a reddish silk cloak over all, and wearing jewellery of great splendour. Her gold signet ring is inscribed ARNEGUNDIS REGINE, which should identify her as Arnegunde, the second wife of Clothar, who died about 570. Two graves beneath Cologne Cathedral belong to the same courtly milieu and are perhaps twenty years earlier. One is of a lady, the other a small boy, probably her son. The jewellery in the woman's grave is among the finest known in Germanic Europe. The little boy, about six years old, was equipped with the panoply of the Frankish warrior in miniature: helmet, sword, axe, spears, shield, and knife. But not all aristocratic Franks were buried in churches. Several richly furnished warrior graves of the sixth and seventh centuries lay within the cemetery at Krefeld-Gellep, far from any obvious ecclesiastical site, and the warrior-chieftain buried at Morken, also in the Rhineland, lay within the ruins of a Roman villa, below a later church, but seemingly unconnected with it. Old habits died hard in the aristocratic barbarian world. Great warriors and their womenfolk must still be buried with grave goods appropriate to their station, long after accepting the Christian faith. Only gradually did burial in churches become the accepted way, and even then grave goods were not entirely abandoned.

Early Frankish settlements reveal a close relationship with late Roman communities,

RECONSTRUCTION OF THE DRESS and arms of Childeric (d. 481) on the basis of his grave-furniture, found at Tournai, Belgium (*left*).

RECONSTRUCTION OF THE DRESS, arms, and horse-equipment of a Frankish noble buried at Krefeld-Gellep: mid-sixth century (*right*).

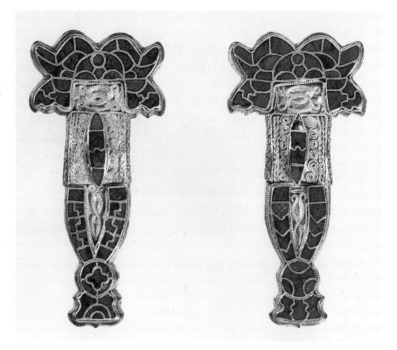

GOLD AND GARNET
JEWELLERY from a richly
furnished woman's grave
below Cologne cathedral: late
sixth century. This is probably
the interment of a royal
Frankish lady.

an unsurprising fact given the strength of many of those communities even in the fifth century. At Berry-au-Bac in Picardy, a Gallo-Roman rural site provided the focus for a group of Frankish *Grubenhäuser* and long halls, probably without any break in occupation. It has long been appreciated that Frankish cemeteries were frequently sited at or near Roman villas in north and central Gaul, giving way in turn to medieval villages centred on a Merovingian or Carolingian church. This suggests a sequence of late Roman villa estate, Frankish settlement and cemetery, and later village, an entirely plausible sequence. But it has not yet been fully revealed on any one site in its entirety. Later Frankish settlements are far from impressive in structure and layout. One of the most extensively examined, at Gladbach near Neuwied, consisted of a number of *Grubenhäuser* grouped around a rectangular hall. At Brebières in the Pas de Calais, a large series of *Grubenhäuser* of the sixth and seventh centuries was connected with various industrial activities and may have been subsidiary to the royal villa at Vitry-en-Artois near by. The residences of the Frankish nobility have not yet been certainly identified in the archaeological record. It is probable that they often lay within Roman towns and cities, thus making recognition a matter of hazard. Even in the countryside, it is clear that knowledge of Frankish settlement is far from representative.

A large tract of eastern Gaul was seized by the Burgundians early in the fifth century. This people had moved far to the west during the previous century, achieving a hold over the Main-Neckar area close to the Roman frontier. But the attraction of land in Gaul was strong and they took part in the mass crossing of the frozen Rhine at the end of 406 under their king Gundohar and settled around Worms, Speyer, and Strasbourg. In 435 they sought to expand their holding by moving north-west into Gallia Belgica, but were pushed back by the Roman commander Aëtius. Later, a Burgundian army, still under Gundohar, was surrounded by invading Huns and destroyed. This disaster effectively ended Burgundian expansion in Gaul, but it led to the Burgundian name being enshrined in later European legend. It provided the germ for the epic poem the *Niebelungenlied*, which beneath a chivalric veneer recounts a confusion of several stories which have their roots in this time of Germanic expansion west of the Rhine.

The Burgundians were still significant enough to earn the status of federates in 443. This gave them a new area of settlement in Sapaudia, south-western Switzerland, and the adjacent parts of France, where they could assist in controlling access to Italy through the Alpine passes. They fulfilled their obligations as federates by fighting against the Huns in 451 and the Suevi in Spain 456. The final collapse of Roman authority in Gaul allowed them to extend towards the Rhône so that they eventually held much of the land between that river and the Alps. But this was the height of their power. They could not withstand the expanding realm of the Franks and soon dwindled in importance, leaving little more than the name of Burgundy on the map of France.

Northern Gaul also received incoming Saxons, a fact often forgotten, chiefly because until recently little archaeological evidence for their presence had appeared. Around Bayeux in Normandy the *Saxones Baiocassini* were established and are twice mentioned

HUN BRONZE CAULDRON,
found at Törtel, Hungary:
fifth century.

by Gregory of Tours. Saxon pottery and metalwork is now increasingly being recognized in the Calvados, for instance in the cemeteries at Giberville and Sannerville. Other Saxons settled in the Somme basin and in the Pas de Calais, and here too their graves are appearing, as at Nouvien-en-Pontieu. Another group had ventured to the west coast of Gaul and settled around the mouth of the Loire. By the late sixth century, these northerners had been absorbed in the culture of Merovingian Gaul.

The Alamanni

The Alamanni did not move towards the Rhine and Danube in strength for some time after the Roman frontier was given up in 260. By about 300, however, groups of settlers were occupying land between the Black Forest and the upper Danube, and before long Alamanni were attacking the upper Rhine valley and eastern Gaul. The emperor Julian campaigned against them in the 350s, defeating them several times, most resoundingly near Strasbourg in 357. They remained a formidable threat to Gaul none the less, and they took part in the great invasion of New Year's Eve 406/7. The terrain which their main body occupied north of the Alps was not conducive to the creation of a unified power. Alamannic forces were usually commanded by more than one king or war-leader, and beneath these, in turn, *reguli* led the forces of lesser septs. The strongholds of these local chieftains are one of the most striking features of the archaeology of Alaman-nic territory. The expansion of the Franks drew closer and closer bonds around the Ala-

GRAVE-VAULT of an Alamannic noble at Gammertingen, Germany: *c.* AD 570 (*left*).

RECONSTRUCTION OF THE GRAVE-FURNITURE of a young Alamannic noble lady at Bülach, Germany: *c.* AD 650 (*right*).

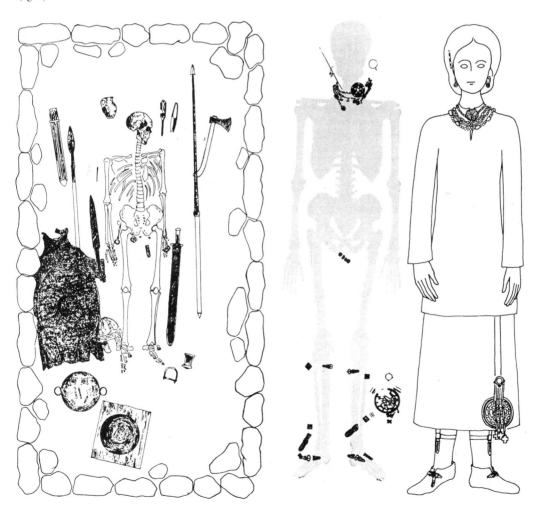

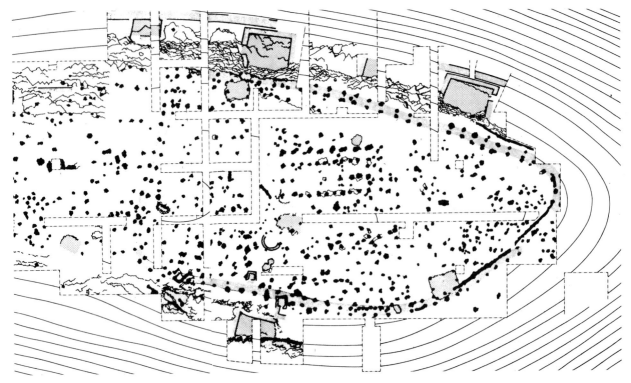

THE ALAMANNIC HILL-TOP STRONGHOLD at the Runder Berg, near Urach, Germany: fourth/fifth century AD.

manni, who thus looked southward to the Alpine valleys and Bavaria for their future. From here they were still able to raid Gaul, Italy, and the upper Danube lands. By 500 they were in control of the best land around the northern Alps, compensation for their exclusion from the Rhineland by Clovis. The lure of Italy was felt by the Alamanni, but they were not strong enough to invade in such numbers as to be able to seize territory there. During the sixth century, the eastern Franks exerted increasing authority over them until eventually Charles Martel took Alamannia into his empire early in the eighth century.

The sites of several major Alamannic strongholds are now known in south-west Germany, the most fully examined being that on the Runder Berg near Urach. This hilltop, only 70 metres by 50 metres at its widest, was girt by a massive timber rampart about AD 300, enclosing many timber buildings of the fourth century. Other structures lay on the lower slopes of the hill, perhaps housing craftsmen under the control of the chieftain who resided here. Other similar strongholds existed at the Gelbe Burg near Dittenheim and the Reissberg near Bamberg. Probably a high proportion of the lesser settlements lie under medieval and modern villages, so that the pattern of settlement as known at present is not representative, as in Frankish Gaul. Some of the old Roman rural sites attracted Alamannic settlers. The villas at Holheim and Praunheim were partially rebuilt by their new masters, and at Baldingen Roman gold coins and a military brooch may be relics of Alamanni who had served in the Roman provinces, or raided them successfully. Alamannic troops in the service of Rome are clearly in evidence at Neuburg on the upper Danube from about 330 onward.

The Vandals

The Vandal invasion of the Empire followed a different pattern from the others. After crossing the Rhine at the close of 406, the Vandals passed through Gaul, reaching the Pyrenees in less than three years. They then swept into Spain, accompanied by Suevi and Alans, and found there rich lands inadequately defended. After a long revel in the peninsula, several Vandal groups came together in southern Spain and briefly established a kingdom in which brigandage and sea piracy were major providers of wealth. The good harbours of Andalusia encouraged adventures across the straits; when even the wealth of Baetica began to fail, the immense resources of Africa sent out an irresistible allure. In May 428, a huge fleet was assembled, manned by Vandals and Alans under the command of Geiseric (or Genseric), one of the most able and ruthless of all barbarian kings. A war-leader of towering authority, he was also a politician of considerable skill, described by Procopius long after his death as the cleverest of men. The Vandal army may have numbered about 20,000 fighting men, as we are reliably informed that the total number who crossed the straits was 80,000. The Roman forces in Africa should have been capable of dealing with an enemy of this size, attacking from the sea. But they were poorly led and never got a chance to deploy in strength against the invaders. From the moment when the Vandals landed around Tangier, serious opposition failed to materialize. The Vandal sweep eastward was breathtaking in its speed and devastating in its effects. Within two years, only three major cities in the coastal belt still held out against them. The invaders did not have to waste time looking for supplies in this rich land. All their energies could be directed towards the seizure of towns and territory. Resisted by few urban garrisons, the Vandals were in full control of the provinces of Mauretania and Numidia in two years. All Rome could do was to offer a *foedus* and hope they would be content with what they already had. But Geiseric wanted more and attacked the wealthy province of Africa, taking Carthage with ease in 439. This gave him a base from which to threaten Italy, and in 440 a Vandal force invaded Sicily. Rome bought off Geiseric with another *foedus* and the Vandals settled back to enjoy the fruits of their north African conquests.

The bulk of the Vandal settlers were probably based around Carthage from 440, although others occupied the fertile land around Cherchel and Tipasa and the plain about the fortress-rock of Constantine. There were widespread confiscations of Roman land and possessions, but many landowners were left in relative peace and some elements of Roman administration were preserved. Some of the leading Vandals even adopted the easy lifestyle and tastes of Roman landed proprietors. But there was still a marked gulf between the mass of Vandal settlers and the provincials. Vandal rule in

Africa was enforced by armed might, and opportunities to raid widely for plunder were usually seized, as in 455 when Spain and Italy were ravaged and Rome itself was sacked. Although the Vandal kingdom is poorly recorded by largely hostile sources, it was patently not the home of a humane and forward-looking regime. Its end came quickly. The Byzantines invaded Africa in 533 and within a few months Vandal power had been shattered for ever.

The Northern Peoples

The peoples of the northern coastlands had long been raiding Gaul and Britain before migration of settler-groups began about AD 400. They included the Frisians of northern Holland, the Saxons of the lower Elbe and Weser region, the Angles of Schleswig, and others from the Jutland peninsula. The stimulus to migration is frequently identified as a worsening of conditions for settlement in the coastal areas, the rising level of the sea rendering wide stretches of land uncultivable. This may have played its part, but an increase of population may have been at least as potent a factor. And the northern peoples will not have been unaware of the increasing difficulties faced by Rome in maintaining her defences in lower Germany and Britain. The name of the Saxons figures most prominently in our written sources, but it is likely that this was a name applied to any raider or migrant who came across the northern seas. The political organization of these peoples is very poorly known. There is no sign that any of them was a strongly centralized power, and the names of their leaders are shadowy at best, if not entirely mythical. The Saxons and others who migrated to Britain and Gaul arrived there as war bands and small settler-groups, only slowly developing as political units after their arrival. This was, then, not a movement like that of the Visigoths or the Vandals, or of the Lombards later, but a piecemeal shift of population over a lengthy period of time, perhaps as long as two centuries. The loose structure of the Saxons continued throughout the fifth century, both in Britain and the north German homeland. This century was a time of considerable change in the coastal regions. Many settlements were given up and never reoccupied. The large cremation cemeteries which provide much of our information on the culture of these people frequently came to an end in the first half of the fifth century; others begin before 500 and continue for three centuries or more. A significant reorganization of population was clearly taking place in response to a number of pressures.

The heartland of the Saxons is usually taken to be the lower valleys of the Elbe and Weser, where some of the best known of their cemeteries have been found. But they extended westward towards Holland and southward towards central Germany. They were in contact with the most important neighbouring peoples, with the Franks of the Rhineland and the Thuringians to the south. The cemetery at Liebenau, near Nienburg in the Weser valley, contains both Frankish metalwork and glass and brooches from Thuringia, relics perhaps of intermarriage as well as of commerce. The Liebenau cemetery is the most fully examined of recent years and is of particular interest as it was continuously used from the early fifth century to the mid-ninth. Pagan burial practices were predominant until the eighth century. They included the separate burial of horses, presumably the mounts of leading warriors. Christian burials without grave goods do not appear before the time of Widukind's baptism in 785, and even afterwards graves could still contain objects for the next world.

The continental Saxons remained a powerful people throughout the sixth and seventh centuries. But like others east of the Rhine they could not withstand the Franks and were finally subjected by Charlemagne in the late eighth century. Their Frisian neigh-

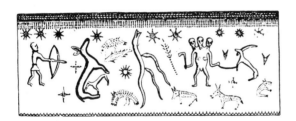

DESIGNS on one of the gold horns from Gallehus, Jutland, Denmark: *c.* AD 400.

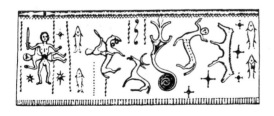

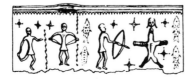

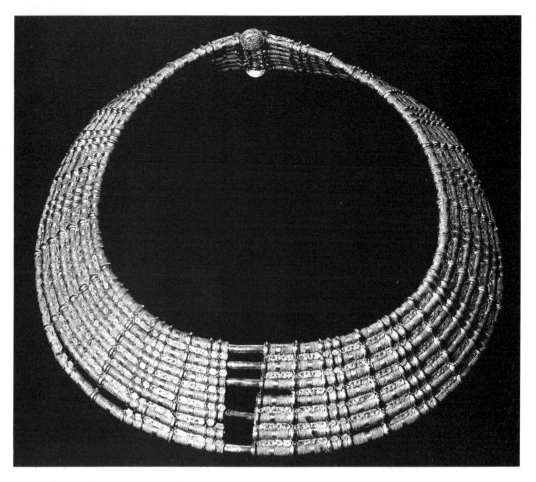

GOLD COLLAR from Möne, Sweden: fifth century.

bours were far less formidable in war, but found an outlet for their energies and sea-manship in the development of a trading network in the northern seas. In this enterprise they were to build a considerable reputation in the following centuries.

The western Baltic lands retained their importance as a centre of power and wealth in the migration period, without receiving intrusions of people from outside the region to any marked extent. The land was productive and what it offered could be exchanged for gold from the eastern Roman world. The stream of gold which reached southern Sweden and the Baltic islands of Gotland and Öland, in particular, was probably partly fed by booty and subsidies paid by Byzantine emperors to the eastern peoples. Those who received the gold in Scandinavia turned it into brooches, spiral rings, magnificent collars, and other ornaments. The largest hoard of the period, from Tureholm in Söder-manland, weighed 12 kilograms of pure gold, while a single ring found at Trolleberg weighs 1.25 kilograms. The Golden Age of Scandinavia is not a misnomer.

Connections between the western Baltic and other parts of Europe, including the

Roman world, were maintained into the migration period. A major centre of trade has long been suspected on the island of Fyn, in the area of Gudme. A rich concentration of precious metal objects was noted here in the nineteenth century and this has been enlarged by recent finds. Many late Roman coins arrived here, along with silver plate, brooches, and other ornaments. The area over which these objects have been found covers 200 hectares, within which a number of settled areas have been located. The emerging picture is of a centre of power which was able to attract portable wealth in great quantity and redistribute it widely in the western Baltic region. This could only be achieved by moving goods by sea and it is not chance that Gudme lies only five kilometres from the coast. There, a port site is known at Lundeborg which has produced further rich finds of Roman imports and migration-period metalwork, including one of the largest gold hoards ever recorded from Denmark. The Gudme and Lundeborg complex may well prove to be a forerunner of the well-known emporia of later centuries, such as Dorestad and Quentovic in the west and Hedeby and Birka in the north.

The peoples of Scandinavia were not well known to the literate Mediterranean world and even the names of the principal groupings are poorly recorded. The most powerful were the Svear (or Sviar) of Uppland in central Sweden and the Gotar to the south of them. A multiplicity of small units may have occupied southern Sweden, where fortified sites exist in their hundreds from the migration period onward. Most of these were small strongholds, surrounded by a single stone wall, one of the largest forts, Gråborg on Öland, being 210 metres across and boasting a wall up to nine metres high. The most completely excavated of these sites, Eketorps Borg also on Öland, was originally a refuge in the late fourth century, but was transformed in the migration period into a highly organized and well-planned settlement, its whole layout indicative of a strong localized authority which was able to dominate the surrounding territory for a lengthy period.

There were centres of much greater power in southern Sweden. At Gamla Uppsala (Old Uppsala), a short distance to the north of the modern city, lie three huge mounds along with hundreds of smaller mounds nearby. Graves excavated within two of the large monuments date to about 500 in one case and half a century later in the other. These are reasonably certainly burials of the ruling dynasty of the Svear, the Ynglingas, known from both Norse and English traditions. The central mound at Gamla Uppsala, not yet excavated, may mark the grave of the founder of the dynasty, Aun, who died in the fifth century. A few miles north of Uppsala is the site of Vendel, where another huge mound still stands, the mound of Ottar, a son of Aun who fell in battle. The date of this structure is uncertain, but it has produced a gold coin of the fifth century. At least one other major political centre in Sweden seems to be identifiable from surviving grave monuments. At Badelunda on the shore of Lake Mälar is a group of large ship-shaped monuments in stone, overlooked by a mound still 15 metres high. Until well into the medieval period, this was the site of a 'Thing' or political assembly.

Two richly furnished cemeteries of the later sixth and seventh centuries, at Vendel and Valsgärde, give some impression of the wealth and external connections of the ruling houses of this part of the northern world. The Vendel graves are ship burials, lying in a group near to the medieval church. Richly ornamented swords, shields, helmets, horsegear, and personal possessions accompanied these members of chieftainly families to the next world, along with horses and dogs sacrificed at their funerals.

Contacts between Scandinavia and a much wider world are still more marked between 500 and 700. East Roman coinage flooded into the Baltic Islands, especially Gotland and Öland. Issues of late fifth-century emperors are commoner on Öland and

BRONZE HELMET, based ultimately on late Roman models, from Vendel, Sweden: early seventh century.

Bornholm, of later rulers on Gotland. The great majority occur in hoards, buried during disturbed times in the sixth century. On the Swedish mainland the Byzantine coins are less frequent, but there is an important concentration at Helgö on Lake Mälär. Sites at Helgö were occupied from the late Roman Iron Age to the Middle Ages and their significance and economic basis altered over that long period. In the period 500–700 this was a major centre of trading activity, imports being received from many parts of Europe and beyond. Glass came in from the Frankish realm, metalwork from several areas of western Europe, fine bronzework from the Mediterranean, a bronze figure of the Buddha from northern India, and a bishop's crozier from eighth-century Ireland. What agency lay behind this astonishingly varied long-distance traffic is not yet satisfactorily explained. Connections with a seat of power are obviously to be looked for, but are still elusive. Helgö was not simply a reception point for exotic imports. Manufacture, especially of metal goods, was carried out here for local markets, and other activities, which leave no archaeological trace behind, were probably also pursued. A cult-centre may also be in question, the Irish crozier being perhaps a relic of a Christian mission to the north. Much is still unexplained about Helgö. All that is certain is that its functions were complex.

The Sixth-Century Migrations

The sixth century saw major invasions from western Russia and from the steppes further east. About 550, the nomad horsemen known as the Avars appeared in the Caucasus and, with the encouragement of the Byzantine emperor, began to attack the peoples of the Black Sea coasts. They quickly moved westward and in the 560s reached the middle Danube, filling the void left by the dispersal of the Gepids. When the Lombards moved south into Italy, the Avars had a free hand to enlarge their sphere of operations and they quickly dominated the middle Danube region, even extending north into the Elbe basin. The power of the Avars was to endure into the early seventh century, but the rising power of the day, the Slavs, was to replace them as the dominant force in east and central Europe.

   The origins of the Slavs are shrouded in uncertainty, made all the more impenetrable by modern interpretations which owe more to political ideology than to dispassionate scholarship. Earlier notions of a Slav genesis within a limited area have now been generally abandoned, though they are still made to appear in some accounts fully formed from the Pripyet Marshes. More plausibly, the Slavs, the *Sclaveni* of Byzantine sources, were an amalgam of cultural groups based between the Dnestr and Dnepr in the east and the Vistula and Oder in the west during the late fifth and earlier sixth centuries. They certainly had links with the Baltic peoples to the north and various Germanic groups to the west. Their movement westward and southward was facilitated by the advance of Germanic peoples into the Danube lands. Within a short time of their recognition in our written sources, Slav settlers had entered Bohemia, passed from there down the Elbe

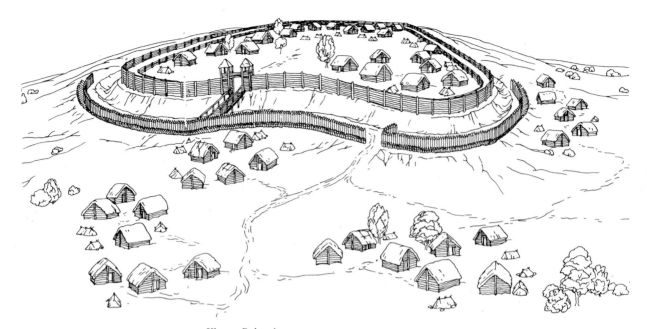

THE SLAV HILL-FORT at Klucov, Bohemia.

valley, extended north into Poland and eastern Germany, and south into the Balkans by way of Bulgaria. Further expansion into western Europe seemed inevitable, but the Frankish advance east of the Rhine brought it to a stop. The Slavs did hold on to the northern Balkans, though their occupation of Greece was ended by the Byzantines in the ninth century. So widespread a dispersal of population inevitably ended in the emergence of numerous Slav states rather than the more unified powers of Germanic Europe.

Among the most shadowy of the migrant peoples were the Gepids, not least because they failed to achieve a permanent settlement either within or outside the Empire. They were early associated with the Goths and may have had similarly mixed origins. They failed to take possession of land in Dacia when it was given up by Rome, and later settled north of that province, to the east of the river Tisza, and remained there until made subject to the Ostrogoths in the fifth century. Their fighting strength was later placed at the disposal of the Huns, the Gepids being close allies of Attila in his invasions of the Balkans and Gaul. But after Attila's death they took a leading part in the revolt against his successors, which broke up the Hun empire. They briefly took hold of the Carpathian basin, but their old opponents the Ostrogoths ejected them and thereafter they failed to find a secure home. The rise of Lombard power in Pannonia was their final undoing. The Gepids were driven out and dispersed after 540; those who hung on were subdued by the invading Avars twenty years later. After that, their name survived but the people disappeared.

The Langobardi or Lombards had long occupied the lower and middle Elbe valley, but had played relatively little part in the invasions of the Roman world before the fifth century. In the 480s, they moved south into northern Austria, and a generation later crossed the Danube to settle in Pannonia, there to become a force to be reckoned with. Under their king Wacho early in the sixth century they maintained friendly relations with Byzantium and with the Franks by means of diplomatic marriages with the royal house. In 552 a Lombard force took part in the last Byzantine campaign against the Goths in Italy. The attractions of the peninsula were not lost on them and at the same time their home in Pannonia was increasingly exposed to the Avars. The new Lombard king, Alboin, decided that the future for his people lay in Italy. In 568 he led a large army towards the Adriatic, drawing in not only Lombards, but also Pannonians, Noricans, Sarmatians, Gepids, and even Bulgars. Behind them, the Avars swept into Pannonia and the Slavs into the northern Balkans. The Lombard army enjoyed a swift success in north-

BELT-MOUNTS OF SLAV-AVAR TYPE from Pohorelice and Dolni Dunajovice, Moravia, and Nove Zamky and Prsa, Slovakia: late sixth/seventh century.

ern Italy. Within a year many of the northern cities were in their hands, along with much of the fertile valley of the Po. The Byzantines and their allies hung on with difficulty to a dwindling number of strongholds, but the Lombards were confident enough to leave them and continue their advance southward, into Tuscany and later to Rome. The land of Italy still offered considerable riches to an invader. The cities made desirable bases for their leaders and there were still productive estates to be plundered. The Lombards had not entered Italy under the terms of a *foedus* but as invaders, and for thirty years they behaved accordingly. No regular system of government was instituted in place of that which they had themselves destroyed. Lombard administration was itself quickly devolved upon a number of military leaders or duces, Alboin and his successor being murdered only a few years after the invasion. The central monarchy was restored in 584, but the military organization of the conquerors remained in place as the administrative framework of the kingdom. The Roman landed order had been largely destroyed and its territory taken by the new masters of Italy. This was much more of a Germanic kingdom than that over which Theoderic had ruled.

The re-establishment of the monarchy led to the consolidation of Lombard power in the north and its extension southward. The principal areas of Lombard settlement, as revealed by cemeteries and place-names, lay north of the river Po, between Piedmont and Friuli. South of the great valley the cemeteries extend thinly to the Romagna hills, but hardly beyond. Some of these can be related to seventh-century land-taking. This is true of the two large cemeteries of Nocera Umbra and Castel Trosino in the duchy of Spoleto. Both were associated with hilltop strongholds in commanding positions. Nocera Umbra contains the graves of several warriors of high rank, charged with the

RECONSTRUCTION OF THE HORSE-GEAR found in a richly furnished Gepid burial at Apahida, Romania: mid-fifth century.

task of guarding the road which linked Ravenna and Rome. Castel Trosino presents a picture of a more mixed community, one in which women's jewellery was recognizably influenced by contemporary Roman and Byzantine fashion. Even in the seventh century barbarians could not escape all influence from Rome.

In the north of Italy several old cities played a significant part in the Lombard kingdom. One of these was Cividale in the north-east, a small town but a favoured early centre. One of the cemeteries outside the town contains graves of men and women who almost certainly took part in the invasion of 568. Another, at the Church of San Stephano, was used as a burial place by a noble Lombard family about 600, by which time they had apparently embraced the Christian faith. There were other noble burials within the walls of Cividale, including one within a church which was probably the grave of a military leader. This kind of noble interment must also be expected at cities like Milan, Verona, and Brescia.

Relations between the Lombards and the Italian population are a complex and much-debated matter. The Roman population of Italy has little voice in the records of the period, but it was clearly not exterminated nor expelled. In the areas under direct Lombard control there appears to have been a fairly effective mingling of barbarian and Roman, which shows itself occasionally in the products of craftsmen and in loan-words. Many of the Lombard loan-words in Italian are of rather humdrum things, while the Lombards seem to have given up their own language by the end of the seventh century, suggesting a fairly rapid integration with the surviving provincials. Lombard nobles who had their seats in the old cities of Italy can hardly have avoided association with the remaining Roman families, even if they wanted to. The Elbe valley, if it was remembered at all, must have seemed a long way off.

From Prehistory to Medieval Europe

It is customary to look for the origins of medieval Europe in the late Roman Empire and the successor kingdoms. The wider contribution of the barbarian peoples to the emergence of later European states must not be underestimated. From the minor tribes settled east of the Rhine came the ancestors of the Franks, the most powerful of the peoples who succeeded to the authority of Rome in western Europe. The motley groups which migrated from northern Germany and Scandinavia would, in due course, create a Germanic culture in Britain which was to deliver the writings of Bede, the *Beowulf* poem, the Lindisfarne Gospels, and the splendours of Sutton Hoo to the European heritage. This is all a long way from the cultural strivings which the earlier chapters of this book record. But there can be no doubt about the continuity of endeavour which is revealed over these many centuries. The divisions which are still widely observed in modern scholarship dissolve in the confluence of the two great streams of barbarian and classical Europe.

Throughout the period under consideration, scarcely any part of barbarian Europe lay entirely beyond contact with the late Roman Empire. The more venturesome, or the more desperate, of the barbarian peoples settled within the remains of that Empire, with varying degrees of success and permanence. The very varied experience of migration and settlement met with by those peoples will be clear from the preceding pages. Some, like the Vandals and Suevi, crossed into the Roman provinces as invaders and adventurers. Some, like the Visigoths, arrived virtually as refugees seeking a new homeland and suffered long hardships before finding it. Others, including some of the early Franks and Alamanni, came first to join the Roman frontier armies, to be followed by others who saw the door to wealth and power swinging open. And there was one people, Theoderic's Ostrogoths, who took their place at the seat of power as a unified force and with the sanction of an emperor.

The great migrations were a complex business. The image of immense hordes tumbling into the Roman world one after another, pushed forward by the Huns and others, must be discarded once and for all. The detailed motivations were various, as were the means of accommodation in new homes. Many of the major migrations were by peoples settled on or close to the Roman frontiers, peoples with long experience of the Empire in one way or another. Analogies with relations between advanced states of the twentieth century and the Third World are not wholly inapposite. Along the extended frontiers of the Rhine and Danube, long contact between Roman and barbarian had brought into being frontier societies which were neither fully Roman nor wholly barbarian. These are most clearly in evidence on the lower Rhine and the upper and middle Danube. The frontier systems of the earlier Empire had greatly altered by the fourth century, and not merely in the character of their fortifications. On the Rhine there emerged a mixed culture of provincial and Germanic elements which was to provide a basis for the culture of the Franks in the fifth century. On the middle Danube, on territory which had witnessed political and diplomatic relations between Roman and barbarian over two centuries at least, a frontier society can be distinguished as early as the third century, in the free circulation of Roman objects of all kinds and in the presence of buildings of Roman style well north of the frontier. Lower down the Danube, commercial and cultural exchange was freely conducted with the inhabitants of the abandoned province of Dacia and the adjacent lands. Frontier societies are known elsewhere in the late Roman Empire, in north Africa and in northern Britain for example, but nowhere else would they play a more historically important part in bringing barbarian and Roman together than on the Rhine and Danube. Behind all this lay the long development of barbarian Europe, drawing on many springs of cultural innovation and never wholly isolated from the peoples of the Mediterranean and the steppe. Those relationships would continue to shape Europe until well into the Middle Ages.

FURTHER READING

1. *The Peopling of Europe*

Interdisciplinary studies are the hallmark of research into the earliest occupation of Europe. Recent overviews which draw the threads together can be found in Clive Gamble, *The Palaeolithic Settlement of Europe* (Cambridge, 1986), and chs. 2 and 3 in the comprehensive survey by Tim Champion, Clive Gamble, Stephen Shennan, and Alasdair Whittle, *Prehistoric Europe* (London, 1984). Graham Richards, *Human Evolution* (London, 1987); Robin Dennell, *European Economic Prehistory* (London, 1983); and Richard Klein, *The Human Career* (Chicago, 1989), provide a longer time-depth on human origins by reviewing the African and Asian evidence that sets the scene for the colonization of the European peninsula. Regional and indeed national overviews are cited in, for example, Derek Roe, *The Lower and Middle Palaeolithic Periods in Britain* (London, 1981). Interpretation and controversy can be found in many edited volumes of which Paul Mellars and Chris Stringer (eds.), *The Human Revolution* (Edinburgh, 1989) and Paul Mellars (ed.), *The Emergence of Modern Humans: An Archaeological Perspective* (Edinburgh, 1991) contain the current debates about fossils and artefacts.

Medieval cave-persons are illustrated by John Friedman, *The Monstrous Races in Medieval Art and Thought* (Cambridge, Mass., 1981), while the expulsion of the Neanderthals from human ancestry and the manœuvring between research schools, which precipitated it in the early years of this century, is dealt with by Michael Hammond, 'The Expulsion of the Neanderthals from Human Ancestry: Marcellin Boule and the Social Context of Scientific Research', *Social Studies Science*, 12 (1982), 1–36. The progress of nineteenth-century research is provided by Donald Grayson, *The Establishment of Human Antiquity* (London, 1983).

The excavation and study of cave sites and stone tools and the way the results have been built into different views of the Palaeolithic can be found in Gamble, *The Palaeolithic Settlement*, chs. 1, 4 and 5; a lively account by François Bordes, *A Tale of Two Caves* (New York, 1972); and Lewis Binford's important work, *In Pursuit of the Past* (London, 1983). Harold Dibble argues a different view of shape changes in stone tools in *The Human Revolution*.

The climatic frameworks which have now been overhauled in the light of the deep-sea record are traced in Gamble, *The Palaeolithic Settlement*, ch. 3; John and Katherine Imbrie, *Ice Ages Solving the Mystery* (London, 1979); Anthony Sutcliffe, *On the Track of Ice Age Mammals* (London, 1986). The role of climate in forcing early humans out of Africa and into Europe is now keenly debated by Clive Gamble, *Timewalkers, the Prehistory of Global Colonisation* (Harmondsworth, 1992), and Brian Fagan, *The Journey from Eden* (London, 1991); while the fossils involved are described in Michael Day's authoritative *Guide to Fossil Man* (London, 1986), and in many of the papers in Mellars and Stringer, *The Human Revolution* and Klein's *Human Career*. Martin Aitken, *Science-based Dating in Archaeology* (London, 1990), charts an understandable course through this vital but sometimes baffling area.

Piltdown continues to fascinate like an unsolved Agatha Christie mystery, Frank Spencer, *Piltdown, a Scientific Forgery* (Oxford, 1990). In my opinion it was Chipper the goose that did it! Look at his photos in this book, hungry for the limelight; something very shifty about his beak. Honest fossils have just as many volumes and papers. None more so than the Neanderthals and what became of them, Chris Stringer and Clive Gamble, *The Neanderthals* (London, 1992); E. Trinkaus and W. W. Howells, 'The Neanderthals', *Scientific American*, 241 (1979), 118–33; and see Mellars and Stringer, *The Human Revolution*.

To gain some insight into recent research about the geographical scale of these early groups I suggest, for raw materials, Wil Roebroeks *et al.*, 'Planning Depth, Anticipation and the Organization of Middle Palaeolithic Technology: The "Archaic Natives" Meet Eve's Descendants', *Helinium*, 28 (1988), 17–34 and for camp-sites Jan Simek, 'Spatial Order and Behavioural Change in the French Palaeolithic', *Antiquity*, 61 (1987), 25–40. For an insight into living areas, or lack of them, look at Paul Callow and Jean Cornford, *La Cotte de St. Brelade* (Norwich, 1986), and Richard Klein, *Ice-Age Hunters of the Ukraine* (Chicago, 1973). The contrasts in the archaeology of the Pioneer phase continue with Philip Allsworth-Jones, *The Szeletian and the Transition from Middle to Upper Palaeolithic in Central Europe* (Oxford, 1986); Paul Mellars, 'A New Chronology for the French Mousterian Period', *Nature*, 322 (1986), 410–11; Robert Gargett's criticisms of Neanderthal burials, 'Grave Shortcomings: The Evidence for Neanderthal Burial', *Current Anthropology*, 30 (1989), 157–77; Philip Chase and Harrold Dibble's investigation of evidence for symbolic behaviour, which sees the demise of bear cults, 'Palaeolithic Symbolism: A Review of the Current Evidence and Interpretations', *Journal of Anthropological Archaeology*, 6 (1987), 263–96; and Iain Davidson and William Noble's discussion of this lack of symbolic behaviour in terms of language origins, 'The Archaeology of Perception: Traces of Depiction and Language', *Current Anthropology*, 30 (1989), 125–55. For an alternative view see Alexander Marshack, 'Early Hominid Symbol and the Evolution of the Human Capacity', in *The Emergence of Human Behaviour*.

Further discussion about the differences the archaeological evidence points to in types of organization and society can be found in Olga Soffer (ed.), *The Pleistocene Old World* (New York, 1987), see ch. by Clive Gamble on 'Man the Shoveller'; Mary Stiner's discussion on Middle Palaeolithic food management strategies, 'A Taphonomic Perspective on the Origins of the Faunal Remains of Grotta Guattari (Latium, Italy)', *Current Anthropology*, 32 (1991), 103–17; and Robert Whallon's contribution on language and colonization in Mellars and Stringer, *The Human Revolution*.

2. *The Upper Palaeolithic Revolution*

The Upper Palaeolithic is not particularly well covered in general textbooks. Probably the best general account is provided in Clive Gamble, *The Palaeolithic Settlement of Europe* (Cambridge, 1986), which sets current perspectives on the European Upper Palaeolithic firmly within the context of more general theoretical approaches to the study of pre-agricultural communities. Rather briefer, but very stimulating accounts, are provided in John Pfeiffer, *The Emergence of Man* (London, 1972) and in Evan Hadingham, *Secrets of the Ice Age* (London, 1980). Some of the earlier textbooks, such as François Bordes, *The Old Stone Age* (London, 1968) and John Coles and Eric Higgs, *The Archaeology of Early Man* (London, 1969) are still very useful for accounts of the general technological succession in the Upper Palaeolithic and (in the case of the latter book) for specific details of some of the major sites. A more 'popular' survey (in French) has recently been provided by Gerhard Bosinski, *Homo Sapiens* (Paris, 1990).

Most of the principal monographs on the Upper Palaeolithic are concerned with the material from specific regions. Denise de Sonneville-Bordes, *Le Paléolithique Supérieur en Périgord* (Bordeaux, 1960) still stands as the most authoritative general account of the 'classic' Upper Palaeolithic sequence in the Périgord and adjacent areas of south-west France. For the central European material we have a range of major monographs: Phillip Allsworth-Jones, *The Szeletian and the Transition from Middle to Upper Palaeolithic in Central Europe* (Oxford, 1986); Joachim Hahn, *Aurignacien* (Cologne, 1977); and Marcel Otte, *Le Gravettien en Europe Centrale* (Bruges, 1981). Further to the East, the Upper Palaeolithic sequence in European Russia has been very fully surveyed in Olga Soffer, *The Upper Palaeolithic of the Central Russian Plain* (Orlando, Fla., 1985), and in two earlier studies by Richard Klein, *Man and Culture in the Late Pleistocene: a Case Study* (San Francisco, 1969) and *Ice-Age Hunters of the Ukraine* (Chicago, 1973) — all, happily, in English, and providing rich and well-illustrated details of the remarkable living structures documented in these regions. The rather sparse evidence for Upper Palaeolithic occupation in Britain is surveyed, in great detail, in John Campbell, *The Upper Palaeolithic of Britain* (Oxford, 1977).

The subject of Upper Palaeolithic art has generated a range of monographs over the past fifty years. Early studies, such as Abbé Breuil, *Quatre cents siècles d'art pariétal* (Montignac, 1952) and Paolo Graziozi, *Palae-olithic Art* (London, 1960) still remain in many ways classic sources, and well worth consulting both for their illustrations and for full accounts of some of the earlier interpretations of the general significance of the art. The most important recent study is André Leroi-Gourhan, *The Art of Prehistoric Man in Western Europe* (London, 1968), which provides not only a wealth of illustrations, but also a full account of his highly con-troversial 'sexual symbolism' interpretations for the art. A shorter account of the same ideas was provided more recently by the same author in *The Dawn of European Art* (Cambridge, 1982). More general studies have been published by John Pfeiffer, *The Creative Explosion: an Inquiry into the Origins of Art and Religion* (New York, 1982) and by Paul Bahn and Jean Vertut, *Images of the Ice Age* (London, 1988)—the latter ac-companied by a range of superb new photographs of the art. The most concise historical survey of differing theoretical perspectives on the interpretation of the art is provided in Peter Ucko and Andrée Rosenfeld, *Palaeolithic Cave Art* (London, 1967); as a general textbook for students, this still remains the most balanced and wide-ranging survey of the whole topic of Palaeolithic art.

Most of the other studies of the Upper Palaeolithic are contained either in articles in a range of specialist journals (such as *L'Anthropologie, Current Anthropology, Proceedings of the Prehistoric Society, Antiquity*, etc.) or in edited conference proceedings. The thorny and highly controversial issues surrounding the origins of *Homo sapiens sapiens* populations, and the related emergence of Upper Palaeolithic cultural patterns, are dis-cussed at length—and from a variety of different theoretical perspectives—in two recent conference vol-umes: Paul Mellars and Chris Stringer (eds.), *The Human Revolution* (Edinburgh, 1989) and Erik Trinkaus (ed.), *The Emergence of Modern Humans: Biological Adaptations in the Later Pleistocene* (Cambridge, 1989). Many of the equally controversial issues of social and economic interpretation in the European Upper Palaeolithic are similarly dealt with in a number of papers in G. Bailey (ed.), *Hunter-Gatherer Economy in Prehistory: A European Perspective* (Cambridge, 1983) and in T. D. Price and J. A. Brown (eds.), *Prehistoric Hunter-Gatherers: The Emergence of Cultural Complexity* (Orlando, Fla., 1985). The problems of recon-structing the general environment of Upper Palaeolithic groups in the glacial landscapes of Europe are very well covered in Karl Butzer, *Environment and Archaeology* (Chicago, 1972) and (with special reference to the French sites) in Henri Laville, Jean-Philippe Rigaud, and James Sackett, *Rock Shelters of the Périgord* (Lon-don, 1980). Finally, some of the special challenges posed by the reconstruction of human behavioural pat-terns over the period of the last glacial maximum in Europe are dealt with (from a regional perspective) in the range of papers in Olga Soffer and Clive Gamble (eds.), *The World at 18,000 BP* (vol. i, *High Latitudes*) (London, 1990).

3. *The Mesolithic Age*

There is an ever-increasing and voluminous literature concerning the Mesolithic. Two very useful intro-ductions are the conference proceedings from the 1985 and 1990 'Mesolithic in Europe' international sym-posia: Clive Bonsall (ed.), *The Mesolithic in Europe* (Edinburgh, 1989) and Pierre M. Vermeersch and Phillip Van Peer (eds.), *Contributions to the Mesolithic in Europe* (Leuven, 1990). These have chapters covering many different sites throughout Europe, regional synthesis, and new analyses of material. They are excellently il-lustrated and the papers concerning the eastern European and Russian material are particularly valuable. An earlier series, Paul Mellars (ed.), *The Early Postglacial Settlement of Northern Europe* (London, 1978) also re-mains a useful collection. A further collection which is essential reading for the later Mesolithic and transi-tion to farming, is Marek Zvelebil (ed.), *Hunters in Transition* (Cambridge, 1986). P. Rowley-Conwy *et al.* (eds.), *Mesolithic North-West Europe: Recent Trends* (Sheffield, 1987) also provides a useful collection of pa-pers ranging from excavation and survey reports to the analysis of faunal assemblages and Mesolithic ceme-teries.

For the methods and results of environmental reconstruction, a very useful book is I. Simmons and M. Tooley, *The Environment in British Prehistory* (London, 1981). The first chapter 'Methods of Reconstruction' summarizes how information about past environments is derived from soils, molluscs, pollen, and plant macro-fossils while the third chapter, 'The Mesolithic' describes how these have been used to reconstruct the environment of the British Mesolithic, although much of it is relevant to northern Europe in general. For a broader European view of early post-glacial vegetation, B. Huntley, 'Europe' in B. Huntley and T. Webb, III (eds.), *Vegetation History* (Brentford, 1988) provides a recent and excellent synthesis.

As will be apparent from this chapter, southern Scandinavia is a particularly important region for Mesolithic studies and J. G. D. Clark's *The Earlier Stone Age Settlement of Scandinavia* (Cambridge, 1975) remains a useful introduction. Lars Larsson has provided an excellent recent synthesis, updating many aspects of Clark's study and indicating new research directions, in 'The Mesolithic of Southern Scandinavia', *Journal of World Prehistory,* 4 (1990), 257–309. Peter Rowley-Conwy, 'Sedentary Hunters: The Ertebolle Example', in G. Bailey (ed.), *Hunter-Gatherer Economy in Prehistory* (Cambridge, 1983), 111–26 provides an excellent case study for reconstructing subsistent-settlement systems and for recognizing the complexity of later Mesolithic societies. I provide a detailed study of Mesolithic hunting patterns in Scandinavia and how decision-making can be reconstructed in *Thoughtful Foragers: A Study of Prehistoric Decision Making* (Cambridge, 1990). An attempt to infer Mesolithic group size for Denmark using artefact distributions is O. Grøn, 'Seasonal Variation in Maglemosian Group Size and Structure. A New Model', *Current Anthropology,* 28 (1987), 303–27. There are three journals which carry most of the reports concerning new finds and analyses concerning the Mesolithic in southern Scandinavia: *The Journal of Danish Archaeology, KULM,* and *Meddelanden fran Lunds Universitets Historiska Museum.* For a speculative model concerning the process of culture change and discussion of complexity in Mesolithic southern Scandinavia, T. D. Price, 'Affluent Foragers of Mesolithic Southern Scandinavia' in T. D. Price and J. A. Brown (eds.), *Prehistoric Hunter-Gatherers: The Emergence of Cultural Complexity* (New York, 1985), 341–63.

Other regions of Europe have also been very well covered by syntheses of existing data. Paul Mellars' 'Settlement Patterns and Industrial Variability in the British Mesolithic' in G. de G. Sieveking *et al.* (eds.), *Problems in Economic and Social Archaeology* (London, 1976) provides a useful summary of the diversity of data, particularly in lithic assemblages in Britain. This is, however, increasingly out of date and a new synthesis of the British material is required. The Mellars chapter should be read with the chapter on the Mesolithic in Simmons and Tooley, *The Environment in Prehistory*, and the Star Carr reports referenced below. Rozoy provides a comprehensive, though very culture history oriented, summary of the data from France in 'Les Derniers Chasseurs', *Bulletin de la Société Archéologique Champenoise* (numéro special, 2 vols., 1988). For Mesolithic adaptations in Northern Spain and Pyrenean France, L. Straus, 'Epipaleolithic and Mesolithic Adaptations in Cantabrian Spain and Pyrenean France', *Journal of World Prehistory,* 5 (1991), 83–104 provides an excellent review. M. Jochim, 'The Late Mesolithic in Southwest Germany: Culture Change or Population Decline', in P. M. Vermeersch and P. Van Peer (eds.), *Contributions to the Mesolithic in Europe* (Leuven, 1990), 183–9, discusses several aspects of the Mesolithic and early postglacial environments in southwest Germany.

Many individual site reports could be noted for further reading. The classic work is J. G. D. Clark, *Excavations at Star Carr* (Cambridge, 1954), which should be followed by later studies which describe changing ideas about the Mesolithic and further analysis of the Star Carr material, notably J. G. D. Clark, *Star Carr: A Case Study in Bioarchaeology* (Addison-Wesley module in anthropology, 10, 1975) and A. J. Legge and P. Rowley-Conwy, *Star Carr Revisited* (London, 1988). For the Scandinavian sites one of the most useful and fascinating site reports is that of Agerod V by Lars Larsson, 'Agerod V: An Atlantic Bog Site in Central Scania', *Acta Archaeologica Lundensia* 8:12 (1983). This is a short report, clearly written and well illustrated giving an impression of the wealth of the Scandinavian sites and the quality of recent excavations. Three reports on sites in Denmark are particularly interesting: S. H. Andersen, 'Tybrind Vig', *Journal of Danish Archaeology,* 4 (1985), 52–69; S. H. Andersen, 'Ertebølle Revisited', *Journal of Danish Archaeology,* 5 (1986), 31–86, and

E. B. Petersen, 'Vaenget Nord: Excavation, Documentation and Interpretation of a Mesolithic Site at Ved-baek, Denmark', in C. Bonsall (ed.), *The Mesolithic in Europe* (Edinburgh, 1985), 325–30. For southern Europe, the report on Franchthi cave in several fascicles is essential reading: T. W. Jacobson (ed.), *Excavations at Franchthi Cave, Greece* (Bloomington, Ind., 1987 onwards). For the nature of small lithic scatters in the Norwegian highlands see S. Bang Andersen, 'Mesolithic Adaptations in the Southern Norwegian Highland', in C. Bonsall (ed.), *The Mesolithic in Europe* (Edinburgh, 1989), 338–50 and for the Polish site of Calowanie, R. Schild, 'The Formation of Homogeneous Occupation Units ('kschemenitsas') in Open-Air Sandy Sites and its Interpretation for Mesolithic Flint Assemblages', in C. Bonsall (ed.), *The Mesolithic in Europe* (Edinburgh, 1989), 89–98. Two volumes which illustrate the extremes of Mesolithic site types are D. Srejovic's volume on *Lepenski Vir* (London, 1972), which describes the remarkable rich material culture and complex settlements of the Danube, and P. Mellars, *Excavations on Oronsay* (Edinburgh, 1987), which describes the equally fascinating, but materially impoverished, Mesolithic shell middens on that small island. Related sites in the Hebrides, such as Bolsay Farm, are described in S. Mithen, 'Excavations at Bolsay Farm, a Mesolithic Settlement on Islay', *Cambridge Archaeological Journal*, 2, 241–52.

The above reports carry considerable information about the subject-areas covered in this chapter. For further reading concerning technology consult R. Jacobi, 'Britain Inside and Outside the European Mesolithic', *Proceedings of the Prehistoric Society*, 42 (1976), 67–84 for detailed discussion of chronological sequences and M. Pitts and R. Jacobi, 'Some Aspects of Change in the Flaked Stone Industries of the Mesolithic and Neolithic in Southern Britain', *Journal of Archaeological Science*, 6, 163–77 for a case-study concerning changing use of raw materials. B. Scar, 'The Scanian Maglemose Site of Bare Mosse II', *Acta Archaeologica* (1989), 87–104 and N. Barton, 'Vertical Distributions of Artefacts and some Post-depositional Factors Affecting Site Formation', in P. Rowley-Conwy *et al.* (eds.), *Mesolithic Northwest Europe, Recent Trends* (Sheffield, 1987), 55–62 provide useful case studies of refitting. A provocative discussion of the evolution of microlith technology in Britain is provided by A. Myers, 'Reliable and Maintainable Technological Strategies in the Mesolithic of Mainland Britain', in R. Torrence (ed.), *Time, Energy and Stone Tools* (Cambridge, 1989), 78–91. For an example of a functional study of microliths as arrowheads see J. Fris-Hansen, 'Mesolithic Cutting Arrows: Functional Analysis of Arrows used in the Hunting of Large Game', *Antiquity*, 64 (1990), 494–504, while D. Clarke's 'Mesolithic Europe: The Economic Basis', in G. de G. Sieveking *et al.* (eds.), *Problems in Economic and Social Archaeology* (London, 1976), 449–82 suggests alternative uses for microliths, such as tools for plant processing. An example of the stylistic analysis of microliths is given by H. P. Blankholm, 'Stylistic Analysis of Maglemosian Microlithic Armatures in Southern Scandinavia: An Essay', in P. M. Vermeersch and P. Van Peer (eds.), *Contributions to the Mesolithic in Europe* (Leuven, 1990), 239–57. A case-study of microwear analysis is given by J. Dumont, *A Microwear Analysis of Selected Artefact Types from Mesolithic Sites at Star Carr and Mount Sandel*, British Archaeological Reports, Oxford, 1988.

Four works providing additional examples of structural remains on Mesolithic sites: J. Coles, 'The Early Settlement of Scotland: Excavations at Morton, Fife', *Proceedings of the Prehistoric Society*, 37 (1971), 284–366; P. Woodman, *Excavations at Mount Sandel* (Belfast, 1985); E. Englestad, 'Mesolithic House Sites in Arctic Norway', in C. Bonsall (ed.), *The Mesolithic in Europe* (Edinburgh, 1989), 331–7; and J. Roche, 'Spatial Organisation in the Mesolithic of Muge, Portugal', in C. Bonsall (ed.), *The Mesolithic in Europe* (Edinburgh, 1989), 607–31.

The works referenced above concerning southern Scandinavia provide further reading concerning subsistence patterns. In addition there is a compilation of faunal remains from Europe in S. H. Andersen *et al.*, 'Making Cultural Ecology Relevant to Mesolithic Research, I, a Data Base of 413 Mesolithic Faunal Assemblages' and in P. M. Vermeersch and P. Van Peer (eds.), *Contributions to the Mesolithic in Europe* (Leuven, 1990), 23–51. A study of bird foraging is C. Grigson, 'Bird Foraging Patterns in the Mesolithic', in C. Bonsall (ed.), *The Mesolithic in Europe* (Edinburgh, 1989), 60–79. For studies of plant remains from Mesolithic sites see J. Hansen, *The Palaeoethnobotany of Franchthi Cave* (Bloomington, Ind., 1991) and J. Vaquer *et al.*, 'Mesolithic Plant Exploitation at the Balma Abeurador, (France)', *Oxford Journal of Archaeology*, 5 (1986), 1–8.

For the reconstruction of Mesolithic settlement patterns see P. Rowley-Conwy, 'Sedentary Hunters: the Ertebølle Example', in G. Bailey (ed.), *Hunter-Gatherer Economy in Prehistory* (Cambridge, 1983), 111–26; H. B. Bjerck, 'Mesolithic Site Types and Settlement Patterns at Vega, Northern Norway', *Acta Archaeologica*, 60 (1989), 1–32; and G. A. Clark, 'Site Functional Complementarity in the Mesolithic of Northern Spain', in C. Bonsall (ed.), *The Mesolithic in Europe* (Edinburgh, 1989), 589–603.

For Mesolithic cemeteries, three reports are particularly important reading: E. E. Albrethsen and E. B. Petersen, 'Excavation of a Mesolithic Cemetery at Vedbæk, Denmark', *Acta Archaeologica*, 47 (1976), 1–28, L. Larsson, 'The Skateholm Project—A late Mesolithic Settlement and Cemetery Complex', *Meddelanden fran Lunds Universitets Historiska Museum* (1983–4), 1–38; and J. O'Shea and M. Zvelebil, 'Oleneostrovski Mogilnik: Reconstructing the Social and Economic Organisation of Prehistoric Foragers in Northern Russia', *Journal of Anthropological Archaeology*, 3 (1984), 1–40. For an interpretation of this data with respect to social organization see G. A. Clark and M. Neeley, 'Social Differentiation in European Mesolithic Burial Data', in P. Rowley-Conwy *et al.* (eds.), *Mesolithic Northwest Europe: Recent Trends* (Sheffield, 1987). A fascinating paper on dog burial is L. Larsson, 'Dogs in Fraction—Symbols in Action', in P. M. Vermeersch and P. Van Peer (eds.), *Contributions to the Mesolithic in Europe* (Leuven, 1990), 153–60. A comprehensive survey of skeletal remains with respect to palaeopathology is R. Newell *et al.*, 'The Skeletal Remains of Mesolithic Man in Western Europe: An Evaluative Catalogue', *Journal of Human Evolution*, 8 (1976), 1–228.

Two works illustrate the use of artefacts to suggest social boundaries in Mesolithic Europe: P. Vang Petersen, 'Chronological and Regional Variation in the Late Mesolithic of Eastern Denmark', *Journal of Danish Archaeology*, 3 (1984), 7–18 and P. Gendel, *Mesolithic Social Territories in Northwest Europe*, BAR International Series, 218, Oxford.

For further reading on Mesolithic art, Azilian painted pebbles are discussed by C. Couaud, *L'Art Azilian, Origene—Survivance* (XX^c supplément à Gallia Préhistoire) (Paris, 1985), while a range of artefacts from southern Scandinavia have been described by L. Larsson, 'Mesolithic Antler and Bone Artefacts from Central Scania', *Meddelanden fran Lunds Universitets Historiska Museum* (1977–8), 28–67. The Levantine paintings have been described and interpreted by A. Beltran, *Rock Art of the Spanish Levant* (Cambridge, 1982), and the art of Lepenski Vir by D. Srejovic's *Lepenski Vir* (London, 1972).

4. *The First Farmers*

The Mesolithic background is covered most recently by C. Bonsall (ed.), *The Mesolithic in Europe* (Edinburgh, 1989) and by P. Vermeersch and P. van Peer (eds.), *Contributions to the Mesolithic in Europe* (Leuven, 1990). A continent-wide synthesis is offered in A. Whittle, *Neolithic Europe: A Survey* (Cambridge, 1985), and another in I. Hodder, *The Domestication of Europe* (London, 1990). There are many regional surveys of varying scope and date. R. Tringham, *Hunters, Fishers and Farmers in Eastern Europe 6000–3000 BC* (London, 1971) and D. Theocharis, *Neolithic Greece* (Athens, 1973) still usefully cover those areas, though inevitably becoming out of date on recent detail. S. Tinè, *Passo di Corvo e la Civiltà Neolitica del Tavoliere* (Genoa, 1983); G. Barker, *Landscape and Society: Prehistoric Central Italy* (London, 1981); and J. Guilaine *et al.* (eds.), *Premières communautés paysannes en Méditerranée occidentale* (Paris, 1987) cover aspects of the Mediterranean; see also J.-P. Demoule and J. Guilaine (eds.), *Le Néolithique de la France* (Paris, 1986).

The Linear Pottery culture is imaginatively treated in P. Bogucki, *Forest Farmers and Stockherders* (Cambridge, 1988); see also, among a vast literature, J. Pavúk (ed.), *Siedlungen der Kultur mit Linearkeramik in Europa* (Nitra, 1982), and J. Rulf (ed.), *Bylany Seminar 1987* (Prague, 1989). M. Gimbutas, *The Goddesses and Gods of Old Europe* (London, 1974) and *The Language of the Goddess* (London, 1989), and N. Kalicz, *Clay Gods: The Neolithic Period and Copper Age in Hungary* (Budapest, 1971) investigate matters of cult and ritual.

All these references will provide guides to a further plethora of discussion and description in journals, conference proceedings, and excavation reports. Among the latter, note especially recent reports on southeast Europe, such as M. Gimbutas (ed.), *Neolithic Macedonia* (Los Angeles, 1976), which is a report on Anza, and C. Renfrew *et al.* (eds.), *Excavations at Sitagroi* (Los Angeles, 1986).

5. *The later Neolithic and Copper Ages*

No single work adequately summarizes the material discussed here; and much of the primary description is in European languages other than English. Also, it must be confessed, this chapter is to some extent a personal view and hence this list begins with some articles by the present writer in which points are argued at greater length. The basic division of the period around 3500 BC is discussed in 'Plough and Pastoralism: Aspects of the Secondary Products Revolution' in N. Hammond, I. Hodder, and G. Isaac, *Pattern of the Past* (Cambridge, 1981), while the interpretation of some of the distinctive pottery types as narcotic-burners or containers for alcohol is discussed in two works: 'Cups that Cheered' in W. H. Waldren and R. C. Kennard (eds.), *Bell Beakers of the West Mediterranean* in the International Series of BAR (Oxford, 1987) and, 'Sacred and Profane Substances: The Ritual Use of Narcotics in later Neolithic Europe', in P. Garwood *et al.* (eds.), *Sacred and Profane Conference Proceedings* (Oxford Archaeological Monographs, 1991).

Broad surveys are available in Alasdair Whittle, *Neolithic Europe: A Survey* (Cambridge, 1985); and Ruth Tringham, *Hunters, Fishers and Farmers in Eastern Europe 6000–3000 BC* (London, 1971) although written a long time ago, is still useful for its systematic exposition. A treasure-house of redrawn illustrations and brief notes on individual sites is available in Hermann Müller-Karpe, *Handbuch der Vorgeschichte* (iii, *Kupferzeit*) and especially the third (plates) volume (*Beck'sche Verlagsbuchhandlung*), (Munich, 1974). An equally comprehensive set of summaries, though still rather undigested, is Jan Lichardus and Marion Lichardus-Itten, *La Protohistoire de l'Europe: le néolithique et le chalcolithique entre la mer Mediterranée et la mer Baltique* (Paris, 1985).

The themes which are raised in the first part of this chapter have been considered in a stimulating essay, which appeared after this chapter was written: Ian Hodder, *The Domestication of Europe* (London, 1990). From another point of view, Peter Bogucki, *Forest Farmers and Stockherders: Early Agriculture and its Consequences in North-Central Europe* (Cambridge, 1988), usefully draws together material from a large area of the North European Plain. A wide-ranging survey of megalithic monuments in Europe (and indeed beyond) is given by Roger Joussaume, *Dolmens for the Dead* (London, 1988), to be read together with A. Sherratt, 'Genesis of Megaliths: Monumentality, Ethnicity and Social Complexity in Neolithic North-West Europe', *World Archaeology*, 22 (1990), 147–67.

Regional surveys are more easily available, and several have been translated into English in the International Series of BAR (British Archaeological Reports), e.g. Henrietta Todorova, *Eneolithic Period in Bulgaria: 5th millennium BC* (Oxford, 1978) is an especially useful guide, though there is fuller information in her *Kupferzeitliche Siedlungen in Bulgarien* (Munich, 1982). Others in the International Series of BAR are: Linda Ellis, *The Cucuteni Tripole Culture: A Study in Technology and the Origins of Complex Society* (Oxford, 1984); D. Ya. Telegins, *Dereivka: A Settlement and Cemetery of Copper Age Horse Keepers* (Oxford, 1986); and a classic piece of field survey, with important consequences for the interpretation of settlement patterns, is Janusz Kruk, *Neolithic Settlement of Southern Poland* (Oxford, 1980). The Varna cemetery and its context is excellently illustrated and described in the catalogue of a recent St Germain-en-Laye exhibition, *Le Premier Or de l'Humanité en Bulgarie: 5è millennaire* (Paris, Réunion des musées nationaux, 1989). The British Isles are well served by another exhibition catalogue and associated essays: D. V. Clarke, T. G. Cowie, and A. Foxton, *Symbols of Power at the Time of Stonehenge* (London, 1985).

This selection no more than scratches the surface of a very rich but forbiddingly diverse literature, which remains to be synthesized into prehistory.

6. *The Palace Civilizations of Minoan Crete and Mycenaean Greece*

The pace of archaeological discovery in Greece during the past thirty years has been so rapid that there are few up-to-date books to provide a detailed overview of Bronze Age civilization. Among the most useful of these are P. M. Warren, *The Aegean Civilizations* (Oxford, 1975; 1990); G. A. Christopoulos (ed.), *Prehistory and Protohistory* (Athens, 1970); and M. S. F. Hood, *The Arts in Prehistoric Greece* (London, 1978). Discoveries in Crete are well described in St. Alexiou, *Minoan Civilization* (Heraklion, 1973) and G. Cadogan, *Palaces of Minoan Crete* (London and New York, 1976), while J. D. S. Pendlebury's *The Archaeology of Crete* (London, 1939) remains basic. Mainland Greece is similarly covered in W. D. Taylour, *The Mycenaeans* (London, 1964; 1983) and J. T. Hooker, *Mycenaean Greece* (London, 1976), which is especially useful for its detailed bibliography for each chapter. J. Chadwick, *The Mycenaean World* (Cambridge, 1977) is an equally valuable survey from a different viewpoint, which links the written evidence from the Linear B archives to the material remains. At the time of writing, R. Treuil *et al.*, *Les Civilizations Égéennes* (Paris, 1989) provides the most up-to-date account of Greek prehistory from the Neolithic to the end of the Bronze Age and an excellent bibliography. An English edition is awaited.

There are many descriptions of individual sites and the finds made there, as well as surveys of different categories of architecture and find, published as monographs or journal articles. The site reports range from A. J. Evans's classic *Palace of Minos at Knossos* (London, 1921–36) to A. J. B. Wace, *Mycenae: An Archaeological History and Guide* (Princeton, NJ, 1949); G. Mylonas, *Mycenae Rich in Gold* (Athens, 1983); C. Blegen, *The Palace of Nestor at Pylos* (Princeton, NJ, 1966); Chr. Doumas, *Thera: Pompeii of the Ancient Aegean* (London, 1983); J. Sakellarakis, 'Drama of Death in a Minoan Temple', *National Geographic*, 159, 2 (Feb. 1981), 204–22; and G. F. Bass, 'Oldest Known Shipwreck Reveals Splendours of the Bronze Age', *National Geographic*, 172, 6 (Dec. 1987), 693–733. J. W. Myers, E. E. Myers, G. Cadogan, *The Aerial Atlas of Ancient Crete* (London, 1992) provides a valuable resource of site descriptions and bibliography, together with a new 'angle' on many sites.

Several lavishly illustrated museum catalogues have recently been published in Greece (though these are difficult to obtain elsewhere) such as *The Mycenaean World* (Athens, 1988), for an exhibition held first in Berlin and then in Athens; M. Ventris and J. Chadwick, *Documents in Mycenaean Greek* (Cambridge, 1973) is the basic guide to the Linear B tablets found at Pylos and Knossos and to their contents, while Chadwick's *Decipherment of Linear B* (Cambridge, 1967) is vital to understanding why we are now certain they are written in an early form of Greek. The philologist L. R. Palmer, often regarded by his archaeologist colleagues as something of a maverick, but always worth reading, first cast doubt on Evans's interpretation of the date of the Knossos tablets and the ramifications of the dispute still continue. His *Mycenaeans and Minoans* (London, 1961; 1965) provides many thought-provoking ideas.

The nature of the palatial economy, increasingly a subject of interest, is examined in a host of works. Examples of these are J. T. Killen, 'The Wool Industry of Crete in the Late Bronze Age', *Annual of the British School at Athens*, 59 (1964), 1–15; C. Shelmerdine, *The Perfume Industry of Mycenaean Pylos* (Göteborg, 1985); P. Halstead, 'On Redistribution and the Origin of the Minoan–Mycenaean Palatial Economies' in E. B. French and K. A. Wardle (eds.), *Problems in Greek Prehistory* (Bristol, 1988), 519–30. The collection in Th. Palaima and C. Shelmerdine (eds.), *Pylos Comes Alive. Industry and Administration in a Mycenaean Palace* (New York, 1984) is particularly useful.

O. T. P. K. Dickinson, *The Origins of Mycenaean Civilization* (Göteborg, 1977) provides the full details of the development of the Shaft Graves and the context in which the Mycenaeans are first recognizable. P. M. Warren and V. Hankey's *Aegean Bronze Age Chronology* (Bristol, 1989) is packed with vital information about relative stratigraphies and the date and context of Greek objects in the Near East, or Egyptian objects in Greece. It also provides a full list of carbon 14 dates for the area. As a reference book it is basic but hard-going for the half-initiated.

Greek prehistoric religion evokes speculation far beyond the limits of the archaeological evidence. A. C.

Renfrew, *The Archaeology of Cult* (Oxford, 1985) provides a vital analytical framework for the identification of cult sites as well as reporting the fascinating discoveries at Phylakopi on the island of Melos. The relationship between the Homeric epics and Bronze Age Greece is best explored in A. J. B. Wace and F. H. Stubbings (eds.), *The Homeric Companion* (London, 1962), though this is in need of updating to take account of recent finds.

7. Earlier Bronze Age Europe

An account of the period which is both readable and authoritative remains to be written, either in English or any other language. J. M. Coles and A. F. Harding provide a region-by-region summary of the major classes of material in *The Bronze Age in Europe* (London, 1979), which is an excellent guide to more detailed studies, but does not in itself provide a coherent picture of the whole. The central and east European parts have been usefully updated by Anthony Harding, 'The Bronze Age in Central and Eastern Europe: Advances and Prospects', *Advances in World Archaeology*, 2 (1983), 1–50. Another interpretative essay, of similar length to the present one, is by Stephen Shennan, in T. Champion (ed.), *Prehistoric Europe* (London, 1983), while M. Rowlands offers a stimulating discussion under the title 'Conceptualising the European Bronze and Early Iron Ages', in J. Bintliff (ed.), *European Social Evolution: Archaeological Perspectives* (Bradford, 1984).

Older accounts, such as Stuart Piggott, *Ancient Europe* (Edinburgh, 1965) or D. L. Clarke, 'Trade and Industry in Barbarian Europe' in *Analytical Archaeologist: Collected Papers of David L. Clarke Edited by his Colleagues* (London, 1979) are well worth reading for their insights, while Marija Gimbutas' vast *Bronze Age Cultures in Central and Eastern Europe* (Mouton, 1965) although unreliable, synthesizes a great deal of older literature.

For a magnificent corpus of undigested illustrations and brief notes on individual sites, the committed reader should consult Hermann Müller-Karpe, *Handbuch der Vorgeschichte* (iv, *Bronzezeit*) and especially the third (plates) volume (*Beck'sche Verlagsbuchhandlung*), (Munich, 1980). Many of the illustrations are taken from individual volumes of the *Prähistorische Bronzefunde* series, from the same editor and publisher, which consist of catalogues of particular types of bronze objects on a regional basis. Other classes of material are less comprehensively published, although textiles—which are far more important than their fragmentary remains would suggest—have recently been splendidly analysed in E. J. W. Barber, *Prehistoric Textiles: The Development of Cloth in the Neolithic and Bronze Ages* (Princeton, NJ, 1991).

Individual aspects of the material discussed in this chapter are considered in popular books such as P. V. Glob, *The Mound People: Danish Bronze-Age Man Preserved* (London, 1974), or Richard Bradley's thoughtful *Passage of Arms: An Archaeological Analysis of Prehistoric Hoards and Votive Deposits* (Cambridge, 1990). The international contacts of the Carpathian basin are discussed in A. Sherratt, 'Warriors and Traders: Bronze Age Chiefdoms in Central Europe', in B. W. Cunliffe (ed.), *Origins: The Roots of European Civilisation* (London, 1987); and some comparable themes are covered by Kristian Kristiansen, 'From Stone to Bronze: The Evolution of Social Complexity in Northern Europe, 2300–1200 BC', in E. M. Brumfiel and T. K. Earle (eds.), *Specialisation, Exchange and Complex Societies* (Cambridge, 1987). Material from the British Isles is unusually well illustrated in D. V. Clarke, T. G. Cowie, and A. Foxton, *Symbols of Power at the Time of Stonehenge* (London, 1985). Stuart Piggott, *The Earliest Wheeled Transport, from the Atlantic Coast to the Caspian Sea* (London, 1984) is not only an excellent piece of scholarship but successfully evokes prehistoric attitudes to this important item of material culture and its economic and social context—as well as being a pleasure to read.

8. *The Collapse of Aegean Civilization*

For a more detailed study of the end of the Mycenaean and Minoan Late Bronze Age, V. R. d'A. Desborough's *The Last Mycenaeans and their Successors* (Oxford, 1964) remains indispensable reading; it was somewhat modified and brought up to date in his introductory chapter to *The Greek Dark Age* (London, 1972), which includes his account of a sub-Mycenaean culture. For a wider ranging but less detailed study, with a concentration on the east Mediterranean, N. K. Sandars, *The Sea Peoples* (London, 1978) cannot be bettered: she has since published a follow-up article 'North and South at the End of the Mycenaean Age: Aspects of an Old Problem', *Oxford Journal of Archaeology* (1983), 43–68. Both authors, and especially the latter, are less enthusiastic than the present author about the role of 'barbarians' in the Aegean around 1200 BC and subsequently. Much more cautious, too, are the conclusions of A. Harding, *The Mycenaeans and Europe* (London, 1984), where most of the evidence is considered. J. Bouzek, *The Aegean, Anatolia and Europe, Cultural Interrelations in the Second Millennium BC* (Lund, 1985) is more partisan, like the present author.

The 'alien' handmade pottery is attracting increasing attention. K. Kilian's 'Mycenaeans Up to Date' in E. B. French and K. A. Wardle (eds.), *Problems in Greek Prehistory* (Bristol, 1988), 127–33 gives a summary account with drawings of vase shapes, distribution maps, and a good bibliography. E. Hallager's 'Aspects of Aegean Long-Distance Trade in the 2nd Millennium', *Momenti Precoloniali nel Mediterraneo Antico*, Academia Belgica (Rome, 1985), 91–101, is especially concerned with the evidence from Chania and favours the view that some of the Sea People's names indicate their place of origin in the west Mediterranean.

References to sites and finds in the Aegean up to 1964 are listed in *The Last Mycenaeans and their Successors*. Subsequent major additions, mentioned in this chapter are, in English accounts, Lefkandi (Euboea), M. R. Popham and L. H. Sackett, *Excavations at Lefkandi, Euboea, 1964–66* (London, 1968); M. R. Popham and E. Milburn, 'The LH IIIC Pottery of Xeropolis (Lefkandi): A Summary', *Annual of the British School at Athens*, 66 (1971), 33–5; and (for intramural burials) J. Musgrave and M. Popham, 'The Late Helladic IIIC Intramural Burials at Lefkandi, Euboea' in the same periodical vol. 86 (1991), 273–91; Tiryns, a summary by K. Kilian in his article referred to above and especially pp. 134–6 and its cited bibliography; Phylakopi (Melos), C. Renfrew *et al.*, *The Archaeology of Cult, the Sanctuary at Phylakopi* (Oxford, 1985); Rhodes, C. Mee, *Rhodes in the Bronze Age* (Warminster, 1982), especially pp. 87–92, and C. Macdonald, 'Problems of the Twelfth Century BC in the Dodecanese', *Annual of the British School at Athens*, 81 (1986), 125–51 with a useful discussion of 'alien' objects; Koukounaries (Paros), D. U. Schilardi, 'The Destruction of the Mycenaean Citadel at Koukounaries on Paros', in J. L. Davies and J. F. Cherry (eds.), *Papers in Cycladic Prehistory* (Los Angeles, 1979), 158–79, and 'The LH IIIC Period at the Koukounaries Acropolis on Paros' in J. A. Macgillivray and R. Barber (eds.), *The Prehistoric Cyclades* (Edinburgh, 1984), 184–206; Palaikastro, Kastri, on Crete, L. H. Sackett, M. R. Popham, and P. M. Warren, 'Excavations at Palaikastro, VI', *Annual of the British School at Athens*, 60 (1965), 269–99. For Serraglio (Cos), there is only the full account in Italian by L. Morricone, 'Coo-Scavi e scoperte nel Serraglio e in localita minori', *Annuario della Scuolo Archeoligca di Atene*, 50–1 (1972–3), 139–397.

Aggression, warfare, and invasions have fallen out of fashion in our post-World War II era, with emphasis now given to natural causes or, more mechanistically, to an inevitable collapse of the social and economic systems existing before 1200 BC. R. Carpenter's *Discontinuity in Greek Civilisation* (New York, 1968) placed the emphasis on drought following a shift in trade winds; it initially gained favour but has not stood the test of time. Earthquakes are currently fashionable and reference to and support for this theory will be found in the article by K. Kilian referred to above. The theory of a system's collapse has several supporters and will be found in books advocating the so-called New Archaeology. An example can be found in A. C. Renfrew, 'Systems Collapse as Social Transformation', in A. C. Renfrew and K. L. Cooke (eds.), *Transformations: Mathematical Approaches to Cultural Change* (New York, 1979), 481–506. A useful review of opinions on the causes of the 1200 destructions, with stress placed on the dire economic consequences they might have had, is given by P. B. Betancourt, 'The End of the Greek Bronze Age', *Antiquity*, 50 (1976), 40–7.

On more specific matters, the idea of northern mercenaries with their alien Naue II type swords was put forward by H. W. Catling, 'A New Bronze Sword from Cyprus', *Antiquity*, XXXV (1961), 115–22. On amber, the standard account remains that of A. Harding and H. Hughes-Brock, 'Amber in the Mycenaean World', *Annual of the British School at Athens*, 69 (1974), 145–80; while the suggestion that the amber beads in the burials at Saggara in Egypt might have been worn by the wives of foreign mercenaries was made by M. S. F. Hood at an international conference on amber held in Czechoslovakia in 1990, the proceedings of which have yet to be published. The possible connections between amber and Italy and the West is considered by H. Hughes-Brock, 'Amber and the Mycenaeans', in J. M. Todd (ed.), *Studies in Baltic Amber*, published as *Journal of Baltic Studies*, XVI (1985), 257–67. References to cremation on Crete and their connection with pyxides will be found in M. R. Popham, 'A Late Minoan Pyxis', *Oxford Journal of Archaeology*, 5 (1986), 157–64. The greaves from Athens were first dated to LH IIIC by P. Mountjoy in 'The Bronze Greaves from Athens, a Case for a LH IIIC Date', *Opuscula Atheniensia*, XV (1984), 135–7.

The division of the IIIC period into three main stages was proposed by A. Furumark, with suggested dates, in 'The Mycenaean Pottery and its Relation to Cypriote Fabrics', *Opuscula Archaeologica*, III, 194–5. The end of LH IIIB is now generally accepted as being later than his 1230 BC, with an approximate date of 1200. Also, his LM IIIB 2 stage is now usually referred to as LM IIIC. For a more detailed, if not always quite convincing, up-to-date study of chronology, see P. Warren and V. Hankey, *Aegean Bronze Age Chronology* (Bristol, 1989).

9. *Reformation in Barbarian Europe*

There is no single book that covers the entire period discussed in this chapter, though J. M. Coles and A. F. Harding, *The Bronze Age in Europe* (London, 1979) deals with the Late Bronze Age aspects, there arranged geographically and not thematically, and stopping short of the Iron Age developments discussed here. A general review of the whole of the first millennium BC is that by John Collis, *The European Iron Age* (London, 1984), while an up-to-date account of current preoccupations in Iron Age studies in continental Europe is Peter S. Wells, 'Iron Age Temperate Europe: Some Current Research Issues', *Journal of World Prehistory*, 4 (1990), 437–76.

Excellent pictures and short discussions of the main themes may be found in *Avant les Celtes: L'Europe à l'age du bronze, 2500–800 avant J-C* (Daoulas, 1988) and in *Au temps des Celtes, V^c–Ier siècle avant J-C* (Daoulas, 1986).

Stimulating discussion of the socio-economic foundations of the period, set in a British context, is provided by Richard Bradley, *The Social Foundations of Prehistoric Britain* (London, 1984), and the same author has discussed many aspects of metalworking and metal deposition in a series of articles culminating in *The Passage of Arms: An Archaeological Analysis of Prehistoric Hoards and Votive Deposits* (Cambridge, 1990). Early glass in Europe has recently been discussed in detail by Julian Henderson, 'Glass Production and Bronze Age Europe', *Antiquity*, 62 (1988), 435–51. Agricultural developments are handled by P. J. Fowler, *The Farming of Prehistoric Britain* (Cambridge, 1983).

Rock art has been the subject of many short articles but few full-length studies: the recent publication by John Coles, *Images of the Past: A Guide to the Rock Carvings and other Ancient Monuments of Northern Bohuslän* (Uddevalla, 1990) serves as much more than just an excellent field guide. Wetland sites, including trackways such as those in the Somerset Levels, are fully discussed (with further references) in Bryony Coles and John Coles, *People of the Wetlands: Bogs, Bodies and Lake-Dwellers* (London, 1989), as well as in their *Sweet Track to Glastonbury: The Somerset Levels in Prehistory* (London, 1986).

10. *Iron Age Societies in Western Europe*

General books on the archaeology of Iron Age Europe are few. J. Collis, *The European Iron Age* (London, 1984) provides an overview while two earlier works, T. G. E. Powell, *The Celts* (1958; repr. London, 1980) and J. Filip, *Celtic Civilization and its Heritage* (1962; repr. Northampton, 1977) are still well worth reading for the lively insights they provide. The relationships between the Mediterranean and the barbarian world are extensively covered in P. S. Wells, *Culture Contact and Culture Change* (Cambridge, 1980) and B. Cunliffe, *Greeks, Romans and Barbarians: Spheres of Interaction* (London, 1988), while the impact of the Celtic migrations is fully considered by H. D. Rankin, *Celts and the Classical World* (Beckenham, 1987). A series of useful detailed papers on aspects of Iron Age society can be found in T. C. Champion and J. V. S. Megaw (eds.), *Settlement and Society: Aspects of West European Prehistory in the First Millennium BC* (Leicester, 1985) and J.-P. Mohen, A. Duval, and C. Eluère, *Les Princes Celtes et la Méditerranée* (Paris, 1988).

The colonizing powers in the Mediterranean are most conveniently dealt with by J. Boardman, *The Greeks Overseas* (London, 1980); D. Harden, *The Phoenicians* (1962; repr. Harmondsworth, 1971); and S. Moscati (ed.), *The Phoenicians* (Milan, 1988).

The themes of Celtic art and religion have produced a massive literature. Among the more useful and accessible introductions are R. and V. Megaw, *Celtic Art* (London, 1989); S. Piggott, *The Druids* (London, 1968); and J. L. Brunaux, *The Celtic Gauls: Gods, Rites and Sanctuaries* (London, 1988).

Regional studies are not prolific, but a few are available including A. Arribas, *The Iberians* (London, 1964); R. J. Harrison, *Spain at the Dawn of History* (London, 1988); P. S. Wells, *The Emergence of an Iron Age Economy* [in Slovenia] (Cambridge, Mass., 1981); B. Cunliffe, *Iron Age Communities in Britain* (1974; 3rd edn., London, 1991); and M. Szabó, *The Celtic Heritage in Hungary* (Budapest, 1971). Finally, there are a number of general illustrated essays on the Celts including V. Kruta and W. Forman, *The Celts of the West* (London, 1985) and B. Cunliffe, *The Celtic World* (London, 1979).

11. *Thracians, Scythians, and Dacians*

There are few up-to-date books available in English; general reading must thus still include the classic works of the earlier part of the century: E. Minns, *Scythians and Greeks* (Cambridge, 1913); M. Rostovtseff, *Iranians and Greeks in South Russia* (Oxford, 1922); S. Casson, *Macedonia, Thrace and Illyria* (Oxford, 1926); and V. Pârvan, *Dacia: An Outline of the Early Civilizations of the Carpatho-Danubian Countries* (London, 1928).

For Greek colonization see J. Boardman, *The Greeks Overseas* (2nd edn., London, 1980) and articles in J.-P. Descœudres (ed.), *Greek Colonists and Native Populations* (Oxford, 1990), especially C. Danov, 'Characteristics of Greek Colonization in Thrace' (pp. 151–5), and Maria Coja, 'Greek Colonists and Native Populations in Dobruja (*Moesia Inferior*): The Archaeological Evidence' (pp. 157–68).

For the Scythians and Sarmatians, more recent works include T. T. Rice, *The Scythians* (London, 1957) and R. Rolle, *The World of the Scythians* (London, 1989); the latter is a slim, un-updated translation of the 1980 German original, but Rolle's firsthand experience of the Scythian material through her own excavations makes this one of the best available introductions (though F. Trippett, *The First Horsemen* in the Time–Life 'Emergence of Man' series (New York, 1974) can also be recommended). Rolle is interesting (though brief) on the question of the Amazons; an early work touching on this is Hermann Ploss's *Das Weib* (1885), most recently edited into English by Paula Weidegger as *History's Mistress* (Harmondsworth, 1986); the quotation by Maria Mies concerning pastoralism and patriarchy is from an article 'Social Origins of the Sexual Division of Labour', in Mies, Bennholdt-Thomsen, and von Werlhof, *Women: The Last Colony* (London, 1988). Also useful are: T. Sulimirski, *The Sarmatians* (London, 1970); Sulimirski's various surveys of Soviet archaeological literature in *BULIA (The Bulletin of the London Institute of Archaeology)* in the late 1960s and early 1970s; T. Sulimirski and T. Taylor, 'The Scythians', in *The Cambridge Ancient History* iii.

2 (Cambridge, 1991)—replacing E. Minns's original chapter of 1935, which may nevertheless still be read with profit; A. I. Melyukova, 'The Scythians and Sarmatians' in D. Sinor (ed.), *The Cambridge History of Early Inner Asia* (Cambridge, 1990); and K. Marčenko and Y. Vinogradov, 'The Scythians in the Black Sea Region', *Antiquity*, 63 (1989), 803–13.

For Thracians and Dacians, the two most accessible books are both by R. F. Hoddinott: *Bulgaria in Antiquity* (London, 1975) and *The Thracians* (London, 1981). Works translated from eastern European languages include D. Berciu, *Daco-Romania* (Geneva, 1978); E. Condurachi, *Romania* (London, 1967); A. Fol and I. Marazov, *Thrace and the Thracians* (New York, 1977); and the more detailed works reproduced in the International Series of BAR (British Archaeological Reports), especially I. Glodariu, *Dacian Trade with the Hellenistic and Roman World* (Oxford, 1976); G. Bichir, *Archaeology and History of the Carpi* (Oxford, 1976); and M. Shchukin, *Rome and the Barbarians in Central and Eastern Europe* (Oxford, 1989). The best study of the Dacians is an unpublished Cambridge Ph.D. thesis by A. Bergquist, 'The Emergence of a pre-Roman State in Dacia: The Archaeological and Historical Sources for Transylvania' (Cambridge, 1989).

In addition to this literature, there is a large and attractive body of articles, books, and exhibition catalogues that deal with Thracian, Scythian, and Dacian art. The catalogues often contain the most up-to-date English-language reviews of research written by eastern European scholars; the best include *From the Lands of the Scythians* (Metropolitan Museum of Art and Los Angeles County Museum of Art, 1976); *Nomads of Eurasia* (Natural History Museum of Los Angeles County, 1989); *Frozen Tombs: the Culture and Art of the Ancient Tribes of Siberia* (British Museum, London, 1978); *Treasures from Romania* (British Museum, London, 1971); *Thracian Treasures from Bulgaria* (British Museum, London, 1976); and *The New Thracian Treasure from Rogozen, Bulgaria* (British Museum, London, 1986). Monographic publications include B. F. Cook (ed.), *The Rogozen Treasure* (London, 1989); I. Venedikov and T. Gerassimov, *Thracian Art Treasures* (London, 1975), and B. Piotrovski *et al.*, *Scythian Art* (Oxford, 1987). More specialized studies include three by T. Taylor: on the influence of Persian metalworking styles on Thracian gold- and silversmithing, in *The Cambridge Ancient History*, Plates to vol. iv, (new edn., Cambridge, 1988); on iconography and symbolism among the Getae see 'Flying Stags: Icons and Power in Thracian Art', in I. Hodder, *The Archaeology of Contextual Meanings* (Cambridge, 1987), pp. 117–32; and on 'The Gundestrup Cauldron', *Scientific American* (1992), 84–9; see also A. Bergquist and T. Taylor, 'The Origin of the Gundestrup Cauldron', *Antiquity*, 61 (1987), 10–20.

David Clarke's concept of 'detribalization' is outlined in 'The economic context of trade and industry in Barbarian Europe till Roman Times', in his collected papers, *Analytical Archaeologist* (London, 1979).

On the reliability or otherwise of Herodotus see the recent studies by F. Hartog, *The Mirror of Herodotus* (Berkeley, 1988) and J. Gould, *Herodotus* (London, 1989). See *Hippocratic Writings*, ed. G. E. R. Lloyd (Harmondsworth, 1978) for the Hippocratic corpus.

12. *The Impact of Rome on Barbarian Society*

Several of the volumes mentioned at the end of Chapter 10 are relevant also to this chapter. As a general guide, B. Cunliffe, *Greeks, Romans and Barbarians: Spheres of Interaction* (London, 1988) provides an outline of much of the early part of the story and K. Randsborg, *The First Millennium AD in Europe and the Mediterranean* (Cambridge, 1991) takes it on. There is much (too much!) to be read on the Roman Empire, but comparatively little to explain the mechanisms by which the state worked. Outstanding, however, are R. Duncan-Jones, *The Economy of the Roman Empire* (Cambridge, 1974); P. Garnsey, K. Hopkins, and C. R. Whittaker (eds.), *Trade in the Ancient Economy* (London, 1983); and K. Hopkins, *Conquerors and Slaves* (Cambridge, 1978). For a view of Roman frontiers S. L. Dyson, *The Creation of the Roman Frontier* (Princeton, NJ, 1985) offers a factual summary and explanations.

Surprisingly little has been written of a general nature of transformations in barbarian society at this time, but G. Alföldy, *Noricum* (London, 1974) and N. Roymans, *Tribal Societies in Northern Gaul* (Amsterdam, 1990) provide insights and systematic explanations. E. A. Thompson, *The Early Germans* (Oxford, 1965) is a classic of textual analysis. The same broad subject-material together with an assessment of the archaeological background is treated in M. Todd, *The Northern Barbarians* (2nd edn., Oxford, 1987). For the conquest of the Dacians and their society see F. Lepper and S. Frere, *Trajan's Column* (Gloucester, 1988).

13. *Barbarian Europe*

General works: B. Kruger (ed.), *Die Germanen* (2 vols.; Berlin, 1976, 1986) is a compendious work, containing a mixture of valuable and unreliable chapters; R. Hachmann, *The Germanic Peoples* (London, 1974) is readable but highly contentious; E. A. Thompson, *Romans and Barbarians* (Madison, Wisc., 1982) contains several important studies of the migration period; W. Goffart, *Barbarians and Romans, AD 418–584. The Techniques of Accommodation* (Princeton, NJ, 1980) is a stimulating and provocative study of the settlement of barbarians within the Roman provinces; and M. Todd, *The Northern Barbarians* (2nd edn., Oxford, 1987) is a survey of the archaeology of the early Germans to the fourth century.

Among recent studies of individual peoples are: R. Christlein, *Die Alamannen* (Stuttgart, 1978); W. Menguin, *Die Langobarden* (Stuttgart, 1986); P. Perin and L.-C. Feffer, *Les Francs* (2 vols.; Paris, 1987); E. James, *The Franks* (Oxford, 1988); H. Wolfram, *History of the Goths* (Los Angeles and London, 1988); J. Werner, *Die Langobarden in Pannonien* (Munich, 1962); J. Campbell (ed.), *The Anglo-Saxons* (London, 1982); M. Gimbutas, *The Slavs* (London, 1971) is to be used with caution; Z. Vana, *The World of the Ancient Slavs* (London, 1983) is a magnificently illustrated survey of recent work; C. Courtois, *Les Vandales et l'Afrique* (Paris, 1955) is still the fullest account of its subject; E. A. Thompson, *The Goths in Spain* (Oxford, 1969) is the best single study of the Visigothic kingdom. W. Ennslin, *Theoderich der Grosse* (Munich, 1945) is a fine biography, not yet fully superseded.

The literature on settlements, material culture, cult, and burial is immense and only a few significant works are noted. On settlement, W. Haarnagel, *Die Grabung Feddersen Wierde II* (Wiesbaden, 1979) is of outstanding importance, as is W. A. van Es, *Wijster. A Native Village beyond the Roman Frontier* (Groningen, 1967). M. Stenberger, *Vallhagar* (Stockholm, 1955) is a fine early study of a migration-period microcosm. On buildings, B. Trier, *Das Haus im Nordwesten der Germania Libera* (Münster, 1969) is useful though now incomplete. On trade connections, U. Lund Hansen, *Römischer Import im Norden* (Copenhagen, 1987) is of exceptional interest. H. W. Böhme, *Germanische Grabfunde des 4 bis 5 Jahrhunderts zwischen unterer Elbe und Loire* (Munich, 1974) is of fundamental importance. An outstanding publication of a major cemetery is R. Pirling, *Das römisch-fränkische Gräberfeld von Krefeld-Gellep* (Berlin, 1966, 1974, and 1979). On cult, H. R. Ellis Davidson, *Gods and Myths of Northern Europe* (London, 1964) covers much ground. On early Germanic art, B. Salin, *Die altgermanische Thierornamentik* (2nd edn., Stockholm, 1935) is a masterpiece, not yet rivalled in a single work. On the nomad peoples, J. O. Maenchen-Helfen, *The World of the Huns* (Los Angeles, 1973) and R. Rolle, *The World of the Scythians* (London, 1989).

CHRONOLOGICAL
TABLES

Table 1. Simplified time chart

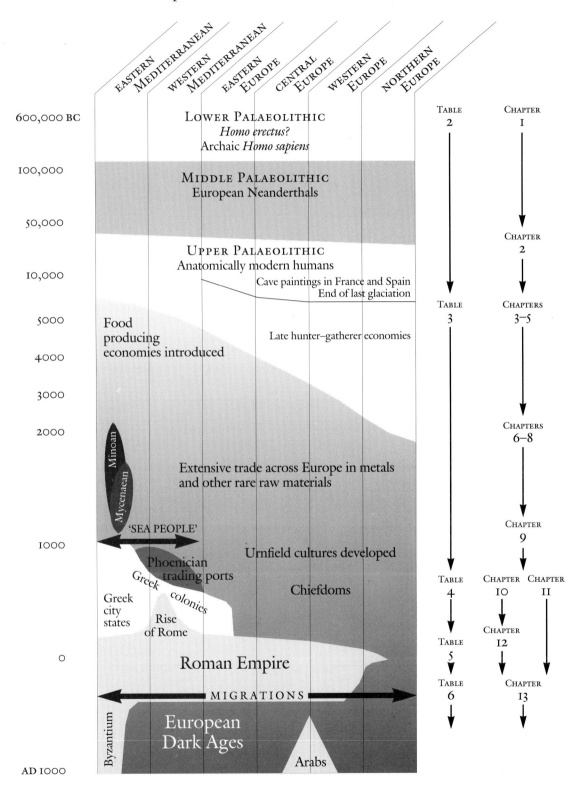

	EASTERN MEDITERRANEAN	WESTERN MEDITERRANEAN	EASTERN EUROPE	CENTRAL EUROPE	WESTERN EUROPE	NORTHERN EUROPE		TABLE	CHAPTER

600,000 BC — LOWER PALAEOLITHIC / Homo erectus? / Archaic Homo sapiens — TABLE 2 — CHAPTER 1

100,000 — MIDDLE PALAEOLITHIC / European Neanderthals

50,000 — CHAPTER 2

UPPER PALAEOLITHIC / Anatomically modern humans

10,000 — Cave paintings in France and Spain / End of last glaciation — TABLE 3 — CHAPTERS 3–5

5000 — Food producing economies introduced / Late hunter–gatherer economies

4000

3000

2000 — Extensive trade across Europe in metals and other rare raw materials — CHAPTERS 6–8

Minoan / Mycenaean

'SEA PEOPLE' — CHAPTER 9

1000 — Phoenician trading ports / Urnfield cultures developed — TABLE 4 — CHAPTER 10 — CHAPTER 11

Greek colonies / Chiefdoms

Greek city states / Rise of Rome — CHAPTER 12

0 — Roman Empire — TABLE 5

MIGRATIONS — TABLE 6 — CHAPTER 13

Byzantium / European Dark Ages / Arabs

AD 1000

Table 2. The Palaeolithic period

BP (years ago)	GEOL. PERIOD	ARCH. PERIOD	CLIMATE	TECHNOLOGY
1.6 million	Pliocene			
800,000	Lower Pleistocene			
700,000	Middle Pleistocene	Lower Palaeolithic		
600,000				
500,000				pebble tool/flake traditions (Clactonian/High Lodge)
400,000				hand axe/flake/scraper (Acheulean/Abbevillian)
300,000				
200,000				
150,000				scraper/flake/point (early Mousterian, Levallois tradition)
100,000	Upper Pleistocene	Middle Palaeolithic		
90,000				
80,000				
70,000				
60,000				knife/small hand axe/scraper/flake/point (Mousterian, Micoquian, late Acheulean)
50,000				
				spread of Upper Palaeolithic technology across Europe 43,000 south-east Europe
40,000				40,000 northern Spain
		Upper Palaeolithic		35,000 south-west France
30,000			Brief occupation of Britain and northern Europe during warmer 'Arcy/Paudorf' interstadial	Gravettian technologies in central and western Europe
20,000			Last glacial maximum	Bi-facial pressure-flaking appears in Early Solutrian
			16,000–13,000 Very cold 'Older Dryas' phase	
			13,000 Start of main later glacial climatic warming	
			12,500 Colonization of northern France, Holland and southern Britain during late glacial interstadial (Allerød)	12,000 Azilian technologies simplified bone and stone tool technologies
10,000 (= 8000 BC)			11,000–10,000 'Younger Dryas'	
			End of last glaciation: spread of forest	

HUMAN TYPE	CULTURE & ACHIEVEMENT	BP (years ago)
		1.6 million
		800,000
		700,000
Homo erectus? Mauer mandible from near Heidelberg		600,000
archaic *Homo sapiens*		500,000
Swanscombe		
Petralona		400,000
Arago		
Bilzingsleben		300,000
Atapuerca		
Steinheim		200,000
European Neanderthals *Homo sapiens*		150,000
Pontnewydd		
Ehringsdorf		100,000
La Chaise		
Biache St. Vaast		90,000
		80,000
		70,000
Le Moustier		60,000
La Ferrassie		
Krapina		50,000
Guattari		
Neander Valley		
Chapelle-aux-Saints		
Saint-Césaire		
	Earliest perforated animal teeth and extensively shaped bone, antler, and ivory artefacts	40,000
Anatomically modern humans	Earliest deliberately manufactured beads and traded sea shells. First naturalistic art forms. Bones incised with possible 'Lunar' notation or tally marks. Circular huts at Arcy-sur-Cure	
Mladec		
Vogelherd		
Les Rois		30,000
Cro-Magnon, etc.		
	Female 'Venus' figurines found across western, central, and eastern Europe. Also animal statuettes manufactured from bone, clay, stone, etc. Mammoth bone houses in central and eastern Europe	
		20,000
	Earliest eyed-sewing needles and antler spear throwers	
	Main florescence of cave painting. Carved stone lamps of Lascaux. Earliest barbed spears in later Magdalenian	
	Earliest definite evidence of wooden bows and arrows at Stellmoor, northern Germany	10,000 (= 8000 BC)

Table 3. Early farming and metallurgy

	NORTHERN EUROPE	WESTERN EUROPE	CENTRAL EUROPE
8000			
	7500 Establishment of Maglemosian technology in northern Europe		
7000			
6000			
5000	Broad blade industries develop in continental Europe		
4500	Appearance of cemeteries and complex hunter–gatherer societies		
4000	First megaliths in Scandinavia	First megaliths in France	Round earthwork enclosures 'Lake villages' in Alpine area
3500	Elaborate tomb building and flint mining	Elaborate tomb building	Cart models Impact of metal designs on pottery
3000	Corded Ware, tumuli, and individual burials	Large passage graves, henges, and stone alignments	Steppe intrusion (tumuli), then fusion
2500			
2400	Flint daggers imitate bronze	Spread of Bell-Beakers to Britain, France, and Iberia	Tin–bronze used: copper ring ingots
2300			
2200			
2100			
2000			
1900			
1800	Beginnings of Nordic spiral style	Wessex Culture, rich burials	Fortification and long-distance trade to the Baltic
1700			
1600			
1550			
1500	Tree trunk coffin burial	Field systems	Expansion of bronze industries and amber trade
1450			
1400			
1350			Start of Urnfield period
1300			
1250			
1200			
1150			
1100		Start of fortified hilltop sites	
1050			
1000			
950		First abandonment of Swiss lake sites	
900			
850		Final abandonment of Swiss lake sites	
800			
750		Start of 'Hallstatt Iron Age'	
700			

Mediterranean	Balkans and Aegean	Steppe	
			8000
			7000
First settled agricultural communities in Greece, the Balkans, and southern Italy			
Gradual adoption by native communities in central and western Mediterranean of pottery, sheep, and other new items of resource			6000
Further development of Greek and Balkan communities (larger tell settlements, copper metallurgy, and other craft skills) and expansion to edge of Steppe zone			5000
Mediterranean becomes more fully Neolithic			
Islands e.g. Malta, colonized			4500
Expansion of agricultural communities into loess areas of central and western Europe			
Extensive trade in obsidian and painted pottery	Pottery decorated in graphite and manganese Development of copper metallurgy	Experiments in horse domestication	4000
Cave burials			
	Vine and olive in Aegean; use of plough	Spread of pit grave tumuli	3500
	Decline in tell settlements; dispersal of villages	Use of cart	
Temples in Malta	Silver extraction in Aegean	Pottery braziers for narcotics	3000
	Some fortification of settlements		2500
Bell–Beakers spread to Sicily	First imports from the Levant	Catacomb graves	2400
			2300
			2200
			2100
	c. 2000 First palaces in Crete		2000
Pithos burials, silverwork		Spread of chariot	1900
			1800
	c. 1700 Linear A script in Crete		1700
	New palaces in Crete		1600
Contact with Mycenaeans in Italy	*c.* 1550 Grave circle A at Mycenae	Diversification of harness equipment	1550
	Eruption of Thera Volcano		1500
	c. 1450 Earliest Mycenaean palaces		
	Destruction of most Minoan palaces		1450
	c. 1400 Destruction of Knossos (high date)		1400
	c. 1350 'Treasury of Atreus' built		1350
	Mycenaean pottery in quantity at Amarna, Egypt		1300
	Kaş wreck		
	c. 1250 Destruction of Knossos (low date)		1250
	Final fortification at Mycenae and Tiryns		1200
	c. 1200 Destruction of Mycenaean palaces		
	c. 1190 Attack of Sea Peoples on Egypt		1150
	1184 Sack of Troy according to Eratosthenes		1100
	c. 1050 Beginning of widespread use of iron in Greece		1050
			1000
			950
			900
			850
	c. 800 Euboean and Cypriot pottery in trading post at Al Mina		800
	776 First Olympic games		750
			700

Table 4. Mediterranean states and temperate Europe

	CENTRAL MEDITERRANEAN	WEST MEDITERRANEAN
800BC	*c.*800 Foundation of Carthage *c.*775 Greek colony of Pithecusae founded on Ischia by Euboeans Cumae founded soon after *c.*735 Euboeans found Naxos on Sicily *c.*730 Corinthians found Syracuse	*c.*800 Phoenician port of Gadir (Cádiz) underway
700	700–600 Orientalizing period in Etruria	
		*c.*630 Kolaios from Samos reaches Tartessos in southern Spain *c.*620–540 King Arganthonios rules Tartessos
600	*c.*615 Etruscans at Rome	*c.*600 Foundation of Massalia by Phocaeans
	*c.*537 Etruscans and Carthaginians fight Phoenicians at battle of Sardinian Sea *c.*530–520 Foundations of Spina and Adria near the mouth of the Po 525 Etruscans at war with Cumae	*c.*560 Foundation of Alalia on Corsica by Phocaeans *c.*550 Rise of Ibiza as Phoenician trading enclave
500	474 Naval battle at Cumae, Etruscans defeated	*c.*500 Carthaginians intensify hold on southern Spain
	415–413 Athenian expedition against Syracuse	410–339 Bands of Iberian mercenaries serve in Sicily and Greece
400	*c.*390 Celtic invasion of northern Italy	
		*c.*330 Pytheas explores the Atlantic seaways
300	306 Treaty between Carthage and Rome 295 Celts defeated at Sentium 285–282 Roman victory over Celtic Sennones in northern Italy 264–241 First Punic War 225 Celtic coalition beaten at Telamon 218–201 Second Punic War	237 Hamilcar Barca lands in Spain 236–219 Carthaginians annex south-eastern Spain Second Punic War
200		211–206 Roman annexation of Spain begins 197–133 Wars in Spain 154 Cities of Nicae and Antipolis in southern France threatened by hill tribes
	149–146 Third Punic War: destruction of Carthage 133 Tiberius Gracchus becomes tribune: social unrest and political fragmentation in Rome intensifies	133 Fall of Numantia 121 Province annexed by Rome *c.*118 Foundation of Roman colony of Narbonne
100		102–101 Marius defeats Cimbri and Teutones
	49 Caesar crosses Rubicon: civil war 47–44 Dictatorship of Caesar 27 The beginning of Empire. Octavian assumes the name of Augustus	47–45 Caesar campaigns in Spain and Africa against the Republicans

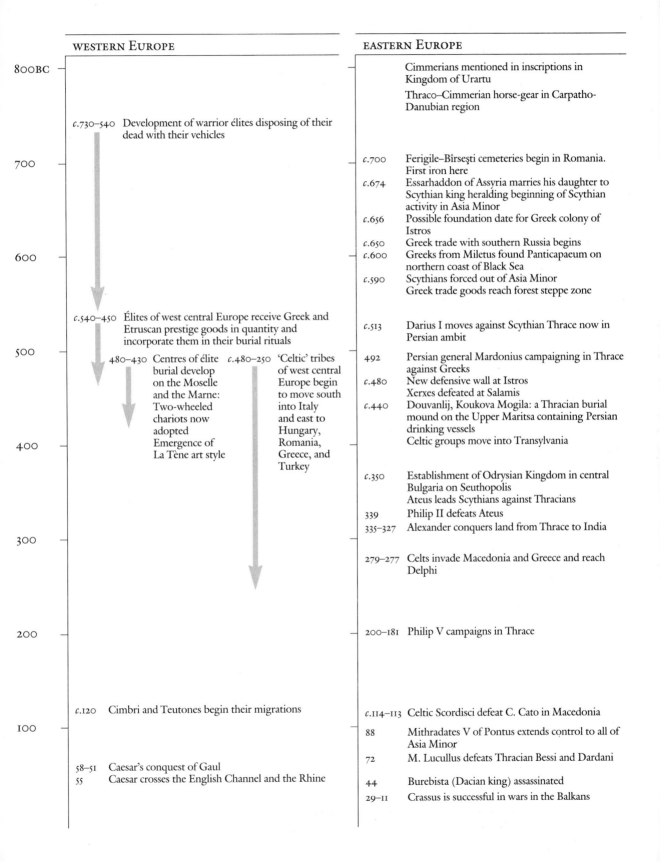

	WESTERN EUROPE		EASTERN EUROPE	

800BC

        Cimmerians mentioned in inscriptions in Kingdom of Urartu

        Thraco–Cimmerian horse-gear in Carpatho-Danubian region

*c.*730–540 Development of warrior élites disposing of their dead with their vehicles

700

*c.*700 Ferigile–Bîrseşti cemeteries begin in Romania. First iron here

*c.*674 Essarhaddon of Assyria marries his daughter to Scythian king heralding beginning of Scythian activity in Asia Minor

*c.*656 Possible foundation date for Greek colony of Istros

*c.*650 Greek trade with southern Russia begins

*c.*600 Greeks from Miletus found Panticapaeum on northern coast of Black Sea

600

*c.*590 Scythians forced out of Asia Minor
        Greek trade goods reach forest steppe zone

*c.*540–450 Élites of west central Europe receive Greek and Etruscan prestige goods in quantity and incorporate them in their burial rituals

*c.*513 Darius I moves against Scythian Thrace now in Persian ambit

500

480–430 Centres of élite burial develop on the Moselle and the Marne: Two-wheeled chariots now adopted Emergence of La Tène art style

*c.*480–250 'Celtic' tribes of west central Europe begin to move south into Italy and east to Hungary, Romania, Greece, and Turkey

492 Persian general Mardonius campaigning in Thrace against Greeks

*c.*480 New defensive wall at Istros
        Xerxes defeated at Salamis

*c.*440 Douvanlij, Koukova Mogila: a Thracian burial mound on the Upper Maritsa containing Persian drinking vessels
        Celtic groups move into Transylvania

400

*c.*350 Establishment of Odrysian Kingdom in central Bulgaria on Seuthopolis
        Ateus leads Scythians against Thracians

339 Philip II defeats Ateus

335–327 Alexander conquers land from Thrace to India

300

279–277 Celts invade Macedonia and Greece and reach Delphi

200

200–181 Philip V campaigns in Thrace

*c.*120 Cimbri and Teutones begin their migrations

100

*c.*114–113 Celtic Scordisci defeat C. Cato in Macedonia

88 Mithradates V of Pontus extends control to all of Asia Minor

72 M. Lucullus defeats Thracian Bessi and Dardani

58–51 Caesar's conquest of Gaul
55 Caesar crosses the English Channel and the Rhine

44 Burebista (Dacian king) assassinated

29–11 Crassus is successful in wars in the Balkans

Table 5. The Roman Empire and beyond

EMPERORS

27 BC–AD 14	Augustus
14–37	Tiberius
37–41	Gaius
41–54	Claudius
54–68	Nero
69–79	Vespasian
79–81	Titus
81–96	Domitian
96–8	Nerva
98–117	Trajan
117–38	Hadrian
138–61	Antoninus Pius
161–80	Marcus Aurelius
180–92	Commodus
193–211	Septimius Severus
212–17	Caracalla
218–22	Elagabalus
222–35	Severus Alexander

EVENTS

15–12 BC	Conquest of the Alpine peoples
12–7 BC–AD 4–5	Conquest of Germany underway
AD 9	Roman armies devastated by Arminius
16	Withdrawal of Roman troops behind the Rhine
43	Conquest of Britain begins
46	Annexation of Thrace by the Romans
50–85	Nomad power increases under Parthians: Dacian state reformed under Decebalus and threatens Moesia
69	The year of the four emperors
78–85	Agricola campaigns in Britain
86–92	Domitian campaigns against the Dacians led by Decebalus
101–6	Trajan conquers Dacia. Suicide of Decebalus. Attempt to stabilize the frontiers. No further advance contemplated.
157–8	Dacians beyond Dacia threaten the Province and are subdued
162	The Chatti, a German tribe, attempt to migrate into Roman held territory and raid south to the Adriatic
167	Marcomanni, Quadi, and Iazyges cross to Danube
168–80	Wars against German tribes

Table 6. The end of the Roman Empire and after

284–305	Diocletian's reforms
306–37	Reign of Constantine I
312	Battle of the Milvian Bridge and Constantine's conversion to Christianity
324	Foundation of Constantinople
c.370	Frankish attacks on the Rhineland
357–9	Julian's campaigns in Gaul against Franks and Alamanni
361–3	Julian's reign as Augustus
367–8	Barbarian attacks on Britain
c.370	Arrival of Huns around Black Sea
376	Visigoths settled in northern Balkans as *foederati*
378	Battle of Adrianople
383–8	Usurpation of Magnus Maximus
391	Pagan temples closed by Theodosius
395–408	Stilicho's ascendancy in the West
395–430	Augustine, Bishop of Hippo
395–410	Alaric, king of the Visigoths
406/7	Invasion of Gaul by the Vandals, Suevi, and Alans
407	Revolt of Britain from Rome
407–11	Constantine III's usurpation
408	Invasion of Italy by the Visigoths under Alaric
410	Sack of Rome by the Visigoths and death of Alaric
418	Settlement of the Visigoths in western Gaul
429	Vandal invasion of North Africa
430–53	Aetius' ascendancy in the West
439	Vandal capture of Carthage
440–6	Hun raids on the Balkans
440–50	Anglo-Saxon invasions of Britain
451	Huns under Attila invade Gaul; Huns defeated at the Catalaunian Fields
453	Death of Attila
455	Vandal sack of Rome
476–80	End of the Western Roman Empire
481	Death of Frankish king, Childeric
488	Ostrogoths under Theoderic invade Italy
490s	Victory of the Britons over the Anglo-Saxons at Mount Badon
486–511	Reign of Clovis, king of the Franks
493	Ostrogothic kingdom founded by Theoderic in Northern Italy
507	Defeat of the Visigoths by the Franks at Vouillé
526	Death of Theodoric
527–65	Reign of Justinian
533	Byzantine reconquest of Africa
535–53	Byzantine reconquest of Italy
558–61	Frankish kingdom united under Clotar I
550–60	Slav penetration of the northern Balkans
560s	Settlement of the Avars in Pannonia
565	Death of Justinian
568	Lombard invasion of Italy
569–86	Reign of Leovigild in Spain
590–616	Reign of Agilulf in Italy
597	Augustine's mission to Kent
626	Avar siege of Constantinople
681	Bulgars invade the Balkans
711	Arab invasion of Spain

ACKNOWLEDGEMENT
OF SOURCES

The editor and publishers wish to thank the following who have kindly given permission to
reproduce the illustrations on the following pages:

6   British Library, H. Knipe,
     'Nebula to Man' (J. M. Dent &
     Sons, 1905)

7   British Library, Add. MS 62925
     f57

10   British Library, J. Boucher de
     Perthes, 'Antiquitès Celtiques et
     Antédiluviennes', 1847

12   Trustees of the British Museum

13   Society for American
     Archaeology, from *American
     Antiquity*, 52; 1, 1987

14   (top) Francois Bordes, 'A Tale
     of Two Caves', © 1972 by
     Francois Bordes. Reprinted by
     permission of HarperCollins
     Publishers

     (bottom) Lewis R. Binford 'In
     Pursuit of the Past' (Thames &
     Hudson, 1983)

23   Trustees of the British Museum

25   John Wymer, 'Palaeolithic Sites
     of East Anglia' (Geo Books,
     Elsevier Science Publishers, 1985)

28 and 29   P. Callow and J. M.
     Cornford, 'La Cotte de St
     Brelade 1961–78' (Elsevier
     Applied Science Publishers,
     1986)

30   G. I. Goretsky and I. K.
     Ivanova, 'Molodova I: Unique
     Moustercian Settlement on the
     Middle Dniestr Region'
     (Nauka, 1982)

32   Trustees of the British Museum

39   The Natural History Museum,
     London

47   F. Bordes, 'The Old Stone Age'
     (Weidenfeld & Nicolson, 1968)

48   Dr Paul Mellars

49   Dr Paul Mellars after Leroi-
     Gourhan and Leroi-Gourhan
     1964

50   (top) Institut für Urgeschichte,
     Tübingen

(bottom) Dr Alexander
Marshack

52   Dr Randall White

55   (left) © Musée de l'Homme,
     Paris
     (right) Prof. B. Vandermeersch,
     Université de Bordeaux I

62   Novosti Press Agency

63   Dr Paul Mellars after Farizy 1988

66   (top left) Novosti Press Agency
     (top right) The Natural History
     Museum, London
     (bottom) M. Mussi, 'On the
     Chronology of the Burials
     found in the Grimaldi Caves',
     Antropologia Contemporanea 9;
     95–104, 1986, courtesy of Museo
     di Archeologia Ligure, Genova-
     Pegli

71   Dr Alexander Marshack

77   F. Bordes, 'Leçons sur le
     Paléolithique', vol. 2, courtesy
     of Madame Denise de Sonneville

88   J. G. D. Clark, 'Excavations at
     Star Carr' (Cambridge
     University Press, 1954)

91   National Board of Antiquities
     and Historical Monuments,
     Finland, photo by A. Äyräpää

92   J. Jensen, 'The Prehistory of
     Denmark', 1982, after E. Brich
     Petersen 1979

93   P. Vang Petersen 'Chronology
     and Regional Variation in the
     Late Mesolithic of Eastern
     Denmark' 1984, *Journal of
     Danish Archaeology*, drawn by
     Eva Koch Nielsen

94 and 95   S. K. Kozlowski, 'A
     Survey of Early Holocene
     Cultures of the Western Part of
     the Russian Plain'

98   S. V. Oshibkina, 'The Material
     Culture of the Veretye-type
     Sites in the Region to the East of
     Lake Onega'

99   figs. 1 & 4 J. G. D. Clark
     'Excavations at Star Carr'
     (Cambridge University Press,
     1954)
     figs. 2, 3, & 5 J. G. D. Clark,
     'The Earlier Stone Age
     Settlement of Scandinavia'
     (Cambridge University Press,
     1975)
     figs. 6 & 8 S. V. Oshibkina,
     'The Material Culture of the
     Veretye-type Sites in the
     Region to the East of Lake
     Onega'
     fig. 7 G. M. Burov, 'Some
     Mesolithic Wooden Artefacts
     from the Site of Vis I in the
     European North East of
     USSR'
     fig. 9 Brandenburghisches
     Landesmuseum für Ur- und
     Frühgeschichte

100 Prof. Lars Larsson

101 Institute of Prehistoric
     Archaeology, Moesgard

102 Prof. Peter Woodman

104 (top) Dr J. C. Chapman
     (bottom) Dragoslav Srejovic
     'Lepenski Vir' (Thames &
     Hudson, London, 1972)

105 Prof. S. H. Andersen and
     Journal of Danish Archaeology 4;
     52–69 figs 18 & 20

108 after Obermaier and Wernert
     1919

110 J. Vaquer *et al.* 'Mesolithic
     Plant Exploitation at the Balma
     Abeurador', 1986

122 Prof. Lars Larsson

124 after John O'Shea and Marek
     Zvelebil, *Journal of Anthro-
     pological Archaeology* 3(1); 1–40
     (Academic Press, Inc.)

128 Institut de Paléontologie
     Humaine. Photo by J. P.
     Kauffmann

130   (top) S. Hallgren/Institute of Archaeology and the Historical Museum, Lund
(bottom left) A. Noll/Institute of Archaeology and the Historical Museum, Lund
(bottom right) Oleneostrovski Mogilnik, N. Gurina 'Materialyi Issledivaniya po Arkheologgi', *SSSR* 47, (Nauka, 1956)

134   A. Beltran 'Rock Art of the Spanish Levant', 1979

141   Prof. H. Todorova/Vladimir Vitanov Agency

143   Volos Archaeological Museum/TAP Service

146   Marija Gimbutas, 'The Gods and Goddesses of Old Europe' (Thames & Hudson, 1974)

147   Dacia NS VII 1963, Institutul de Arheologie, Bucharest

148   Kálmán Kónya

150   Pitt Rivers Museum, Oxford

154   M. Paccard

156   Prof. J. Lüning

159 and 162   Dr Rudolph Kuper, University of Cologne

163   Dr V. Pavúková

173   Trewin Copplestone, *Cambridge Encyclopedia of Archaeology*, 1980, after Todorova

175   after V. M. Masson and N. Merpert 'The Eneolithic of the USSR' (Nauka, 1982)

178   Musée National Suisse, Zurich (P14372 & 13698P)

179   original plan by L. Bonneau and Z. le Rouzic 1916, completed by J. L'Helgouac'h 1965

181   Nationalmuseet, Copenhagen

183   Ashmolean Museum, Oxford

186   Andrew Sherratt after Panayotov and Dergachov

188   Landesamt für Archäologische Denkmalpflege, Sachsen-Anhalt, Halle

189   Claude Masset

191   Nationalmuseet, Copenhagen

194   D. L. Swan

197   Ashmolean Museum, Oxford

198   F. Mezzena, Museo Archeologico, Aosta

203   Ashmolean Museum, Oxford

205   K. A. Wardle

206   Hirmer Fotoarchiv, Munich

209   Ashmolean Museum, Oxford

210 and 212   Hirmer Fotoarchiv, Munich

213   Prof. M. Warren, University of Bristol

215, 218, and 221   Ekdotike Athenon, Athens

222   Hirmer Fotoarchiv, Munich

223   (top) Hirmer Fotoarchiv (bottom) Ekdotike Athenon, Athens

224   National Archaeological Museum, Athens and TAP Service

226   (top) Ekdotike Athenon, Athens
(bottom) Prof. Paul Aström

230   Hirmer Fotoarchiv, Munich

231   (top) Mycenae Archive, University of Birmingham
(bottom) Deutsches Archäologisches Institut, Athens

234   (left) Ecole Francaise d'Athènes, Athens
(right) Mycenae Archive, University of Birmingham

236   Diana Wardle

237   National Archaeological Museum, Athens and TAP Service

239 and 240   Trustees of the British Museum

241   Institute of Nautical Archaeology, Texas. Photo by Donald A. Frey

248   (top) Antikvarisk-Topografiska Arkivet, Stockholm
(bottom) Nationalmuseet, Copenhagen

249   J. Jensen 'The Prehistory of Denmark' (Methuen, 1982) after S. W. Andersen 1981, Nationalmuseet, Copenhagen

252   Salisbury and South Wiltshire Museum

255   Ashmolean Museum, Oxford

257   Landesamt für Archäologische Denkmalpflege, Sachsen-Anhalt, Halle

258   Dr F. Moosleitner, Salzburger Museum, Austria

262   Ashmolean Museum, Oxford

264   Magyar Nemzeti Múzeum, Budapest

265 and 266   Dr Andrew Sherratt

267   Prof. A. F. Harding

269   Ashmolean Museum, Oxford

270   Wiltshire Archaeological and Natural History Society, Devizes

271   Nationalmuseet, Copenhagen

273   Ashmolean Museum, Oxford

284   (*a*) and (*c*) Dr H. W. Catling Archaioligiki Ephemaris 1904/Ashmolean Museum, Oxford

286   (right) The Cyprus Museum

294   (3 items on right) after Dr. C. Macdonald

298   (*c*) The Cyprus Museum
(bottom left) Director of Antiquities and the Cyprus Museum

299   (left) Dr C. Macdonald

300 and 301   The Syndics of Cambridge University Library, Carl Schuchhardt, 'Schliemann's Excavations', 1891

302   (below) Princeton University Press

306   Excavation project 'Feudvar' Vojvodjanski muzej, Novi Sad; Freie Universität, Berlin

307   Dr P. Medovic, Vojvodjanski Muzej, Yugoslavia

308   Musée National Suisse, Zurich

311   (left) Nationalmuseet, Copenhagen
(right) Alinari

312   Musée des Antiquités Nationales, Photo R.M.N.

313   © St Edmundsbury Museums Service, Moyse's Hall Museum

316   Royal Commission on the Historical Monuments of England

318   Bayerisches Landesamt für Denkmalpflege. Photo by O. Braasch

319   Antikvarisk-Topografiska Arkivet, Stockholm

321   Museo Civico Archeologico, Bologna

322   (top) Museum für Ur-und Frühgeschichte, Potsdam
(bottom) © The Trustees of the National Museums of Scotland 1994

323   Dr J. Hrala, Archaeological Institute, Prague

327 National Museum of Wales, Cardiff

328 (top) Somerset Levels Project (bottom) Francis Pryor, Fenland Archaeological Trust

330 (top) Prähistorische Staatssammlung, Munich (bottom) Nationalmuseet, Copenhagen

331 Cambridge University Collection; copyright reserved

333 (top and bottom left) Alinari (bottom right) Dr J. Hrala, Archaeological Institute, Prague

334 Prof. A. F. Harding

342 (top) Museos de la Muralla de Sagunto (bottom) 'I Celti', (Gruppo Editoriale Fabbri, Bompiani, Sonzogno)

346 Landesdenkmalamt Baden-Württemberg. Photo by O. Braasch

347 Stuart Piggot, 'Ancient Europe' (Edinburgh University Press, 1965)

348 (top) Giraudon/Musée Archéologique, Chatillon-sur-Seine (bottom) Lauros-Giraudon/ Musée Archéologique, Chatillon-sur-Seine

349 Württembergisches Landesmuseum, Stuttgart

356 Museo Civico Archeologico, Bologna

360 Alinari

362 National History Museum of SRR, Bucharest

365 The Ancient Art & Architecture Collection

366 (top) Nationalmuseet, Copenhagen (bottom) Ashmolean Museum, Oxford

368 Musée des Jacobins, Morlaix

369 Trustees of the British Museum

382 State Hermitage Museum, Russia

385 (top) Vladimir Vitanov Agency

393 and 396 State Hermitage Museum, Russia

400 Nationalmuseet, Copenhagen

403 (top left) Trustees of the British Museum (centre right) Society of Antiquaries of London (bottom) Nationalmuseet, Copenhagen

406 C. Cichorius, 'Die Reliefs der Traianssäule', 1896–1900/ Ashmolean Museum, Oxford

416 (left) Musée des Antiquités Nationales. © Photo RMN (right) Erich Lessing/Magnum Photos and Musée Archéologique, Dijon

418 Musée des Antiquités Nationales. © Photo RMN

423 Trustees of the British Museum

425 Ashmolean Museum, Oxford

426 Lonchampt-Delehaye/ CNMHS © DACS 1994

428 Musée Calvet, Avignon

432 © The Trustees of the National Museums of Scotland 1994

435 Alinari

436 (left) Istituto Centrale per il Catalogo e la Documentazione, Rome (right) Institutul de Arheologie, Bucharest

449 P. Perin and Laure-Charlotte Feffer, 'Les Francs' (Armand Colin, 1987)

454 W. Haarnagel, 'Die Grabung Fedderson Wierde' (Franz Steiner Verlag, Stuttgart)

455 Kossack, Behre, Schmid, 'Archäologische und Naturwissenschaftliche Untersuchungen an Siedlungen im Deutschen Küstengebiet' (VCH Verlagsgesellschaft, Weinheim)

457 National Museum, Bucharest

458 Archäologisches Landesmuseum der Christian-Albrechts-Universität, Schleswig

464 Musée des Beaux-Arts et d'Archéologie, Troyes, France. Photo by Musées de Troyes

465 P. Perin and Laure-Charlotte Feffer, 'Les Francs' (Armand Colin, 1987)

466 Römisch-Germanisches Museum, Cologne

468 Magyar Nemzeti Múzeum, Budapest

469 and 470 R. Christlein, 'Die Alamannen' (Theiss Verlag, Stuttgart, 1978)

473 M. Todd, 'The Early Germans' (Blackwell, 1992)

474 and 476 Antikvarisk-Topografiska Arkivet, Stockholm

478 and 479 Z. Vana, 'The World of the Ancient Slavs' (Orbis)

480 M. Todd, 'The Early Germans' (Blackwell, 1992)

In a few instances we have been unable to trace the copyright holder prior to publication. If notified the publishers will be pleased to amend the acknowledgements in any future edition.

Picture research by Sandra Assersohn

INDEX